THE GREENWOOD ENCYCLOPEDIA OF
INTERNATIONAL RELATIONS

THE GREENWOOD ENCYCLOPEDIA OF
INTERNATIONAL
RELATIONS

VOLUME IV
S–Z

CATHAL J. NOLAN

Executive Director
International History Institute
Boston University

GREENWOOD PUBLISHING
Westport, CT • London

Library of Congress Cataloging-in-Publication Data

Nolan, Cathal J.
    The Greenwood encyclopedia of international relations / Cathal J. Nolan.
      p. cm.
    Includes bibliographical references and index.
    ISBN: 0–313–30743–1 (set : alk. paper)—ISBN 0–313–30741–5 (v. 1 : alk. paper)—
ISBN 0–313–30742–3 (v. 2 : alk. paper)—ISBN 0–313–32382–8 (v. 3 : alk. paper)—
ISBN 0–313–32383–6 (v. 4 : alk. paper)
    1. International relations—Encyclopedias. I. Title.
JZ1160.N65 2002
327'.03—dc21   2002019495

British Library Cataloguing in Publication Data is available.

Library of Congress Catalog Card Number: 2002019495

ISBN: 0–313–30743–1 (set)
      0–313–30741–5 (vol. 1)
      0–313–30742–3 (vol. 2)
      0–313–32382–8 (vol. 3)
      0–313–32383–6 (vol. 4)

First published in 2002

Greenwood Press, 88 Post Road West, Westport, CT 06881
An imprint of Greenwood Publishing Group, Inc.
www.greenwood.com

Printed in the United States of America

The paper used in this book complies with the
Permanent Paper Standard issued by the National
Information Standards Organization (Z39.48–1984).

10 9 8 7 6 5 4 3 2 1

Sapere aude

For my children,
Ryan Casey and Genevieve Michelle

Contents

Preface

"History," said the American industrialist Henry Ford, "is more or less bunk." Even the great eighteenth-century historian of the Roman Empire, Edward Gibbon, was only slightly more respectful: "history," he declared, is "little more than the register of the crimes, follies, and misfortunes of Mankind." So why bother to consult, let alone write, a multivolume work of international history and international relations such as this? Because history is—whatever Ford thought of it on his good days or Gibbon on his bad ones—the most important of all humanistic inquiries. For modern societies to live with the forces of nature that science has unleashed and that ideological folly or personal vanity threatens to deploy for destructive or oppressive purposes, they first must come to terms with history. Their leaders and citizens alike must understand the ways in which increased material knowledge brings social progress even as it expands conflict and opportunities for war. And they must appreciate that vanity and a lust for power among people of sustained ambition abides still near the center of public affairs and relations among nations and states. In sum, they must realize the profound truth of the matter-of-fact observation, which Albert Einstein once made, that politics is both more difficult, and ultimately far more important, even than nuclear physics.

This work presents readers with the essential continuity of events of their own day with the great ideas, leading personalities, and major developments of the past. Yet, how does any scholar determine what is a key event and who the leading individuals are or identify great-unseen forces and long-term trends that lead to tectonic shifts in the affairs of states and peoples? It is by now axiomatic that historians "know more and more about less and less." That is a particular problem for a work such as this, where the danger lurks of presenting a compendium of "interesting facts" and "more interesting facts," with little coherence and interpretive context. Had a simple compilation of facts been the aim of this work, it might have emerged instead as a multi-author effort wherein dozens of specialists were asked to present their findings about fairly narrow disputes. Instead, it is the work of a single author—albeit, one humbly grateful to hundreds of deeply learned and prolific specialists. Although such an approach presents dangers of interpretive error, it offers opportunities for an expansive exposition that may engage general readers to search out libraries of more specialized histories. Even so, in a work such as this it is more important than usual for readers to know the basis on which historical events and persons were selected for presentation, and the assumptions that underlie its author's judgments about their significance. These criteria and assumptions I have laid out in the paragraphs that follow.

LOGIC OF THE WORK

The first issue to be dealt with is objectivity. In the social sciences and academic history, objectivity springs from conscious emotional, intellectual, and personal detachment from the facts in order to permit them to "speak for themselves." Of course, that is precisely what facts never do. Historical, political, social, and economic statements and assumptions are laden with the values of observers and analysts, even those who honestly strive for detachment rather than merely make a humbug bow in its general direction. This problem is a by-product of the inherent uncertainty of knowledge in these fields. "If you would know history, know the historian" is also sound advice concerning economics and political science. In the final analysis, the best guard against subjective distortion of objective truth is a critical intelligence and skeptical, but not cynical, attitude toward intellectual authority. That does not mean that objective truth is impossible. It does mean, however, that it is hard to attain and that it must never be assumed. In writing this book, I have attempted to achieve a standard of objectivity, which is best summed up in the advice John Quincy Adams lent to all would-be writers of history. "The historian," Adams cautioned, "must be without country or religion." In addition, while alert to issues of human freedom in whatever era, which I must forewarn readers is a high personal value ("if you would know history . . ."), I have tried to avoid reading the values of the present into the past, the better to judge people and events in the light of the imaginative as well as real-world possibilities of their own day.

Passion is also disdained in the modern academy. Yet, it is mostly a virtue in historical writing. One must be scrupulous about facts, of course, and fair-minded. On the other hand, one should not be dispassionate about the Holocaust, or the crimes of Stalin or Mao, or the brutality of the génocidaires who carried out the Rwandan massacres. I have tried, and I hope that I have generally succeeded, to write "without country or religion" in assessing such matters, but that does not mean assuming a position of neutrality on the moral significance of salient people and events. A pose of studied disinterest about the qualities of communism or fascism relative to democracy, or the deeds of Tamerlane, or the meaning of terrorism, is necessarily feigned for any thinking and feeling human being. It is also itself a committed view, whether self-aware that it is so or not. Moreover, to take on a dishonest, because morally masked, position is, to paraphrase Talleyrand, worse than a crime: it would be a mistake. An affectation of detachment from lessons that history teaches about the human condition is both sterile and boring. It is far better for readers to encounter open judgments. On this point, I cleave to the wisdom of the British historian G. M. Trevelyan that in writing about and assessing historical actors and events "the really indispensable qualities [are] accuracy and good faith." Reconstructions of past events and motivations are as accurate as I have been able to make them, though I probably have made errors of fact and interpretation that will require correction in any subsequent edition of this work. As to the rest, I ask readers to accept that I have presented what I believe to be the facts of history, and drawn conclusions about the meaning of those facts, in good faith.

Concerning the comparative length of one entry with another, it is generally true that the further events recede from the present, the more history and historians compress their description. Ideally, that is done because more of the original dross, which always conceals the meaning of human affairs, has been burned away and the right conclusions drawn about what place in the larger story a given historical event or person holds. In reality, it probably more closely reflects a common tendency and need to fix all things in relation to one's own time and point of view. I have made what effort I can to correct for this habit, but I am sure I am as guilty of it as most. As to the length of the overall work, I may only plead in the spirit of Blaise Pascal that I would have written far less, but I did not have the time.

Analytically, this study starts from the straightforward observation that states have dominated international affairs for the past 350 years. Among the nearly 200 states of the early twenty-first century the vast majority are, at most, regional powers or just minor countries. Even so, smaller states sometimes have been quite influential in the larger course of world history, if sometimes solely as objects of aggression or imperial competition. And they are often interesting and important in their own right or concerning issues of regional significance. Thus, all countries currently in existence are covered in this work, as are a large number of extinct nations. Each is treated in an entry that at the least summarizes the main features of its national development and tries to situate the country in the larger contexts of time and region.

It remains true, however, that it is the most powerful states, the major civilizations from which they arise, and the wars in which they are involved that have been the major influences in world history. Even small changes within or among the Great Powers have a more important and long-term impact on world affairs than signal events within or among smaller countries. Comprehensive coverage is thus given to the foreign policies and interactions of the most powerful states and to the dynamics that drive them, including economic, intellectual, political, and social innovation or decay. This includes former Great Powers, now extinct or just declined from the first rank, dating to the Peace of Westphalia (1648) and emergence of the modern states system in seventeenth- and eighteenth-century Europe. Likewise, it is true that even lesser—whether in character or talent—individuals in charge of the affairs of Great Powers have a broad influence on world history and politics. Often, their influence has been weightier than that of even a moral or intellectual titan, if the latter was confined to a Lilliputian land. Therefore, individuals who might be reasonably judged as of little personal consequence are sometimes given their day in this work, owing to the indisputable public consequences of their choices, actions, or omissions while in command of the public affairs of major powers. More than one otherwise mediocre prime minister or president of a Great Power, or unrelieved and appalling dictator, has slipped into significant history via this back door, held ajar for them by the pervasive importance of raw power as a motive and moving force in the affairs of nations. For this reason, most leaders of major powers are profiled, including American, Austrian, British, Chinese, French, German, Indian, Japanese, Ottoman, Russian, and Soviet, along with key military and intellectual figures.

Even the Great Powers pursue grand plans and strategic interests within an international system that reflects wider economic, political, and military realities and upholds certain legal and diplomatic norms. A full understanding of world affairs—which is much more than just relations among states and nations—is incomplete without proper awareness of the historical evolution and nature of this international system (or international society), its key terms, ideas, successes and failures, and the role played in it by numerous nonstate economic and political entities. It is also crucial to appreciate that world affairs manifest cooperative as well as competitive and violent interstate relations and that, since the nineteenth century, complex international relationships have been mirrored in expanding numbers of regional organizations dealing with security, but also economic, social, legal, and even cultural arrangements. Besides the states on the world stage, other actors that demand attention include customs unions, multinational corporations, nongovernmental organizations, and an impressively expanding host—angelic and otherwise—of international organizations. As for individuals, prominent leaders from the lesser powers of Africa, Asia, Australasia, the Americas, and Europe are included according to whether they had a significant impact on international affairs beyond their nation's borders. If they had a major impact on their own society but not on wider affairs, mention of their role is usually made in the national reference alone. Also, United Nations (UN) Secretaries-General are listed, as are many individual Nobel Prize (for Peace) winners.

As with the unique role of the Great Powers, war as a general phenomenon—and great wars among major powers in particular—receives special attention. War is more costly and requires more preparation, effort, sacrifice, ingenuity, and suffering than any other collective human endeavor. There is no greater engine of social, economic, political, or technological change than war and the ever-present threat of war even in times of peace. Moreover, war and the modern state, and the larger international system, clearly evolved together since c. 1500, each greatly influencing the other. World wars—wars that involved most of the Great Powers in determined conflict—greatly compounded these manifold effects. Hence, world wars and protracted Great Power conflicts are covered in detail, including the *Seven Years' War*, the *French Revolution* and *Napoleonic Wars*, *World War I*, *World War II*, and the *Cold War*. Dozens of lesser wars, civil wars, rebellions, and guerrilla conflicts are also recounted, as they constitute a good part of international history and of influential national histories. In sum, war is a major part of international affairs and therefore a core subject of this book.

General developments of world historical significance are also covered, including *industrialization*, *modernization*, *telecommunications*, *total war*, and the *green* and *agricultural revolutions*. Straight historical entries include biographies, major battles, international economic history, national histories, and the history of general international processes and events. Entries attempt to summarize thousands of years when dealing with major civilizations, religions, or economic trends (though with numerous cross references), hundreds of years in the case of the Great Powers and precolonial, colonial, and post-independence history of newer nations. Most listings that are separate from national histories concern the modern era, though some go back much further. The focus is, once again, on the rise of the Great Powers and the course of world civilizations, their formative wars, and their diplomatic, political, and economic relations. This means that the progressive enlargement of the states system through imperial wars, colonialism, and the expansion of commerce and market economics beyond Europe to Africa, Asia, and the Americas has been covered.

In the interest of universality, a serious effort was made to cover regions that, objectively speaking, formed only tributary streams of the riverine flow of world history. Along with something of the flavor of their local histories, it is recounted how such areas were affected by their forced inclusion in the modern state system—often by the *slave trade* or overseas *imperialism*—and by international economic developments. This is particularly true for such areas as the Caribbean, Central America, and the associated states and dependencies of the South Pacific, which are often neglected in more straightforward narrative histories. Along with all modern states, also covered are all extant political entities, whether fully sovereign or not, including *associated states*, *city-states*, small *colonies*, *condominiums*, *dependencies*, *microstates*, and legal oddities such as the *Sovereign Military Order of Malta* (SMOM). Lastly, a fair number of extinct polities are listed, including former empires, kingdoms, federations, failed states, and political unions, such as *Austria-Hungary*, the *East African Community*, the *Ottoman Empire*, *Senegambia*, the *Soviet Union*, and the *United Arab Republic*, among many others. Also included are colonial-era names and relevant descriptions of all newly independent nations.

Although most summaries are confined to the post-1500 period, national histories may include far distant events if these are generally deemed significant in the evolution and/or historical memory of modern nations or provide intimations of the scope and direction of a given people's posture toward the outside world. For instance, the founding and succession of China's divers dynasties receive extended coverage, partly because their accomplishments and failures importantly illuminate modern China's troubled response to external pressures and its twentieth-century struggle with foreign invasion and internal revolution and partly because China remains deeply cognizant of its long and rich history, and this fact has a strong influence on its contemporary foreign policy behavior. Major intellectual revolutions that have had global historical—including not only intellectual, but also legal and political—significance are also discussed, notably the *Renaissance, Protestant Reformation,* and the *Enlightenment*. Although these tumultuous upheavals were originally and primarily European phenomena, they ultimately had profound effects on all international relations down to the present day, such as in their contribution to the development of secularism and the ascendancy of the state as the central principle of political organization. All political revolutions of world historical significance are covered, including the *American Revolution*, the *French Revolution*, the two *Chinese Revolutions* of the first half of the twentieth century, and the several *Russian Revolutions*. Revolutions of more local or regional significance—such as the Cuban, Ethiopian, and Iranian—are also abstracted and their importance assessed.

STRUCTURE OF THE WORK

This work is organized alphabetically. Single-word entries are, therefore, easy and straightforward to locate. But it is not always obvious where a compound term should be listed. For ease of use by readers, compound entries are listed as they are employed in usual speech and writing, that is, in the form in which they are most likely to be first encountered by the average reader. For instance, *natural resources* and *strategic resources* appear, respectively, under N and S rather than R. If readers are unable to find an entry they seek under one part of the compound term, they should have little difficulty finding it under another component of the term or phrase. Additionally, the book is heavily cross-referenced (indicated by italics), with some license taken when cross-referencing verbs to entries, which are actually listed as nouns, such as *annex*, which leads to *annexation*. Readers would be well advised to make frequent use of this feature since cross-references almost always provide additional information or insight on the original entry. Rather than clutter the text unduly with italics, however, common references such as "war," "peace," "surrender," "negotiation," "defeat," "treaty," as well as all country names, have been left in normal font. Yet, all such commonly used terms and all countries have discrete entries. In rare cases, some common terms and specific countries are highlighted, indicating that they contain additional information highly relevant to the entry being perused. To avoid confusion or sending the reader on a fruitless cross-reference search, foreign words and phrases have not been italicized. If they are, then a specific cross-reference to the term or phrase is listed because it has a special and precise meaning for international relations. For example, a textual reference to "the domestic status quo" does not receive italics, whereas "after 1919, Britain was a leading *status quo power*" does, to inform readers that additional information exists under this specialized term. For ease of use, oft-cited acronyms are cross-referenced for quick referral. Thus, *UNGA* redirects browsers to *United Nations General Assembly*, and *WTO* refers readers to the *Warsaw Treaty Organization* and the *World Trade Organization*. Otherwise, entries that readers might have encountered elsewhere in acronym form appear here under the full name of the organization. If a reader does not know the formal title of an international organization, it may be easily located by scanning all entries under the first letter. Thus, if searching for *ECOSOC* without knowing what that acronym stands for, a reader should simply scan entries under E until he or she arrives at *Economic and Social Council (ECOSOC)*. Exceptions to this rule are foreign language acronyms commonly employed in English. These are listed under the acronym itself rather than under a foreign spelling, which is most likely unknown to the English language reader. Hence, the former Soviet security and intelligence agency is listed under *KGB (Komitet Gosudarstvennoy Bezopasnosti)*, rather than the obscure "Komitet."

Crises and wars are inventoried by conventionally accepted names. Readers unsure of a standard name for a war or crisis should simply check a country entry of any known participant. There they will find in the form of a cross-reference the precise term for the entry sought. This method is especially useful for the several wars that even now go by unusual names, or in some cases multiple names, or those conflicts with which a given reader may not be familiar. For instance, someone seeking information for the first time on China's several wars with Japan might reasonably assume that they are called "Chinese/Japanese War(s)" of some given date. In fact, these important conflicts are usually referred to, in English, as the *Sino/Japanese War(s)*. Looking under China or Japan will locate the appropriate cross-reference and guide the reader to the entry that is being sought. Likewise, the several wars involving Israel and various Arab states are listed chronologically under *Arab/Israeli War(s)*, rather than under politically loaded or parochial terms such as "Yom Kippur War" or "Six Day War," although these terms are listed and cross-referenced in consideration of readers who are used to them. In cases of special confusion or a recent change in nomenclature, a guiding cross-reference is listed. For example, the *Iran/Iraq War* was often called the *Gulf War* until that term was usurped by the media for use about the multinational conflict with Iraq over its 1990 invasion and annexation of Kuwait. Readers will find here the entry *Gulf War (1980–1988)*, which explains the shift and redirects them to the newly accepted name of *Iran-Iraq War (1980–1988)*. Below that appears *Gulf War (1990–1991)*, which synopsizes the UN coalition's war with Iraq. Some technical points are as follows:

1. For syntactical reasons, cross-references that begin with a country's name may appear otherwise in the text. For instance, the *invasion of Grenada* may appear in a given sentence, but the entry is found under *Grenada, invasion of*.

2. All civil wars are listed under the country name. Thus, *American Civil War* appears under A and not C. In this case, and some others, the advice of reviewers has been followed to cross-reference wars to their vernacular usages. This allows more general readers to easily find the entries they seek, but has the felicitous side effect of compelling chauvinists or jingoists, of whatever country or stripe, to locate their nation's most boastful conflicts by mere, even humbling, alphabetical order!

3. All dates are from the Common Era (C.E.) unless stated otherwise, in which case the standard designation B.C.E. (Before the Common Era) is used. In cases where ambiguity exists, C.E. is added to ensure clarity.

4. I have for the most part followed the practice of specialists in using the pinyin system for romanizing Chinese personal and place names. However, names that have long become familiar to Western readers under their Wade-Giles form have been left in that form, as in "Chiang Kai-shek" rather than "Jiang Jieshi," with a cross-reference to the pinyin form to avoid causing confusion for younger readers. In some special cases, the alternate form has been provided immediately in parentheses, but this has not been the preferred approach.

SPECIAL FEATURES

Biography

Recent trends in historiography emphasize interactions of whole populations and or social and economic forces. Yet it remains true, as Thomas Carlyle famously noted, that much of international history is accessible through stories of the lives of great men and women caught up in, and to some degree shaping, the tumultuous events of their times. Certainly that remains true of many, even most, states before the nineteenth century and of personal or "charismatic" dictatorships still. Significant lives may serve as beacons, illuminating history. The limitations of space in this work, however, meant that its compact biographies seldom attempt to explain the inner meaning of these extraordinary lives. Readers must explore full biographies to acquire that knowledge and psychological insight into their subject. This work is necessarily limited to the public importance of public lives and is mostly confined to the political sphere, with personal and psychological detail kept to a minimum. Even so, peculiar human elements have not been ignored where they are specially revealing and clearly relevant, as in the mysticism of Nicholas II, the cruelty of Amin, the erratic and callous disregard for life of Mao, the extreme overconfidence of Hitler, or the sadism and near-clinical paranoia of Stalin.

Diplomacy

Entries include key concepts such as *arbitration, conciliation, diplomatic immunity, good offices, mediation*, and *sphere of influence*. Major diplomatic conferences are described, including *Westphalia, 1648; Vienna, 1815; Paris, 1856; Berlin, 1878; Paris, 1919; Washington, 1922; Bretton Woods, 1944; San Francisco, 1945*; and *Helsinki, 1973–1975*. Practices of negotiation, diplomatic functions, and ranks and titles are included. Classic diplomatic terms such as *cordon sanitaire, raison d'état, rapprochement, Realpolitik, Weltpolitik*, and many others are defined and examples of their application provided.

Intelligence

A sampling of major intelligence agencies is included, among them *CIA, KGB, MI5/MI6, Mossad, NSA, STASI*, and *Sûreté*, as well as common terms, jargon, and slang from intelligence tradecraft.

International Law

Listed and defined are numerous international legal concepts, maxims, and specialized terminology, many with illustrative examples, including dozens of entries on subfields such as *international criminal law, international customary law, international public law, laws of war, recognition*, and *sovereignty*. Numerous treaties, from *arms control* to the *Space Treaty* to agreements on the *Law of the Sea* and *Antarctica*, are provided and their terms listed and explained. International law and the attendant politics of *human rights* issues are covered, including *female circumcision, citizenship, refugees, slavery*, and the *slave trade*.

International Organizations (IOs)

All major multilateral bodies and organizations are covered, dating back to the mid-nineteenth century. IOs proliferated with the founding of the *League of Nations* and the *UN*. This work includes entries on all specialized agencies, as well as key committees and commissions of the UN system. There is comprehensive coverage of regional organizations, including several failures, whether organized around economic, political, or security themes. Some prominent nongovernmental organizations are also listed.

International Political Economy

Major economic institutions, such as *GATT, IBRD, IMF*, and the *WTO*, and interstate economic associations, such as *ASEAN, CARICOM, ECOWAS, EEC, EU, NAFTA, OECD*, and *OPEC*, have entries. Some historic multinational corporations have been added, such as the *East India Company* and the *Hudson's Bay Company*, and there are more general entries on foreign direct investment and related economic concepts and specialized language, such as *adjustment, balance of payments, debt rescheduling, deficit financing, First Tranche, free trade agreements, oligopoly*, and *structural adjustment*. Also, international economic history is well-covered in entries such as *world depressions*, the *Bretton Woods system*, the *agricultural revolution, industrialization*, and the *gold standard*.

Maps

Multiple maps are available to readers. Some cover world political divisions on a region-by-region basis. Others illustrate major historical conflicts or events, such as the occupation of Germany in 1945, expansion and contraction of the Japanese Empire, and U.S. intervention in Central America and the Caribbean. Some concern long-standing diplomatic and strategic controversies, such as the *Eastern Question* or the *Straits Question*.

Military History

Included are major concepts such as *envelopment, flanking, mobilization, strategy*, and *friction*. Also listed are entries on military ranks and units and a limited set of entries on major weapons systems, conventional and otherwise. Many wars are synopsized, including discussion of their course, causes, and effects. The crucially important events of *World War I* and *World War II* receive extended coverage. Pivotal battles over the past 500 years of world history are highlighted. Generals and admirals of special accomplishment or failure earned discrete biographical entries.

Political Geography

There are entries on every nation, colony, possession, and protectorate, as well as key geographical features, definitions of strategic regions and geographical concepts, and an overview of select geopolitical theories. Significant minority groups are described, such as *Fulani, Ibos, Karen, Kurds*, and *Zulu*. Some nonsovereign regions are cataloged, especially those with secessionist histories, including *Chechnya*, *Ossetia*, *Nagorno-Karabakh*, *Québec*, and *Shaba*. Country entries provide a synopsis history and description of major foreign policies pursued and alliances and may also list core international associations, population levels, and the quality and size of the national military.

Political Science

Included are major concepts, terminology, and translations into plain English of current thinking in this jargon-laden discipline, which also encompasses academic *international relations theory*. This embraces concepts and terms from theoretical subfields such as *dependency*, *deterrence*, *game theory*, *decision-making theory*, *just war theory*, *liberal-internationalism*, *Marxism*, *perception/mis-perception studies*, *realism*, *strategic studies*, and various *systems theories*. There are also intellectual sketches of key political thinkers on international affairs, among them *Hobbes*, *Bentham*, *Kant*, *Marx*, *Rousseau*, and *Adam Smith*.

Acknowledgments

Dr. Samuel Johnson noted, "The greatest part of a writer's time is spent in reading, in order to write; a man will turn over half a library to make one book." I am keenly aware of that truth and immensely grateful to the hundreds of specialists whose books and articles I have relied upon in such measure. I have not hesitated to add interpretations of my own in areas I know well or where it seemed to me that larger patterns in history were readily apparent and moral and other lessons might be fairly drawn. Even so, writing a work of history such as this is primarily an exercise in synthesis. In a work of this scale and nature, it is simply not possible for a single author to master the primary sources that are the raw ore from which the purer metals of historical truth must be smelted. Instead, my challenge has been to gain sufficient command of the specialty literature in order to provide enough detailed narrative that past events become comprehensible, while also communicating the differing interpretations to which those events may be subject.

If this were a normal monograph, my heavy intellectual debt would be documented in extensive footnotes. That has not proven possible here, since footnotes and related academic paraphernalia would have added several hundred more pages to an already overlong work. However, at the end of longer entries, I have cited direct sources and other recommended books—the latter for various reasons and not by any means always-interpretive agreement on my part. Also, I have added clusters of more general references upon which I have relied in entries of central importance, such as "*war*" or "*international law*" or "*Spanish America.*"

Finally, I have prepared and included a Select Bibliography of works consulted. Neither the end citations nor the bibliography are intended to provide a comprehensive listing of the many important works of specialized history available to scholars. My more limited purpose is to point general readers to a mixture of the best, along with the most recent, scholarship in different fields and to expose them to a variety of interpretive points of view. I fully appreciate that a broad work of this nature is necessarily a mere steppingstone to a far richer understanding of international history, which may be gleaned only from a wider reading of those specialized histories. If this work encourages readers to pursue that search for themselves, its purpose will have been achieved.

On a personal note, I need and wish to express my profound gratitude to those who have assisted me in completing this task. I have taken parts of the past seven years to write this work. In that time, I wrote or edited other books, but this one was always on my mind, its demands pervading my reading and thinking, its conclusions seeping into my teaching. My first thanks must go to my editor at Greenwood, Michael Hermann, who is simply the finest editor with whom I have ever worked. In addition to lifting from me all concerns about production values and the usual mundane matters that accompany production of any book, he has been a frequent and always constructive critic and adviser on issues of content.

Several of my colleagues at Boston University must wish that e-mail had never been invented or at least that I had never been introduced to the technology. For their patience with me and forbearance of my many inquiries, and for their counsel, collegiality, and friendship, I am ever appreciative. My thanks and gratitude to Erik Goldstein and David Mayers, both of whom have been extraordinarily supportive of my work. I look forward to many more years together as colleagues and friends, joined now also by my old colleague and friend from the University of British Columbia, Robert H. Jackson. William Tilchin has been prodigiously supportive of this project and as we have worked together on several other conference and book projects. He has read and commented on numerous entries, often saving me from error and always boosting my confidence whenever it sagged, usually during moments when I realized how absurdly huge a task it was that I had set myself. How may I express the fullness of my gratitude to my friend and colleague, William R. Keylor, with whom I had the privilege of cofounding the International History Institute at Boston University and with whom I am honored to work closely on a daily basis? Had I an entry in this book for "gentleman and scholar," it would simply read, "See Bill Keylor," because there would be no need to say more.

Few have read, commented on, corrected, and laughed at (usually in the places intended) more of the text than my dear friend and former colleague, Dr. Carl C. Hodge of Okanagan University College in Kelowna, British Columbia. I am grateful also for comments on selected entries by Dr. Charles Cogan, Senior Fellow at the John F. Kennedy School of Government at Harvard University; Professor Charles Neu, Chair of History at Brown University; and Professor Tom Nichols of the Naval War College. Many other scholars and specialists have read and commented on one entry or another. I have thanked them individually in private and now do so again here. Min Wu, of the International History Institute, has been particularly helpful in confirming and correcting Chinese personal and place names, as has Sijin Cheng of the Department of Political Science. To them, I also extend my sincere thanks.

My wife, Valerie, read all of the book in manuscript form and has been a constant and sage adviser on language, syntax, and Latin throughout its years of writing. As always, she has remained cheerful and supportive even as I spent far too many hours lost in a book on the Mauryan state in India, or Qing China, or Samori Touré, or ensconced in front of the computer. My children, Ryan and Genevieve, continue to fill our home with laughter, wit, and song. At ages eleven and nine, I am deeply grateful for their cheerful presence and companionship.

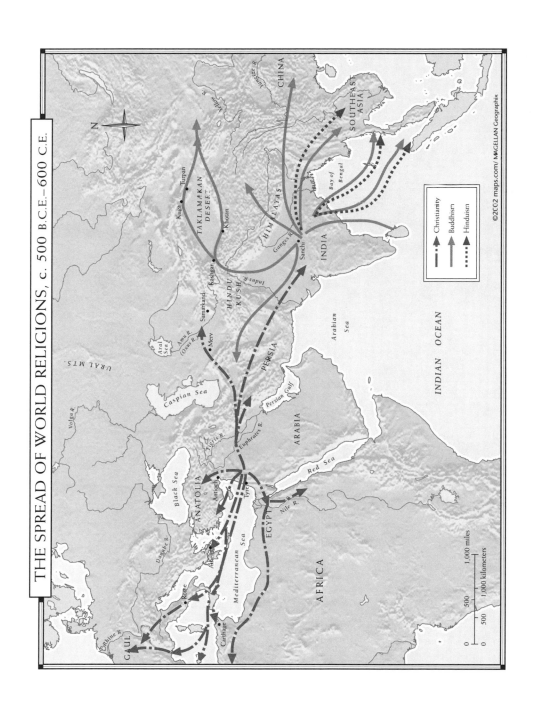

THE SPREAD OF WORLD RELIGIONS, c. 500 B.C.E.–600 C.E.

©2002 maps.com/ MAGELLAN Geographix

Christianity
Buddhism
Hinduism

URAL MTS.

Volga R.

Rhine R.

Danube R.

Black Sea

ANATOLIA

Antioch

Athens

Rome

GAUL

Carthage

Mediterranean Sea

EGYPT

Nile R.

AFRICA

Tigris R.

Euphrates R.

Tyre

Red Sea

ARABIA

Persian Gulf

Arabian Sea

PERSIA

Caspian Sea

Aral Sea

Amu R.
(Oxus R.)

Merv

Samarkand

Kashgar

HINDU KUSH

Indus R.

Ganges R.

Sanchi

INDIA

Bay of Bengal

HIMALAYAS

Khotan

Kuga

Turpan

TAKLAMAKAN DESERT

Tarim R.

Yellow R.

CHINA

SOUTHEAST ASIA

INDIAN OCEAN

N

0   500   1,000 miles
0   500   1,000 kilometers

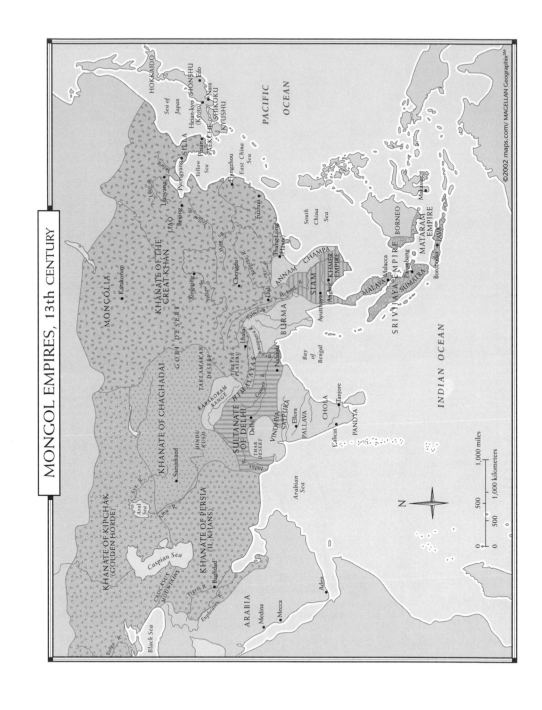

MONGOL EMPIRES, 13th CENTURY

©2002 maps.com/ MAGELLAN Geographix℠

HOKKAIDO

Sea of
Japan

HONSHU
Heian-kyo Edo
(Kyoto)
Pusan Nara
PAEKCHE SHIKOKU
KYUSHU

SILLA
Pyongyang

Liao R.
Liaoyang

Kaesong

Beijing

Yellow
Sea

Gangzhou
East China
Sea

Fuzhou

PACIFIC
OCEAN

MONGOLIA

Karakorum

KHANATE OF THE
GREAT-KHAN

LIAO

GOBI DESERT

Yellow R.

Yongning

Yangzi R.

Chengdu

South
China
Sea

Dali

Thang-Long
Hanoi

BORNEO

TAKLAMAKAN
DESERT

KHANATE OF CHAGHADAI

Lhasa

Tibetan
Plateau

Mekong R.

ANNAM

CHAMPA

MATARAM
EMPIRE

KARAKORAM
RANGE

HIMALAYAS

Salween R.

BURMA

SIAM

Angkor
KHMER
EMPIRE

Malacca

MALAYA

JAVA

Borobudur

Madiun

Brahmaputra R.

SULTANATE
OF DELHI

Ganges R.

Ayutthaya

SRIVIJAYA EMPIRE

Palembang

SUMATRA

HINDU
KUSH

Samarkand

Indus R.

Delhi

Nalanda

Bay
of
Bengal

KHANATE OF KIPCHAK
(GOLDEN HORDE)

Amu R.

Syr R.

Aral
Sea

VINDHYA

SATPURA

Ellora

CHOLA

Tanjore

PALLAVA

Calicut

PANDYA

Narbada R.

THAR
DESERT

Indus R.

INDIAN OCEAN

Caspian Sea

KHANATE OF PERSIA
(IL-KHANS)

Baghdad

Tigris R.

Arabian
Sea

CAUCASUS
MOUNTAINS

Black Sea

Volga R.

ARABIA

Medina
Mecca

Euphrates R.

Aden

N

0   500   1,000 miles

0   500   1,000 kilometers

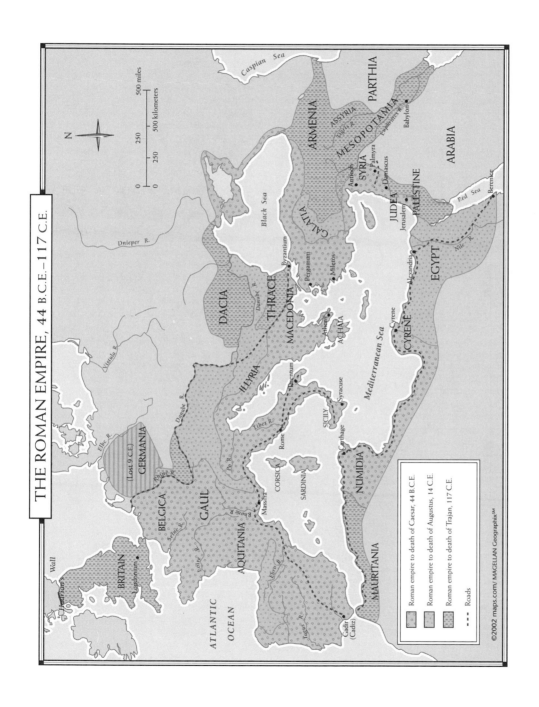

THE ROMAN EMPIRE, 44 B.C.E.–117 C.E.

N

500 miles
500 kilometers
0   250   500
0   250

Caspian Sea

PARTHIA

ARMENIA

ASSYRIA

MESOPOTAMIA

Babylon

GALATIA

SYRIA
Palmyra
Antioch   Damascus

ARABIA

Red Sea

JUDEA
PALESTINE
Jerusalem
Berenice

Black Sea

Dnieper R.

Danube R.

Byzantium
Pergamum
Miletos

THRACE

MACEDONIA

Athens
ACHAIA

DACIA

Vistula R.

Danube R.

ILLYRIA

Brundisium

Cyrene
CYRENE

EGYPT
Alexandria

Nile R.

Mediterranean Sea

Syracuse

SICILY

Tiber R.
Rome

Po R.

CORSICA

SARDINIA

Carthage

NUMIDIA

MAURITANIA

GERMANIA
(Lost 9 CE)

Elbe R.
Rhine R.

BELGICA
Seine R.

GAUL
Loire R.

AQUITANIA

Rhône R.

Massilia

Ebro R.

Tagus R.

Gadir
(Cadiz)

Hadrian's Wall

BRITAIN
Londinium

ATLANTIC
OCEAN

Roman empire to death of Caesar, 44 B.C.E.
Roman empire to death of Augustus, 14 C.E.
Roman empire to death of Trajan, 117 C.E.
Roads

THE SPREAD OF ISLAM, 622 – 750 CE

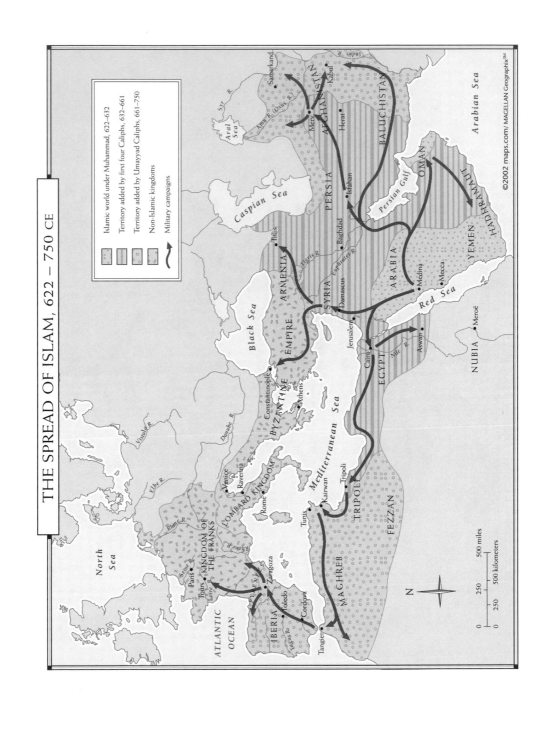

Legend:
- Islamic world under Muhammad, 622–632
- Territory added by first four Caliphs, 632–661
- Territory added by Umayyad Caliphs, 661–750
- Non-Islamic kingdoms
- Military campaigns

©2002 maps.com/ MAGELLAN Geographix℠

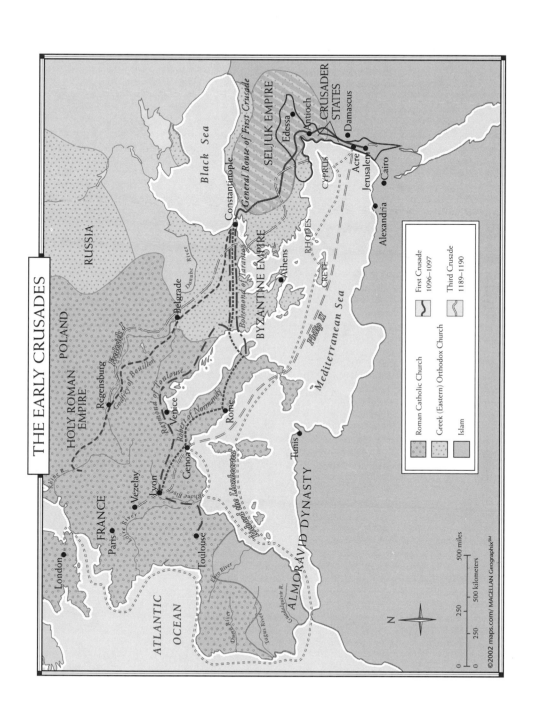

THE EARLY CRUSADES

ATLANTIC OCEAN

London

FRANCE
Paris
Seine River
Vezelay
Lyon
Toulouse
Rhône River

HOLY ROMAN EMPIRE
Regensburg
Weser R.
Rhine R.
Godfrey of Bouillon
Raymond of Toulouse
Robert of Normandy

POLAND

RUSSIA

Frederick I
Belgrade
Danube River

Venice
Rome
Genoa
Bohemond of Tarantino

BYZANTINE EMPIRE
Athens

Constantinople

Black Sea

SELJUK EMPIRE

General Route of First Crusade

Edessa
Antioch
Damascus

CRUSADER STATES

Richard the Lionhearted
Philip II

RHODES
CRETE

Mediterranean Sea

CYPRUS
Acre
Jerusalem
Cairo
Alexandria

Tunis

ALMORAVID DYNASTY

Ebro River
Guadalquivir R.
Duero River
Tagus River

N

0   250   500 miles

0   250   500 kilometers

©2002 maps.com/ MAGELLAN Geographix℠

Roman Catholic Church

Greek (Eastern) Orthodox Church

Islam

First Crusade
1096–1097

Third Crusade
1189–1190

EXPLORATION AND COLONIZATION, c. 1700

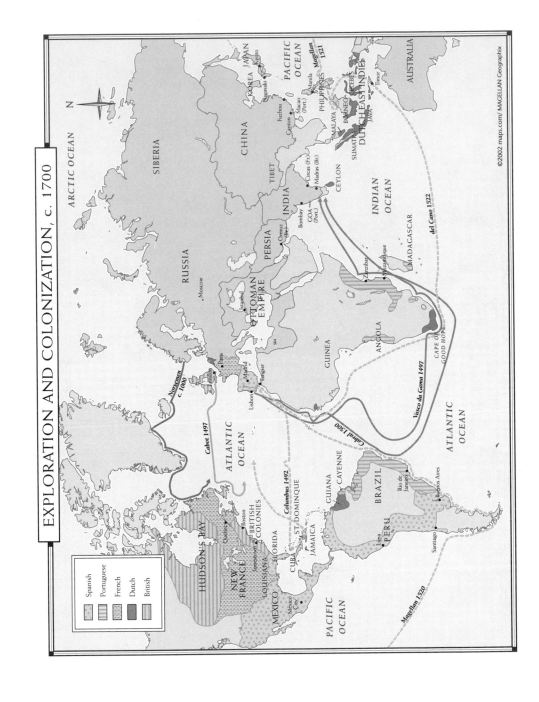

©2002 maps.com/ MAGELLAN Geographix

THE OTTOMAN EMPIRE, 1300–1924

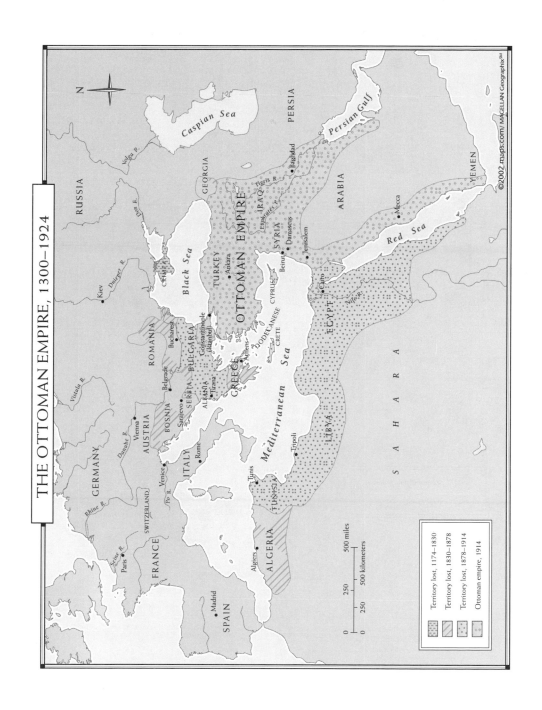

©2002 maps.com/ MAGELLAN Geographix℠

RUSSIA

Caspian Sea

PERSIA

Persian Gulf

Volga R.

GEORGIA

Baghdad

YEMEN

Don R.

Tigris R.

OTTOMAN EMPIRE

IRAQ

ARABIA

Kiev

Dnieper R.

Black Sea

TURKEY

Ankara

Euphrates R.

SYRIA

Mecca

Red Sea

CRIMEA

Damascus

Vistula R.

ROMANIA

Bucharest

Constantinople
(Istanbul)

BULGARIA

CYPRUS

Beirut

Jerusalem

Cairo

EGYPT

Belgrade

DODECANESE

Nile R.

Athens

Rhine R.

Danube R.

Vienna

AUSTRIA

SERBIA

ALBANIA

Tirana

Sarajevo

BOSNIA

GREECE

CRETE

Mediterranean
Sea

S A H A R A

GERMANY

Po R.

Venice

ITALY

Rome

LIBYA

Tripoli

SWITZERLAND

Seine R.

FRANCE

Paris

Tunis

TUNISIA

Madrid

SPAIN

Algiers

ALGERIA

500 miles

500 kilometers

250

250

0

0

Territory lost, 1174–1830

Territory lost, 1830–1878

Territory lost, 1878–1914

Ottoman empire, 1914

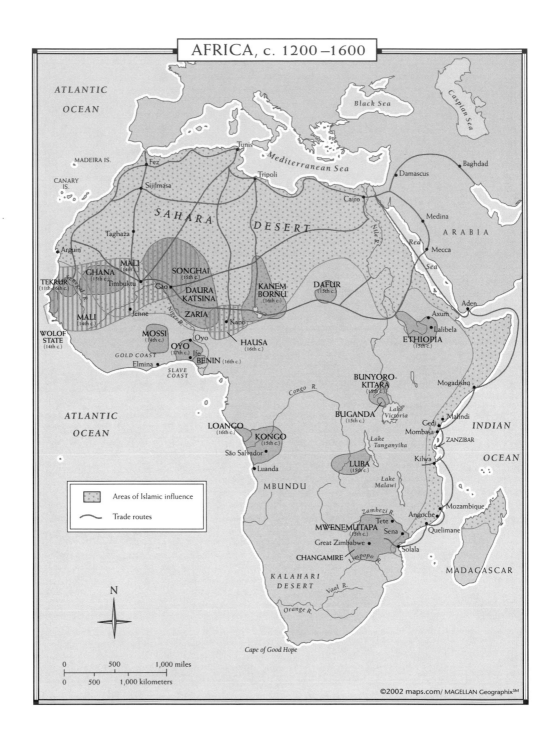

AFRICA, c. 1200–1600

ATLANTIC OCEAN

ATLANTIC OCEAN

Black Sea

Caspian Sea

Mediterranean Sea

MADEIRA IS.

CANARY IS.

Fez

Tunis

Tripoli

Sijilmasa

Baghdad

Damascus

Cairo

Medina

ARABIA

Mecca

Red Sea

S A H A R A   D E S E R T

Taghaza

Arguin

GHANA (13th c.)

MALI (14th c.)

Timbuktu

SONGHAI (15th c.)

Gao

DAURA KATSINA

KANEM BORNU (16th c.)

DAFUR (15th c.)

Nile R.

Aden

Axum

TEKRUR (11th-16th c.)

MALI (14th c.)

Jenne

Niger R.

ZARIA

Kano

Lalibela

ETHIOPIA (15th c.)

WOLOF STATE (14th c.)

MOSSI (14th c.)

Oyo

HAUSA (16th c.)

OYO (17th c.)

Ife

BENIN (16th c.)

Elmina

GOLD COAST

SLAVE COAST

Mogadishu

BUNYORO-KITARA (15th c.)

BUGANDA (15th c.)

Congo R.

Lake Victoria

Gedi

Malindi

Mombasa

ZANZIBAR

INDIAN OCEAN

LOANGO (16th c.)

KONGO (15th c.)

São Salvador

Luanda

Lake Tanganyika

LUBA (15th c.)

Kilwa

MBUNDU

Lake Malawi

Mozambique

Angoche

Quelimane

MADAGASCAR

Zambezi R.

Tete

MWENEMUTAPA (15th c.)

Sena

Solala

CHANGAMIRE

Great Zimbabwe

Limpopo R.

KALAHARI DESERT

Vaal R.

Orange R.

Cape of Good Hope

Areas of Islamic influence

Trade routes

N

| 0 | 500 | 1,000 miles |
| 0 | 500 | 1,000 kilometers |

©2002 maps.com/ MAGELLAN Geographix℠

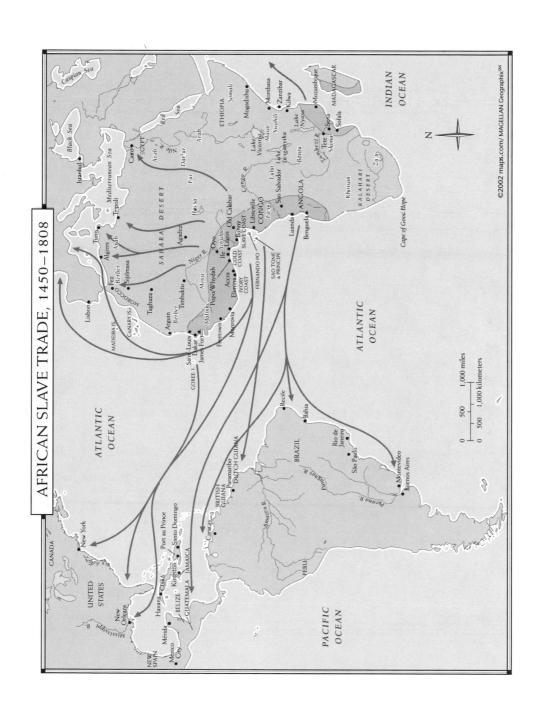

AFRICAN SLAVE TRADE, 1450–1808

Caspian Sea

Black Sea

Istanbul

Mediterranean Sea

Tripoli

Tunis

Algiers

Fez

MOROCCO

Sijilmasa

Berber

Taghaza

SAHARA DESERT

Agadez

Hausa

Arguin

Berber

Timbuktu

Mossi

Malinke

Niger R.

Oyo

Ife

Lagos

GOLD COAST

Popo Whydah

Accra

Elmina

IVORY COAST

Monrovia

Freetown

James Fort

Dakar

Saint-Louis

COREE I.

Lisbon

MADEIRA IS.

CANARY ISS.

Red Sea

EGYPT

Cairo

Nile R.

Arab

Darfur

Fur

Arab

ETHIOPIA

Mogadishu

Somali

Mombasa

Zanzibar

Kilwa

MADAGASCAR

Mozambique

Sofala

Tete

Sena

Shona

Zambezi R.

Lake Nyasa

Lake Tanganyika

Lake Victoria

Masai

Bantu

Swahili

Congo R.

Luba

Lunda

São Salvador

KONGO

Libreville

Old Calabar

Bonny

SLAVE COAST

Yoruba

FERNANDO PO

SÃO TOMÉ & PRÍNCIPE

Luanda

Benguela

ANGOLA

Kwango R.

Khoisan

KALAHARI DESERT

Zulu

Cape of Good Hope

INDIAN OCEAN

ATLANTIC OCEAN

ATLANTIC OCEAN

PACIFIC OCEAN

CANADA

UNITED STATES

New York

New Orleans

Mississippi R.

NEW SPAIN

Mexico City

Merida

BELIZE

GUATEMALA

Havana

CUBA

Kingston

JAMAICA

Santo Domingo

Port au Prince

Caracas

PERU

Amazon R.

BRAZIL

Recife

Bahia

Rio de Janeiro

São Paulo

Montevideo

Buenos Aires

Paraná R.

Paraguay R.

BRITISH GUIANA

DUTCH GUIANA

Paramaribo

N

0   500   1,000 miles
0   500   1,000 kilometers

©2002 maps.com/ MAGELLAN Geographix℠

THE GROWTH OF RUSSIA, 1598–1796

	Russia in 1584
	Acquisitions, 1584–1700
	Acquisitions, 1700–1772 (Primarily Peter the Great)
	Acquisitions, 1772–1796 (Catherine the Great)

0   300   600 miles
0   300   600 kilometers

FINLAND

Archangel

Ural Mountains

Baltic Sea

St. Petersburg

Pskov

Riga

Moscow

Kazan

Smolensk

Vistula River

Minsk

Warsaw

Volga River

Don River

Kiev

Dnieper R.

Odessa

Danube River

Asov

Astrakhan

Caspian Sea

Sevastopol

Black Sea

Caucasus Mts.

N

©2002 maps.com/ MAGELLAN Geographix℠

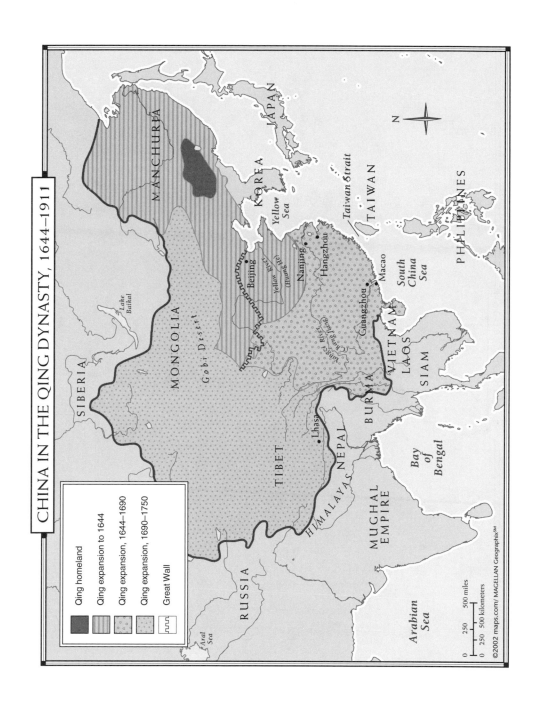

CHINA IN THE QING DYNASTY, 1644–1911

Legend:
- Qing homeland
- Qing expansion to 1644
- Qing expansion, 1644–1690
- Qing expansion, 1690–1750
- Great Wall

Aral Sea

RUSSIA

SIBERIA

Lake Baikal

MONGOLIA

Gobi Desert

MANCHURIA

KOREA

JAPAN

Yellow Sea

Beijing

Yellow River (Huang He)

Nanjing

Hangzhou

Yangzi River

Taiwan Strait

TAIWAN

Macao

Guangzhou

South China Sea

PHILIPPINES

VIETNAM

LAOS

SIAM

BURMA

Xi Jiang

TIBET

Lhasa

NEPAL

HIMALAYAS

MUGHAL EMPIRE

Bay of Bengal

Arabian Sea

N

0   250   500 miles
0 250 500 kilometers

©2002 maps.com/ MAGELLAN Geographix℠

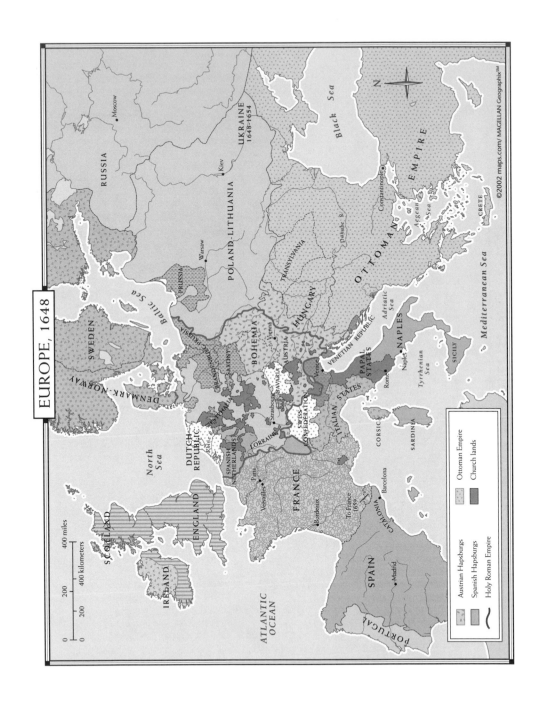

EUROPE, 1648

N

©2002 maps.com/ MAGELLAN Geographix℠

SWEDEN

DENMARK-NORWAY

North
Sea

Baltic Sea

RUSSIA

Moscow

POLAND-LITHUANIA

UKRAINE
1648-1654

Kiev

Warsaw

PRUSSIA

SCOTLAND

IRELAND

ENGLAND

ATLANTIC
OCEAN

DUTCH
REPUBLIC

SPANISH
NETHERLANDS

WESTPHALIA

BRANDENBURG-PRUSSIA

SAXONY

BOHEMIA

Vienna

AUSTRIA

HUNGARY

TRANSYLVANIA

Danube R.

Black Sea

Constantinople

OTTOMAN EMPIRE

Aegean
Sea

Mediterranean Sea

CRETE

Rhine R.

LORRAINE

Strasbourg

SWISS
CONFEDERATION

BAVARIA

ITALIAN STATES

VENETIAN REPUBLIC

Venice

Adriatic
Sea

PAPAL
STATES

Rome

NAPLES

Naples

Tyrrhenian
Sea

SICILY

CORSICA

SARDINIA

FRANCE

Paris

Versailles

Bordeaux

To France
1659

CATALONIA

Barcelona

SPAIN

Madrid

PORTUGAL

0   200   400 miles

0   200   400 kilometers

Austrian Hapsburgs

Spanish Hapsburgs

Holy Roman Empire

Ottoman Empire

Church lands

THE FRENCH AND INDIAN WAR, 1754–1763

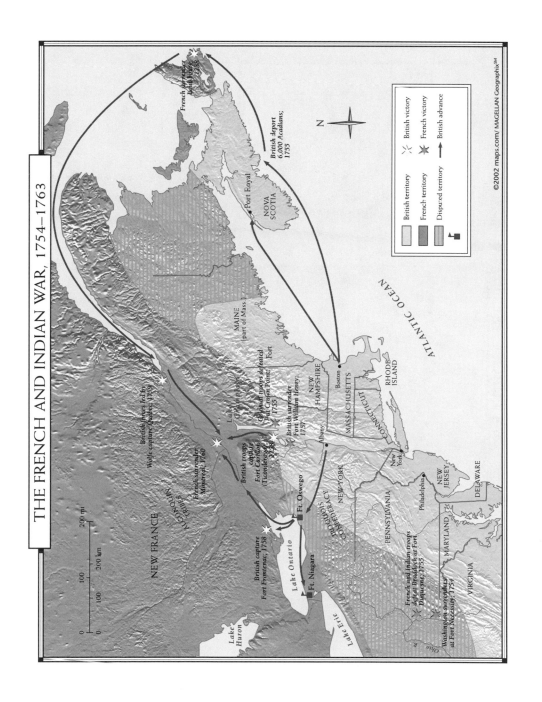

NEW FRANCE

ALGONQUIN ALLIES

Lake Huron

Lake Erie

Lake Ontario

Ft. Niagara

Ft. Oswego

British capture Fort Frontenac, 1758

French and Indian troops defeat Braddock at Fort Duquesne, 1755

Washington surrenders at Fort Necessity, 1754

Ohio R.

VIRGINIA

MARYLAND

DELAWARE

PENNSYLVANIA

NEW JERSEY

Philadelphia

NEW YORK

IROQUOIS CONFEDERACY

New York

Albany

CONNECTICUT

RHODE ISLAND

MASSACHUSETTS

NEW HAMPSHIRE

Boston

MAINE (part of Mass.)

ATLANTIC OCEAN

British troops capture Fort Carillon (Ticonderoga), 1758

British troops defeated at Crown Point, 1755

British surrender Fort William Henry, 1757

British forces led by Wolfe capture Quebec, 1759

French surrender Montreal, 1760

French surrender Louisburg, 1758

British deport 6,000 Acadians; 1755

NOVA SCOTIA

Port Royal

N

British territory
French territory
Disputed territory

British victory
French victory
British advance

Fort

200 mi
200 km
0   100   200
0   100

©2002 maps.com/ MAGELLAN Geographix℠

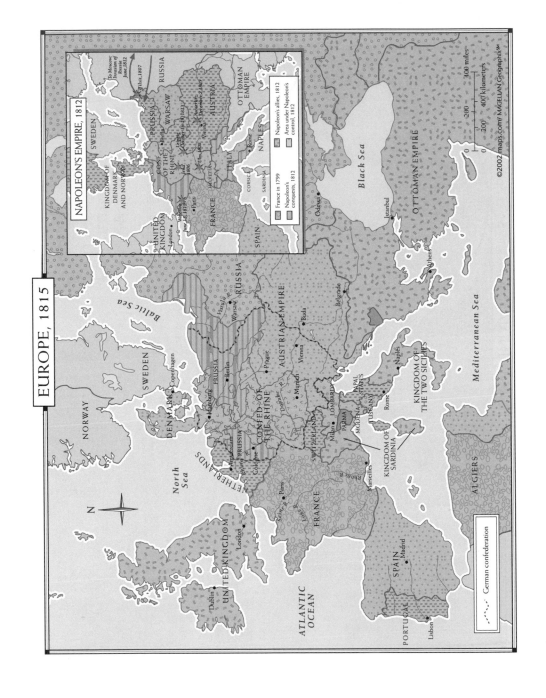

EUROPE, 1815

NAPOLEON'S EMPIRE, 1812

France in 1799
Napoleon's conquests, 1812
Napoleon's allies, 1812
Area under Napoleon's control, 1812

German confederation

©2002 maps.com/ MAGELLAN Geographix℠

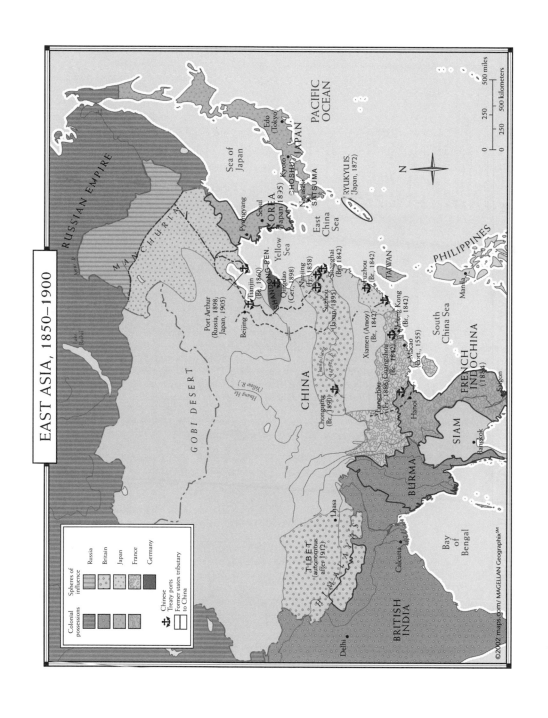

EAST ASIA, 1850–1900

Colonial possessions

Spheres of influence
- Russia
- Britain
- Japan
- France
- Germany

⚓ Chinese Treaty ports

Former states tributary to China

RUSSIAN EMPIRE

MANCHURIA

GOBI DESERT

CHINA

TIBET (autonomous after 1912)

HIMALAYAS

Huang He (Yellow R.)

Lake Baikal

Amur R.

BRITISH INDIA

Delhi

Calcutta

Bay of Bengal

BURMA

SIAM

Bangkok

FRENCH INDOCHINA (1884)

Saigon

Hanoi

Lhasa

Chongqing (Br., 1890)

Yangzi (Chang) R.

Guangzhou (Fr., 1886)

Xiamen (Amoy) (Br., 1842)

Macao (Port., 1555)

Hong Kong (Br., 1842)

Guangzhou (Br., 1842)

South China Sea

PHILIPPINES

Manila

TAIWAN

Fuzhou (Br., 1842)

Shanghai (Br., 1842)

Suzhou (Japan, 1895)

Nanjing (Br., 1858)

Qingdao (Ger., 1898)

SHANDONG PEN.

Tianjin (Br., 1860)

Beijing

Port Arthur (Russia, 1898; Japan, 1905)

Yellow Sea

East China Sea

RYUKYU IS. (Japan, 1872)

Pyongyang

Seoul

KOREA (Japan, 1895)

Sea of Japan

CHOSHU

SATSUMA

Nagasaki

Kyoto

Edo (Tokyo)

JAPAN

PACIFIC OCEAN

N

500 miles

500 kilometers

0   250   500

©2002 maps.com/ MAGELLAN Geographix℠

U.S. INTERVENTION IN LATIN AMERICA, 1895–1940s

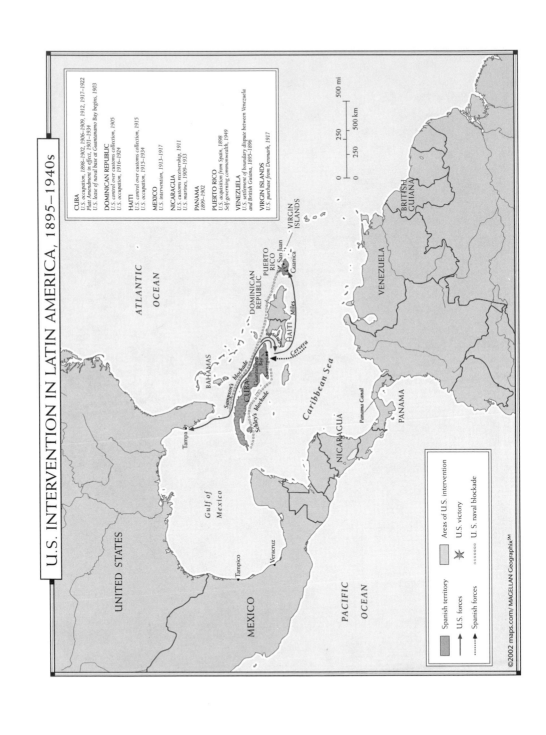

CUBA
U.S. occupation, 1898–1902, 1906–1909, 1912, 1917–1922
Platt Amendment in effect, 1901–1934
U.S. lease of naval base at Guantánamo Bay begins, 1903

DOMINICAN REPUBLIC
U.S. control over customs collection, 1905
U.S. occupation, 1916–1924

HAITI
U.S. control over customs collection, 1915
U.S. occupation, 1915–1934

MEXICO
U.S. intervention, 1913–1917

NICARAGUA
U.S. customs receivership, 1911
U.S. marines, 1909–1933

PANAMA
1899–1902

PUERTO RICO
U.S. acquisition from Spain, 1898
Self-governing commonwealth, 1949

VENEZUELA
U.S. settlement of boundary dispute between Venezuela and British Guiana, 1895–1896

VIRGIN ISLANDS
U.S. purchase from Denmark, 1917

Spanish territory

U.S. forces

Spanish forces

Areas of U.S. intervention

U.S. victory

U.S. naval blockade

©2002 maps.com/ MAGELLAN Geographix℠

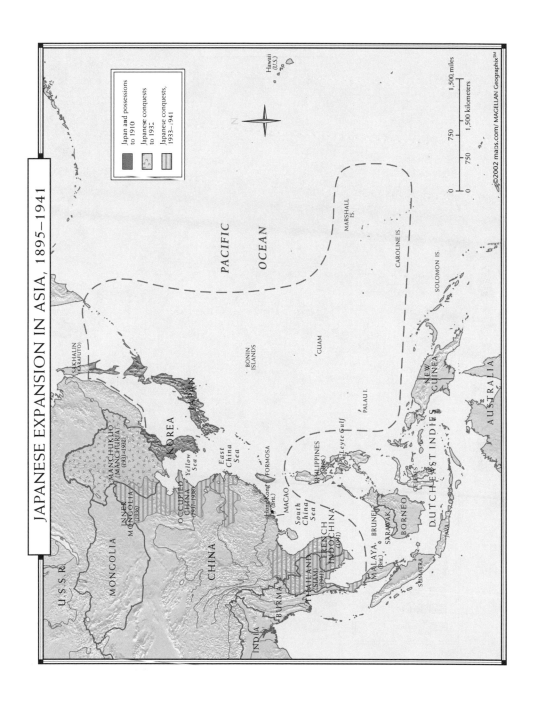

JAPANESE EXPANSION IN ASIA, 1895–1941

Japan and possessions to 1910

Japanese conquests to 1932

Japanese conquests, 1933–1941

U.S.S.R.

MONGOLIA

SAKHALIN
(KARAFUTO)

MANCHUKUO
(MANCHURIA)
(1931–1932)

INNER
MONGOLIA
(1936)

OCCUPIED
CHINA
(1937–1938)

CHINA

KOREA

JAPAN

Yellow
Sea

East
China
Sea

FORMOSA

BONIN
ISLANDS

PACIFIC
OCEAN

Hawaii
(U.S.)

MARSHALL
IS.

CAROLINE IS.

GUAM

PALAU I.

INDIA

BURMA

THAILAND
(SIAM)
(1941)

FRENCH
INDOCHINA
(1941)

Hong Kong
(Brit.)

MACAO

South
China
Sea

PHILIPPINES
(1942)

Leyte Gulf

MALAYA
(Brit.)

BRUNEI

SARAWAK

BORNEO

SUMATRA

JAVA

CELEBES

DUTCH EAST INDIES

NEW
GUINEA

SOLOMON IS.

AUSTRALIA

N

0   750   1,500 miles

0   750   1,500 kilometers

©2002 maps.com/ MAGELLAN Geographix℠

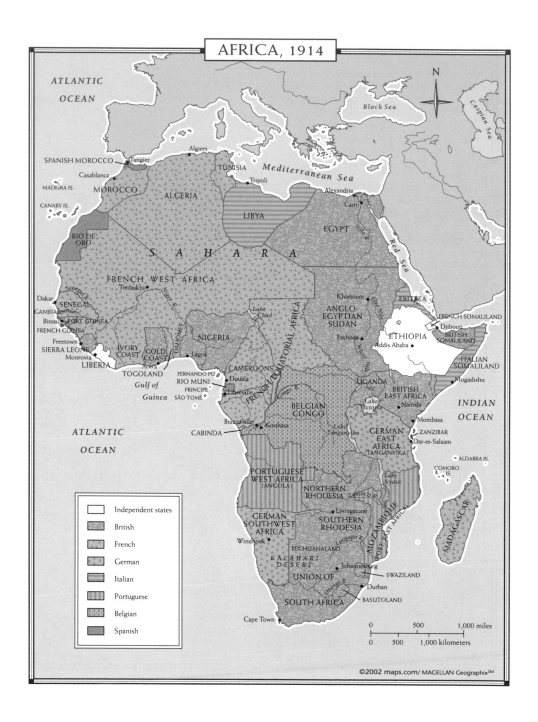

AFRICA, 1914

N

ATLANTIC OCEAN

Black Sea

Caspian Sea

Mediterranean Sea

SPANISH MOROCCO • Tangier
TUNISIA
Casablanca • Algiers
MADEIRA IS.
MOROCCO
ALGERIA
Tripoli
LIBYA
Alexandria
Cairo
EGYPT

CANARY IS.

RIO DE ORO

S A H A R A

Nile R.

Red Sea

FRENCH WEST AFRICA
Timbuktu
Senegal R.
Dakar • SENEGAL
GAMBIA
Bissau • PORT. GUINEA
FRENCH GUINEA
Freetown
SIERRA LEONE
Monrovia
LIBERIA
IVORY COAST
GOLD COAST
Accra
TOGOLAND
Gulf of Guinea
FERNANDO PO
RIO MUNI
PRINCIPE
SÃO TOMÉ

Niger R.
Lake Chad
NIGERIA
Lagos
DAHOMEY
CAMEROONS
Douala
Libreville

Khartoum
Blue Nile
ERITREA
ANGLO-EGYPTIAN SUDAN
FRENCH SOMALILAND
Djibouti
BRITISH SOMALILAND
ETHIOPIA
Addis Ababa
Fashoda
White Nile
ITALIAN SOMALILAND
Mogadishu

FRENCH EQUATORIAL AFRICA

Congo R.
Brazzaville
Kinshasa
CABINDA
BELGIAN CONGO

UGANDA
BRITISH EAST AFRICA
Lake Victoria
Nairobi
Mombasa
ZANZIBAR
GERMAN EAST AFRICA (TANGANYIKA)
Dar-es-Salaam
Lake Tanganyika

INDIAN OCEAN

ATLANTIC OCEAN

ALDABRA IS.

COMORO IS.

PORTUGUESE WEST AFRICA (ANGOLA)
NORTHERN RHODESIA
Zambezi R.
Lake Nyasa
MOZAMBIQUE
PORT. EAST AFRICA

GERMAN SOUTHWEST AFRICA
Windhoek
SOUTHERN RHODESIA
Livingstone

MADAGASCAR

BECHUANALAND
KALAHARI DESERT
Limpopo R.
Johannesburg
SWAZILAND
Durban
Orange R.
UNION OF SOUTH AFRICA
BASUTOLAND
Cape Town

Legend	
	Independent states
	British
	French
	German
	Italian
	Portuguese
	Belgian
	Spanish

0   500   1,000 miles
0   500   1,000 kilometers

©2002 maps.com/ MAGELLAN Geographix℠

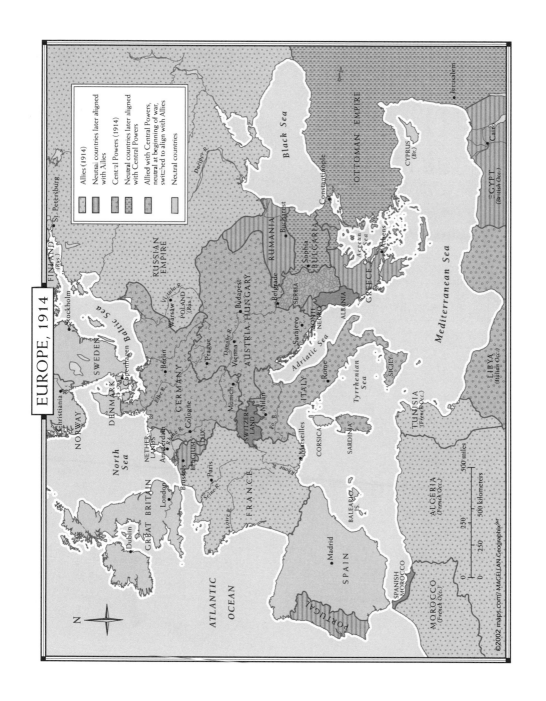

EUROPE, 1914

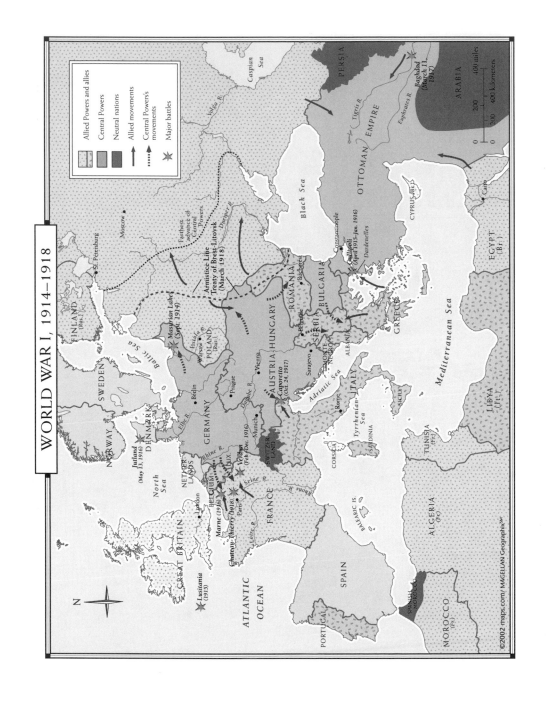

WORLD WAR I, 1914–1918

Allied Powers and allies
Central Powers
Neutral nations
Allied movements
Central Powers's movements
Major battles

St. Petersburg

Moscow

FINLAND (Rus.)

SWEDEN

NORWAY

Caspian Sea

Volga R.

Farthest advance of Central Powers

Armistice Line Treaty of Brest-Litovsk (March 1918)

Dnieper R.

Baltic Sea

Masurian Lakes (Sept. 1914)

Vistula R.

Warsaw

POLAND (Rus.)

DENMARK

Jutland (May 13, 1916)

North Sea

NETHER-LANDS

Berlin

Elbe R.

GERMANY

Prague

Danube R.

Vienna

AUSTRIA-HUNGARY

Caporetto (Oct. 24, 1917)

GREAT BRITAIN

London

Lusitania (1915)

ATLANTIC OCEAN

BELGIUM

LUX.

Rhine R.

Munich

SWITZER-LAND

Verdun (Feb.–Dec. 1916)

Marne (1916)

Chateau-Thierry (1918)

Paris

Seine R.

FRANCE

Loire R.

Rhone R.

ITALY

Rome

Tyrrhenian Sea

SARDINIA

CORSICA

BALEARIC IS.

SPAIN

PORTUGAL

MOROCCO (Fr.)

SPANISH MOROCCO

ALGERIA (Fr.)

TUNISIA (Fr.)

LIBYA (It.)

Mediterranean Sea

SICILY

Adriatic Sea

Sarajevo

MONTE-NEGRO

ALBANIA

SERBIA

Belgrade

Bucharest

ROMANIA

BULGARIA

GREECE

Constantinople

Gallipoli (April 1915–Jan. 1916)

Dardanelles

Black Sea

OTTOMAN EMPIRE

Tigris R.

PERSIA

Euphrates R.

Baghdad (March 11, 1917)

ARABIA

CYPRUS (Br.)

EGYPT (Br.)

Cairo

400 miles

400 kilometers

200

0

©2002 maps.com/ MAGELLAN Geographix℠

EUROPE BETWEEN THE WARS, 1918–1939

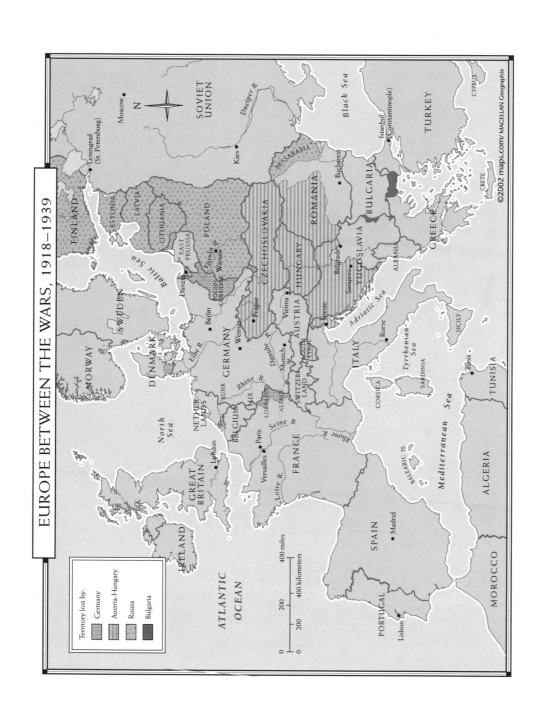

Territory lost by:
Germany
Austria-Hungary
Russia
Bulgaria

SOVIET UNION

Moscow

Leningrad (St. Petersburg)

FINLAND

ESTONIA

LATVIA

LITHUANIA

EAST PRUSSIA

POLAND

Vistula

Warsaw

POLISH CORRIDOR

Danzig

Dnieper R.

Kiev

BESSARABIA

Bucharest

ROMANIA

BULGARIA

Black Sea

Istanbul (Constantinople)

TURKEY

CYPRUS

CRETE

GREECE

ALBANIA

YUGOSLAVIA

Belgrade

Sarajevo

Adriatic Sea

Trieste

HUNGARY

AUSTRIA

Vienna

SOUTH TYROL

CZECHOSLOVAKIA

Prague

Weimar

Berlin

GERMANY

Elbe R.

Munich

Danube R.

SWITZERLAND

RUHR

Rhine R.

LUX.

LORRAINE

ALSACE

BELGIUM

NETHERLANDS

DENMARK

SWEDEN

NORWAY

Baltic Sea

North Sea

IRELAND

GREAT BRITAIN

London

ATLANTIC OCEAN

FRANCE

Paris

Versailles

Seine R.

Loire R.

Rhône R.

ITALY

Rome

CORSICA

SARDINIA

Tyrrhenian Sea

SICILY

Mediterranean Sea

BALEARIC IS.

SPAIN

Madrid

PORTUGAL

Lisbon

MOROCCO

ALGERIA

TUNISIA

Tunis

N

©2002 maps.com/ MAGELLAN Geographix

400 miles
400 kilometers
0   200   400
0   200   400

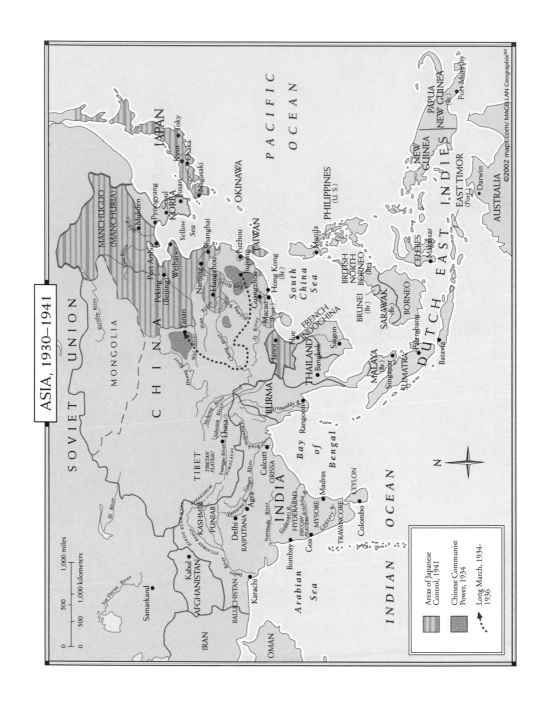

ASIA, 1930–1941

SOVIET UNION

MONGOLIA

MANCHUGUO (MANCHURIA)

CHINA

Mukden
Port Arthur
Peking (Beijing)
Weihaiwei
Yan'an
Nanjing
Shanghai
Hangzhou
Fuzhou
Jiujiang
Guangzhou
Macao (Port.)
Hong Kong (Br.)

Amur River
Keelon River
Ili River
Yellow River
Huang He
Wei River
Yangtze River
Han River
Yalu River
Min River
Xi River

JAPAN
Tokyo
Kyoto
Osaka
Nagasaki

KOREA
Pyongyang
Seoul
Busan

Yellow Sea

OKINAWA

TAIWAN

South China Sea

PACIFIC OCEAN

PHILIPPINES (U.S.)

Manila

BRITISH NORTH BORNEO (Br.)

BRUNEI (Br.)

SARAWAK (Br.)

BORNEO

CELEBES

Makassar

NEW GUINEA

PAPUA NEW GUINEA

Port Moresby (Br.)

DUTCH EAST INDIES

EAST TIMOR (Port.)

Darwin

AUSTRALIA

©2002 maps.com/ MAGELLAN Geographix℠

FRENCH INDOCHINA
Hanoi
Hue
Saigon

THAILAND
Bangkok

MALAYA (Br.)
Singapore

SUMATRA

Palembang

Batavia

BURMA
Rangoon

Irrawaddy R.
Mekong River
Salween River

TIBET
Lhasa
TIBETAN PLATEAU

Tsangpo River
HIMALAYA
KARAKORUM
HINDU KUSH RANGE

KASHMIR
PUNJAB
Delhi
RAJPUTANA
Agra

INDIA
ORISSA
Calcutta
HYDERABAD
DECCAN PLATEAU
Bombay
Goa
Madras
MYSORE
Krishna R.
Cauvery R.
TRAVANCORE
Colombo
CEYLON

Bay of Bengal

Narmada River
Godavari R.
Krishna R.
Yamuna R.
Ganges River
Sutlej River

AFGHANISTAN
Kabul

BALUCHISTAN
Karachi

IRAN

OMAN

Arabian Sea

INDIAN OCEAN

Samarkand

Syr Darya River

Indus River
SULAIMAN RANGE

N

500   1,000 miles
0
0   500   1,000 kilometers

Areas of Japanese Control, 1941

Chinese Communist Power, 1934

Long March, 1934–1936

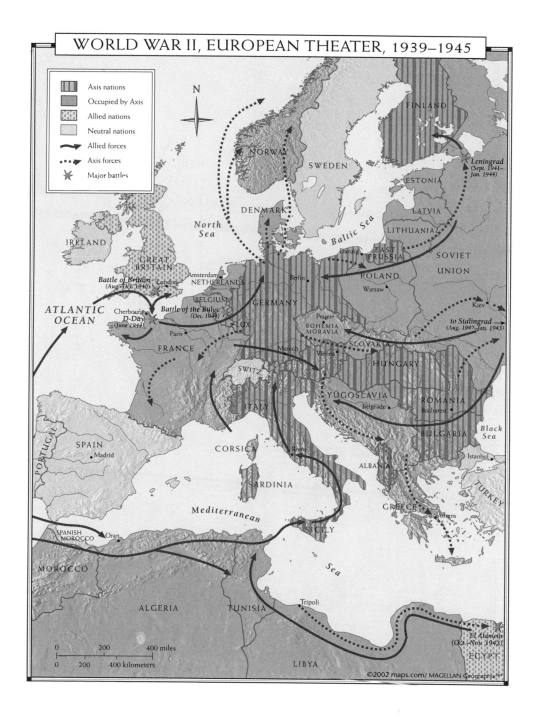

WORLD WAR II, EUROPEAN THEATER, 1939–1945

N

Legend:
- Axis nations
- Occupied by Axis
- Allied nations
- Neutral nations
- Allied forces
- Axis forces
- Major battles

IRELAND

GREAT BRITAIN

Battle of Britain (Aug.–Oct. 1940)
London

Amsterdam
NETHERLANDS

BELGIUM

LUX

Battle of the Bulge (Dec. 1944)

Cherbourg
D-Day *(June 1944)*

Paris

FRANCE

ATLANTIC OCEAN

NORWAY

SWEDEN

North Sea

DENMARK

Baltic Sea

Berlin

GERMANY

Munich

SWITZ

ITALY

CORSICA

Rome

SARDINIA

Mediterranean

SICILY

Sea

FINLAND

Leningrad (Sept. 1941–Jan. 1944)

ESTONIA

LATVIA

LITHUANIA

Danzig

EAST PRUSSIA

POLAND

Warsaw

Prague
BOHEMIA MORAVIA

Vienna

SLOVAKIA

HUNGARY

YUGOSLAVIA

Belgrade

ALBANIA

GREECE

Athens

SOVIET UNION

Kiev

to Stalingrad (Aug. 1942–Jan. 1943)

ROMANIA

Bucharest

BULGARIA

Black Sea

Istanbul

TURKEY

PORTUGAL

SPAIN

Madrid

SPANISH MOROCCO
Oran

MOROCCO

ALGERIA

TUNISIA

Tripoli

LIBYA

El Alamein (Oct.–Nov. 1942)

EGYPT

| 0 | 200 | 400 miles |
| 0 | 200 | 400 kilometers |

©2002 maps.com/ MAGELLAN Geographix℠

WORLD WAR II, PACIFIC THEATER, 1941–1945

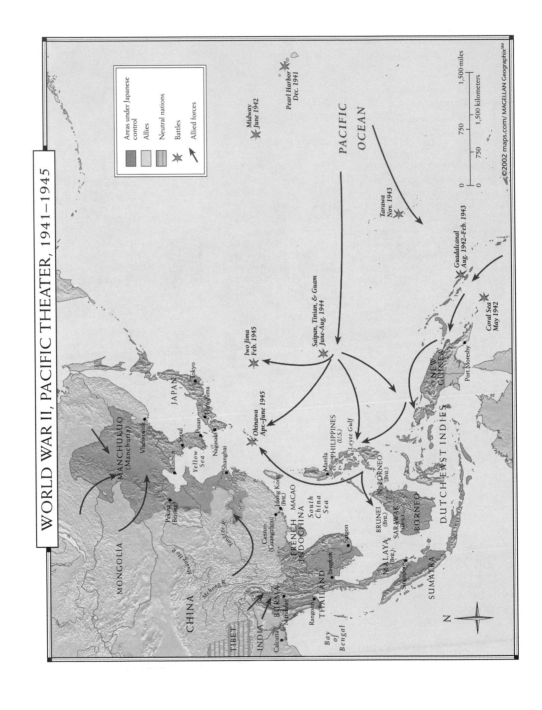

Areas under Japanese control

Allies

Neutral nations

Battles

Allied forces

Pearl Harbor
Dec. 1941

Midway
June 1942

PACIFIC
OCEAN

Tarawa
Nov. 1943

Guadalcanal
Aug. 1942–Feb. 1943

Coral Sea
May 1942

0   750   1,500 miles
0   750   1,500 kilometers

©2002 maps.com/ MAGELLAN Geographix℠

Iwo Jima
Feb. 1945

Saipan, Tinian, & Guam
June–Aug. 1944

Okinawa
Apr.–June 1945

Tokyo

JAPAN

Kagoshima

Seoul
Pusan

Dairen

Vladivostok

Nagasaki

Yellow
Sea

Shanghai

MANCHUKUO
(Manchuria)

MONGOLIA

Peking
(Beijing)

Canton
(Guangzhou)

Hong Kong
(Brit.)

MACAO

South
China
Sea

PHILIPPINES
(U.S.)

Manila

Leyte Gulf

NEW
GUINEA

Port Moresby

BORNEO
(Brit.)

BRUNEI
(Brit.)

SARAWAK
(Brit.)

BORNEO

DUTCH EAST INDIES

SUMATRA

MALAYA
(Brit.)

Singapore

THAILAND

Bangkok

Saigon

FRENCH
INDOCHINA

CHINA

Yangtze R.

Mekong R.

Huang He R.

TIBET

INDIA

Calcutta

BURMA

Mandalay

Rangoon

Bay
of
Bengal

N

INDEPENDENT STATES TO 1991

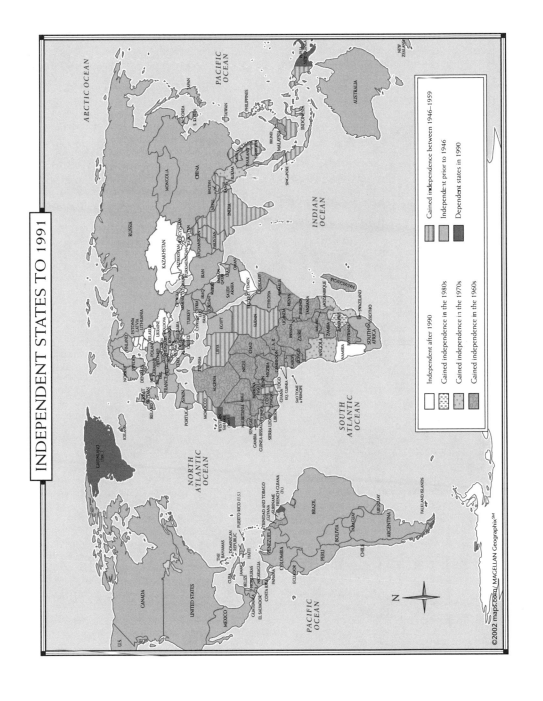

©2002 maps.com/ MAGELLAN Geographix℠

Legend:

- Independent after 1990
- Gained independence in the 1980s
- Gained independence in the 1970s
- Gained independence in the 1960s
- Gained independence between 1946–1959
- Independent prior to 1946
- Dependent states in 1990

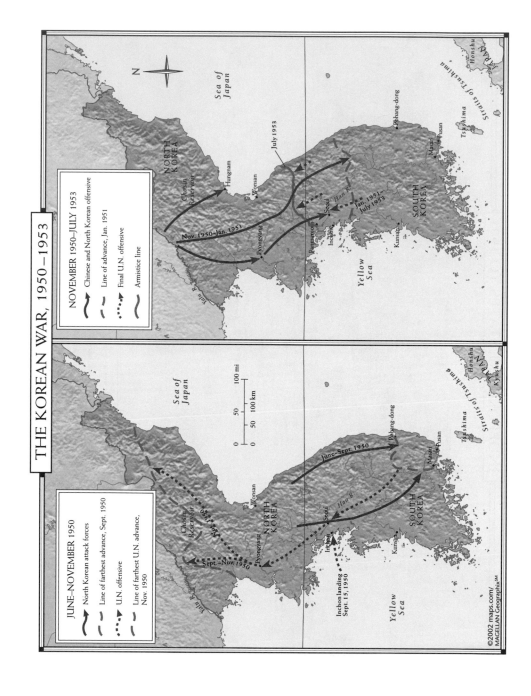

THE KOREAN WAR, 1950–1953

JUNE–NOVEMBER 1950

→ North Korean attack forces
⤳ Line of farthest advance, Sept. 1950
⋯→ U.N. offensive
⤏ Line of farthest U.N. advance, Nov. 1950

NOVEMBER 1950–JULY 1953

→ Chinese and North Korean offensive
⤳ Line of advance, Jan. 1951
⋯→ Final U.N. offensive
⤏ Armistice line

©2002 maps.com/
MAGELLAN Geographix℠

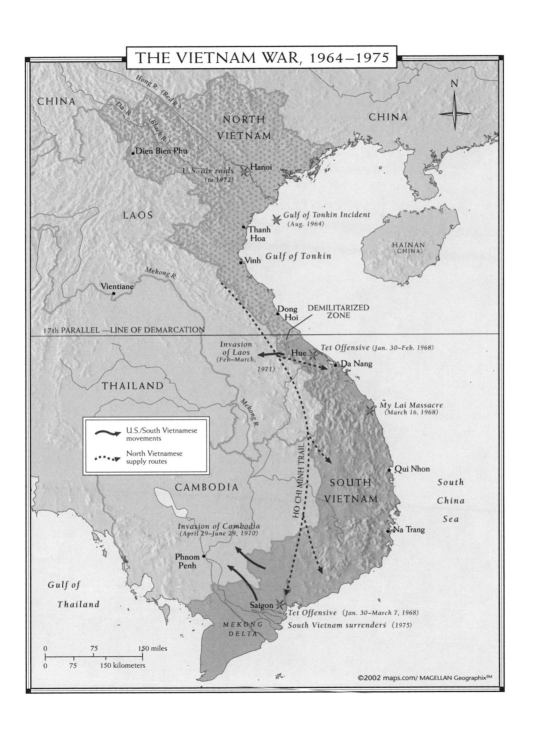

THE VIETNAM WAR, 1964–1975

CHINA

Hong R. (Red R.)

Da R.

Black R.

NORTH VIETNAM

CHINA

N

•Dien Bien Phu

U.S. air raids (to 1972) ✳ •Hanoi

LAOS

✳ *Gulf of Tonkin Incident (Aug. 1964)*

•Thanh Hoa

HAINAN (CHINA)

•Vinh *Gulf of Tonkin*

Mekong R.

•Vientiane

•Dong Hoi **DEMILITARIZED ZONE**

17th PARALLEL —LINE OF DEMARCATION

Invasion of Laos (Feb–March, 1971) •Hue ✗ *Tet Offensive (Jan. 30–Feb. 1968)*

•Da Nang

THAILAND

Mekong R.

✗ *My Lai Massacre (March 16, 1968)*

→ U.S./South Vietnamese movements

⇢ North Vietnamese supply routes

CAMBODIA

HO CHI MINH TRAIL

•Qui Nhon

SOUTH VIETNAM

South China Sea

Invasion of Cambodia (April 29–June 29, 1970)

•Na Trang

Phnom• Penh

Gulf of Thailand

Saigon• ✗ *Tet Offensive (Jan. 30–March 7, 1968)*

MEKONG DELTA *South Vietnam surrenders (1975)*

0   75   150 miles

0   75   150 kilometers

©2002 maps.com/ MAGELLAN Geographix℠

COLD WAR EUROPE, 1946–1990

N

NATO Alliance
Warsaw Pact Nations

ICELAND

ATLANTIC
OCEAN

North
Sea

IRELAND
Dublin

UNITED
KINGDOM

London

NETHERLANDS
Amsterdam

Rhine R.

Brussels

BELGIUM
Bonn

LUX.

WEST
GERMANY

Paris
Seine R.

Loire River

FRANCE

SWITZ.

Geneva

Munich

Po River

SPAIN
(Joined NATO in 1982)

Lisbon
Madrid

PORTUGAL

ALGERIA

NORWAY
Oslo

SWEDEN
Stockholm

DENMARK
Copenhagen

Elbe River

Berlin

EAST
GERMANY

Prague

CZECHOSLOVAKIA

Danube River

Bratislava

Vienna

AUSTRIA

Budapest

HUNGARY

Belgrade

YUGOSLAVIA
Sarajevo

Tiber R.

Rome

ITALY

ALBANIA
(Withdrew from
Warsaw Pact in 1968)

Tirana

Mediterranean Sea

FINLAND

Helsinki

Leningrad

Riga

Vilnius

Minsk

SOVIET UNION

Vistula R.

Warsaw

POLAND

Kiev

Kishinev

ROMANIA

Bucharest

BULGARIA
Sofia

Skopje

Istanbul

TURKEY

GREECE

Athens

0   200   400 miles
0   200   400 kilometers

©2002 maps.com/ MAGELLAN Geographix℠

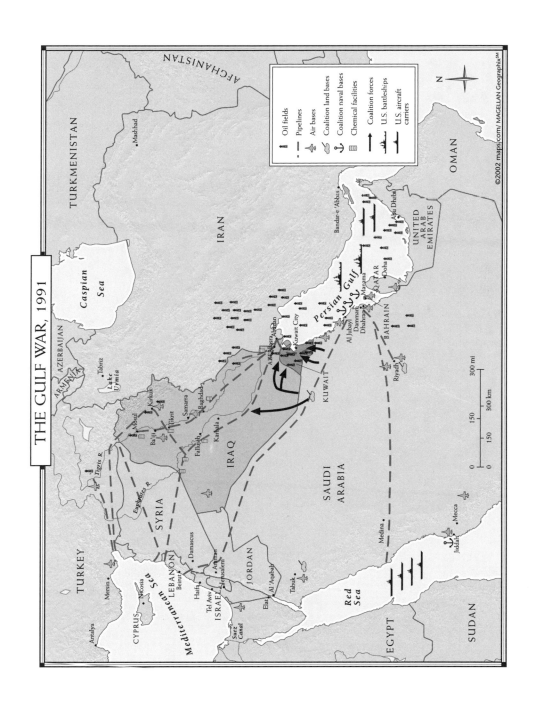

THE GULF WAR, 1991

©2002 maps.com/ MAGELLAN Geographix℠

Legend:
- Oil fields
- Pipelines
- Air bases
- Coalition land bases
- Coalition naval bases
- Chemical facilities
- Coalition forces
- U.S. battleships
- U.S. aircraft carriers

SA. *See Sturmabteilung.*

Saar. A coal-rich valley in western Germany. It was administered by the *League of Nations* as a *condominium*, 1919–1935, when France controlled extraction of its coal resources as *reparations*-in-kind for French mines which the *Reichswehr* flooded while retreating in 1918. It was returned to Germany in 1935 following a *plebiscite* in which 90 percent voted in favor of union—making the Saar the only legal acquisition of territory in *Hitler*'s career. That was achieved through pressure from the *Catholic* clergy, and in good measure also through *Nazi* intimidation and an effective rumor that the Nazis had a way to know how individuals voted. After *World War II* France reoccupied the Saar. It was returned to *West Germany* in 1957.

Sabah. The northernmost part of the island of Borneo (formerly British North Borneo), ruled by a British trading company for most of the nineteenth century and nearly half of the twentieth. With *Sarawak*, it joined Malaysia in 1963. For decades, the Philippines maintained a dormant claim to this territory.

saber-rattling. Explicitly threatening to use *force* to decide a *dispute*, or displaying one's capability for using force (say, by full-scale *maneuvers* near the *frontier*, or by *incursion*) as an implicit threat. *See also gunboat diplomacy; show of force; show the flag.*

sabotage. The destruction of economic or military *infrastructure*. This may occur during an industrial strike, but the term applies especially to damage done by enemy agents or *fifth columnists* to machinery or infrastructure during wartime. Sabotage (of power plants, communications facilities, and so forth) is thus one of the main *tactics* of *guerrillas* or *partisans* in warfare. It may also be the object of *covert action*. It derives from "sabot," which were shoes made from hollowed-out wooden blocks worn by French peasants and early industrial workers. They were sometimes thrown into machinery to wreck its workings, hence "sabotage." *See also Luddism.*

SAC. *See Strategic Air Command.*

sack. When an invading or occupying army is let loose to *plunder* a town, usually employing mass *rape* and killing of civilians. The practice was a common feature of warfare in the era of *mercenary* armies, where such rapine and plunder was held out as a reward for victory. *See also Gulf War; Nanjing; pillage; requisition; retreat from Moscow; Tamerlane.*

Sadat, Muhammad Anwar el- (1918–1981). Egyptian statesman. Vice president, 1969–1970; prime minister, 1973–1974; president, 1970–1981. As a young nationalist, during *World War II* he supported *Nazi Germany* against the British. In 1952 he participated in the *coup* that overthrew King *Faruk.* He was a loyal lieutenant during the long period of *Nasser's* rule in Egypt. Succeeding Nasser, he made major changes in Egyptian foreign policy. He began by breaking with Moscow and expelling 20,000 Soviet advisers. He also planned for the *Third Arab-Israeli War,* which he believed was necessary to break the diplomatic logjam in the Middle East flowing from the preponderant regional power Israel had achieved after 1967 by virtue of its spectacular victory over the Arab states in the *Second Arab-Israeli War.* Sadat's principal aim was to shake Israeli military and security confidence, smugness even, and thereby jump-start a negotiation which would return *Sinai* to Egypt. It worked: although the Israelis overcame their initial surprise and reverses to completely encircle an Egyptian army, when the fighting ended the talking at last began. Armored by a claim to at least partial victory, Sadat called for *peace* with Israel and agreed to fly to Tel Aviv to meet with Israeli leaders. Over time he completed a *reneversement des alliance* which moved Egypt into the American orbit. He then participated in talks at *Camp David* which led to a breakthrough *peace treaty* with Israel in 1979. Disregarding his earlier war making, the world properly honored him with a *Nobel Prize* for Peace. Remembering (and hating) his peacemaking, some of his countrymen plotted to kill him. In 1981 he was assassinated by *fundamentalists* of the *Muslim Brotherhood.* At Sadat's side, and almost killed by the gunfire himself, was the man who succeeded him as president, *Hosni Mubarak.*

Suggested Reading: R. W. Baker, *Egypt's Uncertain Revolutions Under Nasser and Sadat* (1979).

Sadowa, Battle of (July 3, 1866). *See Seven Weeks' War (1866).*

Safavid dynasty. *See Iran.*

safe conduct. A letter granting permission to pass through hostile territory in time of *war*, given to persons such as eminent civilians, *Red Cross* personnel, *neutrals*, *diplomats*, or enemy personnel protected by a *truce*.

safe haven. An area of *civilian* refuge in a *war zone*. Among recent examples, the United States, Britain, and France jointly declared and enforced safe havens for *Kurds* in northern Iraq and "marsh Arabs" (*shi'ites*) in southern Iraq in the aftermath of the *Gulf War*. The *United Nations* declared six safe havens in Bosnia in 1993. In 1994 *NATO* was called in to defend these from Bosnian Serb attack. Also that year, France unilaterally declared and established havens for civilians fleeing *genocide* in Rwanda. *See also DMZ; neutral zone.*

safe house. In *intelligence*, a (presumed) secret location where *cipher* and other *covert* activities can be carried out, or *agents* may hole up or be *debriefed*, confident that the locale is not being watched or bugged by opponents.

Sahara Desert. The world's largest desert, stretching 1,700 miles north to south and 5,000 miles east to west. Physically, the desert has been expanding in girth at least since the days of the *Roman Empire*, when coastal settlement in North Africa was much wider and deeper than today and encompassed areas which have since turned to desert. It was historically important for its salt deposits, which were serviced by *slave labor* and caravans. From the seventh to eleventh centuries, most of its sparse population converted to *Islam*. For many centuries it constituted a huge barrier between the forest and savanna peoples of Africa and the Mediterranean world and sustained harsh slave-raiding empires. It also acted something like *Inner Asia* in its relation to surrounding settled populations: the Sahara was for many centuries the source of *razzia*, conquest, and general disruption by nomads against agricultural and urban peoples. *See also Algiers; Bornu; Fulbe Empire; Kanem; Mali; Morocco; Sahel; sudan; Tripoli; Tuareg.*
Suggested Readings: E. W. Bovill, *Caravans of the Old Sahara* (1933); E. W. Bovill, *Golden Trade of the Moors* (new edition, 1968).

Sahel. The arid, semi-desert region in Africa bordered by the *Sahara Desert* to the north and a true savannah to the south; it is essentially, and historically, the *frontier zone* between the Sahara and the *sudan*. Its peoples are mostly *Muslim*, and mostly extremely poor. For many centuries, indeed for most of the second millennium C.E., its peoples were alternately subjected to slave-raiding, or themselves formed vast *cavalry* empires. From c. 1970 to 2000 the area was severely afflicted by drought, *famine*, and *war*.

Sahrawi Arab Democratic Republic. *See Polisario; Western Sahara.*

Sakhalin (Karafuto) Island. Russian raids were launched against Sakhalin Island, 1806–1807, which then had but a few Japanese settlements. Distracted by the *Napoleonic Wars*, Russia's interest in this large northern island waned until midcentury. In 1858 Japan and Russia agreed to divide Sakhalin. In 1875 Japan gave up its half to Russia in exchange for the *Kurils*. It regained southern Sakhalin in the *Treaty of Portsmouth* in 1905. With Russia gravely weakened by the triple calamities of *World War I*, the *Bolshevik Revolution*, and the *Russian Civil War*, Japan seized the northern half as well. Under American pressure, Tokyo withdrew from northern Sakhalin in 1925, and it reverted to the Soviet Union. Southern Sakhalin was taken from Japan by decision of the *Cairo Conference*, and given to the Soviets by agreement at *Yalta*, after which all Sakhalin was claimed and occupied by Russia.

Sakharov, Andrei Dimitrievitch (1921–1989). Soviet nuclear physicist and *human rights* activist. After helping to design the Soviet *hydrogen bomb* he became a *dissident* under the powerful influence of his wife, Yelena Bonner. He was as morally crushed by the ending of the *Prague Spring* as were the Czechs more literally, and he publicly advocated radical change in the Soviet Union itself. He won the *Nobel Prize* for Peace in 1975. His stature preserved him from the punishment camps at first. However, after he organized a *Helsinki watch group*, wrote to *Jimmy Carter* directly, and criticized the *invasion of Afghanistan* in 1979, the persecution began: he and Yelena Bonner were *exiled* to the gray provincial city of Gorky. His case was prominent on the Western-Soviet *human rights* agenda for many years. In 1986 he was finally released by *Gorbachev*. Given the profile of the Sakharov case, that was both intended and taken as a sign things were truly changing in Moscow. When Sakharov died in 1989 he was given a *state funeral* by the system he had once served, and then as loyally had opposed.

Suggested Reading: Andrei Sakharov, *Memoirs* (1990).

sakoku. "Closed country." Japan under the *Tokugawa shoguns*, during most of the seventeenth through nineteenth centuries. In 1639 the Tokugawa prohibited oceanic voyages, cutting Japan off from western (though not Chinese or Korean) contact; the edict was not lifted until 1853. Toward the end of the Tokugawa period the term was replaced by a call for "kaikoku" ("open country"). *See also Japan; isolationism.*

Salāh-ed-Dīn, Yusuf ibn Ayyub (1137–1193). "Saladin." Sultan of Egypt and Syria. His father was a *Kurd*, and a provincial governor at Tekrit under the Seljuk Turks of Asia Minor. In the service of Nur ad-Din, *emir* of Syria, Salāh-ed-Dīn fought in Egypt, 1167–1168, where he became grand vizier (1169) under the defeated Fatamid *caliphs*. He subsequently deposed the Fatamids (1171) and proclaimed himself the sovereign ruler of Egypt. From his base in Egypt he began to expand westward across North Africa and eastward into the Arabian peninsula. After Nur ad-Din's death he incorporated most of Syria and Palestine (but not the mountain fastnesses held by the *Druse* and *Assassins*) into his empire, along with Mesopotamia. The Seljuks now paid him homage and *tribute*. He had become the leading prince of the Muslim world. Salāh-ed-Dīn next turned to face the *Christian* threat, in the form of the *Crusader* states and occupation of *Jerusalem*. In 1187 he inflicted a massive defeat on a Crusader army at Tiberias. On October 3rd of that year, his troops overwhelmed the remaining defenders of Jerusalem and recaptured the city for *Islam*. Subsequently, he battered down Crusader castles along the Syrian coast, earning respect for both his military skill and his great chivalry. A Christian counterattack, led in person by King Richard I (Coeur de Lion, 1157–1199) of England and King Philip of France, retook Acre in 1191 but was unable to retake the city in two advances against it. Richard defeated Salāh-ed-Dīn at Caesarea and Jaffa, exacted from him a three-year treaty, and departed the Holy Land, only to be captured and held for ransom by the Christian hands of the *Holy Roman Emperor* in Germany. Salāh-ed-Dīn is remembered not merely for his conquests, but for wise and benevolent government, and for economic prosperity and rebuilding of infrastructure, roads, and canals.

salami tactics. A crude (*political science*) metaphor to describe *aggression* which seeks to expand one slice of territory at a time, pausing to digest each territorial meal and to gauge the response of possible opponents. *See also opportunism.*

Salazar, Antonio (1889–1970). Portuguese dictator. Prime minister, 1932–1968; foreign minister, 1936–1947, minister of war, 1936–1944. His quasi-*fascist* dictatorship kept Portugal out of *World War II*, but he fought drawn-out colonial wars in Angola, Guinea-Bissau, and Mozambique. As with *Franco* in Spain, Salazar's domestic misrule kept Portugal out of the mainstream of European economic *integration*, and political and cultural developments, until after his death. *See also corporatism.*

salient. A projection outward from a line of battle, whether caused by tactical design, topography, or exhaustion. *See also Battle of the Bulge; Kursk; Ypres.*

Salisbury, Robert Arthur (1830–1903). "Cecil." Third Marquis of Salisbury. Secretary for India, 1866, 1874–1876; foreign secretary, 1878–1880, 1886–1892, 1895–1900; prime minister, 1885–1892, 1895–1902. Troubled by home questions such as religious tests in the universities (he was chancellor of Oxford, 1869–1874), he was always more comfortable and most interested in foreign policy. He attended the *Berlin Congress* with *Disraeli*. He was entirely devoted to empire and consistently opposed *Home Rule* for India or Ireland. He was a bitter political rival of *Joseph Chamberlain*. To Salisbury is often attributed the policy of *splendid isolation*, but it might be fairer said that he pursued limited cooperation with other *Great Powers* when it suited his sense of Britain's *national interest*. His diplomacy was not therefore *isolationist* so much as ad hoc and pragmatic. He negotiated the *Mediterranean Agreement* in 1887. During the *scramble for Africa* he consolidated several African colonies, though failed to prevent other powers from making serious gains. He faced down France over *Fashoda*, avoiding war but standing firm; and refused to be drawn into war over the *Jameson raid*. He avoided war with the United States over the Venezuela dispute and with Turkey over the first *Armenian genocide* and insurrection in Crete. He was drawn into and isolated by the *Second Boer War*, however. He broke that diplomatic isolation by arranging the *Anglo-Japanese alliance* of 1902. He was deeply committed to maintaining Britain's naval superiority. *See also Anglo-German Naval Arms Race.*

SALT I and II. *See Strategic Arms Limitation Talks.*

salt march (March 12–April 6, 1930). A brilliantly effective protest organized by *Mohandas Gandhi* against the imperial monopoly on salt production, and thus the whole exploitive relationship of Britain in India. With elegant simplicity, and at age 61, he walked some 240 miles to the coast, gathering mass support along the way. There he made salt from the sea and announced his noncooperation henceforth with collection of the imperial salt tax. He was arrested along with tens of thousands of others, including many women, who emerged for the first time as an important part of Gandhi's movement. The main point was made, however, and never thereafter forgotten by Indians or by officials of the British *Rāj*. As usual, Gandhi's arrest provoked unrest and riots. This time, Britain was spurred to call the *Round Table Conference* of 1930.

salvo. A phalanx of *artillery* or rifles fired at once, for maximum destructive and psychological effect. *See also broadside.*

samizdat (sam izdatelstvo). "Self-publishing." Originally, laboriously typed and copied, privately circulated, illegal literature distributed within closed *totalitarian* societies, especially the *Soviet Union*. This method was used by *dissidents* to keep alive ideas, books, and pamphlets which the various *Soviet* bloc and other *communist* states banned. During the *Cold War*, some samizdat literature was smuggled out, published in the *West*, and then smuggled back into the Soviet bloc countries. In Poland in the 1980s, the *Central Intelligence Agency* instead smuggled in computers, printers, and printing presses to *Solidarity* in remarkable quantities. At one point, Solidarity presses were producing 700 regular samizdat periodicals. Samizdat has since become a generic term for banned dissident literature within closed societies, whether communist or not.

Samoa. This Pacific territory was an American-British-German *condominium*, 1889–1900, when it was split into *American Samoa* (United States) and Western Samoa (Germany), with Britain *compensated* with several Solomon Islands. New Zealand captured Western Samoa from Germany in 1914, and after 1919 ran it as a *mandate*. U.S. troops were based there, 1942–1945, when New Zealand returned to govern it as a *trusteeship territory*. *Independence* came in 1962, after a *plebiscite* by which Samoans disenfranchised themselves in favor of a tribal council. Insistence on traditional communal ownership of property overseen by this council discouraged foreign investment and led to considerable corruption and to *International Monetary Fund* controls in the 1980s. Samoa joined the United Nations in 1976. It has ties to Australia and the United States but is most closely oriented to New Zealand. Reflecting even older ties, trade with Germany is still extensive. In a 1990 plebiscite a slim majority reinstated universal adult suffrage. It dropped "Western" from its formal name in 1997.

Samori Touré (c. 1835–1900). West African *warlord*. A Mandingo from Guinea, he received early training as a *mercenary* soldier and at a young age converted to *Islam*. He later became an Islamic teacher and a trader. During the later 1860s and early 1870s he organized an army financed by, and largely organized for, participation in the *slave trade*. He seized control over a wide area in West Africa nearly as large as France, conquering many local tribes between modern Guinea, Mali, and Burkina Faso. He governed with some cruelty and could be ruthless in dealing with prisoners from units of the French *Tirailleurs Sénégalais*, or his own family: he had a son walled up alive and left to die. From 1883 to 1885 he fought against French attempts to conquer his growing empire, but signed a *protectorate* agreement in 1886. That year he established Islam as the faith of his empire, provoking a revolt by its non-Muslim subjects which engaged most of his army to crush, and gravely weakened his state vis-à-vis the French. In 1891 he rejected the treaty with France and launched a series of attacks on French forts and settlements. By 1893 he was forced to resort to guerrilla operations out of Côte d'Ivoire. He invaded Upper Volta (Burkina Faso), 1896–1898, where he raided and *pillaged* widely. He was finally captured by the French in 1898 and exiled to Gabon, where he died. An argument continues among regional specialists as to whether he was an early African nationalist who, had he not been faced with a constant threat from the French, might have constructed a state capable of surviving in the twentieth century, or just a more successful sort of warlord whose personal empire would not have survived the death of its founder. *See also Tippu Tip.*

samurai. The warrior caste of *feudal* Japan, surviving as a class into the later nineteenth century. At their height, hundreds of thousands served as retainers to the *daimyo.* In the decades of the *Unification Wars*, especially under *Toyotomi Hideyoshi*, the samurai emerged as members of *standing armies* and a de facto rural constabulary (or army of occupation) barracked in new "castle towns" which soon marked the main inland routes of Japan. At the same time, separation of the samurai from the land, the feudal basis of their social status and function, combined with the advent of domestic peace under the *Tokugawa* to convert them into a parasitic warrior class enjoying broad legal rights and exemptions and kept at state expense, but also essentially underemployed and socially useless. In return, the samurai were supposed to lead lives of service and ethical example and to adhere to the bushidō ("way of the warrior") code. In the mid-nineteenth century nearly 5 percent of the population, or about 1.9 million people, lived in samurai households. Tied to fixed incomes and the domains of the daimyo system, many were impoverished. With the *Meiji Restoration*, military reform led to commoner armies and rapid decline of the samurai. The Restoration War, 1868–1869, saw the closing epic of the samurai: a *siege* of the castle of Aizu which ended in burning of the city and ritual suicide (seppuku) by several dozen "White Tigers." In 1871 the ban on intermarriage with commoners was lifted; in 1873 national conscription was introduced; and in 1876 samurai pensions were curtailed. Several rebellions followed, culminating in the *Satsuma rebellion*, after which most samurai were tamed, dead, or militarily irrelevant.

sanctions. (1) Specific: Targeted *reprisals* related to a particular good or economic sector of interstate trade, undertaken in order to coerce compliance with an existing trade agreement; or political and diplomatic sanctions undertaken to counter a *delict* against bilateral obligations which does not rise to the level of universal interest or importance. Such sanctions might include travel restrictions, trade and financial restrictions, or suspension of *diplomatic relations*. (2) General: Encouragement and enforcement of another state's obligations under *international law* by means of cultural, diplomatic, economic, or, in the last resort, coercive military pressure or even punishment by other states. Sanctions tend to be applied step by step, both to increase pressures over time and to allow for graduated removal of penalties later. This can be done bilaterally (e.g., the United States against Cuba or Vietnam, or Britain against Rhodesia) or multilaterally (e.g., the *League of Nations* over Italy's aggression against Ethiopia in 1935; the United States, Commonwealth, and

Netherlands sanctions against Japan prior to *World War II*; oil sanctions by *OPEC* against Western allies of Israel in 1973; or *United Nations* sanctions against South Africa, Haiti, Iraq, Libya, and Serbia, among others). Economic sanctions are a major component of the theory of *collective security*. However, there is much dispute over their efficacy. Critics argue that a major change of policy has resulted from sanctions in but a handful of cases, that they tend to unite *public opinion* in the sanctioned state, and that they often have a highly disproportionate impact on the most innocent and vulnerable members of the targeted society. Proponents maintain that there are degrees of effectiveness and cost and benefit, when applying sanctions, as there are with any foreign policy choice. At the least, it is generally true that sanctions are most often used, and are most effective, against weak states and that they are virtually useless, and even counterproductive, when applied against a determined regime or a *Great Power*. Also, the *leverage* one obtains (and the cost one incurs) from sanctions is far greater when they are applied to allies with whom one has extensive relations on other matters—and therefore also many reasons not to impose sanctions—than when they are implemented against openly enemy or hostile states with which one does not have broad ties and against whom sanctions will have correspondingly little effect. Although it is never admitted openly, perhaps the most common reason for imposing general economic, diplomatic, or political sanctions is to satisfy domestic public opinion in participating states that "something is being done," where failure to act might instead lead to increased public pressures for military intervention. However, it should be remembered that in the last resort bilateral or multilateral use of force may be legally applied, under specific conditions, and also constitutes a form of sanctions—indeed, both bilaterally and under the theory of collective security, force remains the ultimate sanction. *See also boycott; coercive diplomacy; compellence; disinvestment; embargo.*

sanctity of treaties. *See* pacta sunt servanda.

Sandinistas. (1) A *guerrilla*-revolutionary movement in Nicaragua led by Augusto Sandino (1896–1934), a nationalist and rebel, active 1926–1934. (2) The Frente Sandinista de Liberación Nacional (FSLN). The FSLN originally was a broad front of opposition to the *Somozas*, 1961–1979. Once it took power in Nicaragua, 1979–1990, it shed its moderate members, some of whom joined the *Contras*, and was increasingly dominated by hard-core *Marxists* gathered around *Daniel Ortega* and his brother. After losing internationally supervised elections in 1990, it participated in a tense coalition government while retaining control of the army and police. In 1994 it gained just 25 percent of the vote. Ortega and the Sandinistas were defeated again in 1996, by José Arnoldo Alemán and the Liberal Alliance. By 2000 the Sandinistas had entered revolutionary middle age as an established opposition.

Sandwich Islands. Former name of *Hawaii*.

San Francisco Conference (April 25–June 26, 1945). The follow-up to *Dumbarton Oaks*, where the main outlines of the *United Nations Organization* had been decided. San Francisco was in many ways the less important, though more public, of the two foundation meetings. Fifty-one nations (including Poland, whose government was in dispute among the *Allies*) attended, in contrast to only the *Big Four* at Dumbarton Oaks. Of these, just nine were European states. In this sense, San Francisco marked the transition from a *Eurocentric* community of states to a true *international system*. After adjusting working proposals to please smaller powers and achieving agreement on the scope of the *veto* among the *permanent members* of the *Security Council*, the conference accepted the *Charter of the United Nations. See also human rights.*

San Francisco system. *See Japan; Japanese Peace Treaty.*

San Marino. A European *microstate* which officially styles itself the "Serene Republic of San Marino." It is located in the eastern part of the Italian peninsula and claims to be the oldest independent country in Europe. It is just 38 square miles in size and has a population of c. 25,000. It had close trade and other connections with Italy after 1862. From 1947 to 1957 and from 1978 to 1986, it was governed by a coalition which included *communists*, as was much of northern Italy.

San Martín, José de (1778–1850). Enigmatic South American revolutionary. A *Creole* from northern Argentina, he led armies against the Spanish in what is modern-day Argentina, Chile, and southern Peru. Less is known of San Martín than of *Bolívar*, his great counterpart to the north. He fought in Europe against *Napoleon*, 1808–1811. He returned to Argentina in 1812 and was put in charge of a campaign to take *Upper Peru*. He determined to take the region via Chile, rather than through the Andes. For this task he prepared for nearly three years, at Mendoza. In 1817 San Martín conducted a brilliant military campaign, including crossing the exceptionally difficult Andes range with 5,000 men, before striking the Spanish in Chile at the Battle of Chacabuco (February 12, 1817) and taking Santiago two days later. There, Bernardo O'Higgins became military dictator (until 1823), while San Martín planned to continue north to Peru. The Spanish counterattacked, however, forcing him to win again near Santiago at the Battle of Maipú (April 5, 1818). For two years more, he planned his assault. He finally struck in 1920, by sea. He captured Lima (July 10, 1821), the heart and capital of imperial power in Latin America, when the Spanish withdrew. The local nobles bowed to reality and proclaimed independence on July 28th, though in fact, of all colonial cities, Lima was certainly the most loyal still to Spain. San Martín immediately abolished Indian *tribute* and slavery and was named Protector of Peru.

He spoke of establishing a unified Latin American *monarchy* and introduced dramatic reforms of the *encomienda* system. By 1824, however, it was clear that separate *republics* would be set up. After meeting secretly with Bolívar, he returned to Argentina and then retired to Europe—leaving to Bolívar the task of completing the liberation of northern Peru. He never returned to Latin America.

Suggested Reading: John Lynch, *The Spanish American Revolutions, 1808–1826* (1986).

sans-culottes. "Without breeches." Named for their distinctive dress, these were the urban poor in Paris who were extreme *republicans* and supporters of *radicalization* of the *French Revolution*. The term passed down to refer to any grassroots, poorer sort of urban revolutionary.

San Stefano, Treaty of (March 3, 1878). This agreement ended yet another *Russo-Turkish War*, this one in 1877–1878. It proclaimed Montenegro and Rumania independent, enlarged Serbia, declared Bulgaria (including Macedonia) *autonomous* within the *Ottoman Empire*, and expanded Russian influence in the *Caucasus*. This alarmed the Austrians and angered the British. *Disraeli* forced revisions of its terms, notably reversing south Slav and Armenian gains, later that year at the *Congress of Berlin*. San Stefano's lasting importance was mainly symbolic: Bulgarians and Serbs never forgot the vainglorious dreams of "Greater Bulgaria" and "*Greater Serbia*" it briefly fulfilled. *See also Eastern Question.*

Santa Anna, Antonio López de (1797–1876). Mexican statesman. This was a man with nine political lives, who used up all of them in spectacular intrigues and gambits. He led a successful coup in 1822. He helped fend off Spanish forces attempting the reconquest of Mexico in 1825, and rode a wave of popularity into the presidency in 1833. In 1836 *Texas* rebelled, and Santa Anna responded by slaughtering a garrison of 183 defenders at the Alamo. He lost his presidency when his army was soundly defeated by General Sam Houston at the Battle of San Jacinto River (April 21, 1836), where Santa Anna was himself captured. In 1838 he lost his leg to a cannon ball while leading a Mexican army to repel French forces, which had landed at Veracruz to force Mexico to pay *reparations* for a variety of minor grievances. In 1839 he was briefly president, and in 1841 led another successful coup. In 1845 he was forced into exile in Cuba. In 1846 he became president again, sailing to Mexico ostensibly as a peacemaker after the United States had annexed California and Texas and war tensions were mounting. He quickly seized control of the army but then faced the humiliation of the *Mexican-American War*, which cost Mexico a vast, resource-rich *hinterland*, and Santa Anna his high office yet again. Once more he sailed into Caribbean exile. In 1853 he returned to the presidency, a supposedly lifetime appointment which was cut short two years later when his political enemies (who were legion) drove him from the country (August 17, 1855). Even his devious skills and secret offers to cooperate with all sides—French, American, and Mexican nationalist—could not bring him back to power during the years of French rule of Mexico under *Maximilian*. He tried to return in 1864, and briefly did so physically, but the French would not deal with him. In 1867 he again tried to invade his own country but was captured and condemned to death. Pardoned, he retired to New York until 1872, when he was given amnesty. He returned to Mexico in 1874 and died there in 1876. His legacy to Mexico was severe truncation of its national territory, fatal weakening of its position relative to the United States, and decades of political instability.

São Tomé and Principe. These Gulf of Guinea islands were a Portuguese *colony* until 1974. The islands were settled after 1490 mainly by Portuguese convicts, as well as by a number of Jews deported or fleeing the Catholic *Inquisition* and other persecution in *Iberia*. The *slave trade* (with *Benin*, and then with *Congo*) became an economic mainstay in the fifteenth century, once a sugar cane plantation economy was introduced to the islands. The plantations of Brazil and the West Indies soon supplanted those of São Tomé and Principe, however, and many of the islands' original planters followed suit. In time, the races melded. In 1975 these territories became a *sovereign* state.

Sapa Inca. "Sole Inca." *See also Inca Empire.*

sapper. A military engineer, usually one employed in building or undermining trenches. *See also trench warfare.*

Saracen. Originally, Syrian nomadic tribes encountered and conquered by the *Roman Empire*. Later, a generic *Crusader* term for any Muslim warrior they faced, especially the grand coalition assembled at the end of the twelfth century by *Salāh-ed-Dīn*, which retook *Jerusalem* and held off the Christian counterattack led by the *Norman* king Richard I (Lionheart).

Sarajevo. Capital of *Bosnia-Herzegovina*. It was the locale of the assassination of *Franz Ferdinand* in 1914, and hosted the Winter *Olympics* in 1988. After Bosnian *independence*, Serb *militia* laid *siege* and shelled it throughout 1992 and 1993. It became a center of United Nations relief efforts and international media attention. In 1993 it was declared a United Nations *safe haven*, though hardly anyone living there noticed until *NATO* enforced this status after 1994.

Saratoga, campaign and battle of (July 6–October 17, 1777). *See American Revolution.*

Sarawak. Located on northern Borneo, this territory is peopled by an eclectic mix of Malays, Chinese, and native Iban. It was a British *protectorate*, 1888–1946, under the "White Rajas," the family Brooke, a merchant family which controlled the Sarawak trade for nearly a century. Their day ended with Japanese invasion during *World War II*. Sarawak was made a *crown colony*, 1946–1963. It was economically tied to Singapore once that *city-state* was founded, a relationship which began Sarawak's *modernization*. With *Sabah* it joined Malaysia, over Indonesian objections. *See also Konfrontasi.*

Sardinia, Kingdom of. This large Mediterranean island was taken from Spain and given to the *Austrian Empire* by the Treaty of Rastadt (1714), following the *War of the Spanish Succession*. It formed the core of an independent Italian kingdom, 1720–1860, along with Genoa (after 1815), *Piedmont*, and *Savoy*. It allied with Piedmont and France to defeat Austria in 1859 and thereafter merged with the mainland of Italy in the general unification of 1861, ceding Savoy to France as part of the price of union. Sardinia was mostly dominated by Piedmont after 1748, and hence the kingdom is usually referred to as *Piedmont-Sardinia. See also Camillo di Cavour; Giuseppe Garibaldi;* risorgimento.

satellites. Following the launch of *Sputnik*, by the early 1960s spy satellites had become a principal means of *intelligence* gathering by technologically advanced nations. They were followed into orbit by large numbers of weather and commercial satellites. While no formal legal regime governed these devices even by the end of the twentieth century, tacit *rules* existed in practice: (1) passes over another nation's territory were tolerated in ways which overflights by aircraft were not (they could not be prevented in any case, without provoking costly retaliation); (2) information of an economic nature such as location of minerals or environmental degradation gleaned by an advanced country's satellites about a non–space-faring nation was, in general, made available to the country concerned; (3) states were liable for harm caused should their satellites crash on the territory of another country. When the U.S. spacecraft Skylab crashed in Australia the United States promptly paid compensation. After years of delay, the Soviet Union finally paid to clean up nuclear contaminants from one of its satellite reactors strewn by a crash across the Canadian arctic. In 2001, Russia took out $200 million in insurance in the event its MIR space station damaged property in South America. It crashed safely into the South Pacific.

satellite state. An astronomical metaphor for when a *state* is nominally *sovereign* but is so controlled in its foreign and domestic affairs by another power it is said to "orbit" (act under the dominant *influence* of) the larger power. *See also client state.*

sati (**suttee**). Ritual immolation of upper-caste, *Hindu* widows. It was abolished by regulation of the *East India Company* in 1829. (When Sir Charles Napier was told sati was an honored Indian custom, he said, "We, too have an honored custom: when men burn women alive, we hang them.") Sati continued—although much less frequently—into the twenty-first century, even experiencing a late twentieth-century revival which prompted a new anti-sati law in 1987. Banning the practice was surely right, but less honorably it was turned by British propagandists (mainly *missionaries*) into a symbol of Indian "barbarism" and "backwardness," which was used to justify a tightening British imperial noose, which was grossly unfair to an ancient and rich culture and civilization. A comparable social problem rooted in ancient Hindu practices and attitudes toward women is "bride burning," wherein dowries (also made illegal in independent India) which are judged inadequate by the groom's family may lead to "accidental" immolation of a new wife.

satisfaction. Under *international law*, when *reparation* is made for nonmaterial *damage* done by some state action.

satisficing. *See game theory.*

Sato Eisaku (1901–1975). Japanese prime minister, 1964–1972. He revised Japan's *security treaty* with the United States and secured the return of *Okinawa*. He also improved relations with South Korea. He utterly disavowed *nuclear weapons* for Japan. He was awarded the 1974 *Nobel Prize* for Peace.

Satsuma rebellion (February 17–September 24, 1877). The last and largest of several failed rebellions by *samurai*, mainly in reaction to their loss of legal privileges, social status, and government income as a result of the *Meiji Restoration* and its attendant military, tax, and finance reforms. Government forces suffered 10,000 casualties (6,000 killed in action), while the rebels lost 18,000 killed and wounded. The rebels failed to rouse commoners to their cause or to unite across old *daimyo* borders. After the rebellion a severe *inflation* set in which took years to control.

saturation attack. Overwhelming enemy defenses in specific areas by mass use of weapons and/or troops.

satyagraha. *See Mohandas Gandhi.*

Saudi Arabia. *Arabia* exploded onto the world stage with the founding of *Islam* in the seventh century C.E. and remained important within the *Islamic world* ever since, under various *caliphates*, then the *Ottoman Empire*, for whom *Hashemite* sharifs governed the holy city of *Mecca*. Saudi Arabia, on the other hand, was founded by *Abd al-Aziz ibn Saud* in 1926. The modern importance of this *feudal* kingdom stems from two facts: (1) it sits atop a major share of the world's known oil reserves, and (2) it contains the *Hejaz*, the spiritual focal point for the Islamic world, constituting one billion members of humanity. The Hejaz has been there for 1,300 years, but the oil was only discovered in 1935, with the first exports in 1938. *Modernization* came slowly under the conservative *sunni* dynasty which ruled the country: the House of Saud. Yet the royal house was more modern than most of the *Wahhabi*, many of whom were purged and killed at Sabila in 1929. *Slavery* was only made illegal in 1962, and laws restricting the public life of women abounded into the twenty-first century. In the 1960s Sheik *Yamani* led Saudi Arabia into OPEC and took over its lead during the 1973 and 1979 *oil shocks*. Saudi Arabia sent contingents to fight Israel in 1948 and in 1973. It intervened in the Yemeni civil war to block a *Nasserite* revolution, supporting royalists fighting against Yemeni radicals and Egyptian troops. That year, *Kennedy* sent token U.S. air forces to Saudi Arabia to deter Egyptian attacks. During the *Cold War* it was nominally *nonaligned*, but in fact deeply anti-Soviet. After the *invasion* of Afghanistan it gave financial and other support to the Afghan *mujahadeen*. It supported Iraq during the *Iran-Iraq War*, a conflict which drove it closer to the West out of fear of radical *shi'ites* in Iran. It broke *diplomatic relations* with Iran in 1988 and agreed to preparations necessary to receive the *rapid deployment force*. In 1990 the Saudis welcomed U.S. and other foreign troops and joined the *Gulf coalition*. It cut back contributions to the *Palestine Liberation Organization (PLO)* after the *Gulf War*, owing to the PLO's support for Iraq. Saudi Arabia then rearmed against possible threats from either Iran or Iraq. It also faced domestic religious and political unrest. In 1980 the Great Mosque in Mecca was attacked by militant shi'ites from the deep desert. Portions were severely damaged when the Saudi military shelled it, leading to much criticism in other Islamic countries. In 1987 shi'ites from Iran and elsewhere rioted, leaving hundreds dead. During the 1990 *haj* nearly 1,500 pilgrims were killed in a crowd panic. In the decade following the Gulf War there developed limited Western as well as increased internal pressure for more political representation and civil and political rights, including for women, but the dynasty continued to adhere to deeply conservative social and political mores.

Savoy (Savoie). A region in southeast France, conquered by *Richelieu*, once part of the Kingdom of *Sardinia*. In 1834 *Mazzini* led an abortive invasion of Savoy. It was ceded back to France in 1860 as part of the settlement permitting the unification of Italy.

Scandinavia. Denmark, the Faeroe Islands, Iceland, Norway, and Sweden (and sometimes Finland). After the age of the *Vikings*, Scandinavia was slowly drawn into European civilization, unusually not by conquest, but mainly by commerce and by conversion to *Christianity* by *missionaries*. After the *Napo-*

leonic Wars Scandinavians turned to *neutrality*. Denmark, Norway, and Sweden all stayed neutral during *World War I*. Only Sweden was able to avoid being attacked by *Nazi Germany* during *World War II*. After the war, Scandinavia emerged as a zone of *social democracy* combined with very high standards of living, unusual political stability, and major advances in social justice.

Scapa Flow. After *World War I*, most surrendered German *warships* were sailed to this British naval base in the Orkney Islands. When it became clear that Britain would seek to retain the fleet to add to its own, the German crews scuttled their ships. Thus, ingloriously, ended the great *Dreadnought* race. *See also Anglo-German naval arms race; Jutland; sea power.*

Scharnhorst, Gerhard Johann von (1775–1813). Head of the Prussian *General Staff*. He was wounded at *Jena-Auerstädt* in 1806, fighting *Napoleon*. He agreed with his subordinates *Gneisenau* and *Clausewitz* on the need for major military reform, and oversaw the great (and partly secret) reorganization of the Prussian Army, which had been so badly beaten in 1806, when the Prussian Army was still nearly half *mercenary* at a time other states were moving toward the *nation-in-arms*. These reforms were thus far more than just military: they incorporated the main lesson of the *revolution in military affairs* brought about by the *French Revolution*, to wit: a basic reordering of society, albeit to the limited degree possible in Prussia, to break the class grip of the nobility on the officer corps and make it instead a meritocracy; to simultaneously end *feudal* treatment of the rank and file; and to make more humane the brutal system of Prussian drill and discipline inherited from *Frederick the Great* (1712–1786). Scharnhorst was killed in battle in 1813, but his new Prussian Army was victorious, 1813–1814, and intervened decisively at *Waterloo* (1815). It also became the prime vehicle of Prussian nationalism in the nineteenth century.

Schengen Agreement (1995). A multilateral treaty permitting citizens of member countries to cross borders without *passports* by removing internal border controls—on land, sea, and in the air—between member states of "Schengenland," and harmonizing *visa* arrangements with some 190 nonmember states. Signed in a village which straddled the French, German, and Luxembourgian borders, it came into effect in July 1995. Initially, the Schengen zone had seven member states (Belgium, France, Germany, Luxembourg, Netherlands, Portugal, and Spain), with associated status for the five members of the *Nordic Passport Union*. Other states signing later included Italy (1990), Greece (1992), and Austria (1995). The United Kingdom chose to remain outside the zone. A clause permitted *hot pursuit* by neighboring police forces, although this treaty right may be suspended for internal security reasons. At the same time, external border controls were made more strict out of concern over increased ease of *smuggling*, drug trafficking, *migrant* labor and potential illegal *immigration*, movement of criminals and other "undesirable persons," and movement of third-country *nationals*. The movement of all non–Schengen zone persons was to be monitored via a shared computer (police and immigration) database known as the Schengen Information System.

schism. A formal division over matters of doctrine within a church or between branches of the same faith, or within a secular *ideology*. *See also Albania; Avignon Captivity (of the papacy); Byzantine Empire; Catholic Church; Christianity; clash of civilizations; communism; Counter-Reformation; Coptic Church; Druse; Ecumenical Councils; Eighty Years' War (1566–1648); Elizabeth I; fundamentalism; Great Schism; Guelphs and Ghibellines; Holy Roman Empire; Internationals; Islam; Martin Luther; Marxism; Old Believers; Old Catholics; Orthodox Church; Papal States; party line; Protestant Reformation; res publica Christiana; shi'ia Islam; strel'sty; sunni Islam; Third Rome; Thirty Years' War (1618–1648); Vatican; Vatican Councils; Western Europe; Westphalia, Peace of.*

Schleswig-Holstein. These duchies on the lower Jutland peninsula were under Danish rule for centuries, despite having a predominantly German-speaking population. Royal-Schleswig and Ducal Schleswig were joined as a result of the *Great Northern War (1700–1721)*. Denmark lost Holstein to the *German Confederation* in 1815, as punishment for having allied with *Napoleon I*. During the upheavals of 1848 Denmark tried to annex the duchies, but popular opposition and Prussian intervention forestalled this. In 1864 *Bismarck* seized the duchies for Prussia in a sharp summer war, annexing Schleswig. To assuage Vienna, a *condominium* was set up in which Prussia administered Schleswig and Austria spoke for Holstein. However, Bismarck never intended this as a permanent settlement. He annexed Holstein to Prussia in 1866, after crushing Austria in the *Seven Weeks' War*. Following *World War I*, the *Treaty of Versailles* set a *plebiscite* for northern Schleswig, where there were many Danes, and the area subsequently voted to join Denmark. After *World War II* the rump of Schleswig-Holstein voted for incorporation in West Germany.

Schlieffen, Alfred von (1833–1913). Chief of the Imperial German *general staff*. He saw action as a young officer during the *Seven Weeks' War* and served as a staff officer during the *Franco-Prussian War*. He oversaw the massive German *arms buildup* on land after 1895. Rejecting the caution of the elder *Moltke* (whose greatest fear had been a *two-front war*) and exalting force over diplomacy—hence his disregard for Belgian and Dutch *neutrality*—Schlieffen devised (1897) and modified (1905) the *Schlieffen Plan*. He worked on it for years, tinkering with railway timetables and calculation of the optimum movement of whole divisions along narrow roadways. Given the enormous French *fortification* effort around and in Paris, he needed to devise a plan able to mass and move enough men with sufficient speed (within 40 days, it was generally agreed, and was so stated in the plan) to achieve a decisive, wheeling victory over France, as was accomplished in 1870—and would be again in 1940. He never solved this problem, since he could not overcome the ineluctable physical absence of a transportation system sufficient to move German troops at the pace and in the numbers required. Again, he might have recalled the advice of the elder Moltke, "No plan survives contact with the enemy for more than 24 hours." *See also* Blitzkrieg.

Schlieffen Plan (1905–1914). Originally drafted by *Alfred von Schlieffen* but significantly modified by the younger *Moltke*, this grand strategic plan of the German *general staff* was premised on the likelihood of a *two-front war*. It proposed a swift blow in the west to knock out France using nearly seven-eighths of the German Army, while remaining strictly on the defensive against Russia in the east. It was assumed that French *élan* and wounded national pride would cause a headlong rush by the bulk of the French Army into *Alsace-Lorraine*. (In fact, France's Plan XVII of 1913 proposed to do exactly that.) Germany would permit the French to advance toward *fortified* positions, defending these with about one-seventh of all western forces while hastening the great bulk of the *Reichswehr* past fortified French border positions in a huge flanking maneuver, which necessarily violated the *neutrality* of the *Low Countries*. That would likely bring Great Britain into the war, under terms of the *Treaty of London* of 1839. The plan noted the likelihood of British intervention but failed to deal with it adequately. Instead, it was merely hoped that the *British Expeditionary Force* (BEF) would not arrive in sufficient numbers to have a decisive effect, at least not before Germany achieved a strategic victory by sweeping past Paris to slam an iron door behind the French Army, now trapped by its earlier advance. All this was to be achieved according to a strict timetable: clear Belgium and reach the French frontier by the 22nd day; reach the Somme and Meuse by the 31st day; and win the war clearly in the west by the 40th day—it was thought Russia could not deliver its vast forces to the *eastern front* before six weeks. With France beaten, Britain would have to withdraw from the continent and perhaps the war. With the *western front* secure, the core of the German Army could be rushed by rail to the east to stop an expected Russian advance into Germany. *Mitteleuropa* would then be constructed in due course. It is seldom noted, though nonetheless true, that besides reckless dismissal of *international law* the Schlieffen Plan ignored the interests of Austria, Germany's principal ally. Vienna was to defend against Russian attack as best it could while Berlin achieved victory in the west.

Schlieffen himself recognized that the plan could not work: there was no way to achieve the decisive numbers needed above Paris in the time allotted, over the roads available. Nevertheless, with modifications (Holland was ignored and troop levels on the eastern front increased), the plan was implemented in 1914. It failed because of civilian panic in Berlin as Russian armies *mobilized* and advanced more quickly than expected into *East Prussia* from the Polish salient, requiring that critical units be withdrawn from the western offensive to defend (or rather, to calm) the home front population. And it failed because the Belgians, British, and French put up more effective resistance than was anticipated, and then counterattacked in force at the first *Battle of the Marne*. It failed mainly, however, because it was logically and logistically flawed from the beginning: for a plan devised by the linear intellectual descendants, and countrymen, of *Clausewitz* it was singularly lacking in appreciation of his concept of *friction*, or of the contingency of battle. This critical flaw meant that the main effect of the plan was to largely determine the initial focus of the Great War, and where the main battle lines would lie until 1918, not through its success but by its failure. Through its arrogant violation of Belgium's neutrality and drawing of the *British Empire* into the fighting, the Schlieffen Plan also greatly expanded and prolonged the conflict. *See also Paul Hindenburg; Erich von Ludendorff; Masurian Lakes; Tannenberg.*

Suggested Reading: G. Ritter, *The Schlieffen Plan* (1958).

Schmidt, Helmut (b. 1918). West German statesman. Minister of defense 1969–1972; minister of finance, 1972–1974; chancellor, 1974–1982. He continued the *Ostpolitik* of his predecessor, *Willy Brandt*, striving to maintain *détente* in the face of deteriorating American-Soviet relations in the latter half of the 1970s. He was the first postwar chancellor of Germany ever to criticize an American president (*Jimmy Carter*) in public. That revealed the rising importance of Germany and frustration with the erratic shifts Schmidt saw in U.S. diplomacy toward Europe during the *Ford*, Carter, and *Reagan* presidencies. He was a strong supporter of responding to Soviet *missile* deployment in the late 1970s with new *NATO* missiles in the early 1980s, and encouraged a reluctant United States to do so. He succeeded in carrying out the policy, but it cost him the support of the left wing of his *Social Democratic Party*, and he was ousted in 1982. He was a prolific and widely respected writer on foreign affairs after leaving office. *See also Helmut Kohl; neutron bomb.*

Schultz, George P. (b. 1920). A Marine Corps veteran of *World War II*, Schultz was later an academic at M.I.T., the University of Chicago (dean of the business school), and Stanford University. He held three cabinet posts in the *Nixon* administration: secretary of labor, director of the Office of Management and Budget, and treasury secretary, where he was highly successful in a most difficult period. He was secretary of state under *Ronald Reagan* and *George H. Bush*, 1982–1989. He was a calming, prudential voice within the first Reagan cabinet, counteracting the coarser ideological bent of Caspar Weinberger and some others. He was also a strong supporter of the *Helsinki Accords* and of *Solidarity* in Poland. He was instrumental in developing Reagan's strategy toward the *Soviet Union* and adjusting to rapid change during the late *Cold War*. He endorsed Reagan's decision to seek a major arms buildup preparatory to engaging in arms control talks with Moscow. With greater reluctance, he also supported Reagan's surprise decision to launch a major research effort into a *Strategic Defense Initiative* (SDI). Schultz then encouraged Reagan to use the leverage gained over Moscow by the arms buildup and SDI, and by support for anti-Soviet *guerrillas* such as the *Contras* and *mujahadeen*, to prise concessions from the Soviets on *arms control*, the *Afghan-Soviet War*, regional conflicts, and *human rights*. He was especially effective in this regard once *Gorbachev* came to power in Moscow, giving Schultz and Reagan someone flexible (and healthy) to work with to end the Cold War. He returned to Stanford (Hoover Institution) after leaving office.

Suggested Reading: George P. Schultz, *Turmoil and Triumph: My Years as Secretary of State* (1993).

Schuman Plan. The plan for building the *European Coal and Steel Community*, proposed by *Robert Schuman* in 1950 and set up in 1952. His intention was to build political *union* not all at once, but by a sustained effort at *integration* of Europe's economies and societies across a broad front of activities, beginning with the vital (to both industrial development and industrial war) coal and steel industries. *See also functionalism.*

Schuman, Robert (1886–1963). French statesman. Minister of finance, 1946–1947; prime minister, 1947–1948; foreign minister, 1948–1952; president of the European Assembly, 1958–1960. A member of the French *Resistance* during *World War II*, he is most famous for devising the *Schuman Plan*, and most praised for forging the Franco-German *alliance* which formed the core of European *integration* after 1950. He also played a role in founding *NATO*. *See also Jean Monnet.*

Schuschnigg, Kurt von (1897–1977). Austrian chancellor. A veteran of *World War I*, in which he was wounded, he was minister of justice under *Engelbert Dollfuss*, becoming chancellor upon the latter's murder during an abortive *Nazi* coup in 1934. A stern *authoritarian*, he was forced from office by the Nazi takeover in the *Anschluss* of Austria and Germany in March 1938. He was incarcerated at *Dachau* during *World War II* until being liberated in 1945 by the American Army. After the war he emigrated to the United States.

Suggested Reading: Kurt von Schuschnigg, *The Brutal Takeover* (1969, 1971).

***Schutzstaffel* (SS).** "Guard detachment." This wholly evil organization began as *Hitler's* elite bodyguard in 1926, a special detachment of the *Sturmabteilung* (SA) founded and commanded by *Himmler*. It surpassed the SA in size and influence after engaging in patricide against its rival in the bloodbath of the *Night of the Long Knives*. It was later subdivided into the Allgemeine (General) SS and the Waffen (Armed) SS, which grew to an astonishing 40 divisions during *World War II*, including many *armored* or SS *Panzer* divisions. The Waffen SS were ideological and battlefield *shock troops* and a pampered rival (better transport, weapons, and supplies) to the *Wehrmacht*. They were drawn from all over the Nazi empire, according to utterly specious criteria of "racial purity." Even so, in the closing days of the war the SS diluted their racial standards in the scramble to recruit fresh *cannon fodder*: the concept of *Volksdeutsche*, for example, was rather desperately extended to include Croatian and other non-German *fascists*. The SS presented itself as a crusading organization in the tradition of the *Teutonic Knights*, which encouraged anti-Slavism and rabid *anti-Semitism* among its members. The SS was also self-consciously pagan and anti-Christian: Himmler and other SS crackpots actively searched for the "Holy Grail," which they thought a Teutonic, not a Christian, icon; and they sent out archeologists to find lost Atlantis, which they believed had been an *Aryan* civilization. The SS carried out the dirtiest tasks of the Nazi regime, including the mass murder of millions of Jews, *Roma*, homosexuals, and other victims of the *Holocaust* (the SS Totenkopfverbände, or "Death's Head Unit," ran the *death camps*). The SS was the main instrument by which the *final solution* was devised, at *Wannsee* by such SS officers as Heydrich and *Eichmann*, and carried out, in SS-supervised death camps like *Auschwitz*. For these actions, SS officers and men were rewarded with the usual perquisites—financial, social, and sexual—which imperial *conquest* always affords such a *praetorian guard*. At *Nuremberg* the SS was named a criminal organization, so that simple membership became a retroactive international crime. *See also* Gestapo; Sicherheitsdienst; *Warsaw Ghetto*.

Schwarzkopf, Herbert Norman (b. 1934). U.S. general. As a young officer Schwarzkopf served two tours of active combat duty in the *Vietnam War*. He was deputy commander during the 1982 *invasion of Grenada*. He came to fame as commander of the United Nations *Gulf coalition* forces which fought Iraq in the *Gulf War*, coordinating operations of more than 500,000 troops drawn from 28 countries. The plans used in Operation Desert Shield and Operation Desert Storm were adapted from contingency exercises he and his staff had designed, and practiced, long before the Iraqi invasion of Kuwait. His loud temper and rages reportedly almost led to his being dismissed from command. His main role was coordinating with Arab allies. His major *tactical* decision was to disapprove proposals for an amphibious landing. He subsequently quarreled with subordinates over who was responsible for permitting the escape of the majority of the *Republican Guard*.

scientism. Preference for pseudoscientific language and aping of the scientific method in nonscientific disciplines, such as the humanities or social sciences. *See also paradigm; political science; rational choice theory; theory; variable.*

"scissors crisis." *Jargon* for the twin dilemma of mounting foreign *debt* at a time of shrinking *export* earnings, leading to a severe crisis for weaker economies by cutting domestic savings and government revenues.

scorched earth. A tactic used by retreating armies in which all land, crops, and housing to be abandoned are torched (and bridges blown up, mines flooded, dams breached, and so forth) to deny them to the enemy. This lengthens an enemy's *supply lines* and forces it to waste troops and resources in *requisition* and resupply, thus slowing any advance. In 1707 *Peter I* of Russia ordered a policy of scorched earth against the invading Swedish army of *Charles XII*, in which he ordered state peasants and *serfs* in the advance of the Swedish Army to flee to the forests; those who would not had their villages burned, and any caught selling food to the Swedes were hanged, and their entire villages also burned even if only a few were guilty. This drew Charles into Ukraine, where his army was destroyed at *Poltava* (July 8, 1709). The Austrians employed scorched earth to hinder the Prussians in Silesia and Bohemia during the wars of *Frederick the Great*; Russia used the tactic again and to great effect against *Napoleon* in 1812; the *Union* used it offensively against the *Confederacy*, 1864–1865; and all sides used it in both directions during *World War II*. Sometimes such destruction is done more from wanton spite than as a stratagem with any military purpose or consequence. Some examples: German troops flooded French and Belgian mines during their final retreat in 1918; *Hitler* had Warsaw destroyed before retreating from it in 1944; Iraqis fired Kuwait's oil wells at the close of the 1991 *Gulf War*.

Scotland. Scotland was for many centuries a decentralized kingdom which was organized around clan (family, but more accurately tribal) loyalties and divided as well by geography into the highland clans (to the west, connected mainly by sea to each other and outlying islands) and the lowland clans and other lowland dwellers (to the south and along Scotland's eastern coast). Not even the *Roman Empire* could conquer these wild tribes of ancient Picts and Gaels who had migrated to Scotland from Ireland. The Emperor Hadrian (76–138, r. 117–138) therefore decreed a line of *fortifications* should be built, from Solway to Tyne, to mark the northern border of the Empire in Great Britain. That left part of northern *England* and all of Scotland (as yet undefined territories whose populations mixed easily and often) on the other side. *Christianity* migrated to Scotland by the fifth century, along Roman roads then over Hadrian's wall, and from Ireland, through the media of regional and local trade and *missionaries*. After the Romans departed from the island of Great Britain, Scotland was divided—as was the rest of the island—into petty and quarrelsome kingdoms and chiefdoms, of varying Scots, Irish, Pictish, and Germanic peoples.

As with the rest of Western Europe after the fall of the great Empire, a general decline in levels of civilization set in, not just in the form of political fragmentation but in terms of declining commerce and literacy. *Feudalization* began, except for the highlands, areas not conducive to intensive agriculture and peasant cultivation, where the thinner population remained loosely organized in traditional clans—fiercely antagonistic and often brutally ruled tribal associations, dressed up as extended kinship groups. Starting in the eighth century, and lasting some 400 years, into this mix was thrown a new foreign element, as Scotland's history became intimately linked to that of Scandinavia—as did that of all the *British Isles*, by the arrival of the *Vikings*. The "Northmen" first arrived as terrifying and murderous coastal raiders and pillagers, but eventually they came in greater numbers as conquerors, and then in family groups as settlers. During the eleventh and twelfth centuries the whole of Great Britain underwent a dramatic restructuring of its relationship to Scandinavia and to the *res publica Christiana* of the Continent, as well as a readjustment of the internal *balance of power* among its various nations and states.

Scotland now began centuries of conflict with neighboring England, troubles which appear almost foreordained by Scotland's thin population, endless and unresolved internal divisions, and partial cultural absorption of its lowland people, especially the Scottish nobles, many of whom had lands and titles on both sides of the border, into the powerful *Norman* monarchy which took shape in England from 1066 onward. The conflict was touched off by the overarching ambitions for conquest of England's Edward I ("Longshanks," 1239–1307), and controversy over the rightful succession to the Scottish throne. Some Scots resisted conquest by Edward, first under the leadership of *William Wallace*, and later of Robert Bruce (1274–1329, r. 1306–1329), crowned king in 1306. Others among the nobles threw in their lot with the English king, however, and many Scots simply cowered before the enormous armies the English repeatedly brought into the lowlands. Still, Bruce ultimately prevailed over the feeble son of Longshanks, Edward II (1234–1327), at the decisive Battle of Bannockburn (June 24, 1314), where a large English army was virtually slaughtered.

In the thirteenth and fourteenth centuries, to keep English armies at bay Scotland allied with Norway, France, and other anti-English powers. Scotland abolished *serfdom* in the fourteenth century, well before England. From the fourteenth through the sixteenth centuries, Scotland cleaved to the "auld alliance" with France, which formed naturally as a result of mutual propinquity to a common enemy, England. This association began to break down when Scotland converted to the new religion during the *Protestant Reformation*, in Scotland's case the dour *Calvinism* of the preacher John Knox (1505–1572), which developed into a national faith and church as Presbyterianism. As France retained the old *Catholic* faith and the *Wars of Religion* swept over Europe in the sixteenth and seventeenth centuries, this historical prop of Scottish independence was kicked away.

Matters came to a head during the reign of *Elizabeth I* of England and the interrupted reign of Mary Stuart, Queen of Scots (1542–1587), who was supported by the Catholic powers of Europe in her claim to both the Scottish and English thrones but was opposed by many of her would-be subjects for her Catholic faith and ties to foreign Catholic powers. Elizabeth kept the fires of dissent alive with money and subversion, and in the end Mary lost the Scottish throne and personal freedom (1567), and then her life to an English executioner (1587). However, her son James (1566–1625), king of Scotland as James VI (1567–1625), mounted the English throne after the childless Elizabeth died in 1603: a *union of crowns* between England and Scotland, and therefore peace along the border, was finally achieved when James VI was also crowned James I of England (1603–1625). Trouble still lay ahead. The lowlands might accept union with the ancient enemy, to which it had grown closer and more alike over the centuries, but the highlands were still wild, hardly governed at all, and fiercely independent. For a time this social and cultural division among Scots was obscured by the dominance of the religious question in Scottish and international politics. Arcane doctrinal and ecclesiastical disputes pulled Scotland deep into England's great civil wars in the middle of the seventeenth century, when Scottish nobles alternately backed the English king, Charles I (1600–1649), then betrayed him to *Cromwell*. Scotland despised the restored king, Charles II (1630–1685, r. 1660–1685), for his Catholicism and welcomed the "Glorious Revolution," which put *William of Orange* on the throne. This left only one loose end: the *Jacobites*, but their bolt was shot, too, after 1746. In the end, Scotland was conquered by English arms, by the depth of England's purse, and by the weight of its greater population and more advanced and organized state and military. This and the compelling fact that the two countries shared many real interests and views—economic, political, security, and even religious—was recognized constitutionally when Scotland's independent monarchy was abolished and it was united with England and Wales in the *Act of Union* of 1707.

In the eighteenth and nineteenth centuries Scotland was even more integrated with England and served as an engine of disproportionate power and influence in British national politics, as it did also in British letters, science, higher education, invention, overseas exploration and empire-building, and domestic *industrialization*. Scots fought loyally in all Britain's wars after the Act of Union. Beginning in the 1930s, however, there developed a democratic nationalist and primarily cultural movement for "devolution," or *autonomy*, and celebration of Scots culture and tradition. Following on the 1970s discovery of North Sea *oil* there arose new demands among a sizable minority of Scots for outright political independence, within the context of membership for Scotland in the *European Union*. By the end of the twentieth century this one-time cultural movement had achieved a devolved Scottish parliament and backed a mass political party devoted to Scottish independence. Scotland's ties to *Ulster* are historically strong. Its modern population, too, remains divided between Catholic and Protestant (with the majority Protestant). The more important social cleavages in its history, however, were and remain those between the lowlands and the highlands; or in more modern terms, between the Edinburgh-Glasgow urban axis on one hand and the countryside on the other, as well as among social classes and class divisions in the larger cities produced over many decades by industrialization.

Suggested Reading: J. D. Mackie, A History of Scotland (1964, 1974).

Scott, Winfield (1786–1866). "Old Fuss and Feathers." He saw his first action as a young officer during the *War of 1812*, during which he was captured by the British, at Queenston. He was freed in a prisoner exchange and soon led the forces which captured Fort George in 1813. Overcoming a slight wound, he participated in the American campaign in *Québec* and the attack on Montréal later that year. Promoted to brigadier general, he led a second invasion of Canada in 1814, during which he was wounded twice more. He served again during the Blackhawk War, prosecuted against Wisconsin's Indians by President *Andrew Jackson* in 1832. In 1836 he fought in another of Jackson's Indian wars, against the Seminoles of Florida. Scott was next sent to Maine to *show the flag* to the British and Canadians during the *Aroostook War,* which he helped ensure remained a more comic than deadly confrontation. He was promoted to commanding general of the U.S. Army in 1841.

His major military exploits came during the *Mexican-American War*. Not content with defending Texas and the western United States, he proposed and carried out an invasion of Mexico, landing at Veracruz on March 9, 1847, and capturing Mexico City on August 7th. Despite his great victory, for the second time in his career he was charged with official misconduct, and for the second time was cleared of all charges. The scale and swiftness of the victory made him a national hero. Seeking to capitalize on this reputation, he ran for the *Whig* nomination for president in 1848. He was defeated by another hero of the recent Mexican war, *Zachary Taylor*. Scott ran for president again in 1852 but was soundly defeated. He sensed early on that the *American Civil War* was coming, and designed a grand strategy to win it for the Union. He proposed a naval *blockade* of the South (this became the Anaconda Plan), along with a war of *attrition* on land. After many fits, starts, and failures, the Union would eventually adopt the essentials of Scott's plan and press it home to victory. Scott was himself too old and ill to command, however, and resigned his post as the head of the army in 1861. He was replaced by the excessively cautious and ultimately disastrous dandy George B. McClellan.

Suggested Reading: John Eisenhower, Agent of Destiny (1997).

"scramble for Africa." The rapid, competitive *Great Power* partition of Africa during the latter third of the nineteenth century, in which formal and informal *spheres of influence* were converted into *colonies* by *annexation* or *conquest*. At its beginning, about 1876, some 90 percent of Africa was still under the control of indigenous rulers—some of them truly appalling and interested mainly in slave raiding, but Africans nonetheless. By its end, about 1912, only isolated pockets of Africa remained free of European military occupation and control. It arose in part from the late entry of Italy and Germany—themselves only just unified within Europe—into the game of colonial acquisition, and partly from the development of river steamships and inland *railways* which made commercial penetration of Africa's interior viable for the first time. Also contributing was French desire for *prestige* through empire, to compensate for its humiliation in the *Franco-Prussian War* (1870–1871). The British were largely drawn into the scramble by concern over gains by other European powers and by unscrupulous or driven individuals; but of all the imperial powers, Great Britain was the least interested in exchanging informal for formal empire in Africa, and was the major strategic loser when it was all over.

The scramble was thus caused largely by extant European interests in Africa, which the course of circumstance then helped stimulate arguments for further intervention to protect. Among such arguments, the continuance of indigenous *slavery* within Africa made odd bedfellows of *missionaries* and anti-slavery humanitarians with romantic imperialists, who formed a ménage a trois with hardheaded geopolitical strategists. It was sparked, though not caused, by Belgian King Leopold II's personal claim to the *Congo*. In 1881 France captured *Tunis*; in 1882 Britain took *Egypt*, after France failed to join in a double intervention. *Bismarck* then made it an all-out Great Power competition by his sudden reversal on colonial policy from 1883 to 1885, when he proclaimed *German Southwest Africa*, *German East Africa*, *Kamerun*, and *Togo* to be German *protectorates*, and convinced Britain to recognize these claims in return for Egypt. In 1885, in response also to the French annexation of Dahomey (1883), Britain proclaimed an Oil Rivers Protectorate over the Niger delta.

The *Berlin Conference* (1884–1885) was called by Bismarck and was attended by 13 European powers, with the United States present as an observer. It drew and confirmed Africa's colonial borders with attention solely to imperial interests, with the major geostrategic effect of blocking British expansion along the Congo and up the Niger. Britain (under *Salisbury*) responded by making a protectorate of *Bechuanaland* (1885), increasing pressure on the *Boer* republics of *Transvaal* and the *Orange Free State*, and backing *Cecil Rhodes* in his various machinations and plots in *Rhodesia*. In 1890 Salisbury agreed with Bismarck to a series of boundary understandings wherever British and German colonies touched, and confirmed British control of *Zanzibar*. In exchange, Germany acquired *Heligoland*. In 1891 Portugal's claim to *Nyasaland* was confirmed, along with Britain's claim to Rhodesia. *Madagascar* became a French protectorate in 1885 and a colony in 1896. In 1893 *Côte d'Ivoire* became a French colony, as did *French Guinea*. *Dahomey* was made a French protectorate in 1893 and a colony in 1900. In 1895 the composite colony of *French West Africa* was established. In 1896 Britain overran *Ashante* from its colony in the *Gold Coast*, but in the east Italy was repelled and humiliated by *Abyssinia* in the *First Abyssinian War*. Ethiopia then doubled its territory by conquering small African chieftaincies to its south. In 1898 *Sudan* was reconquered by the British, out of Egypt, after the bloody and decisive *Battle of Omdurman*. That same year, French forces finally defeated *Samori Touré* in the *French Soudan* and claimed *Niger* from the *Fulbe* and *Tuareg*.

The scramble had by now become so intense, and the prestige stakes so high, that Britain and France nearly tumbled into war at *Fashoda* in 1898 before backing away. The last Bunyoro resistance in *Uganda* was overcome by British forces in 1899. Direct control of northern *Nigeria* was instituted by London in 1900, although Kano and other *Hausa* cities were not occupied until 1902. With conquest of the Boer republics during the *Second Boer War* by Britain, also in 1902, only *Liberia* and Abyssinia remained independent south of the Sahara. In 1910 Britain consolidated its southern colonies in the *Union of South Africa*. In North Africa, in 1911 Italy invaded *Tripoli* but could not pacify it until the 1930s. The struggle to control *Morocco* led to two major crises which threatened all Europe with war, in 1905 and 1911. In 1912 Morocco was peacefully *partitioned* between France and Spain, with *compensation* given to Germany in Kamerun. The scramble thus ended just in time for the competitive European empires to descend together into *World War I*, which began the process of unraveling what they had only just stitched together in Africa. Peace proved an illusion in Morocco, too, as the *Rif Rebellion* later broke out there, 1921–1926. *See also Agadir; imperialism; Frederick D. Lugard; First Moroccan Crisis; pan-Islamicism; Henry Morton Stanley; Swahili Arabs; Tippu Tip.*

Suggested Readings: Eric Axelson, *Portugal and the Scramble for Africa, 1875–1891* (1967); John Hargreaves, *West Africa Partitioned*, 2 vols. (1974); Lawrence James, *Savage Wars: British Campaigns in Africa, 1870–1920* (1985); D. M. Schreuder, *The Scramble for Southern Africa* (1980).

"scramble for concessions" (in China). *See spheres of influence.*

scuttle. To deliberately sink one's own ship to deny its use to the enemy. The most spectacular example occurred when the entire surrendered German battle fleet was scuttled by its crews at *Scapa Flow*, in Scotland, after *World War I*.

SD. *See Sicherheitsdienst.*

SDECE (*Service de Documentation Extérieure et de Contre-Espionage*). As the name suggests, it is the *counterespionage* service of France. *See also Sûreté.*

SDI. *See Strategic Defense Initiative.*

Seabed Treaty (1971). It proclaimed the seabed under the *high seas,* beyond the *twelve-mile limit,* to be a *nuclear weapons free zone,* which it was already, and was likely to remain in any case. Since it was largely symbolic, it was adhered to by most states. Note: The treaty said nothing about *boomers* which operate beneath the oceans. Hence, during the *Cold War* even the Soviet Union and United States *ratified* it, seeing it as mostly harmless.

sea mine. An explosive capable of damaging or sinking a passing ship. They are laid by ship, plane, or *submarine.* Floating mines detonate on contact. Others may be tethered below the surface, or rest on the seabed, to be triggered by sound or by magnetic attraction. They were first used during the *American Civil War.* The *Hague Convention* of 1907 prohibited floating mines as indiscriminate in nature and required *belligerents* to notify all other governments of the existence of minefields at sea. In practice, these provisions were disregarded. Huge minefields were laid in the Baltic and North Seas during *World War I* and *World War II,* by Germany and Britain, including illegal minefields in parts of the *high seas* and, with regard to Norway before it was invaded by Germany in 1940, in the *territorial waters* of a *neutral.* The United States used sea mines to clog Democratic Republic of Vietnam (DRV) harbors during the *Vietnam War.* Nicaragua's harbors were mined in peacetime by the *Reagan* administration, which sought to bottle up the *Sandinista* regime. The Persian Gulf was heavily mined by both sides during the *Iran-Iraq War,* which eventually led to an international minesweeping operation by several of the world's leading navies, including cooperation between the Soviet and U.S. Navies

sea power. (1) A nation which is in the first rank in naval strength. (2) A synonym for naval strength, implying an ability to project force far beyond one's own shores. (3) A theory developed in its most sophisticated form by *Alfred Thayer Mahan* and others, which says the key to dominant or even world power is naval strength, and views the oceans as avenues of contact rather than barriers between continents. This theory also makes cultural assumptions about the effects of sea power. It sees continental or *land powers* as *conservative* and often *authoritarian,* where the army is the senior service and economies tend toward *self-reliance.* In contrast, maritime powers are seen as *liberal,* with the navy and *merchant marine* driving the economy through overseas commerce. For thousands of years, until the fifteenth century *revolution in military affairs* and *gunpowder revolution,* war at sea was merely a continuation of war on land: coast-hugging warships, almost always steerable *galleys,* were used to transport shock troops or to board and grapple with troops on other ships. Guns changed everything: warships became mobile *artillery* platforms, with ever-larger sailing vessels able to bring firepower to bear against hostile coastlines or ships. This doomed the galley, which was swept from the seas in the sixteenth century by *caravels, frigates,* and *men-of-war.* During the seventeenth century navies composed of huge, and hugely expensive, *ships-of-the-line,* including some *privateers,* employed new fleet tactics such as *line ahead, broadside,* and *raking.* They were so expensive to build and maintain (requiring not just the ships, but permanent docks, crews, and dredged harbors) that they required new kinds of states, bureaucracies, and professional services to support them, so that trade, exploration, and maritime warfare blended into a nearly continuous blur of interstate conflict, commerce raiding, and state-sanctioned *piracy.* The next major change came with the nineteenth-century invention of the *ironclad* and *turret* and the twentieth-century *Dreadnought* revolution. By the twenty-first century the decisive weapons of sea power were the *aircraft carrier* and *submarine. See also air power; Anglo-German Naval Agreement; Battle of the Atlantic; Battle of Tsushima Straits; battleship; Black Sea Fleet; blockade; boomer; Bosphorus; capital ship; convoy; Coral Sea; cruiser; Dardanelles; destroyer; English Channel; Exploration, Age of; Fisher; Five-Power Naval Treaty; flag; flota; geopolitics; Gibraltar; Gulf War; Jutland; Leyte Gulf; London Naval Disarmament Conference; Halford Mackinder; mercantilism; Midway; mutiny; Nine Power Treaty; Panama Canal; Pearl Harbor; Rimland; George Rodney; Royal Navy; Scapa Flow; show the flag; sloop of war; Spanish Armada; Straits Question; Suez Canal; Trafalgar; Tsushima Straits; two-power standard; U-boat; unrestricted submarine warfare; wolf pack; world island; World War I; World War II.*

Suggested Readings: Bernard Brodie, *Naval Strategy* (1942); Colin Gray, *Leverage of Sea Power* (1992); John Guilmartin, *Gunpowder and Galleys* (1975); Alfred T. Mahan, *The Influence of Sea Power upon History* (1890); Daniel O'Connel, *The Influence of Law on Sea Power* (1975); P. Padfield, *Guns at Sea* (1973); E. Potter, *Sea Power* (1981); Clark Reynolds, *Navies in History* (1998); Clark Reynolds, *Command of the Sea* (1974).

search-and-destroy missions. A term used by the U.S. military during the *Vietnam War* to refer to its main *military objective* (1965–1968) of searching out the enemy's larger-scale armed forces and destroying them, rather than trying to take and hold territory from National Liberation Front (NLF) *guerrillas.* It was aptly described as a tactic to "find, fix, and finish" enemy forces. *Infantry* was used to locate the enemy, who was then to be destroyed by U.S. *artillery* and *air power.* The NLF and the People's Army of Vietnam (PAVN) countered by close-in fighting ("cling to their cartridge belts," as one NLF commander put it) to annul the U.S. firepower advantage. In the media and in *public opinion,* "search-and-destroy" was misunderstood and became associated with scenes of GIs burning out Vietnamese villages and other *depredations* against civilians, and even came to mean something akin to *atrocity.* This image was reinforced by the reported (but unconfirmed) remark of a U.S. officer about his unit's firing on the village of Ben Tre in 1968: "It became necessary to destroy the town in order to save it." *See also liberation; My Lai massacre; pacification.*

search and seizure. *See visit and search.*

Sebastopol. Capital of the *Crimea.* Founded by *Potemkin,* it was besieged for a year by the British, French, and Piedmontese during the *Crimean War.* In the *Treaty of Paris* (1856), it was *demilitarized.* Russia refortified it, 1870–1871, making it again the main base of the *Black Sea Fleet.* It was bombarded and captured by Germany in 1942 but later liberated. It was presented as a "gift" to Ukraine by Russia in 1954. In mid-1993 the Russian parliament claimed the city, but *Boris Yeltsin* disavowed the land grab as a "shameful act." When Ukraine subsequently agreed to Russian possession of the Black Sea Fleet, it agreed to lease the fleet's historic Sebastopol base to Russia.

secession. Formal withdrawal from a political *union* or *federation.* Most secessions face forceful resistance and may be treated as criminal rather than political movements. A few are peaceful. While encouraged by the principle of *self-determination,* they face fundamental hostility from a states system which is inherently conservative about the survival of its extant members. Generally, it takes *intervention* by some outside power in the form of military *aid* or troops for secession to be realized. Yet there are just enough bloody, self-won successes (such as Eritrea) and sufficient ethnically or otherwise repressive regimes to encourage more attempts. *See also American Civil War; American Revolution; Biafra; Basques; Chechnya; Congo; East Timor; Eritrea; Kalistan; Katanga; Kosovo; Kurds; Panama; Québec; Taiwan; Tamil Tigers; Tibet.*

secondary sector. A conventional category describing economic *production* which manufactures or processes products. A huge increase in the number of workers in this sector of the economy occurred with the *industrial revolution,* reaching nearly half the workforce in some economies. In the most advanced economies this trend reversed after *World War II,* with more workers moving into service jobs in the *tertiary sector. See also primary sector; structure.*

Second Empire. France, from the declaration of empire by *Napoleon III* in 1852, to his capture at *Sedan* and abdication in 1870. *See also France.*

second front. The *World War II* demand from the Soviet Union, and the promise made repeatedly by the Western *Allies,* to relive pressure on the *eastern front* by attacking Germany in the west. It was mainly delayed by a lack of landing craft and transports and by the prior necessity of winning the *Battle of the Atlantic.* The British were more reluctant than the Americans to proceed, having experienced the horrors of *Passchendaele* and the *Somme* in *World War I,* and the more near-term disaster at *Dieppe.* Also, *Churchill* remained convinced that the *Balkans* were the "soft underbelly of Europe" through which a saber thrust might end the war more quickly and additionally, cut the Soviets short of entering Central Europe. As the term referred to operations in France and northwest Europe, landings in North Africa, Sicily, and Italy did not satisfy American demands for a quick opening of a second front, or allay Soviet suspicions that the Western Allies were determined to fight Germany to the last Russian. The second front was established on June 6, 1944 (D-day). *See also Ardennes Offensive; Dwight D. Eisenhower; Bernard Montgomery; Normandy campaign; George Patton; strategic bombing; thousand bomber raids; two-front war.*

Second International. *See International (Socialist).*

Second Moroccan Crisis. *See Agadir.*

Second Republic. France, from the *Revolution of 1848* to the proclamation of the *Second Empire* by *Napoleon III* in 1852.

second strike. Launch of a retaliatory strike of *nuclear weapons* which survive an enemy's *first strike.*

second-strike capability. The capacity to retaliate with a devastating *nuclear* strike even after suffering colossal damage from a *first strike*. It has been often, but wrongly, argued that second-strike capability distinguished the *superpowers* in the *Cold War*. In fact, Britain and France also had second-strike capability: once their *deterrent* was *submarine*-based it was not subject to a first strike, even should both home countries be utterly destroyed. *See also sufficiency.*

Second World. A synonym for the *communist* states during the *Cold War*, with the partial exception of *Yugoslavia* after 1947, China after the *Sino-Soviet split*, and *Albania* after 1958. *See also First World; Fourth World; Third World; Soviet bloc.*

Secretariat. The *executive* or administrative body of an *international organization*. In the *United Nations* it is the division which houses the main corps of international civil servants, headed by the *secretary general*. Appointments are frequently made based on country of origin or *caucus group*, as well as merit. In the mid-1980s pressure from major donors, especially the United States, which began to withhold its subventions, led to trimming of the budget of the UN Secretariat. A good deal of fat and administrative corruption was eliminated.

secretary general. (1) Chief administrative officer of an *international organization*, such as the *League of Nations* or the *International Labor Organization*. (2) The chief administration officer of the *United Nations Organization*, who heads its *Secretariat*. Election is by a two-thirds vote of the *United Nations General Assembly (UNGA)*, following a recommendation by the *Security Council*, for a term of five years; reelection is possible. During the *Cold War* most secretaries general were compromise candidates agreed to by the *superpowers*. After 1990, elections in the UNGA became more complex and fluid. Beyond administrative functions and performance of specific tasks set by the Security Council or UNGA, the secretary general may bring to the attention of the United Nations any matter regarded as a threat to international *peace* and *security*. To date, the personality of the various secretaries general has been a key determinant in how active or passive, and effective, the office has been. By date of first election, the secretaries general have been *Trygve Lie*, Norway (1946); *Dag Hammarskjöld*, Sweden (1953); *U Thant*, Burma (1961); *Kurt Waldheim*, Austria (1972); *Javier Pérez de Cuéllar*, Peru (1982); *Boutros Boutros-Ghali*, Egypt (1992); and *Kofi Annan*, Ghana (1997).

secretary of defense. In the United States, the *cabinet* officer in charge of the Department of Defense (*Pentagon*), the *Joint Chiefs*, and all military matters relating to national security. Until *World War II* this office was "secretary of war."

secretary of state. In the United States, the *cabinet* officer in charge of the *State Department*, formally (but not always actually) responsible for formulating and overseeing implementation of American *diplomacy*; elsewhere called *foreign minister*.

secret diplomacy. For some in the *intelligence* business, this euphemism is preferred to *covert action*.

secret police. A euphemism for political police, which are secret and powerful services used in dictatorial and *totalitarian* societies to repress dissent and/or instill terror in the populace, as a deterrent to opposition to the government's policies. *See also* Gestapo; KGB; NKVD; Stasi; Truth Commission.

secret service. (1) In general: an alternate for *intelligence services*, as in "the British secret service." (2) In the United States: the arm of the *Department of the Treasury* which is responsible for combating counterfeiters and for protecting the president, vice president, visiting *heads of state* or *government*, cabinet officers, and former presidents and their families.

secret speech. It was delivered by *Khrushchev* before the twentieth Congress of the *Communist Party* of the Soviet Union, in February 1956, during which he stunned the assembled *apparatchiki* by denouncing *Stalinism*. He criticized *Stalin* directly and by name, a man hitherto the center of an extraordinary *cult of personality*. The charges against him were (1) gross failures of policy, domestic and foreign, all the while claiming infallibility and *purging* and *liquidating* dissenters who were loyal members of the Party; (2) assuming that conflict with the *capitalist* world was inevitable and must necessarily lead to war; and (3) not permitting *socialist* parties in neighboring countries to adapt *communism* to local conditions, rather than toe the *party line* set by Moscow in all things. Khrushchev proposed to permit a domestic thaw, to substitute for the assumption of war a new policy of *peaceful coexistence* which took account of the nuclear age, and to relax tensions with other socialist countries by permitting them a degree of *autonomy*. In practice, he failed to carry out these policies, largely because easing repression and allowing national autonomy soon proved to threaten the Soviet empire and even the Soviet Union itself, as in the *Hungarian Uprising* and the *Sino-Soviet split*. His own recklessness meant he also plunged the world into repeated crises. The speech was released to the "New York Times" by American and Israeli intelligence and published on June 4, 1956. It created a worldwide sensation. In China, it helped spark the *Hundred Flowers campaign* (1956–1957).

"secret treaties." Historically, most treaties were negotiated in secret and some or all of their *terms* kept secret, facts which were accepted as standard and necessary to the conduct of *diplomacy* for centuries. "Secret treaties" is a modern pejorative, which gained currency in reference to the alliance commitments among the *Great Powers* before *World War I*: the exact terms of prewar alliances were secret, which some later thought affected the course of the *mobilization crisis* and contributed to outbreak of the war. Secrecy took on a strongly pejorative connotation with the rise of democratic objections, primarily in the United States and in the *liberal peace program* during *Woodrow Wilson*'s presidency. Revelations of secret wartime agreements among the European Allies which ran counter to the *Fourteen Points* (including the *Treaty of London*, the *Constantinople Agreement*, and the *Sykes-Picot Agreement*) caused a sharp reaction after the war which amounted to proposals for revolution in diplomatic affairs, captured in Wilson's call for a new, *open diplomacy*. Secrecy in treaty-making still thrived among dictatorships, however, as in the *Nazi-Soviet Pact*. It has become much more difficult—though not impossible—for most democracies. *See also transparency.*

secularism. A social and political philosophy which rejects all *religion* as inappropriate when applied to public affairs. It is a prominent characteristic of the industrial and post-*Enlightenment* age, whether openly admitted or not by *modernizing* political movements, which must contend with organized religious belief in every society. The most radical secularists ever to take power gave the world the *Terror* during the *French Revolution* and the multiple horrors of twentieth-century *communism*. Yet it is a mistake to confuse secularism with repression of *liberty*, just as it is to assert the reverse: secularists in many nations have worked to free social and public policy from the strictures of fanatical religious *ideologies*. In most instances, they were compelled to compromise with the public forms, if not the essence, of local religious faith. By the end of the twentieth century secularists coexisted fairly easily with tamed religious communities in the West and elsewhere, but remained in perpetual tension and conflict with all proponents of religious *fundamentalism*. *See also clash of civilizations.*

secular trends. Decades-long statistical patterns in the world economy which mark periods of prolonged *inflation, growth,* and/or economic contraction. The *price revolution* of the seventeenth century was one such trend. Similarly, an inflation set in following the vast expense of the *War of the Austrian Succession* (1740–1748), the *Seven Years' War* (1756–1763), and the *American Revolution* (1775–1783), which contributed to a global recession and to the fiscal crisis in France which came to a political head in 1789. During the *Napoleonic Wars* prices rose all over the world, in large part due to the direct cost of the fighting but also its interference with normal trade. From 1815 to 1850 the price trend reversed under the impact of the technological innovation of the *industrial revolution* and new modes of cheap transportation. In the 1850s prices rose in response to *gold rushes* in *California* and Australia and the costs of the *Crimean War.* In 1873 a severe *deflation* and *world depression* set in which, combined with the advance of *railways* and Germany's shift to *protectionism,* depressed world prices until new gold strikes were made in the Yukon, Siberia, and Southern Africa, which stimulated another round of global inflation prior to *World War I. See also business cycle.*

security. *See environmental security; international security; national interest; national security; security dilemma.*

security analyst. A specialist in *national security* issues. Traditionally this meant almost exclusively attention to matters of *defense* and *strategy,* but during the latter part of the *Cold War* it expanded to involve questions of the economic basis of national strength, and post–Cold War, such nonmilitary issues as *environmental security.*

security community. A loose term for a depth of mutual interaction, *integration,* and security confidence which surpasses a mere *alliance* commitment to the point of virtually eliminating considerations of *force* from the conduct of foreign policy. For instance, relations between or among Australia–New Zealand; Canada–United States (and increasingly Mexico); Norway–Sweden; and within the *European Union. See also complex interdependence; democratic peace.*

security complex. Social science *jargon* for a grouping of states whose proximity and interests make them necessarily factors in each others' foreign and security policy. *See also regionalism.*

Security Council. The main organ of the *United Nations*, above the other five *Principal Organs*. It is charged with maintenance of *peace* and *security*, and is a lawmaking body when it passes *binding resolutions*. It was originally made up of the five *permanent members*, plus six nonpermanent members drawn on a rotating basis from the *United Nations General Assembly*. The latter group was subsequently increased to 10 members. From the 1990s, there was discussion of elevating Germany and Japan to the first group, although that poses serious constitutional and political problems, for each of them and for the United Nations. All decisions, whether procedural or substantive, require an affirmative vote of nine members, while substantive questions and binding resolutions must not have among the negative votes (must not be *vetoed* by) any of the five permanent (P-5) members, although they may receive abstentions by one or more of the P-5 without suffering failure. The Security Council was blocked from effective action during most of the *Cold War* by American and Soviet vetoes on various issues, especially wars and crises, which concerned them, but additionally by disagreement over the status of China and on *decolonization* issues by British and French vetoes. From 1988 to 1993 it enjoyed a remarkably active period in which not one veto was cast, though China frequently abstained, a record broken by a Russian veto on the relatively trivial and nonideological question of funding for *peacekeeping* operations in Cyprus. The Security Council thus showed tentative signs of emerging from its Cold War doldrums to become the serious forum for resolution—and not just discussion—of *international security* issues which its founders intended. *See also collective security; Gulf War; Korean Conflict; Kosovo; Palestine; Resolutions 242, 338, 660, and 678; sanctions.*

security dilemma. The "theory" that under conditions of international *anarchy* when one *state* seeks to improve its defenses those improvements will be seen as threats by other states, which must assume the worst. An *arms race* may result, as other states match the first increase in military preparedness. This in turn will be seen as a threat by the first state, which thinks its defensive intentions are obvious and therefore that its neighbors are arming without cause, or to attack. So it raises the ante and arms some more, and so on. As an observation of an aspect of international relations in times of high global tension, this idea has some merit. For instance, each move made by Imperial Spain under *Philip II* to preserve the status quo of the extant world order was instantly interpreted as aggressive and threatening by powers on the anti-*Habsburg* side of the fence. Similarly, during the early *Cold War* the Soviet Union and United States routinely assumed aggressive motivations on the part of each other, even where later historians have shown fear of loss to be more prevalent. On the other hand, in its pure form as a theoretical *model* employed by social scientists the idea of the security dilemma ignores that in the real world states constantly assess intentionality, and not just capability. Thus, the American arms buildup during the Cold War did not lead to counterarming by Canada, Mexico, Britain, or France, because those states saw no intended threat to themselves. However, it did contribute to arms procurement in countries such as Cuba, which perceived a definite threat. In contrast, the simultaneous arms buildup by the Soviet Union led most of its neighbors to counterarm. Why? Because they feared (or at least doubted) Soviet aggressive intentions. The concept is therefore subject to gross misapplication to real-world events and may utterly misconceive subject matter in a strained search for a *rational choice* model of human behavior. For example, one study of the arms race in the Middle East—arguing from the idea of a security dilemma and "rational choice model" of how "actors" behave under "conditions of international anarchy," rather than from known facts about key personalities and time-lines—seriously argued that *Saddam Hussein* was "forced" to develop nuclear weapons in the 1980s because although he had signed the *NPT*, Israel had not, and this must surely have increased his sense of insecurity. Furthermore, Israel had attacked his nuclear reactor and nuclear weapons research program (June 7, 1981), and this meant Hussein was compelled to regard Israel as an enemy state and arm against it. Only a methodology predisposed to crudely cutting and pasting reality to fit into theory, rather than utilizing theories (general observation of patterns of behavior) to illuminate important aspects of reality, could compose such a convoluted and ahistorical treatment of *causation* and thereby arrive at the *reductio ad absurdum* conclusion that Saddam Hussein's motives were defensive.

security studies. A specialization within the academic discipline of *international relations* which concentrates on issues of *national security*, and increasingly, also *international security*. See also *security analyst*.

security treaty. An agreement between or among *states* undertaking mutual military support in the event any signatory is attacked by a nonsignatory. Some compacts will specifically name the third country or countries, and may or may not also delineate precise conditions under which the *treaty* may be invoked.

Sedan, Battle of (September 1, 1870). The key battle of the *Franco-Prussian War*, in which French resistance was broken (20,000 dead), the main French army (80,000) *surrendered*, and *Napoleon III* himself was captured. The *Second Republic* was proclaimed three days later, the *Paris Commune* was established, and the road to Paris left open to the Prussians. Paris was then besieged by the Prussian Army from September 19, 1870 to January 28, 1871.

sedes materiae. In *international law*, the locale of settlement.

sedition. Inciting a population to disloyalty or rebellion against an established government.

Seeckt, Hans von (1866–1936). He served as a *staff officer* in *World War I*, then headed Germany's secret *rearmament* program, 1919–1926. Although politically neutral, his secret training of the *Reichswehr* in the Soviet Union built the core of an armed force which proved rapidly expandable by *Hitler* after 1933, in the form of the *Wehrmacht*. Just before his death he was a military adviser to the *Guomindang* in China.

segmentary state. A concept developed to account for the fact that in Indian and other premodern history, numerous states and statelets existed which did not conform either to the modern conception of the *unitary state* or to the *feudal* conception of political authority loosely organized through a system of *tribute* and vassalage. In a segmentary state system there are many centers of political and economic power, or political communities, and many political actors, but only one *legitimate* king (*sovereign*), who is usually acknowledged by lesser centers of power through ritual and religious ceremony.

seisen. "Holy war." A Japanese belief before and during *World War II*, flowing from the emperor myth and idea of *kokutai*, that military service was in a divine cause and Japan was a nation touched by Providence to lead all other Asian peoples.

seizure. Detention of *contraband* or other cargo, pending judgment in a *prize court*.

Sekigahara, Battle of (September, 1600). Nearly 200,000 men met in this climax of a century of *feudal* warfare, in which *Tokugawa Ieyasu* led a coalition of eastern *daimyo* in finally establishing firm control over most of Japan. Sekigahara was the culminating battle of the *Unification Wars*. Ieyasu finished the job of unification at Osaka in 1615.

Sekou Touré, Ahmed (1922–1984). *See Guinea.*

self-defense. A fundamental international legal principle (with domestic parallels) upholding the right of a state to take a range of measures to protect its other legal rights or to redress infringements of those rights by other states. This right is customarily limited by a requirement of *proportionality*. Historically, self-defense has been interpreted expansively to mean defense of the *national interest*, howsoever defined according to time and circumstance, not just against a direct threat of one's territory. Article 51 of the *Charter of the*

United Nations recognizes a right of "individual or collective self-defense if an armed attack occurs against a Member." Article 51 was cited in founding extra–United Nations *alliances* such as *NATO*, to justify UN military aid to South Korea in the *Korean Conflict*, and to Kuwait in the *Gulf War*. However, the right of self-defense is logically, morally, legally, and historically prior to the UN Charter, and thus may be invoked outside the restrictions of the Charter. This is not always understood among journalists or the general public, or by all political scientists. Most states prefer not to do this for reasons of *prestige* and political precedent, but if their *vital interests* are at stake they will surely invoke a right of self-defense in this more fundamental sense. *See also abatement; aggression; Entebbe; preventive strike.*

self-determination. (1) Legally accepted: The right of a *sovereign* entity (*state*) to its preferred political institutions and form of government. (2) Controversial: The right of all *peoples* to separate, sovereign states. (3) In practice: Proclaimed as an international right of all peoples by *Woodrow Wilson* in the *Fourteen Points*, and again at the *Paris Peace Conference*, the idea of self-determination based on *popular sovereignty* was upheld against the defeated empires of the *Central Powers* (Austria, Germany, and the *Ottoman Empire*) but rejected (a) as to the subject *nations* of Russia (an erstwhile ally of the victorious *Allied* powers); and (b) for the colonial populations of European *empires*, other than Germany's. German colonies and Ottoman provinces were converted into *mandates*. Paradoxically, this "right" was invoked to sanction the legitimacy of *Czechoslovakia* and *Yugoslavia*, which were themselves *multinational* states but which had broken free of the defeated *Austro-Hungarian Empire* in the last days of the war. After *World War II* self-determination was endorsed by the United Nations as expressing the right of colonial peoples to *independence* from Western empires, but denied to those such as *Biafrans* or *Kurds* who subsequently wished to exercise it against extant *Third World* nations. Acceptance by the United Nations in 1993 of self-determination by *Eritrea* was an exceptional case, as that state had a prior existence distinct from Ethiopia and clearly and effectively established its *de facto* sovereignty by force of arms over the course of a 30-year conflict. The same held true for *East Timor*, which became independent in 2002. Self-determination was asserted by the *successor states* of the *Soviet Union* and Yugoslavia but not granted to all such claimants (see *Chechnya, Kosovo*). It is unclear if the principle will continue to be applied in the twenty-first century as an accepted international political norm or if it will be denied out of revulsion toward the violence, and from fear of the disorder, which so often attends its realization. Another unanswered question is whether political self-determination conflicts overmuch with market efficiencies and regional *integration*, or is facilitated by those forces. *See also absolutism; American Revolution; colonialism; decolonization; divine right; French Revolution; human rights; imperialism; liberty; revolution; secession; slavery; trusteeship system.*

self-governing territories. (1) Any *territory* not fully *sovereign* but enjoying domestic *autonomy*. (2) In the *Middle East*: the *Palestinian* lands formerly part of the *occupied territories*, which were progressively surrendered to Palestinian control by Israel beginning in 1994, including *Gaza* and parts of the *West Bank*, but excluding *Jerusalem*. The process was interrupted by renewal of the *Intifada* in 2000.

self-help. (1) In *international law*: the claim that as enforcement of rights is ultimately up to the victim of a violation, *unilateral* or *multilateral* action may be taken to redress certain legal wrongs without resort to a court. In ascending order of effectiveness, or at least of warning, peaceful self-help devices (also known as *measures short of war*) available to states include *diplomatic protest*, *recalling the ambassador*, breaking *diplomatic relations*, *withdrawal* (from *international organizations*), *retorsion*, *reprisal*, *embargo*, *sanctions*, *pacific blockade*, and *occupation*, if undertaken with both an announced and real intention not to proceed to *annexation*. Of course, the ultimate self-help device is *war*. (2) In international relations *theory*: some analysts see an assumed, underlying condition of international *anarchy* as dictating that each state must always look to its own *security*, making self-help an ineluctable characteristic of the *international system*. In this view, use of unilateral force by states and general non-cooperation and conflict are seen as structural features of world politics. *See also self-defense*.

self-preservation. Under *international law*, this plea may be used to defend undertaking what otherwise would be *illegal acts*. *See also necessity; self-defense; self-help*.

self-reliance. A national economic policy which aims at *self-sufficiency* in low-technology manufactured *goods*, especially for *Third World* countries, to lessen dependence on outside powers or global market forces. It involves *import substitution* and state-directed industrial development (*dirigisme*). *See also autarky*.

"self-strengthening" movement (in China). An effort at internal reform by the *Qing dynasty*, following the great upheavals of the *Taiping* and *Nian Rebellions* and the imposition of the *treaty port system* on China as a result of its humbling and defeat in the *Opium Wars*. It took place under the Dowager Empress *Cixi* but was mainly the product of provincial officials who had been decisive in saving the Qing by local actions during the rebellions, who sought to restore internal order and external greatness by reviving China's core *Confucian* traditions and values. *See also Sino-Japanese War*.

self-sufficiency. The attempt by a single nation or state to develop economically based on its internal resources and without major connections to world financial markets or trade. *Dependency theory* advocated this option as the only means of "breaking free" of the structural ties of the *world capitalist system*. In extreme form, self-sufficiency amounts to *autarky*, as in North Korea after 1953. However, the term also describes efforts to preserve or develop national control over key industries or markets, without necessarily implying a withdrawal from world trade and finance. China tried self-sufficiency under the *Qing*, and again under *Mao* after the *Sino-Soviet split*, emerging from this extremism only under *Deng Xiaoping*. Japan attempted self-sufficiency from the West under the *Tokugawa shoguns*, although it remained open and economically connected to China and Korea. India tried a less pronounced form of self-sufficiency until c. 1995, when it reoriented toward *free trade* and global markets. *See also isolationism; mercantilism; neo-mercantilism.*

sellers' market. One where the prices of *goods and services* are high. The antonym is *buyers' market*.

semiperiphery. In *dependency theory*, areas occupying an intermediate position between the *core* and the true *periphery* and possessing certain economic and political characteristics of both.

Sendero Luminoso. "Shining Path." A *Maoist*, *terrorist* organization in Peru founded and led for two decades by an eccentric former philosophy professor, Abimael Guzmán. During the 1970s and 1980s it waged disruptive, indiscriminate bombing campaigns in the cities and conducted numerous assassinations of government officials, police, and judges. Into the 1990s it retained solid control of portions of the countryside, often in cooperation with *drug cartels*. Guzmán was captured without resistance in 1992. That curtailed, but did not end the violence. By 2001 Shining Path guerrillas and violence had returned to large parts of the Peruvian countryside.
    Suggested Reading: David Scott Palmer, *The Shining Path of Peru* (1992).

Senegal. The Wolof of Senegal were a *tributary* state of the *Mali* empire into the fourteenth century, but then broke free. The Senegal coast was first probed by the Portuguese in the fifteenth century (1444), but it was France which *colonized* Senegal in the seventeenth century. Lost to France during the *Napoleonic Wars*, it was reoccupied in 1817. Penetration of the interior was slow but deliberate after 1854: France aimed at a huge colonial empire, for which the Senegal River would serve as the Nile of West African commerce. Independent *sheikdoms* in the interior, and the *Tukolor Empire*, resisted French rule until 1893. In 1895 Senegal was joined to *French West Africa*. During *World War II* the French in Senegal supported *Vichy*, leading to British shelling of Dakar, the capital and main port. The *Free French* took control in 1942. In 1958 it became *autonomous* within the *French Community* and gained full *independence* in 1960, after a year joined with Mali in the abortive

"Mali Federation" under the leadership of *Léopold Senghor*. In 1982 Senegal joined with Gambia in *Senegambia*, but this confederal experiment was abandoned in 1989. A revolt in Casamance, in the southeast, broke out in 1982 and festered into the next century. Persecution of ethnic Senegalese by Mauritania resulted in a spillover of refugees, 1988–1989, and an undeclared border war-cum-skirmish in 1990. Relations with Mauritania remained tense into the mid-1990s. France continues to guarantee Senegal's security.

Suggested Reading: J. F. A. Ajayi and Michael Crowder, eds., *History of West Africa*, 2 vols. (1974).

Senegambia. A *confederation* formed by Senegal and Gambia in 1981. It shared federal institutions and aimed at common defense and monetary policies. It was dissolved in 1989.

Senghor, Léopold (1906–2001). President of Senegal, 1960–1980. Senghor was a noted poet, member of the Académie Française, cultural leader, statesman, and a founder of the *négritude* movement to revive and celebrate traditional African culture. Drafted into the French Army in 1939, he spent part of *World War II* as a *prisoner of war* in a German prison camp. In 1945 he was elected to the French Constituent Assembly as a delegate from Senegal. The next year he was elected to the National Assembly. A proponent of *pan-Africanism*, his several attempts at regional *federation* came to naught, partly because they conflicted with the territorial and national state vision of *Houphouët-Boigny*. Instead of his *conservative* accommodation with France in a large, federal union, *French West Africa* broke into discrete territorial states, each weak and effectively dependent on France. Senghor thereupon became president of Senegal, in 1960, leading his predominantly Muslim nation for 20 years despite his personal Catholicism. He survived a *coup* attempt in 1962, and thereafter ruled as a benevolent authoritarian. Senghor maintained close economic, political, and security ties between Senegal and France. He was among the first—and the few—postcolonial African leaders to leave power gracefully, departing in favor of an effort to establish multiparty democracy. This was perhaps his greatest legacy, achieved despite his having run a *one-party state* for much of his tenure as president. *See also* Rassemblement Démocratique Africain.

Senkaku (Diaoyu, or Tiao-yu-tai) Islands. Located north of Taiwan, between China and Japan, their ownership is disputed by all three countries.

sensitivity. Used to describe a level of *interdependence* where *internal affairs* in one *state* react easily to events within other states, especially on economic matters such as sudden changes in *interest rates* or *stock* prices. Societies also may be sensitive to political or cultural trends in neighboring states, or in states with similar ideological-political systems (as was shown by the toppling of successive east European *Communist* governments, 1989–1990). *See also domino theory.*

sentry. A soldier or military unit placed on guard at the extremes of a set position.

separate opinion. When a justice on an international court agrees with a *judgment* but submits a discrete opinion providing different reasoning.

separate peace. When one member of an *alliance* negotiates an exit from a *war* without consulting its allies, looking solely to its own interests. Austria and Russia several times made separate deals with France during the *Napoleonic Wars*. In 1918, Russia's bending to the German *diktat* at *Brest-Litovsk* threatened and deeply embittered the *Allied and Associated Powers*, prompting their armed *intervention* in North Russia during the early part of the *Russian Civil War*. During *World War II*, France (*Vichy*) made a separate peace with *Nazi Germany* in 1940, Italy made a separate peace with the *Allies* in 1943, and Finland and several minor *Axis* states attempted to negotiate exits from the war as Germany itself was invaded, 1944–1945. The *Arab League* expelled Egypt for making a separate peace with Israel in 1978. And so on.

separatism (*séparatisme*). A synonym for *secession*. Those who advocate this are sometimes called "separatists." In Canada the politically correct wince at this usage, when applied to those from *Québec* who wish to form their own country. There, the term of art and preference is the uniquely awkward "sovereigntists."

sepoy. Native soldiers, especially in India. They were first introduced in India by the Compagnie des Indies Orientales of France in 1740. Subsequently, hundreds of thousands trained and enlisted in the private army of the British *East India Company* and were later attached to the British Army in India. *See also Robert Clive; Indian Army; Indian Mutiny; tirailleurs.*

Sepoy Rebellion. *See Indian Mutiny.*

September 11, 2001, terrorist attack on the United States. On September 11, 2001, nineteen *terrorists* of the *al Qaeda* network, working in well-timed coordination, hijacked four civilian airliners in the United States. They used simple box cutters to slit the throats of flight attendants to intimidate the passengers, and then to kill the pilots and crews. Two of the planes were then flown into the World Trade Center twin towers by *kamikaze* pilots (it was later learned from the mouth of the plot's mastermind, *Usama bin Laden*, that not all the hijackers knew it was to be a suicide mission). This ultimately collapsed both buildings due to the intense heat produced by the ignited jet fuel, which melted their supporting steel skeletons, causing the towers to implode. Nearly 3,000 people were killed, spanning some 80 nationalities. Even so, the victims were mostly American civilians, including nearly 500 emergency workers killed when the towers collapsed, who had rushed to the site upon learning of the twin impacts so that they might lend aid in evacuation and provide medical assistance to the many injured and dying. A third plane was flown into a wing of the Pentagon, killing more than 100 more Americans, both civilian and military. The fourth plane crashed in a field in rural Pennsylvania, possibly because several passengers rushed the cockpit once they learned via cell phone that three other hijacked aircraft already had been used as flying bombs. This act likely spared the *White House* or the Capitol from destruction.

Taken together, the multiple attacks constituted the worst assault on the American homeland in the country's history. They caused over $100 billion in damage to physical infrastructure. The core of Manhattan was gutted, much of New York City remained closed for days, and whole sections of the subway system were blocked for many months. The New York Stock Exchange closed for an unprecedented span and saw prices plunge to historic lows in the week after it reopened, totaling over a trillion dollars in lost market capitalization. The attacks caused hundreds of thousands of people in many dozens of countries to lose their jobs, as the United States and much of the trading world headed deeper into a recession already underway, but which was greatly aggravated by the fear and uncertainty engendered by the events of September 11th. The United States was prompted to reconsider its force commitments and procurement policies, its deterrent posture and policies, and its active defenses and neglected homeland security. The attack immediately provoked Washington and its core allies to adopt a proactive, anti-terrorist stance of hunting down and destroying terrorist threats with global reach wherever they appeared anywhere in the world, a policy shift encapsulated in the *Bush Doctrine*. Just as two generations before, after *Pearl Harbor*, Americans again proved defiant in the face of early defeat, resolute in prosecuting an unasked-for war to ultimate victory, and enormously magnanimous toward the long-suffering peoples of soon-to-be overturned despotic regimes, as in Afghanistan. Many other powers rallied to this effort, to one degree or another. China remained most detached, but Russia made a historic shift toward long-term accommodation with the West.

The first overt counter-blow by the United States was struck on October 7, 2001, when Washington launched Operation Enduring Freedom to liberate Afghanistan from the *Taliban*, as a prerequisite to destroying al Qaeda training bases and hunting down thousands of its members who were being harbored by the atavistic, oppressive regime which had misgoverned that country since 1996. The attacks of September 11th, and then the forceful and concerted U.S. response, stimulated the first extra-area military deployments by Germany and Japan since *World War II*, perhaps setting a precedent for the ever-greater involvement of those wealthy but still relatively timorous democracies in global governance involving future multilateral military operations. In addition to U.S. forces, military assets were deployed in the Afghanistan campaign from a number of other states, including significant numbers from the United Kingdom, along with mostly symbolic deployments by Australia, Canada, the Czech Republic, France, Germany, Italy, Japan, New Zealand, Poland, Russia, and Turkey. Finally, the attack triggered seriatim proclamations of alliance commitments to the United States: Australia upheld its obligations under the *ANZUS treaty*; for the first time ever, *NATO* invoked Article 5 of its Charter, formally asserting that the destruction of the World Trade Center and attack on the Pentagon constituted an attack on all members of the alliance; and Latin American states proclaimed their willingness and obligation to cooperate in hemispheric defense under terms of the *Rio Treaty*.

September massacres (September 2–6, 1792). *See French Revolution.*

Serbia. A *feudal* Serb state was long an outer *tributary* province of the *Byzantine Empire*. It was decisively conquered by the Ottomans (at the Battle of Kosovo) in 1389. Serbia then became a tributary of the *Ottoman Empire*. Upon the fall of *Constantinople* (1453), and with a succession crisis underway in Serbia, it was re-invaded and overrun by *Muhammad II*, 1456–1458, and lost all prior *autonomy*. Serbia remained a discontented Ottoman province until the nineteenth century. A Serb revolt from 1804 to 1813 broke down in *civil war*. However, Serbia won renewed autonomy by 1817, as a Russian *protectorate* still formally within the Ottoman Empire. It benefited again in 1830 from the general weakness occasioned by the *Greek War of Independence* and the Egyptian revolt of *Mehemet Ali*, and by renewed pressure from Russia, the great *Orthodox* power to which Serbs henceforth looked for aid. Following the *Crimean War*, Serbia became a multinational protectorate, although the Ottoman Empire remained as *suzerain*. Serbia went to war with the Ottoman Empire in 1876, looking to expand into *Bosnia-Herzegovina*. It failed to achieve that goal, but its disastrous military showing provoked Russian and then other Great Power intervention. The Great Powers had other ideas about how to answer the *Eastern Question*: Britain gained bases in Cyprus and Austria received Bosnia-Herzegovina as *compensation* for Russian gains at Turkey's expense. With this Great Power intervention, Serbia was *recognized* as fully *independent* in the *Treaty of San Stefano*, a status confirmed in the *Congress of Berlin*, both in 1878.

In 1885 Serbia fought Bulgaria over a minor territorial issue, laying out a pattern of future conflict in the Balkans driven by Serb insistence on regional expansion; it was not alone in that foreign policy, but it was the most persistently aggressive of the new Balkan states. After 1903 Belgrade was ever more assertive about building *Greater Serbia* out of ethnically Serb lands then held by Austria and Turkey. The 1908 annexation of Bosnia-Herzegovina by

Austria-Hungary provoked an aggressive Serb response: formation of the *Balkan League*. During the first two *Balkan Wars* which followed, Serbia gained large amounts of territory. On the other hand, in 1914 its continually provocative and reckless policies led to a direct confrontation with Austria, which triggered the *mobilization crisis* and then *World War I*. In that war most of Serbia was overrun and occupied by Austrian and German troops (1915), and its army was forced to evacuate the country, to Corfu. In 1918 Serbia joined Croatia and Slovenia in the unlikeliest of federations: the *United Kingdom of the Serbs, Croats, and Slovenes*, which was recognized at the *Paris Peace Conference* (1919–1920) and renamed *Yugoslavia* in 1929. That was an association it dominated for the next decade.

Membership in the *Little Entente* did not deter the larger *fascist* states: Yugoslavia was attacked by Nazi Germany on April 6, 1941, and Serbia was occupied. The Nazis set up a *puppet state* in Serbia, as they did in Croatia and other parts of Yugoslavia, run in Belgrade by Serb fascists and *collaborators*. Serbia saw hard fighting during *World War II* until liberated by *Tito's* communist *partisans* and royalist *Chetniks*, whom Tito then *liquidated* in a short but extremely bloody Serbian civil war. While Tito lived he completely dominated Serbian politics—within the context of the Yugoslav Federation. In the succession struggle and final breakdown of Yugoslavia which followed his death, Serbian nationalists again set out to construct "Greater Serbia." Led by *Slobodan Milošević*, they took over subregional governments in *Voivodina* (October 1988), *Montenegro* (January 1989), and *Kosovo* (February 1989). After June 1991, they supported militia attacks on Slovenia and Croatia and taught the world a new and ugly term for an old and brutal policy: *ethnic cleansing*. In 1992–1993 the war spread to *Bosnia*, and Serbia was increasingly identified as the clear aggressor: Milošević made a secret deal with Franjo Tudjman (1922–1999) to *partition* Bosnia between Serbia and Croatia. All *Security Council* resolutions were ignored, as were U.S. and *European Community* warnings. Serbia was placed under *sanctions* by the United Nations on May 30, 1992, but still refused to accept the *Vance-Owen peace plan* or other attempts to broker a peace that recognized Bosnian *sovereignty*.

By June 1993, the Vance-Owen plan was dead. Serbia had, *de facto*, attached to itself large parts of Bosnia and eastern Croatia. It had done so at great cost: that year, its inflation hit 1,900 percent per month (an annualized rate of four quadrillion percent), and Serbia's *central bank* issued a 500 billion dinar note. This forced the government to issue a new currency in 1994, *pegged* to the deutschmark. A UN *blockade* and sanctions followed, although they proved fairly porous. In 1995 *NATO* intervened to preserve Bosnia from Serb and Croat aggression, though mainly to preserve itself from inter-alliance dissension. Nonetheless, from Belgrade's point of view this meant an enforced peace, which it accepted in the *Dayton Peace Accords* of 1995. Milošević then turned on Kosovo, where low-level *guerrilla* activity provided an excuse to ethnically cleanse another region of historical importance to Serbs, but long since occupied by another resident people. This provoked a NATO bombing campaign, ultimately against civilian *infrastructure* in Serbia proper, and then a ground occupation of Kosovo. This military defeat brought out the anti-Milošević opposition, which defeated him in 2000 elections. Milošević tried to ignore the elections but was driven from office by mass demonstrations. The next year he was handed over for international trial for *war crimes* at The Hague, and UN sanctions against Serbia were finally lifted.

Suggested Readings: Branimir Anzulovic, *Heavenly Serbia: from Myth to Genocide* (1999); John K. Cox, *The History of Serbia* (2002); Barbara Jelavich, *Russia's Balkan Entanglements, 1806–1914* (1991); David MacKenzie; *Serbs and Russians* (1996); Leften Stavrianos, *The Balkans Since 1453* (1958).

serfdom. *Feudal* servitude of the peasantry which could amount to effective *slavery*, extant in parts of Europe into the early nineteenth century and in Russia to 1861. In general, the pattern of peasant life was far more brutal in Eastern Europe and Russia than in Western Europe. After the ninth century, peasants in Western Europe began to extend their freedom from the feudal bondage of the "manorial system." They were required to give the landlord fewer days of free labor, some became free-holding or rentier tillers, and they could even earn reasonable real wages for their labor. This trend was accelerated after the twelfth century with the development of growing market centers in the towns and cities and new cottage industries in the countryside, partly as a consequence of the *Black Death*. Scotland abolished serfdom in the fourteenth century, well before England. Most Scandinavian countries abolished serfdom in the late eighteenth century. In France, Belgium, and the Rhineland, liberation of the peasantry arrived with the *French Revolution's* confirmation of the independence of peasant farmers, other than in the *Vendée* where recalcitrant *Catholic* peasants were slaughtered, in the name of liberty, from 1794. In contrast, Prussian serfs were emancipated in 1807 but lost most of their lands in consequence. Serfdom was abolished within the *Austrian Empire* after the *revolutions of 1848* in Vienna and Hungary. In Eastern Europe lack of market forces and rising real wages combined to fatally weaken the peasantry's ability to resist being forced back into virtual *slave labor* conditions. There were, as a result, many peasant revolts over the succeeding centuries, some with more lasting effects than others. On the whole, peasants in Eastern Europe and Russia were unable to throw off their shackles until the late nineteenth century. In important cases (Prussia in 1807, Russia in 1861), serfdom was abolished as part of larger, modernizing reforms forced on a regime by defeat in a foreign war. In other cases (Austria in 1848), abolition resulted from the threat of internal revolution.

In Russia under *Peter I*, about half the peasants were serfs who belonged to their landowners and could be bought and sold like slaves; another 40 percent were "state peasants" who were not owned but owed onerous labor and military service and had to pay heavy taxes. Fully one-fifth of these peasants were owned by the *Orthodox Church*. There were also about 10 percent outright slaves, indentured as debtors. Peter actually expanded serfdom by eliminating slavery, since he wished to bring that nontaxed portion of the population under obligations of service to the state. On the other hand, the uniform view of *Marxist* historians that Russian peasants were all utterly immiserated has been successfully challenged by broader-minded research. Peasants had some rights, such as to choose their own village representatives, and the fact that they were greatly needed by the landlords gave them some influence. Conditions also varied by region and by time: in some historical periods hardship was much greater than in others. Also, the Russian state under the tsars was so grossly inefficient that it was effectively a nonfactor in the daily lives of most peasants and serfs, outside the unfortunates who were *conscripted* for a lifetime of military service. And if all else failed, peasants could and did run away en masse to the vast forests or to the open steppe lands of the south, to become robbers or join with the *Cossacks* or otherwise evade the tsarist system. Lastly, it should be noted that the Russian nobility was also bound to the state by onerous obligations of military service and heavy taxation. And Peter ordered many thousands of nobles to relocate to *St. Petersburg*, often at ruinous levels of personal expense. *See also Alexander II; encomienda; Nicholas I.*

Suggested Reading: J. Blum, *Lord and Peasant in Russia* (1961).

services. *See goods and services.*

servitude. When the exercise of *sovereignty* over a *territory* is limited by a binding legal obligation to other states to permit specific limited uses of that territory (such as on *coastal states* concerning innocent passage transit rights, or on those states through which run international *canal zones*), or on itself not to use it for express purposes (as in the ban on military uses of the *Aland Islands*, or *no-fly zones* imposed by the United Nations on Bosnia and Iraq). Servitudes are not normally affected by *state succession. See also intervention.*

settlers/settlement. Settlement of new populations in lands newly *discovered, conquered,* or *annexed* was a standard policy of *imperial* powers from Rome to Imperial China, from the European states in the Americas and selected parts of Africa, to *Hitler's* dreams of *Lebensraum* to the east and Chinese seeding of *Tibet* with *Han* after 1960. For the myriad effects of the settlement form of *colonialism* on the fortunes of empire, *diffusion* of technology and of *world religions,* as well as political and social ideas, stimulus to creation of *cash crop* economies and integration of entire continents with global markets, see individual country entries. *See also Algerian War of Independence; American War of Independence; Angola; Christianity;* colons; *Creoles; encomienda; Indian Wars; Islam; Mozambique; Rhodesia;* slavery; slave trade; *South Africa; White Highlands.*

"Seven Sisters." The seven largest *oil* companies, which, before the formation of *OPEC*, colluded to set oil prices and control supply. The proliferation of national companies (e.g., Petrobras in Brazil, Petrocan in Canada) and policies, the emergence of OPEC in the 1970s, and multiple mergers in the 1990s meant that these *multinational corporations (MNCs)* no longer controlled the same market share or enjoyed the influence they once did.

Seven Weeks' War (June 15–August 23, 1866). "Austro-Prussian War." *Bismarck* employed his usual precise, manipulative political skills to deliberately start this war between Prussia and the *Austrian Empire*. His central aim was to finally win the competition with Austria for control of *Germany*, which he knew would also set the stage for a war with France over who would be *preponderant* in Europe. He wanted the war so he could annex the northern tier of the *German Confederation* and expel Austrian influence from southern Germany as well. Having secured French neutrality and a secret alliance with Italy (*Piedmont-Sardinia*), he ordered *Moltke* to attack. The combat was mercifully brief. The Prussians—armed with the first *rifled bore*, rapid-fire breech-loaders (the famous Dreyse rifles, or "needle-guns")—occupied several German states within days (June 16th), and only then *declared war* on Austria (June 22nd). That gave the Prussians several days advantage, as the Austrian Army began to march north. The outmoded and ill-equipped Austrians were crushed at Sadowa (also known as Königgrätz, July 3rd). The brevity of fighting was also Bismarck's doing: once he achieved his main goals he held back those Prussian dogs of war, the king and his generals, who most strained at the leash, insisting that Austria must be invaded. Bismarck was magnanimous at the peace table, too. In the Treaty of Prague (August 23, 1866) which formally ended the war, Austria lost no territory other than the cession of Venetia to Italy (a small reward for Italian support of Prussia). The German Confederation was broken apart, and Frankfurt, *Hanover*, Hess-Cassel, Hesse-Nassau, and *Schleswig-Holstein* were *annexed* to Prussia, while all the south German states once within Austria's *sphere of influence* were attached to Prussia by *secret treaties*. At a blow, Austria ceased to be a German or Italian power and was turned instead toward the *Balkans*. The shift was accelerated by the *Ausgleich*, which followed the defeat, giving Hungary an equal status with Austria within the empire and a large share in imperial policy. In sum, for Berlin this war set the stage for the even more decisive *Franco-Prussian War* and Bismarck's creation of the *Second Reich*. For Vienna, however, it marked the transition point from being an imperial power to becoming a political question.

Suggested Reading: Geoffrey Wawro, *The Austro–Prussian War* (1996).

Seven Years' War (1756–1763). It began with a *diplomatic revolution* in 1756 in which France set aside centuries of opposition to the Austrian *Habsburgs* and allied with Austria, Russia, Saxony, the *Holy Roman Empire*, and Sweden to fight Prussia and its new ally, England. This was a double climax, first of Anglo-French imperial competition overseas and next of a determination by older continental powers to push the upstart Prussia, and its brash king *Frederick II (the Great)*, out of the ranks of the *Great Powers* back among the middling powers. Austria, Russia, and France secretly allied to attack and divide Prussia, but Frederick struck first, invading Saxony and Bohemia (1756–1757). He lost badly at Kolin (June 18, 1757), near Prague. As he withdrew north, the French overran Hanover, Russian *Cossacks* pillaged *East Prussia*, and an Austrian corps captured and looted *Berlin*. Frederick recovered for Prussia with an overwhelming victory over French and Imperial forces at Rossbach (November 5, 1757) and another over the Austrians at Leuthen (December 5, 1757). He could not obtain the peace he desperately wanted and needed. In 1758 he fought defensively, fighting Russia to a bloody draw at Zorndorf (August 25, 1758) but losing to Russia and Austria at Hochkirch (October 14, 1758).

The European *balance of power* now began to work in Frederick's favor. Under *William Pitt*, England used its huge advantage in *sea power* to *blockade* France economically, while pressing a hard attack under *Clive* on land in India, where the French were ultimately reduced to the tiny *enclaves* of *French India*. The *Royal Navy* and its *privateer* allies drove the French from several Caribbean islands, including Guadeloupe (1759). English victories in India, the West Indies, West Africa, and on the *Plains of Abraham* made 1759 the "annus mirabilis" for Pitt. The stage was set for the rapid conquest of all *Québec*, which rendered the rest of *New France* strategically untenable. Also, the *Iroquois Confederation* abandoned its *neutrality* to join the English side. In 1760 the English captured Montreal, and sealed the French failure in the Americas in 1762 with the capture of Grenada, Martinique, and other island possessions. In Europe, Frederick was still encircled by enemies determined to crush him once and for all. At Kunersdorf (August 12, 1759) the Prussian Army was routed, suffering its worst defeat of any of Frederick's wars. He recovered with victories at Liegnitz (August 15, 1760) and Torgau (November 3, 1760). The Russians he could not stop, however, and they burned Berlin that same year. The British either could not or would not send a large army to aid their continental ally, which Frederick must have seen in terms of that famous later damnation of supposed English treachery, "Perfidious Albion!" Spain then joined the war against England in 1762, in a "family compact" with *Bourbon* France, and immediately lost Havana and Manila to Royal Navy action. Both were subsequently returned, although Florida was not.

What saved Frederick and Prussia was blind chance: the death of the Tsarina Elizabeth (1709–1762) and the brief ascent to the throne of Peter III (1728–1762). Peter was a romantic and uncritical admirer of all things German, and of Frederick in particular. He called off the war on a bizarre and prejudiced whim, signed a *peace treaty*, and even offered to ally with Prussia against Austria! He was quickly assassinated, but Frederick and Prussia had been spared invasion and total defeat. Sweden next made peace with Russia, and with near-bankruptcy all around, Austria's isolation, and England's continuing mastery at sea, the war began to wind down. The new balance of power in Europe and extraordinary English gains in North America and India were alike confirmed in the *Treaty of Paris* (1763). The Seven Years' War was a portent of the modern wars to come, in showing how warfare was growing more costly with each passing decade: Prussia had lost a half million dead; Austria lost 300,000; Russia and France lost comparable numbers. It was, in a real sense, the first truly world war. It rearranged core alliances within Europe and demonstrated to all concerned that Britain had achieved maritime supremacy virtually everywhere else. *See also East India Company.*

Suggested Readings: Fred Anderson, *Crucible of War* (2000); Robert Asprey, *Frederick the Great* (1999); James C. Riley, *The Seven Years' War and the Old Regime in France* (1986).

Sèvres, Treaty of (1920). The agreement with Turkey to formally end *World War I*, negotiated at the *Paris Peace Conference,* signed but never *ratified.* It would have created independent states in Armenia, Mesopotamia, and Syria, and called for cession of swaths of Turkish land to Greece (including *Smyrna*). It also would have created an independent Kurdish homeland (*Kurdistan*). It was rejected by the Turks, who were able to wait out Allied unity and gain the more favorable terms of the *Treaty of Lausanne* in 1923. *See also reparations.*

Seward, William (1801–1872). U.S. secretary of state, 1861–1869. A former *Whig* governor of New York, he tried but failed to win the presidency in 1860. He was an important *Republican*, nonetheless, and so joined *Abraham Lincoln's* cabinet. During the *American Civil War* he was the most important cabinet officer on the *Union* side. He recovered Lincoln's error in declaring a *blockade* of the *Confederacy*, and otherwise deflected foreign powers from granting *recognition* to the South. That contribution to the war effort was worth several battlefield victories, at least. His most delicate diplomacy came during the *Trent Affair*, in which he fashioned a compromise solution which avoided a disastrous war with Great Britain. He protested vehemently, however, against British outfitting of Confederate *commerce raiders*, such as the CSS Alabama. He stayed on after the war in *Johnson's* cabinet and supported *Reconstruction*. These were not happy years, at home or abroad. In foreign policy he was an isolated *expansionist* in a nation thoroughly exhausted of "guts and glory," and which remembered that the Civil War had roots in the acquisition of territory from Mexico in the 1840s: when Seward purchased *Alaska* from Russia in 1867, the public dismissed the move as "Seward's Folly." Whatever his failings, he served the nation masterfully in the hour of its worst crisis. For that, he is widely regarded by historians as the greatest of U.S. secretaries of state.

Seychelles. Occupied and colonized by France from 1768, these islands were seized by Britain during the *Napoleonic Wars* (1794). They were jointly ruled with Mauritius from 1814 until 1903, when they became a Crown Colony. *Independence* was granted in 1976 but was not accepted entirely willingly. In 1979 the country became a *one-party state*. In 1981 a group of white *mercenaries* tried to overthrow the government but were foiled (with the help of Tanzanian troops) and fled to South Africa. Democracy was established in Seychelles over the course of the 1990s.

Shaba. (1) An important copper and iron mining region of East Africa, where around the end of the first millennium C.E. an important iron-age culture developed which spread to surrounding areas in the following centuries. A Nyamwezi empire, under Msira, held out in Shaba against the Belgians until 1891. (2) An alternative name for *Katanga* province of Congo. *See also Congo crisis.*

Shah. The title taken by the Pahlavi *dynasty* in Iran. *See also Muhammad Reza Pahlavi; Reza Shah Pahlavi.*

Shaka Zulu (1787–1828). A military genius as well as mad butcher, Shaka raised the *Zulu* from clan to nation and made himself their king. He spent his adolescence in poverty and shame, as he and his mother lived as outcasts. As a man and a king, Shaka was devoted to his mother to the point of insane and murderous rages against those he thought had given her offense in his youth. Trained as a regimental commander under Dingiswayo (r. 1800?– 1818), king of the Mthethwa, in 1816 Shaka became chief of the small Zulu clan, of which he was a member of the royal family. When he took power the Zulu numbered fewer than 2,000, among whom just 400 were warriors. He utterly transformed the fighting style of the Zulu impi (regiments) and expanded from this small base to organize a loose collage of small neighboring tribes into a martial society with himself as supreme commander and absolute ruler. He changed impi tactics from loose assemblies to tight and controlled formations, and weaponry from thrown spears to the assagai—a stabbing spear with an 18-inch blade, which required direct hand-to-hand combat to be employed with effect. This altered the character of warfare all over southern Africa, changing it to the degree its weapons allowed toward a concept of *total war.*

Shaka's refinements to the extant idea of fighting in regimental units were revolutionary: he introduced age-grade regiments which made for easy assimilation of newly conquered recruits; and his demanding training gave the barefoot impi (Shaka eschewed the traditional Zulu sandal) extraordinary speed and mobility, which frequently also gave them the advantage of surprise. Most of all, Shaka turned the Zulu into a nation and the nation into a *standing army*, with a people attached to it. He also changed the purpose of

Zulu war, from ritual display and intimidation to the permanent conquest and physical annihilation of enemies. These tactical and strategic innovations swept aside all local resistance. He killed any who opposed him, politically or militarily, and assimilated the rest into his growing army and empire. Over the course of his reign he may have killed over a million Africans. His chosen method of execution—and he murdered hundreds of thousands of his own people as well as prisoners and hostages—was impalement. This was the *Mfecane*, a wildly rapid conquest of the *Nguni* peoples of southern Africa, many of whom were subsumed into the Zulu imperium.

Shaka's rage and personal lust for revenge for his youthful humiliations was unbound with the death of his mother in 1827. In the end, even leading Zulu companions who had most benefited from Shaka's rule had enough: Shaka was assassinated by some of his generals and two half-brothers. In an earlier age, the *imperialism* of Shaka and the Zulus might have led to creation of a vast empire, though whether this entity could have survived and stabilized after the death of its charismatic founder is doubtful. In the end, Shaka spared almost no one from his mad rages. He destroyed and depopulated much of southern Africa, and he built no state or cultural monument which lasted. The Zulu then ran into the competing and technologically superior imperialism of the northward-expanding *Boers*, and later of the British, and were themselves made a subject people before the end of the nineteenth century. See *Zulu wars*. See also *Nurhachi*.

Suggested Reading: E. A. Ritter, *Shaka Zulu: The Rise of the Zulu Empire* (1957).

Shamir, Yitzhak (b. 1915). Israeli foreign minister 1980–1983, 1984–1986; prime minister, 1983–1984, 1986–1992. He was a member of the *Irgun*, then the *Stern Gang*. From 1948 to 1965 he worked for *Mossad*. He opposed the *Camp David Accords*, supporting instead a creeping *annexation* via new settlements on the *West Bank*. During the *Gulf War* he agreed to U.S. requests for restraint in the face of unprovoked Iraqi *missile* attacks. Later, however, he refused to abandon his settlements policy or to join *peace talks* sponsored by the *Bush* administration. Shamir thus presided over the most precipitous deterioration in U.S.-Israeli relations since the wartime crisis in October 1973. In 1992 he was defeated at the polls, and his policies on settlements and negotiation were both reversed.

Shandong (Shantung) peninsula. Also known as Jiaodong peninsula. A large, strategically located region in northern China which contained the *leasehold* and attendant *sphere of influence* seized by Germany from the *Qing* in the *concession diplomacy* of 1898. Its *Christian* converts and *missionaries* were the first targets of anti-foreign violence during the *Boxer Uprising*. It was seized by the Japanese in 1914, and its retention was part of the *Twenty-one Demands*. At the *Paris Peace Conference*, on April 30, 1919, it was decided by the *Big Four* that Japan should retain possession of Shandong. That decision led to massive anti-foreign demonstrations four days later (*May 4th Movement*), and a nationwide *boycott* of Japanese imported goods. Japan retained Shandong until 1922, when it withdrew under terms negotiated during the *Washington Conference* in the *Nine Power Treaty*. It retook the area by force in 1938, holding it until defeated in 1945, when it reverted to China. *See also Kiaochow incident; Yuan Shikai.*

Shanghai communiqué (February 28, 1972). A joint declaration issued by the United States and China at the conclusion of *Richard Nixon's* historic visit to hold direct talks with *Mao Zedong* and *Zhou Enlai* in the People's Republic of China (PRC). It fudged on the ongoing conflict of the *Vietnam War* and the older conflict over the status of the two Koreas in order to lay the basis for a key *rapprochement*, or at least the beginning of new working understanding and arrangement, over the question of the independent status of *Taiwan*. It thereby set in motion a process which led to *normalization* of Sino-American relations, including reseating of the PRC instead of Taiwan in the *United Nations*, and culminated in formal *recognition* of the PRC by the United States in 1979.

Shanghai Cooperation Organization. A group composed of China, Russia, and several Central Asian republics, formed in 1997 as the successor to the "Shanghai Five," whose principal aim is to coordinate resistance to *terrorism* and *Islamist* political movements in the Central Asian region and western China. *See also Uighurs.*

Shanghai massacres. (1) May 30, 1925: Guards at a Japanese mill in Shanghai killed a Chinese worker during a strike. In the demonstrations that followed on May 30th, British police fired on the Chinese crowd, killing eleven demonstrators in support of the strike against the Japanese-owned firm. Massive protest strikes spread up and down the Chinese coast, including *Hong Kong*. On June 23rd, British troops killed fifty-two Chinese students in Guangzhou (Canton). These shootings and demonstrations significantly strengthened the *Guomindang* in the coastal areas by speaking directly to its building nationalist rhetoric and agenda. Organizational efforts were also assisted by a follow-on *boycott* of all British goods. (2) April 1927: Chinese *communists* were massacred by the Guomindang in several Chinese cities, starting in Shanghai, where "Green Gang" underworld thugs and businessmen organized goon squads to join in the killing of workers and trade unionists. The purge came after *Chiang Kai-shek's* victory over the main northern *warlords*, and was followed by a virtual reign of *white terror* in the cities. *Mao, Zhou Enlai,* and other Communists fled to *Yenan*. The massacres thus marked the start of the long and bloody *Chinese Civil War*.

sharia. Traditional *Islamic* law, based on al Qur'an (the Koran) and the sunna, or interpretations of the life of the Prophet Muhammad. It is not universally codified. Interpretation usually rests on classical Islamic jurisprudence, of which there are several schools, such as the Hanafi, invocation of explicit injunctions in the Koran, and the example of the life of Muhammad. It can apply, by modern standards, draconian punishments for criminal and civil offenses, including stoning for adultery, flogging for consumption of alcohol, and amputation of the hand for theft. Its introduction by *fundamentalist* regimes tends to alienate more moderate Muslims, non-Muslims, and all *secular* citizens. At times, introduction of the sharia has led to large-scale resistance and bloodshed, as in Afghanistan, Iran, Nigeria and Sudan.

Sharon, Ariel (b. 1928). Israeli general and prime minister. Sharon became a national hero in Israel owing to his genuine military achievements during the *First, Second,* and *Third Arab-Israeli Wars.* During the *Fourth Arab-Israeli War,* Sharon commanded the Israeli thrust which crossed the *Suez Canal* and encircled the Egyptian Third Army, converting a near defeat into a dramatic victory. Afterward, he moved into politics as a member of Likud, serving under Prime Ministers *Yitzhak Rabin* and *Menachem Begin.* In 1981 he was named Israeli defense minister. From that position he oversaw the initially militarily successful but politically disastrous and domestically highly divisive invasion of Lebanon in 1982. The Israeli Army followed his orders to shell Beirut, driving the *Palestine Liberation Organization* (PLO) from Lebanon, before retiring to an enlarged "security zone" Tel Aviv had proclaimed five years earlier. Overseas, the image of Israeli *artillery* shelling Beirut, and an attendant massacre of Palestinian civilians—including many women and children—at the Shabra and Shatilla *refugee camps* by Lebanese Christian *militia* allied to Israel, soured relations with many traditional supporters in the West. In 1983, under heavy pressure and criticism, Sharon resigned. By 1985 Israel had enough of this *Vietnam War*–like *quagmire,* in which radical *shi'ite* militia could not be defeated or accommodated, and pulled its troops back to a more limited, defensible "security zone" which straddled its border and southern Lebanon. Sharon, meanwhile, had returned to government almost immediately, but in much less sensitive portfolios. Fourteen years later, in 1999, Sharon was selected by Likud as its new leader, following the electoral defeat of Benjamin Netanyahu by the *Labor Party* under Ehud Barak. Sharon clearly provoked—whether he caused or not is another matter—the "second" *Intifada* to break out in the *West Bank* in 2000, by ostentatiously visiting a site of shared veneration but disputed ownership among Jews and Muslims, the Al Aksa Mosque and Temple Mount in *Jerusalem.* His assertion of sole Israeli *sovereignty* led to an immediate and violent Palestinian response, and within weeks if not days the peace process collapsed. Sharon then led Likud back into office, and toward a far tougher line concerning future territorial concessions to the PLO.

Sharpeville massacre (March 21, 1960). South African police fired on a crowd of peaceful black demonstrators, most of them schoolchildren, killing 72 and wounding 186. The massacre led to an international outcry, became a rallying term for efforts to introduce *sanctions*, and convinced many hitherto peaceful opponents of *apartheid* that the system would have to be resisted with force. *See also African National Congress; Nelson Mandela; Pan-African Congress.*

Shatt-al-Arab. A waterway flowing into the *Persian Gulf*, lying between Iran and Iraq and formed by the junction of the Tigris and Euphrates Rivers. It contains several small islands and *oil* drilling and processing facilities, and it controls riverine passage into the heart of the Persian Gulf. In 1975 the two nations agreed it should form their common *border*. On September 17, 1979, *Saddam Hussein*, dictator of Iraq, unilaterally denounced the agreement and five days later his troops suddenly attacked Iran. The *Iran-Iraq War* (1980–1988) which followed took upwards of one million lives. Hussein then threw away any small gains he had made, at such great cost, by invading Kuwait in 1990. Hemmed in by the *Gulf coalition* and United Nations *sanctions*, that year he surrendered to Iran all territory taken in the earlier war.

sheikdom. A *state*, or more often a statelet, ruled by a sheik (Muslim prince).

shell shock. A *World War I* term for *battle fatigue*, or any of the psychological disorders associated with sustained *artillery* barrages or other exposure to fire. It is today called *post traumatic stress disorder*.

Shenyang incident. *See Mukden incident.*

Sherman, William Tecumseh (1820–1891). He graduated from West Point in 1840 as an *artillery* officer. He fought in the Seminole wars and in the *Mexican-American War*, mainly in California. In 1850 Sherman resigned from the army to try his hand at business, but failed repeatedly. He found modest success as a teacher in Louisiana. He rejoined the army with the outbreak of the *American Civil War*, seeing action at First Bull Run (July 21, 1861). He took command of Union forces in Kentucky, and moved farther west in 1862, serving under *Ulysses S. Grant*. Sherman commanded brilliantly at the bloody and desperate battle of Shiloh (April 6–7, 1862), and again during Grant's Mississippi campaign which culminated in the pivotal victory at Vicksburg (July 4, 1863), which secured the West for the Union. When Grant departed to command the Army of the Potomac, Sherman succeeded him as commander of the Army of the Tennessee. His first victory came at Chattanooga (November 24–25, 1863). In March 1864 he was given overall command in the west, taking charge of the Armies of the Cumberland and the Ohio, as well as the Tennessee. With the bulk of this combined force he marched on

Atlanta, coordinating his advance with Grant's steady drive toward Richmond. He fought several small battles against desperate Confederate defenders before capturing Atlanta on September 2, 1864. Like so many other wooden cities in the nineteenth century, such as Berlin (1806) and Moscow (1812), Atlanta burned under military occupation. Whether or not Sherman ordered the fire, he appreciated its effect: he was among the first to see that the way to beat the *Confederacy* was to wage *total war* against it. On November 16, 1864, he began his famous (infamous, in the South) "march to the sea," occupying Savannah before turning north to punish South Carolina. There, his troops exacted a special revenge on the first Southern state to secede from the Union, whose militia had fired the first shots of the war at Fort Sumter. While Sherman marched north to close off routes of escape, Grant pursued *Robert E. Lee* until surrender of his army at Appomattox Court House on April 9, 1865. After the war Sherman moved west, where he was a ruthless Indian fighter. In 1869 Grant named him commander of the army, a post he held until his retirement in 1884. *See also war.*

Shevardnadze, Eduard Amvrosiyevich (b. 1928). Soviet foreign minister, 1985–1990; president of Georgia 1992– . He was a major figure in ending the *Cold War*, freeing Eastern Europe from Soviet and Russian domination, and negotiating major *arms control* agreements. He resigned in dramatic fashion before the Supreme Soviet while warning *Gorbachev*, who sat stiffly behind him, that he was consorting with enemies of *glasnost* and *perestroika* and drifting to dictatorship. As president of Georgia, in early 1992 he faced growing unrest, *secession* in *Ossetia* and *Abkhazia*, and a widening *civil war*. In 1992 he also converted to *Orthodoxy* from agnosticism—whether sincerely or not may be reasonably doubted; perhaps, as with *Henri IV* and Paris, for some even Tbilisi might be "worth a mass." Shevardnadze accused Russian troops of aiding Ossetian rebels. He was almost killed by an assassin on July 4, 1993, and thereafter accepted *CIA* security assistance training for his guards. As the war went badly for Georgian forces, he was compelled to accept a Russian military presence. He was again nearly assassinated in 1998. In 2000 he won reelection with a suspiciously high, almost Soviet, percentage of the vote. In 2001 he faced a mutiny by elements of the army, and he hinted that Georgia might seek *neutrality* rather than *NATO* membership.

Suggested Readings: Cathal J. Nolan, ed., *Ethics and Statecraft* (1995); Eduard Shevardnadze, *The Future Belongs to Freedom* (1991).

shi'ia Islam. "The Party (of Ali)." The major sect within *Islam* which early on broke with the *sunni* majority to develop its own forms of piety and follow its own historical path. Shi'ites accept as *legitimate* three *caliphs* whom they agree with sunnis correctly succeeded the Prophet Muhammad, as well as Muhammad's son-in-law, Ali (d. 661 C.E.), the fourth caliph. However, they reject the caliphs who in fact—historically—followed Ali. Thus, they deny legitimacy to the fifth caliph, Mu'awiya, founder of the sunni dynasty known as the Umayyad Caliphate (661–750), who followed Ali's assassination, and all of his sunni successors. Shi'ites proclaim only the descendants of Ali and Fatima, or the family of Muhammad, as the rightful—that is, anointed by Allah—successors to the Prophet and ruler of all Muslims. These shi'ia shadow candidates became known as "Alids." There are variants on this position, of differing subtlety or obscurity. A deeply eschatological, quasi-messianic variant called "Twelfth-imam shi'ism," or colloquially just "Twelvers," recognizes eleven specially anointed imams who have already lived, while awaiting the arrival (future return) of the twelfth, or "Hidden Imam," who is said to be the true caliph. In contrast, *Ismailis* (Fatamid) are sometimes called "Seveners" because they believe the rightful succession stopped in 765 C.E. with the death of the sixth caliph, the last visible to earthly eyes after Muhammad. Some Ismailis (Nizari) divide further, following only until the fourth caliph. All of this represents theological adjustment to historical reality, in which the devout are encouraged to believe that Muhammad's true successors exercise hidden influence in the interest of the community of believers. Shi'ism thus became the main repository of Islam's original highly apocalyptic vision (quite similar to that of *Christianity, Judaism,* and *Marxism,* too, for that matter), after the first several generations waited in vain for the great and promised transformation. This tradition is embodied in the idea of the *mahdi,* a quasi-cult notion which looks to the arrival of a divinely guided, heroic figure—the true or hidden imam—who will transform and end all history.

Over the centuries, this had great political significance: it is possible to create great turmoil and conflict in devout Islamic societies if some claimant to political power can, sincerely or not and legitimately or not, assert a claim to an Alid nature and candidacy. Shi'ite communities also have displayed a repeated tendency toward exclusivity, indeed a real elitism that is contrary to the great spiritual leveling which made original Islam so attractive to so many, and still does. This flows from a temperamental tendency in its theology which holds the larger mass of faithful sunni (let alone non-Muslims) in some degree of disdain, as nonprivileged by—and perhaps even incapable of—the highest truths of the faith. A *fundamentalist* variant of shi'ism thus utterly rejects the right of Muslims to select their own rulers. It is not enough for a community of believers to establish laws based on the Koran or the faith, say such fundamentalists. Muslims must also have among them the physical presence of a true imam, one in genuine (Alid) descent from the Prophet, who must be received as the spokesman of the divine will on earth. Only such a ruler is truly fit to govern Muslims, because only such a man (women are wholly excluded) is anointed by Allah. Any leader not within this tradition, however devout, is to be scorned as a usurper. Such radical believers historically would, from time to time as circumstance permitted, challenge Muslim leaders they regarded as not part of the Alid tradition, or whom they declared to have supplanted the legitimate rule of a true imam. In the modern world, fanatics within this tradition of self-perception as an elite vestige of the true faith work to replace *secular* regimes with "Islamic" ones, even when the secular regimes strive to be representative democracies and otherwise give voice to the moral concerns and interests of their Muslim citizens. And they sometimes seek to accomplish such change by violent means. Despite this much more vehement political tradition, the great corpus of shi'ia doctrine is akin to sunni doctrine and practice. However, among Muslims shi'ites come closest to following an interpretive priesthood ("mujtahids") and have the most highly developed and distinctive mystical traditions (Sufism). *See also ayatollah*; Hezbollah; *Iran*; *Iraq*; *Islam*; *Ruhollah Khomeini*; *Mecca*.

Suggested Readings: John Esposito, ed., *Oxford History of Islam* (1999); Marshall Hodgson, *The Classical Age of Islam* (1974).

shi'ite. An adherent of *shi'ia Islam*. They are found mainly in Iran, southern Iraq, parts of Lebanon and Pakistan, and Yemen.

Shimonoseki, Treaty of (April 17, 1895). This, the most damaging of all *unequal treaties* signed by China in the nineteenth century, formally ended the *First Sino-Japanese War* (1894–1895). It confirmed Korea's nominal independence, but in fact made it a Japanese *protectorate*. Other provisions ceded *Taiwan*, the *Pescadores*, and the Liaodong peninsula to Japan. It also forced China to pay a large *indemnity*, permitted Japan right of passage on the Yangzi River, and granted it rights to set up factories in Shanghai. Two weeks later, in the *Triple Intervention* Russian (and other *Great Power*) intervention voided the clause on the Liaodong peninsula, which included the highly strategic *Port Arthur*.

Shining Path. *See Sendero Luminoso.*

Shinto. The indigenous folk religion of Japan, emphasizing ancestor worship and harmony with nature. For centuries it coexisted with *Buddhism*, often sharing temples and shrines, and organized mostly locally. This changed in 1868, when Shinto was officially and closely identified with the exalted position of the Japanese *emperor* during the *Meiji Restoration* ("State Shinto") to sustain imperial claims to descent from the sun goddess and provide political support to Meiji reformers. The shrines were given a hierarchical organization under close government supervision. By 1884 an official cult of "Great Teaching" was established which amalgamated Shinto lore and Buddhist practice. Shinto was even imposed on Korea and Taiwan after 1895. During *World War II* Shinto priests accompanied Japan's armies to affirm the "divine mission" of the Japanese race and state. The close association of Shinto with the state was broken after 1945, when Emperor *Hirohito* publicly disclaimed his divine ancestry to satisfy *occupation* demands to sever his ties to Japan's militarist past, and as part of the price to be paid to avoid charges of *war crimes*. Freedom of belief and disestablishment of Shinto were then enshrined in the postwar constitution, leading almost overnight to a remarkable new diversity in Japanese religious practices and beliefs. There was renewed (though brief) international controversy over the revival and use of Shinto ceremony to invest Hirohito's son, *Akihito*, in the first open display of the old rites at a government level since 1945.

ship-of-the-line. Any *warship* in the age of sail powerful enough (at least double rows of cannon, totaling no fewer than 60) to join a *line ahead* formation in battle alongside the most powerful warships, without constituting a weak point in the line. Ships-of-the-line were the sail equivalent of twentieth-century *battleships*. *See also frigate; galleon; man-of-war; sloop of war.*

shock treatment. A semi-slang term used about the choice to rapidly, rather than gradually, displace a *central planned economy* with the mechanisms of a *market economy*. Essentially, it involves eliminating *subsidies* to state industries and allowing prices to find their market levels, while controlling *inflation* by not printing extra *currency* or raising public-sector wages to keep them level with prices. This was done most deliberately (and successfully) in Poland after 1989, and in Hungary and several other former *Soviet bloc* states.

shock troops. (1) Military units specially trained and equipped to strike sudden, stunning blows against an enemy position. *Napoleon I* used *cavalry* this way, to great effect. (2) The first line of troops sent in during an assault, used to absorb the maximum shock force of enemy defensive fire.

shogun ("Sei-i-tai-shogun"). "Great barbarian-subduing general." From the eighth century until the triumph of the Minamoto clan in the twelfth century, this was the title of generals commanding *pacification* campaigns against the *Ainu* to the north. Under the Minamoto it became a hereditary title for the head of the great warrior households. From the Minamoto the shogunate passed to the Ashikaga clan (1333–1603), then to the *Tokugawa* (1603–1868). With the Tokugawa, warrior rule was ascendant in Japan: the 15 shoguns of Edo ruled in fact while a succession of *emperors* reigned in Kyoto as figureheads, though some were more beholden to the *bakufu* than were others. The shogunate ended with the *Meiji Restoration* in 1868. *See also* generalissimo; *Japan.*

short-term capital account. An accounting system which seeks to measure the flow of all short-term *investments* and payments made by a national economy.

show of force. Making a display of one's military capabilities in order to deter or coerce an opponent into taking some desired action. *See also demonstration; compellence; coercive diplomacy; deterrence; gunboat diplomacy; mobilization; prestige; saber-rattling; show the flag.*

show the flag. A *demonstration* of military presence or capability in a disputed area, either to support a client government, display resolve around a given policy position, or signal a desire to be involved in any settlement of the questions at stake.

show trial. A rigged legal proceeding, staged for *propaganda* purposes and to get rid of political enemies. *See also Gang of Four; purge trials; Stalin; strel'sty.*

shrapnel. Explosive shells containing Minie balls, nails, or metal fragments, designed to explode above or among enemy troops to cause maximum damage and shock. Loosely, the fragments of any exploding shell.

shuttle diplomacy. A term coined about *Henry Kissinger*'s repeated trips to and within the Middle East in search of a negotiated settlement, following the *Fourth Arab-Israeli War*. It later entered general use regarding any sudden flurry of face-to-face diplomatic activity by top leaders, especially during a *crisis.*

Siam. *See Thailand.*

Sian incident. *See Xi'an incident.*

Siberia. The Asian portion of Russia, from the Ural Mountains to the Pacific. Russian expansion into this huge land was comparable to the settlement of the west in North America, except it took over 300 years. This was viewed by Russians almost as defensive expansion, since Russia had been repeatedly invaded by *Inner Asian* nomads through Siberia. As in the Americas and elsewhere, *indigenous peoples* were conquered and assimilated, pushed aside to marginal areas, or simply exterminated. Siberia's vast reserves of *natural resources* were exploited by the Russian and later the Soviet empire. Both empires also used Siberia to host their vast prison camp system, and for internal *exile* of dissidents. After the breakup of the Soviet Union in 1991 eastern Siberia, in particular, became more economically independent, looking not to Russia but to China, Japan, and the wider world for investment funds and export markets. Some early talk was even heard of the political *independence*, or at least *autonomy*, which Siberia tasted briefly during the *Russian Civil War.* *See also conscription; GULAG; Alexander Kolchak.*
Suggested Readings: G. Lensen, *Russia's Eastward Expansion* (1964); W. Bruce Lincoln, *Conquest of a Continent* (1994); A. Wood and R. French, *Development of Siberia* (1989).

Siberian intervention (1918–1922). *See Czech Legion; Russian Civil War.*

Sicherheitsdienst **(SD).** The *intelligence* department ("Security Service") of the *Nazi Party* and the *SS*. It was created by *Himmler*, joined in the *Night of the Long Knives*, and worked closely with the *Gestapo*. Under *Heydrich*, the SD was heavily involved in the *"final solution to the Jewish problem,"* directing the "Einsatzgruppen" (mobile death squads), which murdered one million victims of the *Holocaust*. In June 1944 the SD absorbed its rival, the *Abwehr*, exacting a terrible vengeance on Abwehr officers suspected of involvement in the *July Plot* to assassinate *Hitler*. At *Nuremberg*, the SD was among the Nazi groups found by the court to be a criminal organization. *See also* Schutzstaffel; Sturmabteilung.

Sicily. *See Casablanca Conference; Camillo di Cavour; Charles V; Ferdinand and Isabella; friendly fire; Giuseppe Garibaldi; Italy; Joachim Murat; Benito Mussolini; George Patton; population; Reconquista; Renaissance; second front; Two Sicilies, Kingdom of; World War I; World War II.*

"sick man of Europe." (1) The *Ottoman Empire*, so called by *Nicholas I* just before he tried to *annex* several portions of it, leading to the *Crimean War*. (2) After *World War II*, a term applied to several nations, notably Italy and then Britain, in reference to the poor relative performance of their national economies.

Sidra (Sirte), Gulf of. An inlet of the Mediterranean off the Libyan coast. *Muammar Quadaffi* asserted *sovereignty* over these waters, proclaiming a *line of death* across its mouth. However, the United States and other nations affirm it as international waters. The U.S. Navy challenged Libyan claims with flyovers and ship transits. Several times in the 1970s and 1980s there were clashes with the Libyan Air Force or Navy, neither of which fared well against the Americans.

siege warfare. Surrounding, isolating, and attacking a *fortified* position or city with one's military forces to cut the enemy's *lines of supply*, then *bombarding* or starving the defenders into submission where a direct attack would be too costly in lives or would prove ineffective. Napoleon revolutionized eighteenth-century warfare, which was dominated by endless sieges, by simply isolating or ignoring fortified positions, a feat made possible by the expansion in the scale of his army owing to the *revolution in military affairs* and *levée en masse*. *See also Dien Bien Phu; fortification;* guerre mortelle; *poison; Sedan; trench warfare; Sébastien de Vauban.*

Siegfried Line. (1) In *World War I*: A set of trenches and fortifications to which the German Army fell back in 1917, not in retreat but for *tactical* reasons. (2) In *World War II*: German defensive works facing the *Maginot Line*, constructed during the 1930s. Many of its guns were stripped away, 1940–1944, to feed then-active fronts, so that it posed a lesser obstacle to *Allied* advance in 1944 and 1945 than was feared in the West or hoped in Berlin. It was known in Germany as the "West Wall."

Sierra Leone. Freetown colony was established by Britain in 1787 as a haven for freed *slaves* from England (where a court ruled 15 years earlier that any slave arriving on its shores would win freedom) and Canada. It failed, but a second try was made from 1792. Other freed slaves arrived in later years, from the United States and the Caribbean. Freetown became a Crown Colony in 1808, the year after Great Britain declared the *slave trade* illegal and while Britain was in great need of a West African base for its warships then engaged against France in the *Napoleonic Wars*. From this point, much larger numbers of freed slaves were settled in Freetown, perhaps 60,000 by 1870. During the nineteenth century some other British colonies in West Africa were administered by the governors in Freetown, making it a center from which British influence diffused throughout the region. The interior, which was already heavily populated by Africans, was made a British *protectorate* only in 1896, during the latter years of the *scramble for Africa*. The two administrative regions were joined as Sierra Leone (named for the lion-shaped mountain that dominates Freetown) in 1951 and became independent in 1961. The 1960s and 1970s were marked by political instability and a decaying and corrupt economy. In the 1980s economic and social frustrations led to outbreaks of tribal violence. In addition to its *Creole* population, Sierra Leone gained a sizable Lebanese commercial class, which grew larger still as a result of the *Lebanese Civil War*. However, its civil society and then its infrastructure both collapsed into civil war in the 1990s, fueled by illicit trade in the region's diamonds and a spillover of fighting from the long civil war in Liberia: in 1992, having destroyed most of Liberia, the *warlord* Charles Taylor invaded Sierra Leone, ravaging and destabilizing it. The conflict was characterized by repeated atrocities by a large and particularly vicious rebel group, the Revolutionary United Front (RUF), which killed indiscriminately and employed punishment amputations of limbs, including of children. *ECOMOG* intervention forces entered the conflict in 1997 and chased the rebels from the capital but took heavy casualties (over 1,000 Nigerian soldiers were killed). United Nations *peacekeepers* followed, but, being poorly led and armed, hundreds were taken *hostage* by the rebels and many were brutally killed. In 2000, British marines were sent to defend Freetown from a fresh assault by the rebels. They then stayed to assist the United Nations train national police and an army and to defend reconstruction, even as the war spread to neighboring Liberia and Guinea.

Suggested Reading: Christopher Fyfe, A *History of Sierra Leone* (1962).

sigint. *See signals intelligence.*

signals corp. *See flag; flag of truce.*

signals intelligence. Any and all information gathered by intercepting and listening to signals, or secure messages, sent by foreign governments, their *diplomats*, military, or *spies*. It is also concerned with the protection of one's own decryption and transmission of secure messages. *See also cabinet noirs.*

signature. Provisional acceptance of a *treaty* by one or more contracting *states* or other *international personalities*. It is preceded by *negotiation* and followed (though not always) by *ratification*, and only then does the treaty enter into force. Note: Signature alone does not make a treaty binding on the state concerned; a treaty must also be ratified (fully consented to) in order to be legally binding.

Sihanouk, Norodom (b. 1922). Cambodian statesman. King, 1941–1955, 1993– ; prime minister, 1955–1970; president of a *government-in-exile*, 1978–1992. He was installed as a nominal king by the French, but then he collaborated with the Japanese *occupation* in the hopes of achieving independence. In 1955 he abdicated to become prime minister following the *Geneva Accords*, which he helped negotiate. As war dominated the peninsula, he was ousted in 1970 by a pro-U.S. military *coup* led by *Lon Nol* while he was outside the country making one of his many films. Sihanouk returned to Cambodia in alliance with the *Khmers Rouges* in 1975 but was soon placed under detention. He resigned as *head of state* in April 1976. He was released in 1978 and went into *exile* in China. In 1993 he returned to Cambodia following United Nations–brokered elections. He was greeted as the only candidate all Cambodian factions could agree to install as an interim head of state. He was then made a constitutional *monarch* again, with his son as prime minister.

Sikhism. A blend of *Hinduism* and *Islam* which developed in the *Punjab* and that over time became a distinct religious tradition. It was founded by Nānak (1469–1538), its first guru, as a syncretic union of Islamic rejection of the Indian *caste system* but retention of many other Hindu beliefs. It was broadly tolerant and rejected the religious extremes of India: the radical asceticism and self-abnegation found in Hinduism and Islam alike on the one hand, and the highly ritualized and rigid caste system which engulfed most Indians on the other. *Akbar* donated land in Amritsar to the Sikhs, who built the Golden Temple on it. It acquired a martial character later, under Guru Gobind Rai (1666–1708), as Sikhs responded to persecution by the Mughal emperor and Muslim zealot *Aurangzeb*. Gobind Rai formed an "Army of the Pure" to defend Sikhs, taking the surname Singh ("Lion"), which all Sikhs used thereafter, and instituting other distinguishing features of Sikh men, including beards, turbans, and carrying of a comb and ceremonial dagger. In 1710, as Mughal power waned, a Sikh kingdom was set up in the Punjab. Maharaja Ranjit Singh (1781–1839) governed this "Land of the Five Rivers," 1799–1839, signing a treaty of border demarcation with the *East India Company* in 1809 and seizing *Kashmir* from the Afghans in 1819. The *Sikh Wars* ended in 1849 with "John Company's" conquest of the Sikh kingdom in the Punjab.

Many Sikhs thereafter took up service in the *Indian Army*, where they proved to be among the most loyal *sepoys* during the *Indian Mutiny*. Sikhs participated separately from Hindus or Muslims in the *Round Table Conferences*, 1930–1932. They were not given a separate homeland, as were (some) Indian Muslims. Instead, when Punjab was partitioned between India and Pakistan in 1947, many Sikhs joined desperate Hindus in fleeing to India. In the 1970s a movement for *secession* from India and creation of a Sikh homeland to be called Kalistan ("Land of the Pure") built support, including within large émigré communities in Britain and Canada. Radical proponents engaged in *terrorism* and *assassination*, provoking violent government repression in the Indian Punjab. In 1984 the main Sikh holy site, the Golden Temple in Amritsar, was taken over by militant *separatists*, who killed hundreds of moderate Sikhs and Hindus to advance their secessionist cause. They were bloodily assaulted right inside the Temple by *armor* and Indian Army troops, an act of perceived contempt and desecration that killed thousands, destroyed ancient Sikh archives and holy books, outraged all devout Sikhs, and led directly to the assassination of *Indira Gandhi*. That assassination, by her Sikh bodyguards, in turn led to horrific and indiscriminate immolations and other brutal murders of thousands of Sikhs by outraged Hindus and *Congress* supporters in Delhi and other cities.

Suggested Readings: J. S. Grewal, *The Sikhs of the Punjab*, rev. ed. (1998); W. H. McLeod, *Sikhism* (1997).

Sikh Wars. (1) 1845–1846: Following the *East India Company*'s humiliating defeat in the First *Afghan War*, and taking full advantage of a succession struggle after the death of Maharaja Ranjit Singh (1781–1839), the British turned on both Sind and the Punjab. Incidents along the Punjab border grew between 1843 and 1845. In December 1845, the British struck, capturing Lahore after several fierce battles in which 20,000 Sikhs and *sepoys*, and some British troops, were killed. The war ended after just three months, in a treaty surrendering *Kashmir* (which had been betrayed to the British by a Sikh chieftain) and other territories to *British India*. (2) 1848–1849: *Dalhousie* broke this treaty before its ink had fully dried, in order to invade the rump of the lands still in Sikh hands. In several bloody battles in 1849 the Punjab was taken by the British, although it was not fully *pacified* until 1850.

Sikkim. A former British *protectorate* bordered by Bhutan, Nepal, and Tibet, forming a gnat of a nation (with just 350,000 people) in the midst of the elephantine states of India and China. Sikkim was transferred to Indian protection in 1950. In 1975 it was made a state of India in a general reorganization of India's northern frontier administration.

Sikorski, Wladislaw (1881–1943). Polish prime minister, 1920–1926. He commanded in the *Polish/Soviet War* and was prime minister until his former comrade-in-arms, *Pilsudski*, forced his retirement. Until his (accidental) death in 1943, he headed the Polish *government-in-exile* in London during *World War II*. He was supported by *Roosevelt* and *Churchill*, but after the *Katyn massacre* the Soviets refused all further dealings with the London Poles, and his influence waned.

Silesia. A mineral-rich, historically German province in Central Europe, long a *Habsburg* possession and part of the *Holy Roman Empire*. It was for centuries a theater of struggle between medieval Austria and Poland, and later between Prussia and Russia. Wracked by the *Protestant Reformation*, it was a major battleground of the great *Wars of Religion* of the sixteenth and seventeenth centuries. As the majority of its population converted to *Lutheranism*, it allied with *Gustav II* during the *Thirty Years' War*. Subsequent occupation by the *Austrian Empire* saw reconversion of many Silesians to *Catholicism*. *Maria Theresa* of Austria lost the territory to *Frederick the Great* in the *War of the Austrian Succession*. She tried, but failed, to retake it during the *Seven Years' War*, after which it was under permanent Prussian control. With the exception of the *Napoleonic Wars*, when *Napoleon* altered the makeup of Germany at will, it remained attached to Prussia, then to Imperial Germany. After *World War I* a Polish rebellion and *League of Nations* plebiscite *partitioned* Silesia, with portions going to the reemerged state of Poland and the new state of Czechoslovakia, with the rest remaining in Germany. At the *Munich Conference* (1938), the Czech portion was repartitioned between Germany and Poland. All Silesia was occupied by Nazi Germany during *World War II*. After the war the major part of Silesia was given to Poland by virtue of decisions, made at *Yalta* and confirmed at *Potsdam*, to reset the German-Polish border at the *Oder-Neisse line*. Its ethnic German population was forcibly expelled and replaced by Polish *refugees*, some of them from eastern Polish provinces annexed by the Soviet Union.

Silesian Wars, First (1740–1742) and Second (1742–1746). *See Frederick the Great; Maria Theresa; War of the Austrian Succession.*

Silk Road. The major overland *trade route* from western China (Xinjiang), traversing the Pamirs and Central Asia, passing into and through northern India and on to the Middle East, and thence by ship to the markets of the Roman Mediterranean. The end of the Western *Roman Empire* led to a significant decline in regional and world trade. Commerce slowly revived as the

Byzantine Empire clung to existence and small successor kingdoms took shape in Western Europe. Along this prosperous route grew up magnificent cities, such as Samarkand, which were seats of advanced ancient learning and great civilizations. Such rich trade in silk, spice, porcelains, and precious metals also drew in brigands, bandits, and nomadic raiders. The worst of these were the *Mongols*, but once their empire was established (even Mongol order was better than none) the Silk Road became once more a major route of travel between European and Asian lands. The *Black Death* also traveled this road, in the fourteenth century. After the Mongol Empire collapsed the Silk Road again became too dangerous to traverse, and Arab and Indian traders resorted instead to cartage by sea. The overland path was made mostly obsolete by the *Age of Exploration*, which opened up oceanic trade routes between Europe and Asia.

silo. An underground launch facility and its crew and *missile(s)*. Silos are usually *hardened* against attack.

Simla Agreement (June 1972). *See Ali Bhutto; Kashmir.*

Sinai. An Egyptian peninsula lying east of the *Suez Canal*. It was captured by Israel in 1956 but was returned to Egypt as part of the 1957 *cease-fire* agreements. UNEF *peacekeeping* forces were in place, 1957–1967, when *Nasser* ordered them out. Sinai was captured by Israel again in 1967. It was all returned to Egypt by April 1982 under *terms* of the *Camp David Accords* and subsequent *peace treaty*. Those agreements succeeded despite a 1979 Soviet *veto* of a United Nations buffer force. It was replaced by a non–United Nations "Multinational Force of Observers." *See also Arab/Israeli Wars; Anwar Sadat.*

Sinai War. *See Second Arab-Israeli War (1956).*

Sinatra doctrine. A startlingly humorous reference in early 1989 by the (until then, publicly) dour Soviet spokesman Genadi Gerasimov. He was asked whether Moscow still believed in the *Brezhnev Doctrine* for its Eastern European *satellite states*. He said that the Soviet Union would henceforth follow the "Sinatra doctrine: they can do it their way" (in reference to the hit song "My Way" by the American crooner Frank Sinatra). On one level a trite quip, this remark nonetheless was widely read as an important signal to *communist* regimes and reformers within the *Soviet bloc*, and especially in East Germany, that Moscow would not intervene to prevent the decommunization of erstwhile allies. *See also Revolutions of 1989.*

Singapore. A largely undeveloped island was taken over by the *East India Company* in 1819, when Sir T. Stamford Raffles purchased a lease from the Sultan of Johor and founded the modern settlement. It was run by Company governors, 1826–1867, in combination with Penang and Malacca as the composite colony *Straits Settlements*, during which time it grew into a major port servicing the *British Empire* in Asia. It was also a major British military and naval base in the first half of the twentieth century. However, its large British and *Indian Army* garrison surrendered to *Yamashita* on February 15, 1942, following an overland attack which took Singapore from the rear. A famous myth later grew that Singapore's defenses faced seaward and thus could not be brought to bear on the Japanese. In fact, the guns could face landward, but they were useless because they had been supplied with the wrong ammunition. Still, *Churchill* and other British leaders were blameworthy for this huge disaster, as they had underestimated the Japanese. Some 75,000 British and Commonwealth troops were captured. Some Indian nationals among the prisoners later joined *Subhas Bose* to fight alongside Japan against Britain in the *Indian National Army*. Singapore reverted to British control upon Japan's surrender in 1945. In 1959 it became independent. In 1963 it joined the Malaysian Federation, but left and became independent once more in 1965. It then concentrated on economic *growth*, becoming one of the so-called *Asian Tigers* under *Lee Kuan Yew*, who governed Singapore via a paternalistic, *one-party* system (People's Action Party). Its diplomacy is coordinated with that of ASEAN. In August 1993, it held presidential elections under a new constitution, but the usual suspects from the People's Action Party won again, as most expected. *See also Sarawak.*

Suggested Readings: Nicholas Tarling, ed., *Cambridge History of Southeast Asia* (1992); Lee Kuan Yew, *From Third World to First* (2000).

Single European Act (1987). As proposed in 1986, it suggested further *integration* of the *European Community (EC)*, saying that by 1992 there should be a fully integrated market and a community "without frontiers," where *capital*, *goods*, and people moved freely. France, Greece, and Ireland objected to the speed of the proposals, and Britain, France, and Germany all worried about the integrated market's effect on their national economies. It was in the end a compromise agreement which had few penalties for not meeting the deadlines for *integration*. Italy, Denmark, and Greece at first refused to sign. It was delayed until late in 1987 owing to a *referendum* in Ireland, ordered by the Irish courts because it was thought that the Act violated Irish *neutrality*. It revised the original EC *treaties* and reflected the rising power of the *European Council* over the *European Commission* and *European Parliament*. In 1992—the "Year of Europe"—uncertainty caused by the reunification of Germany meant the times were more confused than celebratory. *See also qualified majority voting.*

single integrated operational plan (SIOP). A U.S. contingency plan developed during the *Cold War* for waging war with the Soviet Union following a failure of *deterrence*. It included the use of *nuclear weapons*.

single market. *See European Union.*

Sinification. To influence by, or make like or characteristic of, Chinese culture and values, including veneration of the emperor, ideographic writing, and *Confucianism*. This was classical imperial policy: Chinese emperors sought unity in all things, including culture and religion. Whenever the Chinese Empire expanded it was policy to sinify conquered or vassal peoples, such as the Vietnamese, Koreans, Tibetans, and some *Inner Asians*. This was part bureaucratic convenience and part "civilizing mission" undertaken by a confident, and often also genuinely superior, culture. *See also mission.*

Sinn Féin. "Ourselves alone." A nationalist, mainly Catholic movement founded in 1902 and active before and during the *Irish War of Independence*. It split badly over the *peace treaty*, leading to the *Irish Civil War*, and ceased to dominate Irish politics. A faction reemerged as a crudely *Marxist* party fronting for the *Irish Republican Army* (Provos) in *Ulster* after 1969. Under Gerry Adams and other "moderates," in the 1990s Sinn Féin was accepted by London as a legitimate negotiating and governmental partner in Northern Ireland. In 2001, continuing IRA refusal to surrender weapons led to a breakdown in the process of political reform and normalization; this changed with the *September 11th terrorist attack on the United States*.
    Suggested Reading: Peter Taylor, *Behind the Mask: The IRA and Sinn Féin* (1998).

Sino-Japanese War, First (1894–1895). China increasingly fell under the sway of foreign powers under the *unequal treaties* during the second half of the nineteenth century. It then emerged from the extraordinary upheavals of the *Taiping* and *Nian Rebellions*, recognizing its need for *modernization*. It tried to accomplish this through a "self-strengthening" movement which looked to update its great *Confucian* traditions. However, what China only reluctantly and half-heartedly attempted, Japan enthusiastically carried through: in the *Meiji Restoration* it forged ahead with modernization on all fronts, including of its army and navy, fully determined to become in Asia the equal of the European *Great Powers*. Tokyo's penetration of *Korea* after 1875, its annexation of *Okinawa*, and a punitive expedition to *Taiwan* set the path toward conflict with China. By 1894 Japan was ready to employ its new forces directly against China. Internal unrest and factionalism in Korea provided the pretext, as first Japan then China intervened. The Japanese defeated a Chinese army at Pyongyang and destroyed a Chinese fleet in the Yellow Sea—eliminating China's *blue water navy* for decades to come. The Japanese routed additional Chinese armies sent in as reinforcements, winning victory after victory to great popular acclaim at home. They occupied Port Arthur and the Liaodong peninsula, where Japanese troops committed appalling atrocities against Chinese civilians and *prisoners of war*. Tokyo then imposed on China the severe terms of the *Treaty of Shimonoseki*. So complete was the Japanese military triumph and so harsh their political *diktat*, other Great Powers undertook the *Triple Intervention* to reverse certain territorial gains Japan had made in which they also had an interest. This "stolen victory" enraged Japan and further alienated it from the Western nations. At the same time, nationalist opinion in Japan lost its ancient respect for China and Korea, a shift which prepared the way for Japanese aggression and far worse atrocities to come in the twentieth century. Meanwhile, a fatally wounded China sloughed toward the *Boxer Rebellion* and made a desperate invitation to Russia to enter Manchuria, in a last-ditch effort to balance the rising power of Japan. China's weakness thus put Japan on a collision course with Russia in Manchuria, which shortly thereafter led to the *Russo-Japanese War* (1904–1905).

Suggested Readings: Marius Jansen, *Japan and China* (1975); Morinosuke Kajima, *The Diplomacy of Japan, 1894–1922*, vol. 1 (1976).

Sino-Japanese War, Second (1937–1945). The Japanese took six years to digest *Manchuria* after their invasion in 1931, which proceeded from the *Mukden incident*. In 1932 heavy fighting broke out in Shanghai, where Japanese and Chinese fought to an effective standstill. In early 1933, in anticipation of criticisms in the *Lytton Commission* report, the Japanese pushed deeper into northeastern China. After heavy fighting, the Chinese agreed to the Tanggu Truce in May 1933. The Japanese again crept toward, then into, China proper in 1936, skirmishing and extending their control. A border skirmish on July 7, 1937, the *Marco Polo Bridge Incident*, was seized upon as a *casus belli* by the *Guandong Army*, which later that month attacked and quickly overran most of northern China, without a *declaration of war*. The Chinese chose to respond to the south against a major Japanese garrison dug in at Shanghai. *Chiang Kai-shek* ordered an all-out effort. This was a huge mistake: nearly 250,000 of China's best troops were lost, August–October 1937, or close to 60 percent of the Nationalist Army as it then stood. Japan next captured and sacked the Republican capital in the infamous *Rape of Nanjing*, December 1937–January 1938. The Japanese then continued their advance down the coast, seizing China's major ports, while other units moved inland along the *railways*, taking city after city until most of China's population was under what turned out to be almost everywhere—not just Nanjing, though that was the worst—a vicious and murderous Japanese occupation. However, things did not always go the way the Japanese planned: at Wuhan, in April 1938, Chinese forces killed perhaps 30,000 Japanese troops, and Chiang ordered the dikes holding back the Yellow River to be blown up.

Thus, Japan found it had entered "the China quagmire," as its national historians tend to describe the war that now evolved. This war required Japan to attempt the occupation of all China, a nation many times its own size and population. That was not the more limited—though still wholly aggressive—war for natural resources and *Lebensraum* that Japan's top leaders had discussed and planned. Instead, it was a military and economic effort driven by the most fanatic *militarists* among the officer corps of the semi-independent Guandong Army. And it was a wider war which the Japanese Army and nation would not—and likely also could not—win. Still, it was the Chinese who did most of the suffering and dying. The Japanese Army garrisoned any areas it controlled with thousands of strong points (blockhouses) and settled in to exploit the land—or so they hoped. However, Chinese forces repeatedly attacked Japanese positions, compelling Japanese commanders to send out raids or conquer and *pacify* new areas, further stretching their forces. On the other hand, the Chinese were internally divided between the *Guomindang* under Chiang Kai-shek and the *Communists* under *Mao* and *Zhu De*, as well as numerous semi-independent commanders and erstwhile or would-be *warlords*. These multiple antagonists united to fight the Japanese, but only nominally and under great duress after the *Xi'an incident*. China's cause was viewed sympathetically in the United States, but most of Europe was wholly preoccupied with events being driven toward war, clearly from 1938, by *Nazi Germany*. Private aid and American volunteers arrived (the *Flying Tigers*), and some government help as well. Probably more important, Soviet pilots flew as "volunteers" with the Chinese Air Force. The Japanese attempted to ease their logistical and occupation problems by breaking China into large blocs on the model of their *puppet states* in *Manchukuo*. Each region—Inner Mongolia, Taiwan, the "Republic of China" (north China), and central China—was ostensibly governed by a Chinese government. These puppet regimes were, of course, merely fronted by *collaborators*. The most infamous of these traitors was *Wang Jingwei*, who presided mainly over the mass graves of his butchered countrymen and women from his "capital" at Nanjing. In 1940 the Communists launched a "hundred regiments" campaign, which was initially successful, but was then overwhelmed by a fierce Japanese counterattack order called the "Three Alls" ("kill all, burn all, destroy all").

In January 1941 Communists and Nationalists began fighting each other again when Chiang ordered an attack on the Communist New Fourth Army. The renewed civil war and the war against Japan then merged into the even larger conflict of *World War II*, with the Japanese attack on *Pearl Harbor*. With the aid of war matériel and supported by some *air power* provided by the United States and Britain, the Chinese suffered defeat after defeat but still kept large formations of Japan's land forces tied down in occupying a vast and ever-resistant land. Meanwhile, American and ANZAC forces "island-hopped" toward Japan preparatory to bombing its *home islands* into rubble from bases in the Pacific. The first major raids were actually made, in June 1944, from airfields in southern China. The Japanese retaliated with their southern or Ichigo ("No. 1") offensive, which aimed at taking out the Allied air bases. This greatly relieved pressure on the Communists in the north, by drawing off Japanese troops, while further decimating the Nationalist armies. The Sino-Japanese war ended simultaneously with World War II, actually in August and legally with Japan's formal surrender on September

9, 1945. By then it had tilted the balance within China: for years the Nationalists had been harried and cut off from their urban base, while the Communists—saved from extinction by the Japanese intervention in 1937—had grown more powerful among the peasants. When the *Chinese Civil War* resumed, the Communists were more than equal to the Guomindang, despite U.S. aid to the latter. *See also Burma Road; China War; Neutrality Acts.*

Suggested Readings: John Boyle, *China and Japan at War, 1937–1945* (1972); F. Dorn, *The Sino-Japanese War* (1974); Peter Duus et al., eds., *The Japanese Wartime Empire, 1931–1945* (1996); James Morley, *The China Quagmire* (1983).

Sinologist. An analyst who studies the economics, history, politics, and other features of China's culture, governmental system, and foreign policy.

Sino-Soviet split. From the ascension to power of the Chinese *Communist Party* (CCP) in 1949 to the death of *Stalin* in 1953, Sino-Soviet relations were increasingly embittered by the old dictator's predilection to condescend and lecture the Chinese on how to construct *socialism* in their country. Chinese *communists* also recalled Stalin's disastrous *party line* command to ally with the *Guomindang*, which had led to the *Shanghai massacres* in 1927. Other irritants included special Russian privileges in China, including retention of *Port Arthur*, some exacted by Stalin as the price for his attacking the Japanese in Manchuria at the end of *World War II*. These Russian holdings—along with Hong Kong and Macau—were the last foreign *concessions* in China, and thus grated painfully on memories of 150 years of humiliating *capitulations* to foreigners. In addition, the leadership began to disagree over the appropriate path to internal development. Militating against embitterment was *Mao Zedong's* personal and tactical devotion to Stalin. From 1953 to 1958 the Chinese were accorded more status by Moscow and received technical aid, but they were still treated as subordinates. Then *Khrushchev* denounced Stalin in his *secret speech* in 1956, without consulting or forewarning Mao. Just before this denunciation of Stalin, the Chinese delegate had delivered a speech in praise of the old tyrant. Insult was thus added to the injury perceived by Beijing.

The main cause of the split was disagreement over how much risk could be run in confronting the capitalist world in an era of *nuclear weapons*. Where the Soviets were fearful of nuclear war and proposed *peaceful coexistence* with the Western powers, Mao made wild and reckless assertions that he desired such a war—for instance, over *Quemoy and Matsu* in 1958—even if 300 million Chinese died in it, so long as the capitalist nations were wiped out. In 1957 Moscow agreed to supply nuclear weapons technology to China. It was a bad faith offer, however, intended as part of a strategy to withhold such weapons from China in exchange for U.S. agreement to deny them to *West Germany*. When this switch occurred in 1959, Beijing reacted with vehement denunciation of the Soviet Union. The split was real from this point, and it deepened in mid-1960 when the Soviets, without warning, withdrew from China all their advisers and industrialization blueprints. Western statecraft hardly noticed, adjusted, or tried to take advantage of this huge shift within the communist world. Although the fundamental clash was competition between rival imperial *nationalisms*, it was also an ideological contest between "*revisionists*" and "left-wing adventurists"—the respective recriminations of the Chinese and Russian leadership of each other. In 1962 this struggle over leadership of the communist world was symbolized by competition for the loyalty of Albania, which shifted toward China, and to a lesser degree over the position of Yugoslavia. These minor communist states soon became proxies for mutual public criticism by the communist Great Powers.

By 1964, with a small *détente* underway between the United States and the Soviet Union, the Soviets considered China the gravest threat to their regime. *Marxist-Leninist* rhetoric about ineluctable conflict with the capitalist West was one thing; Chinese missiles, atomic weapons, and extreme ideological hostility was quite another. In 1966 and again in March 1969, elements of the *Red Army* and the *People's Liberation Army* clashed along the disputed Amur/Ussuri River border. During the second crisis the Soviets indirectly asked *Richard Nixon* what the U.S. response would be to a *preemptive strike* against China's nuclear facilities and weapons. Nixon warned off the Soviets and indicated the United States would intervene. That shattered some of the ideological barriers to improved Sino-American relations and laid the basis for a partial *rapprochement* between Beijing and Washington, despite their continuing deep disputes over the *Vietnam War* and the status of *Taiwan*. The discrete *Cambodia-Vietnam War* (1977–1991) was, on one level, a *proxy war* that flowed from the Sino-Soviet split (although its principal causes lay deep in Indochinese history and in the darker recesses of the twisted mind of *Pol Pot*). Sino-Soviet relations did not recover until just before the collapse of the Soviet Union, when both sides were looking to counterbalance the clearly emerging preponderance of the United States. *Gorbachev* visited Beijing, signaling a fresh beginning. Unfortunately, his visit coincided with demonstrations that culminated in the *Tiananmen Square massacre*. Within two years, the Soviet Union itself was *extinct*. After 1991, Russian-Chinese relations improved on the basis of mutual interest in trade and as a means of balancing against perceived U.S. *hegemony*.

Suggested Reading: Gordon Chang, *Friends and Enemies* (1990).

Sino-Vietnamese War (February 17–March 5, 1979). Long-term causes included Vietnam's mistreatment of its ethnic Chinese minority (Hoa), a simmering border dispute over which negotiations broke down in 1978, and Hanoi's alliance with the Soviet Union, which aggravated the *Sino-Soviet split*. The immediate causes were intensification in 1978 of the *Cambodia-Vietnam War* for which China sought to "punish" Vietnam (hence Beijing's nomenclature: the "Punitive War"), and China's resolve to demonstrate military prowess and assert itself as a regional *hegemon*. Beijing's largely infantry attack was directed by *Deng Xiaoping*. It met fierce resistance from border troops but advanced 10 miles by February 22nd. People's Army of Vietnam (PAVN) divisions were recalled from Laos and Cambodia to meet the incursion. On March 5th, having advanced 40 miles, China announced it would withdraw. Chinese casualties probably totaled 65,000 (26,000 killed in action); Vietnam's were likely 62,000 (30,000 killed in action). China's military weakness, rather than reserves of strength, had been exposed and few of its goals accomplished: Vietnam remained in Cambodia, retained its alliance with Moscow, stepped-up persecution of the Hoa, and still disputed the border.

SIS. Secret Intelligence Service. The main *intelligence service* of Britain. It was one of the most active and important during the *Cold War*. See also MI5/ MI6.

situational factors. *Jargon* for the facts of the *balance of power*, *capabilities*, *national interest*, and intentions of allies and opponents which a *statesman* must consider when making a foreign policy decision.

Sitzkrieg. For the full meaning of this famous *World War II* pun compare *Blitzkrieg* and *Phony War*.

Six Day War. *See Third Arab-Israeli War.*

size. The actual, geographical extent of a *state* or an *empire*. Size matters, but sheer size does not guarantee a nation great power: witness the historical experiences of Australia and Canada. A state must also have the requisite population and technological means to exploit the abundant natural resources which great physical size usually brings, and convert them into economic and military power and diplomatic influence. Large size can even reduce national power by bringing a country into contact with many adversaries. Thus, the size of the Soviet Union gave it multiple borders, while its policies ensured each of these was hostile. Still, small size is more likely to handicap a country that seeks to expand its power and influence than is largeness. That is so simply because of the material reason that if a country is big, ambitious leaders are more likely to have available to them a large population, plentiful resources, and a solid economic base.

Skaggerak. The German name for the *Battle of Jutland*.

skirmishers. Light *infantry* used to harass regular columns of troops. The Austrians used *partisans* as skirmishers in their wars with *Frederick the Great*. Colonial *militia* similarly harried the British in the *American Revolution*. Noting this, *Napoleon* used skirmishers innovatively, to break up rigid enemy formations before a full attack by his massed infantry or *cavalry*. *See also irregulars.*

slash and burn. A land-clearing technique used by very poor, itinerant farmers in virgin forest areas. It leaves soil badly depleted and open to erosion after just a few crops are taken. It is of international concern because it threatens common environmental interests in the rain forests, especially in the *Amazon basin.*

Slav. Any of the Balkan or East or Central European peoples related by culture, ethnicity, or language: (1) Eastern Slavs: Byelorussians, Moldavians, Russians, Ruthenians, and Ukrainians. (2) South Slavs: Bulgars, Croats, Serbs, and Slovenes. (3) Western Slavs: Czechs, Moravians, Poles, and Slovaks. The generic term derives from "slave," reflecting the horrific condition of these varied peoples during the Middle Ages and under the *Mongol* Khanates. *See also* Lebensraum; *Mamluks; pan-Slavism; Slavophile; Yugoslavia.*

Slave Coast. The West African coast from the Niger delta to the Volta, named for the "primary product" taken from there during the sixteenth through the nineteenth centuries. From ports such as Porto Novo and Lagos, vast numbers of *Yoruba* and other slaves departed for plantations in the *New World.* Nearby sections were known as the *Gold Coast* and *Ivory Coast. See also Ashanti; slave trade.*
  Suggested Reading: C. W. Newbury, *The Western Slave Coast and its Rulers* (1961).

slave labor/slavery. The ownership of one person by another for purposes of exploiting their unpaid toil. Slavery is an institution as old as recorded history, appearing in some form in virtually every known ancient society and many modern ones, irrespective of race or locale. Slavery has existed as an indigenous social and economic institution almost everywhere, in Africa, Asia, Europe, and the precolumbian Americas. Indeed, slave labor at one time or another supported most pre-industrial agrarian civilizations. At least 40 percent of the population of Italy was enslaved under the *Roman Empire*, a figure which also held true for the *Confederacy* nearly two thousand years later. A leading historian of slavery, Seymour Drescher, points out that to the end of the eighteenth century "personal bondage was the prevailing form of labor in most of the world. . . . Freedom, not slavery, was the peculiar institution."
  Slave-dependent societies were most often religious and/or military dictatorships, whether overt or hidden, whose more privileged members lived in relative comfort but also fear of bloody revolt. And not without reason. From 73 to 70 B.C.E., a former gladiator (slave) named Spartacus led a great slave rebellion against Rome which was suppressed only with a major military effort and massive brutality. Russian peasants, who became effective slaves at several points in history, rebelled frequently and often with enormously pent-up and

savage violence, and frequently also with religious undertones. The slave population of Haiti successfully rebelled in 1791, the only *New World* slaves to do so, winning their freedom—of a sort—in 1804. Their success gave nightmares to slave holder families throughout the Americas in the nineteenth century.

Many slave societies allowed concubinage and even intermarriage: in South Africa, throughout the *sudan*, in Nubia, Ethiopia, Egypt, and in the Middle East, and especially in Latin America, slave concubinage helped produce, over several generations, distinctly mixed-race populations. The Dutch took slaves from south India to the *Spice Islands*, and from Java to *Cape Colony*. After the end of the *slave trade*, the British transported indentured Indian labor throughout their empire. In some times and places the mixed communities which resulted were accepted; at other times in other places they were not. In India, slavery coexisted with the *caste system* of *Hindus* and was unquestioned by Muslim overlords, who practiced it in India as they did everywhere else. The *East India Company* tolerated traditional Indian slavery, and in many ways relied on it, even past the ostensible liberation of all slaves within the *British Empire* in 1833. Some slave systems permitted occasional manumission, usually for military services rendered. Some literature depicts indigenous slavery, such as under the *Ottomans* or in parts of Africa, or within *Islamic* countries in general, as less harsh than slavery in the New World. To a degree, this was true: Old World slaves might even rise to positions of real authority, trusted by rulers who would not entrust potential clan or ethnic rivals with power. It remains true that forced labor in all societies and times was still hard and personally unrewarding (that is, forced) labor, and that even less physically onerous service in a "big house" (or casa grande, or harem, or palace guard) remained unfree.

Columbus began the enslavement of the peoples of the New World, on *Hispaniola*, where he introduced the *encomienda* system. Indian slavery failed, however, mainly due to destruction of the Indian population by epidemic disease, and hard conditions on farms or in the mines. It was also opposed by *missionaries*, including the *Jesuits*, as a violation of the natural freedom of New World peoples. By the 1560s–1570s these settlements looked for a new supply of forced labor, which the few remaining Indians could not fill, to Africa, where indigenous slavery was endemic—but was also calibrated by many local rulers so that the loss of laborers it entailed did not severely damage their economies—and where Europeans had already established it in several offshore plantation economies. From 1500 to the middle of the nineteenth century Africa as a whole suffered huge demographic losses to slavery. The losses were uneven: many African societies found it rewarding to commit fully to the slave trade, and devoted themselves to slave-raids against weaker neighbors—few Africans were actually captured by European or even *Swahili Arab* traders. Others exchanged war captives with coastal traders in return for firearms, which were then used to overturn the inland *balance of power* and acquire more captives, while still larger African states and empires employed huge numbers of slaves to work their own economies (more than 16 million firearms were imported by Africans in the nineteenth century).

Even at the peak of the African slave trade, the awful truth is that more Africans were likely toiling as slaves in Africa, owned by other Africans, than were hauled away by sea or across the desert by camel caravan. The *Hausa* forced nearby pagans into slave villages which surrounded and sustained their *city-states*; *Benin* and the great *Yoruba* cities also enslaved weaker tribes, raiding westward and throughout the great Niger delta; *Songhay* expanded its use of slaves in the sixteenth century, raiding far afield and south of the Niger bend; the *jihads* of the *Fulbe* in part justified and supported enslavement of sudanese pagans, and so forth. For all these peoples and empires, the horse was an important instrument of slaving: *cavalry* on the sudan and savannah easily ran down helpless villagers during slave raids hundreds of miles from Africa's coasts, caravan routes, and imperial capitals. The introduction of firearms in the sixteenth through the eighteenth centuries worsened the situation and dramatically changed the balance of power: guns made slaving easier but war more costly, requiring still more slaving to pay for the new war technology which now sustained or overturned political power. Firearms strengthened formerly weak coastal and forest tribes, who obtained them first from European traders, against the traditionally dominant slave-raiding states of the savannah and desert, which since the thirteenth century had relied on armored cavalry.

In Africa and elsewhere, whole empires rested on military slaves. *Mamluks* from south Russia and the Caucasus sustained Muslim caliphs for centuries, and as a slave dynasty themselves ruled Egypt, Palestine, and Syria from 1250 to 1798. The trade went both ways: several of the tsars, including *Peter I* and *Catherine the Great*, kept black slaves at court; one of the poet Pushkin's ancestors was a Petrine slave. The Ottomans used a partial slave force, the *Janissaries*, to defeat the Mamluks and help govern their vast empire. Military slaves were also commonplace in medieval India, where other Mamluks briefly achieved supreme power. And as had been the case in Rome and ancient Persia, off the shores of the Ottoman Empire into the nineteenth century tens of thousands of slaves chained to their oars rowed fleets of *galleys* on missions of trade or war. On a lesser scale, the *Barbary pirates* reserved their galleys for Christian slaves while importing African women and children as slave concubines and household servants. Morocco in the seventeenth and eighteenth centuries relied on sudanese slaves to stock its military and to conquer Songhay. Brazil fought the *War of the Triple Alliance* (1864–1870) using slave soldiers, whose performance led to partial abolition of slavery in 1871 and full abolition in 1888. In several conflicts in the late twentieth century a form of military slavery was revived: in Angola, Mozambique, and among the *Tamil Tigers*, child slaves were ripped from their families and trained (severely deprived and then brainwashed) and widely employed as cold-blooded killers, often while high on narcotics. In China under the late *Ming dynasty*, children could be indentured as servants, and young girls were sold in markets feeding the sex trade.

Two countries were founded by freed slaves: *Sierra Leone* (Freetown) in 1787 and *Liberia* in 1822. Other free black colonies were founded in emulation of Freetown: on Fernando Po and at Libreville in Gabon. Slavery (as opposed to the slave trade) was ruled illegal in England in 1772; it was made illegal within the British Empire in 1833. This had the unintended consequence of increasing demand for, and export of, Indian and Chinese "coolie" and indentured labor to various parts of the Empire, including *British North America* and *Natal*, as well as sparking the *Great Trek* of the *Boers* away from anti-slavery laws and in search of new supplies among the *Nguni* peoples. Slavery was abolished in the French Empire in 1848 but continued in practice in several French colonies in Africa for decades more—the French colonial army greatly depended on native troops and rulers, some of whom saw enslavement of prisoners and captured women as legitimate war *booty*. Paris moved to enforce an end to slavery within its African colonies only in 1905, when about one million slaves were freed. In many cases their lives improved little, as they remained in indentured servitude under local rulers. The Ottomans abolished slavery within their empire (except for the *Hejaz*) in 1857. The *Roma* were enslaved in Rumania until 1864. In the New World, slavery was legal in the United States until 1865 (abolished by the Thirteenth Amendment), in Cuba (under Spain) until 1886, and in Brazil until 1888.

Despite nineteenth-century efforts to abolish slavery internationally (including at the *Berlin Conference* of 1884) it existed into—and indeed expanded during—the twentieth century. It was reintroduced to Western Europe (from whence it had been banished during the late Middle Ages) by *Nazi Germany*, which enslaved millions and literally worked them to death. Slavery was reintroduced to Russia by the *Bolsheviks* and was expanded on a mass scale under *Stalin*: millions of Soviets were enslaved and worked to death in a giant forced labor and prison camp system known as the GULAG *archipelago*. The *Khmers Rouges* and other radical movements in Southeast Asia in the 1970s and 1980s used mass slave labor alongside *terror* to control entire populations; and uncounted millions more drudged in slavelike conditions in China's vast, secret prison and work camp system during the decades of *Mao's* misrule, and after. Saudi Arabia made slavery illegal only in 1962. As many as 100,000 black slaves labored for Moorish masters in Mauritania into the 1980s, and, despite international pressure, as "indentured servants" toiled and suffered into the twenty-first century. In war-torn Sudan slavery grew in the 1990s, feeding off old religious and ethnic bigotry and the misery of a 30-year civil war. Well-intentioned souls outside Sudan bought some of these slaves to free them, which probably increased incentives for slave-kidnappings.

In Latin America "debt peonage" systems kept generations of poor families in effective bondage through much of the twentieth century, and into the twenty-first century in more remote areas. Near-slave conditions (including for children) may be found still in illegal "sweat shops," debt-bondage systems, and houses of prostitution in major world cities on every populated continent. And in a band of hostility that crosses Africa still, from the west coast through Nigeria to the Sudan, slavery's legacy of conflict and mistrust lingers among the descendants of those who once raided, and those who were taken. Civil wars and ethnic conflicts broke out in the late twentieth century in many countries which straddle this zone, often with roots in the deep hatreds and slave wars of times past. In 2001, the *International Labor Organization (ILO)* estimated that some 25 million children were effectively enslaved in Africa as indentured servants or sex slaves, with others sold to buyers in the Middle East and Europe. Yet for all that record of immiseration and persecution, in general the practice of slavery underwent a secular decline after 1800, so that for the first time in history it is no longer legally acceptable or widely practiced in civilized societies. *See also Azores; Canary Islands; crimes against humanity; Abraham Lincoln; Madeira; nongovernmental organizations (NGOs); piracy; rachat; serfdom; V-1; white slavery; William Wilberforce; zeriba system.*

Suggested Readings: D. Davis, *The Problem of Slavery in Western Culture* (1966); Seymour Drescher, *From Slavery to Freedom* (1999); Paul Lovejoy, *Transformations in Slavery: A History of Slavery in Africa* (1983).

slave states. The 15 states of the American union where *slavery* was legal until the *American Civil War* finally settled the issue, and the Thirteenth Amendment at last cleansed the land of an ancient evil: the 11 states which seceded and formed the *Confederacy* (Alabama, Arkansas, Florida, Georgia, Louisiana, Mississippi, North Carolina, South Carolina, Tennessee, Texas, and Virginia), as well as four *border states* (Delaware, Maryland, Kentucky, and Missouri), which remained within the *Union.* Kentucky and Missouri split, with Confederate *governments-in-exile* moving south upon military occupation by the Union. West Virginia, originally part of Virginia, refused to remain part of a slave state. After war began, it seceded from Virginia to remain in and side with the Union. *See also free soil.*

slave trade. The transport of persons from one locale to another in order to sell them into *slavery.* Beginning around 1100 C.E. and lasting for another several centuries, a specialized trade in slaves ran from Europe to Africa and the Middle East and India, which all imported *Slav* and Caucasian military slaves to supply regiments of *Mamluks.* However, from the sixteenth through the nineteenth centuries the modern transatlantic slave trade developed. This was mainly a trade in captives from West and Central Africa, brought to the *New World* to labor on plantations or in mines, and in general to exploit the vast resources of the Americas and West Indies for the benefit of Europe and of settler populations. The Spanish began importing African slaves to New

Spain as early as 1501 to replace Indian laborers who were dying en masse from exposure to measles, smallpox, and typhus and whose souls the *Jesuits* insisted on saving. In 1542 "New Laws" were promulgated by *Charles V* forbidding enslavement of Indians and ostensibly ending the *encomienda* system. This provoked rebellion among hacienda owners in Peru. The real cause of decline in Indian slavery was the dramatic fall in Indian numbers due to disease, which had the long-term effect of substantially increasing demand for African slaves. By 1600 a majority of people living in the West Indies were of African or mixed-race descent. The Portuguese also imported large numbers of African slaves to Brazil, and English settlers brought black slaves to the American South.

The transatlantic slave trade reached new levels from the 1630s, when it was taken over north of the equator by the Dutch, as a result of their seizures of Portuguese territories in Africa, and briefly also in Brazil during the *Eighty Years' War* (1566–1648). Intense scholarly work was done in the last quarter of the twentieth century to more precisely measure the number of slaves taken across the Atlantic from Africa. Assuming an average loss of life of some 15 percent en route during the transoceanic passage attendant on this vile trade, the consensus—though not wholly undisputed—figure is nearly 12 million Africans (predominantly males, at a ratio of about 2:1) taken across the Atlantic to forced labor in the Caribbean and the Americas. The United States, Brazil, and the Caribbean and South American plantation economies continued to import African slaves into the middle of the nineteenth century. The racial differences involved in the Atlantic slave trade made it a particularly pernicious variant of an ancient scourge, which still mars race relations all through the Americas.

East Africans were also taken away in a branch of the slave trade which predated the Atlantic trade and outlasted it. This trade dealt in smaller numbers of slaves overall, with anywhere from 5 million to 7 million Africans taken from East Africa, and since the drain occurred over 1,200 years, starting in the eighth century if not earlier, the numbers in any given year were smaller than those of the Atlantic trade and the impact was thus more drawn out, though hardly less dramatic in terms of retarded demography and social, economic, and political development, in addition to raw human suffering. The East African trade was run at first by Muslim (Arab) slavers operating from *Zanzibar*, then briefly by the Portuguese out of Zanzibar and Mozambique, then again by the Arabs of *Oman*, and finally by *Swahili Arabs* and freelancers such as *Tippu Tip*. It served slave markets in Arabia and India and was not closed down until 1873, with some slaves being sold secretly into the early twentieth century.

Finally, there was an even older overland slave trade dating at least to the ninth century C.E., and possibly earlier, which crossed the *Sahara Desert* via several well-established routes to the bazaars of the Mediterranean coast in *Morocco, Tunis, Algiers,* and *Egypt*. This trade is less well documented, but it is likely that it took some 9–10 million more Africans, predominantly women and children from the *sudan*, savannah, and forest zones, on the hard trip by foot across the great desert. None of those figures, as awful as they are, account for the nameless numbers of innocents who died at the hands of ruthless slavers—surely among the hardest and cruelest occupations ever devised, requiring the destruction of whole communities and daily ripping apart of loving families, along with beatings and killings of any who resisted—before they reached markets where they could be sold into bondage.

Toward the end of the eighteenth century a humanitarian movement developed opposed to continuation of slavery and the slave trade. It caught hold most powerfully in the northern United States and Britain, where it was guided by a reformist Christian philosophy and the driven personality of *William Wilberforce*. The antislavery movement was also connected to the rise of new industries which saw slavery and the agrarian interests it sustained as retrograde, and to industrial workers' movements which saw slavery as depressing wages. In 1792 Denmark banned the slave trade within its empire, and in 1805 it banned participation by its subjects in the slave trade anywhere. In 1807 Britain followed suit, banning the trade within the *British Empire*. However, abolition of the slave trade did not mean the end of slavery: Britain abolished the practice of slavery within its Empire only in 1833— nearly three decades after it banned trading in slaves—and it did so with full *compensation* to owners for the loss of their "property." The United States made importation of slaves illegal in 1808, but its *slave states* winked at the practice in reality and protected the institution of slavery in law until the issue was decided by the *American Civil War*. Trade in human cargoes was condemned (but not made universally illegal) by the *Great Powers* gathered at the *Congress of Vienna*. As only Britain had the naval power to enforce a global ban and other nations were loath to permit rights of *visit and search* to London for other reasons, the slave trade remained an internationally legal trade except for unilateral bans secured or imposed by the major slaving nations.

Britain thus pursued bilateral ban agreements which permitted the *Royal Navy* to search other nations' ships with their express and prior permission, and began unilateral enforcement. France banned the slave trade in 1818, but not the practice of slavery within its empire, so that the trade and practice continued internally into the twentieth century within many French possessions. In 1815 Portugal restricted slaving to south of the Equator (it banned slavery in all its possessions in 1838); in 1817 Spain did the same. Spain and Portugal banned the trade completely in 1820. The Dutch, otherwise long the most liberal (and capitalist) of peoples in Europe, did not ban it until 1863—which strongly suggests that the abolition movement led to slavery's decline, and not the reverse, as some argue. Yet banning the trade did not stop the evil business per se. Trade in slaves continued just as long as slavery as an institution and economic system still thrived in the Americas, North

Africa, the Middle East, and elsewhere. In fact, at first banning the sea trade actually made the passage more lucrative for the slavers and vastly more dangerous for slaves, who were the prime evidence of illegality should a slave ship be boarded. More brutal slavers resorted to tying their captives together and weighing them down to ensure they would sink when thrown overboard upon the approach of a British warship. This heinous practice continued until laws were amended making the apparatus of slavery (chains, berths, whips) in themselves sufficient evidence for conviction.

The end of the slave trade meant a dramatic decline in trade between Africa and the rest of the world, such that the Danes withdrew from trading forts they had occupied for two centuries in the Gold Coast (1850); the Dutch followed suit in 1872. The larger imperial powers had broader interests in Africa and remained in place. The slave trade had been so disruptive of African life that it must be identified as the single greatest force of change within Africa from c. 1650 to 1850, underlying most of its wars and state building, as well as the destruction of several African empires, and underpinning almost all economic relations. Against that proposition, however, must be laid the fact that the end of the external slave trade during the second half of the nineteenth century did not bring with it a corresponding diminution of slavery or slave raiding within Africa itself. As a result, humanitarians joined forces with imperialists and other romantics to identify the continuation of slavery in Africa as a justification for establishing *direct rule* by European empires. Thus, in the last third of the nineteenth century arguments against slavery reinforced reasons of prestige and global strategy to provoke the *scramble for Africa*. All that was left was to call in the lawyers: the Convention of St. Germain (1919) made trading slaves on land or at sea a crime under *international law*; it was reinforced by another convention in 1926, a special *protocol* in 1953, and another supplementary convention in 1956. *See also Madeira; triangle trade.*

Suggested Readings: Roger Anstey, *The Atlantic Slave Trade and British Abolition, 1710– 1810* (1975); Herbert Klein, *The Atlantic Slave Trade* (1999); Daniel Mannix, *Black Cargoes* (1978); David Northrup, *The Atlantic Slave Trade* (1994).

Slavophile. A Russian intellectual and cultural tradition maintaining that values drawn from *Slav* culture and institutions are superior, and more appropriate for Russia, than are Western values and institutions imported by figures such as *Peter I, Alexander II,* or even *Mikhail Gorbachev* and *Boris Yeltsin.* This tradition sometimes prefers harsh autocrats such as *Ivan IV* (the Terrible), *Nicholas I,* and *Stalin,* but also throws up populist reformers such as *Herzen* and the *narodniki. See also Orthodox Church;* Pamyat; *Russification; Third Rome; Westernizer.*

sleeper. A *penetration agent* left inactive for years.

sloop-of-war. A mid-size *warship* in the age of sail, with cannon on just one deck; comparable to a *cruiser*. *See also man-of-war.*

Slovakia. Formerly a province of the *Austro-Hungarian Empire*, after *World War I* it became part of *Czechoslovakia*, sharing the twists and turns of that country's fate until the end of 1992. The only interlude came during *World War II*, when a Nazi *protectorate* was set up in Slovakia under Josef Tiso (1887–1947). In 1941 it *declared war* on the Soviet Union and then on the United States, in tandem with the German declarations. The Slovak population did not so readily embrace these policies, however. In 1944 Slovak *resistance* fighters rose against the Germans, declaring "Free Slovakia" and hoping for help from the approaching *Red Army*. They were wiped out, and Slovakia was not liberated until the arrival of Russian troops in 1945. The traitor Tiso was found hiding in a cellar and was shot. Slovakia resumed its prewar status as part of Czechoslovakia until that *federation* broke up at the turn of January 1, 1993. After independence it remained reliant on heavy industries and *armaments* manufacture, which had been disproportionately located on its territory, and rapidly fell behind the more consumer-oriented Czechs. In 1993 it arranged its first *International Monetary Fund* loan. That year, heavily *Catholic* Slovakia also saw a rise in open discrimination against its *Roma* minority, led by the prime minister and president, which ultimately provoked criticism and a legal response from the *OSCE* and the *European Union*. The anti-Roma ("Gypsy") drive had *fascist* overtones. Slovakia has a Hungarian minority of some 500,000. By 2001 Slovakia was still making slow progress in adjusting to the new realities of the post-Soviet era in Europe.

Slovenia. It was part of the *Austrian Empire* from the fourteenth century. Along with other non-German provinces, it witnessed a rise in national consciousness after the *Revolutions of 1848*. It became a constituent republic of *Yugoslavia* at the end of *World War I*, with the *extinction* of the old empire. During *World War II* it was partitioned between Nazi Germany and *fascist* regimes in Hungary and Italy. It was restored to Yugoslavia in 1945, sharing that larger state's fate under *Tito* and *communist* rule. It proclaimed independence in June 1991. After fighting and winning an intense but only 10-day battle with Federal Yugoslav Army forces (essentially, the Serbs), it was recognized by the *European Community*, at Germany's urging, on January 15, 1992. Given its physical remove from Serbia, and because it contained very few Serbs—who therefore did not act as *fifth columnists* as they did elsewhere in the Balkans—it escaped the worst of the *Third Balkan War*, during which it was shielded from Serbia and from fighting in Bosnia by the interposition of a crescent of Croatian territory. Slovenia has minor territorial disputes with Italy, pertaining to lands acquired by Yugoslavia after World War II, and with Croatia, over unresolved border demarcation following the breakup of Yugoslavia. It began membership negotiations with the *European Union* in 1998.

slump. An ill-defined but widely used term for a temporary decline in economic activity, often affecting a single *service* or *commodity*. In some usages, this retraction is less pronounced than in a *recession*; in others it is a synonym for recession.

small powers. A self-explanatory term for those *states* which rank near the bottom in size or in relative economic and military power. *See also Great Powers; microstates; middle power; regional power; world power.*

small states. *See dwarf states; microstates.*

smart weapons. Originally, any weapons with a "fire-and-forget" capability to seek out precise targets (some select targets themselves) and destroy them while doing minimum *collateral damage*. They were first used, highly effectively, by the United States to interdict the Democratic Republic of Vietnam's (DRV's) conventional invasion of the Republic of Vietnam (RVN) in 1972. They were extensively used in the *Gulf War* (1991) and in *Kosovo* (1998). The U.S. air campaign in Afghanistan following the *September 11, 2001, terrorist attack on the United States* saw a spectacular display of air combat superiority born of global positioning satellites and targeting systems, laser guided munitions, photographically detailed ground maps prepared in advance by satellite and high-altitude aerial reconnaissance, advanced radar, 24-hour battlefield monitoring by robotic aircraft, heat and motion detector nighttime fighting capabilities, and moving-target tracking indicators. This meant that, in contrast to *carpet bombing* techniques of past wars, or even the relative precision bombing of the Gulf War, during the Afghanistan campaign the United States required on average just two smart bombs to destroy one target. At the start of the twenty-first century, major military powers were working on, inter alia, "smart *armor*" designed to deploy only when under fire, satellite-guided munitions for *artillery*, and advanced lasers. *See also bomb; cruise missile; just war tradition; missile; revolution in military affairs; terrain contour matching; Vietnam War.*

Smith, Adam (1723–1790). Scottish political economist of the *Enlightenment* period. He is widely regarded as the founder of the discipline of *economics*, although he pursued a far more sophisticated *political economy* approach than do many, more narrowly quantitative, modern economists. He was a moral philosopher of note who held a professorship in that position at Glasgow and wrote widely on astronomy, language, ancient sciences, and logic. His enormously influential book "Inquiry Into the Nature and Causes of the Wealth Of Nations" (1776), which pioneered *liberal* economic theories on the division of labor, operation of markets, money, and wages, was actually conceived as the first installment of a much larger work, which he never completed, of inquiry into the broad gamut of moral philosophy (other parts were to consider law, ethics, and politics). Smith was a fierce critic of *mercantilism* as a state policy, depicting it as interfering with the natural economic liberty which was the birthright of all humanity, and as leading to irrational and inefficient distribution of economic resources. He criticized the natural tendency of merchants to pursue monopolies, which he believed operated against the public interest. He proposed as a general solution *free trade*, so that specialization and an international division of labor among nations might produce wealth for all trading partners, pointing out as well to Britain's imperial masters that "fleets and armies are maintained, not with gold and silver [the mercantilist view], but with consumable goods." This argument that Britain's war-making capacity would be enhanced by free trade had great appeal, impressed *William Pitt* mightily, and appeared confirmed in the aftermath of the *American Revolution* (1775–1783), when Anglo-American trade not only resumed but expanded.

On the other hand, Smith challenged another basis of past British martial success, reliance on the *national debt* to deficit finance wars with larger continental powers, by arguing that Great Britain ought to finance future wars by direct and heavy taxation. His semi-subversive, progressive purpose in that proposal was to increase the pain of war for ordinary "consumers," and thereby shorten wars. In that, he again anticipated much of nineteenth-century *liberalism*. He would surely have been appalled by the deficit financing of wars carried out by the free-trading United States in the second half of the twentieth century. He called for virtually unregulated markets and policies of broad social *laissez-faire* as being most conducive to freedom—although he was never a full-throated proponent of the extreme version of that doctrine which developed later, not directly from his theories but out of radical application of utilitarian principles to social policy in the mid-nineteenth century. He begrudgingly accepted the *Navigation Acts* as being necessary to national defense, but otherwise he opposed all restrictions on international commerce, which he believed would support not just prosperity for all but also peace among nations. His ideas were hugely influential, even more so after his death, when they heavily affected British foreign economic policy and social legislation in the 1820s and thereafter. *See also classical school; comparative advantage; "decline of the West"; Immanuel Kant; liberal-internationalism; physiocrats.*

Suggested Reading: R. L. Heilbroner, *The Worldly Philosophers*, 7th rev. ed. (1999).

Smithian growth. A term of art among economic historians for the phase or era of world economic history preceding the *Industrial Revolution*, which saw formation and integration of markets in *commodities, land, capital,* and *labor.* Their concerns include comparative study of legal, cultural, and institutional variations among national economic systems, and how these may have affected the "great divergence" between European and non-European economies as first identified by *Adam Smith.* The duration, character, and subsequent effects of this period are broadly disputed. Secondarily, the term has acquired currency in discussions of the necessary preconditions for sustained growth by any modern economy.

Suggested Readings: Marshal Hodgson, *Rethinking World History* (1993); David Landes, *The Wealth and Poverty of Nations* (1998); Kenneth Pomeranz, *The Great Divergence: Europe, China, and the Making of the Modern World Economy* (2000).

Smithsonian Agreement (December 18, 1971). The first effort at agreement on *currency* realignment by the *Group of Ten*. It was drawn up in response to the *Nixon shocks*.

Smoot-Hawley Tariff (1930). A high *tariff* wall against nearly all imported *goods*, enacted by the U.S. Congress in response to the *Great Depression*. This *neomercantilist* policy greatly exacerbated the depression by erecting barriers to world trade just as expanded trade became essential to economic recovery. It provoked a round of retaliatory *tariffs* from all other major trading states. It most severely damaged trade with Canada and Latin American countries and with Germany. Along with *reparations* and *war debts* quarrels, this greatly contributed to the nearly complete breakdown of the international economy in the 1930s.

smooth-bore. A musket or *cannon* with a bore which is not rifled (grooved) but smooth, giving it far less accuracy and range than a rifled weapon: estimates are that early smooth-bore muskets, which fired 1-ounce lead balls about 300 meters, inflicted just one casualty for every 200–500 aimed shots. Smooth-bore weapons were the norm during the *Napoleonic Wars*, when their limited range and accuracy was a key to *infantry* tactics such as use of massed formations and advances which concluded with attack by *bayonet* and saber. They were displaced in Great Power armies by *rifled-bore* firearms beginning with the *Crimean War* and the *American Civil War*. Generals were slow to adapt, however, which contributed to numerous massacres of charging *infantry*, who now could be accurately fired on at 10 times the previous range. That shift so advantaged defenders that those wars both ended in ugly and costly *attrition* and *trench warfare*. When rapid-fire ability was later added to rifled weapons, as in *machine guns* and then also *artillery*, the carnage which resulted from attacking a prepared enemy position became unprecedented, as was demonstrated repeatedly during horrific *World War I* battles such as the *Somme* and *Verdun*. Rifled weapons became standard issue in all armed forces during the twentieth century. Smooth-bore muskets (as opposed to shotguns, which are short-range smooth-bore weapons) survived in less advanced areas and in private hands much longer: this author saw newly hand-manufactured smooth-bore guns, whose technology was unchanged from the nineteenth century, in use by *Tuareg* in northern Nigeria and central Niger as late as 1980.

smuggling. To *import* or *export* goods in violation of local law, especially if done to avoid payment of *excise*. *See also BfV; contiguous zone; Continental System; contraband; drug cartels; INTERPOL; Nikita Khrushchev; kulaks; Vladimir Ilyich Lenin; representation;* samizdat; *Schengen Agreement; War of Jenkins' Ear.*

Smuts, Jan Christian (1870–1950). South African general and statesman; British field marshal. Trained as a lawyer, Smuts joined the *Afrikaner* cause after *Cecil Rhodes* organized the infamous *Jameson raid.* He took a general command in 1900 during the *Second Boer War* and proved a brilliant *guerrilla* commander. He invaded *Cape Colony* itself in 1901, but after initial victories he was driven back. Smuts then helped negotiate an end to the conflict. He played a major role in establishing the Union of South Africa in 1910. He commanded a British, Belgian, and Portuguese invasion of *German East Africa* in 1915. He negotiated (unsuccessfully) with Austrians who were looking for a *separate peace* in 1916. He joined the Imperial War Cabinet in 1917, represented South Africa at the *Paris Peace Conference*, and signed the *Treaty of Versailles.* He was prime minister of South Africa, 1919–1924, and again, 1939–1948, and led a reluctant South Africa into *World War II.* He later played an active role in formation of the *Commonwealth*, and at the *San Francisco Conference.* He was highly regarded and often consulted by *Winston Churchill*, a fact which gave Smuts influence far beyond his country's capacities. *Apartheid* was formally legislated in the country only in 1949, after Smuts was defeated and left office. Although he expressed sympathy for South Africa's disenfranchised populations, he never devised lasting solutions to their plight, or the country's.
    Suggested Reading: W. K. Hancock, *Smuts*, 2 vols. (1962, 1968).

"Soccer War" (1969). The American term for what is known internationally as the *"Football War."*

Social Charter. The labor and social policy code of the *European Union. Conservatives*, in Britain in particular, objected to it as too "socialistic." It was passed into law nonetheless.

social contract. In political philosophy, an imaginary bargain which takes place in the *state of nature* in which individuals contract with each other to form *states*; these provide security and social welfare and set laws which regulate social relations. By extension, it is said by some theorists that no social contract is necessary or possible among states, and therefore there can be no escape from the *anarchy* said to characterize the *international system. See also harmony of interests; Thomas Hobbes; Immanuel Kant; Leviathan; Jean-Jacques Rousseau.*

social Darwinism. Intellectually crude and false association, by analogy, of the raw mechanisms of biological evolution theorized by Charles Darwin (1809–1882) with the political, social, and economic realms of human endeavor and interaction. This quarter-baked, misapplied notion was especially widespread among intellectuals and journalists after 1890, most notably among early anthropologists, who eschewed knowledge of the history of the "new" societies they studied in Africa and Asia in preference for pseudobiological and cross-cultural approaches. It drew as well on the sociological work of Herbert Spencer, who (rather than Darwin) employed the phrase "survival of the fittest." Thus, Darwin's seminal "Origin of Species by Natural Selection" (1859) and "The Descent of Man" (1871) were misread—and as often, merely misquoted or alluded to—by nonbiologists to support whatever crackpot thesis they clung to for other reasons. Social Darwinism thereby reinforced extant urges to *imperialism* with pseudoscientific rationalizations for domination, including by liberal-democratic societies, as a supposed consequence of "natural selection"—through war and colonial expansion—among competing civilizations. It played especially well among those already enamored of *militarism* and competitive *nationalism*. At its worst, it ultimately lent support to the spurious "race" theories of the *Nazis* by supporting claims to special privileges for the "*Aryan* race" and justifying the subjugation and *liquidation* of "inferior races," especially Slavs and Jews, who stood in the way of *Lebensraum* for the *Volk*. Its other major impact was to spur Japanese, Chinese, and other non-European nationalists to attempt radical—and usually also dictatorial—social, economic, and military reforms in an effort to stave off the political "extinction" of their countries. Everywhere, the antidote to the poisonous teachings of social Darwinism is historical study, which shreds the claims of all racists and hardly ever supports the assertions of even softer nationalists that their community embodies unique virtues or harbors fewer vices than others. *See also* Geopolitik; Herrenvolk; *liberalism*; *positivism*; *mercantilism*; Cecil Rhodes; Weltpolitik.

social democracy. The parliamentary, and usually nondoctrinaire, political philosophy of modern *socialist* parties. Social democracy was originally orthodox *Marxist* in its analysis of social and economic conditions, but it was also rooted in parliamentary and union reform movements, from the "Chartists" in England to the CGT in France, and the German union movement which grew up in the last half of the nineteenth century. Social Democrats therefore eventually left more doctrinaire Marxism behind and came to stress the utility and justice of economic regulation and the benefits of a *mixed economy*. They took power peacefully in most Western countries, including Britain, Canada, France, Germany, and nearly all of Scandinavia. The United States was a notable exception. There, unions were less powerful and faith in market forces more widespread. Still, social democratic ideas merged with "New Dealism" in the 1930s and continued to influence the *Democratic Party* during most of the latter twentieth century. In fact, by the end of the twenty-first century "liberalism" in the United States had become a surrogate term for what is in substance, and elsewhere identified as, social democracy. In part this unique usage developed out of the *Cold War*, during which few American politicians wished in any way to be identified with socialism, even of the perfectly respectable democratic type. *See also Eduard Bernstein; Willy Brandt; Gro Harlem Bruntland; Friedrich Ebert; Jean Jaurès; Olaf Palme; Helmut Schmidt; social fascism; Weimar Republic.*

Suggested Reading: Dietrich Orlow, *Common Destiny* (2000).

social dumping. The idea, and sometime accusation, that *developing countries* compete unfairly with *OECD* and other developed economies by denying basic worker rights and decent wages in their home markets, which has the effect of dumping their social costs onto *First World* workers and consumers. In response, developed country labor movements have focused on implanting environmental and "fair wage" conditions in trade deals, often translating into support for *protectionist* legislation. Thus, *NAFTA* passed the U.S. Congress only after the *Clinton* administration agreed to negotiate side agreements on the environment and workplace conditions in Mexico, a move supported by Canadian unions as well.

social fascism. A spurious charge, made by the *Comintern* in the 1930s, that *social democracy* was not a rival for working class support on the left but instead was "the left-wing of *fascism*." This sort of tunnel vision delayed, or prevented, *Popular Front* governments from forming and thus helped real fascists take power in several countries, including Germany.

social imperialism. When *nationalism* plays a unifying rather than a divisive role in a society by deflecting class and social tensions outward in the form of an assertive, even *aggressive*, foreign and military policy.

socialism. (1) In general: an economic and political theory or system which advocates heavy regulation of economic and political affairs with the fundamental aims of more equality in wealth distribution and ending class distinctions and privileges. To varying degrees, socialists posit communal ownership, not of all property but of the *factor endowments* of a national economy. Few, if any, modern socialists entirely reject private property. As distinct from *communism*, most variants of socialism developed within a broadly democratic and parliamentary tradition. (2) In orthodox *Marxism*: the intermediate stage between *capitalism* and communism, where the *proletariat* takes control of the *means of production* and establishes a socialist *mode of production*, but where the pure, classless society of communism is still distant and workers must therefore rely on the coercive apparatus of the *dictatorship of the proletariat. See also African Socialism; anarchism; Ba'ath Party; Eduard Bernstein; Ernest Bevin; Léon Blum;*

Willy Brandt; Brezhnev doctrine; Bernt Carlsson; collectivization; Congress Party; Édouard Daladier; Friedrich Ebert; Franz Fanon; five-year plans; Alexander Herzen; International (Second); Labor Party; François Mitterrand; mixed economy; nationalization; Olaf Palme; Andreas Papandreou; Paris Commune; peaceful coexistence; permanent revolution; Popular Front; privat-ization; proxy wars; Russian Revolution, March (February) 1917; secret speech; Helmut Schmidt; Sino-Soviet split; social democracy; socialism in one country; soviet; Soviet legal thought; Soviet Union; Spanish Civil War; stab-in-the-back; Sun Yixian; Taiping Rebellion; utopian socialism; world socialist system.

"socialism in one country." Orthodox *Marxist* predictions of general revolution in the *capitalist* nations following the *Bolshevik Revolution* in Russia failed to come to pass, creating a predicament for *Bolshevik* theory. The slogan "socialism in one country" was devised by *Stalin* to justify concentration on consolidating control over the *Russian Empire* during the power struggle within the *Communist Party* which followed *Lenin's* death, reflecting the reality that after 1918 capitalist countries had not fallen like *dominoes* pushed over by the inevitability of *communism*. *Trotsky* and the "Left Position," in contrast, championed the doctrine of *permanent revolution*. A third faction proposed to continue the *New Economic Policy* indefinitely. Stalin argued that it was possible to construct socialism in a Russia insulated from outside threats and influences, not least because of the huge size and abundant resources of the old empire inherited from the tsars. Only much later would he tie world revolution to expansion of the Soviet Union's territorial base and geopolitical prominence. Stalin triumphed, largely because he controlled most of the Party *apparat*, and "socialism in one country" thus became the *party line* at the Fifteenth All Union Congress of the CPSU in December, 1927. All who had opposed Stalin's will on this subsequently were *purged*.

Socialist International. *See International, Second.*

socialist realism. The oppressive Soviet aesthetic doctrine that all art, literature, and culture must help build *socialism*, in the orthodox *Marxist* sense of that term. It was a euphemism for thought control by the *Communist Party* and the state. Some otherwise fine artists, such as Maxim Gorky, accepted its stultifying confinements. Others were driven to despair, and even to suicide (V. V. Mayakovsky). One Chinese writer, Lu Xun, scathingly noted that the Soviet notion of a model poem was: "Oh, steam whistle! Oh, Lenin." *See also cultural revolution; party line; samizdat.*

social overhead capital. The physical *infrastructure* of a national economy, plus those socially provided assets such as healthcare, education, and technological skills, which enable human beings to make maximum productive use of *capital goods*.

soft currency. Money not freely convertible to other mediums (*hard currency* or precious metals), and thus not held in *foreign exchange* reserve accounts for use in trade or *money market* intervention. Smaller economies are often soft currency economies, in which *black markets* in hard currency coexist with the official *exchange rate*.

soft goods. Those with a limited life expectancy, such as processed food or clothing. *See also durable goods.*

soft loan. (1) Money lent to a *developing nation* on terms lower than market rates and with an easier repayment schedule; (2) such a loan made repayable in the local *soft currency*.

soft power. Something of a synonym for *influence*, implying complete abstinence from the use of *force* or other coercive means, in favor of a national example of economic or ideological success which others seek to emulate and which garners *prestige*, along with persuasion and financial rewards for approved state behavior.

Sokoto. *See Fulbe (Fulani) empire.*

soldiers. *See artillery; brevet promotion; cavalry; chemical agents; civilian primacy; conscription; Geneva Conventions; guerrilla warfare; Hague Conventions;* hors de combat; *infantry; Janissaries; just war; mercenaries; military ranks; military units; missing in action (MIA); mutiny; neutral rights; officers; partisans; peacekeeping; pillage; plunder; posttraumatic stress disorder; prisoner of war; prohibited weapons; rape; Red Cross; resistance; samurai; sentry; sepoy; standing army; superior orders; trench warfare; voting with their feet; war; war crimes;* and various wars.

Solidarity (*Solidarnosc*). This Polish trade union and nationalist movement began in the 1970s in *Gdansk* and grew to include 25 percent of all Poles. Led by *Lech Walesa*, it pressed ever-greater demands until the *Soviet Union* threatened *intervention*, as it previously carried out in *Czechoslovakia* and *Hungary*. The Polish Army, under *Jaruzelski*, then stepped in to impose *martial law*, and Solidarity was banned (1982). It was re-legalized in 1989. With the collapse of *communism*, to which it made a major contribution—and not solely in Poland—it reemerged as a political movement. In 1990 it won a massive victory in free elections, making Walesa president of Poland. As a broad nationalist movement, it subsequently fractured under the duress of policy disagreements about how to proceed with Poland's adjustment to *market economics*, and moved into opposition. Walesa then resigned his membership. In 1994 it called its first post-*communist general strike*.
Suggested Reading: Timothy Garton Ash, *The Polish Revolution* (1983, 1991).

Solomon Islands. Although sighted by the Spanish in 1568, the first Europeans settled only in 1870. Germany settled some of the islands from the 1880s. Britain made the Solomons a *protectorate* in 1899, administered from Fiji. In 1900 a regional settlement among the United States, Germany, and Great Britain split *Samoa* into *American Samoa* (to the United States) and *Western Samoa* (to Germany), with Britain *compensated* by Germany with several of its holdings in the Solomon chain. After *World War I,* the island of *Bougainville* and some other small islands in the chain remained with the Papua New Guinea *mandate territory.* The Solomons were *occupied* by Japan, 1942–1943, but were liberated by the U.S. Marine Corps, with a particularly fierce fight over Guadalcanal (August–February 1943). Returned to Britain after the war, the Solomons received *autonomy* in stages between 1952 and 1970. *Independence* came in 1978. They opposed *nuclear* testing in the South Pacific and supported independence for *Kanaky.* In 1984 they seized U.S. fishing boats within their claimed *Exclusive Economic Zones.* The United States responded with a brief *embargo,* which was lifted in 1985. The *dispute* was settled in a 1987 *treaty.* In 2000 the Solomons were wracked by ethnic conflict among native and immigrant islanders.

Solzhenitsyn, Alexandr (b. 1919). Russian novelist and nationalist. As a young officer in *World War II* he was taken from the lines and sent to the prison camp system of the *GULAG* for the most minor of indiscretions in his personal correspondence. He did not come out again until the amnesty which followed *Stalin's* death in 1953. During a brief literary and cultural "thaw" under *Khrushchev,* Solzhenitsyn published his autobiographical novel "One Day in the Life of Ivan Denisovich" (1962), the first honest depiction of camp life under *Stalinism* ever seen in Russia. His subsequent novels ("Cancer Ward, August 1914") and his magnum opus, "The GULAG Archipelago," were banned in the Soviet Union but published in the West, and earned him the *Nobel Prize* for Literature in 1970. He was not permitted to leave to collect his prize. However, in 1974 he was arrested, accused of *treason,* and deported (from his own country) into exile. Widely regarded as a great and heroic figure by Western liberals, he next startled—and to a degree also alienated—some Western audiences with harsh criticism of democratic *capitalism.* He then settled into a reclusive life in Vermont, occasionally firing off missives giving vent to radical *Slavophile* and *Orthodox* views. In 1994 he returned to Russia with his family after 20 years of foreign exile.

Somalia. Somalis were in trade contact with Arabia from ancient times. Most converted to *Islam* in the tenth and eleventh centuries. They spent the next several centuries variously under the control of Ethiopia and the Muslim states of the Gulf, Muscat and Oman, and local sultans. *Somaliland* was divided into diverse *protectorates* within the British, French, and Italian empires after 1884. The French portion ultimately became *Djibouti.* All three protectorates faced *guerrilla* raids for nearly 30 years, led by the "Mad Mullah," Muhammad Hassan (1864–1920), whose prolonged struggle fathered an early Somali nationalism among a people historically sharply divided into numerous clans. *Italian Somaliland* was overrun by the British in 1941 and occupied by them until 1949. In 1950 it was declared a United Nations *trust territory*, the only one to be managed by a defeated *Axis* power (Italy). In 1960 it united with *British Somaliland* to form Somalia, which also asserted ethnic and historic claims to portions of Ethiopia, Kenya, and Djibouti. In 1969–1970 a *Marxist* military faction led by General Muhammad Siyad Barre took power and opened port facilities to the Soviet Union. In 1974 an even more radical group took power in Ethiopia, and the Soviets shifted to support this new *client state* to the west in the war with ethnic Somali *guerrillas* fighting for *secession* of the *Ogaden* region. In 1977 the *Ethiopia-Somalia War* broke out. After Somalia was beaten, largely by Cuban troops who intervened on the side of Ethiopia, it expelled all *Soviet bloc* advisers and asked the United States for aid. Washington supported Barre, whose Marxism looked increasingly tattered and inconvenient, rather than threatening, and in exchange took over Soviet-built naval facilities at Berbera. Throughout the 1980s border skirmishes continued with Ethiopia, producing a mass of *refugees* and contributing to endemic *famine* and disease. A peace agreement was reached in 1988, propelled mainly by the exhaustion of both countries. Civil war then broke out in Somalia among territorially based clans. In 1990, with *Cold War* imperatives no longer at stake, American aid was cut and the U.S. base at Berbera was closed. Barre fled at the start of 1991. In light of this, in 1991 former British Somaliland seceded from Somalia and sought international *recognition*, which it did not receive, although it proved relatively peaceful and stable compared to the rest of the country. Clan divisions intensified during the succession struggle which followed in the rest of Somalia, leading to both a catastrophic famine and a United Nations intervention, 1991–1995. By the end of 1993 most of the country outside the capital showed signs of reconstruction, but famine and a return to *anarchy* remained real threats to the population. Mogadishu remained uncontrollable by any one party, and a political solution eluded all. It then sank back into chronic *warlordism* and virtual anarchy. During the rest of the 1990s Somalia was identified by the United States as a base of international *terrorism* and aggressive Islamic *fundamentalism*. In fact, it had ceased to exist as an effective *state*. See also *failed state; Quasi state*.

Suggested Reading: I. M. Lewis, *Modern History of Somaliland*, 2nd ed. (1979).

Somalia, United Nations intervention in (1991–1995). The United Nations *intervened* in Somalia in March 1991 in an effort to negotiate a *cease-fire*, to directly help 200,000 *refugees* hemmed into Mogadishu, and to bring food relief to some 4.5 million Somalis threatened with *famine*. Immediate relief was to be followed with a "reconciliation conference" hosted by Nigeria on behalf of the *OAU*. However, the famine grew worse with the closing of most ports by gunmen from rival factions and a withdrawal of the *United Nations*. UN Secretary General *Boutros Boutros-Ghali* therefore asked the United States to intercede to provide a minimum of security for food and medical convoys. After months of hesitation, while a UN consensus was built which accepted the use of U.S. troops for purposes of *armed humanitarian intervention* in Africa, the troops disembarked in December 1992. This was the first time in 47 years that the UN dispatched troops with liberal *rules of engagement* (essentially, shoot anyone interfering with the humanitarian mission), and it did so without asking permission of the Somalis. The long-term plan was still for the OAU to play a role in mediating a settlement. In April 1993, the clans agreed to establish a 74-seat Transitional National Council. The United Nations committed 28,000 troops to replace the U.S. force; and the United States for the first time agreed to provide a contingent (some 4,000 marines) under UN command. In July, the United Nations became engaged in a bloody battle with the *militia* of General Muhammad Farrah Aideed following an ambush which killed 24 Pakistani peacekeepers. The fighting raised frictions between Italy and the United Nations when the Italians (the former colonial power) and some Arab states objected to the use of extensive force against Aideed. In subsequent fighting hundreds of Somalis and dozens of UN peacekeepers were killed—the worst United Nations casualty rate since the *Congo crisis*. Television coverage of some Somalis gleefully mutilating American corpses rapidly eroded public support in the United States for continued involvement in the UN effort, and the *Clinton* administration—with its finger, as ever, on the pulse of public opinion polls—withdrew all U.S. forces. The rest of the UN mission followed by 1995. This experience was so searing for the United Nations and the Clinton administration that both balked at providing aid even on receiving advance warnings of a coming *genocide* in *Rwanda*. *See also Bosnia; Kosovo; peace enforcement; peacemaking; war crimes trials.*

Somaliland. The East African coastal region divided into *British Somaliland, French Somaliland,* and *Italian Somaliland.* The British and Italian portions eventually formed modern Somalia, while the French section became Djibouti. Somaliland has been retained as the internal name of northern Somalia. It declared itself an independent state in 1991. Despite bringing peace to its inhabitants and becoming strategically important to landlocked Ethiopia, "Somaliland" garnered no international *recognition.*

Somme, Battle of (July 1–November 18, 1916). For the British (and Canadians, and troops of several other Commonwealth nations), the Somme was the single most terrible battle not just of *World War I,* but in all their military history. This summer offensive was made against the center of the German salient on the western front. It was launched in support of a French offensive on the flank which had already failed—and led to the appalling carnage of the French and German armies at *Verdun*. The attack went ahead in spite of available intelligence that the Germans had recently reinforced the opposing trenches, which in any case defenders had improved on for nearly two years. The British, under *Douglas Haig*, sent 19 divisions marching shoulder-to-shoulder toward the German lines. They suffered astonishingly high casualties: on the first day alone 20,000 British troops were killed and 40,000 more were wounded. Over the next four months of fighting the front line advanced no more than 10 miles deep along a 20-mile front, with over 1.2 million casualties on all sides.

The British used tanks at the Somme, for the first time in the war. Their appearance caused initial panic in the German lines, but the British squandered this tactical advantage by failing to mass their *armor*, so that their tanks bogged down or were picked off one by one as the Germans quickly learned how to defend against them. Of the 49 slow and cumbersome Mark I tanks sent into the attack, fully 36 were disabled. Haig learned almost nothing from the carnage on the Somme, and continued to launch additional frontal assaults through 1917. That failure of command imagination—combined with the casualties, lack of advance, and hence apparent futility of further attacks—contributed to the *French Army mutinies* and mutiny by elements of the *British Expeditionary Force* during 1917. The image of the carnage along the Somme was seared into the memory of the British governing classes, and nation, for several succeeding generations. It indirectly affected British strategy in *World War II*, away from a direct assault on *Hitler*'s "Fortress Europe" toward flanking operations in Greece, North Africa, Sicily, and the Balkans and a concentration on *strategic bombing* of Germany in lieu of an early invasion of the continent.

Somoza, Anastasio (1896–1956). Nicaraguan dictator. In 1933 he headed the National Guard, which was trained by the United States to replace the marines it had kept in Nicaragua for nearly 20 years. It was these troops who killed the rebel Augusto Sandino and who propelled Somoza to power in a 1936 *coup*. His was a corrupt, personal dictatorship which *kowtowed* to the United States in foreign affairs and repressed efforts at rural reform. He was assassinated in 1956. His sons, Luis Somoza and *Anastasio Somoza Debayle*, followed him into the family business—dictatorship. *See also Sandinistas.*

Somoza, Anastasio Debayle (1928–1980). Nicaraguan dictator. Son of *Anastasio Somoza*. President, 1967–1972, 1974–1979. He inherited his father's National Guard, while his older brother, Luis, became president. When Luis died in 1967 Debayle won a rigged election, something at which his family was well practiced. His regime was so corrupt that international earthquake relief funds were pirated to his personal and family use. This undercut his *legitimacy* and undermined the effort to defeat leftist *guerrillas*. By 1979 the

Army and National Guard were defeated by a broad and popular front led by the *Sandinistas*, and he fled. He was assassinated in Paraguay in September 1980.

Sonderbund. A league of seven *Catholic* cantons, formed in 1845 out of opposition to federal reforms in Switzerland. It fought a losing civil war in 1847 against more *liberal* Swiss cantons. *See also Jesuits.*

Sonderfall. *See Switzerland.*

Sonderweg. "The special path." There are several versions of this highly deterministic thesis about the course of German history, but all share the notion that *Nazism* was the only possible and logical outcome of prior German history. Hence, the argument is made that the great events in that history—the *Reformation*; the long-postponed unification of the nation; and the rise, internal development, and ultimate domination of Germany by *Prussia*—were all of a piece and led more or less "inevitably" to *Hitler* and Nazism. Among many problems with this thesis are that it ignores that Hitler was an Austrian and that Nazism started in Bavaria, not Prussia. In the 1990s a version of this thesis was relaunched by Daniel Goldhagen, who argued that German history contained an "eliminationist *anti-Semitism*" which led inexorably to the *Holocaust*.

Song dynasty (960–1279). The *Tang dynasty* collapsed in 907, leaving China fractured among various *warlord* states for more than 50 years. In 960 the military command of the last of the Five Dynasties in north China elevated their leader to power as the first Song emperor, inaugurating the Northern Song (Qidan Liao) dynasty, which lasted from 960 to 1125. The founder of the Song was Zhao Kuangyin (reign name Taizu, d. 976). He completed the conquest of eight of the Ten Kingdoms of southern China, and his successor added the last two. China was more or less unified again under the Song, except that the Sixteen Prefectures in the north, all inside the boundary of the *Great Wall*, were ruled by the Qidan Liao dynasty in a creatively ambiguous relationship with Song China. Still, China's population reached 120 million, and the period was marked by a cultural, intellectual, and bureaucratic efflorescence. China also faced threats from *Inner Asian* tribes all along its northwest frontier and from the northern Liao Empire. Pressure from Liao was superseded by invasion by Jürchen (Ruzhen) warriors. Despite this constant military pressure from Inner Asia, Song rulers encouraged and sponsored learning and the arts, and further entrenched and expanded China's hugely influential scholar-elite examination and bureaucratic systems. This involved codifying a state-sponsored "Legalism" or neo-*Confucianism*, which remained influential into the early twentieth century.

Most specialist historians consider the Song dynasty to represent the pinnacle of classical Chinese civilization. Despite a massive Song *standing army*, however, the original Song capital, Kaifeng, was overrun in 1126 by Jürchen, who established the Jin Empire (1115–1234) in north China, with its capital at Yanjing (Beijing). The Song sought to *appease* the Jin by paying *tribute*, and were forced to move their capital and empire southward in a long, fighting retreat, beginning with the humiliation of the Jürchen capture of a Song emperor in 1127. The Song were pressed south of the Yangzi by the Jürchen advance, there establishing the Southern Song as a tributary of the Jürchen Empire. It survived in the south of China from 1127 until the *Mongol* conquest of all China in 1279. Meanwhile, the Jürchen Empire was greatly disturbed by another in the periodic sudden shifts in the course of the Yellow River (1194). This led to a final war with the Southern Song (1206), before they faced their own invasion at the hands of Chinggis (Ghengis) Khan's (1162–1227) Mongol horde, starting in 1211. The Mongols hammered at the border until they overran the Jürchen Empire in 1234. The great khan's successors conquered the Southern Song by 1279.

Suggested Reading: Morris Rossabi, *China Among Equals* (1983).

Songhay. Also known as Songhai. This *Mande*-speaking, West African empire straddled the great bend of the Niger, profiting as middleman in the trans-Saharan salt, *gold*, and *slave trade* since the time of ancient *Ghana*. Like that of *Kanem*, its original ruling house claimed to have Yemeni roots, although this was more likely a propaganda effort to gain *legitimacy* within the *Islamic* world after the conversion of its population. Songhay was briefly a *tributary* of *Mali*, which cut it off from the desert trade in the thirteenth century. It broke free of Mali in the fourteenth century, and then—resurgent under a military innovator and conqueror, Sunni Ali (r. 1464–1492) it utilized mounted knights to expand into several former Mali provinces, slave-raid, and in general displace Mali as the major power in the region, 1464–1484. Songhay captured Timbuktu from the *Tuareg* in 1469 and took Jenne with a riverine fleet in 1473. Songhay greatly expanded *slavery* in the local economy, raiding south of the Niger to replenish its slave population. Under Muhammad Ture (r. 1493–1528) it expanded westward and northward and raided in force as far south as the *Hausa* states. Muhammad Ture was deposed by his sons in 1528, and thereafter Songhay was deeply divided between animist and Muslim parties.

In 1591 Songhay was invaded and extinguished by a Moroccan army equipped with firearms—which made an extraordinary trek across the desert to capture Timbuktu—for which Songhay's spear-cavalry and bowmen simply were no match. The original Moroccan conquerors were at first reinforced, but the tie to Morocco was effectively broken in 1618 when the fruits of conquest failed to meet expectations in Marrakesh. The Moroccan soldiers abandoned in Songhay clung to power, and over time they came to form an ethnically distinct ruling class called, prosaically enough, the "arma" (gun-men). In the 1660s a succession crisis in distant Morocco led the arma to formally repudiate the Moroccan tie. Steeped in desert mysticism, they were intolerant of the older and alternate Muslim intellectual tradition of Tim-buktu. For another 200 years the "Moors of Timbuktu" ruled over an area centered on the old Songhay cities of Gao, Jenne, and Timbuktu, but not much else of what had been the Mali and Songhay empires. The Moors taxed Saharan salt and gold mined by Mande slaves, and sold other slaves into the Arab markets on the coast, but built nothing and blocked others from doing so as well by occupying the great trade and cultural centers of the Niger Valley. A rump of old Songhay existed in Dendi, but overall the region that had always been someone's empire fell into permanent and disastrous decline. The old idea of a single sudanic empire thus expired with Songhay. The Moors were then themselves overrun by firearms technology married to a much harder will, that of al-Hajj Umar (c. 1795–1864), leader of the third great *jihad* by the *Fulbe* in the nineteenth century and founder of the unstable and short-lived *Tukolor Empire*.

Suggested Reading: David Conrad, *The Songhay Empire* (1998).

Sonnenfeldt Doctrine. In 1976 a senior counselor in the *State Department*, Helmut Sonnenfeldt, voiced an idea which *diplomats* had discussed but not broached in public: that the West's real interest was orderly Soviet "manage-ment" of Eastern Europe and the inner Soviet empire. He suggested that *NATO* ought to hope not for the destruction of the *Soviet bloc* but for de-velopment of an "organic" relationship within it. When these private remarks to European ambassadors were reported in the press they caused a diplomatic tempest in a samovar. The *revolutions of 1989* rendered them moot. *See also* Pax Sovietica.

South. (1) A nebulous term coined to allow the politically correct to avoid saying, with no more accuracy, *Third World*. It generally is used to refer to the *developing countries* of Africa, Asia, and Latin America, as opposed to the affluent *North* or *OECD* states. (2) An American colloquialism for the *Con-federacy* in the *American Civil War*.

South Africa. This land had a rich tribal mix before the arrival of European settlers: Khoi ("Hottentot"), San ("Bushmen"), *Swazi*, Sotho, *Xhosa*, and *Zulu* numbered among the major *ethnic groups*. These tribes had their own long history of warfare and conquest, culminating in the early nineteenth-century *mfecane* under *Shaka Zulu*. European settlers came in two distinct waves. Dutch (and some French *Huguenots*) settled at *Cape Colony* after 1652, slowly melded into the *Boer* people and began a *migration* inland which included extermination or enslavement of the Khoi and San, whom they overran. In

1770 the Boers first faced the more powerful *Nguni* peoples, across the Fish River. During the late eighteenth and early nineteenth centuries they fought a fierce set of wars with the Xhosa and Zulu (then migrating south, also at the expense of the Khoi) in the so-called "Kaffir Wars." The British took Cape Colony from the Dutch in 1795, and for good in 1814. British government and settlement then *encroached* on Boer lands in the early nineteenth century. So the Boers moved on, under Andries Pretorius (1799–1853) in the *Great Trek*, to found three republics beyond the reach of British law: *Natal* (annexed by Britain in 1845), *Orange Free State*, and *Transvaal*, under *Paulus Kruger*.

In 1867 huge diamond deposits were discovered, launching a shift in the basis of southern Africa's economic and social life from agrarian to industrial. This accelerated with the discovery in 1886 of *gold* in the *Rand* (Transvaal). That exacerbated a three-cornered (British, Boer, and Nguni) competition over land. The British won all the wars that followed, the three *Zulu Wars* and both *Boer Wars*, the second of which foreclosed Boer independence. However, on May 31, 1910, the Union of South Africa was created from Cape Colony and the erstwhile Boer states. Utterly excluded from this union of the two "white races" of southern Africa, two years later blacks formed the *African National Congress* (ANC). Under *Louis Botha, James Hertzog*, and *Daniel Malan*, South Africa lived uncomfortably with its British connection, but it sternly repressed and exploited its disenfranchised black majority and Indian and "Coloured" minorities. Under General *Jan Smuts* the tie to Britain was more positive and the hand of the state somewhat less heavy. A miners' revolt in the Rand in 1922 reaffirmed that the color bar in South Africa had deep support among whites and was rooted in economic exploitation. Internationally, South Africa fought alongside Britain in both world wars, although in 1914–1915 a minor Boer rebellion had to be suppressed.

In 1949 South Africa took a hard turn to the right: victory of the *National Party* meant the introduction of *apartheid* and the start of several decades of progressive isolation for all South Africans. Following the *Sharpeville massacre* (1960), the *African National Congress* and the *Pan-African Congress* reconsidered their nonviolent policies and began to prepare for *guerrilla warfare*. In 1961 prime minister Hendrik Verwoerd (1901–1966) took South Africa out of the Commonwealth and made it a *republic*. In the 1960s the first of a series of ever-tighter *sanctions* began to bite into the economy, although the strains would not show until the 1980s. In 1971 the *International Court of Justice* declared South African refusal to surrender control of *Namibia* to the United Nations an illegal usurpation. Meanwhile, South Africa lent aid to the white minority *UDI* regime in *Rhodesia* and to the Portuguese fighting guerrillas in Angola and Mozambique. Its mid-1970s creation of the *Bantustan* system was both ridiculed and rejected by the *community of nations*. Once all regional allies bowed to the inevitable (the Portuguese in 1974–1975 and Rhodesia in 1980), South Africa was truly isolated. After 1976 Soweto and other black townships became hotbeds of unrest and resistance. Domestic casualties mounted even as Balthazar Johannes Vorster (1915–1983), prime minister, 1966–1978, took the country into a drawn-out *intervention* in the Angola and Mozambique *civil wars*, including extensive combat with Cuban troops. Domestic controls were tightened even more in 1986, while *nuclear weapons* were built in secret.

The country was fast becoming ungovernable domestically due to violence and civil disobedience in the townships and the rise of openly *fascist* movements among extremist whites. After decades in *laager*, things finally began to change when *F. W. de Klerk* took office in 1989: Namibia was let go, the troops came home from foreign wars, the *nuclear weapons* were dismantled as secretly as they had been built, *Nelson Mandela* was released from 28 years in prison, and the ANC was unbanned. Sanctions ended in 1993 after whites agreed to a multiracial constitution (69 percent voted yes to full democracy in the last whites-only *referendum*). A Multiracial Council took charge in September and a new constitution was adopted. Free elections were held in April 1994, leading to an ANC majority and to Mandela's presidency over a coalition, reconciliation government. South Africa rejoined the Commonwealth in 1994 and made tentative moves into United Nations *peacekeeping*, in the Rwanda crisis of that year. Its transition to democracy was greatly facilitated by the work of its innovative *Truth and Reconciliation Commission*.

Suggested Readings: Roger B. Beck, *History of South Africa* (2000); T. R. H. Davenport and Christopher Saunders, *South Africa: A Modern History* (2000); W. M. MacMillan, *Bantu, Boer and Briton* (1964); Anthony Sampson, *Mandela* (1999); Monica Wilson and Leonard Thompson, eds., *Oxford History of South Africa*, 2 vols. (1969–1971).

South America. That portion of the *Americas* below the Panamanian isthmus.

South Asia. The countries between *West Asia* and *Southeast Asia*: Bangladesh, Bhutan, India, Maldives, Nepal, Pakistan, Sikkim, and Sri Lanka.

South Asian Association for Regional Cooperation (SAARC). It was formed in 1985 by Bangladesh, Bhutan, India, Maldives, Nepal, Pakistan, and Sri Lanka. Its *secretariat* was located in Kathmandu in 1987 and serves as a regional center for political communications, and potentially for economic and security cooperation. As with all regional associations, it is both hampered and made necessary by the great diversity, different *development* strategies, and ethnic, environmental, and geopolitical conflicts among its membership. Ten SAARC summits were held by 1998, but none was called for several years following the India-Pakistan conflict in the Kargil region in 1999. Progress resumed in 2001, however, when a separate Indo-Pakistani summit was held. In 2001 SAARC broadened its mandate to consider social problems, such as the plight of children in the region.

South China Sea. Located within the circle of China, Malaysia, the Philippines, Taiwan, and Vietnam, this shallow sea contains several disputed island chains and archipelagos, including the *Spratlys* and *Paracels*.

Southeast Asia. The countries east of India and south of China, to wit: Brunei, Cambodia, Indonesia, Laos, Malaysia, Myanmar (Burma), the Philippines, Thailand, and Vietnam. By convention, Papua New Guinea is usually situated in the *South Pacific*. Historically, Southeast Asia was home to several advanced civilizations, especially the *Khmer Empire*, builder of the exceptional Angkor Wat temple complex which is situated in modern Cambodia. Most of the region's population settled along great peninsular river valleys, including the Irrawaddy and Mekong, which were friendly to intensive subsistence cultivation of rice and hence could sustain large populations. Larger urban settlements also grew up in the great archipelagos and islands which dominate the seas of the region. Southeast Asia straddles the major *trade routes* and shipping lanes between China and India and between China and Europe. *See also Northeast Asia; Oceania; South Asia.*

Suggested Reading: Nicholas Tarling, ed., *Cambridge History of Southeast Asia*, 2 vols. (1999).

Southeast Asia Treaty Organization (SEATO). A regional *security* organization set up in 1955 to carry out a *security treaty* signed on September 8, 1954, by Australia, Britain, France, New Zealand, Pakistan, the Philippines, Thailand, and the United States to extend protection also to Cambodia, Laos, and the Republic of Vietnam (RVN). It had no standing military force and never became involved in the key wars and other conflicts of the region. Pakistan pulled out in 1973 and France left in 1974. SEATO was dissolved in 1977.

Southern Africa. The southernmost region of Africa, and island extensions, comprising the states of Angola, Botswana, Lesotho, Madagascar, Malawi, Mozambique, Namibia, Seychelles, South Africa, Swaziland, Zambia, and Zimbabwe.

Southern African Development Community (SADC). Initially an association of the *front line* states and other states from Southern Africa: Angola, Botswana, Lesotho, Malawi, Mozambique, Swaziland, Tanzania, Zambia, and Zimbabwe. It was formed in 1980 as the Southern African Development Coordinating Conference to coordinate *development* efforts and promote *integration* in selected sectors which might lessen its members' collective dependence on South Africa, then still a white-ruled, minority regime. It had limited success before the collapse of *apartheid*, but it showed more promise as South Africa emerged as a powerful and cooperative partner in, rather than a hostile obstacle to, regional economic cooperation.

Southern African Development Coordinating Conference (SADCC). *See Southern African Development Community.*

Southern Song dynasty (Jin Empire). *See Song Dynasty.*

South Korea. *See Korea, Republic of.*

South Pacific. The island states and *dependencies* of the south and central Pacific Ocean, including some north of the equator, such as the *Micronesian* states. The term generally excludes those islands, such as Hawaii or the Easter Islands, which are under clear control of states from outside the region, although it includes several disputed French possessions. It contains sovereign ex-*colonies*, states in *free association* with former colonial powers, as well as *protectorates*, dependencies, and *Trust Territories*.

South Pacific Commission (SPC). A regional association established in 1947 by Australia, Britain, France, the Netherlands (later withdrew), New Zealand, and the United States. Eight island states joined between 1965 and 1980. In 1983 all remaining *South Pacific* states and self-governing *territories* were admitted, making it the only body which gathered together all regional governments. Before 1989 political matters were excluded from the agenda. That encouraged creation of the *South Pacific Forum* and led to rivalry and tension between the two associations, with the Forum at one point seeking to take over the Commission. Tensions eased after 1991. The Forum emerged as the region's political organization, while the Commission served as a conduit for extraregional *aid* and as a cooperative cultural, economic, and technical association. Britain withdrew from the SPC in 1995 over concerns about its politicization, but rejoined in 1997.

South Pacific Forum (SPF). *See Pacific Islands Forum.*

South Seas Bubble (1720). A financial "bubble" (speculative fever) in shares of the South Seas Company, which had been chartered by the English state to aid in alleviation of the *national debt* that had grown up during the wars against *Louis XIV*. When the bubble burst, vast fortunes in the new paper currency were wiped out and for much of the 1720s and 1730s, under *Robert Walpole*, Great Britain concentrated on conservative fiscal reform rather than expensive wars.

South Vietnam. *See Vietnam, Republic of.*

Southwest Africa. Former name of *Namibia*, 1918–1990, changed in 1918 from *German Southwest Africa*.

South Yemen. *See Yemen.*

sovereign. (1) A condition of legal *independence* enjoyed by a *recognized* state. (2) A *monarch*, whether actually exercising or merely symbolically representing a state's *international personality. See sovereignty.*

Sovereign Military Order of Malta (SMOM). Order of the Hospital of St. John of Jerusalem or "Knights Hospitallers." A military and religious order founded during the *Crusades* (1099) in *Jerusalem* to provide succor to and protect *Christian* pilgrims on the way to and in the *Holy Land.* It was recognized by the pope in 1113. When Jerusalem was recaptured for *Islam* in 1187 by the Muslim warrior-prince *Salāh-ed-Dīn*, the Knights Hospitallers retreated to Acre and, on further defeats, to Cyprus (1291). In 1310 they conquered and moved to Rhodes. They remained militarily active in the eastern Mediterranean against the *Ottoman Empire*: in 1344, in alliance with *Venice*, they captured Smyrna; in 1365 they took Alexandria. In neither case could they hold what they had taken. They were overrun on Rhodes by the Ottomans in 1522. In 1530 *Charles V* gave them *sovereignty* over Malta, which they thereafter held as a fortified Christian outpost in a mostly Ottoman and Muslim eastern Mediterranean, but they also had outposts as distant as St. Croix in the Virgin Islands. The *Protestant Reformation* led to suppression of their branches in most Protestant countries and confiscation of their great estates. In 1798 they were overthrown by *Napoleon*, who was en route to Egypt; some of the knights moved to *St. Petersburg* to find refuge from the French under the protection of the *Orthodox* sovereign Paul I. *Nelson* retook Malta, but the British government declined to restore the Order. Malta formally became a British possession at the *Congress of Vienna*. In 1834 the Order was displaced to Rome, where it remained. In 1994 SMOM became a permanent observer at the United Nations, where it was formally regarded as an "entity" but not a *state*. In 2001 SMOM had c. 12,000 "knights" worldwide, including the king of Spain and several former Italian prime ministers, and was formally *recognized* by the *Vatican* and several other "Catholic powers" (including Cuba) as *sovereign*, although it had fewer than 80 citizens and occupied less than two acres of land. It enjoyed rights of *extraterritoriality* accepted by the Italian state. Some countries recognize its postage stamps, although they do not recognize SMOM itself. Membership is generally hereditary, though "knighthoods" are also offered on merit and in exchange for an annual fee.

   Suggested Readings: E. Bradford, *The Shield and the Sword* (1973); Jonathon Riley-Smith, *Hospitallers: History of the Order of St. John* (1999).

sovereignty. Sovereignty is a moral as well as a legal construct. It is an assertion of collective rights based on a notion of unique community, be it real, aspirational, or merely administratively convenient. It represents a modern (*Westphalian*) compromise between the age-old problem of order and the equally ancient aspiration to justice in political affairs. It is also the prerequisite for full membership in the *community of nations*. In modern form, it emerged first in Europe: as warfare became more expensive (requiring, for instance, *standing armies* and navies) the price of independence for a minor noble became unsustainable. Political, administrative, and military consolidation occurred, first in France and England, roughly followed by Spain, Sweden, Prussia, and Russia, and later by Austria, Germany, and Italy. Ideas of *raison d'etat* and later, of the *nation* and the *national interest*, displaced older notions of universal faith, *feudal* allegiance, and the *res publica Christiana*. This great change marked the Italian *Renaissance* and was codified more generally in the *Peace of Westphalia* following the *Thirty Years' War*. It was broadened and radicalized by the wholly innovative idea of *popular sovereignty* during the *Enlightenment*, the *American Revolution*, and most importantly, the *French Revolution*. As a historical institution sovereignty has never been as clear-cut as princes (or international lawyers) might like, and it still takes various and complex forms in the modern world.

Political sovereignty is actual freedom from foreign control. On rare occasions prior to 1900, though more commonly in the twentieth century, *recognition* was withheld from a government with such *de facto* (real) control of a given *territory*, as in the initial Western refusal to recognize the *Bolshevik* regime which won the *Russian Civil War* in 1921, or the communist regime which won the *Chinese Civil War* in 1949, or the Vietnamese *puppet regime* in Cambodia, 1978–1992. Legal sovereignty is formal, recognized *independence* under *international law*. States may retain *de jure* (legal) status even without de facto control of territory, as when most states refused to recognize illegal *annexations* such as the 1940 Soviet takeover of the *Baltic States*, or Iraq's 1990 annexation of Kuwait, both reversed in 1991. Full sovereignty is a condition in which de facto control of a territory exists and is also recognized and accepted in law by other states, thus creating a community of states with shared and binding legal obligations, one to another. This is the ideal, and also the most normal, condition. However, weak states—and increasingly, strong states, too—have found that even full sovereignty does not mean they are free from all outside influences in economic or political decision making.

Note: *Civil wars* or *secessions* ineluctably raise questions of recognition and sovereignty. It is an open secret that no matter how vehement are initial objections, other states will, in the fullness of time, recognize whichever side wins the struggle for physical and political control of a given territory. For specific rules and effects of sovereignty see *abatement; airspace; anarchy; armed humanitarian intervention; associated state; autarchy; autonomy; border; boundary; cannon-shot rule; co-imperium; colonialism; common heritage principle; commonwealth status; complex interdependence; condominium; dependency; diplomatic relations; domain; empire; equality; failed state; federation; Finlandization; free association; freedom of the seas; frontier; functionalism; hard shell thesis; high seas; Home Rule; hot pursuit; human rights; humanitarian intervention; imperialism;*

independence; internationalize; international law; international personality; international society; intervention; jurisdiction; kowtow; *law of the sea; laws of war; liberation; mandate system; Montevideo Convention; Moon Treaty; multinational corporation; noninterference; nonintervention; Outer Space Treaty;* par in parem; *partition; piracy; pooled sovereignty; popular sovereignty; privateer; protectorate; puppet state; quasi states; realism; representation;* res communis; *reservation; satellite state; self-defense; self-determination; self-help; servitudes; Soviet legal thought; state immunity; statelet; state obligations; state of nature; territorial integrity; territorial sea;* territorium nullius; *three-mile limit; tribe; tributary; tribute; trusteeship system; twelve-mile limit; ultimatum; unincorporated territory; union of sovereign states; withdrawal.*

Suggested Readings: Gerhard von Glahn, *Law Among Nations*, 6th ed. (1992); F. H. Hinsley, *Sovereignty*, 2nd ed. (1986).

Soviet bloc. The *Soviet Union*, its *satellites* and *Communist* allies, and *client states*, 1945–1989. The bloc centered on *Eastern Europe* but included Afghanistan (1978–1988), Albania (until 1968), Angola (after 1975), Bulgaria, Cambodia (after 1978), China (until the *Sino-Soviet split*), Cuba, Czechoslovakia, East Germany, Ethiopia (after 1974), Hungary, Laos (after 1975), Mozambique (after 1975), Mongolia, Nicaragua (after 1979), Poland, Rumania, Somalia (1969–1977), Vietnam (the Democratic Republic of Vietnam only after 1955; all of Vietnam after 1975), South Yemen (after 1979), and Yugoslavia (but only loosely, and only until 1947). The ties that bound dissolved in the *revolutions of 1989*, followed by the *extinction* of the Soviet Union itself in 1991. *See also Comintern.*

sovietize. To make similar to the social, economic, and political forms of the *Soviet Union*, especially its *one-party, communist* political system and centrally *planned economy.*

Soviet legal thought. The *Soviet Union* took several distinct positions on matters of *international law*. Initially, Soviet thinkers dismissed the whole notion as an international class construct intended to preserve *capitalist* supremacy, and therefore not binding on *socialist* states. However, they slowly adjusted to the practical realities of living in a world of states, and sought to develop a distinct legal theory. Among their more important—though not intellectually persuasive or consistent—innovations, Soviet writers and Soviet practice tended to divide law among *nations* into three types: (1) Law among *communist* states, where the *Brezhnev Doctrine* was applied in practice long before it was promulgated as a principle of Soviet *diplomacy*. (2) Law among "bourgeois states," or traditional international law. The Soviet Union proclaimed disinterest in this category but actually participated more or less as a traditional power, largely adhering on a pragmatic basis to the established corpus of law, and (mostly) negotiating and keeping its agreements in *good faith*. (3) Law between communist and bourgeois (and other non-communist) states. In this last class, the Soviets played a double game: they elevated the notion of *sovereignty* to an absolute when it came to the affairs of the socialist camp, insisting on *nonintervention* and *noninterference*. Yet not only did they simultaneously advocate a legal right to aid *rebellion* and *revolution* against Western states or colonial empires, they actively promoted *disinformation, propaganda, wars of national liberation*, and other forms of *subversion*. In spite of all this arcane theorizing, with the exceptions noted, the Soviet Union in general behaved as did most other states, and certainly most *Great Powers*: correctly observing international law on most matters and keeping its treaty commitments on the whole, while preserving outside the reach of international law those matters it deemed to concern its *vital interests*. *See also peaceful coexistence.*

Suggested Reading: Gerhard von Glahn, *Law Among Nations*, 6th ed. (1992).

sovietologist. A scholar or *intelligence* analyst who studied the history, economics, and politics of the *Soviet Union*. One school of interpretation in the West viewed the Soviet system as irredeemably *totalitarian*. It saw the roots of this tendency firmly planted in *Leninism* in addition to (and not solely in) *Stalinism*, and the choking vine of tyranny entwined throughout Soviet history. In the 1970s and 1980s a *revisionist* school rejected totalitarianism as a major explanation of Soviet behavior, along with the implicit comparison of the Soviet Union to *Nazi Germany* that "totalitarian" implied. It looked instead for social bases of support for the regime and emphasized the supposed discontinuity between the Stalinist and post-Stalinist eras. Although the debate continues, the weight of (still incomplete) archival evidence and ex-Soviet testimonial has begun to accumulate on the side of the scale depicting the Soviet Union as akin to Nazi Germany in its savage ideology and levels of internal—including mass murderous—repression, though also as more *opportunistic* in its *aggression* than was *Hitler's* Germany. After 1991 most sovietologists, of whichever view, restyled themselves as Russian or area specialists.

Soviet (Petrograd). The *Russian Revolutions of 1917* witnessed a revival of the *St. Petersburg Soviet* of 1905. Under *Trotsky*, the Petrograd Soviet—and its sister-*soviets* in dozens of other centers—was an intense rival to the *Provisional Government* throughout 1917. Established in March in the old *Duma* building, it was dominated until autumn by doctrinaire, orthodox *Marxists*. They did not try to either share power with, or wrest it from, the liberals and "bourgeoisie" of the Provisional Government, thinking that the historical moment for *socialism* had not yet arrived on the highest tide of history. The Soviet played an important role in the demoralization and collapse of the army, especially by issuing a decree that *officers* would have to answer for their commands to a committee of soldiers. An all-Russian Congress of Soviets met in June but failed to act decisively. *Lenin* thought the moment was ripe and struck for power. He was wrong: an attempted *Bolshevik* coup in July failed, and Lenin was forced to flee to Finland. As the political situation in Russia and the military situation on the *eastern front* continued to deteriorate, he returned. Delay and factionalism within the Soviet proved fatal (in time, literally, to many the Bolsheviks would later have killed): an undertow of unrest pulled moderates from control of the Soviets, and power was seized by the more radical, opportunistic Bolsheviks. By November (October) the Bolsheviks controlled the Petrograd Soviet and used it to propel themselves into power via a second, successful *coup d'etat*.

Suggested Reading: Alexander Rabinowitch, *Prelude to Revolution: The Petrograd Bolsheviks and the July 1917 Uprising* (1991).

soviets. (1) Originally, broad councils of workers and soldiers in Russia; (2) similar councils briefly established after *World War I* in Hungary and parts of Germany, and even more briefly in Guangzhou (Canton) in December, 1927; (3) the people of the Soviet Union (though many objected to being referred to this way, essentially as "committees"). *See also Béla Kun; Jiangxi Soviet; Petrograd Soviet; St. Petersburg Soviet.*

Soviet Union. The *Russian Empire*, 1918–1991, with the formal name change made in 1922. Forged in the fires of the *Russian Civil War*, the Soviet Union suffered *extinction* on December 25, 1991. Fifteen *successor states* were formed at its breakup: *Armenia, Azerbaijan, Belarus (Byelorussia), Estonia, Georgia, Kazakhstan, Kirghizstan, Latvia, Lithuania, Moldova (Moldavia), Russia, Tajikistan, Turkmenistan, Ukraine,* and *Uzbekistan.* Although the Soviet Union was much more than just Russia, or even its empire, for continuity's sake and readers' convenience the main outlines of, and most cross-references to, Soviet history are provided under *Russia: Soviet Russia 1918–1991, Russian Civil War,* and *Russian Revolution, 1917.* Much additional information may be located under *Cold War* and *World War II.* See also entries on constituent republics, select national leaders, and autonomous regions, but especially: *Leonid Brezhnev; collectivization; communism; Communist Party; Mikhail Gorbachev; Andrei Gromyko; GULAG archipelago; KGB; Nikita Khrushchev; Vladimir Ilyich Lenin; Marxism-Leninism; Vyacheslav Molotov; NKVD; OGPU; purge trials; Sino-Soviet split; Soviet bloc; space race; Josef Stalin; Stalinism; Leon Trotsky;* Yezhovshchina; *Giorgii Zhukov; Gregori Zinoviev.*

space age. The present era, which perhaps really began on October 3, 1942, the day German scientists first test-launched a *V-2* rocket at *Peenemünde*, but which most clearly dates to the launch of *Sputnik* by the Soviet Union on October 4, 1957.

space race. An intense technological, military, nationalistic, and *prestige*-driven competition between the United States and the Soviet Union to achieve a sequence of "firsts" or "longests" in space; inter alia: first artificial *satellite*; first animal in space; first animal to survive being in space; first man to orbit Earth; first man to walk in space; first two-man mission; first docking by two spacecraft; first unmanned probes to the Moon and various planets; first spacecraft to orbit the Moon; first man on the Moon; first space station; longest mission; longest continuous human habitation in space; longest-lasting space station; and so on. It was initiated by the launch of *Sputnik* on October 4, 1957. The public American and Soviet space programs were essentially by-products of secret, and more primary, military research into *ICBM* development and satellite reconnaissance essential to the *Cold War*, both for a war-fighting capability and in *verification* by *national technical means* of the other side's military capabilities or compliance with *arms control* agreements.

The space race became a matter of deep public interest and full-fledged international competition for prestige when *John F. Kennedy* declared that the United States would seek to land a man on the Moon and return him safely to Earth before the close of the 1960s. In 1969, in an exercise whose political justification was enhanced American standing through a demonstration of scientific and technical prowess, but which also spoke to general human urges to exploration and satisfaction of intellectual curiosity—with its Apollo 11 mission the National Aeronautics and Space Administration (NASA) landed two men on the Moon, while a third remained in lunar orbit in a sister craft. The Lunar Lander (LEM), named the Eagle and running critically low on fuel, was manually set down by pilot Neil Armstrong in the Sea of Tranquility at 22.18 GMT, July 20, 1969. The first words broadcast to a listening world from a foreign celestial body were, "Houston. Tranquility Base here. The Eagle has landed." A few hours later, Armstrong stepped onto the surface of the Moon, making "one small step for [a] man, one giant leap for Mankind." Six more Apollo missions to the Moon followed, numbered 12 through 17. Apollo 13's mission was aborted mid-flight on the way to the Moon when an onboard explosion caused a critical loss of power and oxygen, and a watching world held its breath for several tense days waiting to see if the crew could jerry-build the spacecraft's systems and land safely home. They did, but barely so. After Apollo 17 lunar exploration ceased for the remainder of the twentieth century, not because there was no good reason to continue—there were many—but because the public's interest had waned, and domestic and foreign policy troubles in the United States distracted attention from the Moon and other exploration and research.

The Soviets had earlier landed several unmanned probes on the Moon, but once beaten to a manned landing by Apollo 11 they abandoned their lunar exploration program and never attempted a manned landing of their own. In other areas of the space race the Soviet Union excelled, including early unmanned planetary exploration (by probe) and building a long-lasting, if rather primitive, space station (MIR). During the *détente* of the early to mid 1970s a brief period of *superpower* collaboration in space occurred, but overall the space race retained a central, secretive military component for both sides. Even with the end of the *Cold War* Earth-orbital space research and exploitation remained at base a matter of geopolitics and *national security*. Military experimentation and research continued, mostly out of the public eye. There was also a new emphasis on economic possibilities, such as multinational cooperation to develop space-based technologies and unique materials, which centered on the international space station, Freedom. All along, at lower levels of activity, pure science research was also continued.

Meanwhile, Japan, the European Union, China, and India had also emerged as space powers. Japan's first rocket went up in 1955, but its program sputtered for decades after that. The EC set up a modest space program in the mid-1960s and established the European Space Agency (ESA) in 1975. It was the only major agency to emerge from commercial interests rather than as an offshoot of military research. By 2000 the ESA rivaled NASA in both unmanned planetary exploration and commercial rocket launches. China launched its first "Long March Rocket" and satellite in 1970, and by the end of the twentieth century had developed ambitious plans for manned missions and planetary exploration. India launched its first military rocket in 1963; India commenced commercial satellite launches only in 1999. Brazil and several smaller nations had rudimentary programs in place by century's end. And, for the first time, private groups and economic interests began to seriously invest in space exploration and exploitation, partly motivated by an interest in potential profit but in part due to growing impatience among scientists and the interested public with the glacial pace and massive inefficiency of many government space programs. *See also Werner von Braun; Moon Treaty; Outer Space Treaty; Strategic Defense Initiative; V-1 and V-2 rockets.*

Suggested Readings: William Breuer, *Race to the Moon* (1993); Walter A. McDougall, *The Heavens and the Earth: A Political History of the Space Age* (1997).

Spain. In 711 C.E. Moors from North Africa swept into Iberia, a poor and arid peninsula with few natural resources, claiming most of it for *Islam*. For the next eight centuries Iberia witnessed a see-saw battle between Christian and Muslim rulers and states in the long and culturally formative *Reconquista*, with the fortunes of war eventually favoring the Christians. In 1469 the union of Aragon and *Castile*, through the *dynastic marriage* of *Ferdinand and Isabella*, set the stage for the final battle. In 1492 the last surviving Moorish state (*Granada*) fell to their *Crusading* armies. They then sent *Columbus* west to search for a strategic back door to China and thence to the Holy Lands of the Middle East. In 1493 the *line of demarcation* gave Spain a monopoly over most of the *New World*. Accompanying this expansion abroad, at home there was severe persecution of Jews and Moors by the monarchy and by the *Inquisition*, as Catholic, *Habsburg* power now centered on a united Spain. Its powerful *infantry* dominated warfare for 150 years, supplemented by *mercenary* armies bought with the *plundered* gold of the Aztec and Inca Empires. In the sixteenth century Spain enjoyed a "golden age" of prosperity, internal (though not external) peace, and artistic achievement. It also built a vast overseas empire, even beyond the Americas, the first "world empire" in history. It thus became *primus inter pares* among the *Great Powers* in Europe as well.

Imperial Spain faced no threat to the south, but was badly overstretched north to the *Spanish Netherlands*, east into Italy and parts of Germany, and west across the Atlantic to the Americas, and even beyond far into the Pacific. Enjoying the "precocious modernity" of a semimodern state, religious uniformity in an age of doctrinal upheaval following its expulsion of Jews and Moors, benefiting from a "power vacuum" in Europe caused by prolonged internal disorder in France, drawing on American silver and a deep cultural mentality of the crusading state, sixteenth- and seventeenth-century Spain was perhaps the first true world power and presence. *Philip II* repeatedly sent Spanish (Castilian) armies into Europe and the *Spanish Armada* against England—then an upstart, *pirate* nation in Spanish eyes—in 1588. Spain annexed Portugal in 1580 and held it to 1640, making it the first global empire. He made Madrid the capital in 1561. His son and grandson, both also named Philip, completed Spain's economically and intellectually disastrous expulsion of its most educated and commercially advanced classes, which had begun in 1492: they expelled all Jewish "Conversos," who were joined in enforced *exile* by suspect converts from Islam ("Moriscos"), 1609–1614. Spain's long decline—which was underlain by economic backwardness, *inflation*, military and fiscal mismanagement, and pursuit of an unsustainable *Weltpolitik* rooted in ancient European visions of universal empire—had started with the breakaway of the Netherlands in the *Eighty Years' War*. It was greatly advanced by naval defeats at England's hand and by truly definitive defeat by *Richelieu* and France in the *Thirty Years' War*, though the overlapping Franco-Spanish conflict actually continued to 1659, ending with the *Treaty of the Pyrenees*. Why these prolonged, losing wars when on several occasions a better peace might have been had? The answer was essentially ideological: an empire which God had given to Spain, or so it was thought, could not be rejected or turned over to heretics.

The fall by Spain into subservience to France was completed with the *War of the Spanish Succession* (1701–1713), which began when *Louis XIV* placed an infant *Bourbon* on the Spanish throne (Philip V, 1700–1746) and established a "family compact" between Bourbon Spain and France. The utter nadir of Spain's humiliation came with the dictatorship of Manuel Godoy (1767–1851; dictator, 1792–1808) and its invasion and conquest by *Napoleon*. The Spanish court had worked with Napoleon to invade Portugal with a Franco-Spanish army in 1807, forcing that country's monarch, John VI, to flee on a British warship to Rio de Janeiro. British forces landed in Portugal in August 1808 to help the Portuguese hold the highlands. The war spread to Spain when Napoleon cavalierly forced his brother Joseph onto the Spanish throne as King José I, deposing King Ferdinand VII, who was taken as a prisoner to

France, where he remained until the defeat of Napoleon in 1814. That utter humiliation of a former world power sparked a national revival: Spaniards of all classes took to *guerrilla warfare* and fought back against the French in the *Peninsular War* (known in Spanish history as the War of Independence). A national *junta* was formed (September 1808) which declared itself the *legitimate* government of Spain and its world empire. In 1810 the junta yielded some power to a new Cortes (parliament) which met in Cadiz, a city Spanish forces still held, while the French held court in Madrid. The Cortes of Cadiz had representatives not just from Spain but also its overseas colonies, and in 1812 produced Spain's first written, and also liberal-democratic, constitution. Yet the French occupation cost Spain most of its empire: Madrid's moment of captivity and weakness, and the opening for debate in the Cortes of fundamental issues of *sovereignty* and *legitimacy*, stimulated the revolutionary upheavals and wars of independence waged against Spain in Latin America, 1810–1825. Latin American *republicans* now struck for independence, largely achieving it everywhere on the South American continent by 1825, leaving *Spanish America* reduced to Cuba and Puerto Rico. Even the Haitians took from Spain, controlling all of *Hispaniola* to 1844.

The *Carlists* forced a succession struggle which led to civil war in Spain, 1834–1837, and again, 1870–1876. This quarrel kept Spain separate from the political currents which were leading Europe into the *Revolutions of 1848*, but it also held Spain back from faster economic *modernization* and from liberal reform. A domestic revolution shook the country in 1868. The remainder of its empire was stripped away by another newcomer, America, during the *Spanish-American War*. Reduced by the "Disaster of '98" to its home shores—save for a few remnants of empire in form of minor North and West African colonies—Spain entered the twentieth century backward, uncertain, defeated, and unstable. The *reactionary* conservatism of King Alphonso XIII (1886–1941; king, 1902–1931) frustrated liberal reform efforts and encouraged dictatorship. Spain stayed out of *World War I* but faced an internal political crisis, 1917–1921. It was humiliated and then brutally repressed by, the *Rif Rebellion* in Morocco (1921–1926). The price was military dictatorship under *Primo de Rivera* after 1923. The Second Republic was established in 1931, upon Alphonso's abdication in disgrace. Spain was next convulsed by mass movements of *anarchism* and *fascism*, forces that collided violently and returned it briefly to international attention during the *Spanish Civil War*, which destroyed the Second Republic. It was quasi-*neutral* in *World War II*. It sent the *Blue Division* to fight the Soviets and gave the *Nazis* naval intelligence and other assistance, as it remained under the iron hand of *Franco*, 1939–1975. When Franco died Spain enthusiastically embraced democracy and modernity. After 1980 it enjoyed rapid growth and prosperity. King Juan Carlos I (r. 1975–) gained great stature for helping to thwart an anti-democracy coup attempt in 1981 and for facilitating nonviolent acceptance of a socialist government in 1982. Spain also joined NATO that year; it entered the *Eu-*

ropean Community in 1986. *See also* audiencia; *Basques; Black Legend; Simón Bolívar; Ceuta;* conquistadores; *Council of the Indies;* encomienda; *ETA; Falange; Falkland Islands; Gibraltar; Melilla; New Granada; New Spain;* real patronato; requerimiento; *José de San Martín; Túpac Amaru.*

Suggested Readings: Raymond Carr, ed., *Spain* (2000); Raymond Carr, ed., *Spain, 1808–1975*, 2nd ed. (1982); J. H. Elliot, *Imperial Spain, 1469–1716* (1964, 1970); H. Kamen, *Imperial Spain* (1983); Stanley Payne, *Fascism in Spain, 1923–1977* (2000).

Spanish America. (1) Historically: all New World possession of the Spanish Empire, c. 1500–1898, governed by the "Spanish Monarchy," as the empire was known, and later by the Spanish Republic. At their greatest extent these stretched from Mexico (then including Arizona, *California,* the Floridas, New Mexico, and *Texas*), through Central America to *New Granada,* and select Caribbean islands, notably Cuba, Puerto Rico, and most of *Hispaniola.* It included all South America except for Brazil, which was Portuguese. However, in the political sense it included Brazil, too, from 1580 to 1640, once *Philip II* annexed Portugal and its overseas empire to Spain. Spanish America in this sense existed in some form or other from 1492 to 1898, although it was severely truncated and reduced to a few minor colonies after c. 1825, having fractured in 1808 during the French invasion of Spain (*Peninsular War*), leading to the emergence of distinct national movements in Spain itself as well as in the colonies by 1825. It came to an end with the *Spanish-American War.* (2) Today: the mainly Spanish-speaking areas south of the United States, to wit: Central America (except for Belize), South America (except for Brazil and French Guiana), and parts of the Caribbean. *See also* audiencia; *Aztec empire; Black Legend; Simón Bolívar; Christopher Columbus;* conquistadores; *Council of the Indies;* encomienda; *Inca; Maya;* real patronato; requerimiento; *José de San Martín; Túpac Amaru.*

Suggested Readings: Kenneth Andrien and L. L. Johnson, *Political Economy of Latin America in the Age of Revolution, 1750–1850* (1994); D. A. Brading, *The First America: The Spanish Monarchy, Creole Patriots, and the Liberal State, 1492–1867* (1991); J. H. Elliot, ed., *Hispanic World, Civilization, and Empire* (1991); J. H. Elliot, ed., *Imperial Spain, 1469–1716* (1964, 1970); John Kicza, ed., *The Indian in Latin American History* (1993).

Spanish-American War (1898). The United States had long maintained an interest in Cuba. Thus, *insurrectionists* against Spanish rule could fairly easily provoke and steer American public sympathy for their cause. The *Protestant* religious press and the *yellow press,* in particular the Hearst chain, also stirred anti-Spanish and anti-*Catholic* sentiment. Even so, William Randolph Hearst (1863–1951) much exaggerated his influence over U.S. foreign policy when he cabled an artist in Cuba: "You furnish the pictures and I'll furnish the war." Spain's image and cause were also hurt by genuine cruelties it committed, including use of *concentration camps,* and by occasions when U.S. and Spanish warships exchanged fire. The *Republican Party* contained the lion's share of *jingoists* and *imperialists,* but this did not include President *William*

McKinley. His fatal flaw was an inability to withstand the building sentiment for war, especially after the *U.S.S. Maine* was sunk in Havana harbor. Perceiving an intolerable stalemate in Cuba, the United States issued an *ultimatum.* That brought appeals by Spain to other European powers, but although most thought the United States was in the wrong none was willing to help. Madrid thus decided to concede on all points except complete Cuban *independence.* That offer came just too late: Congress was determined on war, and McKinley went along rather than divide his party. To great fanfare and public delight, the United States inflicted defeat upon defeat on the ill-equipped and already half-beaten Spanish. The Americans were aided by Cuban troops, who had badly weakened the capabilities and morale of the Spanish even before the arrival of *Theodore Roosevelt* and the "Roughriders." The United States also took the opportunity to strike at Spain wherever it found Spanish targets, not just in Cuba. Within 10 weeks, the American public therefore found that its small crusade to free Cuba from *colonialism* had conceived an unwanted (by most) colonial *empire;* to wit: the United States found it now controlled *Guam,* the *Philippines,* and *Puerto Rico,* as well as Cuba. At a blow, the Spanish empire in the Americas was finished and the United States was transformed into an imperial *republic* with far-flung Pacific interests. It soon also faced a *guerrilla war* against its colonial control of the Philippines. *See also white man's burden.*

Suggested Readings: Louis L. Gould, *The Spanish-American War and President McKinley* (1982); G. F. Linderman, *The Mirror of War* (1974); Ivan Musicant, *Empire by Default* (1998). Louis Pérez, *The War of 1898* (1998).

Spanish Armada (1588). "Enterprise of England." Dispatch of an invasion fleet by *Philip II* of Spain against the England of *Elizabeth I* was a decision long in the making, and long argued for by Philip's allies and subordinates. In 1685 Pope Sixtus V called on Philip to undertake a *Crusade* for the *Counter-Reformation* of the *Catholic Church* against *Protestant* England. Philip demurred, as he was preoccupied with his war against the Dutch—the *Eighty Years' War* (1566–1648)—among several other expensive and difficult conflicts. When Sir Francis Drake (c. 1540–1596), an English *privateer,* raided the Galicia coast, Philip finally decided to undertake the conquest of England. Methodical as always, he commissioned a study of previous invasion attempts and learned that, since the *Norman* invasion of 1066, England had seen nine governments fall or seriously weakened by invasions from the sea, seven additional landings of armies in Britain, and dozens of successful coastal raids. Philip eventually settled on a plan of attack which involved combining all his ships into a single grand armada and sending this to the Netherlands to collect troops from the Army of Flanders, thence directly to England to land an armed host which would march directly on London. Knowing more or less what was coming, from 1685 Elizabeth intrigued with the sultan of the *Ottoman Empire,* though to little avail, commissioned new *ships-of-the-line,* and embargoed all other vessels that might be converted to warships from leaving English ports, and sent Drake to enter Spanish ports with his squadron and destroy all ships he found there. On April 29, 1587, Drake entered the harbor at Cadiz and destroyed or captured 24 Spanish ships, and burned the docks and warehouses, confirming Philip's determination to deal once and for all with England. The cost of the Spanish invasion plans was so fearsome, however, that he had to sell his wife's jewels to pay for it.

Elizabeth, too, was feeling stretched: she had an army guarding the Scottish frontier and another she could ill-afford in Flanders, allied with the Dutch. And her ambassador in Paris, Sir Edward Stafford, was in fact a spy for Philip. While Elizabeth's spies were similarly well-placed—one delivered to her an exact copy of the Spanish invasion plans—the sheer disparity of forces was such that when the Spanish Armada hove to at Calais on August 6, 1588, it looked as though Philip's "grand strategy" might well succeed. Then *friction* took a hand, even as Spanish troops began to embark onto troop transports, some 200 flat-bottomed barges which were to be escorted by the Spanish *galleons* and *frigates*. On August 7th the English sent fireships into the Armada, which was awaiting the troop ships at anchor. This scattered the fleet, forcing it out of harbor. English ships were armed with heavier and more rapid-firing cannon (probably at a ratio of three shots to every Spanish round). They therefore closed with the Armada, and the two entangled fleets were carried on the prevailing wind into the North Sea, fighting desperately along the way. Through collisions at sea, groundings, and getting lost in the Channel fog, the Spanish lost a squadron of galleys and four *ships-of-the-line* before the two main fleets even engaged, on August 8th off Gravelines.

In that battle, the English sank one Spanish ship-of-the-line and forced two Portuguese galleons to ground, losing no ships themselves in any engagement other than the eight small fireships which they had expended to try to break up the Spanish fleet. At Gravelines, the Spanish fought in a traditional crescent-shaped line, whereas the English used new *line-ahead* and other tactics. The key, however, as suggested by most military historians, was gunnery: the Iberian ships lacked heavy artillery and had inferior gun carriages, which made even their smaller guns cumbersome to reload and fire. They also carried a motley crew of calibers. That may well have befitted the convoy escort assignment for which Philip intended the Armada, but it ill-served a battle fleet engaged with the well-trained and better-armed Elizabethan navy, which commanded larger-caliber weapons with a three-to-one greater rate of fire. Nor did any of the 20,000 soldiers the Spanish ships carried in order to close and board the enemy actually manage to do so: not a single one of the more maneuverable and better-crewed English ships was boarded, making the on-board Spanish troops merely targets for English *grapeshot* and snipers. On the dismal voyage back to Spain, made via Scotland and Ireland due to the winds and English pursuit, the Armada lost another third of its complement, or about 50 ships and 15,000 men. *See also Trafalgar.*

Suggested Readings: D. Goodman, *Spanish Naval Power, 1589–1665: Reconstruction and Defeat* (1996); C. J. Martin and Geoffrey Parker, *The Spanish Armada* (1988); Geoffrey Parker, *The Grand Strategy of Philip II* (1998).

"Spanish Captivity" of Portugal (1580–1640). *See Brazil; Eighty Years' War (1566–1648); Philip II; Portugal.*

Spanish Civil War (1936–1939). It began as a revolt of elements of the colonial army, led by *Franco* and supported by the *Carlists* and *Falange*, conservative Catholics and the church hierarchy (but not all priests), and captains of industry. On the Republican side was the *Popular Front* coalition, drawing on an eclectic mix of peasants, workers, *democrats*, *socialists*, *communists*, *anarchists*, and assorted and imported romantic adventurers. While Franco's forces said they fought for church, tradition, and fatherland, the watchword of the anti-clericals and social reformers on the Republican side was "it is better to die on your feet than to live on your knees," a slogan of *Zapata*, made famous in Spain by the female anarchist revolutionary "La Passionaria." The Western democracies declared *neutrality*. In Britain and France, many saw the Republic as a reprise of *Kerensky's* ill-fated regime in Russia, and worried about national and private assets there, should "the Left" win the war. They also feared being drawn into a repeat of 1914, when a regional quarrel had escalated into all-out *Great Power* war. The *fascist* states of Europe, on the other hand, eagerly *intervened*. They sent arms—including air force units—and tens of thousands of "volunteers" to fight alongside Franco and the *Falange*. The *Soviet Union* counter-intervened, becoming the main backer of the Republican side, along with Western volunteers in the *international brigades*. In all, some 750,000 died, many in tit-for-tat massacres. When the Soviets suddenly cut off aid to the Republic in 1939 as part of the *reneversement des alliance* with Nazi Germany leading to the *Nazi-Soviet Pact*, Republican forces collapsed. Terrible retribution followed: perhaps 200,000 Republican prisoners were murdered by Franco. Within just weeks, Britain and France had cause to rue the fact they had not helped a struggling fellow democracy survive a fascist takeover: Nazi Germany attacked Poland on September 1st, beginning *World War II*, that far larger and more desperate contest against fascism. *See also Condor Legion; Fifth Column; Guernica; League of Nations; Neutrality Acts.*

Suggested Readings: Hugh Thomas, *The Spanish Civil War* (1961). The international flavor of the Spanish war was well captured, in English, in Ernest Hemingway's *For Whom The Bell Tolls* (1940), but especially in George Orwell's contemporaneous *Homage to Catalonia* (1938).

Spanish Fury (1576). *See Eighty Years' War (1566–1648).*

Spanish Inquisition. *See Inquisition.*

Spanish Main. The Caribbean coast of Mexico and the United States, from the sixteenth through the eighteenth centuries, from whence treasure ships in *convoy* (*flota* and *galeones*) plied their way to Spain initially filled with *plunder*, and later with the slave-mined silver and gold of the Americas. These treasure ships were preyed upon by English *pirates*, French *buccaneers*, and in times of war (which was virtually constant in the seventeenth and eighteenth centuries) also by commissioned French, Dutch, or English *privateers*.

Spanish Monarchy. *See Spanish America.*

Spanish Netherlands. The southern half of medieval Burgundy (*Flanders*), which remained mostly *Catholic* during the *Reformation* and hence split from the rebellious *Calvinist* United Provinces during the *Eighty Years' War*. This territory was a perpetual battleground between France, Spain, and the Dutch Republic over repeated efforts at expansion by *Louis XIV*. The Treaty of Rastadt (1714) converted the Spanish Netherlands to the *Austrian Netherlands*. *See also Treaty of Utrecht (1713).*

Spanish Road. The main *Habsburg* supply route from *Castile* to the *Spanish Netherlands*. It was of vital strategic and economic importance during the *Eighty Years' War* (1566–1648) and the *Thirty Years' War* (1618–1648), especially in those periods when French or English naval power denied Spain the coastal sea route to its northern possessions. It ran through Lombardy, several Swiss cantons, and into the *Rhineland*. One of its most critical choke points was *The Grisons*. It included a remarkable postal service, a "pony express" of early modern Europe dating to 1504 when the Taxis family first created a chain of 106 relay stations supplied with fresh mounts to connect territories bound together by the new *union of the crowns* of Burgundy and Castile. In 1516 the young *Charles V* signed a contract with the Taxis family guaranteeing delivery times, and in 1518 Charles and King Francis I (1494–1547) of France agreed to extend *diplomatic immunity* to all official couriers using this mutually advantageous service. *Philip II* deployed similar services connecting his new capital at Madrid with Rome and Vienna.
  Suggested Reading: Geoffrey Parker, *The Army of Flanders and the Spanish Road, 1567–1659* (1972).

Spanish Sahara. Also known as Rio de Oro. A West African *colony* of Spain. It was invaded unsuccessfully by Morocco in 1957. It was given up by Spain in 1976 and was immediately divided between Mauritania and Morocco. *See also Western Sahara.*

Spartacist Uprising (1919). The Spartacists were German *communists*, led by *Rosa Luxemburg* and Karl Liebknecht (1871–1919), who tried to seize control of *Berlin* at the end of *World War I* as a base for a wider German social and political revolution. The revolt was put down not by *Weimar* authorities but by units of *Freikorps*, who murdered Luxemburg and Liebknecht after taking them prisoner. The name referred, with the heavy romantic self-consciousness typical of Rosa Luxemburg, to the gladiator and *slave* revolt in the *Roman Empire* in 73 B.C.E. led by Spartacus (d. 71 B.C.E.).

Spearhead Group. *See Melanesian Spearhead Group.*

Special Drawing Rights (SDRs). The main unit of account in the *International Monetary Fund* (IMF), as well as several other international financial institutions, including the *International Bank for Reconstruction and Development* (IBRD). All IMF voting and lending is by SDR shares. SDRs serve as a backup international *liquidity* reserve which is available to member states of the IMF. Set up in 1969, they were first made available in 1970 as a supplement to national reserve assets. SDRs are allocated by reference to fund contributions and are designed to supplement other sources of global liquidity. Their value (and interest rate) is calculated with reference to a basket of international currencies, so that SDRs constitute artificial *currency* made up of a basket of national currencies, which is reviewed every five years and updated as need arises. Interest rates are updated weekly.

special economic zones. *See export processing zones.*

special envoy. An *envoy* sent on a specific mission or tasked to perform a set function on behalf of the *Secretary General* of the *United Nations* or some other *multilateral* body.

special forces. Highly trained, specially armed and equipped, elite units maintained within most modern militaries for use in intelligence gathering; small-unit tactical operations; other *covert operations*; advisory assistance to local regular forces; anti-hijacking and anti-terrorist actions; and other special missions, including "snatch-and-grab" and sabotage missions, weapons pathfinding for bombers and artillery, sniping, and so forth. The British keep perhaps the single most professionally respected force, the Special Air Service (SAS). The United States maintains multiple specialized units, including the super-elite Delta Force and Navy Seal teams, as well as more numerous army special forces such as the Rangers and Green Berets. Russia, China, France, Germany, Israel, India, and every other significant military power trains and maintains similar elite military and covert special operations units.

special interest section. An ad hoc arrangement between states that wish (or need) to maintain some contact, or even *relations officieuses*, in the absence of full *diplomatic relations*. These are usually set up within the *embassy*, and under the custodianship, of a *neutral* power. For example, during the long, twilight struggle between the United States and Cuba after the ascent to power of *Fidel Castro*, relations were conducted in each country through special interest sections hosted by Switzerland. On occasion the old national embassies may be used, but they are downgraded in status and renamed as special interest sections. Officials of such special sections are not usually covered by full *diplomatic immunity*. *See also agency; good offices.*

specialized agencies (of the United Nations). The *functional* organs designated in Article 57 of the *United Nations Charter* and later additions, to wit: *Food and Agriculture Organization (FAO)*, *International Bank for Reconstruction and Development (IBRD)*, *International Civil Aviation Organization (ICAO)*, *International Development Association (IDA)*, *International Finance Corporation (IFC)*, *International Fund for Agricultural Development (IFAD)*, *International Labor Organization (ILO)*, *International Maritime Organization (IMO)*, *International Monetary Fund (IMF)*, *International Telecommunication Union (ITU)*, *United Nations Educational, Scientific and Cultural Organization (UNESCO)*, *United Nations Industrial Development Organization (UNIDO)*, *Universal Postal Union (UPU)*, *World Health Organization (WHO)*, *World Intellectual Property Organization (WIPO)* and *World Meteorological Organization (WMO)*. Related organizations not usually included in this list are the *General Agreement on Tariffs and Trade (GATT)*, the *International Atomic Energy Agency (IAEA)*, and the *United Nations High Commission for Refugees (UNHCR)*. *See also UNICEF.*

special membership. Some organizations (for instance, the *Commonwealth*) grant this status to *microstates* to enable them to enjoy full benefits of membership without incurring the costs of attending all meetings or making donations. *See also Nauru; Tuvalu.*

special relationship. An unofficial term widely used when a *Great Power* wants to flatter an ally by signaling that it is *primus inter pares* among all allies. Or it may be used by a small power to try to bind a larger power, through ingratiation, more closely to the small state's interests and agenda. For some (*Winston Churchill's* idea of the "English-speaking world," France's *la francophonie*, Russia's *CIS*, Germany's alliance with Austria, or South Africa's support for Rhodesia), the term also carried ethnic and cultural connotations. Britain and the United States used it to express their exceptionally close *alignment* during the first half of the twentieth century. After *World War II*, however, it was invoked—by Britons far longer than Americans, for whom it ceased to have much substance after the *Suez Crisis*—largely to compensate for the rapid decline in geopolitical weight and importance of the shrinking *British Empire*, through its attachment to the still-rising power of the United States.

Speer, Albert (1905–1981). Nazi minister for armaments and munitions, 1942–1945, and *Hitler's* personal architect and toadying admirer. He joined the *Schutzstaffel* (SS) early and rose to oversee staging of the *Nuremberg Rallies*. He then joined the staff of *Rudolf Hess*. He consulted with Hitler on grandiose, deeply pretentious (and second-rate) plans for the reconstruction of *Berlin* and for building a new Nazi capital at Nuremberg in a neoclassical, *fascist* style. As armaments minister he was exceedingly able, as well as ruthless. He probably single-handedly extended *World War II* by putting Nazi Germany on a full war economy footing: Hitler had delayed mobilizing women, for example, due to short-war expectations and Nazi *Volkisch* ideology. In so doing, he made extensive use of *slave labor* from the *concentration camps*. During the final *Battle of Berlin*, he secretly countermanded Hitler's orders to destroy all infrastructure in Germany. All his wartime actions except that latter act brought him before the tribunal at *Nuremberg* as an accused "major war criminal." He pleaded guilty and received a sentence of 20 years, which he served alongside Hess in Spandau Prison. He once admitted—oblivious to the moral content of the statement, as he had been oblivious to the moral content of the *Third Reich*—that the only time in his adult life, or during the war, that he ever cried was on learning of the death of Adolf Hitler. He later published his war diary and other books. They provide a cold, but unique, first-hand account and insight into the daily operations of the Third Reich.

Suggested Readings: Dan van der Vat, *The Good Nazi: The Life and Lies of Albert Speer* (1997); Albert Speer, *Inside the Third Reich* (1970).

sphere of influence. (1) An area of small or weak states or portions thereof, dominated by a larger power purposefully or by virtue of its proximity, resources, and expanded appreciation of self-interest. (2) An area declared by a *Great Power* to be its exclusive region of interest, where it will act with force if pressed, to defend its dominance and to exclude other Great Powers. (3) An area of *terra incognita* to which states make legal claim in order to preempt the claims of other states; e.g., the infamous 1493 *line of demarcation* between Portugal and Spain. By the late twentieth century, mainly because of the acute sensitivities of *liberal-internationalism* and of newly independent states, spheres of influence were no longer called that in diplomacy or public rhetoric, although they were no less real "on the ground" than in prior eras. *See also Brezhnev Doctrine; CIS; concession diplomacy; Congress of Berlin; Eastern Question; empire; Greater East Asia Co-Prosperity Sphere; hinterland; Manchuria; mare nostrum; Monroe Doctrine; Nazi-Soviet Pact; near abroad; Open Door; Poland; Potsdam; propinquity; protectorate; scramble for Africa; Shandong; sphere of interest; Sykes-Picot Agreement; Tilsit; Twenty-one Demands; unequal treaties; Yalta.*

sphere of interest. A tighter concept than *sphere of influence*, implying a narrow, even territorial aspect. In colonial times, these were the areas of *hinterland* deemed to directly affect coastal settlements, and were claimed as an extension of them. *See also Fashoda crisis; propinquity.*

Spice Islands. Former name of the Moluccas group, once a Dutch colony and then part of postcolonial Indonesia. First encountered by the Portuguese in 1512, they were the key prize in the great sixteenth-century contest for control of the *spice trade*. In 1529 Spain renounced its claim in return for a heavy payment from Portugal. The islands were later seized by the Dutch. *See also Age of Exploration; slavery; Indonesia.*

spice trade. For more than a millennium spices from Asia (cloves, various peppers, curry, cinnamon, and others) were a major part of international trade, which flowed from China and the Indonesian archipelago through Central Asia and India, to the Middle East and on to Western Europe. Arab dealers—and in a sense Arab civilization too—thrived and depended on this trade. In the Mediterranean, *Venice* controlled the trade, which made Italy rich and in the economic realm underwrote and sustained the Italian *Renaissance*. This changed with the *Ottoman Empire's* conquest of *Constantinople* in 1453. That calamity (from Europe's point of view) stimulated a frantic search for a new way to the fabled spice lands of the east. The Portuguese slowly but steadily circumnavigated Africa, bypassing Venice and contributing to its decline, and reaching the Indian Ocean (accomplished by Vasco da Gama) in 1497. Meanwhile, in 1492 a Genoese adventurer, *Christopher Columbus*, sailed west in search of the riches of Asia and—from *Isabella's* perspective, more importantly—to find a strategic route to attack the infidel via the backdoor to the Holy Land. In the *line of demarcation* papal decision of 1493, Portugal was given a monopoly over the eastern spice trade by the Pope. Lisbon was never able to secure effective control of the sources of the spices. Over time it lost its monopoly over knowledge of the trans-African trade routes, and then lost the *Spice Islands* to the Dutch. The spice trade was, for the better part of two centuries, the major motive behind European expansion and warfare in Asia. *See also East India Company; Fugger, House of.*
Suggested Reading: Kristof Glamann, *The Dutch-Asiatic Trade* (1958).

spies. Spies are members of the second oldest profession. As with members of the oldest profession, the activities of spies are routinely condemned as unacceptable in polite society, as sneaky, dishonorable, immoral and reprobate. And just about as routinely as with that other profession, they are employed, paid off, rewarded, and cosseted by the same government officials who castigate other states for doing likewise. This habitual hypocrisy on the part of states is a standard part of the game of *espionage* in an era of mass public opinion, but an absence of sound public education about the nature and practices of international relations. In fact, most states regard espionage as an entirely legitimate, though necessarily secret, part of politics among nations—not just when they are doing it themselves, but even to a remarkable degree when spying is carried out by opponents as well. All states engage in spying, at least on an ad hoc basis, to whatever degree their resources (human, financial, and technical talents) permit. Spying was a function of the earliest modern *diplomats*, during the *Renaissance* and thereafter, and even modern spies frequently operate under "diplomatic cover." Again, that is widely known and roughly tolerated by host states. Information purchased from local informants in some foreign court, or from some unhappy or ambitious servant privy to darker and more personal princely secrets, was used to supplement official conversations and other open information gathering, in order to further the political analysis essential to survival in the wolf-like system of European nation-states. Such "inside information" became so valued by all parties that peacetime spying among states ever after became more or less openly tolerated, in a curious application of the idea of the general international principle of *reciprocity*. That is, spies might well be known and not immediately arrested or otherwise interfered with, as long as their activity was not so blatant it embarrassed the host country, or so threatening to real *national interests* (such as fomenting rebellion or plotting assassinations, as many a Spanish spy did in the court of *Elizabeth I*) that it forced a host to take drastic immediate countermeasures.

Over time, modern states slowly developed professional, secret *intelligence services* dedicated to gathering otherwise hard-to-obtain information abroad, along with *counterintelligence* services to place limits on foreign *agents* doing the same in one's own court, or military establishment, or foreign ministry. In addition to keeping foreign spies away from potential domestic traitors and critical secrets, counterintelligence officers whenever possible also seek to misinform such agents so that they transmit *disinformation* to their sponsoring governments. They also watch identified agents to see who among one's own people they contact, and who might be disloyal or subversive. Modern states do, of course, try to block other states from spying to the greatest degree possible (which frequently is not very far, especially in open and democratic societies). Most often, however, they will not maim or kill a foreign spy in peacetime, again on the basis of the principle of reciprocity. On the other hand, most states will readily execute their own nationals who are caught spying for foreign powers. A special practice concerns spying in wartime: although wartime espionage is not prohibited under the *laws of war*, it is so threatening to one's war effort, and hence *vital interests*, that wartime spies are nearly always denied the status of *prisoners of war (POWs)* and are instead *summarily executed*, "pour encourager les autres" ("to encourage the others"), as Voltaire dryly put it about English Admiral John Byng, who was court-martialed and shot for cowardice in 1757. *See also active measures; agent of influence;* agent provocateur; *agitprop; assassination;* attaché; cabinet noir;

cipher; covert action; cryptology; dead letter drop; debrief; double agent; double cross; economic espionage; elint; Klaus Fuchs; Alger Hiss; honey trap; humint; illegal agent; intelligence; legal agent; listening post; mole; overt-covert action; penetration agent; persona non grata; psychological warfare; Ethel and Julius Rosenberg; safe house; sabotage; satellite; secret diplomacy; sigint; station; surveillance; tradecraft; wet affair.

Suggested Reading: Christopher Andrew, *Intelligence and International Relations* (1987); F. H. Hinsley, ed., *British Intelligence in the Second World War* (1979); *Jane's Intelligence Review* (1991–).

spillover. In *integration* theory, the suggestion that successful cooperation among states in one *functional* area encourages cooperation in others, builds trust and mutual interest, and one day, perhaps, may conduce to full political union.

"splendid isolation." A misleading term, partly because it was often used by *Salisbury* about his own diplomacy. It is more accurate to say Britain under Salisbury followed a policy of limited arrangements and commitments, befitting a fluid situation. In its narrowest meaning, it suggested Britain's unique ability to stand on the strength of the *Royal Navy* and *British Empire* without formal allies, at least until its severe isolation during the *Boer War* encouraged it into the *Anglo-Japanese Alliance* of 1902. The term should not be taken to mean Britain stood aloof from international disputes or *Great Power* rivalry in Europe, on anything like the earlier American *isolationist* model. *See also Trafalgar.*

split states. *See Alsace-Lorraine; China/Taiwan; Cyprus; East Germany/West Germany; Ireland/Ulster; Italia irridenta; North Korea/South Korea; Palestine; partition; Rhineland; Somaliland; Vietnam.*

spot market. One where buying or selling takes place at the market price of the day, in cash or cash equivalent, and for immediate delivery. For instance, the spot market for *oil* is constantly active and is an influential indicator during times of crisis. *See also forward market.*

Spratly Islands (a.k.a. *Nansha, Truong Sa*). An archipelago of 500 coral reefs, *islets*, and *islands*, only 30 of which are substantial in size. Their control or ownership is contested by six nations: Brunei (which claims only *territorial waters* and an *Exclusive Economic Zone*, not islands per se), China, Malaysia, the Philippines, Taiwan, and Vietnam. Previously, France (before leaving *French Indochina*) and Japan (until its defeat in *World War II*) maintained claims. This sprawling archipelago straddles a busy sea lane connecting the South China Sea to the Pacific and Indian Oceans. Its waters contain rich *fisheries*, and it is thought that a major *oil* field lies beneath the surrounding *continental shelf*. The main tension is between China and Vietnam, each of which claim all the islands, reefs, and territorial waters. In 1974 they fought an air and naval battle over the Spratlys and *Paracels*. China pushed Vietnam out of the latter in another clash in 1982. In 1988 Chinese *warships* and marines took six of the Spratlys from Vietnam, leaving an estimated 100 Vietnamese dead. Vietnam had a military presence on 21 islands in 1992. China occupied seven, but in 1992 attacked and captured two more Vietnamese-held islands. China does not keep troops on these at all times. Instead, it maintains "sovereignty posts" and dispatches regular naval patrols. Taiwan makes the same claims as the People's Republic of China (*mainland China*) and occupies the largest of the Spratlys, Ito Aba (Taiping). It kept some 400–500 troops there after 1958; these soldiers sometimes fired on Soviet and Vietnamese aircraft. In one of the more curious results of these overlapping claims, Taiwan said that it would come to China's aid against Vietnam—adding, unnecessarily, that China did not appear to need its assistance. Malaysia claims three islands, on which it keeps small garrisons. In 1992 it acquired Russian *MIGs* to provide improved air cover to support its claim. The Philippines lays claim to eight islands, which it calls the Kalayaan Archipelago. It has an air base on Pagasa (Thitu on world maps). Concern over these tensions led in 1992 to Indonesia's call for a 10-nation conference on the future of the Spratlys, and *ASEAN* called for creation of a *Zone of Peace, Freedom, and Neutrality* (ZOPFAN), but no nation renounced its claims. In 1993 China and Vietnam opened talks on resolving this dispute, and other talks over oil exploration in the Gulf of Tonkin.

Sputnik. "Fellow Wayfarer." The first earth-orbital, artificial *satellite*, launched on October 4, 1957, by the Soviet Union. Its elementary signal, audible by radio as it circled the globe, shocked and seemed to threaten the West. This gave a huge boost to the international *prestige* of the Soviet Union and also induced misplaced confidence within the Soviet Union. By sparking fears (fed by false charges by *Kennedy*) of a "missile gap," it contributed to a new *arms race* and stimulated the *space race*.

Suggested Reading: Robert Divine, *The Sputnik Challenge* (1993).

Sri Lanka. This island nation was called Ceylon until 1970. Its *indigenous people* were conquered by *Buddhists* from India c. 545 B.C.E. Descendants of these Buddhist conquerors, and of long-since assimilated indigenous peoples, constituted 80 percent of the Sinhalese population in 2000. The remaining 20 percent were ethnic Tamils and *Hindus*, concentrated mainly on and around the *Jaffna peninsula*. In 1505 Portuguese traders appeared along the coast. In 1515 Vasco da Gama secured the Ceylon trade for Portugal, but the Portuguese eventually lost the competition to establish a *spice trade* monopoly to the Dutch *East India Company* (VOC). The Dutch were displaced from Ceylon by English traders from the British *East India Company* (John Company), who seized and claimed Dutch coastal towns in 1796. Britain formally acquired Ceylon in the *Treaty of Amiens*. The English only slowly penetrated the interior of the island, and their *conquest* was not completed until 1814. From 1815 to 1947 Ceylon was an English *colony*, supplying much of the *British Empire's* tea and rubber from its plantation economy. Local representation was permitted after 1920, and the first elections under universal male suffrage were held in 1931. Ceylon became an independent *dominion* in 1947. Solomon West Bandaranaike (1899–1959; prime minister, 1956–1959) was a Sinhalese nationalist who alienated the minority Tamils, reduced the British presence, closed naval bases, and moved Ceylon into the *Nonaligned Movement*. Buddhist *fundamentalism* played a key role in his assertion of Sinhalese nationalism from the mid-1950s, and contributed to the protracted war which broke out with the Tamil minority. Bandaranaike's widow, Sirimavo Ratwatte Bandaranaike (1916–2000), was prime minister, 1960–1965, and again, 1970–1977. In 1978 ethnic and religious tensions contributed to *terrorist* attacks by the *Tamil Tigers*. In 1983 the conflict flared into bloody *civil war*. A *state of emergency* was declared as the Tigers made early gains and seized control of the Jaffna peninsula. In 1987 some 50,000 Indian troops *intervened* as ostensible *peacekeepers*, but they quickly found themselves fighting the Tigers. They were withdrawn, after taking and inflicting heavy casualties, in 1990 as *peace talks* began. In 1993 the talks stalled and heavy fighting resumed. In 1994 Chandrika Kumaratunga, daughter and heir to the Bandaranaike *dynasty*, was elected prime minister. She was reelected in 1999. In 1995 the Sri Lankan Army briefly captured Jaffna but was forced out by renewed fighting as the war resumed. By 2000, at least 60,000 were dead after nearly two decades of civil war.

Suggested Reading: Chandra de Silva, *Sri Lanka: A History*, 2nd rev. ed. (1997).

SS. *See Schutzstaffel.*

St. Bartholomew's Day Massacre (August 23–24, 1572). *See Henri IV.*

St. Germain, Treaty of (September 10, 1919). Negotiated at the *Paris Peace Conference*, this was the *peace treaty* formally ending *World War I* for Austria. It was based on Points 10 and 11 of the *Fourteen Points*, which forced Austria to renounce all claims to non-German areas of its erstwhile *empire*. It went against the principle of *self-determination* by simultaneously stripping Austria of about one-third of its German population. Moreover, any *Anschluss* with Germany was prohibited. The non-German portions of the old empire either became independent (Hungary), part of the new state of *Yugoslavia* (Bosnia-Herzegovina, Dalmatia, and Slovenia), or were incorporated into existing states (Bohemia and Moravia to Czechoslovakia, Bukovina to Rumania, Galicia to Poland, and South Tyrol to Italy). At a blow, the treaty confirmed the end of the ancient *Austrian Empire*—which had been teetering since its defeat in the *Seven Weeks' War* in 1866 and the subsequent *Ausgleich* which formally converted it into the Austro-Hungarian Empire—and that Austria had become a minor power. *See also war guilt clause.*

St. Helena. A British possession in the South Atlantic. *Napoleon* spent his second *exile* there from 1815 until his death in 1821. Examination of a hair sample (his corpse lies embalmed in the Invalides in Paris) performed in the 1980s suggested that someone might have slowly poisoned his food with arsenic, probably his personal valet rather than the British.

St. Kitts (Christopher) and Nevis. Discovered by *Columbus* in 1493, these islands were colonized by Britain, which settled them in 1624 as a trading base and to grow tobacco. France sought possession of the islands until its defeat in the *War of the Spanish Succession* in 1713. In 1882 Britain abolished the Nevis parliament and joined it to St. Kitts. The territories were part of the Leeward Islands Federation, 1871–1956, and then the *West Indies Federation,* 1958–1962. They became *associated states* with Great Britain in 1967, and fully independent in 1983, with Nevis enjoying limited *autonomy.* They supported the *invasion of Grenada* by the United States and OECS. The islands have similar populations, largely composed of the descendants of black *slaves.* Nevertheless, in 1998 a majority of Nevis's 4,000 or so voters voted yes in a *referendum* on *secession* from St. Kitts. However, the tally fell just shy of the two-thirds majority constitutionally required to break the *union.*

St. Laurent, Louis (1882–1973). Canadian statesman. Minister for external affairs, 1946–1948; prime minister, 1948–1957. Strongly anti-Soviet, he was a supporter of the formation of *NATO* and Canadian-U.S. defense cooperation in *NORAD.* He led Canada into the *Korean Conflict* and agreed to build the *St. Lawrence Seaway.*

St. Lawrence River/Seaway. In the sixteenth through eighteenth centuries the St. Lawrence was a scene of prolonged and violent conflict. Along with the southern gateway of the Mississippi, it was a main route into the interior of North America for traders, explorers, and military expeditions. France controlled the mouths of both rivers until the *Peace of Paris* (1763), which transferred *Québec* to English control. The St. Lawrence was charted for the *Royal Navy* by *James Cook*, 1768–1771. The Seaway, a vast system of locks and canals connecting the commercial centers of the *Great Lakes* with the Atlantic *trade routes*, was a joint construction venture of Canada and the United States, 1954–1959. It is today administered by both powers.

St. Lucia. An eastern Caribbean island ceded to Britain by France as part of the settlement of the *Napoleonic Wars* at the *Congress of Vienna*, 1814–1815.

It was given *autonomy* in 1967 as an *associated state*, and *independence* in 1979. It supported the *invasion of Grenada*.

St. Petersburg. It was founded as the new Imperial Russian capital by *Peter I (the Great)* on May 16, 1703, to serve as his "window on the West." Double shifts of 20,000 conscripted laborers were employed, under armed guard, and nobles were ordered by the thousands to relocate there and build stone houses at their own expense. The city was intended to serve as a more open northern port than Archangel, which was frozen shut much of the year. The rigors of its construction went some way toward laying a basis for official police power in Russia, as Peter insisted on regulation and punishment for the least offense, from littering to failing to clear snow from in front of buildings. For 200 years this Petrine city served as the political and cultural capital of the Russian Empire (1703–1917). The *St. Petersburg Soviet* was established there in 1905. Its name was changed to Petrograd in 1914, to make it sound less German. The *Petrograd Soviet* then proved key in the events of the *Russian Revolutions of 1917*. The name was changed again, to Leningrad, in 1924 by the *Bolsheviks*, and it ceased to be the main Russian capital, which moved back to Moscow, the old capital of the Muscovy tsars and seat of the *Kremlin*. Leningrad was defended valiantly during a *Nazi* siege which lasted nearly 900 days (December 1941 to January 1944) and led to widespread *famine*, cannibalism, and one million deaths. At the behest of its population it was renamed St. Petersburg in September 1991, just before the collapse of the *Soviet Union*.

Suggested Reading: W. Bruce Lincoln, *Sunlight at Midnight: St. Petersburg and the Rise of Modern Russia* (2001).

St. Petersburg Conference/Declaration (1868). *See just war tradition; prohibited weapons.*

St. Petersburg Soviet (1905). Its precise origins remain murky, due to conflicting claims (or blame) for its creation which resonate still in Russian politics. Even so, it seems to have arisen fairly spontaneously from Workers' Unions, and then was aided and joined by professional revolutionaries. It first met in October and was chaired by the *Mensheviks*. It came increasingly under the influence of the more radical socialist intelligentsia, including the *Bolsheviks* and the then still-independent revolutionary *Trotsky*. It was emulated by smaller *soviets* in more than 50 provincial cities and some rural areas. Its real importance lies not in 1905, but in the precedent it set for a revival of the soviets in 1917, with all that meant for Russians, the subject peoples of the *Russian Empire*, and later the world at large. *See also Russian Revolution, 1905.*

St. Pierre et Miquelon. The two largest of a group of small islands off *Newfoundland* which form an *overseas department* of France. Overlapping *Exclusive Economic Zone* claims, especially regarding *fish* stocks, led in the 1980s to diplomatic controversy and even some comically pretentious *saber rattling* by Canada toward France.

St. Vincent and the Grenadines. Discovered by *Columbus* in 1498, possession was disputed by Britain and France until the *Seven Years' War (1756–1763)*, during which the islands were seized by Britain. They became an *associated state* in 1969, and independent in 1979. They supported the *invasion of Grenada*.

STABEX. "Stabilize Exports." Created under the *Lomé Conventions*, this agency seeks to stabilize export earnings from certain key commodities. It established a *compensatory financing* fund paid into by *European Union* members which makes *soft loans* or grants credits to *ACP Nations* when commodity prices fall below set trading levels. *See also* COMPEX.

stability. (1) In *economics*: When an economy is productive and growing within a steady range for a sustained period, without wide fluctuations in the *business cycle*. (2) International: When the *Great Powers* in a given period, or *regional powers* in a given region, accept the existing *balance of power* and work to preserve it. (3) In politics: When a *regime* seems safe from any fundamental change or challenge, either because it enjoys *legitimacy* with most of the population or because it is effective at repression.

stabilization program. After borrowing passes the *First Tranche*, the *International Monetary Fund* (IMF) may decide to impose certain conditions on further borrowing which aim at stabilizing a national economy so that repayment is a real possibility. Such programs vary from *state* to state, but they usually share three main components: (1) *devaluation* of the national currency to cheapen *exports*, earn *foreign exchange*, and improve the *balance of payments*; (2) cuts in government spending to curb consumer demand, decrease *inflation*, and boost domestic staple producers; and (3) price liberalization through cuts in consumer *subsidies* and elimination of *price controls*, even on staples, in the hope this will stimulate domestic production while lowering government expenditures. This program was designed for application to *OECD*-type economies, where it had great success. It enjoyed less success or favor in the *Third World*, where it was often unevenly applied, exports suffered from *inelasticity* of demand, and cheapness did not so much increase volume of exports as lower revenues.

"stab in the back." An accusation by the far right in Germany holding that by signing the *Armistice* the *liberal* and *socialist* politicians of the *Weimar Re-*

public, and the Jews, but not the *Reichswehr*, lost *World War I*—in short, that the German Army had been "stabbed in the back" as it had stood, unbowed and undefeated, in foreign fields. That was patent nonsense, of course: the Reichswehr had in the summer of 1918 refused to fight any more offensive battles on the *western front* and then had been thrown back by a great *Allied and Associated Powers* counteroffensive. Yet the accusation had plausibility for troops who in July 1918, just before the second *Battle of the Marne*, had stood astride one-third of Russia, much of the *Caucasus*, and the *Baltic States*; were across the Italian frontier and within shell-shot of Paris; and who with their allies controlled all the *Balkans* and much of the *Middle East*. All that was really a great chimera: Austria and Turkey were both exhausted and collapsing, and the gains in Russia depended on the outcome on the western front. Most important, the German Army was clearly beaten in the west by September 1918, was in headlong retreat, and had whole units which no longer obeyed orders to fight. Finally, it was the Reichswehr, in the enlarged form of *Hindenburg* and *Ludendorff*, who told the *kaiser* and the civilians in Berlin to *ask for terms*. All that notwithstanding, the *Nazis* and other rightists made much of this bitter thesis, feeding off the wounded *nationalism* of millions of soldiers (and their families) who had not themselves surrendered or felt defeated. Partly to avoid a repeat of this myth, at the *Casablanca Conference* the *Allies* of *World War II* demanded *unconditional surrender* from Nazi Germany and agreed on its prolonged military *occupation* after the war. *See also mutilated victory.*

staff officer. One who works in a headquarters, helping higher-level, senior command officers with administration, battle plans, and logistics. *See also line officer.*

stages of growth. (1) A general idea that *economies* progress from less advanced to more advanced levels of *development*, organization, and sophistication. (2) An argument about *modernization* of the *Third World* based on *capitalism* and scientific *technology* and modeled on the Anglo-American experience with *industrialization*. It was made most forcefully and famously by the economist W. W. Rostow in his influential book "The Stages of Economic Growth" (1960). Rostow said that economies progressed to the point that *takeoff* (toward sustained *growth*) occurred. He identified five stages along the path to a "mature economy": traditional (subsistence), transitional (preparation for takeoff), actual takeoff, progress toward maturity, and finally arrival at full maturity as an industrial, consumer society. *See also dirigisme; Marxism; sustainable growth.*

stagflation. The combination of slow or stagnant economic *growth* with high *inflation*. This occurred on a wide scale in the early 1970s, in the wake of the *oil shocks* and *Vietnam War*, and led to *beggar-thy-neighbor* policies and *protectionism*.

stagnation. When economic *growth* falters as production fails to expand. It is attended by rising unemployment, business failures, and also rising public debt due to increased social welfare spending occasioned by higher unemployment rates.

stalemate. A military outcome in which no side is the clear victor. When this occurs, the immediate *postwar* settlement may lead to a *peace* which is merely a period of disguised rearming and refitting for *war*. Or it may help both sides recognize the futility of further attempts to win a disputed point by force. For example, after the effective stalemate of the *Russo-Japanese War*, Russia and Japan reached a series of secret accommodations dividing *Korea* and *Manchuria*, the very *territories* over which they had fought so bitterly and bloodily in 1904 and 1905. *See also defeat; victory.*

Stalingrad, Battle of (September 5, 1942–January 31, 1943). Stalingrad was the largest of the many Soviet cities named for the great tyrant, *Josef Stalin*, who ruled Russia with the mailed fist of the *NKVD* and the firing squad, and who fought there during the *Russian Civil War*. (It had been called Tsaritsyn; after Stalin it would be renamed Volgograd.) The German and Russian high commands both chose to emphasize the symbolic importance of this sprawling, mostly wooden, industrial city which spanned the Volga and threatened the flank of the German armies sent to conquer the Caucasus. Stalin gave the order, "Not one step backward!" *Hitler*, too, would refuse a request by his commanders to permit a fighting retreat. And so neither side gave *quarter* in this battle of bloody and unmerciful *attrition* which raged around, through, and over the city for five awful months, scattering or squashing its population like so many disturbed ants. Much of the fighting was hand-to-hand. As logistics ultimately became the decisive factor, the tide slowly turned in favor of the Soviets, who had shorter *lines of supply*. The German Sixth Army, under General Friedrich von Paulus (1890–1957), asked Hitler for permission to retreat but was ordered to stay and fight. *Göring* boasted that the *Luftwaffe* could resupply the *Wehrmacht* in Stalingrad, but it failed miserably to do so, and the men of Sixth Army were encircled and progressively slaughtered. With 100,000 already dead, only 110,000 frozen men lived to see von Paulus disobey his orders and *surrender*.

Hitler had just promoted von Paulus to field marshal, knowing that no officer of that high rank had ever surrendered in German military history—in short, in the hope that he would commit suicide. Paulus made propaganda broadcasts for the Soviets during the remainder of the war and was finally released from a Soviet prison in 1953. He spent his last years as a lecturer to the East German military. Most other Germans who surrendered at Stalingrad were not so lucky: after years of hard imprisonment and *forced labor*, nine out of ten German *prisoners of war* never returned to Germany. In 1992 it was revealed that Russian casualties at Stalingrad were far higher than previously reported, at a staggering 1.3 million. Still, for the first time in the war, German soldiers had tasted bitter defeat on the *eastern front*. After Stalingrad, a cruel worm began to burrow in the mind of the German nation that it could, after all, lose the war. For that reason and others, the battle was one of the great turning points in *World War II*, and indeed in the history of the twentieth century.

Suggested Reading: Antony Beevor, *Stalingrad* (1998).

Stalinism. Of or like the political style and system of *Josef Stalin*, to wit: rigid, absolute control from the top; centralization of all *decision making* and *collectivization* of the economy; political paranoia, accompanied by *purging* and *liquidation* of perceived enemies; strenuous efforts at thought control; a doctrinaire *ideology* which yet shifts with tactical needs; crushing all internal party and bureaucratic resistance with a hammer of textual manipulation pounded on an anvil of orthodoxy; and all supported by a pervasive *cult of personality*. See also *five-year plans*; *kulaks*; *purges*; *show trials*; *totalitarianism*; Yezhovshchina.

Suggested Readings: G. Gill, *Stalinism* (1990); Roy A. Medvedev, *Let History Judge* (1989); Robert C. Tucker, ed., *Stalinism* (1977); Chris Ward, *Stalin's Russia*, 2nd ed. (1999).

Stalinization. Forcible conversion of a social and political order to make it conform to the principles and practices of *Stalinism*. See also *de-Stalinization*.

Stalin, Josef Vissarionovich, né Dzhugashvili (1879–1953). "Koba." Soviet dictator. A poor Georgian by birth, an *Orthodox* seminarian by training, and a Great Russian nationalist and *Marxist-Leninist* by conviction. His childhood was brutal. His father, an alcoholic shoemaker who was killed in a street brawl in 1890, beat the boy often. His mother fawned on him, however. At age 14 she sent him for training as an Orthodox priest. Stalin hated the seminary and by age 19 was already an active organizer in revolutionary politics. He was brutal in his later family life, too: he drove his wife to suicide, his son to drink, and his daughter Svetlana into *exile* from Russia. In 1903 Stalin joined the *Bolshevik* faction of the Russian Social Democratic Party, where his code name, Stalin, meant "Man of Steel" (he had many code names, including Koba, an initial nom de guerre taken from a hero of Georgia's nationalist past). Twice sentenced to exile in *Siberia* for political crimes, Stalin still rose steadily within the party. He returned from exile when the *Russian Revolutions of 1917* broke out. He was commissar for nationalities, 1921–1922, and general secretary, 1922–1953. Using his control of the Party administrative apparatus Stalin forced *Trotsky* out of office in 1927, and out of the country in 1929. He later had him killed. Stalin eliminated lesser rivals by murder or *purge*, clearing the way for an unchallenged personal dictatorship.

Stalin's policies were *socialism in one country*, centralized *five-year plans*, and forced *collectivization*. In the process, he called for "liquidation of the *kulaks* as a class," created a deliberate *famine* in Ukraine which consumed millions of lives, and launched the *Yezhovshchina* and other terrible purges. Western estimates placed the total number of Stalin's non-wartime victims at 20 million dead, a claim much criticized in certain circles during the *Cold War* for supposed gross exaggeration. In 1989 official Soviet figures placed the number of victims at closer to 40 million dead, 1929–1953. In either case, the numbers make Stalin the greatest mass murderer in human history, surpassing even *Hitler's* staggering body count; only *Mao's* figures may yet rival Stalin's, depending on what the still-closed Chinese *archives* one day reveal. In foreign relations, Stalin first followed a policy of *isolationism*, but then sought to form a front with the United States against Japan after 1931. He did not achieve that goal, but did *normalize relations* in 1934. That same year he took the Soviet Union into the *League of Nations*. Stalin also tried to form a front against Hitler, but *Neville Chamberlain* and other Western leaders showed little interest or trust in his diplomatic feelers. After the *Munich Conference*, Stalin moved to negotiate a separate *spheres of influence* deal with Germany. The *Nazi-Soviet Pact* divided Eastern Europe between the two great tyrants, with Stalin attacking Poland on September 17th, by prior agreement with Hitler. He then attacked Finland, without Hitler's agreement, on November 30th. In 1940 he fulfilled the terms of the pact by annexing the *Baltic States* and parts of Rumania.

Stalin ignored warnings about *Barbarossa* from the West, and from his own *intelligence* and *frontline* troops. He was stunned by the fact and the fury of the German onslaught. With *Lend-Lease* and his own factories behind the Urals, he recovered and directed the Soviet *counterattack* and drive to *victory* in *World War II*. To do so, Stalin compromised many revolutionary principles to the expedient needs of the wartime moment, reintroducing *military ranks*, opening the doors of the churches, and appealing to Russian *nationalism* as a more powerful motivator than communist *internationalism*. He negotiated at *Tehran*, *Yalta*, and *Potsdam*—probably in bad faith—with enormous consequence for the course of the *Cold War*. Just as Stalin had done immediately before World War II, right after it ended he abandoned his earlier caution and pursued an opportunistically aggressive foreign policy. From 1944 to 1949 he set up *puppet regimes* throughout Eastern Europe, while at home he maintained the *Red Army* at wartime strength and speeded the Soviet *nuclear weapons* program.

Stalin then grew cautious again, refusing at first to be drawn into the *Korean Conflict*, but eventually backing and supplying North Korean *aggression* and encouraging *Mao Zedong* to intervene directly, and himself supplying thousands of pilots and *MIGs*—disguised by Chinese markings—and pilots to fly them. Stalin made himself the center of a grotesque *personality cult*, and by all accounts was an utter paranoid constantly planning *purges* to forestall plots, real or imagined. For this he was denounced by *Khrushchev* in his *secret speech* (1956). Despite all the terror and bloodshed of his reign, decades later—after the fall of the Soviet Union—Stalin still retained a following among old true believers in the army and *Communist Party*. Nor did Stalin always receive from historians the full moral disapprobation his extraordinarily monstrous life and acts deserved. *See also Alexander I; biological warfare; Ivan the Terrible; Peter I; Stalingrad; Stalinism; Stalinization; de-Stalinization.*

Suggested Readings: Alan Bullock, *Parallel Lives: Hitler and Stalin* (1991); Robert Conquest, *Stalin: Breaker of Nations* (1991); Vojtech Mastny, *The Cold War and Soviet Insecurity* (1996); R. C. Raack, *Stalin's Drive to the West, 1938–1945* (1995); Robert C. Tucker, *Stalin as Revolutionary* (1974); Robert C. Tucker, *Stalin in Power* (1990); Adam Ulam, *Stalin: The Man and His Era* (1989).

standard. A *norm* which may be adopted as a binding *rule* into a *treaty*. For example, a treaty which agrees to use *jus soli* as the basis for *naturalization*.

standard of living. An *indicator* of social and economic *development* which attempts a statistical representation of the grade of material wealth, and comfort and concomitant well-being, enjoyed by individuals, classes, or whole societies. It is a complex, composite measure of the availability of *consumer goods* and *public goods*, individual *purchasing power*, and access to social resources such as education and employment.

standard operating procedure (SOP). The pattern of routine implementation by which a bureaucracy carries out decisions made at a higher level. Its implication for foreign policy is that SOPs may skewer decisions in ways unforeseen by policy makers, especially when routine procedures are applied in crises.

standards of civilized behavior. Moral standards from which a *derogation* may be asserted only if a fair claim is substantiated that the requirements of war-making warrant such a waiver. This is a main pole of tension in the *just war tradition*; the other is *necessities of war*.

standing army. "Militum perpetuum." The permanent, professional army of a nation which is not *demobilized* in times of peace. It is usual not to count in this regard *reserves* or *militia* or potential (as opposed to actual) *conscripts*. The development of standing armies is historically quite recent, and parallels the rise of centralized monarchies and *nation-states*, starting in England and France during the *Hundred Years' War* (1337–1453). In 1444 the French king Charles VII (1403–1461) finally brought roving *mercenary* bands under control and into his pay, after which all officers were in service to the crown. The next step was taken by the Dutch Army during the *Eighty Years' War* (1566–1648). Dutch success against Imperial Spain encouraged imitation, which came in the form of the new Swedish Army of *Gustavus Adolphus* during the *Thirty Years' War* (1618–1648). Across the *English Channel*, also numbering among the first of the modern and standing armies was the republican force raised against the king by *Oliver Cromwell* during the First and Second English Civil Wars (1642–1649). From c. 1650 to 1700, virtually every power in Europe moved to adopt standing armies, in part to reduce reliance on untrustworthy mercenaries, but more to concentrate military power under the *sovereign*. By 1713 *Louis XIV* had put 400,000 men into the field. However, such forces could not be sustained by the eighteenth-century state, and for much of the remainder of that century standing armies of the European Great Powers fell back to 40,000 to 60,000 on average. Further afield, as well as deeper into the past, the *Ottoman Empire* had a standing force based on an imperial model in form of the *Janissaries*. The *Mamluks* in Egypt were also a permanent force, and Imperial China maintained a standing army dating to the *Song dynasty*. And of course, the *Roman Empire* and the *Byzantine Empire* maintained large, permanent armies. The *Mongols* under the great khans were not much more than an army with a people attached to it. The *samurai* of Japan were a permanent force, too, but were organized on *feudal* rather than modern professional lines. The development of professional standing armies after c. 1560 was a critical component of the early modern *revolution in military affairs* and contributed to subsequent world dominance by various European powers. The importance of a standing army was also clearly demonstrated by the rise of *Prussia* over the course of the seventeenth and eighteenth centuries, due in large measure to the determination of successive dukes and kings to maintain the highest quality standing army but also to husband its use. *See also banner system*; *Frederick the Great*; Junkers; *Philip II*; *Shaka Zulu*.

Standing Committee. *See Politburo.*

Stanley, Henry Morton, né Rowlands (1841–1904). British explorer. A lifelong adventurer, he served as a volunteer in the *Confederate* Army and later in the U.S. Navy. He accompanied Charles Napier to Abyssinia as a journalist. In 1869 he was sent to "find Livingstone." He dallied, witnessing the opening of the *Suez Canal* before traveling to Turkey and India. Finally, in 1871 he left Zanzibar to find Livingstone at Ujiji, and with him explored the *Great Lakes* region. From 1874 to 1877 he made the second ever European crossing of Africa. He started with an exploration of then little-known Uganda in 1874, and then traced the Congo River to its outlet at the sea. In 1877 he traveled down the Lualaba with *Tippu Tip*. His real importance emerged after 1879, when he was hired by King *Leopold* of Belgium to map the territory of what is now *Congo* preparatory to its conquest by the king, an act which set off the *scramble for Africa*. Stanley attended the *Berlin Con-*

ference (1884–1885) and was active in *pacification* campaigns in the Congo Free State in the late 1880s.

stare decisis. "Standing for things already settled." The general legal rule that courts should apply prior legal *judgments* (precedent) in cases of a similar nature. In *international law*, this rule is only weakly applied. *See also persuasive precedent; transformation.*

START I and Start II. *See Strategic Arms Reduction Treaties.*

"Star Wars." *See Strategic Defense Initiative.*

Stasi. The *secret police* and main *intelligence agency* of *East Germany*. At its height, it had 95,000 full-time agents, twice as many as the *Gestapo* had to torment four times the population. Its massive archive of files destroyed lives and careers even after 1989, as they revealed who had collaborated by informing on family, friends, workmates, even spouses. It kept files on over half the population and used one citizen in seven as informers. It sought what it called "decomposition," or blocking citizens from any activity or free association not controlled by the state. It nearly achieved this, by quiet but blanket coercion, intimidation, blackmail, and *torture*. Its hated headquarters was stormed by an angry crowd after the *Berlin Wall* fell in November 1989. Public release of Stasi files caused a moral and political dilemma in Germany after reunification, since so many former East Germans (and also some West Germans) were implicated by the files in its unsavory activities. *See also HvA.*

state. The quintessential modern political entity which occupies a defined *territory*, has a permanent *population*, and enjoys *independence* and *sovereignty*. Where once states had significant competitors for ethnic, tribal, and political loyalties, they increasingly came to dominate world affairs over the past 500 years. It is a common, but basic, mistake to consider the modern state as *the* state, for states in some form have, of course, existed for millennia among most (though not all) premodern cultures and societies. Small states, more powerful ones, and great empires have from time to time existed in India, China, the Middle East, Europe, West Africa, and Central and South America well before the invention of the modern state. In their modern form, however, states were shaped principally by early modern European history and most clearly defined by *international law*. They became clearly recognizable and ever more dominant within the *international system* during the sixteenth century, as they performed better than any other form of organization the two essential tasks of international politics: keeping *order* and making *war*. By the end of the eighteenth century—through the mechanisms of *empire* and *colonialism*—states had displaced virtually all other, more traditional, forms of political organization, except for parts of Amazonia, Australia, and south central Africa, where some *stateless* societies were extant.

The modern states then collectively defined only their characteristic institutions as legitimate under international law, a claim they maintained through a long-asserted and subsequently progressively implemented legal monopoly on the use of force, and mainly by their superior organizational capability. Together, the states have divided the continents and regulated the seas, the sky, space, and all of teeming humanity, and determined ownership and/or stewardship of all other species as well. They have made themselves the sole political entities with a legal right to wage *war* (with minor exceptions) or maintain *standing armies* and navies—although it is an open secret that if some sub-national or other nonstate group wages an "illegal" war successfully, by which it secures a defined territory and population, it will ultimately be accepted as a new state, *de facto*. Even then, to gain all the rights and incur all the duties (as defined under *state obligations*) of statehood one must receive *recognition* by other states, *de jure*. By 2000 there were nearly 200 recognized states in the international system, ranging from the surely absurdly small (8,000 people), to the possibly unmanageably large (1.2 billion). Of those nearly 200 states, fully one-half had fewer than eight million people (the equivalent of a single large city) and a *GNP* less than $10 billion—about the size of the national economy of Luxembourg. "State" is also used as a synonym for a government or *regime*. *See also associated state; border; boundary; city-state; civil war; colony; community of nations; dependency; empire; extinction; failed state; frontier; global commons; microstate; Montevideo Convention; nation; nation-state; occupation; protectorate; quasi state; secession; segmentary state; self-determination; state creation; state obligations; state succession.*

state capitalism. (1) A version of *capitalist* development with a high degree of government ownership of the nation's *factor endowments*, and centralized direction and regulation of *capital* and *labor* markets. (2) A fashionable, but inaccurate, dismissal of the *Marxist* origins of the *Soviet* system, by those who still wish to avoid the intellectual discomfort which would be occasioned by an attempt to reconcile Russia's dingy historical experience with *Marx's* sparkling theoretical elegance. *See also dirigisme.*

statecraft. The art of conducting the public affairs of a *state*. Specific to *international relations*, it is a near synonym for *diplomacy* but more clearly implies the direction of domestic policy and *war* as components of foreign policy, as well as peaceful *negotiation*. *See also foreign policy.*

state creation. The process of founding new *states* from the dissolution of *empires*, via *secession*, or through the *extinction* of previous *international personalities*. *See also successor states.*

State Department. *See Department of State.*

state funeral. *See funerals.*

state immunity. From antiquity, *sovereigns* were regarded as immune from harm in their persons, if not their office, and treated as such by each other. In the Middle Ages in Europe, personal immunity was extended to *ambassadors* and then to state property, for the same, pragmatic reasons of avoiding *reprisals* and facilitating communication. It is now established tradition that diplomatic communications are inviolable in law, with the exception, in practice, of *espionage* against them. It is also accepted that diplomatic ships cannot be boarded or *embassies* entered or searched. Also, diplomats and embassies are free of taxation, may not be sued, and are not subject to civil or criminal prosecution. Efforts have been made to restrict this right, yet it is still widely regarded as absolute. Still, administrative restrictions have grown more common during recent years. In general, a distinction has been drawn between activities related to diplomatic functions and the private activities of diplomats. One example: In 1993 the United States began using administrative sanctions and penalties to limit the abuse of immunity from civil fines by which many diplomatic missions obstructed traffic and parking in New York and Washington. *See also* persona non grata; *Vienna Conventions.*

state interest. Anything declared by a given *state* to be of foreign policy concern to it. *See also vital interests.*

statelessness. When an individual is without *citizenship* of a *state*. Historically, persons, *tribes*, and even whole peoples were stateless, existing (happily or not) in prestate patterns of social and political organization. This was true for pre-Roman Britain and medieval Ireland, tribal Germany, aboriginal Australia, *Inner Asia*, most of the Americas, New Guinea, and Africa. The expansion of the state system, which originated in Europe in the fifteenth and sixteenth centuries, meant that most areas of the globe came under state *jurisdiction* by the mid-nineteenth century, although large parts of Africa remained stateless until being absorbed later in the century into European colonial empires. International *human rights* law now declares against statelessness, so this condition of legal limbo affects mostly *refugees*, and even in their case is supposed to be temporary. While some subject peoples, such as the *Kurds* or exiled *Palestinians*, may seem to be stateless, legally speaking their membership "belongs" to one state or another. *See also Fridtjof Nansen; nationality; Westphalian system.*

statelet. An informal term of no legal significance, used to describe small territories which are not legally *sovereign* but are instead nominally part of a larger country, but which nonetheless often act as if they enjoyed sovereign status and powers. Modern examples include *Chechnya*, *Dagestan*, and *Ossetia*.

state obligations. *States*, as *sovereign* members of the *community of nations*, have legal obligations toward, as well as rights against, other members of that community. They must abstain from illegal *intervention* and *subversion*. They are required not to pose a threat to international *peace* and good order, to abjure the use or the threat of the use of *force* as a means of settling *disputes*, and in general to conduct their affairs in *good faith* and in accordance with the accepted principles and *rules* of *international law*. When judged to have injured an *alien*, they must agree to pay *damages*. If members of the United Nations, they have additional duties under the *Charter of the United Nations*: they must advance the aims declared in the charter, including *nonintervention*, *noninterference*, and (paradoxically) respect by all for fundamental *human rights*; they must not aid any state targeted by the United Nations for *sanctions* or other penalty or enforcement mechanism; they must take measures to pre-vent *counterfeiting* of coins, bills, or postal stamps of other states; and they must refuse to *recognize* any *territorial* acquisition obtained through *aggression*, such as Iraq's *annexation* of Kuwait. Other, quite extensive duties may be voluntarily incurred through *consent* to particular *treaties*. Of fairly recent vintage, and deriving mainly from treaty obligations, is an emerging inter-national duty not to unduly harm the environment of the *global commons* or pollute the air, soil, or water of adjacent states or states with which one's ships, planes, or spacecraft (when they crash, often indiscriminately spewing radioactive materials) may come into contact and pollute.

state of emergency. A suspension of normal legal rights and privileges in the interest (or just the name) of *national security* and restoration of order. Such decrees may accompany *insurrections*, as in Sri Lanka in the 1980s or, more problematically, Canada in 1970; serve to repress dissent, as in the Philippines under *Marcos* or South Africa under *apartheid*; or in response to natural dis-asters, mostly to re-establish public order and deter looting. *See also martial law*.

state of nature. A hypothetical condition posited by political theorists as a means of illustrating arguments about the origins and nature of social and political formations prior to the invention of governments or structured social relations. It presumes perfect freedom for the individual (in *Rousseau's* famous depiction, "Man is born free, yet everywhere we find him in chains"). Opti-mists about human nature, such as Rousseau, tend to view the subsequent construction of social and political order as necessary but also as suffocating natural freedoms, and they seek ways of lightening the heavy hand of the *state* on human affairs. For these thinkers the state is the main obstacle to recovering human freedom and happiness, and for the most *radical* it is an unnecessary evil. Pessimists, such as *Hobbes*, refer to the state of perfect human freedom by another name: *anarchy*. In the Hobbesian view, life in the state of nature is "solitary, poor, nasty, brutish and short" in which "all war against all" ("Bellum omnium contra omnes"). The construction of a *unitary state*, or *Leviathan*, and closely regulated social relations, however crippling of personal freedoms, is the only means to a modicum of personal security. Government is an evil entirely necessary if one is to escape the greater dangers of unadulterated liberty.

state of war. *De facto*, an actual condition of *armed hostilities* between or among *nations*, with or without legal form and character. *De jure*, a legal condition of armed hostility which engages the *laws of war*, and historically was begun and ended by the formal legal acts of a *declaration of war* and a *peace treaty*. Whether or not a state of war exists in the classical de jure sense, the 1949 *Geneva Conventions* come into effect once an armed conflict exists, which was not the case with the 1929 conventions or the *Hague Conventions*. In an innovative move, in 1994 Israel and Jordan ended a 46-year legal state of war with a joint *declaration* before negotiating a peace treaty. *See also Korean Conflict; Treaty of Versailles.*

statesman/stateswoman. (1) In polite company: any person responsible for the conduct of *diplomacy*, or other public affairs, at the highest levels of *decision making* and political responsibility. (2) In the judgment of *history*: a person who conducts diplomacy or other public affairs wisely.

states' rights. In the United States, all rights not vested in or forbidden to the federal government by the Constitution, which are thus retained by the separate states of the union. "States rights" was the rallying cry of the *Confederacy*. Later, it was the slogan used by *isolationists* who objected to *ratification* of United Nations covenants or other "entangling alliances," and behind which southern racists defended segregation. *See also nullification.*

state succession. In *international law*, the doctrine that a state following another on the same *territory*, or part thereof, inherits all or some duties and *treaty* obligations of the state which has suffered *extinction*, including the set of *rules* and procedures used to bring state succession to pass. Generally, state succession occurs via mutual agreement (*decolonization*), violent seizure of *independence* by a *dependent* territory from a controlling (colonial or imperial) power, *annexation* or *cession* of territory by agreement between controlling powers, formation of a *union* or *conquest*, and *subjugation*. There are two basic types: (1) Universal: When one state completely absorbs the *international personality* of another by conquest, merger, or *federation*, the rights and obligations of the absorbed state(s) totally end. (2) Partial: This is more complex. While public property passes forward without *compensation*, private property rights are unaffected. Foreign *debt* may cause trouble, as *successor states* are often reluctant to assume old burdens, particularly if the new state has a *revolutionary* government which rejects the *ancien régime* as illegitimate. Bilateral treaties remain in effect only by agreement of the new power, but *servitudes* are not generally affected. In 1978 and 1983, the International Law Commission of the United Nations drafted two conventions governing the treaty and property aspects of state succession. *See also Czechoslovakia; devolution agreement;* pacta sunt servanda; *Soviet Union;* uti possidetis; *Yugoslavia.*

state system. *See international system.*

state terrorism. (1) When a state provides logistical or other support to terrorists to further certain foreign policy goals. In the 1990s the United States designated certain states as purveyors of *terrorism* (among them, Iran, Iraq, Libya, Syria, and Yemen), and in several cases applied unilateral *sanctions* against them. In 1993 the United Nations applied mandatory sanctions against Libya for its refusal to *extradite* two suspects in the bombing of a Pan Am airplane over Lockerbie, Scotland, which killed hundreds. These sanctions were lifted in 1999, after Libya surrendered two of its *intelligence* officers suspected of planting the bomb, who then faced trial in The Hague. Afghanistan under the *Taliban* was also sanctioned, and most states also refused *recognition* to that *fundamentalist* regime. (2) The use of repressive police power within a state, or when, as in the practice of *ethnic cleansing*, it directly seeks to intimidate a *civilian* population for political purposes. *See also terror.*

station. An *intelligence* unit, usually set up in a foreign trade mission, *embassy*, or some other legal cover, which "runs" *legal* and/or *illegal agents*.

status mixtus. A condition of muted hostility and conflict existing somewhere in the twilight zone between real *peace* and open *warfare*. This notion is not yet an accepted part of *international law. See also* inter bellum et pacem; *quarantine; reprisal.*

status quo ante bellum. Political, social, and economic conditions before a war. Psychologically, and often politically and diplomatically as well, after a great war there is almost always a broad public desire to attempt to return affairs to their prior state. This phrase captures that impulse.

status quo post bellum. Changes in political, social and economic conditions resulting from a war. When a return to the prior state of affairs is impossible, whether due to lingering enmities, damaged lives and property, or a new distribution of power resulting from a war, a diplomatic settlement may seek to lock the outcome of the war into a *treaty* or political arrangement.

status quo **power.** Any state, but usually a *Great Power*, which seeks to preserve the political and *territorial integrity* of a given *peace* settlement or established *balance of power*. The cardinal values of such a state or policy are prudence, stability, and a desire to preserve the existing international order. The main vices are resistance to demands for political or diplomatic revision based on claims for greater international justice, a reluctance or inability to adjust to shifts in the balance of power, and great touchiness about issues of *prestige*. The antonym is *revisionist power*. *See also revolution.*

stealth technology. In general, stealth technology seeks to make aircraft (or *submarines* or ships) virtually undetectable through use of nonreflective materials and unusual angular designs which reduce profile on enemy imaging systems. In designer jargon, stealth aircraft have "low observables" in their contrails, infrared, noise, optical visibility, radar, and smoke. A crude version of stealth technology was developed by Germany for use in *World War II*, to conceal the conning towers of *U-boats* from Allied radar. Another early form was used in American *U-2* spy planes. Stealth technology was a closely guarded secret until late in the *Cold War*. It was first widely seen in public in the late 1980s: the "stealth fighter," or F-117A and its sister craft, was first used in combat during the U.S. invasion of Panama in 1988. It was employed extensively during the *Gulf War*, where it proved highly effective and suffered no losses. An F-117A was later shot down over Bosnia, however. Stealth technology is extremely expensive: due to cutbacks which reduced the expected *economies of scale*, but mainly due to the sheer complexity of the technology, the U.S. B-2 *strategic bomber* cost over two billion dollars each (in 2001 dollars).

Stern Gang. Founded in 1939 by radical *Zionists* led by Abraham Stern (1907–1942), it employed *terror* tactics against the British in *Palestine* and against the *civilian* Arab population. Some members later merged into the Israeli Defense Force. Those who showed themselves incapable of adjusting to peace were repressed. *See also Count Folke Bernadotte; Yitzhak Shamir.*

Stimson Doctrine. *See Hoover-Stimson Doctrine.*

Stimson, Henry L. (1867–1950). U.S. statesman. Secretary of war, 1911–1913, 1940–1945; governor of the Philippines, 1927–1929; secretary of state, 1929–1933. In 1927 he mediated an uneasy *peace* in Nicaragua (the Tiptitapa Agreement). He tried to alert *Hoover* and others to the rising danger of Japanese *aggression*, but due to the opposition and influence of *isolationists* was unable to elicit more than the rhetorical commitment of the *Hoover-Stimson Doctrine* to the "*territorial integrity*" of China." He attended the *London Naval Disarmament Conference*. In 1939–1940 he strongly backed *Franklin Roosevelt's* preparedness measures and supported *Lend-Lease*. Although he had previously served three *Republican* presidents, he was appointed secretary of war by Roosevelt. During *World War II* he supported most administration policies, including the decisions to bomb *Hiroshima* and *Nagasaki*. He also served *Harry Truman* briefly in 1945.

stock. Ownership of a corporation or other enterprise, normally divided into shares represented by certificates (stocks) which may be bought and sold on the *stock exchange*.

stock exchange (stock market). An organized and regulated marketplace where *capital* may be raised for a variety of purposes, by the exchange of *stocks* and bonds (securities). Major stock markets are located in Frankfurt, Hong Kong, London, New York, Paris, Tokyo, and Zurich. Of rising importance are markets in Beijing and Seoul, and many others exist among numerous financial centers in nearly every country which is already a *market economy*, or is moving in that direction. A "quote-driven" market is one where buy-sell prices are displayed by "market makers" (for example, NASDAQ), whereas in an "order-driven" market previous trades are used to calculate the price spread (for example, NYSE).

stock market crash. *See Black Tuesday.*

STOL (short takeoff and landing). A genus of military aircraft designed to operate without full-length airfields. They were used highly effectively by Britain during the *Falklands War*, in the *Gulf War*, and by other powers in other conflicts.

Stolypin, Peter (1862–1911). Russian minister of the interior, 1906; prime minister, 1906–1911. He savagely repressed mass peasant unrest in the wake of the *Russian Revolution* (1905), then introduced privatization of landholding which "wagered on the strong" among the peasants by allowing consolidation of small strips into larger farms. His reforms opened the way for entrepreneurial peasants (the *kulak* class) to rise. However, he was a vicious anti-*Semite* who also encouraged a new wave of bloody *pogroms* which were destructive of lives, property, social order, and economic good sense. He would not agree to U.S. concerns about treatment of Jews. A year after his assassination that willfulness led to abrogation of a 72-year-old *commercial treaty*, a breach in ambassadorial appointments, and the nadir of relations between the United States and tsarist Russia, nearly on the eve of *World War I*.

storm troopers. The *Sturmabteilung* (SA), or any private *militia* or gang of political street thugs comparable in its character and makeup to the SA. *See also death squads;* Freikorps; Schutzstaffel (SS).

straight baseline. Since *UNCLOS I* (1958), an increasing number of *states* have taken advantage of a variation on the *baseline* method of determining the *territorial sea*, which was first designed to accommodate the peculiarities of Norway's deep coastal indentations (the fjords). Instead of hugging the shoreline, the straight baseline method permits states to determine the outer limit of their territorial waters from a straight line drawn across the outer points of land, following the overall contour of the shore. This has the effect of marginally increasing the area of the *high seas* claimed as home waters for highly irregular coastlines. However, it greatly increases the territorial sea when applied to more normal coastlines; for instance, in the claims made by Canada for its *Arctic* shore, or by Libya in drawing the so-called *line of death*.

strait. A natural passage, not a canal, which links two seas, oceans, or other large bodies of water. The 1982 *UNCLOS III* agreement recognized more than 100 international straits through which ships of all *flags* have a right of passage.

Strait of Hormuz. A narrow *strait* connecting the *Persian Gulf* and the Gulf of Oman. Three small islands there were seized by Iran in 1971. In 1980 Iraq attacked to regain these islands and additional territory, beginning the *Iran-Iraq War*. Any effective *blockade* of the strait would shut down tanker traffic from the *Gulf States*, as well as from southern Iraq and Iran.

Straits Question. The long dispute among the *Great Powers* over passage of *warships* through the *Dardanelles* and *Bosphorus*. Throughout the nineteenth century successive tsars sought to compel the *Ottoman Empire* to close the straits to all warships save Russian. The British wanted the straits kept closed to the Russian *Black Sea Fleet*, bottling it in its home port and denying Russia access to the Mediterranean. In 1833 Russia signed a *secret treaty* ("Unkiar Skelessi") with Turkey granting Moscow all it sought. This gain was reversed by the Straits Convention of 1841 agreed to by Austria, Britain, France, Prussia, and Russia. The issue contributed to tensions leading to the *Crimean War*. In the *Treaty of Paris* (1856), the straits were closed to all warships in times of peace, and the Black Sea was *demilitarized*. The arrangement so disadvantaged Russia it could not last, and so was amended in 1871, and again at the *Congress of Berlin* (1878), to account for Russia's remilitarization of the Black Sea. The changes permitted transit to all navies if the sultan was unable to defend the status of the narrows. The straits were closed by Turkey (with the support of Russia) to Britain in 1885, and to Russia (with British help) during the *Russo-Japanese War*. After *World War I*, which led to the *extinction* of the Ottoman Empire, the *Treaty of Lausanne* demilitarized the straits but allowed free passage of all warships when Turkey was at peace, provided any force sent north was not larger than the Soviet Black Sea Fleet. The *Montreux Convention* of 1936 was even more advantageous to the Soviet Union. During the *Cold War*, Soviet naval traffic through the straits was closely monitored by *NATO*.

Suggested Reading: Barbara Jelavich, *The Great Powers, the Ottoman Empire, and the Straits Question, 1870–1887* (1973).

Straits Settlements. Three colonies run by the *British East India Company*—of Penang, *Singapore*, and Malacca (Melaka)—were united under company administration in 1826, under the name Straits Settlements. In 1858 it was taken over by the British government, and in 1867 became a *crown colony*. Labuan was separated from 1906 to become the fourth territory in the Straits Settlements. The colony was broken up, 1946–1948, with Singapore becoming a separate colony, while Penang and Malacca were attached to the Federation of Malaya. In 1963 *Malaya* joined with *Sabah* and *Sarawak* to form *Malaysia*.

stratagem. Any artifice, plan, scheme, or ruse designed to surprise or deceive an enemy or opponent.

Strategic Air Command (SAC). The command structure within the U.S. Air Force responsible for *strategic* (including nuclear-armed) bombers and *ICBMs*. The Soviet equivalent in the early years of the *Cold War* was Long Range Aviation. *See also strategic bombing.*

Strategic Arms Limitation Talks and Treaties (SALT I and II). Two sets of nuclear *arms control* agreements during the *Cold War*, spanning a decade of negotiation: (1) SALT I: Talks between the United States and the Soviet Union were held, 1969–1972, aimed at heading off a full-scale *arms race* in defensive weapons systems, expansion of the *Partial Test Ban Treaty*, and placing limits on offensive *strategic nuclear weapons*. An *Anti–Ballistic Missile, Missile (ABM) Treaty* was agreed, and agreement was reached limiting the number of *launchers* each side could deploy. However, setting the limit above extant levels and not including a ban on *MIRVs* undercut the entire agreement by subsequently encouraging a buildup to the permitted limits and thereby rendering each launcher far more threatening than in pre-MIRV days. (2) SALT II: More talks were held, 1973–1979. They focused on resolving the MIRV problem and on placing a permanent cap on *strategic weapons*. A second treaty was signed, but it ran into opposition within the U.S. Senate even before the Soviets invaded Afghanistan, due to concern over Soviet *adventurism* in the Horn of Africa and other regional conflicts, and a sense that the United States had slipped behind Russia in the nuclear arms race. With the Soviet invasion of Afghanistan in December 1979, *Jimmy Carter* withdrew from Senate consideration a treaty he knew had no chance of achieving the required two-thirds consent. Even without formal acceptance, however, both sides observed most of the provisions of the agreement through the 1980s, when the changing dynamic of U.S.-Soviet relations made a *START* agreement possible.

Suggested Reading: Philip Towle, *Arms Control and East-West Relations* (1983).

Strategic Arms Reduction Treaties (START I and II). Agreements to reduce, not just limit, the nuclear arsenals of the United States and Soviet Union, and from December 1991, the *successor states* of Russia, Ukraine, Belarus, and Kazakhstan. It was delayed by Soviet insistence on including French and British *nuclear weapons*, to which Paris and London would not agree; but Moscow ultimately accepted a bilateral deal. (1) START I: negotiations began in 1982 looking to make major cuts in *superpower* nuclear arsenals. An agreement was reached in 1991. *Verification* was through *national technical means*. START I's precise reductions were quickly overtaken by events in the early 1990s, as each side made unilateral cuts to their arsenals, which meant the treaty needed an overhaul just to keep pace. (2) START II: It was signed by *George H. Bush* and *Boris Yeltsin* in January 1993. In combination with START I, it committed the United States and Russia to a reduction of stocks of strategic nuclear *warheads* from roughly 22,000 each to 3,500 each by 2003, with all MIRVed missiles on land to be destroyed and SLBMs reduced significantly. That gave Russia formal nuclear equality with the United States despite the fact that it would have had to reduce anyway, given its grave economic distress. Yeltsin indicated that if Ukraine failed to ratify START I, Russia would not be bound by either START treaty. Ukraine repeatedly promised to ratify, but held off until it extracted funding and other concessions from the United States. That threatened U.S. *adherence* to START II, as the U.S. position was premised on Russia becoming the sole nuclear successor to the defunct Soviet Union. Talks then began about a possible START III.

strategic bombing. Targeting the general war-making capacity of an enemy state, including by *World War II* not just industrial plant but also workers' homes and civilian morale, for destruction from the air. This doctrine grew out of revulsion for the experience of *trench warfare* during *World War I*, in which massive amounts of war matériel and millions of men were destroyed without bringing about decisive *victory* for either side, at least not quickly. It became clear that it was vital to destroy the means of resupply to such giant armies and not just the armies and navies themselves. At its most ambitious this idea was touted as a substitute for direct combat. However, World War II produced countermeasures (effective day and night fighters, radar, anti-aircraft guns, and dispersed and underground production) which severely limited the effectiveness of strategic bombing. Even more limiting was the inaccuracy of most mid-century bomb sights, a fact which restricted tactics to *carpet bombing* of city-sized targets. Once "strategic fighters" (long-range fighters equipped with additional external fuel tanks, which could be dropped as combat commenced) were developed, the *Luftwaffe* was chased from the skies over Germany. By 1943, Allied bombing of Germany—in its concentration of German effort in defense, and its impact on war production—constituted a *second front* in a very real sense. Subsequently, no country has relied on the idea of strategic bombing as an alternative to ground warfare more than the United States. During the *Cold War*, reliance on a military doctrine in which strategic bombers were a main deterrent threat led the United States to build a vast fleet of B-52s for use as a strategic (*nuclear* and *conventional*) bomber. These were heavily used as conventional bombers during the *Vietnam War*, and again in fewer numbers during the *Gulf War*. They were supplemented by the more advanced B-1 bomber in the 1990s. The B-2 was an even more fabulously expensive, intercontinental bomber which employed full *stealth technology*. Some critics worried it might be so effective it would be perceived by the Soviets as a *first-strike* weapon. Budget cuts reduced actual production to just 20 planes, raising per-plane costs to over two billion dollars each. The Soviets deployed a medium-range bomber, the so-called Backfire Bomber, which was controversial during the *SALT II* negotiations because Western *intelligence* thought it had a secret strategic (that is, intercontinental) capability. *See also air power; thousand bomber raids; stealth technology.*

strategic considerations. Anything related to a nation's overall *power*, whether economic, military, or political.

Strategic Defense Initiative (SDI). "Star Wars." A prematurely ambitious *ballistic missile defense* (BMD) research program announced by *Ronald Reagan* in 1983. It originally sought to launch a research program into a total defense against *strategic nuclear weapons* and *ICBM* systems. It called for a complex, integrated structure of nonnuclear, land, air, and space-based defensive systems, most of which were yet untested, designed, or developed. SDI proposed to intercept missiles and *warheads* at all four stages of their flight path: boost, postboost, midcourse, and terminal. At each stage, enemy weapons which "leaked" through the previous stage would be further "attrited." In this early version, SDI was widely criticized as being unrealistic, even unscientific, and that it would be destabilizing of *MAD* since it would encourage an offensive arms race in an effort to retain one's deterrent posture. (One of the more curious features of the policy debate was how some longtime critics of *Cold War* arrangements for mutual *deterrence* suddenly found *assured destruction* a virtuous doctrine when faced with the prospect of SDI research.) SDI proponents responded by reducing the promised scope to a defense of the U.S. nuclear deterrent force, arguing that would reinforce MAD, not undermine it. Others—notably *Edward Teller*—went far beyond the original conception, and in the opposite direction from Reagan's original vision, to suggest a new reliance on space-based *nuclear weapons* platforms: Teller proposed the addition of space-based, *charged particle beam* weapons (with the beams to be generated by narrow channeling of the explosive forces of a *hydrogen bomb*) as the best defense against multiple warheads and dummies. Research continued at decreasing levels of funding for 10 years. In 1993 the *Clinton* administration scaled SDI back to a limited, strictly ground-based and non-nuclear BMD program but continued to fund research and testing. *George W. Bush*, however, immediately increased research in BMD, making it a strategic priority.

strategic doctrine. The complex of fundamental military and geopolitical assumptions and *targeting doctrine* which make up a country's war-fighting strategy.

strategic envelopment. An offensive military doctrine in which one side seeks to draw out, engage, and destroy the armed forces of the other side in a *battle of decision*, or sequence of such battles. It was conceived by *Helmuth von Moltke* as involving a gigantic and continuous maneuver, from *mobilization* through to final victory, in which the strategic aim is to outflank the enemy on both sides, enveloping his forces, and then destroying them.

strategic forces/weapons. Long-range forces/weapons which respond directly to the highest command levels in a war, and which permit the high command to strike at targets of strategic value to an enemy; that is, those targets constituting the main sources of an enemy's military and/or political power which are necessary to its prosecution of the war. Examples of modern strategic forces include a *blue water navy*, *ICBMs*, *submarines*, and long-range bombers. The need to focus on the underlying sources of military power and not just its forward deployments and manifestations, of targeting the war-making system and productive capacity of an enemy state so as to eliminate its ability to replace battlefield losses, was perhaps the primary lesson taught by war in the industrial age. *See also air power; strategic bombing.*

strategic materials. Foodstuffs, minerals for making high-tech alloys, *oil*, and all other items necessary to run a modern *war* or *economy*. *See also strategic stockpiles.*

strategic nuclear parity. *Essential equivalence* in the *nuclear weapons* systems of the Soviet Union (now Russia), and the United States, or some other pairing of *nuclear states*, as measured in *launchers*, *warheads*, or *megatonnage*.

strategic nuclear response. The launch of *strategic nuclear weapons* in response to an enemy's *first strike*. A synonym for *retaliation*. *See also second strike.*

strategic nuclear weapons. *ICBMs* capable of striking multiple targets on a different continent, whose launch would signal Armageddon. The technical line between *strategic* and *tactical* is blurring, as once short-range weapons systems increase in strike ability.

strategic plans. Those concerning the ability to strike an enemy at the sources of its military or political power, and relating to the game of ruse and discovery of military *stratagem*.

strategic stockpiles. Reserves of *strategic materials*, especially *oil*, considered vital for national economic or military performance in case of *war* or *boycott* or *embargo*.

strategic studies. An academic and military discipline which seeks to identify the patterns and possibilities of varying *strategic* interests and policies, with particular attention to how states achieve long-term political goals.

strategic triad. The three launch modes of *nuclear weapons*: land-based missiles, ship- or *submarine*-based ICBMs, and *strategic bombers*. During the latter part of the *Cold War*, having all three was said to reinforce *deterrence* between the United States and the Soviet Union. France maintained an independent triad system into the 1990s, when it commenced redeployment to a primarily submarine-based deterrent. *See also* Force de Frappe.

strategy. A grand plan designed to obtain an ultimate military or political goal, by whatever means—political, economic, military, or diplomatic; as in "it was *Bismarck's* strategy to keep Germany preeminent by isolating France." Strategy in this, its fullest sense refers to the art and science of using the largest-scale *capabilities* of a nation to secure its defense, advance its *foreign policy* goals, or win its *wars*, by the best possible means (those least wasteful of lives, treasure, or other *national interests*). Strategy thus involves a great deal of planning over a long period and employs the full resources of the military, *intelligence*, and *diplomacy*. A narrower sense of the term is the employment of armed force to reach specific military objectives in a war, as in "the United States adopted an island-hopping strategy in the Pacific war." Clausewitz defined strategy in this narrow sense, as "the theory of using battle for the purposes of war." *See also geostrategic; grand strategy; tactics.*
Suggested Readings: MacGregor Knox et al., eds., *Making of Strategy* (1994); Edward Luttwak, *Strategy* (1990); P. Paret, *The Makers of Modern Strategy* (1986).

strel'sty. "Musketeers." A class of non-noble servicemen employed by the *tsars* as the traditional guard of their household. They owed the crown military service rather than taxes, and could not own *serfs*. In wartime, they were organized into armed units which formed the core of a tsarist army that otherwise comprised masses of ill-trained peasant *conscripts*. Many strel'sty were

Old Believers who became ever more alienated from the tsarist court after the *schism* within the Russian *Orthodox Church* following the reforms of Patriarch Nikon (1605–1681). Four regiments of strel'sty revolted in 1682, butchering some 40 officers and unpopular government officials inside the *Kremlin* whom they believed were exerting "German influence." The 10-year-old *Peter I* was deeply affected—an uncle was among those murdered. In 1689 Peter believed the strel'sty were coming to kill him and fled Moscow. Age seventeen, he returned the next month to depose his older sister, Sophia, as regent and assume his duties as tsar. He later crushed the *boyars* and strel'sty, who revolted again in 1698 while he was abroad, slaughtering many (some stories relate that he personally cut off the heads of several). From 1698 though 1700 he conducted strel'sty *show trials* and public executions: nearly 1,200 died; another 600 were flogged and deported to do forced labor in Siberia. Peter banished all strel'sty from Moscow after symbolically shaving their beards to show there was no going back to their old, *Slavophile* ways. He replaced them at the Kremlin with a hand-picked *praetorian guard*, an elite which evolved into two of Russia's most famous regiments: the Preobrazhensky and Semenovsky Guards. The banishment order backfired, however, by spreading discontented strel'sty around the empire. In 1705 Old Believer strel'sty in Astrakhan rebelled, massacring Russian troops and government officials.

Stresa Front. At a conference held April 11–14, 1935, Britain, France, and Italy agreed to oppose *Hitler's* declared intent to rearm Germany. They also stated their support for *Locarno* and their opposition to any *Anschluss* with Austria. The front was soon gutted, however, by the separate *Anglo-German Naval Agreement* and then by the *Second Abyssinian War*, which began later that year. Never again before *World War II* would these former *World War I* allies stand together against Hitler.

Stresemann, Gustav (1878–1929). German statesman. Chancellor, 1923; foreign minister, 1923–1929. Domestically, he repressed armed rebellions in Saxony and Thuringia, and put down the *Beer Hall Putsch* of *Adolf Hitler*. Internationally, he sought accommodation on Germany's western border. He advocated meeting Weimar Germany's commitments under *Versailles*, and thereby achieved a further reduction in *reparations*. He accepted the *Locarno Pact*, led Germany into membership in the *League of Nations* in 1926 (which Hitler disavowed in 1933), agreed to the *Dawes* and *Young Plans*, and secured American loans necessary to German economic recovery. He was awarded the *Nobel Prize* for Peace in 1926 (with *Aristide Briand*). He was less accommodating concerning the German lands lost to Poland in the peace settlement, but could not and did not take forceful action to recover them. Policy toward the Soviet Union was among his principal concerns and led to secret military cooperation, but circumstances permitted no major breakthroughs.

Stroessner, Alfredo (b. 1912). General and dictator of Paraguay, 1954–1989. As a young officer he fought in the *Chaco War* (1932–1935). He led a *coup* in 1954, took the presidency in a rigged election, and set up a strict, even brutal, regime. Backed by the army, he stayed in power by proclaiming anti-*communism* in domestic and foreign affairs and practicing "Stronismo," a policy of fear-or-favor, severe punishment or great reward. He essentially governed on behalf of commercial and landowning interests, but carried out enough in the way of social programs to stave off outright revolt. However, in 1989 he lost his grip on Paraguay as a movement toward representative government swept across Latin America, and the United States placed more overt emphasis on *human rights* concerns in its regional *aid* policies. Toppled by a coup, he fled into *exile* in Brazil.

structural adjustment loans. Money provided, usually by the *International Bank for Reconstruction and Development* or the *International Monetary Fund*, to see a country through a period of basic economic reform, or adjustment of the *structure* of its economy. Such loans are given in accordance with certain *macroeconomic* policies specified by the lender. *See also conditionality; stabilization program.*

structural determinism. When a *theory* concludes that the *structure* or *architecture* of a given international system is what solely decides the behavior of the states ("units") in the system, and thus unduly dismisses the role played by *free will* or the *volition* of decision makers. *See also dependency theory; Marxism; neo-realism.*

structuralism. *See dependency theory; world system theory.*

structural realism. *See neo-realism; realism.*

structure. (1) In logical and historical argument: the underlying forces and considerations which may largely predetermine outcomes, regardless of the efforts of individual *agents* to impress their will on the course of events. (2) In economics: the complex relations among the three main sectors of an economy: the *primary sector*, *secondary sector*, and *tertiary sector*. (3) In international relations *theory*: the shape of the *international system* as defined by the "distribution of power" among the states. Some theorists simply assume an underlying absence of structure, or *anarchy*, at the most basic level of interstate reality. Others employ descriptions which focus on the number of concentrations of power (*unipolar, bipolar, multipolar*). *Marxists* and *dependency theorists* see the system as determined by class relations and an international division of labor. The *classical school* refers to the *balance of power* and *international society*. *See also causation; systems analysis.*

"struggle for power." A classical *realist* phrase, associated closely with Hans J. Morgenthau, suggesting that no matter what the final ends states or other political *actors* aim at in political interaction, the struggle to increase one's relative *power* is always the immediate aim. This thesis has sometimes been misconstrued as arguing that the struggle for power in politics among nations is an end in itself, and then roundly condemned as amoral or immoral. Yet the phrase does little more than state the truism that all political actors strive to increase their *influence*, so that they may better achieve ("maximize") their interests. What the medium of power is (money, *prestige*, votes, or brute force) depends on specific circumstances, just as what interests are advanced depends on specific players, their values, constituencies, wit, wisdom, or stupidity.

Sturmabteilung **(SA)**. "Storm Battalion." Also known as "Brownshirts," from the color of their *paramilitary* uniforms, which were first acquired as surplus-issue uniforms for German troops in Africa during *World War I*. The SA grew out of the *Freikorps* movement. They were used by various Nazi leaders, most especially *Hitler*, to carry out political thuggery and murder during the 1920s and 1930s. In 1933 the SA reached a strength of 400,000, or four times that permitted the *Reichswehr* under the *Versailles Treaty*. The ambition of its leader, the brutal radical Ernst Röhm (1887–1934), was for the SA to displace the *Wehrmacht*. During the *Night of the Long Knives* Röhm was murdered on Hitler's order, partly because as a homosexual he displeased the German officer corps, but more to eliminate him as a potential rival to Hitler himself and to appease the Wehrmacht by emasculating the SA as an alternative military force. As Hitler resumed unchallenged control of the party, the SA devolved into a tamed force which fell under the shadow of the far more sinister *Schutzstaffel* (SS), to which the SA willingly but also unwittingly had given birth in 1926. Unlike the SS and the *Sicherheitsdienst* (SD), which were declared criminal organizations at *Nuremberg*, the SA was not later judged to have been a criminal organization, although it had always counted many criminals among its membership.

subcontinent. The great peninsula of Southwest Asia comprised of modern Bangladesh, Bhutan, India, Nepal, Pakistan, and Sikkim; also the large adjacent island of Sri Lanka, and numerous small coastal islands. *See also Deccan.*

subconventional war. Alternate military *jargon* for *unconventional warfare*. *See also guerrilla war; partisans; resistance.*

subject. Someone under the *sovereign* control of a monarch or state. In monarchies, subject is still often used in preference to the historically republican connotations of *citizen*.

subjects (in international law). Any entity with *international personality*, but mainly the *states*. See also *object*.

subjugation. The complete military suppression of an enemy, entailing utter destruction of all *state* apparatus and *extinction* of the *international personality* of the *defeated* state, following suppression of all armed and civil resistance, at home and abroad. This goes further than *conquest*, which it must follow. See also debellatio.

Sublime Porte. "Bâbâli" ("High Gate," or "Gate of the Eminent"). A diplomatic and *protocol* term for the government of the *Ottoman Empire*, taken from the High Gate that led into the central government complex in *Constantinople* which included the courts of justice, the foreign ministry, and from the seventeenth century also the palace of the *Grand Vizier*. See also *Foggy Bottom; Forbidden City; Kremlin; Quai d'Orsay; Whitehall; White House.*

submarine. A submersible *warship* capable of navigation and weapons firing underwater, and of *espionage*. The first-ever submarine attack was launched by American rebels against the British during the *American Revolution*, using a one-man vessel called the Turtle. It was unsuccessful. A nine-man crew of a moderately less primitive *Confederate* submarine, the Hunley, rammed a powder charge into a *Union* warship on February 17, 1864, becoming the first submarine to sink an enemy ship (the U.S.S. Housatonic). That act led to its own loss with all hands. It was raised in 2000, and the remains of its crew buried onshore in 2001. American-Irish *Fenians* built the first effective submarine, used to attack British shipping in the *Great Lakes*. Well into the twentieth century subs were viewed by most naval strategists as a curiosity, or at best as reconnaissance boats, rather than the *strategic weapons* they ultimately proved to be. France was the first major power to build a fleet of submarines, bitterly known to French seamen as "iron coffins" because their gasoline engines fouled the air supply and asphyxiated some crews. Germany built U-1, the first *U-boat*, in 1906. Britain, too, built submarines, to keep pace in the *Anglo-German naval arms race*, but the focus of the *Royal Navy* remained on its great *Dreadnought* fleet. Still, Britain had far more subs than Germany (74 to 28) when *World War I* began. The U-boats quickly proved effective as *commerce raiders* and even as a threat to British *capital warships*. Meanwhile, the High Seas Fleet stayed bottled into port both before and after *Jutland*. It was Germany's *unrestricted submarine warfare*, recommended in 1917 in a vain but close-run effort to choke off Britain's economy and food supply, which brought about U.S. *belligerency*.

Submarines were neglected again between the world wars by navies enamored still of *battleships*. They truly came into their own during *World War II*. Once again, German surface raiders were bottomed by the British (1939–1940) or chased back into sheltered harbors, but the Kriegsmarine's U-boat fleet inflicted enormous damage on the *merchant marine*. The U-boat assault in the *Battle of the Atlantic*, and in the Mediterranean and North Sea, was not beaten back until mid-1943 by a combination of *convoys* making use of breakthroughs in *signals* intelligence to avoid known locations of *wolf packs*, advances in sonar, mass production by the Allies of destroyers and corvettes to escort the convoys, ocean minefields, land-based *bombers*, and deployment of large numbers of small escort *aircraft carriers*. In the Pacific, American (and some British) submarines also launched unrestricted warfare and took an even more massive toll of Japanese shipping, effectively limiting Japan's merchant marine and naval resupply to home waters by late 1944 and strangling the Japanese economy to the point of impending defeat. Although comprising just two percent of the U.S. fleet, submarines accounted for 65 percent of all destroyed Japanese shipping.

During the *Cold War*, American and Soviet (and later, also British and French) nuclear-powered, *missile*-bearing submarines emerged as the most powerful weapons yet constructed by the twisted genius of humanity. On the other hand, for that reason they also were the principal instrument of late Cold War stability and mutual *deterrence*, since they provided *assured destruction*. Each nuclear missile boat represented a multi-billion-dollar investment, reached the size of World War II *battleships*, and was capable of independent delivery of many dozens of nuclear *warheads*, so that a single *boomer* contained more destructive power than was expended by all the armies, air forces, and navies of all nations in the prior history of warfare. At its height, the Soviet Navy deployed about 500 submarines, to the 130 of the U.S. Navy. The Americans lost two nuclear submarines at sea; the Soviets lost at least seven. In 1968, in the largest *covert operation* since the *Manhattan Project*, the United States used a hollowed-out ship and hoist system to try to raise a Soviet nuclear submarine lost in the deep Pacific. They got the wreck near the surface, when it cracked and the pieces sank. Nearly 10 years after the Cold War ended, the Russian Navy lost its newest missile boat with all hands, the Kursk. *See also Anglo-German Naval Agreement; hunter-killer; innocent passage; London Naval Disarmament Conference; Nine Power Treaty; Alfred von Tirpitz; Trident.*

Suggested Readings: Erminio Bagnasco, *Submarines of World War Two* (2000); J. B. Hervey *Submarines* (1994); *Jane's Fighting Ships* (1897–); Sherry Sontag and Christopher Drew, *Blind Man's Bluff* (1998).

submarine-launched ballistic missile (SLBM). *ICBMs* based on and launched from *boomers*.

submission. A brief to an international court.

subnational forces. Cultural, economic, and social groups or forces within existing national societies which threaten their political disintegration, or major reorganization on nontraditional lines. This became a topic of much contemporary research focus with the breakup of the Soviet Union, Yugoslavia, and Czechoslovakia in the 1990s, and the rising number of *failed states* in Africa. *See also ethnic cleansing; ethnic group; guerrilla warfare; nationalism; rising expectations; technology; tribe; secession; self-determination; separatism.*

subrogation. The assumption of an *extinct* state's rights and duties by a *successor state*.

sub-Saharan Africa. Africa below the *Sahara Desert*, distinguished ethnically and culturally from the Arab and Berber nations to the north. This is the preferred form, especially among the politically correct, for what once was called "Black Africa," even though the diverse peoples of the Sahara itself have for many centuries played a key and integral role in the development of North Africa and of the *Sahel* and *sudan*.

subsidiarity. The idea that policy making in a *union of states*, such as the *European Union*, should take place at the lowest level commensurate with effective governance.

subsidiary. A firm owned and controlled by another firm, often a foreign-based *multinational corporation*.

subsidies. (1) Payments made in support of domestic producers which bring no *hard good* or *service* in return, but are made anyway for political (e.g., *protectionism*) or *strategic* (e.g., to preserve defense industries) reasons. (2) Payments made by larger states to smaller ones, to sustain a friendly regime in power or to underwrite other foreign policy objectives. For example, massive Soviet subsidies to Cuba kept the *Castro* regime afloat; U.S. subsidies to Israel and Egypt facilitated the *Camp David Accords*. (3) Payments made to allies in wartime to sustain their armies in battle and uphold their will to fight. For instance, *William Pitt* (the Elder) used subsidies to sustain *Frederick the Great* in the *Seven Years' War* (1756–1763). His son, and other British prime ministers, did likewise to heavily underwrite the various alliances they assembled to wage the *Napoleonic Wars*, marrying British industrial and commercial wealth to the larger reserves of manpower in Austria, Prussia, and especially Russia.

subsistence economy. One in which the basic economic activities of the majority of people consist of agricultural labor to produce food crops rather than *cash crops*, industrial manufactures, or *services*.

substantiation. The formal *justification* offered for an international legal claim.

subsystem. *See* (1) *region;* (2) *systems analysis.*

subversion. In law and political perception, the effort by one *state* through *covert action, disinformation, propaganda,* or funding *guerrillas* or *terrorists,* to undermine, destabilize, or promote *insurrection* or *treason* against another state or its government. *See also* Comintern; *Radio Free Europe.*

succession of states. *See state succession.*

successor states. *States* which emerge on *territory* where a prior *international personality* has suffered *extinction.* For example, the following arose in whole or in part from the extinction of larger states in the course of the twentieth century: (1) *Austro-Hungarian Empire,* 1918–1920: Austria, Czechoslovakia, Hungary, Poland, Rumania, and Yugoslavia (and part of Italy). (2) *Ottoman Empire,* 1918–1922: Turkey, Egypt, and most modern Arab states, although several were delayed on the path to independence by transit through the *mandate* system of the League *of Nations.* (3) *Soviet Union,* 1991: Armenia, Azerbaijan, Belarus (Byelorussia), Estonia, Georgia, Kazakhstan, Kirghizstan, Latvia, Lithuania, Moldova (Moldavia), Russia, Tajikistan, Turkmenistan, Ukraine, and Uzbekistan. (4) *Czechoslovakia,* 1992: Czech and Slovak Republics. (5) *Yugoslavia,* 1991– : Bosnia, Croatia, Macedonia, Slovenia, Serbia and Montenegro. *See also capitulations; state succession;* uti possidetis.

sudan (French, *soudan;* Arabic, *al-sudan*). That part of Africa lying south of the arid and drought-stricken *Sahel,* but north of the tropical forests of Central Africa.

Sudan. Five times as big as France, Sudan is physically divided by the White and Blue Niles, which join at Khartoum, the city founded by *Mehemet Ali* in 1824. It is greatly diverse, with more than 50 ethnic groups (tribes) and 600 identifiable linguistic groups. About half its population, located mostly in the north, are Arab and Muslim. Ancient Sudan was known as *Nubia* to the Egyptians, the fabled land of the "Queen of Sheba." For centuries it was heavily influenced by the *Coptic Church* and other Egyptian institutions. When most Egyptians converted to *Islam,* northern Arabic Sudanese closely tied to Egypt followed suit. The ethnically African south remained animist and Christian. That ethnic and religious division is fundamental to Sudan and has led to prolonged religious conflict at the center of Sudanese life. Between 1300 and 1500 Sudan was overrun by nomadic Muslim tribes, fragmenting the older Christian kingdom of *Alwa.* Central Sudan was controlled by the *Funj Sultanate,* a cavalry-based military power, from the sixteenth through the nineteenth centuries. From c. 1760–1790, internal revolts wracked and weakened the Funj; they were overthrown by Mehemet Ali in 1821–1822. Egypt then cruelly exploited Sudan, extracting military slaves and other produce for decades, and driving south into Ethiopia in the 1870s. Southern Sudan thus became a prime source of supply for the late Arab *slave trade*, a fact which continues to bedevil its relations with the Arab-dominated northern portion of the country. It was as well itself a center of slave-raiding parties which forayed as far south as Buganda and Bunyoro (in modern Uganda).

Northern Sudan revolted against Anglo-Egyptian control under the *Mahdi* and his successor, "Khalifa" Abdallah, 1881–1898. They inflicted a severe defeat on the British under *Charles Gordon*. Meanwhile, from 1885 to 1898, southern Sudan rebelled against Muslim control. In 1898 the north was conquered, by *Kitchener*, at *Omdurman*, and Sudan was reorganized as an Anglo-Egyptian *condominium*. The south was not fully subdued until the 1920s. In 1924 the British governor was assassinated by an Egyptian nationalist, and London reacted by expelling all Egyptians from Sudan's military and bureaucracy. The British then instituted *indirect rule* and governed north and south separately for several decades. This inadvertently exacerbated historic regional differences. In 1951 Egypt abrogated the condominium agreement. The subsequent deterioration in Anglo-Egyptian relations, leading to the *Suez Crisis* of 1956, determined London on a course of rapid decolonization of Sudan.

Sudan thus became independent in 1956, years—even decades—before most observers expected it would. Within months, a military *mutiny* in the south caused by endemic ethnic and religious conflict propelled Sudan into *civil war*, which soon became chronic. In 1958 a northern military dictatorship under General Ibrahim Abboud increased persecution of southerners and northern Christians. In 1969 another *coup* brought General Muhammad Jaafar el Nimeri to power. He imposed a harsh military order by 1972, ending the civil war by granting southern *autonomy*, while introducing the *sharia* legal code in the north. In 1983 Nimeri extended Islamic law to the animist and Christian south, provoking a renewal of the civil war. He was overthrown in 1985 in a bloodless coup. Elections were held in 1986, but in 1989—just as the civil war looked about to end—a coup brought a militantly *fundamentalist* regime to power in Khartoum, under General Omar Bashir. It adopted policies of forced conversion and even *genocide*, which aggravated the horrors of civil war and the *famine* which had begun in 1983. The regime formally declared *jihad* its foreign and domestic policy.

Throughout the 1990s Sudan was accused by both Egypt and the United States of fomenting *state terrorism*, notably that purveyed by the *Muslim Brotherhood*. In 1992–1993 the military balance in the civil war shifted in favor of the north. The SPLA alliance of southern Christians and animists split, opening up a three-way conflict. The government, under Bashir, insisted that sharia must be applied to all Sudanese, of whom only 70 percent are Muslim. This drew in the *Vatican*, which wanted Sudan's 3.5 million Christians exempted. Other than human rights *nongovernmental organizations*, few spoke on behalf of Sudan's five million animists. A more moderate Muslim group failed to take power in an uprising in 1995, against a government which armed and supported Arab militia in conducting slave raids into the south akin to those of prior centuries. In 1997, facing a war-weary northern population and a country in which half the people had fled their homes, the radical Islamists in Khartoum hinted at self-determination for the south, to permit them to impose a still harsher Islamic regime in the north. The conflict deepened instead, aggravated by a major *oil* discovery in the south. By 1998 millions of southerners, Christian and animist alike, faced death from manmade *famine* and increased fighting. International pressure was building against the war when the *Clinton* administration fired *cruise missiles* into Sudan, targeting what it said was a *chemical weapons* factory in Khartoum. That gained unexpected sympathy for its pariah regime. By 2000 the civil war had claimed two million lives, making it the most deadly of Africa's postcolonial conflicts.

Suggested Readings: Y. F. Hassan, *The Arabs and the Sudan* (1967); P. M. Holt, *The Mahdist State in the Sudan, 1881–1898* (1958); Ann Lesch, *The Sudan* (1998).

Sudetenland. Before 1945, this was the ethnically German area of western Bohemia. It was part of *Czechoslovakia* from 1919. From 1933 to 1938 local *Volksdeutsche* organizations fronting for the *Nazis* lobbied for an *Anschluss* with the *Third Reich*. Although the Sudetenland contained the main Czech defensive fortifications and natural frontier, it was handed over to *Hitler* at the *Munich Conference* in 1938. After *World War II* it was returned to Czechoslovakia; two and a half million Germans were then expelled by the Czechs, the innocent alongside the guilty. After the reunification of Germany in 1989, the issue of compensation soured Czech-German relations. Also, *European Union* rules led to a slow resettlement of the region by the descendants of the expelled Germans, with their attendant historical claims for compensation.

Suez Canal. The great and vital canal across the Suez isthmus which connects the Mediterranean and Red Seas. It is 107 miles long. It was built between 1859 and 1869 by the controversial French engineer Ferdinand de Lesseps (1805–1894). Its opening, and a shift to steam from sail power, cut travel time from Bristol to Bombay to just three weeks from three months, greatly increasing trade as well as facilitating white settlement in parts of India and East Africa. In 1875 Britain bought a controlling interest in the Suez Canal Company from the khedive of Egypt. In 1888 a *convention* was agreed by the *Great Powers* declaring the canal open to all even in wartime. In practice, Britain denied access to its enemies in wartime and on occasion to the enemies of its allies as well, such as the Russians, who were refused passage for their Baltic fleet on its way to the *Battle of Tsushima Straits* with Japan. An *Ottoman* assault on the canal was repulsed by Britain during *World War I*. Its strategic importance contributed to heavy fighting in North Africa during

World War II. In 1956 the canal was *nationalized* by *Nasser*, unilaterally ending a long *servitude* on Egypt but also thereby precipitating the *Suez Crisis*. Egypt denied Israel access to the canal before 1967, when the canal was blocked by sunken ships from the *Third Arab-Israeli War*, after which opposite banks were held by Egyptians and Israelis. It was dredged, mine swept, and reopened after 1975 as part of the *Camp David Accords*. In 1980 it was widened and deepened to oblige larger modern ships.

Suez Crisis. President *Nasser* nationalized the Suez Canal Company on July 26, 1956, to claim its revenues to build the *Aswan Dam*, for which he had been refused Western loans. It was learned in London and Paris that Israel, for reasons pertaining to the origins of the *Second Arab-Israeli War*, was planning to attack Egypt. On September 1st Israel was informed that France would welcome a joint attack. From October 22 to October 24, British, French, and Israeli representatives met at Sèvres, where they agreed to intervene in follow-up to an Israeli advance to the canal under the pretext of separating Israeli and Egyptian forces in the canal area. Israel attacked on October 29th, seizing *Gaza* and sending tank columns deep into the *Sinai*. Two days later Britain and France piggybacked their attack onto the Israeli thrust, with the United Kingdom asserting a right to intervene in accord with the 1954 Anglo-Egyptian treaty. There was an immediate international outcry against the triple *invasion*, including fierce Soviet and American opposition. *Eisenhower* was especially angry at the distraction of world attention from the *Hungarian Uprising*.

The crisis became deadly serious when the Soviets threatened to use force to expel the invaders from its client, Egypt, and publicly threatened rocket attacks (which implied the use of nuclear weapons) on London and Paris: the Soviets were alternately hopeful that Suez would break up *NATO* and fearful that the crisis in Hungary would destroy the *Warsaw Pact*. Eisenhower decided that a Soviet move into Suez would have to be met by U.S. armed forces, and he worried that this latest *Cold War* crisis was escalating toward a nuclear confrontation. He made it patently clear that the United States vehemently opposed the invasion, and insisted Britain and France accept a UN proposal for a *peacekeeping* force interposed in the Sinai. All three invading countries were thus forced to cease military operations within a week. The British and French later withdrew in disgrace; both governments soon fell. Israel pulled back too, but kept the Sinai until 1957. It was the last time during the Cold War that either Britain or France tried to act as a *Great Power* in a globally strategic region without advance clearance from Washington. And it marked the entrée of the United States and the Soviet Union into the morass of Middle East politics, which meant dragging the Cold War as well into a region already suffused with conflict and animosities.

Suggested Readings: Diane Kunz, *Economic Diplomacy of the Suez Crisis* (1991); Keith Kyle, *Suez* (1991); William Louis and Robert Owen, eds., *Suez: 1956* (1989).

sufficiency. An idea introduced into U.S. *strategic doctrine* by *Richard Nixon*, in which a *first-strike capability* was disavowed, and research, development, and deployment aimed only at providing weapons sufficient to guarantee *deterrence*.

Sufism. *See shi'ia Islam.*

Suharto, Radan (b. 1921). Indonesian dictator, 1968–1998. He fought alongside the Japanese in *World War II*, then as a *guerrilla* leader against the return of Dutch rule, 1946–1949. During the attempted *coup* by the *Partai Kommunis Indonesia (PKI)* in 1965 he led the government forces that massacred as many as 600,000 suspected PKI members. He displaced *Sukarno* from power in early 1967, ending the *Konfrontasi*. He formally assumed the title of president the next year. He and his extended family immediately began building a corrupt financial and corporate empire. Under his leadership Indonesia moved to support the United States in the *Cold War* while still maintaining an official stance of *nonalignment*. It seized *East Timor* in 1975, after which Suharto's military conducted a sustained campaign of severe and violent repression which in the view of some amounted to near-*genocide*. Suharto also staked out an Indonesian claim to the *Spratlys*. Domestically, he tolerated little opposition to a rough, *authoritarian* style of government. He and his family and political cronies were thereby free to govern Indonesia as a *kleptocracy*, until the *Asian financial crisis* of 1998 led to massive popular unrest, and he was forced from office. After much delay, he was finally charged with corruption in 2000, but the charges were not pressed due to assertions that he was in failing health.

Sui dynasty (589–618). Following the *North-South Disunion* (220–589), China was reunited by a Xianbei aristocrat from north China, Yan Jian (Wendi), founder of the Sui dynasty. The *Buddhist* Sui intermarried with *Inner Asian* nomads, which greatly enhanced their military position by allowing them to tap into the raw military energy and cavalry organization of the nomads. They also inherited a strong northern China already united under the last of the Sixteen Kingdoms, and from this base they incorporated south China into their empire by direct conquest, 587–589. Under Wendi the famous *Confucian* bureaucratic examination and degree system began to develop. The tax system and Imperial Army were reorganized, mainly with an eye to centralizing control. The *Grand Canal* was also extended under the Sui, along with a network of additional canals under the Sui emperor Yangdi. However, Yangdi also attempted to conquer Korea, only to be repulsed with great loss, 612–614. This was seen by many Chinese to have lost the *mandate of heaven* for the dynasty, and it was overturned by a widespread rebellion inside China. The Sui were succeeded by the *Tang dynasty*.
  Suggested Reading: Arthur Wright, *The Sui Dynasty* (1978).

Sukarno, Achmad (1901–1970). Indonesian president, 1949–1968. He was imprisoned by the Dutch, 1929–1931, for his early political activity. He collaborated with the Japanese during *World War II*, but as Japanese resistance to the *Allies* collapsed across Asia he unilaterally declared Indonesian *independence* (August 1945). In 1949, after four years of *guerrilla warfare*, the Dutch finally accepted him as first president of an independent Indonesia. He hosted the *Bandung Conference* in 1955 but never emerged as a key leader of the *Nonaligned Movement*. As the economy declined, 1956–1965, his *authoritarian* tendencies came to the fore. In 1963 he began the *Konfrontasi*, which almost led to war with Malaysia. In 1965 he was partly pushed aside by General *Suharto*, who savagely put down an uprising by the *Partai Kommunis Indonesia*. He lost real power in 1967 but retained the title of president for about a year after that.

Sulawesi. *See Indonesia.*

Suleiman I (1494–1566). "The Magnificent." *Sultan* of the *Ottoman Empire*, 1520–1566. Immediately upon becoming sultan Suleiman launched a campaign of conquest against the surrounding Christian states in the *Balkans*. He conquered the Serbs, capturing Belgrade in 1521, and defeated the Greeks on Rhodes in 1522. The Hungarians first surrendered to him in 1526, then recanted. Although Suleiman expended vast amounts of blood and treasure to complete the conquest of Hungary, he was never able to do so. In the interim, he also attacked eastward, into Asia Minor and Persia. In 1538 he sent his navy westward to make war on *Venice*, threaten Italy, and raid the Mediterranean coast of Spain. He tried but failed to capture Malta. Suleiman repeatedly intrigued with European powers, taking advantage of the new division within Christendom occasioned by the *Protestant Reformation* and *Wars of Religion*. Suleiman was a lifelong patron of arts, culture, and building; his instincts were primarily imperial and martial, however. He met his end doing battle against the Hungarians in 1566.

sultan. Arabic: "sovereign." (1) The *sovereign* (monarchical) ruler of an Islamic nation, such as Oman. (2) A traditional Islamic ruler, ranked above an *emir*, such as the sultan of *Sokoto* in Nigeria. (3) The ultimate title of rulers of Muslim *empires*, including the *Ottoman Empire* to 1923, and implying authority over all *Muslims*. It has not been claimed by any significant leader in that sense since the fall of the Ottomans. *See also caliph.*

sultanate. A *territory* ruled by a *sultan*, as a secular prince, religious authority, or both. *See also caliphate.*

Sumatra. A large island comprising an important province of modern Indonesia.

summary execution/summary justice. Execution or other penalty carried out "on the spot," after instant judgment, with no appeal permitted, and often without formal legal proceedings of any kind, or at best following a drumhead court martial.

summary procedure. When, by agreement of the *states* party to a case, resolution by an international court follows a simplified and abbreviated judicial process.

summit meeting (summitry). Meetings and talks, sometimes including real *negotiations*, among those at the "summit" of political power. Although *heads of state* or *heads of government* sometimes met in prior centuries, problems of time, distance, and personal security militated against regular summitry until the twentieth century. Even at such high-level gatherings as the *Congress of Vienna* or the *Congress of Berlin*, not all states were represented by their *sovereigns* or top political leaders. The first American president ever to leave the country while in office to personally conduct diplomacy was *Woodrow Wilson*, and he was heavily criticized for going to the *Paris Peace Conference*. In a new age of high-tech communications, mass media, and democracy, the importance of summitry rose alongside the need to handle public relations and build political support for one's foreign policies. In general, peacetime summits are rarely more than ceremonial occasions and photo opportunities, and they may be mere and deliberate distractions for a leader in political trouble at home. On the other hand, summits permit activist leaders to take direct and personal control of diplomacy, bypassing their own and the other side's bureaucracies (this is a mixed blessing). Wartime summits are another matter, because the stakes are much higher and the issues are in need of immediate top-level decision. There were several critical *World War II* summits: *Casablanca, Tehran, Yalta,* and *Potsdam*. During the 1950s and 1960s Soviet-U.S. summits were rare and rarely successful. After *Richard Nixon* held several important summits with Chinese and Soviet leaders summitry was viewed by the media and public as a sign of positive relations and was seen, mostly incorrectly, as a critical mechanism for advancing *arms control* and ending the *Cold War*— which to some people, appeared to amount to the same thing. Subsequently, presidents were sharply criticized if they did not arrange summits with Soviet counterparts, even if such meetings were barren of diplomatic effect. Note: The U.S. press tends to use the term "summit" mainly in reference to presidential meetings with Russia or China, or at most the G-7. In fact, any formal meeting of any top national leaders qualifies as a summit. *See also funerals.*

Sunda (Soenda) Islands. An important group of large islands in the Malay archipelago, including Borneo, Java, Celebes, Sumatra, and Timor.

sunni **Islam.** The main body of believers in *Islam*. It accepts the historical succession of *caliphs* and honors the Sunna, or Tradition (life example) of the Prophet. There are four streams of accepted interpretation within sunni Islam, each reasonably tolerant of the others: (1) Hanafi, officially sanctioned by the *Ottoman Empire* and dominant in Central Asia, India, Iraq, Syria, and Turkey; (2) Maliki, predominant in North and West Africa and Sudan; (3) Shafii, spread through Arabia, East Africa, Egypt and Southeast Asia; and (4) Hanbali, the official doctrine of the Saudis. *See also Ismaili*; shi'ia *Islam*.

Sun Yixian (Sun Yat-sen, 1866–1925). Chinese revolutionary. Sun was born in China but grew up in an *overseas Chinese* family in Hawaii. He was educated (as a medical doctor) in Hong Kong. From an early age he agitated in favor of overthrowing the *Qing dynasty,* founding the Revive China Society in Hawaii in 1894. The next year he tried to lead an insurrection from *Hong Kong*—he was a consistent plotter of revolution by force of arms—but his plan was discovered and he was forced to flee to Japan, and thence to the United States and Great Britain. Through *propaganda* and political organizing he brought together most of the factions opposing the Qing by proclaiming "Three Principles of the People" and of the Chinese revolution: *democracy, nationalism,* and "people's livelihood" (*socialism*). He tried to take advantage of Qing weakness during the *Boxer Uprising,* but his ad hoc effort at rebellion was easily repressed. In 1905 Qing agents tried to kidnap him in London, turning him overnight from a fairly obscure dissident into an international celebrity. He moved to Japan, where he was greatly influenced by the *Meiji* reforms, and where he formed the *Revolutionary Alliance* (or League) in 1905, which he led in renewed efforts to subvert the Qing. Sun also founded the *Guomindang* as a broad-based nationalist movement. He returned to China from the United States when the *Chinese Revolution* broke out in late 1911.

Sun was briefly the provisional president of China in 1912, but he stood down in favor of *Yuan Shikai*, who subsequently again drove him into exile in 1913. He founded another, more radical and secret organization in Tokyo in 1914, the Revolutionary Party. He now tried to obtain Japanese help to overthrow Yuan Shikai the same way he had previously sought Tokyo's aid against the Qing. Having seen the Republic deteriorate into dictatorship and *warlordism*, he abandoned the idea that China was ready to become a democracy. Instead, in the 1920s he remade the Guomindang along *Leninist* lines—his new Revolutionary Party had failed to win much support. He proposed a militarized party rule (*vanguard*), which over time (and in vague ways he did not elucidate) would shift China toward truly representative government. In the 1920s Dr. Sun made collaborative approaches to the Chinese *Communists*, set up close ties to the Soviet Union, tried to work with some of the warlords, and cooperated with the Green Gang of criminals in Shanghai which were also of core importance in the career of *Chiang Kaishek*. At best, he did this seeking to secure Chinese national unity and avoid civil war; but it is also possible he was moved by more personal ambitions. In 1922 he briefly had to flee Guangzhou (Canton) when he fell out of favor with the local warlord. Upon his return he experimented with his theory of a military "vanguard" party. Little came of this. Still, his death in 1925 left China without any unifying figure, and as his old lieutenant Chiang Kai-shek stepped into that breach China continued in the internecine carnage which Sun had so feared and lamented.

Suggested Reading: Harold Schiffren, *Sun Yat-sen and the Origins of the Chinese Revolution* (1970).

Super 301 procedures. Deriving from the 1988 Omnibus Trade and Competitiveness Act, this was a *protectionist* mechanism that permitted U.S. trade officials to unilaterally identify as "priority countries" states deemed to be trading "unfairly." They could then force trade negotiations or impose high *tariffs* after three years. Most U.S. trading partners regarded the 301 law as a violation of *GATT*.

superior orders. The claim "I was just following orders" issued by a superior officer, made to mitigate one's responsibility for *war crimes*. This defense was rejected at the *Nuremberg* and *Tokyo war crimes trials* and does not find favor within most modern systems of moral reasoning. However, it is as old as soldiering: "We know enough if we know we are the King's men. Our obedience to the King wipes the crime of it out of us." [Shakespeare, "Henry V," Act 4, Scene I]. *See also command responsibility; "dirty war."*

supernational. Movements or ideas which span national loyalties and divisions by appeal to some arguably higher, or at least wider, community, for example, *communism; liberal-internationalism; pan-Africanism; pan-Arabism; pan-Slavism. See also supranational.*

superpower. A term in use during the *Cold War* to distinguish the Soviet Union and United States from all other powers, including other *Great Powers*. The term was mostly intuitive, speaking to the declared global reach and interests of those two states, and no clear definition was ever achieved. One offered by social scientists—that the superpowers were those states which possessed a *second-strike capability*—did not account for the fact that Britain and France also had this capability once they, too, acquired *submarine*-based *nuclear weapons* delivery systems. After the collapse of the Soviet Union there developed a regrettable abuse of this term, as in "Nigeria is a West African superpower," or "Japan and Germany are economic superpowers." What is really meant by such statements is that Nigeria is a significant *regional power* and that Japan and Germany have rejoined the ranks of the Great Powers, at least according to some measurements of *power*. The term is sometimes used retroactively, as in "Britain was a nineteenth-century superpower," or "the *Roman Empire* was the superpower of the ancient world." In those particular usages, at least, such retroactive appellation seems appropriate. *See also hegemon; hegemonic stability; hyperpower; preponderant power; primus inter pares.*

supply. The availability of *goods and services* in a given economy. Demand is the appetite for consumption of these goods and services. *See also elasticity.*

supply lines. *See lines of supply.*

supply-side economics. A qualified return to *laissez-faire* notions in economic theory, in comparison to *Keynesian* economics. Where *John Maynard Keynes* suggested that governments attempt to manage demand (consumption), "supply siders" argue for greater attention to supply (production). They believe *deficit spending* by governments to satisfy demand causes gross distortions in national economies. Their preferred means of managing supply is to stimulate production by cutting taxes—in particular high marginal rates, which they see as having the greatest impact on economic behavior—which Keynesians, it was charged, raised too high on the path to social redistribution of demand. Supply-side economics emerged as a leading theoretical school in the 1970s, partly reflecting rising concern with that decade's runaway *inflation* as opposed to an earlier generation's concern with the *deflation* and unemployment crisis of the 1930s. Supply-side prescriptions were partly implemented by the *Reagan* and *Thatcher* administrations in the 1980s, along with policies of *monetarism*.
    Suggested Reading: Robert L. Heilbroner and Lester Thurow, *Economics Explained*, rev. ed. (1998).

supranational. Organizations or processes which are in some sense "above" the individual *state*, by virtue of networks of *functional* connections: for instance, some facets of the *European Union*. *See also integration; supernational.*

Supreme Allied Commander in Europe (SACEUR). The commander-in-chief of *NATO*. Throughout the *Cold War* this position was always held by an American, with *Eisenhower* as the first. The command now rotates among the major *allies*.

Supreme Command, Allied Power (SCAP). A coordinating committee headed by *Douglas MacArthur* in post–*World War II* Japan. It had several thousand employees. Peopled with "New Dealers" as well as more pragmatic and hard-headed military men, it successfully *repatriated* and *demobilized* Japanese troops who had surrendered all over the Pacific theater, as well as Japanese civilians. It oversaw the dismantling of Japan's war industries and the *zaibatsu*, conducted the *Tokyo war crimes trials*, enfranchised Japanese women, forbade state support of *Shinto*, oversaw a massive land reform program, and drafted and set up Japan's new Peace Constitution.

Supreme Headquarters of Allied Forces in Europe (SHAPE). *NATO's* theater headquarters, located in Belgium.

Supreme Soviet. The bicameral (Soviet of the Union and Soviet of Nationalities) legislature of the Soviet Union. It was a rubber-stamp body for decisions made in the *Politburo* by the *Central Committee* of the *Communist Party*.

Sûreté. The French security and foreign *espionage* service. In addition to political and security *intelligence* gathering, it was among the first services to turn to *economic espionage*. Long before the *Cold War* was over, it was already spying on corporations in the United States and other allied countries, and handing such technological and other trade information to French companies and state corporations.

surface-to-air. Weapons fired by ground units or surface ships against aircraft or other *missiles*.

surface-to-surface. Weapons fired by ground units or surface ships against ground targets or surface ships.

surface-to-underwater. An anti-*submarine* weapon, whether a *missile* or a torpedo, fired from a surface ship to dive and seek its submerged target.

"surgical strike." (1) Conventional: The idea that targets can be removed (destroyed) without *collateral damage*. (2) Nuclear: Attempting to use precise and low-yield *nuclear weapons* for *counterforce* attacks.

Suriname. Formerly Dutch Guiana. It has cultural and political connections to the Netherlands, and ethnic (Javanese) ties to Indonesia. The Netherlands acquired this colony in 1667 from England in a trade for New Amsterdam (New York), at the end of the Second *Anglo-Dutch War*. It was run as a giant plantation, using African *slave labor*. Once the slaves were freed, indentured wage laborers were brought in from the *Dutch East Indies* (Java) and from India. Time and basic human impulses blended these diverse communities and gave Dutch Guiana a distinctive *Creole* population, but without eliminating all ethnic divisions and animosities. In 1954 the colony was incorporated directly into the Netherlands in a constitutional *union*. The minority Indian population opposed independence out of fear for their civil rights, and many migrated to Holland before the area was given outright independence, as Suriname, in 1975. In 1980 a military *coup* ended *democracy*. After years of economic decline, political instability, and low-level *insurgency*, elections were held in late 1987. Suriname has an ongoing *border* dispute with Guyana, which has harbored Surinamese *guerrillas* at times. In 1994 it increased economic and cultural ties with Indonesia and began extensive exploitation of its *Amazon* interior. Domestically, it was rocked by corruption and election scandals throughout the 1990s.

surplus value. In *Marxism*, the difference between wages and the value of the *good* which a worker produces. This is supposed to reflect the sole source of *profit* to a *capitalist*, who "expropriates" the "surplus value" of the workers. This idea coarsely ignores other factors besides *labor* which go into production, such as *capital*, management, *technology*, risk, and interest. *See also Chinese Revolution (1949); collectivization;* kulaks; *Russian Revolution (1917).*

surrender. (1) In the field: yielding to a superior military force in the expectation that *quarter* will be given and of becoming a *prisoner of war*. (2) Among states: submission to demonstrated superior military force, which thereby concedes one's case in the legal *dispute(s)* considered *casus belli* to final decision by the dictates of an opponent's *force majeure* and conscience (if possessed). It may mean agreeing to legal limitations on one's subsequent claims or action, such as cession of territory or paying *reparations* or an *indemnity*, which go well beyond the original points at issue. *See also defeat; stalemate; unconditional surrender; victory.*

surveillance. In *intelligence*, keeping secret watch on the activities, contacts, mail, and so forth of a foreign *agent*, *terrorist*, potential *defector*, or other target.

suspension. (1) Of a *treaty*: Placing a treaty in temporary abeyance, but not renouncing or abrogating it. (2) From an *international organization*: A rare punishment for egregious behavior by *states*, whose fellows are normally a most tolerant sort, having much to tolerate in themselves. In the United Nations, suspension requires a majority vote of the *United Nations General Assembly* following a recommendation by the *Security Council*. The procedure has never been used. *See also expulsion; withdrawal.*

suspensive condition. In *international law*, a future event which, if it occurs, will have the effect of creating a legal right.

sustainable development. The idea that *appropriate technologies*, moderation of national consumption patterns, and bringing the rate of *exploitation of natural resources* into balance with their renewal are essential measures for future economic development. It posits that practices common to *modernization* and *industrialization*, as they have evolved to date, cannot be sustained for much longer without destroying the resource and environmental base which supports them. This approach searches for equilibrium between exploitation and replenishment of renewable resources and for conservation of nonrenewable resources. *See also debt-for-nature swaps; environmental security; growth; green loans; transferable development rights (TDRs).*

sustainable growth. (1) A long-term rise in national per capita incomes. (2) In theories of the *stages of growth*, the stage which follows *takeoff.*

Suvorov, Alexander Vasilyevich (1729–1800). Tsarist general. He was the leading soldier in Russia's several wars with the *Ottoman Empire, Prussia,* and *Sweden.* He fought in the *Seven Years' War* (1756–1763), two wars with Poland, and two more with Turkey. He also led *Catherine II's* troops in the *partitions of Poland* and repressed a Polish *rebellion* in 1795. He had considerably less success against *Napoleon I* in Italy in 1799.

suzerain. The ruler of a semi-independent *state*; not a full *sovereign. See also Holy Roman Empire; Kuwait; Mehemet Ali.*

Swahili. A linguistic grouping of various *Bantu* peoples, especially of coastal East Africa.
    Suggested Reading: Thomas Speer, *The Swahili* (1985).

Swahili Arabs. Arabic: "Sahel," or "coastal." Sometimes called Congo Arabs, this was a mixed-race population of Swahili, whose *Bantu* language also contained many Arabic words, and Arabs from Oman and Zanzibar, long established on coastal East Africa. Predominantly Muslim, from the sixteenth century they fell into fierce and often bloody competition with Portuguese traders and Christian *missionaries.* Their plantation economy demanded slaves from the interior, which they took by force. Their commercial empire also penetrated deep into the East African interior during the nineteenth century, overrunning small and less well-organized or armed Lunda, Luba, and Songye kingdoms with small armies organized as hunting and raiding parties in search of *ivory, slaves,* and *tribute.* An alliance with Britain and imported *mercenaries* from Baluchistan allowed Seyyid Said (r. 1806–1856), Imam of Muscat and Oman and overload of the coastal Swahili Arab settlements, to conquer Zanzibar. After his death, Swahili Arab interior ascendancy peaked, and then passed, with the career of *Tippu Tip.* In 1885 *Bismarck* proclaimed a protectorate over most of their coastal territory. Three years later, a Swahili Arab rebellion against the German East Africa Company (a *concessionaire company*) led to direct German intervention, aided by Sudanese mercenaries.

SWAPO. *See Namibia.*

Swaziland. The Swazi, a *Nguni* African people, have been ruled by the same dynasty for more than 400 years. Like the *Zulu,* in the late eighteenth century the Swazi responded to regional overpopulation by organizing into regiments and establishing a strict military structure. The territory they occupied shifted in 1820, however, when they were forced to migrate to their present lands by the looming threat of *Shaka* and the *Mfecane*. Swaziland was guaranteed independence by Britain and the *Boers* until the end of the *Second Boer War*, when it was made a British *protectorate*. Until the 1960s, the Union of South Africa maintained a claim to Swaziland. However, it became fully *sovereign* in 1968, as a constitutional monarchy under King Sobhuza II. In 1973 the king overthrew the constitution and reigned as an *absolute monarch* until his death in 1982. During the later struggle against *apartheid* in South Africa, the large, powerful neighbor which nearly engulfs it, Swaziland allied itself rhetorically with the *frontline states* but out of necessity moderated its policy and continued close economic links with the racist republic. It is still governed according to its traditional African kingship system, where a council of elders advises but cannot restrain a near-absolute monarch.

Sweden. Sweden was an ancient *Viking* kingdom with extensive interests throughout the Baltic and in Russia, where ancient Swedes ("Varangians") were the likely founders of the first Russian state, *Kievan Rus*. Sweden fell under Danish control in 1397, in the *Union of Kalmar*. It broke this *union of crowns* in 1523 with the ascension of Gustav I to the throne, and rose to become an important power by the mid-sixteenth century. It was badly beaten in the Kalmar War with Denmark, 1611–1613, which was ended by bribing the Danes to peace. In the *Thirty Years' War*, under *Gustavus Adolphus* (Gustav II), Sweden intervened with great impact. It lost its great king in battle, but it emerged from the war as one of the top military powers in Europe and was identified as the champion of the *Protestant* cause. During the seventeenth century Sweden was numbered among the *Great Powers*, with an empire which rivaled Russia's. Beneath its surface power, however, it had but a small population and a still weak and underdeveloped economy. Provoked by *Peter the Great* during the *Great Northern War* (1700–1721), the young King *Charles XII* launched a disastrous invasion of Russia in 1708, losing his whole army at *Poltava* (June 27, 1709). After 1716 Sweden's power was spent and it lost its outlying possessions to the rising Great Powers of Prussia and Russia. Charles, who had been forced to spend several years as a "guest" of the *Ottoman* sultan, was killed by a musket ball while fighting the Danes in Norway (December 11, 1718).

In 1809 Sweden was forced to cede Finland and the *Aland Islands* to Russia. It joined in the *War of the Fourth Coalition*, but it was not a major contributor to the defeat of *Napoleon I* and therefore made no great gains at the *Congress of Vienna*. In fact, it lost Pomerania to Prussia, although in exchange it received Norway from defeated Denmark. Under *Charles XIV*, and within the *Concert of Europe*, its ambitions were tamed. Sweden grew content as a *regional power*, isolated from armed conflict (it has not been at war since Napoleonic times) and enjoying its Nordic prosperity and security. It also evolved its Viking parliament into a modern democratic institution, and gave Norway *independence* in 1905. Sweden has always taken its *armed neutrality* seriously. It is a heavily armed country which maintains effective *deterrence* and is actively jealous of its *territorial* rights—it regularly attacked intruders, including Soviet *submarines* illegally traversing its *territorial seas*. Its flexible diplomacy has appeared to some as *appeasement*, as during *World War II* when it continued to supply Nazi Germany with iron ore. It really had no choice, since the invasion of Norway in 1940 strategically surrounded Sweden with German forces. Others regard Swedish policy as a model of how *neutrality* can be made to work when given steel teeth and enacted as more than a policy of platitudes. To maintain its military independence it became a significant *arms exporting nation*. Despite this, in the 1960s and 1970s it acquired a global reputation for supporting *disarmament*.

Sweden's *Social Democratic Party* held power for over four decades after World War II. Many on the democratic left throughout Europe and North America came to see Sweden as a model of social engineering and as a working welfare state, and it gained much *prestige* from this. In the late 1980s, however, Sweden too began to make cuts in social programs owing to budget *deficits* and a building citizen tax revolt. In 1994 it was the only Western state to warn of direct military action should Russia attempt to reassert imperial control over the *Baltic states*, which Sweden proclaimed part of its own *near abroad*. It accepted, via a *referendum*, to become a full member of *European Union* on January 1, 1995.

Suggested Readings: Ingvar Andersson, *A History of Sweden* (1975); Gwyn Jones, *A History of the Vikings* (1968, 2001); M. Roberts, *The Swedish Imperial Experience, 1560–1718* (1979).

Switzerland. This strategically located alpine state was organized as a loose association of several independent cantons from the late thirteenth century. The Swiss won their independence when squares of axe men defeated the armored knights of Austria at Morgarten (1315), Laupen (1339), and Sempach (1386). Swiss *pikers* defeated Burgundy's finest, 1476–1477, securing the home cantons, after which the Swiss were ever in demand and for hire in other people's wars, including the *Wars of Religion* and the *Thirty Years' War*, during which the *Grisons* in particular were of great strategic importance. From the fifteenth through the eighteenth centuries Swiss *mercenaries* served in many foreign armies, including that of the popes, where a remnant of that ancient tradition survives still as the Swiss Guard at the *Vatican*. The *Peace of Westphalia* (1648) confirmed *de jure* the *de facto* independence Switzerland had long since won on the field of battle, separating it formally from the *Holy Roman Empire*. From 1798 to 1802 a French *puppet state*, the Helvetic Republic, was assembled by *Napoleon* out of conquered Swiss cantons. At the *Congress of Vienna* the *Great Powers* agreed to respect a Swiss proclamation of *neutrality*, which was backed by a ban on Swiss any longer serving as mercenaries, other than for the popes.

Switzerland has not been involved in a foreign war since then, partly because of repeated international reaffirmations of its neutrality, and partly because it learned to appreciate and cleave to its new tradition, which the Swiss call the Sonderfall ("special path"). The larger reason for this long peace was Swiss pragmatism: Switzerland *appeased* potential invaders by offering valued services, but it also practiced *armed neutrality* by requiring all fit males between 18 and 55 to serve two years in the military, followed by one month of active duty per year. As a result, within 48 hours Switzerland could put c. 800,000 well-equipped and well-trained troops into the field. Of course, it also historically enjoyed tremendous natural defenses on all its frontiers: the Alps.

The internal union of the Swiss cantons did not occur without conflict, however: a brief *civil war* (the *Sonderbund*) was fought in 1847. Switzerland's present constitution of self-governing cantons within a loose federation dates from 1848. Women were excluded from the national franchise until 1971, and in the 1980s one canton's male voters still refused women the vote in a local *referendum*. Switzerland was first among the late-industrializing nations in Europe (second half of the nineteenth century), and only established an internal *customs union* in 1850. It has a long tradition of support for cooperative international organizations despite not joining the United Nations in 1945 (its voters turned down UN membership again in a 1986 plebiscite): it is home to the *Red Cross*; Geneva was the main seat of the *League of Nations*; and Geneva and other Swiss cities host many additional UN agencies and commissions. Switzerland is also active within the *OSCE*, the *International Monetary Fund* (IMF), and the *World Trade Organization* (WTO).

On the whole, however, most Swiss remain deeply and contentedly neutralist: they voted in national referenda (the Swiss hardly do anything of public purpose without holding a plebiscite!) against joining the *European Community* (1993) or participating in UN *peacekeeping* operations (1994). And, the work of the Red Cross notwithstanding, Switzerland is not a country that is overly fond of *refugees* or immigrants. It is, however, a global banking and financial center and has one of the world's top *hard currencies* and an enviably high *standard of living*. Its *citizenship* is therefore one of the most sought-after and difficult to obtain. In the 1990s those banking interests caused considerable embarrassment, as it was documented that Swiss bankers had withheld assets from survivors of the *Holocaust*, or the descendants of victims of the Nazi *genocide*.

Suggested Readings: Frederick W. Dame, *History of Switzerland* (2001); J. L. Murray, *History of Switzerland* (1985).

Sykes-Picot Agreement (1916). A secret understanding between Mark Sykes (for Britain) and George Picot (of France) to *partition* most of the *Ottoman Empire* at the end of *World War I*. It undercut promises made to the *Arabs*, then fighting the Turks, and conflicted with *Woodrow Wilson's* championing of *self-determination*. It was among the *secret treaties* published by the *Bolsheviks* in 1918. It promised most of *Arabia, Iraq, Palestine*, and *Transjordan* to Britain, while giving France parts of Asia Minor, as well as *Lebanon* and *Syria*. See *Arab Revolt; Lawrence (of Arabia)*.

synthesis. (1) General: combining disparate analytical elements into a single, whole explanation of *causation*. (2) In Hegelian method: a higher truth resulting from a clash of *thesis* and *antithesis* which gives rise to a new thesis. *See also dialectic.*

Syria. Civilization in what is today Syria dates to before the Seleucid Empire, which predated the *Roman Empire*. Western Romans were followed by the *Byzantines*, then came the *Arab* conquest and *Islamicization*, an age of great *caliphates* and imperial power based in Damascus, and centuries of struggle with rival centers of Muslim power: Baghdad in Mesopotamia, Cairo in Egypt, and Qom in Persia. After the Arabs came the *Mamluks*, and after them the *Mongols*, who ravaged Syria in 1400–1401, under *Tamerlane*. The *Ottomans* ruled Syria as a prized province for 400 years (1516–1918), holding in check the Bedouin and safeguarding the *haj* route to Arabia. Ottoman power was displaced in all but name by Egyptian overlordship under *Mehemet Ali*, 1831–1839. Ottoman control was then broken on the wheel of *World War I*, with Damascus falling to the *Arab Revolt* in October 1918. Unbeknownst to the Arabs who fought their way past and through the Turkish guns, Syria had already been secretly awarded to a French *sphere of influence* under terms of the *Sykes-Picot Agreement*. When this became known, it was contested by *Faisal I* on behalf of the Arabs. Nonetheless, Syria was turned into a French *mandate* in 1920. This too was contested by Arab leaders, and from 1925 to 1927 by the *Druse*, who rebelled and briefly took Damascus from the French. In 1936 *Léon Blum* promised Syrian independence, but his government fell before that decision could be carried out. During *World War II* Syria was a battleground for *Vichy* and *Free French* forces, until the latter won out.

After the war the French sought to return to the *status quo ante bellum*, and fought Syrian nationalists until April 1946. Then France withdrew and Syria became fully independent. Syria joined the fight against Israel in the *First Arab-Israeli War*. It aligned with the Soviet Union during most of the *Cold War*, from which it obtained Soviet arms it used to fight Israel again in the *Second, Third*, and *Fourth Arab-Israeli Wars*, losing most badly in 1967 and 1973. It failed to unite with Egypt in the *United Arab Republic*. Domestically, that failure propelled the *Ba'ath Party* to seize power (March 1963) under *Hafaz al Assad*, who instituted a brutal personal dictatorship which lasted for three decades. Assad and Syria became embroiled in the *Lebanese Civil War*, especially after 1976. In 1980 the army was called out to apprehend a budding insurrection in several cities. In June 1982, Syria almost went to full-scale war with Israel again over control of southern Lebanon, but in the end the fighting remained localized in Lebanon. Also that year, the Syrian Army destroyed the city of Hama, killing at least 20,000 *sunni* Muslims whom the regime found mortally threatening: Assad was from the Alawi sect, a ninth-century offshoot of Islam and a social group that had close ties to the French colonial power.

In 1986 Britain broke *diplomatic relations* with Damascus, accusing Syria of *state terrorism*. In 1993 the United States listed Assad's regime as a sponsor of international terrorism. Syria nonetheless established its dominance over most of Lebanon, with Western acquiescence, in the dual wash of the collapse of its Soviet patron and the *Gulf War*, to which Damascus sent 20,000 troops to fight Iraq. In 1992 it participated in multilateral *peace talks*, for the first time negotiating directly with Israel over the return of the *Golan Heights*. Domestically, it was politically unstable for much of the 1990s. Assad, enfeebled for many of his final years, finally died in 2000. He was succeeded by his son.

Suggested Readings: Youssef M. Choueiri, *Arab Nationalism, A History: Nation and State in the Arab World* (2000); Albert Hourani, *History of the Arab Peoples* (1997).

systematic interpretation. Reading clauses of a *treaty* with careful reference to their overall context.

systemic. Affecting the whole, or flowing from the root *structure* of the *international system*.

systemic war. A general or *world war* involving all or most of the *Great Powers*. In modern times, they involved and/or affected all other states in the *international system* to some degree. By consensus, since 1500 the systemic wars have been the *Thirty Years' War*, the *War of the Spanish Succession*, the *Seven Years' War*, the wars of the *French Revolution*, *World War I*, and *World War II*. Such all-out wars among the Great Powers may be no longer possible, or at least they may be no longer winnable, since they are no longer survivable even by the Great Powers in an age of *weapons of mass destruction*. The *Cold War* (which perhaps should be seen as a systemic war by other means) demonstrated a considerable awareness of this reality among the elite leadership of the United States and the Soviet Union.

System of National Accounts (SNA). First developed in 1968, this is a *macro*-level system of reporting on national income (whole economies). The original system was praised for its handling of basic features of buying and selling *goods and services*. It was criticized for failing to take proper account of nonmarket economic activity, such as household consumption and government provision of services such as health and education; for inadequately measuring the value of *investment* in basic research and product development;

and for excluding sources of natural wealth such as *land* and *natural resources*. The new system was introduced in 1994, after 10 years of consultation among EUROSTAT, the accounting arm of the *European Union*, the *International Bank for Reconstruction and Development* (IBRD), the *International Monetary Fund* (IMF), the *Organization for Cooperation and Development* (OECD), and the *United Nations*. It treats nonmarket activities as part of the overall economy, although it still could not account for in-home services such as housework, which do not usually involve payment. It introduced reporting on national wealth in land and resources but did not calculate long-term environmental damage or short-term disasters against national income.

systems analysis/theory. An approach to the study of *world politics* which looks primarily at the *structure* and processes of what it sees as an *international system*, rather than to internal events in particular states or other *actors* within that system. A system is taken to be any whole, or set of relationships, in which the parts are *interdependent* in the sense that changes in one "*variable*" (a given cause) bring about variations (effects) in combinations of other variables. Systems may be loose or tight, may be stable or unstable, and may contain subsystems, such as the Middle East *balance of power* as a subsystem of the global balance of power system, or the *EFTA* as a subsystem of the world economy. The brand names, or "*taxonomies*," applied by systems theorists to their shifting speculations continue to proliferate (cascade, some might say). A sampling: action, analytical, concrete, *hegemonic*, homeostatic, mechanical, steady-state, and so on, seemingly ad infinitum. The proffering of various systems theories as *grand theory* has been widely criticized for exhibiting some or all of the following: apolitical content, conservatism about the possibility of systemic change, excessive *abstraction*, celebrating form over substance, strained assumptions, tautological argument and—this author's personal favorite—*Procrustean* amputation of the facts. *See also anarchic; bipolar; city-state system; endogenous; events data; exogenous; multipolar; neorealism; sensitivity; unipolar; vulnerability; Westphalian system; world capitalist system.*

T

tacit alliance. When states informally coordinate their foreign policies on matters of mutual interest.

tacit consent. Silence on an international legal matter may be taken as implicit *consent*. See also *acquiescence*.

tactical (considerations). (1) The use of *force* on a limited scale, with a limited purpose in mind. (2) Relating to battlefield concerns and interests alone, not to longer-range *strategic plans* or considerations.

tactical weapons. (1) Conventional: Any weapon which is subject to countermeasures at the point where it is used, and which targets not the war-making system or productive capacity of an enemy state but only specific products of that system, such as tanks, ships, aircraft, or soldiers. At its most elementary, the distinction between tactical and strategic targeting is a matter of scale, with enemy tactical targets or forces being those immediately confronting one's own military. (2) Nuclear: Short-range *nuclear weapons* systems for use against sizeable enemy military formations, say, an *armored* division or spearhead, at something like a 200-mile (300-kilometer) range. They may be delivered by aircraft, short-range missiles, or longer-range *artillery*. They are not intended for use against enemy *intermediate* or *intercontinental* systems which threaten one's *strategic* bases of *power*. See also *air power; neutron bomb; strategic weapons.*

tactics. The primary sense is short-range considerations relating to the details of deployment and use of troops or weapons systems in combat. *Clausewitz* defined tactics this way, as "the theory of the use of armed forces in battle." The term is also used to refer to the ploys, *stratagems*, and ruses of political or diplomatic maneuvering. *See also counterattack; entrench; feint; flanking maneuver; pincer movement; retreat; strategy.*

Taft, Howard (1857–1930). *Republican* president of the United States, 1909–1913. In 1900 Taft was made president of the Philippine Commission. In 1901 he became the first U.S. governor of the Philippines. He was thus in-country during the Filipino rebellion led by Emilio Aguinaldo (1870–1964), which was put down with often rough methods by U.S. troops. From 1904 to 1908 he was secretary for war under *Theodore Roosevelt*, whom he then succeeded as president of the United States, 1909–1913. "Dollar diplomacy" is a sometime description of the foreign policy of President Taft, in which economic incentives were substituted for the use of unilateral force to maintain local stability. This was attempted both in Central America and in policy toward China. He also secured an agreement with Canada which significantly freed bilateral trade, though not the full free trade deal proposed in 1911 which brought down the Liberal government in Ottawa. He was defeated in the 1912 elections after quarreling with Roosevelt, who then ran on an independent "Bull Moose" ticket, thereby splitting the Republican vote and sending *Woodrow Wilson* to the White House. From 1921 Taft served as chief justice of the U.S. Supreme Court.

Taft-Katsura Agreement (July 1905). An exchange of *diplomatic notes* between the United States and Japan suggesting mutual acceptance of American possession of the Philippines and Japanese suzerainty over Korea. *See also Root-Takahira Agreement.*

Tahiti. *See French Polynesia.*

Taiping Rebellion (1850–1864). "Taiping Tianguo" ("Heavenly Kingdom of Great Peace"). This was the largest of several major revolts within China between 1850 and 1873. It climaxed as an all-out *civil war* which became the most destructive armed conflict anywhere in the nineteenth century. Before it was over, fighting spread to 16 of *Qing* China's 18 provinces, and the dynasty's hold was near fatally weakened. The rebellion cut deeply into Chinese trade, as well (for instance, India displaced China as the main supplier of tea to Britain). The dominant personality was Hong Xiuquan (Hung Hsiu-ch'üan, 1811?–1864), a half-mad, *Hakka* visionary from Guangdong Province. He dwelled upon personal visions born of crude *Christian* teachings and a vaporous, lingering *Confucianism*: Hong four times failed China's famous Confucian examinations, which would have made him a Qing bureaucrat. These blended in religious/hallucinatory ecstasies from which he concluded that he was the literal son of god and, specifically, the younger brother of Jesus Christ. Hong's messianism merged with a vague but austere socialist idealism, and powerful anti-*Manchu* sentiments in the wider population, to form a Taiping ideology which ultimately attracted millions of adherents. Hong's divinely inspired mission was to overthrow the Qing and remake China into a *utopian* theocracy.

The Taiping movement drew strength from the Hakka, as well as millions of peasants dispossessed by rising prices and population with no corresponding rise in land reclamation or employment, as well as by once-and-future bandits and *pirates*. These were then led by Taiping radical utopians; that is, by severe moral puritans and extreme egalitarians in the mold of Hong himself, who called for communal ownership of property and money and severely puritanical social mores, including segregation of women. Taiping men cut off the Manchu queue or wore their long hair unbound to mark off their rebellion, while many Taiping women served in (segregated) public office and others fought in all-women regiments. Property and revenues were ostensibly held in common, and the Taiping were organized in near-*totalitarian* fashion down to the neighborhood and family level.

On January 11, 1851, Hong declared himself ruler of the "Heavenly Kingdom." This finally attracted *Qing* attention, just as the transition was being made from Emperor Daoguang (d. 1850) to Emperor Xianfeng (r. 1851–1861). It was much too late to avoid large-scale violence. After defeating *banner troops* sent to suppress them in their southern mountain base, a small but efficient and well-led Taiping army captured Yongan in September 1851. Feeding off economic dislocation and fear of foreign influence, the uprising spread up and down the Yangzi valley and then coursed over much of south and central China in 1852 and 1853. In December 1852, the Taiping captured a major military depot. An army of 500,000 Taiping, now equipped with *artillery*, captured Wuhan in January 1853 and took the Imperial capital at Nanjing (or Tianjing, as it was known to the Taiping) two months later. At Nanjing, the Taiping exhibited a *genocidal* intent, singling out for butchery all identified as Manchu civilians. Major punitive and conquering expeditions were sent out, 1853–1855, and again, 1856–1863. For nearly 10 years the part of China which relied on the Yangzi was under the effective rule of the Taiping. A palace coup against Hong failed in 1856 and was followed by a great *purge*. Afterward, bereft of his key lieutenants, Hong grew increasingly distant and mystical. Meanwhile, the Taiping agrarian revolution failed, while Taiping troops ravaged the provinces around their base in Nanjing.

After the *Second Opium War*, in order to protect the valued gains of the *unequal treaties* which had been imposed on China, Great Britain supported the Qing—who signed those treaties—in their internal war against the Taiping. In the end, however, it was not traditional Qing banner troops or intervention by foreign *mercenaries* of the Ever Victorious Army led by "Chinese Gordon," but provincial militia under local Chinese gentry command—most notably the conscript Xiang Army from Hunan—which crushed the rebellion and saved the dynasty. In this task they were greatly aided by the internal discontent in the Taiping areas which inevitably arose from disappointed utopianism. Thus began a militarization of the rural areas which would lead, ultimately, to *warlordism* in the early twentieth century. Nanjing fell after a *siege* in 1864, during which Hong either committed suicide or was killed. The fanatic nature of the core of the Taiping cult was revealed in an extraordinary mass suicide by the Taiping in Nanjing. Taiping elsewhere were hunted down and slaughtered. Perhaps 20 million lives had been lost in the Taiping rebellion and its aftermath, making it the bloodiest civil war in all history. *See also Nian Rebellion; Tonkin Wars; White Lotus Rebellion.*

Suggested Readings: Philip Kuhn, *Rebellion and Its Enemies in Late Imperial China, 1796–1864* (1970); Jonathan Spence, *God's Chinese Son* (1996); Jen Yuwen, *The Taiping Revolutionary Movement* (1973).

Taiwan (Republic of China, on). The large island of Taiwan, or *Formosa*, off the Chinese coast, was originally peopled by Polynesian *aborigines*. They fiercely defended their independence to the degree their less advanced military capabilities permitted. Settlement from the Chinese mainland was further discouraged by the fact that Japanese *wakō* preyed on ships in the Taiwan Strait and East China Sea well into the seventeenth and even the eighteenth centuries. Small-scale Chinese migration began under the *Ming* and continued as refugees fled the *War of the Three Feudatories* (1663–1681). However, at various times Ming and *Qing* mainland governments actually forced their population away from the coast to prevent interchange with *pirates* and immigration to Taiwan. Coastal Taiwan was ruled by the Dutch, 1624–1662, who expelled a small Spanish force—an Asian appendage to the *Eighty Years' War* (1566–1648)—and the wakō, both by the 1640s. The Dutch were then expelled by a Taiwanese *filibusterer* (Koxinga) in 1662. Taiwan was invaded by *Kangxi* and thus fell under Qing control as of 1683 and became a prefecture of the province of Fujian. A revolt in 1721 led by Zhu Yigui was quickly put down. In the 1780s a millenarian group called the Heaven and Earth Society (or Triads) rebelled and occupied several of the larger cities in an admixture of civil war among Chinese immigrants and apocalyptic religious fervor. It was repressed and its leaders executed in 1788. Taiwan was opened to Chinese immigration by the 1850s and was made a full province of the Qing empire in 1885. Taiwan was ceded to Japan 10 years later under terms of the *Treaty of Shimonoseki*, which ended the *First Sino-Japanese War* (1894–1895). Resistance to Japan was intense: the Japanese Army's *pacification* of Taiwan took many years and cost it 60,000 troops, more than it lost in the war with China. Nonetheless, Taiwan was occupied by Japan as a colony until 1945.

Upon liberation from Japan at the end of *World War II*, the *Guomindang* (KMT) reclaimed Taiwan for China. Local Taiwanese might be forgiven for hardly noticing a difference: the Nationalists severely repressed the local population and persecuted remaining Polynesian *aborigines*. In February 1947, a Nationalist *pogrom* killed perhaps 10,000. In 1949 all remaining local resistance was overwhelmed as some two million Guomindang party and family members (including one million soldiers) retreated to Taiwan after suffering defeat in the *Chinese Civil War*, still claiming legitimacy to rule all China. From 1949 to 1975 *Chiang Kai-shek* was president of Taiwan, or the Republic of China (ROC), which existed in tense stand-off with the *communist* People's Republic of China (PRC) on the mainland. *Mao* was planning to invade Taiwan in 1950, when his forces and attention were drawn away by the outbreak of the *Korean Conflict*, which also led the United States to interpose its 7th Fleet between Taiwan and the mainland. The most dangerous subsequent crises came over the coastal islands of *Quemoy and Matsu* in 1953 and 1958.

In 1954 Taiwan signed a security treaty with the United States. American economic aid flowed to Taiwan until 1968, and military aid continued thereafter. An economic boom in Taiwan in the 1960s was fueled by its service as an American air and naval base during the *Vietnam War*. Taiwan held the China seat on the *Security Council* and the *United Nations General Assembly*—upheld by U.S. *veto* of the PRC's credentials—until its UN delegation's *letters of credence* were rejected in October 1971, with the *Nixon* administration abstaining on the procedure so that the PRC could be seated instead. Taiwan also lost the China seat within the *International Monetary Fund* and the *International Bank for Reconstruction and Development*. That led to anti-American riots by an aroused public. However, the Taiwanese elite understood that their country had no choice but continued reliance on unofficial U.S. security guarantees, along with Taiwan's own heavy and advanced armaments. Despite the U.S. shift, which was emulated by most other Western countries which had not previously recognized the PRC, a number of countries continued to recognize the ROC and called for its readmission to the United Nations. Of these, the most loyal were poor and small, as in the case of Central America, where Taiwanese aid and investment purchased diplomatic support from all seven republics in the 1990s. Chiang Ching-kuo (1910–1988), son of Chiang Kai-shek, held power for 10 years, 1978–1988. Taiwan prospered in that time, emerging as one of the *Asian Tigers* and a valued trade partner of many nations, despite its deep and continuing formal diplomatic isolation.

In 1987 four decades of *martial law* was finally ended. That same year, a *Central Intelligence Agency mole* in the Taiwanese military research program stole vital documents which prevented Taiwan from completing development of *nuclear weapons*. After 1988 Taiwan moved toward multiparty democracy, even though that opened old wounds between native Taiwanese and immigrant Nationalists and their descendants. In 1981 China proposed "peaceful reunification" on the *Hong Kong* model of domestic *autonomy* within a Taiwan Autonomous Region. After 1991 Taiwan shifted its policy toward the PRC, under the new slogan "one country, two political entities." It retained close ties to the United States, which in 1992 approved advanced *fighter* sales to Taipei, displaying a continuing commitment even at the expense of warm relations with Beijing. Taiwan makes the same total claim to the *Spratly Islands* as does the PRC. In early 1993 it made tentative, "unofficial" diplomatic contact with the PRC, where its businessmen had become important investors. This reversed decades of following the so-called "Three Nos" (no contact, no compromise, no negotiation). The two Chinas then met formally for the first time later that year, at an *APEC* summit in Seattle. However, that did not prevent China from continuing to block UN membership for Taiwan or from conducting a *show of force* in the Taiwan Strait, with ostentatious missile-firing displays, 1994–1995, in a concerted effort to intimidate the ROC electorate into voting against a pro-independence party, the Democratic Progressive Party (DPP). In 1996 Lee Teng-hui was elected president. In the 2000 presidential election the KMT candidate was defeated by the DPP's Chen Shui-bian, leading to a war scare and public threats of invasion by the PRC should Taiwan formally declare itself independent. This contributed to a sharp deterioration in U.S.-PRC relations under the new *George W. Bush* administration in 2001. Later that year the DPP displaced the KMT from its majority in the national assembly. *See also drift net fishing; overseas Chinese; two-Chinas policy.*

Suggested Reading: Marie-Luise Näth, ed., *The Republic of China on Taiwan in International Politics* (1998).

Taiwan Strait. It connects the East and South China Seas. For the Crises of the Taiwan (or Formosa) Strait, *see also Quemoy and Matsu.*

Tajikistan. Over the centuries this area was overrun by successive waves of nomadic invaders from Persia and then eastern Asia, including by the *Mongols*. In the seventeenth and eighteenth centuries it was home to small, independent khanates (*Bukhara, Khiva*) which existed uneasily between the contracting *Persian Empire* and the expanding *Russian Empire*. In the nineteenth century these khanates succumbed to the latter. With the *Russian Revolutions of 1917*, the Tajiks rebelled, but were forcibly held in the Russian Empire by the *Bolsheviks* following the *Russian Civil War* (1918–1921). Tajikistan was joined loosely with Uzbekistan within the *Soviet Union* in a 1924 reorganization of the "nationalities problem" arranged by *Stalin*. In 1929 it was split from Uzbekistan to form the Tajik (Tadzhik) ASSR. That was a purely administrative change at the time, but one which left it an independent nation following the *extinction* of the Soviet Union in December 1991. After *independence* the local *communists* clung to power, opposed by democratic reformers and Islamic *fundamentalists* alike. By December 1992, ethnic and religious conflict drove 60,000 *refugees* into Afghanistan. The United Nations later oversaw *repatriation* of some of these refugees. In the first six months of 1993 more than 100 border *incursions* took place, by Tajik rebels and anti-communist Afghans fighting the government in Dushanbe. Russian troops were drawn into the fighting, and some were killed. Russia then agreed to a Tajik request to station troops as a unilateral *"peacekeeping* force" in Dushanbe, later *sanctioned* by the United Nations, which bent to a fait accompli by Russia. Tajikistan also agreed to monetary union with Russia, which already provided half its national budget, bringing into question its effective independence from Moscow within the *near abroad.* Civil war continued throughout the 1990s, taking perhaps 50,000 lives, but drawing to an uneasy conclusion in 2000.

Suggested Reading: Martha B. Olcott, *Central Asia's New States* (1996).

Tajiks. A Central Asian people forming the majority of the population of Tajikistan, but also forming a significant ethnic minority population in northern Afghanistan.

takeoff. In various theories of the *stages of growth,* that stage preceding mature, *sustainable growth* and the critical point denoting the transition from traditional economic modes to a modern economy.

Taliban. The term originally meant "religious students," in reference to their origin in Saudi-financed madrassa (Koranic schools) located mainly in Pashtun refugee camps within the frontier provinces of western Pakistan, where youths were indoctrinated in the radical tenets of the *Wahhabi* (Saudi) and Deobandi (originally, Indian) interpretations of *Islam.* Under Mullah Mohammad Omar, they first came to power in Kandahar in 1996 in the wake of a general chaos that was the legacy of the *Afghan-Soviet War* and of a return to traditional *warlordism,* and hence a general longing for peace and order throughout Afghanistan. This desire arose from the fighting among *mujahadeen* factions which, having defeated the Soviet Union, after 1989 had reverted to an even more destructive *civil war.* UN efforts to mediate failed, and the fighting had moved into Kabul and other major cities—destroying much that had remained relatively unscathed during the *holy war* against the Soviets and their allies, the Afghan *communists* under Muhammad Najibullah. As warlords and tribes contended for power with rifle, tank, and artillery after the defeat of the communist regime in 1992, some 30,000 were killed in Kabul alone.

In 1994 the Taliban entered this fray, which had by then spread across the whole country. They were mostly young men who had never known peace or permanent homes and had been filled with *fanatical* fervor by stay-at-home old men, the mullahs who ran Saudi-funded madrassa in Pakistan. These fighters were also aimed at Kandahar and Kabul by Pakistani intelligence (the Inter-Services Intelligence Directorate, or ISI). The ISI funded and armed the Taliban partly because of the latter's Pashtun origin, and hence familial and political connections in Pakistan itself. Islamabad's larger intention appears to have been to end the tribal fighting in Afghanistan and thereby pacify its own aroused—and potentially also *irredentist*—Pashtun minority, as well as to extend its influence deep into a neighboring state. The Taliban proclaimed and launched a *jihad* which first gave them control of the main Pashtun city of Kandahar in 1996. The movement grew rapidly, fed by the misery of several million Afghan refugees straddling the border region with Pakistan, and of millions more Afghans desperate to accept any unifying force which promised to end the long civil war. Spreading Saudi and Pakistani cash bribes to local mujahadeen commanders, they imposed their Wahhabi theology, reinforced by quasi-prophetic appearances by Mullah Omar ("Leader of All the Faithful") in the fabled cloak of the Prophet. The Taliban bought or fought their way into control of about two-thirds of the country by 1998. That year, they won their key military victories, driving the last Northern Alliance opposition into mountain fastnesses in the far north.

From the start, Taliban rule was characterized by radical persecution of women; draconian enforcement and summary punishment of violations of *sharia* law by religious police and courts; and utter isolation from modern cultural, political, and economic currents and affairs. They were financed by Saudi money and by the heroin trade (under the Taliban, Afghanistan supplied more than 90 percent of world heroin, despite occasional anti-poppy campaigns). Their cruel, extraordinarily repressive and atavistic rule drew little world attention, however, until they defaced and then blew up the world-famous *Buddhist* sculptures and monuments at Bamian. These were several millennia old and were certainly of world cultural significance. Such radical iconoclasm and readily revealed barbarism aroused global condemnation, including by most other Muslim states. The Taliban ignored all foreign pleadings, however, convinced that such art works were "un-Islamic" and hence forbidden representations of both human and divine forms. This extreme Wahhabi radicalism—which essentially sought to return to presumed seventh-century Islamic standards of public behavior—isolated Afghanistan from virtually all outside influences, including most of the Islamic world. Persecution of the minority *shi'ite* Hazara additionally brought the Taliban into conflict with the shi'ite fundamentalists governing neighboring Iran and almost led to war with that state in 1998.

By 2001 the Taliban controlled some 95 percent of Afghanistan. As early as 1996 they had invited the serpent influence of thousands of *Afghan Arabs*, or non-Afghan members of the *terrorist* organization *al Qaeda*. Taliban support for the anti-Western terrorists of al Qaeda, and for other *Islamist* guerrillas operating throughout Central Asia and south Russia (Chechnya) and China (Xianjiang), so set them at odds with the whole international community that only Pakistan, Saudi Arabia, and the United Arab Emirates formally recognized their regime. Then came the *September 11, 2001, terrorist attack on the United States*, by al Qaeda. Under *George W. Bush*, a U.S.-led coalition responded with calibrated but devastating military power directed into Afghanistan. The U.S. supported seriatim ground offensives by the opposition Northern Alliance of mostly Tajiks and Uzbeks, the *shi'ite* Hazara of the central highland range who had suffered grievously under the discriminatory *sunni* (Wahhabi) Taliban, and various Pashtun and other ethnic warlord-led groups who read the script on the cave wall and knew the Taliban's days were numbered. Acting severally and together, these forces combined to the end of overthrowing the Taliban regime—a feat accomplished in less than three months as Taliban forward trenches abruptly collapsed after the sustained application of U.S. *air power*. Retreating Taliban troops either negotiated surrender deals with advancing Afghan ground forces or simply fled home to their villages, while the senior Taliban leaders scattered to alpine hideouts. A broad coalition government was installed in Kabul in December 2001, under UN auspices, and was protected there by an International Security Assistance Force composed of troops from more than 20 nations, led by Britain and supported by the United States. The Taliban left behind them a legacy of persecution and destruction, depopulated cities, two million refugees, and another six million Afghans verging on starvation and dependent on foreign aid for simple survival. *See also Afghanistan.*

Suggested Readings: Michael Griffin, *Reaping the Whirlwind* (2001); Ahmed Rashid, *Taliban: Militant Islam, Oil, and Fundamentalism in Central Asia* (2000).

Talleyrand, Charles Maurice de (1754–1838). French statesman. This wily, one-time bishop had one of the most storied careers in all *diplomacy*. He supported anti-aristocratic and anti-clerical forces in the early stages of the *French Revolution*, even backing confiscation of church property in which he lost his own see (in 1791), for which he was excommunicated by the pope. He served as ambassador in London, but left for the United States during *The Terror*. He returned to serve the conservative *Directory* as foreign minister, 1797–1799, launching the ill-fated expedition to Egypt. After *Napoleon*'s coup, Talleyrand agreed to stay on as foreign minister, 1799–1807. He was instrumental in arranging the *concordat* with Rome, negotiating the *Peace of Amiens*, and helping Napoleon control Germany through establishment of the *Confederation of the Rhine*. He once wisely told Napoleon that policy should be guided by the principle that, in peace, nations should do each other the most good possible, and in war, the least harm necessary.

Talleyrand grew ever more concerned over Napoleon's limitless hubris, and left the foreign ministry after *Tilsit*. He secretly communicated, and sometimes actively plotted, with Napoleon's enemies. In 1814 Talleyrand managed to switch sides yet again, facilitating, joining, and serving the *Restoration*. He represented France brilliantly at the *Congress of Vienna*, avoiding direct occupation while gaining agreement to its 1792 borders and that it be treated as one of the *Great Powers*. Those gains were thrown away by the advent of Napoleon's *Hundred Days*. Talleyrand next encouraged a growing split in the *coalition* which had defeated France, parlaying this into enhanced influence with Great Britain. In 1830 he turned against the *Bourbons*, helping to install the *July Monarchy*, which he served as ambassador to London, 1830–1834. At the end of his life this irrepressible opportunist even managed to reconcile with the church. One may only wonder what deals he has since made with the deity, and how long secret talks have been underway with the emissaries of Hades. Attributed remark: "War is much too serious a matter to be entrusted to the generals." *See also Borodino; XYZ Affair.*

Suggested Reading: Duff Cooper, *Talleyrand* (1932, 2001).

Tamerlane, né Timur (1336–1405). Conqueror and *pillager* of Central Asia and India. Tamerlane began as a bandit, in the tradition of the nomadic *Tartars* of Central Asia in the fourteenth century. In 1369 he succeeded his father as emir of Samarkand. After securing his home base, in 1381 he invaded Persia, following this with brief invasions and conquests of Armenia, Azerbaijan, and Iraq (Mesopotamia). His major enemies were to the north, however, in southern Russia. As he attacked these areas, rampaging and slaughtering throughout Ukraine and parts of *Mongol*-occupied Russia proper, rebellions broke out in his recently conquered provinces in Central Asia, and he was forced to return to and reconquer these lands. Thus was set in play a bloody but ultimately futile pattern of shifting personal and martial dominance, in which he ruled so harshly that in his absence rebellion frequently sprang up, to be met with reconquest and retribution. Millions may have died. This left whole regions underpopulated and economically depressed, literally for centuries more. In 1397 Tamerlane savagely repressed a rebellion in Persia. The next year, he invaded India. Once again, slaughter and *pillage* was the order of the day. Tamerlane captured Delhi, which he *sacked*, in 1398. He then abandoned India, satisfied with opening it to pillage, rape, and murder by his army rather than adding it to his empire.

In 1400 Tamerlane invaded Syria, wiping out an entire *Mamluk* army. He rewarded his troops by letting them sack Aleppo and Damascus, before moving on to take and sack Baghdad. Tamerlane then had Baghdad razed as retribution for a brief Arab revolt. In 1402 he invaded Anatolia, defeating the *Ottoman* sultan himself at Ankara. This left Tamerlane master of the Middle East and Central Asia: by 1405 he was receiving *tribute* from the Ottomans, Byzantines, Egyptians, Syrians, and various small khanates of Central Asia and southern Russia. Tamerlane's appetite for bloodshed and plunder remained unsatiated, however: he was planning a massive invasion of China when he took ill and died. Like so many of his Mongol and Turkic nomad forebears, Tamerlane took much from many more settled civilizations, but gave back nothing. His great-grandson, Babur, later invaded India more permanently and founded the *Mughal Empire*. In the immediate post–*Cold War*

period Tamerlane's memory was exhumed and he was celebrated as a hero in Mongolia, where he is still known as "Amir Timur," or "Timur the Great."
Suggested Reading: Beatrice Manz, *The Rise and Rule of Tamerlane* (1989).

Tamil Tigers. "The Liberation Tigers of Tamil Eelam." *Guerrillas*, and *terrorists*, based mainly in the *Jaffna peninsula*. They conducted a long war of *secession* of Eelam from Sri Lanka. Originally favored by the British, the Tamils found themselves a minority in Sri Lanka (Ceylon) after its independence. They had considerable support from the largely *Hindu*, Tamil population of Jaffna, some voluntary and some heavily coerced, as well as the more numerous Tamils in India. Their fight was against the mostly *Buddhist*, Sinhalese majority. It began in 1983 when Tamil violence in the north provoked massive anti-Tamil, Sinhalese massacres in the south. Led by a vicious but cunning *fanatic*, Vellupillai Prabhakaran (b. 1956), the Tigers demanded one-third of the island as their homeland. *Rajiv Gandhi* sent 50,000 Indian Army troops against the Tigers, 1987–1990, but they were bloodied by fierce resistance and withdrew.

The Tigers terrorized the Tamil civilian population, murdering Tamil dissenters as well as on occasion defending them from Sinhalese retaliation which Tiger atrocities did much to provoke. They also employed a form of military *slavery* of children. In 1991, in Madras, a Tiger killed Rajiv Gandhi and a dozen bystanders, with a suicide bomb strapped to her body. In early 1993 talks began on a negotiated settlement based on a new federal system, with guarantees of Tamil *autonomy* and removal of special status for the Sinhalese language from the constitution. However, this offer was deemed insufficient by the hard men in charge of the rebellion in Jaffna. At the end of 1993 the Tigers returned to the gun. In 1995 they lost the city of Jaffna to a major Sri Lankan Army offensive, but over the next several years they won several major encounters with Sinhalese forces, and in 2000 they retook most of the Jaffna peninsula. Their war—which killed perhaps 60,000 by 2001— now took on the autonomous purpose of keeping the Tigers in control of whatever areas they held, and tyrannized. The goal of statehood and social justice for Tamils receded with each broken truce and rejected compromise.
Suggested Reading: Chandra de Silva, *Sri Lanka: A History*, 2nd rev. ed. (1997).

Tanganyika. For 1,000 years its coastal region was exploited as a source of the Arab *slave trade* and later the ivory run to *Zanzibar*. Only in the eighteenth century was the interior penetrated, mainly by *Swahili Arabs* from Zanzibar and the coast. In the mid-nineteenth century *Nguni* refugees from the *mfecane* entered southern Tanganyika, where they took control of the indigenous tribes (as in Hehe). *Bismarck* proclaimed a German *protectorate* over Tanganyika, and this was confirmed at the *Berlin conference* (1885). It thus formed part of the composite colony of *German East Africa*. It was convulsed, at the same time as *German Southwest Africa* was experiencing the *Herero-Nama War*

(1904–1907), by the Maji-Maji Rebellion (1905–1906), a famine-provoked upheaval which was brutally repressed by German troops. After *World War I* the colony was renamed Tanganyika Territory and converted into a British *mandate*. In 1945 it was made a United Nations *trusteeship territory*. It was given *independence* in 1961, and in 1964 formed a *union* with Zanzibar. *See also Tanzania.*

Suggested Reading: John Iliffe, *A Modern History of Tanganyika* (1979).

Tang dynasty (618–907). After the disaster of the *Sui* emperor's defeat in Korea, 612–614, and attendant massive domestic rebellion, the last Sui Emperor, Yangdi, was murdered (618) and the *Buddhist* Tang dynasty claimed the *mandate of heaven* in China under Li Yuan (Gaozu). The Tang reformed the bureaucracy, entrenching the examination system begun under the Sui, and reorganized the government into six cardinal ministries—a system which survived in China until the twentieth century. Gaozu began the disestablishment of Buddhism. This move encouraged a revival of *Confucianism* as the state religion, though *Daoism* was also correspondingly elevated. The reign of Emperor Taizong (r. 626–649) is often depicted as a golden age of prosperity and culture. Peace awaited a new border war with Turkic invaders, who were repulsed with effect by Taizong in 628. The second Tang emperor then re-invaded Korea and expanded as well into northern Vietnam (*Tonkin*) and Central Asia by 657. The third Tang emperor, however, was overawed by his wife, the former concubine Wu, who ruled in his stead and then as *Dowager Empress*, 654–705. From 690 she took the throne as Empress Wu (625–705, r. 690–705). In 676 Wu sent armies to conquer Pyongyang and forced the northern Koreas into a *tributary* status. Facing invasions by Turkic tribes and from Tibet, she was forced to abdicate in 705.

The Emperor Xuanzong (r. 712–756) presided over a genuine Chinese renaissance in art and culture, as well as extended China's empire deeper into Vietnam, below Tonkin to *Annam*, and accepted tribute from the Buddhist kingdom of Tibet. On the other hand, to the north the Uighur were constructing an empire of their own in Mongolia. In 751 a Tang army was defeated by an Arab force near Samarkand, and various *Inner Asian* peoples settled across the northwest frontier. In 755 the Tang general, An Lushan (d. 757), rebelled. For eight years a savage civil war raged which the Tang finally won, with Uighur aid, but which left them permanently weakened vis-à-vis their own provincial military commanders. Large parts of the *frontier* were lost to Tibet and the Uighur Empire, which lasted to 840. In 845 the fervent Daoist and Tang Emperor Wuzong (r. 840–846) formally repressed Buddhism, acting against wealthy monasteries in particular. In the late Tang, China fell into utter chaos, suffused with *mutiny* in the Imperial Army and widespread provincial rebellion. One bandit *warlord*, Huang Chao, waged hugely destructive raids along the coast, 878–884. He was but one of many warlords, Chinese and Inner Asian, who continued to ravage China during the post-Tang, Five Dynasties period, before the return to imperial authority under the *Song*.

Suggested Reading: Woodbridge Bingham, *The Founding of the T'ang Dynasty* (1970).

Tangier. This Moroccan city facing *Gibraltar* fell to the Portuguese in 1471. It was part of Spanish Morocco, 1912–1923, when it was *neutralized* and declared an *international city*. It was governed by a seven-nation *condominium*, 1923–1940. It was then occupied by Spain, 1940–1945, during *World War II*. It was reinternationalized after the war, until 1956, when it was joined to newly independent Morocco.

tanistry. When political succession is decided by election of an heir from a pool of candidates from within a *dynasty*, rather than by primogeniture or other direct hereditary rule.

tanks. *See armor.*

Tannenberg, Battle of (1410). *See Livonian Order; Lithuania; Teutonic Knights.*

Tannenberg, Battle of (August 26–31, 1914). The Russians launched their initial attack of *World War I* from the great salient of Poland and penetrated deep into Germany with a massive *infantry* and *cavalry* force. This unexpectedly rapid deployment and advance by the Russian Army caused panic in Berlin, upset the careful timetable of the *Schlieffen Plan*, which had not anticipated Russian readiness before the 40th day of the war in the west, and forced the *High Command* to pull back badly needed troops from the great German offensive against France. However, German *intelligence* enabled *Ludendorff* and *Hindenburg* to deploy inferior forces to encircle an entire Russian army. The *Reichswehr* then met the much larger Russian offensive forces in a sequence of battles in *East Prussia*, meeting and *defeating in detail* a numerically superior foe. They killed more than 50,000 Russians and took 92,000 prisoners. The disgraced Russian commander, Samsonov, shot himself. Hindenburg named the battle for Tannenberg, site of the great defeat of the *Teutonic Knights* in 1410 by a Slav army. This victory bought Germany time in the east while it pressed its offensive in the west—ultimately, however, to failure and the agony of *trench warfare*. The Russians recovered quickly, to fight again at the *Masurian Lakes*. Although beaten at Tannenberg, their early invasion of Prussia helped save France from defeat, though at a tragically high cost in Russian lives, even as it revealed a fatally divided Russian high command structure and primitive logistical system.

Suggested Readings: Dennis Showalter, *Tannenberg: Clash of Empires* (1991); Norman Stone, *The Eastern Front* (1976). A fictionalized but powerfully evocative account is *Alexandr Solzhenitsyn's* historical novel, *August 1914.*

Tanzania. This state was formed in April 1964, from a *union* of *Tanganyika* and *Zanzibar*. From 1964 to 1985 it was led by *Julius Nyerere*. A moderate *socialist*, Nyerere nonetheless set up a *one-party state* and exhibited a paternalistic political style which often shaded into a milder sort of *authoritarianism*. He attempted to implement a vision of "African socialism" which he claimed rested naturally on historic, communal property patterns, the principles of which he laid out in the (at the time) widely influential and much admired, in certain circles, *Arusha Declaration*. When peasants disagreed, by seeking to remain in their traditional villages and continue their historical patterns of production, force was used to *collectivize* the countryside. By the 1970s the national economy was failing, in part due to the fact Tanzania was surrounded by regional conflicts, but mainly to the incompetence of Nyerere as an economic theorist and manager. Tanzania was a leader of the *frontline* states in their opposition to *apartheid* and to *UDI* in Rhodesia, but was forced by geographical and economic reality to deal with South Africa on a practical basis. In 1970 it was one of only four African states to recognize *Biafra*. From 1970 to 1975, with Chinese help, it completed the Tan-Zam railway linking it to Zambia and reducing its export dependence on South Africa. In 1979 Nyerere approved an *invasion* of Uganda and the overthrow of *Idi Amin*, after Ugandan troops had crossed the border in *hot pursuit* of anti-Amin *guerrillas*. In 1981 Tanzanian troops helped Seychelles repel an invasion by *mercenaries*. After 1985 Tanzania has changed course. It now sought to build a *market economy* and a multiparty democracy. In 1993 a serious constitutional issue erupted with the discovery that Zanzibar had secretly joined the *Islamic Conference* in violation of the country's *secular* constitution. The crisis was so deep it threatened the union. Nyerere was brought back to *mediate*.

Suggested Reading: J. D. Fage, *A History of Africa* (1995); John Iliffe, *A Modern History of Tanganyika* (1979).

tanzimet. "Restructuring." A sustained effort at *modernization* and internal reform within the *Ottoman Empire*, c. 1840–1878. The reforms proved insufficient to forestall the continuing disintegration of the Empire, to prevent *defeat* in yet another *Russo-Turkish War*, or to avoid general worsening of the *Eastern Question*. *See also* perestroika.

targeting doctrine. Any principles set in advance to govern the selection of targets, the order of attack, and the weapons to be used in case of *war*. These principles may or may not incorporate reasoning from the *just war tradition*.

tariff. (1) A tax on *imports*. (2) Very rarely, a tax on *exports*. Tariffs are used to raise revenue for governments and as a mechanism of *protectionism*. *See also common market; customs union; free trade; free trade area; GATT; new protectionism; nontariff barriers; peak tariff; preferential tariff; protective tariff; quota.*

Tartar (Tatar). A generic term for the *Mongol* and Turkic peoples who overran much of the south Russian steppes and the *Caucasus* during the Middle Ages. They established Khanates in Astrakhan, Kazan, and the Crimea and waged war along the southern border of Muscovy for several centuries, marauding in search of *booty* and *slaves*. The Tartars were helped by Turkish *Janissaries* and counted the *Ottomans* as allies. Muscovy gained the upper hand beginning in the reign of *Ivan IV (The Terrible)* and ultimately subdued the Tartars and annexed their lands. Even so, a Tartar army from the Khanate of the Crimea captured Moscow briefly, and sacked it, in 1571. That khanate remained independent of Russia until the eighteenth century. In 1945 *Stalin* expelled 200,000 Crimean Tartars (but not the Kazan Tartars) to Siberia, unjustly accusing them en masse of *collaboration* with the Nazis. After the collapse of the Soviet Union they began to migrate back to the *Crimea*, where the Ukrainian government initially welcomed them as diluting the local Russian majority and thereby reinforcing Ukrainian claims to the peninsula. However, relations with local authorities soon cooled as Tartars competed with Ukrainians and others for housing, jobs, and land.

task force. A momentary gathering of divers military units under a single command for purposes of fulfilling a single major task, such as an *invasion*.

Tasmania. *See Aborigines; Australia; James Cook; Penal Settlements; Van Diemen's land.*

Tatar. *See Tartar.*

tax haven. A country which deliberately maintains very low corporate or income tax levels and other incentives to attract foreign corporate headquarters or *subsidiaries* or private savings. This permits *multinational corporations* in particular to avoid heavy taxes in their home countries. Switzerland has played this role for centuries. Some Caribbean nations, such as the Bahamas, joined the game in the late twentieth century.

taxonomy. A $100 bit of *jargon* for the dime-a-dozen term "classification," self-consciously adapted by the social sciences from its origin in the natural science of classifying organisms. *See also scientism; systems theory.*

Taylor, Zachary (1784–1850). U.S. general and *Whig* president. He fought in the *War of 1812*, serving mainly on the western frontier. He fought again in the Blackhawk War in Wisconsin in 1832 and against the Seminoles in Florida, 1837–1840. He led U.S. troops into *Texas* when that territory was *annexed* in 1845. In March 1846, he took a force of some 4,000 U.S. regular Army to fortify positions along the Rio Grande, in a clear provocation to Mexico which constituted the opening phase of the *Mexican-American War*.

The Mexicans crossed the river to attack him at Ft. Brown; he defeated them in two sharp battles, May 8–9, 1846, and crossed over the Rio Grande to take Matamoros. In September he took Monterey from its defenders. He then signed a local *armistice* with Mexican commanders, but his act was repudiated by President *James Polk*, who seems to have withheld reinforcements out of fear that Taylor, who was a Whig, might prove too successful and become a major political rival after the war (he did). Taylor then divided his forces, sending half to support *Winfield Scott's* landing at Veracruz and the assault on Mexico City. He himself faced *Santa Anna's* army of 21,000 with just 5,000 volunteers, at the Battle of Buena Vista (February 21–22, 1848), inflicting a bloody and decisive defeat on the Mexicans. Taylor rode his success into political office, winning the presidency on the Whig ticket later that year, on a platform which favored admission of *California* to the union as a *free soil* state. This was opposed by, among others, his son-in-law, *Jefferson Davis*. Taylor served for just a year before dying of natural causes.

technical intervention. *See intervention.*

technocracy. A theory of government advocating that decisions regarding industrial policy, the form and character of government, and economic arrangements should be made by "rational" technicians following the dictates and findings of science and *technology*, rather than be left to the appetites and vicissitudes of human desire and human nature. *See also command economy*; dirigisme; *five-year plans*; laissez-faire; *market economy*; *planned economy*.

technocrat. A person who advocates or practices *technocracy*.

technology. The knowledge of how to do, or make, something. Applied sciences such as ballistics, computing, or chemical, genetic, and mechanical engineering, along with navigation on the seas or in space, are all leading examples of the application of science to *production* and problem solving which is the core of modern technology. While changing but slowly in earlier epochs, technology has been extremely dynamic in the modern period, since about the middle of the eighteenth century, driving enormous changes in social and political organization and underlying much of *modernization*. Some economic historians argue that technology was far and away the decisive factor in economic *development* during *industrialization*, though that claim is hotly disputed by others. Technology has always been important for developing or sustaining national *power* and wealth. For most of the nineteenth century Great Britain was the leading power in part because of its technological lead not just in military technologies, but more because of its significant lead in exploitation of coal as new energy supply sustaining an early mastery of steam power, which supplemented rather than supplanted water, wood, and animal power, and in the cotton, textiles, and iron industries.

Technological innovations also greatly affect *warfare* by giving one side a (usually temporary) advantage or by increasing the scale of destructiveness of weapons. However, *diffusion* may later lead to a *stalemate* or war of *attrition* and mass slaughter. That was as true of the invention of the stirrup as of high explosives and ballistic science, the *machine gun*, aircraft, or *ICBMs*. What was new from the mid-nineteenth century onward was that *Great Powers* finally recognized this link between technical knowledge and national power and so began to pour vast sums into basic and applied research which they hoped would provide or sustain some military, economic, or other strategic advantage. *See also mode of production; revolutions in military affairs; technology transfer.*

Suggested Readings: Martin van Creveld, *Technology and War From 2000* B.C. *to the Present Day* (1989); M. Duffy, *The Military Revolution and the State, 1500–1800* (1980); J. F. C. Fuller, *Armaments and History* (1946); D. Headrich, *Tools of Empire* (1981); Joel Moykr, *Twenty-Five Centuries of Technological Change* (1990).

technology transfer. When productive (or military) activity and actors in one *nation* gain access to, and take advantage of, *technology* hitherto available only abroad. Technology may be transferred by importing advanced *goods* or *services*, *foreign direct investment*, *foreign aid*, student and professional exchanges, openly published scientific literature, *economic espionage*, or theft. A famous example of concerted effort at technology transfer was the "window on the West" policy of *Peter the Great*; another famous, and far more successful, example was the great *modernization* of Japan after the *Meiji restoration* in 1868. Access to technology is limited by secrecy inherent to military and competitive economic activity, modern patent law and industrial competition, and explicit export technology restrictions imposed by leading industrial and scientific nations. *See also COCOM; diffusion; revolution from above; turn-key factory; WIPO.*

Suggested Readings: David Jeremy, *International Technology Transfer, 1700–1914* (1991); Dietrich Schroeer and Mirco Elena, eds., *Technology Transfer* (2000).

Tehran Conference (November 28–December 1, 1943). *Stalin* finally agreed to meet with the other major *Allied* leaders, something *Churchill* eagerly accepted and *Roosevelt* had long wanted. The major issues discussed were the date for opening the *second front*, Russian entry into the war against Japan, and the basic shape of the *United Nations Organization*. While disagreements existed over the future of *Poland*, the *Baltic States*, and the *Balkans*, none emerged so clearly into the open that the *United Nations alliance* was threatened. This was still a meeting of wartime allies preoccupied by the immediate needs and purpose of prosecuting the war, but for the first time also clearly confident of winning it, and therefore beginning to look ahead to their plans (and potential future divisions) in the *postwar* world. *See also Potsdam; Yalta.*

telecommunications. *See International Telecommunications Union (ITU); piracy; radio.*

telegraph. *See C³I; Cable Network News; James Dalhousie; Ems Telegram; globalization; Indian Mutiny; International Telegraph Union; Kim Il Sung; Kruger Telegram; Long Telegram; Helmuth von Moltke; revolution in military affairs; war plans; Zimmermann Telegram.*

Teller, Edward (b. 1908). Nuclear physicist. He worked closely with *J. Robert Oppenheimer* on the *Manhattan Project,* 1941–1946. He always refused to accept that there may be overriding moral implications to any *nuclear weapons* research. When Oppenheimer refused to press ahead on the *hydrogen bomb,* Teller was chosen to head the project, bringing it to fruition in 1952. In 1954 Teller's testimony against Oppenheimer was decisive in the revocation of the latter's security clearance, and hence the end of his research career. A Hungarian-born, Jewish refugee from *Nazism,* Teller was also a lifelong and fierce anti-*communist* who seemed forever in search of a "technical fix" to the *Cold War* political problem of what to do about Russia. As head of research and chief guru of the Lawrence Livermore Laboratory, which was second only to *Los Alamos* in terms of U.S. nuclear weapons research, he was enormously influential over several decades. It was Teller, for instance, who personally convinced *Ronald Reagan* to authorize research funds for *SDI,* circumventing entirely *Defense Department* channels through his direct access to the president. Where Reagan hoped and called for a non-nuclear shield against incoming *ICBMs,* Teller privately hoped for, and planned to incorporate, new-generation nuclear weapons into SDI as a power source for *charged particle beam* defenses.
  Suggested Readings: Richard Rhodes, *The Making of the Atomic Bomb* (1986); Richard Rhodes, *Dark Sun: The Making of the Hydrogen Bomb* (1995); Edward Teller, *Memoirs* (2001).

tension. A widely used physical and psychological metaphor describing a state of affairs when relations between or among *states* are strained by serious unresolved *disputes,* especially if there lurks in the background the possibility of one or other using *force.* Tension will then be described as "building toward a *crisis*" if the disputes at issue are not addressed or eased.

terminal defense. The *active defense* of a single target at its terminus or end location.

terminal guidance. Making corrections to the flight path of *missiles* during the final approach to target. *See also ballistic missile; cruise missile; terrain contour matching.*

termination of treaties. *See treaty.*

terms, ask for. A request for enumeration and explanation of the conditions under which a *surrender* will be accepted and an armed conflict terminate. This is the first, essential step in negotiating an end to a *war*.

terms (of an armistice or treaty). Point-by-point declarations of the principles upon which the armistice or *treaty* rests, enumeration of all main and subordinate rights and agreements made by the parties, and at times explicit postponement of specific disagreements, fixed conditions which come into effect under the treaty, whether mutually agreed or imposed by one of the signatories, and any mechanisms of dispute resolution specific to enforcement of the treaty. *See also functus.*

terms of trade. The ratio of the price of *imports* to the price of *exports*. Terms of trade suggest the general direction of the *purchasing power* of a national economy: purchasing power rises if the value of exports outpaces that of imports. When import prices outpace exports, an economy suffers declining terms of trade. For instance, *natural resource* exporters have often found export prices falling steadily compared to the manufactured and high-technology, value-added goods they must import.

terrae dominum finitur, ubi finitur armorum vis. "Dominion over the earth ends where the cannon's fire stops." This so-called *cannon-shot rule* was a practical measurement of enforceable *sovereignty* over *territorial waters* as measured by the effective range of a cannon fired from a shore battery. It governed determination of maritime boundaries before the modern revisions to the *law of the sea* made in *UNCLOS III*. *See also three-mile limit; twelve-mile limit.*

terra incognita. "Unknown land." A term from the *Age of Exploration* for lands hitherto undiscovered, at least from the point of view of Europeans concerning large parts of Africa, the Americas, Asia, and the Pacific. *See also discovery; line of demarcation; sphere of influence.*

terrain contour matching. Advanced computer guidance systems allow *missiles* to match the terrain they overfly with high-quality maps, thus permitting mid-course corrections and ensuring greater accuracy. These course shifts may be substantial for *cruise missiles*. This does apply to *ballistic missiles*.

territorial defense. A defensive posture centering on protection of the homeland and showing little forward or offensive capability. *See also BMD; fortification; Great Wall; Maginot Line; Mannerheim Line.*

territorial integrity. An international legal principle holding that *sovereignty* is indivisible and that existing states should be broken apart or their *borders* significantly rearranged only in extremis. *See also Open Door; uti possidetis.*

territoriality (of criminal law). An international legal doctrine that *municipal law* may concern itself only with criminal offenses committed inside the *territorial jurisdiction* of the state concerned. *See also conflict of laws; jurisdiction; extraterritoriality; servitudes; universality of criminal law.*

territoriality principle. A general principle of *international law* which argues that a state should restrict its regulatory and other legal rule-making to goods, vehicles, and firms which, or persons who, reside within or cross into its territory. *See also alien; conflict of laws; extraterritoriality; jurisdiction; municipal law; servitudes; universality of criminal law.*

territorial jurisdiction. The legal competence of a *state* over the *territory* recognized as belonging to it. *See also jurisdiction; extraterritoriality; servitudes.*

territorial sea (territorial waters). Adjacent waters of a *coastal state*, between the *baseline* and the *high seas*. Formerly confined to the *three-mile limit*, it was extended by *UNCLOS III* to a maximum of a *twelve-mile limit*. A special case is the *Arctic*, where several nations have claimed sectors defined by points drawn from the Pole to the furthest east-west extremities of their northern *territory*. A unilateral claim was made by Indonesia (and some other archipelagic nations) for an "archipelagic regime," in which all waters within a designated perimeter surrounding an archipelago were claimed as *internal waters*. In UNCLOS III a compromise was struck, placing a limit of 100 nautical miles on archipelagic baselines. A unique case is North Korea's unilateral declaration of a 50-mile military zone projected from its baseline, in which it insisted upon exclusive economic and military rights. *See also contiguous zone; straight baseline.*

territorial supremacy. The legal freedom of *recognized* members of the *community of nations* (states) to *noninterference* and *nonintervention* in their *internal affairs*, and inter alia: to regulate entrance and egress from their national territory of persons, goods, and vehicles, subject to other rights, duties, and provisions of *international law*; to regulate rights to property and *nationality* of its own subjects or citizens; to regulate the rights, permissions, and limitations to visitation, residence, or work on the part of *aliens*; and to exercise supreme authority over all formal and legal relations with other states.

territorium nullius. "No one's land." *Territory* not under the *sovereignty* or *jurisdiction* of any *state*. This claim was frequently made, and sometimes was true—in the case of distant, unpopulated islands—by colonizing powers in the age of *imperialism*, in justification of new territorial claims. Modern examples include *Antarctica*, the *Moon*, planets, and other celestial bodies, and the deep *seabed*. *See also Navassa; uti possidetis.*

territory. A marked area under *jurisdiction* of a *state* or, rarely, some other *international personality*, including its airspace, inland waters, minerals, and subsoil. If a *coastal state*, it also has claims to an *Exclusive Economic Zone* corresponding to its *continental shelf* and to *territorial waters*. Territory can be acquired, legally or not, by the following means: *accretion, annexation, cession, conquest, discovery, occupation, peace treaty, prescription, union*, or *secession*. Normally, additions or subtractions to territory caused by annexation or cession do not affect the underlying international personality which governs the territory; that is not the case with conquest, occupation, union, or secession. *See also global commons;* territorium nullius.

terrorism. The use of indiscriminate violence to cause mass fear and panic to intimidate a population and advance one's political goals, whatever they may be. This was a classic instrument of *conquest* and governance of subject populations employed by forces as varied as the *Mongols* and Spanish *conquistadores*. Contemporary usage is limited to acts of terrorist violence by private (*nonstate*) groups which aim at advancing *revolutionary* (or *reactionary*) political goals. When governments use or support terror as an instrument of foreign policy, the preferred term is *state terrorism*. Very often, private groups contain a more prosaic criminal element and motivation, for which stated political aims provide cover and perhaps psychological justification. Though seldom without purpose or internal rationality, terrorism is nonetheless always outside the norms of civilized society. Indeed, it explicitly violates the *just war* principle of immunity for *noncombatants* in order to achieve mass psychological effects. In terms of international law, with the rise in the incidence of international terrorism from c. 1970, the scope of the concept of *political offenses* to which extradition did not apply was narrowed, so that performance of terrorist acts usually made perpetrators subject to extradition.

Terrorists have been found along the entire political spectrum. In the nineteenth century, *anarchists* (notably Russians and Spaniards) were the dominant group engaged in terrorism. During the 1920s and 1930s most terrorists in Europe came from the extreme, *nationalist* right-wing. The *League of Nations* drafted the first international convention on terrorism in 1937, which never came into force. That was a response to the *assassination* of *Alexander I of Yugoslavia* by a Macedonian nationalist, who fled to, and had support from, *fascist* Italy. In the 1960s, 1970s, and 1980s, active terrorists were mainly on the radical left or had agendas derived from the several conflicts in the *Middle East*. They were met by *death squads* and right-wing *militia* which employed tactics of counterterror ultimately indistinguishable from their guerrilla and urban terrorist enemies, and in Latin America, also far more deadly in numbers of total victims. The *United Nations General Assembly* and several regional organizations responded with conventions making terrorism a crime. The main UN instrument came into force in 1977. Other conventions followed in the 1980s. In the 1990s the general nature of political terrorism was blurred by the adoption of terrorist methods by organized international criminal groups, from *drug cartels* in Colombia to Italian, Russian, Vietnamese, and Chinese triads or mafias. Extensive use of terrorism by *ethnic groups* also was prevalent in Bosnia, Burundi, Rwanda, Chechnya, East Timor, other parts of Indonesia, and many additional areas. *Fundamentalists* adopted terrorist tactics in Algeria, Egypt, Sudan, and elsewhere in the *Islamic world* in the 1990s, often provoking mass violence, torture, and killing by the state, especially in Algeria.

Throughout the nineteenth and twentieth centuries terrorists seldom, if ever, achieved their stated political goals. Instead, they more often than not damaged the chance for reform and delayed implementation of political agendas which more civilized people otherwise might have viewed as having some merit. As the twentieth century drew to its close, security analysts most worried about terrorist use of ever more sophisticated and damaging weapons, including potential access to *weapons of mass destruction* by apocalyptic cults and/or fundamentalist religious *fanatics*, with or without state sponsorship. Even when using conventional weapons, the incidence of terrorist attacks and the number of deaths and injuries related to terrorism rose significantly in the second half of the twentieth century, until it numbered tens of thousands per decade globally—still a minuscule figure compared to even a small war, but not unworthy of serious security measures or analytical attention. Terrorism then leapt up the scale of individual state and civilized world concern with the unprovoked *September 11, 2001, terrorist attack on the United States*. The impact of the attack was unprecedented, by several measures. It was the greatest single loss of American civilian lives ever inflicted; it caused over $100 billion in damage to physical infrastructure; it led to hundreds of thousands of people in many dozens of countries losing their jobs as the world headed into a sharpened recession post–September 11th; and it prompted the greatest power on Earth at the start of the twenty-first century to fundamentally reconsider its force commitments and procurement policies, its effective deterrents, defenses, and homeland security, and to adopt a proactive, antiterrorist stance of hunting down and destroying terrorist threats with global reach wherever they appeared anywhere in the world. *See also anarchism; assassin; Baader-Meinhof; Black Hand; Black September; Usama bin Laden; George W. Bush; Bush Doctrine; destabilize; Entebbe raid; Euzkadi Ta Askatasuna; Freikorps; Front de Liberation du Québec; guerrilla war; Hamas; hijacking; hostage taking; insurgency; Irish Republican Army (IRA); Irgun; Khmers Rouges; narco-terrorism; Nazis; Olympic Games; Palestine Liberation Organization; al Qaeda; Red Brigades; Red Terror; SD; SS; Sendero Luminoso; Shanghai Cooperation Organization; Stalin; Stern Gang; Taliban; Ulster.*

Suggested Readings: Bruce Hoffman, *Inside Terrorism* (1998); Walter Laqueur, *Terrorism* (1977); Jessica Stern, *The Ultimate Terrorists* (1999); Jonathan R. White, *Terrorism: An Introduction*, 3rd ed. (2001).

tertiary sector. Economic activity which neither draws products from nature nor directly manufactures or processes goods, but is instead exclusively concerned with providing a wide range of *services*. After *World War II* this sector of the economy expanded enormously in advanced, industrial societies. *See also primary sector; secondary sector; structure.*

Teschen. Part of Silesia, ruled by the Habsburgs, 1772–1918. In the confusion engendered by division of the Austro-Hungarian lands in the closing days and aftermath of *World War I*, it was simultaneously claimed by Czechoslovakia and Poland. There was some fighting between those states into 1919. In 1920 it was *partitioned* by the *League of Nations*, leaving both sides discontented and posing an obstacle to collaboration within the *Little Entente*. After the *Munich Conference* (1938), the Czech portion was claimed by Poland. Following *World War II* and the incorporation of both Poland and Czechoslovakia into the *Soviet bloc*, Moscow reimposed the old 1920 to 1938 border.

Test Ban Treaty. *See Partial Test Ban Treaty.*

Tet Offensive (January 30–February 24, 1968). An attack on the cities of the Republic of Vietnam (RVN, South Vietnam) by the *Viêt Cong* (VC), or National Liberation Front (NLF), which coincided with the Tet, or lunar, holiday—a traditional period of *cease-fire*. (There was precedent for this: the Tây Són leader, Nguyên Huê or Quang Trung, defeated the *Manchus* in a series of battles launched during Tet in 1789, ending a Chinese invasion.) Some NLF entered the cities disguised as Army of the Republic of Vietnam (ARVN) troops, on U.S. military transports. Others were already there, *fifth columnists* lying in wait and long-prepared to lead an expected "general uprising" of the civilian population. U.S. military intelligence knew an attack was planned, but misjudged its timing and scale. Many ARVN troops were home for the Tet holiday. Of 44 provincial capitals, 36 were attacked, as were 5 more large cities, 64 smaller cities, and 50 "strategic hamlets." Saigon was a prime target, but the fiercest fighting was in Huê, where the NLF slaughtered 5,000 civilians before being overcome. ARVN and U.S. forces retook the cities after heavy fighting which inflicted massive losses on the NLF (50 percent total casualties, including 37,000 killed and 6,000 captured). This was followed by ARVN reprisal massacres of some NLF prisoners and suspected supporters.

Such huge combat losses, and the follow-up massacres, finished the NLF as an effective fighting force, and it was subsequently replaced in the field by North Vietnamese (PAVN, People's Army of Vietnam) regulars. While Tet thus was a major military disaster for the NLF, it resulted in an unexpected strategic victory for the Democratic Republic of Vietnam (DRV) and was a decisive turning point in the war. Occurring just after the *Johnson* administration gave assurances that the war was nearly won, the sheer scale of the offensive undermined years of optimistic claims by the administration and field commanders that the enemy was near defeat. The televised onslaught by thousands of NLF—including fighting inside the American Embassy compound in Saigon—also shook general press and public confidence in the administration's truthfulness. Tet made victory look ever more distant, and so many Americans turned against further prosecution of the war. Two months later, Johnson called a halt to bombing of the north and refused *Westmoreland's* and the Joint Chiefs' request for an additional 200,000 troops to finish the job of mopping up the remaining NLF in the countryside. Soon after that, the *Paris Peace Talks* began. *See also Clark Clifford; Robert McNamara; pacification; Vietnamization.*

Suggested Reading: Stanley Karnow, *Vietnam* (1984); Don Oberdorfer, *Tet!* (2001).

Teutonic Knights. Order of the Knights of the Hospital of St. Mary of the Teutons in Jerusalem. A *crusading* military order founded in 1191 in *Jerusalem* during the Third Crusade. With the failure of the Crusader states in the *Holy Land*, the Order moved into eastern Europe. It briefly fought for Hungarian Christians in Transylvania and then ravished Courland, Poland, Russia, and western Prussia, all under the absolution of the *Catholic Church* and in the name of the *Holy Roman Empire*. The Knights then settled in the conquered areas as a landed aristocracy, vacillating in *feudal* allegiance among the Empire, the king of Poland, and the popes. They united with the *Livonian Order*, 1237–1525. While the Knights maintained a strict feudal regime for peasants, driving many into virtual *slavery*, a number of Baltic cities within the Order's sphere were permitted to join the *Hansa*. The Knights frequently fought the Poles and Lithuanians, on whose territories their own bordered, and who at that time formed a large *condominium* dominating most of eastern Europe and western Russia. The Knights were defeated badly by a combined Polish-Lithuanian army at Tannenberg in 1410. In 1466 the Teutonic Order lost West Prussia to Poland and was compelled to transfer its capital from Marienburg to Königsberg (*Kaliningrad*). In 1525 the Grand Master of the Order, Albert of Brandenburg, converted to *Protestantism* and was invested as the Duke of Prussia. The Livonian Order broke away as one result. The remaining Catholic elements of the Teutonic Order survived in Germany, a landless and powerless ceremonial shell of their former presence, until 1809. *See also Crusades; East Prussia; Germany; Junkers; Kaliningrad exclave; Knights Hospitallers; Knights Templars; Orthodox Church; Poland; Prussia.*

Texas. Originally part of *Spanish America*, it became part of Mexico in 1821 upon Mexico's independence from Spain. In 1826 a so-called "Fredonia Republic" was declared by some misfit American settlers, but it was put down the following year by Mexican forces. Although Texas remained sparsely populated, after 1830 fighting between Mexicans and American settlers broke out again, this time on a larger scale and leading to a proclamation of *independence* by the latter in 1836. The great myth of Texas nationalism was birthed at the Alamo, whose 183 defenders were slaughtered by Mexican forces under *Santa Anna*. A few months later, a Texas army under Sam Houston (1793–1863) defeated the Mexican Army under Santa Anna, at San Jacinto (April 21, 1836), securing independence for Texas as an independent republic. In 1845 Texas was *annexed* by the United States, an act not accepted by Mexico until after its defeat in the *Mexican-American War*, which that annexation, and the related machinations of President *James Polk* to acquire *California*, provoked. Texas—which joined the American union as a *slave state*—later seceded from the Union (over Governor Houston's objection) to join the *Confederacy*. It was cut off from the Confederacy east of the Mississippi during the *American Civil War*. It was not occupied during the war, and in 1865 was the last part of the Confederacy to surrender its arms and rejoin the federal union. In 1901 *oil* was discovered in Texas, permanently altering its importance to the U.S. economy and leading to a boom in its population.

textiles. Woven fabric, or any fiber (jute, wool, etc.) capable of being woven. The cloth industry has long been a mainstay of economic activity. It was the most widespread of all industries in medieval Europe and continued to be of central importance well into the nineteenth century. In several distinct periods, textile production greatly expanded and benefited from technological innovation. The first was during the twelfth century, with the introduction of a pedal-operated loom, water-powered mills, and the spinning wheel. Another peak of great innovation and enhanced *productivity* came during the *Industrial Revolution*, with the application of steam and mechanical power to the tasks of carding, spinning, and weaving. Until the *Uruguay Round* of *General Agreement on Tariffs and Trade* (GATT), international trade in textiles was managed under the exceptionally complex Multi-Fibre Arrangement; but that was phased out, 1994–2004. Under *World Trade Organization* law, textiles are distinct from clothing, which is any manufactured garment rather than just fabric, to which a different schedule of *tariffs* may apply. Textiles and clothing both remain labor-intensive industries, though far less so than in previous centuries. This makes them crucially important to economies and exporters whose main *comparative advantage* is cheap labor. For the same reason (the high number of associated jobs), they were long and heavily protected by *Organization for Economic Cooperation and Development* (OECD) countries. *See also NAFTA.*

Thailand. As the Kingdom of Siam it was a power in Indochina for centuries, combating the Khmer Empire (Cambodia) and later contesting for *hegemony* with Vietnam. The Siamese were pushed from Cambodia by Vietnam in 1623. They reinvaded Cambodia in 1717, expelling the Vietnamese from the north and forcing the Khmer to switch allegiance and *tribute*. Vietnam expanded deeper into Cambodia, 1755–1760. Siam, at war with Burma at that time, was unable to intervene. From 1769 to 1773 Vietnam and Siam fought again, with Siam retaining most of Cambodia. From the sixteenth century Siam and Vietnam maintained a *condominium* over Laos. After the Tây Són Rebellion, Siam invaded the Mekong. The Tây Són destroyed the Siamese (1785), ending Siam's designs on southern Vietnam. Siam survived the Imperial Age without being colonized by a European power, the only southeast Asian nation to keep its *independence*. Siam did not escape unscathed: serving as a *buffer* between the British in India and the French in Indochina, Siam was stripped by France of its *vassal states* in *Cambodia* and *Laos*. Around the turn of the twentieth century it began to both *modernize* and *westernize*, while retaining its absolute *monarchy* until a bloodless revolt in 1932 converted it into a constitutional monarchy. In 1938 that reform was overturned by Pibul Songgram (1897–1964), who moved toward dictatorship during his first premiership, 1938–1944. Siam changed its name to Thailand in 1939. In 1940–1941 Thailand took advantage of the Japanese takeover of *French Indochina* to wage an undeclared war with France for border provinces lost to Laos in 1904 and Cambodia in 1907.

Thailand was occupied by Japan in 1941, by agreement with Pibul Songgram who briefly recovered Thailand's Indochinese territories from France under the *fascist* New Order in Asia (five provinces gained in 1941 were returned to Laos and Cambodia in 1945). While his government supported Japan, many Thai *guerrillas* joined the *resistance* to the Japanese. After a *coup*, Songgram returned as prime minister, 1948–1957, *aligned* with the Western powers against local Asian *communist* movements, and took Thailand into *SEATO*. During the American phase of the *Vietnam War*, Thai bases were used by the United States to bomb the Democratic Republic of Vietnam (DRV, North Vietnam), the *Hô Chí Minh Trail*, and *Khmers Rouges* positions in Cambodia. In 1967 Thailand joined ASEAN. During the 1980s Khmers Rouges settled along the border and sometimes just inside Thailand, from where they conducted guerrilla operations against the Vietnamese-backed government in Cambodia. That kept *tensions* high with Vietnam. With peace in Indochina, Thailand sought to more closely coordinate its diplomacy with other ASEAN members. In the 1980s it enjoyed an economic *boom*, though in the early 1990s there was some retrenchment from uncontrolled *growth*. In 1993 a *cease-fire* was signed with rebels in the Kachin region, who had been fighting the central government since 1961. Five other *ethnic groups* continued fighting, with the most significant *rebellion*, among the *Karen*, dating back to the 1940s. Thailand was hard hit by the *Asian financial crisis*, 1997–1998.

Suggested Reading: Rong Syamananda, *A History of Thailand* (1981).

thalweg. In *international law*, the rule that on a navigable waterway the *boundary* between two states shall run down the middle of the main channel, thus giving each state equal access to commercial uses, traffic, and so forth. If *accretion* occurs, the boundary shifts to track the center of the channel. If *avulsion* takes place instead, the original boundary remains in place.

Thatcher, Margaret, née Roberts (b. 1925). British stateswoman; prime minister, 1979–1990. Thatcher fundamentally changed the *Conservative Party* and Britain, not merely moving it to the right domestically and in foreign affairs, but permanently altering the underlying structure of its political economy. For the most part she focused on domestic policy, where she emphasized *monetarism, privatization* of major industries *nationalized* by earlier governments, cutting tax rates, general reversal of *Keynesian* governmental habits of intervention and regulation of the economy, and curtailment of the power of trade unions—she broke the Welsh coal miners' union by refusing to bend before a prolonged, bitter, and even nationally divisive strike. In foreign policy, she was deeply suspicious of connecting British *diplomacy* to the *European Community*, much preferring a *special relationship* with the United States and a close, personal cooperation with *Ronald Reagan*, over whom she had considerable *influence* on *Cold War* policy. She led Britain during the *Falklands War* and supported the U.S. bombing of *Libya* in 1986. On the other hand, she was deeply angry over the U.S. *invasion of Grenada*, on which she was not consulted despite Grenada being a member of the *Commonwealth*. She also faced sustained criticism from within the Commonwealth over her refusal to impose mandatory, comprehensive *sanctions* against South Africa. She led the West in recognizing that *Gorbachev* was different from other Soviet leaders, declaring "I can work with this man." Her opposition to the *European Union*, combined with an unpopular poll tax proposal, led to an internal *Tory* "coup" which forced her resignation in 1990. In April 1993, from her new seat in the House of Lords, Lady Thatcher called for *intervention* by *NATO* in Bosnia. That momentarily shook Western leaders, but did not influence their policy in any meaningful way. Thatcher's real legacy was in moving not only her own party to the right, but also moving the *Labour Party* from its long dalliance with the hard-line left closer to the center, and even to the right, by winning three general elections in a row, which had not been accomplished since the days of *Liverpool*. Nothing so concentrates the political mind as defeat, however, or clouds it like victory: in the 1990s a reformed Labour Party under *Tony Blair* won back-to-back majorities against a decimated and demoralized Conservative Party.

    Suggested Reading: Eric J. Evans, *Thatcher and Thatcherism* (1997).

thaw. A journalistic, but not inaccurate, metaphor describing improvements in interstate relations which are less than a full *rapprochement*, but notably warmer (less tense) than a preceding period of chilly relations or *cold war*.

theater nuclear weapons. Systems limited in range to one region or *theater of war*.

theater of war. (1) In combat: A strategically and geographically distinct area within a larger conflict, as in "the Pacific theater during *World War II*." (2) In *international law*: the locale(s) where *acts of war* may lawfully be carried out.

theocracy. Rule by a priesthood, acting as deputies (soi-dissant) of the deity. *See also Bhutan; Byzantine Empire; caliph; Enlightenment; Fulbe Empire; fundamentalism; Inquisition; Iran; mandate of heaven; popular sovereignty;* real patronato; res publica Christiana; *secularism; Sudan; Taiping rebellion; Taliban; two swords; White Lotus rebellion.*

theory (in international relations). In normal discourse about world affairs a theory is any statement about economic, political, social, and historical facts pertaining to *states* and the *states system*, which purports to explain causal relationships among some or all of these facts. In contemporary international relations theory it usually means a working hypothesis or theorem (a proposition capable of being deduced from the assumptions of a theoretical system) put forward by an academic who then seeks to "test" it by reference to empirical "data" (by which is most often meant the facts of *history*, however badly or shallowly read or understood). Alternately, academics use "international relations theory" in reference to some systematic view, or body of theorems, which they have collectively assembled. These will then be upheld by this or that clique within the academy as universal explanations of state behavior. Basic flaws, contradictions of the real world, and other obvious problems will simply be reclassified as "lacunae in the literature," or "matters for further empirical investigation and research," phrases which perhaps should be read as meaning: "I intend to seek another grant," and "possible dissertation topic for one of my research assistants here." Alternately, the colloquial sense of "theory" is "an unproven assumption," which may be nearer the mark in describing most putative academic theories about international relations.

In fact, many ideas asserted to be theories in post-1950 social science literature about world affairs are, upon even the most cursory inspection, revealed to be little more than exaggerated metaphors (e.g., *bicycle theory* or the widely cited notions of *bipolarity, multipolarity,* and other variations on analogies to magnetic attraction). Other so-called theories are well-known, obvious, indeed trite observations, overdressed as sophisticated—but usually just sophistic—analysis. Perhaps the most basic error made by social scientists who seek a formal theory of international relations is the deeply false assumption that the facts of history as collected or gathered by historians are (1) mere data, and (2) already established as objective truths. Such uncritically accepted "empirical data" is then strained (in both senses of the word) through sieves of mathematical or other formalistic analysis by political scientists, so that a general and theoretical meaning may be divined. This ignores the epistemology of history, which is itself profoundly theoretical, often to the point of being heavily overladen with psychological, sociological, economic, political, and other causal assumptions and explanations imposed on facts by the historians who peer at them from inside the prison (they would say, prism) of their own times.

On the other hand, there is a body of international relations theory called the *classical school* which is deeply humanistic and steeped in knowledge of the intricacies and limitations of historical and human *agency* and the complex normative, legal, and other operations of what it calls *international society*. On specific theories of international relations and political economy, and related topics, *see also behavioralism; causation; collective security; communism; critical theory; decision theory; decision-making theory; dependency theory; deterrence; Albert Einstein; game theory; falsification; geopolitics; grand theory; hegemonic stability theory; idealism; imperialism; international law; just war tradition; Keynesian economics; labor theory of value; liberal-internationalism; long-cycle theory; macro; Maoism; Marxism; Marxism-Leninism; mercantilism; micro; modernization; monetarism; mood theory; neorealism; outlier; pacifism; paradigm; parsimonious theory; postbehavioralism; postimperialism; postmodernism; qualitative analysis; quantitative analysis; rational choice theory; rational decision-making; realism; scientism; structuralism; supply side; systems theory; traditionalism.*

Thermidor (July 27, 1794). (1) A conservative *reaction* and *coup* which marked the end of *The Terror* in France and of rule by the *Committee of Public Safety* and the start of the *Directory*; it was named for the 11th month of the *French Revolution* calendar, or Thermidor, July 19–August 17. (2) Any comparable *conservative* reaction to preceding, revolutionary events.

thermonuclear bomb. *See hydrogen bomb.*

thesis. (1) A proposition to be considered against logical or empirical objections raised against it. (2) In Hegelian method, a proposition capable of generating an opposing proposition (*antithesis*). *See also dialectic.*

"The Terror." In April 1793, the *French Revolution* took a radical turn under the Committee of Public Safety. In October, the *Girondins* were overthrown and many were guillotined by the even more radical *Jacobins*. During 1793 and 1794 the main Jacobin leaders, *Robespierre* and *Danton*, then struggled to control the Revolutionary Convention. With Robespierre's ultimate victory, Danton and his supporters were put to death and "The Terror" entered a crescendo phase. Nearly 13,000 were guillotined in the cities, while in the *Vendée* a virtual *genocide* took place against *Catholic* priests and their peasant followers. Its essential, modern spirit was captured by Louis Saint-Just (1767–1794), a 27-year-old *fanatic* bombast who, among other ridiculous ideas, proposed with Robespierre that French boys be removed from their mothers at age seven and raised to serve the state: "The Republic," he pronounced, "consists in the extermination of everything that opposes it." "The Terror" ended after July 28, 1794, with the arrest and guillotining of Robespierre and about 100 of his closest followers (including Saint-Just) by those who feared a new purge might sweep them into the prisons or to the guillotine. In its day, this orgy of state organized political violence shocked, and shook, the conscience of Europe. By modern standards of state murder the number of its victims seems almost modest: the death toll of "The Terror" barely equals, for example, a single day of murders of Jews by the *Nazis* at the height of the *Holocaust*. *See also Cultural Revolution; Red Terror; Yezhovshchina*.

think tank. A quasi-private, non-teaching academic and policy institute usually, though not always, affiliated with a major political party. At best, they can be generators of legislative and foreign policy ideas. More often, they are career parking places for potential officials in a new administration who are affixed to the party currently in opposition.

Third International (COMINTERN). *See International (communist)*.

Third Reich. *See Germany; Adolf Hitler; National Socialism; Reich*.

Third Republic. France, from the *defeat* of 1871 to the defeat of 1940. Legally, it survived until the creation of the *Fourth Republic* in 1946; politically, however, it effectively ended with its displacement by *Vichy*. *See also Léon Blum; Georges Clemenceau; Édouard Daladier; Charles de Gaulle; Dreyfus Affair; Jules Ferry; France; Franco-Prussian War; Free French; Paris Commune; Tonkin Wars*.

Third Rome. A Russian *Orthodox* doctrine with deep *nationalist* undertones, first formulated in the sixteenth century, which maintained that responsibility for the "True Church" and Christian faith had passed to Russia, where Moscow was the Third Rome, or rightful capital of the Christian world. The logic of the succession was this: the original Christian capital at Rome was lost when the *Roman Empire* in the West succumbed to pagan invaders in the fifth century (the Orthodox, in *schism* from the *Catholic Church*, did not acknowledge the claims of, and ignored indignant protests by, distant popes who claimed to govern the faithful all along, from Rome); the Second Rome was said to have been *Constantinople*, which was overrun by the Muslim Ottoman Empire in 1453. *Peter I* was the first *tsar* to take up this claim and use it as cudgel against the Ottomans, by claiming to be the liberator of the Orthodox and other Christian peoples of the Balkans and a protector of the *Holy Places* in *Jerusalem*. It fed into *Slavophilism* with its none-too-subtle suggestion that Russia might seek to liberate the Second Rome from the Muslim Turk. Certainly this was its primary meaning during the *Russo-Turkish Wars*.

Third World (*tiers monde*). A term coined by French theorists but popularized by *Nehru* and used to describe the political *neutrality* of most *developing nations* with regard to the *Cold War* contest between West (*First World*) and East (*Second World*). It later evolved to mean more the economic conditions of poverty and *dependence* of the majority of African, Asian, and Latin American nations. By c. 1970, it referred to the fact that their economies and living standards did not rank with the *OECD* nations, while their non-*communism* or *non-alignment* (true in most, but not all, cases) also positioned them outside the *Soviet bloc*. However, some Third World countries de facto joined the Soviet camp, while others sided openly with the West. The term therefore eventually assumed a primary, economic sense as a nearly exclusive connotation. During the 1960s and 1970s it took on an additional imputation, one of Western responsibility to help meet the socioeconomic needs of Southern peoples, based upon moral claims growing out of complaints about *imperialism* and *neocolonialism*. By the 1980s, however, imagery had shifted and "Third World" evoked a sense of harsh, corrupt, and abusive regimes which denied *basic rights* to impoverished populations even while also failing to satisfy their *basic needs*. In the 1990s it was displaced by *South* as a term of preference among those analysts who wished to escape from under some or all of these negative meanings, though it remained in wide, popular use. *See also ACP nations; appropriate technology; ASEAN; Bandung; debtor cartel; debt crisis; dependency theory; development; Fourth World; G-77; Generalized System of Preferences; graduation clause; International Bank for Reconstruction and Development; International Monetary Fund; Lomé Conventions; multinational corporation; modernization; NIEO; NWICO; Nonaligned Movement; North-South issues; OAS; OAU; Pacific Islands Forum; quasi states; regional banks; rising expectations; South Pacific Commission; STABEX; stabilization program; UNCTAD; UNDP; United Nations General Assembly.*

Thirty Years' War (1618–1648). The first half of the seventeenth century in Europe was riven with crisis: economic, political, social, intellectual, and religious. This ferment was both reflected in, and worsened by, the Thirty Years' War, which was not really one war but several, and which did not really begin in 1618 or end in 1648. Yet, those conventional dates cover well a series of related wars, mostly centered in or fought over Germany. The main protagonists at first were *Catholics* and *Protestants* and the states each controlled, but *mercenaries* too were important participants, while princes of different faiths ultimately schemed with each other against their co-religionists. Moreover, the war ended not with the triumph of one religious party over the other, but with a great compromise based on entirely *secular* principles. In its course and destructiveness it took the religious question out of European and *Great Power* politics (at least, as a major subject of *diplomacy*), jolted the convictions of princes even as it shook the land, and reorganized the states system around agreement that members should conduct their affairs based upon *raison d'etat*, rather than differences of opinion on such questions as transubstantiation or the transmigration of souls. In short, it was nothing less than a *revolution* in the affairs of states which had lasting, and global, significance.

(1) Bohemian phase, 1618–1625: It began with a Protestant challenge to the Catholic (*Habsburg*) rulers of Bohemia, including the humorous (to Protestants) and sacrilegious (to Catholics) Defenestration of Prague, in which two imperial ambassadors were pushed out a second story window, to land alive but humiliated in a dung heap. The Protestant rebellion which followed threatened the religious balance among the Electors who chose the *Holy Roman Emperor*: Bohemia held the decisive seventh vote, since the first six were divided among three Catholic and three Protestant electors. The revolt thus struck at the heart of Habsburg and Catholic power in Germany, just as it was also being challenged doctrinally by criticisms of *Martin Luther* and constitutionally by German princes during a contested imperial election. This confluence of events encouraged one brash, young, Protestant prince, Frederick of the Rhineland (the "Winter King"), to intervene in support of Protestantism in Bohemia, in hope of securing the province for himself. Catholic Europe responded with a *coalition* which overthrew Frederick, employing mainly Spanish troops hardened in the *Reconquista* and conquest of the Americas and full of a *fanatic* fire against Protestantism stoked by the *Inquisition*. The Imperial Army crushed the Bohemian rebels at the *Battle of White Mountain* (November 8, 1620). The Empire then imposed a draconian punishment on all Bohemia, instituting the full weight of the *Counter Reformation* and the cruel *tortures* and doctrinal rigors of the Inquisition to root out heresy and strip rebels of their lands, freedoms, and often also of their lives. The war spread, however, to the Palatinate next, where it continued into 1623 and Catholic victory.

(2) Danish phase, 1625–1629: The King of Denmark, Christian IV (1577–1648), wanted an expanded domain, fresh new lands for his son to rule. He saw the chance to play upon Protestant (and French) fears of Catholic Spain, whose reach extended now into Germany. A Protestant coalition failed to form around him, however, and after four years of fighting which devastated north Germany, Christian and Denmark were alike beaten into submission. Catholic and Imperial power was now ascendant, and the great Habsburg armies and generals, the imperial officer *Tilly* and the mercenary *Wallenstein*, seemed unassailable. It was a time for grace and magnanimity if the spate of war was to end. Instead, Emperor *Ferdinand II* tried to turn back a century of compromise with Protestantism by an edict which would have forced Protestant princes and Free Cities alike within the Holy Roman Empire to yield traditional freedoms—dating to the 1555 *Peace of Augsburg*—to imperial authority, and even to convert back to "the one true Faith" (from the other one). Even many Catholic princes saw this as a narrow Habsburg grab for *hegemony* in Germany, rather than as a Catholic policy.

(3) Swedish phase, 1630–1635: The Imperial edict brought Protestant Sweden and Catholic France together, in defense of local *autonomy* against Imperial authority and Spanish hegemony. Now *Gustavus Adolphus* intervened, seeing an expansion of Swedish power as nicely linked to the Protestant cause in Germany. Though he died in battle, his intervention altered the whole course of the war—and modern history. It saved the Protestant cause, but also converted the conflict into a raw struggle for political power, regardless of faith. Catholic France, led by a prince of the church, Cardinal *Richelieu*, entered the war not on the side of the Catholic cause but in alliance with Protestant princes in Germany and Sweden, and even the Ottoman *Sultan*, to fight Catholic Austria and Spain.

(4) General phase, 1635–1648: For thirteen more years Catholic, Protestant, and private armies battled, mostly marauding over Germany, sacking cities and terrorizing the populace as they battened on the land. Now, too, Catholic fought Catholic and Protestant killed Protestant, while both murdered, raped, tortured, and burned out each other, spreading *famine*, pestilence, *refugees*, cruelty, and death through the heart of Germany and Europe. Huge mercenary armies did not so much fight strategic battles as constantly maneuver, plunder, and forage, all the while collecting their wages of death. Entire cities were put to the sword out of revenge or *reprisal*. Most famously, Magdeburg was sacked by the Imperial Army on May 20, 1631. Its 25,000 inhabitants were butchered—man, woman, and child, without distinction—while the entire city was razed to the ground, except for the cathedral, the sole surviving building whose aspirational spires looked out over the smoking ruin of Christian mercy and the mock tradition of *just war*. That left some areas of Germany and Bohemia denuded of half their population, while other provinces paid huge ransoms to approaching armies—of whichever side—to deflect the war elsewhere, escape with their lives, and keep towns, livestock, and farms intact.

Relief finally arrived in 1648, in the form of the *Peace of Westphalia*, that great set of agreements which settled the religious question in Germany once and for all, and on a secular basis, and which thus conventionally and reasonably demarcates the emergence of the modern state system. Another major consequence of the war was to leave Germany weak and divided (more than 300 distinct German entities were *recognized* at Westphalia), and so on the margins of world history and politics for another 150 years. The general mêlée had amounted to a fundamental crisis in European civilization, in its final phase witnessing a transition from an era of war between religious communities to a new era of war among princes and states, for raison d'état. The age of "horizontal loyalty" to popes and the Holy Roman Empire was about over, though the full transition would take many more years. The new age of "vertical loyalty" to centralized states and monarchs was well underway, driven far down that road by a prolonged war which had speeded advanced state-building and political and administrative centralization, as necessary in order to sustain wartime taxation and finances and thereby keep enlarged armies in the field. *Primus inter pares* among the myriad states and statelets of Europe for the next two centuries was France, the preeminent Great Power of the second half of the seventeenth century and the greatest single beneficiary of the Thirty Years' War. Thus did an originally German conflict, stemming from an odd confessional confrontation, become a European-wide war—and in essence also a global war, with naval battles waged as far afield as Brazil and Ceylon—which reshaped the whole international system, and replace a declining Imperial Spain at the pinnacle of the state system with the rising power of France.

Suggested Readings: Ronald Asch, *The Thirty Years' War* (1997); Geoffrey Parker, ed., *The Thirty Years' War* (1987); S. H. Steinberg, *The "Thirty Years' War" and the Conflict for European Hegemony, 1600–1660* (1966).

Thirty Years' War (1914–1945). A term gaining acceptance among historians to point out the interrelatedness of the two major conflicts which scarred and dominated the first half of the twentieth century: *World War I* and *World War II.*

thousand bomber raids. Massive air raids against German cities and industrial plant, mounted by the United Kingdom and United States during *World War II.* The first raid hit Cologne on the night of May 30–31, 1942. The British subsequently bombed Germany by night. At first the Americans bombed it by day, unescorted by fighters until the long-range P-40 Mustang was developed much later in the war. However, they suffered plane and crew losses so heavy that the U.S. Air Force, too, switched to night bombing. The raids pulverized *Hitler*'s cities. They were, in fact, specifically intended to "de-house" German workers and provoke a political revolt against the misery they produced. It is less clear what damage they did to war production, as most German factories had already moved underground or further east, out of range. Allied losses lightened in late 1944 and in 1945, as long-range escort fighters became available, *air superiority* was established, and *Luftwaffe* pilot losses became irreplaceable. Not even Hitler's introduction of the first jet fighters, one of his vaunted "secret weapons," could compensate for a severe pilot shortage and inexperience.

Paradoxically, these raids raised German *national morale*, rather than shattering it as hoped. After the war, they were criticized on *just war* grounds as disproportionate and *indiscriminate*. The cruel truth is that, at the time, they provided grim satisfaction to Allied publics who more or less believed that Germans (and in the Pacific, the Japanese) deserved a taste of what they had rained down on others. The tone was set by hard men on all sides, such as Britain's Arthur "Bomber" Harris, in charge of Bomber Command. After Royal Air Force bombers totally destroyed 780 acres of German city, and its inhabitants, he rather callously remarked that the damage done "squared our account" for the earlier German bombing of the cathedral city of Coventry. Such is war. By the time it all ended, in May 1945, Anglo-American bombing of Germany had killed 600,000 civilians and seriously injured nearly a million more. Among the dead, some 20 percent were children, whereas the vast majority of the remainder were those unable to flee the cities: women, the old, the infirm or poor. The United States bombed Japan in similar fashion, to even greater effect. There, strategic bombing of the *home islands* ultimately brought the whole Japanese economy and population to its knees, even before the atomic bombings of *Hiroshima* and *Nagasaki* incinerated the last vestiges of a will to resist further in the name of the god-emperor, *Hirohito*.

three-mile limit. The minimum extension of *territorial waters* agreed upon before *UNCLOS III*. It originates from the *cannon-shot rule* championed by the Netherlands in the seventeenth century, in opposition to a Danish view that the territorial sea should have an agreed upon, gauged width. Three nautical miles out (from low tide) was a nice compromise between these positions. *See also twelve-mile limit.*

throw weight. Discounting fuel and rocket weight, throw weight is the *payload* carried by a *missile*. It includes all *penetration aids*, single reentry vehicles or MIRVs, *warheads*, and release and guidance devices.

Thucydides (c. 460–400 B.C.E.). *See Peloponnesian Wars.*

thugi (thuggee). "Dacoity." Ritual murder (by strangulation) and robbery, as part of a devotional cult to the *Hindu* goddess Kali. Some thugs claimed a right to this practice as a *caste* profession. The thugs often preyed on travelers, which interfered with trade. The practice was banned by the *East India Company* in 1835.

Tiananmen Square incident (April 4–5, 1976). Tiananmen Square had emerged as the key site of nationalist and student demonstrations during the *May 4th movement* demonstrations in 1919. It had also witnessed the extraordinary demonstrations of the *Red Guards* during the *Great Proletarian Cultural Revolution*. In 1976 it again took center stage in Chinese history, as tens of thousands of initially peaceful protestors gathered at the memorial to the heroes of the *Chinese Revolution* which dominates the Square. They had come to pay homage to the recently deceased *Zhou Enlai*. Ultimately, the Beijing police moved in and made mass arrests; these were followed by *show trials*. At the level of the *Politburo*, the incident was used by *Mao* and the *Gang of Four* to *purge* key enemies, most notably *Deng Xiaoping*.

Tiananmen Square massacre (June 4, 1989). In 1988 the pro-democracy movement in China led to a revival of the *Democracy Wall* movement. Mass student demonstrations in Beijing followed the death of reformer *Hu Yaobang* (April 15, 1989), provoking much hesitation and fierce debate about what to do among central authorities in the *Chinese Communist Party* (CCP). International media attention was enormous as a result of the presence in Beijing of hundreds of reporters gathered there preparing to cover a historic state visit by *Mikhail Gorbachev*, which clearly signaled the end of the *Sino-Soviet split*. Some students began a hunger strike, and the Square filled on certain days with a million or more ordinary Chinese, workers, and residents from Beijing and nearby towns and cities determined to show support for the students. Some demonstrators began calling for resignations of the top CCP leaders. On May 20th, *martial law* was declared, but in the two weeks which followed the demonstrators' and strikers' ranks grew. This was a direct challenge to the state and the CCP. Finally, *Deng Xiaoping* (perhaps remembering the worst excesses of the *Great Proletarian Cultural Revolution*), *Li Peng*, and other top CCP leaders ordered in the *People's Liberation Army* (PLA).

The first units, from near Beijing, refused to enter the Square. Deng called up more distant units, however, and on June 4th hundreds of Beijing's students and citizens were indiscriminately shot or were crushed to death under PLA tanks. That act of callous barbarism was watched on live international television, until the signal was cut off. A thousand or more may have died (all bodies were buried in secret), as the PLA fanned into the city killing more students and onlookers. Some PLA soldiers were literally torn apart by enraged crowds, who had watched children mown down without warning or just cause. Violence spread to other cities, but was contained by similarly tough methods. Thousands were arrested, and many were executed. Others were sent to *reeducation* camps. Some escaped abroad, after months in hiding, to become international critics of the regime. China was universally condemned and briefly withdrew into wounded, xenophobic *isolationism*. The formal end of the *Cold War* in 1990 and the general thrust of reform already underway in China meant the massacre only temporarily interrupted its historic economic and diplomatic opening to the wider world. However, it led to many more years of political repression than might have been the case had the "moderate" faction in the *Politburo* not been overruled by Deng and his octogenarian comrades, for the crisis led directly to the rise of *hard-liners* to leadership positions, including Li Peng and *Jiang Zemin*, who repressed demonstrators in Shanghai. The West considered *sanctions*, but in the end the massacre led only to rejection of Beijing's bid to host the 2000 *Olympic Games* (it later won the 2008 Games), a feeble if well-intentioned moral gesture. *See also Flying Tigers; May 4th movement; Tiananmen Square incident.*

Tibet. Tibet moved in and out of Chinese control over the centuries, according to the strength of the emperors and the politics of *Inner Asia*, especially concerning the *Mongols*. Tibet was the key to control of Mongolia at least since the time of the great Khans in the thirteenth century. As an Inner

Asian dynasty themselves, the *Qing* (Manchus) understood this, and thus Emperor *Kangxi* occupied Lhasa in 1720, beginning an era of Chinese military intervention in Tibetan affairs. Thereafter Kangxi's successors both supported and manipulated "Yellow Hat Lamaism" to better control the population. An uprising occurred in 1750 that was quickly suppressed. *Gurkhas* from Nepal invaded Tibet in 1790, but they were defeated by *banner troops* sent in by the Qing Emperor *Qianlong*. After the *Boxer rebellion* (1900), the Manchus were a moribund political force in China, and Tibet correspondingly broke free of *Han* control. Lord *Curzon* attached it to the *British Empire*, via an unprovoked invasion, in 1904. This was accepted by Moscow, which during the *Great Game* had flirted with supporting Tibet against China and Britain, in the *Anglo-Russian Entente* of 1907. The *Chinese Revolution* of 1911 also wracked Tibet, causing the Dalai Lama to flee. Tibet's de facto independence from China was confirmed in 1913 when the *Dalai Lama* returned from exile (in India) to reign under a newly proclaimed British *protectorate*.

Britain's power in Asia ebbed steadily and was on the wane even before it took charge in Tibet. And British attention, energy, and resources were all drawn back to Europe by two world wars. Finally, by 1949 China was again ascendant in the region, and after the *Chinese Revolution* of 1949 it was under an aggressively nationalist and *communist* regime which was determined on "reunification" of Tibet with China. In 1950 China invaded Tibet, declaring that it was simply recovering a long-lost province. Nine years later Tibetans rose against China, then in the midst of the chaos of the *Great Leap Forward*. They were defeated after heavy fighting and much bloodshed, and widespread destruction within Tibet. The Dalai Lama fled into *exile*, from where he lobbied a mostly cautious, though not wholly indifferent, world to support Tibetan independence. The *Indo-Chinese War* of 1962 was indirectly caused by China's effort to assimilate Tibet. In 1965 Tibet was made an "autonomous region" within China. During the *Great Proletarian Cultural Revolution* it was harshly treated, with Buddhist temples closed and even destroyed by rampaging *Red Guards*, and thousands of monks and others killed. In 1988 and 1989, widespread unrest was again savagely repressed. China deliberately encouraged Han *immigration* into Tibet to reinforce its claims and suffocate local nationalism. This cynical policy worked: by 2000 native Tibetans were an ethnic minority in their own land.

Suggested Readings: Christopher Beckwith, *The Tibetan Empire in Central Asia* (1987); Tsering Shakya, *Dragon in the Land of Snows* (1999).

tied aid. Attaching procurement "strings" to grant *aid*, so that the money either goes directly to purchases from local producers in the *donor country* or later recycles back to the donor economy for follow-up *services*. It is criticized for undercutting the *development* impact of aid by converting it into a manufacturing export support or job program for the donor economy and by forcing recipients to purchase inappropriate or expensive *goods*. Its proponents argue that it helps sustain a domestic constituency for aid which otherwise might dry up. Most donor nations have agreed to significantly reduce the percentage of their aid which is tied; a few have even done so.

tied loan. A loan where the borrower must spend the monies solely in the lending country. It has the same benefits to the lender, and the same problems for the borrower, as experienced with *tied aid*.

Tientsin (Tianjin), Treaty of (1858). China was forced to sign this humiliating agreement with Britain (quickly followed, on the basis of the *most-favored nation* principle, by similar *unequal treaties* with France, Russia, and the United States) after a display of British *gunboat diplomacy* during the *Second Opium War*. It permitted a British ambassador to take up residence in Beijing, opened ten more coastal cities to foreign trade as *treaty ports*, allowed foreigners to import opium for sale to Chinese addicts, gave additional *Qing* guarantees and access to the interior of the country for traders and Christian *missionaries*, and set disadvantageous *tariff* terms.

Tientsin (Tianjin), Treaty of (1885). Signed during the *Tonkin Wars* between France and China, by this treaty China renounced *suzerainty* over Vietnam and *recognized* it as a French *protectorate*.

Tigre (Tigray). A province of *Ethiopia*, bordering *Eritrea*, where in the 1970s and 1980s a *secessionist* movement fought a *guerrilla war* in conjunction with Ethiopia's other wars in Eritrea and with *Somalia*. The Tigreans—led by quixotic *Leninists* who admired *Enver Hoxha*—led a coalition to victory under Meles Zenawi, who later pushed them from central power.

Tilly, Count Johan (1559–1632). *Catholic* and Imperial field marshal in the *Thirty Years' War*. A *Habsburg* subject born in the *Spanish Netherlands* (*Flanders*), Tilly was raised by his *Jesuit* teachers to the service of the Church militant. He first saw combat at age fifteen and spent the remainder of his life in military service. He fought in behalf of the *Holy Roman Empire*, 1600–1608, against the *Ottomans* in Hungary. In 1610 he hired out to the Catholic League. He led a Catholic coalition army into Bohemia in the first phase of the Thirty Years' War, crushing the Bohemian Protestants at the *Battle of White Mountain* (November 8, 1620). Throughout the 1620s he was one of two principal Habsburg generals, along with the great *mercenary* of the Age, *Immanuel Wallenstein*. Tilly again led a Catholic army to a major victory, over the forces of Christian IV of Denmark, in 1626. It was his army which was responsible for the most famous atrocity of the Thirty Years' War: the *sack* of Magdeburg. Tilly was beaten badly in 1631 during the spectacular intervention in the war by *Gustavus Adolphus* of Sweden and was driven all the way back to Bavaria. He was mortally wounded in April 1632. *See also* *Ferdinand II.*

Tilsit, Treaties of (July 8, 1807). These treaties were signed after *Napoleon I's* occupation of Prussia in October 1806, during the *War of the Fourth Coalition*, and defeat of the Russian Army at Friedland on June 14, 1807. Negotiated directly by Napoleon and *Alexander I*, two treaties—one open and one secret—set up French and Russian *spheres of influence* in Europe and proclaimed a mutual defense pact. The two emperors met, with studied drama, on a raft in the middle of the River Niemen. In the public treaty, Russia accepted French domination of Europe west of the Elbe, reduction in half of its defeated ally Prussia, creation of a French *vassal state* (the Grand Duchy of Poland) on its own doorstep, reorganization of Germany into a French-controlled Confederation of the Rhine, and *recognition* of three of Napoleon's brothers as kings of Naples, Holland, and Westphalia. In the secret accord Alexander agreed to join Napoleon's *Continental System* on the condition (which was fulfilled) that Britain refused to make *peace* with France, and to join the war against England. In turn, France agreed to *partition* the European possessions of the *Ottoman Empire* with Russia, should the Turkish sultan not make peace with the tsar. Russia was also granted a claim on Finland, which it forced Sweden to cede two years later. The agreements were soon violated by both sides: Russia remained neutral in the war with England and secretly continued to trade outside the Continental System, while France gave no help in the war against the Turks. In 1812, Napoleon tossed aside what was left of Tilsit and invaded Russia, beginning a mortal contest which ended only with his defeat and overthrow in 1814 and again in 1815.

tilt. A journalistic, but not inaccurate, term for when a state's foreign policy gradually changes from one of *neutrality* to one of favoring a given side in a *conflict*, or changes slowly from supporting one side to supporting the other.

Timbuktu. *See Fulbe; Mali Empire; Songhai; Tuareg.*

Timor. Largest of the Lesser *Sunda Islands*. It was first colonized by the Portuguese. The Dutch laid claim to part of the island in 1613. The dispute was resolved in a treaty (1859; renegotiated and implemented in 1914), which set the border between Dutch and Portuguese claims. Indonesia inherited the Dutch half after *World War II*. Portugal clung to *East Timor* until 1975, when it was illegally annexed by Indonesia. After many years of *guerrilla war*, it became independent in 2000.

Tippu Tip, né Muhammad bin Hamed (c. 1830–1905). Also known as Tippu Tib. A *Swahili Arab* from Zanzibar who from the 1860s to 1890s united much of eastern Africa by military force, and in service of *slave* and *ivory* trading, under the nominal authority of the Sultans of Zanzibar. He took for himself the title "Sultan of Utetera." He met *Stanley* in 1877 and accepted to become a governor for King *Leopold*, based at Stanley Falls, 1877–1892. He realized that the *Great Powers* were about to invade his and surrounding territory, which until then had been largely free of direct contact with Europe. In 1883 he tried to rally eastern Congolese to accept the authority of Zanzibar to forestall European entry, but this claim was dismissed at the *Berlin Conference*. He retired to Zanzibar in 1893.

Suggested Reading: Heinrich Brodie, *Tippu Tip* (2000).

tirailleurs. (1) Originally, French sharpshooters and *skirmishers* during the *Napoleonic Wars*. They were made famous by their innovative use by *Napoleon* to break up the opposing line, before hitting it with his *cavalry* and *infantry*. The term was later used for non-French troops who adopted comparable tactics. (2) Units of native troops organized by the French colonial army especially in Senegal and West Africa, but also used in *French Indochina*.

Tirailleurs Sénégalais. A famous West African native force first organized by the French in 1857. Along with European *mercenaries* in the *French Foreign Legion*, it did most of the fighting, conquering, and dying as France constructed its vast empire in West Africa in the second half of the nineteenth century. It cost France almost three times as much to maintain a French soldier in Africa as it did to hire an African mercenary in the Tirailleurs Sénégalais. Also, the death or maiming of one of the latter in battle did not arouse the same anti-imperialist opposition in France as white battle deaths did. In the 1890s the French expanded the force through use of the *rachat* system, or purchase of domestic slaves. Other Tirailleurs Sénégalais were recruited from the detritus of the army of the collapsed *Tukolor Empire*. Other European powers did much the same: the British held most of their imperial possessions in West Africa with the King's African Rifles, founded in 1902; Germany used all-white mounted troops in *German Southwest Africa*, but elsewhere employed African "askaris"; the Italians, too, used "ascaris" in Somaliland and their several invasions of Ethiopia. In *World War I* some 180,000 Tirailleurs Sénégalais served with the French Army, part of a contingent of nearly 850,000 colonial troops France used in the Great War.

Tirpitz, Alfred von (1849–1930). German grand admiral and ultranationalist. He persuaded *Kaiser Wilhelm II* to build a great battle fleet to challenge Britain at sea, not so much by promising a German *victory*—though at a planned ratio of 2 to 3 that was conceivable—but by denying Britain its clear predominance ("the Tirpitz Plan" or "risk theory"). This enormously destabilized international relations before *World War I*. Although early on he cavalierly dismissed *U-boats* as ineffective, once they proved themselves by sinking warships and merchant vessels he quickly converted to vigorous support of a policy of *unrestricted submarine warfare*. He resigned, in a Prussian huff, in 1916 when temporarily overruled on that issue. He later became a leading propagandist for German *revisionist* history about the origins and nature of the war and was active in far-right politics during the *Weimar Republic*. *See also Jutland; "stab-in-the-back."*

Titoism. Archaic. It meant the assertion of the *national interests* of a communist *state* against the international interests of the *communist* movement, as defined by Moscow. It derived from the practice of *Tito* of *Yugoslavia*. Once the Soviet Union became *extinct*, and Yugoslavia broke apart, the term assumed solely historical significance.

Tito, né Josip Broz (1892–1980). *Partisan* general and Yugoslav marshal and dictator. Born in Croatia, during *World War I* Josip Broz served with a Croatian unit in the Austro-Hungarian Army, fighting on the Serbian front. Already a radical *socialist*, he was imprisoned for subversion until 1915. He returned to the front, where he fought well. After his unit was moved to the Russian front, he was severely wounded and taken prisoner. He was freed during the *Bolshevik Revolution* and joined the *Red Army* in Siberia during the *Russian Civil War*. He returned to his homeland, now part of the newly formed state of *Yugoslavia*, in 1920. He joined the Yugoslav *Communist Party*, rising to membership in its *Politburo* by 1928. He was imprisoned, 1928–1934. During the 1930s he worked for the party, under the code name "Tito." In 1935 he returned to Moscow as part of his work for the *Comintern*. He barely survived the *Yezhovshchina* in the late 1930s and returned to Yugoslavia.

Like many *communists*, Tito did not oppose the *Nazis* overtly even after Yugoslavia was invaded by Germany. His anti-German activism dated instead to *Hitler's* invasion of Russia, in June 1941. Tito's military experience now came into play: he organized a large partisan force and led it into Bosnia and Croatia in 1942. In December 1943, he announced formation of a *provisional government*. Tito won British backing and *recognition* after his forces inflicted some damage on the Germans, though nowhere near as much as wartime or postwar propaganda made out. Overall, Tito's partisans in fact suffered mostly bloody defeats and took heavy casualties. In 1944, therefore, Tito was forced to retreat out of Montenegro and ultimately to flee to British-occupied Italy. He was later returned to Yugoslavia aboard a *Royal Navy* vessel. Tito then traveled to Moscow to visit *Stalin* and gave his assent to Stalin's plan for *Red Army* units to cross into Yugoslavia from Rumania. Tito was hailed by many as the liberator of Yugoslavia, but it is now accepted by most historians of World War II that the country was in fact liberated from Nazi occupation not by Tito's partisans but by the arrival of the Red Army.

At war's end, Tito established an independent communist regime without Soviet aid: Stalin actually kept his promise to Tito and withdrew all Red Army units. Tito showed his brutal side by immediately *liquidating* surrendered

Chetniks and remaining *Uštaše*: as many as 200,000 died upon his orders to wreak vengeance and clear the way to dictatorship. In 1948 he broke with Stalin and later became a leader within the *Nonaligned Movement*. Although he *normalized relations* with Moscow in 1955, he never accepted marching orders from the Soviets the way other Eastern European states and leaders did. He publicly criticized the crushing of the *Hungarian Uprising* and rejected the invasion of *Czechoslovakia* in 1968 and the *Brezhnev Doctrine* employed to justify it. Domestically, he generally favored the Serbs, but not so much as to cause the breakup of the *federation*. He ruled with an iron hand, crushing efforts at reform, but allowed each of the regions relative autonomy along ethnic lines. After his death Yugoslavia soon flew apart: its major ethnic groups sought full independence once Serbia reversed Tito's internal policy and instead began to *ethnically cleanse* the outlying provinces of non-Serb populations. *See also guerrilla warfare.*

Suggested Readings: Jasper Ridley, *Tito* (1994); Richard West, *Tito: And the Rise and Fall of Yugoslavia* (1995).

Tlatelolco, Treaty of (1967). Treaty for the Prohibition of Nuclear Weapons in Latin America. An agreement declaring the Latin American region a *nuclear weapons–free zone*, signed by 14 states in February 1967 and in effect as of April 1968. By 1990 almost all Latin American states had adhered, and all then declared *nuclear states* accepted to honor the zone. However, that did not account for *near-nuclear states*, including Argentina and Brazil, which were secretly researching *nuclear weapons* until the 1980s. Like all such agreements to date, it offers no safeguards against cheating or altered geopolitical circumstance. Nonetheless, it is widely touted as a useful regional supplement to the *Nuclear Non-Proliferation Treaty*.

Tocqueville, Alexis de (1805–1859). French historian and the single most astute observer of American politics and society. De Tocqueville ran for the Chamber of Deputies in 1837 and lost, but was elected in 1839. As a political *liberal* he was impressed by the republicanism of the *Revolutions of 1848*, but as an economic liberal he was off-put by demands for state welfare and market (price controls) regulation. After 1848 he was a noted foe of *socialism* and radical republicanism in France. In 1849 de Tocqueville became first vice president of the National Assembly and then briefly France's minister of foreign affairs. He retired to his estate and to writing upon the ascent to power of *Louis Napoleon*, whose constitution (in both senses of the word) and despotism he despised. De Tocqueville's fame arises not from his life's acts, however, but from his writing. In all his works he attempted to reconcile the remnants of the *ancien régime* in France, from which he himself sprang, having been born into an old *Norman* landed family, to the rise of mass *democracy* which was progressing apace within France over the course of the nineteenth century.

De Tocqueville rose to fame early in life when he went to the United States in 1831 with a commission to report on its prison system. He traveled all over America, a vast and difficult undertaking in the 1830s, and rather than a bureaucratic memo produced a large and classic work, "Democracy in America" (1835–1840). Written at age thirty, this was a masterpiece of instruction in democracy to de Tocqueville's countryfolk, drawing upon what he observed to be the nature and workings of what was then the world's only popular democracy. At the same time, it constituted an artful compendium of insights into American government, civil society, and national character. Its central concern was how American society then (and ever since) was attempting to reconcile two of the great themes of the *Enlightenment* and the *French Revolution* in practice: liberty for all to advance according to their merits and the inequality that must result from liberty as a "natural aristocracy" arises within a generation or two of any leveling revolution. In addition, de Tocqueville had much to say about the enormous social, political, and moral tensions caused by a *liberal* revolution in a land which still had several million *slaves*, along with millions more deeply impoverished laborers in town and country.

Among de Tocqueville's core observations were that anarchic tendencies produced by political equality gave rise to centralizing government, which in turn restrained personal liberty. He noted the profound religiosity of many individual Americans, while pointing out the driven materialism of American society. He took special cognisance of the fluidity of the American class structure and the ease—relative to Europe—with which American citizens moved up, or down, in social standing. De Tocqueville admired this greatly, but observed that it also placed the burden of explanation of success or failure in life on individual talent, character, hard work, and fortitude, and therefore that Americans tended to be less sympathetic than his countryfolk were toward personal failure, even as they more sincerely respected and encouraged personal success regardless of class origin. He was impressed by the way the American middle classes acted as a break on revolutionary ferment and located the success of American democracy firmly in its *bourgeoisie*, whose industry and "common sense" temperament made them supportive of representative government but skeptical of, and therefore resistant to, demagoguery. As for culture, de Tocqueville reflected on the fact that mass democracy was likely to produce a mean mass culture, as not just the political wishes of the majority but also its bourgeois tastes found public expression. He had much that was prescient to say, as well, about the workings of mass democratic politics, the party system, and other core features of American life.

Wittily presented, de Tocqueville's writings on America are, as the cliché goes, "indispensable reading." Less well known are his writings about English life, prompted by many visits to England and no doubt also the fact that he married an Englishwoman. In "Journeys to England and to Ireland" (1835) he explained to the French that despite deep class differences the English nation had a degree of cohesion and genuine solidity and solidarity that the French nation lacked, as it continued to struggle still with the consequences of the internal class warfare let loose in 1792 and again in 1848. This was prescient about the ferocious division to come in the *Paris Commune* of 1870–1871 and subsequent class struggle in France. His great work on France in general is "The Ancien Régime and the Revolution" (1856). *See also rising expectations.*

Togo. This West African coastal area was combed for *slaves* from the fifteenth to the eighteenth centuries. It became a German *colony* called *Togoland* in 1884 and remained so until 1919, when it was divided into British and French *mandates*. The French portion became modern Togo in 1960. It quickly fell into the familiar, postcolonial African pattern of military *coups* followed by creation of a *one-party state* as a cover for personal and *tribal* dictatorship. As the *Cold War* closed and Western *aid* budgets tightened after 1990, it appeared to move in the direction of political openness. Then, President Gnassingbé Eyadéma claimed a 96.5 percent victory in a farcical, rigged election in 1993 which was roundly condemned by international observers. The same thing happened in 1999.

Tōgō Heihachirō (1848–1934). Japanese admiral. He defeated the Russian Imperial Navy twice during the *Russo-Japanese War* (1904–1905), first at *Port Arthur* and then at *Tsushima Straits*. He was chief of naval staff during the early years of the *Dreadnought* revolution and a principal architect of Japanese policy and the pre–*World War II* Japanese Navy at the *Washington* and *London Naval Conferences*.

Togoland. A German *colony* in West Africa, 1884–1919. The western part was made a British *mandate*, 1922–1946, and *trusteeship territory*, 1946–1957, when it joined the Gold Coast (Ghana). The eastern part was a French *mandate*, 1922–1946, and trusteeship territory, 1946–1960, when it became *Togo*.

Tōjō Hideki (1885–1948). Japanese general; extreme nationalist and dictator. Vice-minister for war and chief of the *secret police*, 1937–1939; minister for war and prime minister, 1940–1944. Although he saw actual fighting only once in his military career, in 1937, Tōjō was the driving personality in the "war party" of the Japanese political elite, pushing for an aggressive policy in China as early as 1931. He helped plan both the *Mukden incident* and the *Marco Polo Bridge incident*. In 1937–1938 he was chief-of-staff in the *Guandong Army*. He was determined to establish Japan as the *preponderant power* in Asia, which meant expelling the Western empires from China and southeast Asia and most likely fighting the old enemy, Russia. He successfully pressured the French, Dutch, and British empires in Asia into making concessions, such as closing the *Burma Road*, in support of Japan's *aggression* against China. Unlike the more cautious and moderate Admiral *Yamamoto*, Tōjō argued aggressively for war with Britain, the Netherlands, and the United States in 1941. He replaced *Konoe* as prime minister in October 1941. Once he was convinced by the majority in the navy to strike south (the "south party") rather than do as the Japanese Army wanted and strike against the Soviet Union (the "northern program"), he moved with alacrity to order the attack on *Pearl Harbor*. That decision was made easier by a severe defeat inflicted on the Japanese Army by *Zhukov* and his Siberian divisions in a short, undeclared war in August 1939. When the larger war in the Pacific went badly, Tōjō lost *Hirohito's* confidence and was compelled to resign (July 9, 1944). After Japan's *surrender* he was arrested by the *Allies*. He attempted to commit suicide with a revolver, but managed only to wound himself in the chest. He was tried, convicted, and condemned as a major war criminal at the *Tokyo war crimes trials*, where he steadfastly refused to implicate Hirohito. He was hanged. *See also Doolittle raid.*

Tokelau. It was a South Pacific *dependency* of Great Britain in the nineteenth century. It was administered by New Zealand after 1925. Despite its paucity of numbers (fewer than 2,000), after *UNCLOS III* was promulgated it claimed a 200-mile *Exclusive Economic Zone*, under the *island* rule.

Tokugawa Ieyasu, né Matsudaira Motoyasu (1542–1616). Founder of the *Tokugawa shogunate*. Given by his father as a *hostage*, at age four, to a neighbor *daimyo*, he was captured en route by a rival daimyo and held to age seven. When freed, he returned to his original destination to resume his obligation as hostage, remaining there to age eighteen. In 1560 he allied with *Nobunaga Oda*, only later to pay that *warlord's* loyalty-price of killing his own wife and ordering his son to commit seppuku. The alliance paid him well, however: by 1583 Ieyasu controlled five full provinces. This raised him to a level worthy of political alliance with *Hideyoshi*, which he secured by taking the latter's sister in marriage. In 1590 Ieyasu helped Hideyoshi besiege Odawara and subdue the northeast. He was ordered to relocate north and chose to settle at Edo (Tokyo). Busy with his new domain, he was not involved in Hideyoshi's costly 1592 invasion of Korea. He was appointed one of five regents for Hideyoshi's son, and subsequently led an eastern coalition to victory at *Sekigahara* in 1600. From 1603 to 1605 he was *shogun*, but thereafter raised a son to that ceremonial office while he exercised power from behind the scenes. Ieyasu made peace with Korea in 1605, formalized in the Treaty of Kiyu (1609). In 1615 he besieged and reduced the last daimyo stronghold, the great castle town of Osaka. The realm united, he died in 1616.

Tokugawa shogunate. *See* bakufu; daimyo; *Japan; Tokugawa Ieyasu; tribute;* sakoku; samurai; *Unification Wars.*

Tokyo Round (1973–1979). The seventh round of GATT talks. The unpropitious context was *stagflation*, uncertainty in the *currency* markets, and *recession*. Tokyo continued the basic thrust of *tariff* reduction, but also addressed *nontariff barriers* (NTBs) and tried to speak to *LDC* concerns and bring agricultural products into the GATT process. It succeeded in further reducing *tariffs* and in somewhat adjusting to LDC interests. It was most significant for beginning to limit NTBs such as manipulation of technical standards, import *licensing*, and *customs* regulations. It completely failed to bring *agriculture* under the GATT. *See also Uruguay Round.*

Tokyo war crimes trials. They began in May 1946, under the occupation authority of *Douglas MacArthur*, and did not end until 1948. Eleven judges for the International Military Tribunal were drawn from Australia, Canada, Nationalist China, New Zealand, the Philippines, the United States, and the Soviet Union. Twenty-eight senior Japanese leaders were tried as Class A war criminals on charges ranging from *crimes against humanity* and *war crimes*, such as inhumane treatment of *prisoners of war* and the wounded, to the more controversial charge of *crimes against peace*, which rested on citation of the ban on *aggressive war* to which Japan adhered in the *Kellogg-Briand Pact*, along with the—somewhat more dubious—theory that Japan had deliberately and methodically planned a war of conquest in China. Unlike the *Nuremberg war crimes trials*, simple majority rule was used to decide judgment and sentences. Among the most important political defendants were former prime ministers *Tōjō*, Koiso Kunaki, and Hirota Kōki. *Konoe* committed suicide before he could be tried. Military figures tried and hanged included Generals Matsui Iwane, for presiding over the *Rape of Nanjing*, and Itagaki Seishirō. In all, seven were condemned to hang. At MacArthur's insistence, *Hirohito* was never charged. It was feared that convicting Hirohito would do irreparable harm to the occupation and rehabilitation of Japan, even though there was much sentiment to proceed against him among jurists and the populations of other Allied powers. Seven of the Class A defendants were sentenced to death, including Tōjō and Hirota. Several thousand lesser (Class B and Class C) war criminals were tried by lesser courts or by separate tribunals in the Philippines and other liberated countries; up to 900 of these were executed. In 1960 the United States paroled the last 100 or so convicted Japanese war criminals still in its charge. *See also superior orders; Yamashita.*

Tone, Theobald Wolfe (1763–1798). Irish patriot. *See also United Irish Society.*

Tonga. Tongolese kings ruled much of *Polynesia* before arrival of the first European settlers in 1826. King George Tupou I converted to *Christianity*, unified Tonga, and over the course of his long rule in the nineteenth century held the colonizing powers at bay via balancing treaties with Britain, France,

Germany, Spain, and the United States. Tonga was a British *protectorate* from 1901, but retained significant *autonomy*. Queen Salote ruled, 1918–1965. In 1970 Tonga became independent, while still ruled by *authoritarian* monarchs. It refused to sign the *Treaty of Rarotonga* and welcomed nuclear ships to its ports. Its relations with Fiji were troubled by overlapping claims to the Minerva reefs. Tonga did not join the *United Nations General Assembly* until 1999, but it participated in United Nations *specialized agencies* before that. It is the only South Pacific state to maintain a formal *alliance* with the United States, via an 1888 treaty, which was reaffirmed upon its centenary.

Tonkin. A historic Vietnamese empire, but also sometime *tributary* state of China, located in northern *Indochina*. For centuries it waged defensive wars against various dynasties in China to its north; at other times it was compelled to pay tribute. Meanwhile, it also fought *expansionist* wars southward against its neighbors *Champa* and *Annam*, and westward against the *Montagnards*, Khmers, and Siamese. It was conquered by the French after heavy fighting from 1882 to 1885 (*Tonkin Wars*). It was then merged into *French Indochina* in 1887. *Pacification* took longer, as Tonkinese resistance to the French persisted. Tonkin and its traditions of fierce independence and southward expansion lay at the heart of the Democratic Republic of Vietnam (DRV, North Vietnam) during the *Vietnam War*. It is today a key region in northern Vietnam. Demarcation of the Gulf of Tonkin, an adjacent bay, is disputed by China and Vietnam.

Tonkin Gulf Resolution (August 7, 1964). A joint resolution of Congress which presented President *Lyndon Johnson* with a "blank check" to use force in support of the Republic of Vietnam (RVN, South Vietnam). It followed an attack by North Vietnamese (DRV, Democratic Republic of Vietnam) patrol boats on the destroyers USS Maddux and USS Turner Joy in the Gulf of Tonkin, alleged to have occurred on the nights of August 2nd and 4th. Hanoi admitted the first attack, defiantly asserting it was proper *retaliation* for U.S. assistance to ARVN (Army of the Republic of Vietnam) PT boat and *commando* raids against its coast, but it denied the second incident ever took place. Although it seems likely there was no second attack, there is no evidence that the Johnson administration faked the August 4th incident, as some later charged. Instead, Johnson took advantage of initial and genuine confusion to extract from Congress a "blank check" to intervene in Indochina. He was authorized, by a vote of 416 to 0 in the House and 88 to 2 in the Senate, to "take all necessary steps" in pursuit of security and opposition to *aggression* in southeast Asia. In public, Johnson said: "We still seek no wider war." In private, he compared the Tonkin Gulf Resolution to "granny's nightshirt—it covers everything." Congress repealed the resolution in 1970.

Suggested Reading: E. Moïse, *Tonkin Gulf* (1996).

Tonkin Wars (1882–1885). After the *Taiping Rebellion* (1850–1864) in China, armed Taiping *refugees* moved into *Tonkin* where they reorganized as the White, Yellow, and Black Flag armies. The Black Flags supported the Imperial court at Huê and fought the *Montagnards*. In 1882 the Black Flags, now also supported by China, clashed with the French. Early in 1884 China agreed to withdraw. With the French dividing their forces and fighting deep inside Tonkin, China and the Black Flags resumed the fight. Little *quarter* was given on either side, with atrocities performed even on the dead and few prisoners taken. The *French Foreign Legion* was heavily involved in the fighting. France also sent a naval expedition to Taiwan in 1884 which savaged a Chinese fleet. The *Treaty of Tientsin* was signed in 1885, making Tonkin a French *protectorate*; Chinese regulars and Black Flags alike then withdrew into China.

topography. The relief features of a surface area. Topography, in combination with location, has historically had a great effect on international relations, in both military and political realms. *Tactics* frequently depend heavily on the terrain of a battlefield, and even *grand strategy* must account for physical barriers. For example, the *Schlieffen Plan* sought to avoid the forested Ardennes region and invade France via the lowland plains of Belgium and the Netherlands, even though that meant triggering a wider war with Great Britain; flat topography explains much of Russia's historic fear of *invasion*, and therefore something of its policy of defensive expansion, as it also does Poland's inability to resist invasion for long; the *Grisons* owed their strategic value to the fact they constitute an alpine pass along the *Spanish Road*; all island nations enjoyed unique advantages before the invention of *air power* and the *ICBM*, the *English Channel* gave England a spectacular advantage over continental rivals for nearly a millennium, as did two oceans for the United States during its first century. Topography does not explain all, however; culture and choice remain key factors. Thus, an irregular, alpine topography may permit ethnic groups to live side by side in compartmentalized *peace*, as in Switzerland or along the Andes spine before the erection of the *Inca Empire*; or it may allow them to grapple for each other's throats, should they so choose, fighting for every piece of high ground or defensible valley, as later in the Andes, in the situation on Israel's northern border with Lebanon, or in the Balkans. *See also Deccan; natural frontiers.*

Tordesillas, Treaty of (1494). *See line of demarcation.*

torpedo. A self-propelled, underwater missile. The first primitive torpedoes, which appeared during the *American Civil War*, were not self-propelled. Instead, they were spar weapons made up of a bomb on an elongated pole, intended to be rammed into an enemy ship. The British later invented the self-propelled torpedo, the progenitor of all modern weapons. In turn, they led to the invention of torpedo boats to deliver the new weapon against *capital warships*. The countermeasure to that was the torpedo-boat destroyer, later shortened to "destroyer." The torpedo also served as the principle weapon of *submarines* prior to those warships mounting *missiles*.

torpedo boat. *See torpedo.*

tort. An unjustified breach of international legal obligations. *See also delict.*

torture. Deliberately inflicting great physical pain or mental anguish as a means of coercion, punishment, extraction of information, or just sadistic pleasure. Its use increased greatly in the twentieth century. *Amnesty International* reports annually that the majority of states still use a range of barbaric tortures on an almost daily basis. The *United Nations General Assembly* passed a nonbinding *Declaration* on Torture in 1975, and some regional organizations (*European Union, Organization of American States*) banned the practice in law. A major United Nations *convention* came into force in 1987, making torture a crime under *international criminal law*. Torture may also be a *war crime*, if it accompanies a war. In the late 1990s international tribunals also defined *rape* as a form of torture.

Tory. (1) An English political party from the seventeenth century to c. 1832, which tended to favor the *monarch* over the rights of Parliament, and preservation of a social order based upon aristocratic landholding. Its hold was eroded by the progressive self-assertion of Parliament and the arrival of the *Industrial Revolution*, which raised up new, middle- and working-class interests against it. It was succeeded by the *Conservative Party*. (2) A common nickname for broadly *conservative* parties in English-speaking, parliamentary democracies, or (lower case) for individuals who advocate conservative political principles. (3) A royalist (Loyalist) in the *American Revolution*. With delicious, multiple irony, the term "tory" derives from Gaelic ("tōraidhe") for "highwayman," which in Irish history was a synonym for a landless, persecuted peasant.

totalitarianism. Absolute control by the state of most aspects of the daily lives of its citizens, usually according to the dictates of a ruling party which professed some exhaustive ideology (such as *fascism* or *communism*) which eroded, and ultimately obliterated, normal distinctions among private life, civil society, and the state. It may also be said to exist where a tyrannical cult or priesthood interprets a *fundamentalist* religious vision as the basis of government policy, as well as political, social, family, and individual morality and interactions. In the twentieth century totalitarianism was particularly identified with *Nazi Germany* and the *Soviet Union*. In both those countries during the 1920s and 1930s normal social and moral cohesion broke down, partly as a result of the carnage, dispiriting, and ultimately decivilizing experience of *World War I*. Into that vacuum poured false hopes based on false solutions purveyed by deceitful and evil ideologues, who also were prepared to use street violence and then state *terror* on a massive scale to eliminate public dissenters, and brutalized all other citizens into ritualized expressions of social, political, and ideological conformity. The term is therefore also associated with *Mao's* China, particularly during the extraordinary excesses of the *Great Proletarian Cultural Revolution*, and with the savage regime of *Pol Pot* in Cambodia. It is not usually associated, however, with somewhat milder fascisms, such as those in Italy and Spain, where significant pockets of civil society continued to function outside state control, and in some cases contrary to the will and whims of the state.

Totalitarian systems generally exerted control over society and individuals via the umbrella mechanism of a mass political party, such as the *Communist Parties* of the *Soviet bloc*, China, Cuba, Cambodia, Vietnam, and elsewhere, or the *National Socialist Party* in Germany. Particular attention was paid to youth, which was organized in separate clubs and associations such as the Hitler Youth or the *Red Guards*. Children were indoctrinated into Party ideology even from preschool ages, and older children were encouraged to report any overheard conversations to Party superiors, or some *secret police* such as the *Gestapo* or *NKVD*, which might reflect political heresy on the part of teachers or even siblings or parents. There was, of course, total state control of all news media and heavy reliance on censorship and *propaganda* at the national level. At the neighborhood level, control was maintained even street-by-street by low-level *cadres* or neighborhood committees. In addition, totalitarian systems sought to control art and music—in China, Jiang Qing (Mao's wife) forbade performance of any but a small menu of approved "revolutionary operas," whereas in the Soviet Union the stultifying doctrine of *socialist realism* drove good artists and poets abroad, underground, or in some cases to suicide. All of this aimed at legitimating the regime in general, but much effort also went into inculcating a *cult of personality* (or the *Führerprinzip*, or some similar idea) among the mass population. This elevated the leader to a combination of tribal chieftain, high priest, and *warlord*, in each case making any decision seem infallible and hence unquestionable, even when stark physical evidence of the leader's failure might be staring an individual citizen in the face in the form of an enemy soldier's rifle barrel, or a bomb falling from on high, or a collapsing economy, or just an empty rice bowl.

The essence of all this activity was an utter contempt for genuine *democracy* and for any and all individualism and initiative, all mixed with a strong puritanical streak—in China, not only was *opium* addiction forcibly suppressed, street and village committees enforced bleak codes against disapproved fashions and hairstyles and a ban on wearing makeup by women. The sole exceptions made to this secular prudery was for Party cadres or *nomenklatura*, along with total indulgence of the unchecked personal quirks, and usually also deep perversions, of the Chairman (or General Secretary, or Füh-rer, or Great Leader, or Supreme Guide). Elections were a frequent occur-rence, with citizens required by law to vote and expected to cast ballots en masse for the *party line* candidate or position, in endless *referenda* which pro-vided a veneer of *popular sovereignty* over the abject reality of brutal coercion, *kleptocracy*, rank nepotism, and/or cronyism, and often gross incompetence as well.

Apparently unable to distinguish between legitimate delegation of govern-ing authority via elections and its naked usurpation, some "scholars" make a specious assertion of *moral equivalence* between democratic states and totali-tarian regimes. They suggest that democracies have much in common with totalitarian systems since they, too, control the apparatus of the state "be-tween elections," utterly ignoring the conditional and temporary nature of the exercise of power in the first instance versus its inherently coercive char-acter in the second, and overlooking the full range allowed civil society in democracies but not in any totalitarian society. As George Orwell once re-marked in a different, but related context, "That's so stupid only an intellec-tual could believe it." Other scholars more reasonably object to lumping of diverse political ideologies and historical regimes under a single rubric of "totalitarianism." Still others, including this author, maintain that although important national and ideological differences surely existed and warrant de-tailed attention, even so there were fundamental traits in domestic character shared by modern terror dictatorships.

However, it is important to note that the way totalitarian states treated their own people was not a sure predictor that an aggressive foreign policy also would be pursued, although that was widely and uncritically assumed at times. Thus, although Mao's China frequently used or threatened force to "reunite" with the "motherland" territories it regarded as part of China (*Que-moy and Matsu, Tibet, Taiwan*), its use of force against neighbors was fairly limited, as in the *Sino-Indian War* (1962) or the *Sino-Vietnamese War* (1979). That could not be said about the insatiable appetite for new territory displayed by Nazi Germany against virtually all of its neighbors from 1938, or the Soviet Union's opportunistic aggression as the *Red Army* advanced into eastern Europe from 1944 and into the Far East in 1945. *See also Lord Acton; anar-chism; authoritarianism; Bolshevism; conscientious objection; Iran; laissez-faire; liberal-internationalism; Maoism; Marxism-Leninism; Nazism; North Korea; passport; Red Terror; samizdat; Stalinism; Sudan; Taiping Rebellion (1850–1864); Taliban; theocracy.*

Suggested Readings: Among the most penetrating insights into totalitarianism are those of George Orwell in the brilliant fictional satires of the Soviet Union, *Animal Farm* (1946) and *1984* (1949), and Hannah Arendt's pathbreaking *The Origins of Totalitarianism* (1951). Also see Abbott Gleason, *Totalitarianism* (1995); A. James Gregor, *The Faces of Janus: Marxism and Fascism in the Twentieth Century* (2000).

total war. A *war* fought with unlimited means, on a vast scale, and for limitless *strategic* purposes. A related meaning is the modern tendency of whole societies to become part of the war effort, which engages popular passions and makes civilian populations targets of enemy attack while encouraging retaliation against enemy civilians, until virtually no one is considered a *noncombatant*. This contrasts with the age immediately preceding the modern, when combat and most killing was limited to armed forces. War then was less destructive, partly because of the skittishness of *mercenary* armies, but more because *limited wars* engaged the passions and the fate only of dynasties, monarchs, or local *warlords*, but rarely of mercenaries and still less whole *peoples* or *nations*. *Clausewitz* recognized this developing trend, emerging from the *French Revolution*, in his concept of "absolute war." A later Prussian, *Erich von Ludendorff*, gave it the name "total war" in 1935, in response to *World War I* in which the inconclusive campaign of 1914 had not led sovereigns to make a quick peace, but instead roused popular anger, expectations, and demands for *victory* such that the slaughter of *trench warfare* continued for four years more.

As modern as total war in this sense is, it should be recalled that earlier ages and wars, too, sometimes arose from passionate ideologies and deep and lasting hatreds which encouraged levels of murder and destruction beyond even the normal horrors found acceptable—thus, the *Crusades* and *Thirty Years' War*. Also, some medieval and ancient peoples (Athenians at Melos, the *Romans* at Carthage, and the *Mongols* wherever their horses took them) waged war with ruthlessness and savagery, if not destructive efficiency, which approached the blood lust of moderns. In other words, just as not all modern wars are total, not all total wars were modern. Even so, a permanent change in the nature of warfare occurred with the development of modern bureaucracy and its capacity for organization of people and war economies on a vast scale. When this was married to the rise of *nationalism* during the French Revolution, a transformation reflected in the *levée en masse*, war changed dramatically. This was first seen in the greater scale and new destructiveness of the *Napoleonic Wars* and the character of *Napoleonic warfare*. In the nineteenth century, processes of *industrialization* and technological advance, which first found large-scale military expression in the *Crimean War* and the *American Civil War*, again expanded the scale of firepower, manpower, and general destruction of war.

In the twentieth century growing class hatred in enlarged urban centers, specious and pernicious theories such as *social Darwinism*, the rise of virulent *ideologies* (*communism* and *fascism*), new techniques of *propaganda*, and the advent of *air power* all advanced war toward totality of means and ends. For most observers, World War I and especially *World War II*—which saw *carpet bombing* of cities, the first use of *nuclear weapons,* and exterminationist campaigns by Germany in Europe and Japan in China—appeared to confirm that all modern wars would be total wars. However, the *Cold War* ended with a whimper not a bang, leading most theorists to assert that the era of major wars among large powers was over. In practice, Western militaries and publics thereafter grew used to fighting only limited wars with highly precise means (*Gulf War*, *Kosovo*), which deeply affected their willingness to directly participate in war and hence may signal a shift away from a totality of aims. *See also Carthaginian peace; eastern front; "final solution"; Josef Goebbels; home front; militarization; Morgenthau Plan; Peloponnesian Wars; Shaka Zulu; Tamerlane.*

Suggested Readings: Raymond Aron, *The Century of Total War* (1954); Peter Calvocoressi et al., *Total War* (1989); Arthur Marwick, *War and Social Change* (1974).

tourism. Touring, for pleasure's sake. Once the preserve of the high-born and wealthy, with the new affluence created by the expansive wealth brought about by *industrialization* and modern *capitalism*, international touring became a middle-class activity around the mid- to late-nineteenth century. It expanded even into the working classes in the twentieth century. Today it is a large *service* industry and an important part of the world economy. It provides significant economic benefits to those countries receptive to tourists (and not all are). Tourism is additionally important as a major vehicle for the spread of ideas, cultural awareness—or sometimes misunderstanding—and disease.

Toussaint L'Ouverture (1743–1803). Born into *slavery* in Haiti, in 1791 he joined and then led slave insurgents against French rule. In 1797 he was made commander-in-chief on the island by the French and subsequently drove out the British and Spanish, establishing a working government. In 1800 *Napoleon* decreed that slavery be re-established in Haiti, but L'Ouverture refused to comply. Defeated and then betrayed, he died after a year in a French dungeon. His followers gained *independence* for Haiti in 1804.

TOW. Tube launched, Optically tracked, Wire-guided *missile*. With it, even illiterate *infantry* can undercut a sophisticated enemy's advantage in *air power*, as many *mujahadeen* did in the *Afghan-Soviet War*.

tracer. Ammunition, often for antiaircraft guns, containing chemical compounds which emit light or smoke when ignited (by firing the shell). That allows the shooter to observe where the *ordnance* flies or falls and to adjust aim.

trade. The buying, selling, or barter of *goods and services* within or among nations. Trade among distant political communities is known to have existed for the earliest recorded civilizations. Areas as far removed (and in ancient times, these distances were enormous) as the *Roman Empire* and South India are known to have conducted an extensive trade—Roman coins have been found in southern India dating back two millennia. The fall of Rome broke up one terminus of the great world *trade route* which had sustained the *Silk Road*, however, and thereafter world trade declined as overland routes became ever more insecure, lying open to brigands and nomadic raiders. The explosion of *Islam* into the Mediterranean basin further disrupted trade, as warfare rather than commerce characterized what had once been called by Romans *mare nostrum*. Trade henceforth became more regionalized. *Venice* acted as monopoly middleman for Arab and *Byzantine Empire* trade with *Christendom*, but this reached nothing like the old Roman levels of intercommunal commerce across the Mediterranean. Also feeding into this trade was a discrete trans-Saharan trade in salt (in 200-pound blocks, two per camel), *gold*, and *slaves*, which reached the coast at several termini in Morocco, Algiers, Tripoli, and Egypt.

Also a key influence on world trade from the seventh century was the *haj*, which carried goods as well as people from all over the *Islamic world* to the central terminus of *Mecca* in the *Hejaz*. By the twelfth century, the northern European towns of the *Hansa* conducted a vigorous and multifaceted international trade that reached into Scandinavia and southern Russia, to England and to Italy, and then to the Arab world. That interaction was disrupted, however, with the fall of *Constantinople* in 1453, a tsunami event in world history which sent shock waves through the Mediterranean and European economies, which Portuguese and Genoese explorers rode around the coasts of Africa, and then westward, in search of new routes to India and Cathay. Meanwhile, the Chinese were trading extensively with Japan, Korea, and parts of Indochina, though often under the guise of *tribute*. However, their large internal (and bureaucratically controlled market and prices) and *Confucian* anti-commercial values and Imperial anti-naval attitudes restricted this activity. India, on the other hand, was wracked by seemingly endless cycles of war, empire-building, collapse into competitive states, and more wars among partial empires.

Back in Europe, as banking services developed and expanded during and after the *Renaissance,* so too did international trade, which both prompted and rode along with explorers and adventurers to the four corners of the world during the *Age of Discovery*. Trade then followed *imperialism* and *colonialism*, developing along *mercantilist* lines. Before the nineteenth century, most world trade was highly concentrated in small, high-value items such as spices, fine oils, slaves, firearms, *ivory*, or precious metals. This was partly due to the rudimentary nature of limited economies, but mostly because bulk trade faced high transportation costs and *tariff* barriers. In some cases, trade was strictly limited or even forbidden, such as under the *Tokugawa* shoguns of Japan. The *spice trade*—first overland via the Silk Road, later by sea around India and Africa—was an important early link among China, India, the Middle East, and Europe. The *slave trade* was extant in the Indian Ocean for 1,000 years; its trans-Atlantic counterpart grew hugely in importance after 1500 as markets demanded more sugar, cotton, tea, and coffee from North and South American colonies. Yet, world trade in most bulk commodities, and related services, remained insignificant before c. 1800.

World trade expanded dramatically in the nineteenth century as Great Britain led in the movement toward *free trade* and as steamships and steel production reduced costs and time at sea. By the early twentieth century a world economy was developing in which the principle of *comparative advantage* formed the basis of international trade theory and, increasingly, also actual practice. In 1913 more than 60 percent of all international trade occurred inside Europe; contrary to *liberal* hopes and expectations, that fact did not prevent the most destructive war to that point in history, from breaking out in 1914. Trade contracted sharply during the *Great Depression*, as it had in other *world depressions*. After 1945, world trade expanded enormously, under a new free trade regime initially established at *Bretton Woods*, and for half a century sustained and led by the United States as world trade increasingly came under international standardization and regulation and was conducted according to the *most-favored nation* principle of the GATT. By the start of the twenty-first century most major trading nations were members of the *World Trade Organization*. See also *Physiocrats*; *protectionism*; *Adam Smith*; *treaty ports*.

Suggested Readings: William Ashworth, *A Short History of the World Economy* (1987); Gang Deng, *Chinese Maritime Activities and Socioeconomic Development* (1997); J. Foreman-Peck, *History of the World Economy* (1983); Xinru Liu, *Ancient India and Ancient China: Trade and Religious Exchanges* (1994).

trade agreement. A *treaty* specifying the conditions regulating *trade* in *goods and services*. See also *FTA*; *GATT*; *NAFTA*.

trade balance. A measurement of the movement of *goods and services* between one economy and all others. See also *balance of trade*.

trade barrier. See *free trade*; *GATT*; *new protectionism*; *nontariff barriers*; *protectionism*; *tariff*; *quota*.

trade bloc. Any group of states whose members concert their trade policies. This may take the form of a *preferential tariff*, a *free trade area*, or a *customs union*. See also *European Union*; *imperial tariff*; *Mercosur*; *NAFTA*; *Lomé Conventions*; *STABEX*.

tradecraft. The various techniques used in the conduct of *intelligence* or how intelligence gathering is actually carried out by professionals in the field. Well-known examples include use of *cryptology*, *penetration* or *double agents*, *false flag recruitment*, or setting a *honey trap*. More mundane knowledge includes how to conduct and/or evade *surveillance* and use of *ciphers*, *listening posts*, and cabinet noir.

trade deficit/surplus. *See balance of trade.*

trade-related investment measures (TRIMs). Local content and equity requirements, restrictions on *remittance* of *profits*, *export* requirements, and *technology transfer* measures. An effort was made to bring these into the *Uruguay Round*, representing the first venture by *GATT* into *investment* issues which pertain to *trade*.

trade route. Any overland trail or sea-lane used to carry international trade (and along which historically also flowed armies, culture, religion, and technology). Arab power in the Middle Ages was largely based on the wealth derived from controlling the overland routes from Asia to Europe, which also aided the spread of *Islam*. Developments in shipbuilding and navigation permitted Venetians, Portuguese, and others to bypass the *Middle East*, sending the Arab economy and civilization into a centuries-long decline. Much of the history of *colonialism* is the story of the consolidation and protection of the trade routes to India and China from Europe, from the discovery of the Americas to securing the Cape of Good Hope as a way station to India, or the *Sinai* to build a canal to end the need to circumnavigate the Cape, with guard post colonies at *Aden, Malta,* and *Gibraltar.* Modern transportation has made trade routes more varied and less individually important. Still, some routes (such as those through the *Panama* and *Suez Canals,* or the *Straits of Hormuz*) remain key choke points of global commerce. *See also Black Death; Gur states; Mamluks; piracy; Sahara Desert; Silk Road; slave trade; spice trade; triangle trade.*

trade war. Intense conflict arising from disputes over *trade*. To avoid trade wars, after 1945 the leading trading nations set up *General Agreement on Tariffs and Trade* (GATT), later the *World Trade Organization* (WTO), to establish agreed-upon standards and procedures for mediation and conflict resolution. *See also Anglo-Dutch Wars; East India Company.*

traditionalism. An approach to the study of world affairs which stresses the study of diplomatic *history,* *international law,* and political and moral philosophy and rejects most *quantitative* analyses as arid, amoral, misplaced (unable to deal with volition in human affairs), and/or *reductionist.* In general, that which the *revisionist* finds sophisticated, *cutting-edge,* or "pioneering," the traditionalist will likely see as tendentious, misdirected, obtuse, and far-fetched. *See also behavioralism; classical school; critical theory; postbehavioralism; postmodernism; rational choice theory; qualitative analysis.*

Trafalgar, Battle of (October 21, 1805). The most decisive battle in the history of naval warfare. Twenty-seven British *ships-of-the-line,* the heart and soul of the *Royal Navy* under the command of Admiral *Horatio Nelson* aboard the HMS Victory, met a combined French and Spanish fleet of 33 ships-of-the-line under Pierre de Villeneuve, south of Cadiz off Cape Trafalgar. There they fought the turning-point naval action of the *Napoleonic Wars*. Nelson famously signaled to his fleet crews as the battle commenced: "England expects every man will do his duty," and ordered his captains to close with the enemy line. British tactics and discipline were vastly superior and proved decisive. Of great assistance also was the flintlocks rather than fuses used by the English cannon, which provided immediate (and hence more accurate) discharge as well as a more rapid rate of fire; that more than made up for the enemy's advantage of some 500 guns. Departing from accepted practice, Nelson separated his squadrons into two shorter columns which crossed the enemy *line ahead* formation, instead of following the expected stratagem of paralleling it. Although this exposed the British ships to punishing fire as they made their initial approach, it also temporarily reduced the effective advantage in French ships and guns by separating the top third of the Franco-Spanish line and forcing it to maneuver, and enabled his own ships to *rake* the enemy's prows and sterns with intense short-range fire.

The Franco-Spanish line broke apart and a mêlée ensued, as ships scattered and engaged in pairs or threes, and panic and courage alike were seen among the burning decks and bloodied crews. The British lost none of their ships, and just over 400 men. Prime among the losses was Nelson himself, felled by a French sniper in the hour of his triumph. The French and Spanish lost 20 ships sunk or taken, nearly two-thirds of their complement, some 4,500 killed, and 20,000 prisoners. A victory on that scale guaranteed that Britain continued to dominate the seas and to finance and lead coalition after coalition against *Napoleon*. He would later say of his frustration with the Royal Navy: "Wherever wood can swim, there I am bound to find this damned flag of England!" *Mahan* wrote of Trafalgar: "The world has never seen a more impressive demonstration of the influence of sea power upon history." More than helping to decide the *Napoleonic Wars*, Trafalgar was so huge a victory it left Britain the preponderant *sea power* for the next 100 years. In so doing, it played a role in Britain's post-1815 turn away from Europe toward the *splendid isolation* of preoccupation with protecting its worldwide imperial interests. *See also Battle of the Atlantic; Jutland; Leyte Gulf; Midway; Spanish Armada.*

tragedy of the commons. In economics, when each consumer of a common resource overuses it in the short-run, to the long-term detriment of all.

Trail of Tears. The forcible deportation of the Cherokee nation from Georgia, South Carolina, and Tennessee during 1838. This shameful act (what would later be called *ethnic cleansing*) was ordered by President *Andrew Jackson* and carried out under the command of General *Winfield Scott*. It was marked by much brutal treatment of, and death among, the Cherokee. It was the culmination of Jackson's campaign to remove all the east coast Indian nations to reservations beyond the Mississippi.

transatlantic. Crossing or spanning the Atlantic Ocean, whether in interests, ideas, threats, or *trade*.

Transcaucasia. The portion of *Caucasia* lying south of the Caucasus Mountains. Once the eastern half of the *Byzantine Empire*, it was overrun by Turkic *tribes* in 1071. It is a patchwork of *nations*, as well as ethnic and religious hatreds. In 1993–1994 *wars* or *rebellions* were underway in *Abkhazia, Ajaria, Armenia, Azerbaijan, Georgia; Nagorno-Karabakh, Ossetia,* and *Turkey.* Iran, Russia, and Turkey are historic, *regional powers*.

Transcaucasian Soviet Federated Socialist Republic (SFSR). A composite "republic" within the *Soviet Union*, created in 1922 from *Armenia, Azerbaijan,* and *Georgia.* It was broken apart by *Stalin* in 1936, who made certain that ethnic *enclaves* were left isolated so that they would have to turn to Russia as mediator and referee of all regional conflicts. The world lives with that legacy still: *see also Nakichevan* and *Nagorno-Karabakh*.

Trans-Dniestra. A region in eastern *Moldova*, across the Dniester River, occupied mainly by ethnic Russians and Ukrainians. After Moldova's *independence* on December 25, 1991, rebels in Trans-Dniestra drew support from the Russian 14th Army. In 1993 they also received some diplomatic support from Russia. The CSCE became involved in an attempted *conciliation*, but low-level fighting broke out. Russian troops remained in the area, as did CSCE monitors, into 2001. Stakes were raised by a *referendum* held in 1995, in which the population voted massively for independence from Moldova. A peace accord (1997) gave Trans-Dniestra autonomy within the Moldavian union.

transferable development rights (TDRs). The idea that landowners in areas designated for environmental conservation should retain limited *development* rights but not exercise these on-site. Instead, they could be sold (transferred) for application to nondesignated areas. Proponents argue for the artificial creation, via legislation, of a global market for TDRs as a means to *sustainable development. See also debt-for-nature swaps; environmental security; green loans.*

transformation. In British legal thinking, the doctrine that changes in *international law*, because it lacks a strong sense of *stare decisis*, can be directly incorporated into domestic law even in the absence of legislation by Parliament expressly recording the change.

transgovernmental. Relations, ties, or connections among governments, but at levels of civil service connection, below the political. *See also complex interdependence; functionalism.*

Transjordan. Originally part of *Arabia* when that area was a province of the *Ottoman Empire*. It was later used by Britain to link Egypt with Iraq and was part of the *mandate of Palestine*. In 1949 the larger portion was renamed *Jordan* after seizing the *West Bank* during the *First Arab-Israeli War*.

transnational. *Nongovernmental organizations*, activities, connections, loyalties, or transactions crossing national *boundaries*, including any private *actors* with interests in foreign countries. In international relations literature, the main concern is with the transnational character and influence of *multinational corporations*, but some have written cogently as well on the role of ideas, culture, religion, and professional connections, ideologies, communications, and travel.

transnational corporation. *See foreign direct investment; multinational corporation.*

transpacific. Spanning the Pacific Ocean, whether in interests, *influence*, threats, or *trade*.

transparency. (1) In *arms control*: The notion that agreement on *Confidence and Security Building Measures* (CSBMs) in an otherwise hostile relationship reduces possibilities of miscalculation and *accidental war* by making military capabilities and intentions plain. (2) In *economics*: Standardized accounting procedures and clear regulations which expose some of the inner workings of corporate governance and financial markets, to ensure enhanced investor confidence and avoid financial bubbles or catastrophic bank failures. (3) In *international relations theory*: The idea that access to information which in earlier times was secret, the spread of democratic institutions, and the advent of global communications, has overturned obstacles to information access and thus enhanced prospects for *globalization* and the *democratic peace*. *See also CNN; open diplomacy; secret treaties.*

transportation. (1) A penalty of enforced *exile* in *penal settlements* meted out to common criminals, political *dissidents*, and rebels by several European states which possessed overseas colonies, notably France and Great Britain. (2) On the role of transportation systems in world economic history, *see Age of Exploration; railways; trade route.*

Transvaal. During the *Great Trek* this *Boer* state was established "Across the Vaal River" in 1852. It was *recognized* by Britain, but *annexed* in 1877 by agreement with impoverished Boers then in need of protection from *Zulu* war parties. This drew Britain into the *Zulu Wars*. British administration chafed the Boers and contributed to the outbreak of the *First Boer War*, after which Transvaal became fully independent again by 1884. In 1886 a massive *gold* strike was made in Witwatersrand, inundating this rural, conservative republic with miners, traders, wealth, and all the other non-*Calvinist* wildness and queer folk who always attend an unexpected economic boom. Transvaal was reannexed by Britain after the *Second Boer War*, but again was given considerable *autonomy* in 1906. It was joined to the *Union of South Africa* in 1910.

Transylvania. A region between Hungary and Rumania (within modern Rumania) and constantly a subject of dispute between them. It was ruled by the *Ottomans* and then the *Habsburgs*. After the *Ausgleich*, it became part of Hungary. In 1916 Rumania was bribed into *World War I* on the side of the *Allies* by a secret promise of gaining possession of Transylvania, which it later did via the *Treaty of Trianon*. In 1940 *Hitler* imposed a settlement dividing the province between his two east European allies—a rare instance, indeed, of Hitler as peacemaker. In 1947 the entire region was ceded to Rumania. During the *Cold War* friction continued between what were ostensibly *Soviet bloc* and *Warsaw Pact* allies. In the 1980s Rumania openly persecuted its ethnically Hungarian minority. Once the *Pax Sovietica* no longer applied after 1989, the issue of ownership re-emerged. In 1993 Hungary hinted that it might no longer accept the Trianon borders, thereby reopening the historic question of ownership of Transylvania. That same year, Rumania granted minority language rights to the 1.7 million Hungarians in Transylvania.

traveaux préparatoires. Work done preparatory to a *treaty*, used to clarify later interpretations.

treason. Betrayal of the core interests of a *state*, or other political community, by one of its *citizens*. What constitutes betrayal is, of course, a slippery and partly subjective idea. As such, the charge of "treason" often has been used by states to intimidate dissenters and thereby suppress political opposition or even directly eliminate those identified as enemies of the public (or merely dynastic, sectional, or regime) interest. Many states do not count peacetime espionage as treasonable, merely criminal. Others define treason so broadly it becomes indistinguishable from dissent. The usual penalty upon conviction, in either case, is death. In the twentieth century, *Nazi Germany* and the *Soviet Union*, foremost among *totalitarian* states, had extraordinarily broad definitions of treason. They thus executed many of their own militaries and *purged* party members en masse. They executed tens, and even hundreds, of thousands of ordinary people on trumped-up charges as the concept was applied carte blanche to entire ethnic and other despised populations. Post-Soviet Russia continued to define treason with spectacular illiberality, as in the 2001 sentencing to four years imprisonment of a military journalist who exposed nuclear waste dumping by the Russian Navy, thereby embarrassing certain officers and the government. Similarly, into the twenty-first century, China continued to define treason with a breadth that permitted little dissent and sometimes treated even the holding of forbidden private religious beliefs as a subversive and treasonous act.

At the other extreme lies the United States, which defined treason in Article III, Section 3, of its Constitution—the only crime listed therein. It is an exceptionally narrow definition which sees as treason solely acts of making *war* against one's own country or aiding and abetting the enemy in wartime. This curtailment of the far broader standard common in Europe in the eighteenth century befitted the document's drafters, who themselves had been accused (and surely were guilty) of treason, more broadly defined, against Great Britain just a dozen years earlier, and who were philosophically inclined to preserve large areas of individual liberty against the state. It has been argued that the definition covers peacetime *espionage* in behalf of an enemy state (under the "adhering to . . . enemies" clause). Others dispute even this minor widening. In any case, the U.S. definition proved so restrictive in practice that treason, more amply understood as a political crime, was almost never prosecuted there—fewer than 30 cases in 225 years, to 2001. Among the more distinctive U.S. cases were: *Benedict Arnold*, who escaped to Britain in 1779 and therefore never stood trial; Aaron Burr (vice president, 1801–1805), who was tried on a charge of treason in 1807 but was acquitted by Justice Marshall of the Supreme Court; Thomas Dorr, who was convicted of treason for leading an uprising against the governor of Rhode Island in 1844, but who was pardoned the next year; John Brown and six others, who were executed for treason and other crimes against Virginia in 1859–1860 after their attack on the Federal Armory at Harpers Ferry; a German-American, Max Haupt, convicted of treason for having harbored his Nazi *saboteur* son (who nonetheless had been caught and executed in 1942); and a Japanese-American, Tomoya Kawakita, condemned to death for joining the Japanese armed forces in World War II and for torturing U.S. *prisoners of war*, but whose sentence was commuted by *Eisenhower* in 1953. At the end of 2001, charges of treason were mooted for a young American, John Walker Lindh, discovered fighting for the *Taliban* and *al Qaeda* in Afghanistan after the *September 11, 2001, terrorist attack on the United States. See also Pierre Laval; Vidkun Quisling; Ethel and Julius Rosenberg; Wang Jingwei; war treason.*

treaty. A binding, written agreement between or among *states*, or with other *international personalities*, enumerating *rules* and establishing mutual and binding rights and obligations under *international law*. Treaties may, but need not, establish ad hoc or even permanent mechanisms for resolving *disputes*. They always require *consent*, with the rare but notable exception of a *diktat*. They may and do cover virtually any subject, from the usual concerns with *security* and *commerce* to migratory bird protection and long-term disposition of the mineral resources of the *Moon*. Treaties are created and undergo *adoption* by a four-step process: *negotiation, signature, ratification,* and, finally, entry into force. Subsequently, they may or may not be offered for *registration*. When points of disagreement arise, they are addressed by one or more of these methods of interpretation: *grammatical, historical, logical, restrictive,* and *systematic.* Nomenclature used for treaties is varied, but of minor consequence. There are two truly important distinctions among treaties: (1) Treaties are "executed" or "executory." The first are precise and have an agreed time frame or specific object in view, and once their designated task is completed they pass into history. The second are not time bound, govern ongoing transactions, and may anticipate and accommodate future conditions and developments. (2) Treaties are self-executing or non–self-executing. The first do not require implementing legislation to take effect in domestic law; the second do (but note, if signed and ratified, but not implemented, the failure to implement domestically does not absolve the state concerned from incurring an international *delict*). Lastly, treaties may be terminated (abrogated) in a variety of ways: (a) fundamentally altered circumstances which render them moot; (b) in accordance with *terms* of the treaty itself, such as completing the object in view or reaching a specified date for termination; (c) mutual consent; (d) *violation*; (e) *war*; and (f) *extinction* of one of the parties, though even in this extreme case certain obligations and rights may accrue to the *successor state*(s). The most recent codification of treaty procedures was the *Vienna Convention on the Law of Treaties* (1961). *See also accession; adherence; archive; bilateral;* clausula rebus sic stantibus; *convention; covenant; declaration; derogation; executive agreement; Final Act; friendship treaty; functus; illegal act; instrument of ratification; judicial legislation;* jus cogens; *law-making treaties; multilateral; nonaggression pact; notification; pact;* pacta sunt servanda; *peace treaty; protocol;* obscuritas pacti nocet; *reservation; resolution; secret treaties; security treaty; state succession; suspension; trade agreement; tribe; understanding; validity; verification regime.*

treaty port system. Specified Chinese coastal cities were designated as ports of entry for Western trade under various *unequal treaties* after the first *Opium War,* which ended in 1842. This put an end to the *Cohong* system. The first five, set up under the *Treaty of Nanjing,* were Guangzhou (Canton), Fuzhou, Ningbo, Shanghai, and Xiamen (Amoy). Eventually, nearly 80 of China's major coastal cities were designated "treaty ports" in agreements such as *Tientsin* and *Shimonoseki.* Within these areas, foreign powers enjoyed extensive *extraterritorial* rights, the import *tariff* was extremely low, and some Chinese enjoyed a rare freedom from control by their *Confucian* scholar-elite and emperor. The treaty ports thus funneled not merely foreign goods, but also modern technology and new political and social ideas into China and gave rapid rise to a merchant class not under the control of the emperor or bureaucracy. This aggravated growing divergences between the *Qing dynasty* and China's more modern social classes and between the growing urban economy and the stagnant and increasingly impoverished rural economy. Western powers forced similar treaty ports and concessions on Korea and Japan, until with the *Meiji Restoration* Japan joined the ranks of the *Great Powers*, took over Korea, and itself imposed concessions on China. In the 1920s the "Rights Recovery movement" aimed at regaining full *sovereignty* for China, but this effort was diverted in the 1930s by the *Chinese Civil War* and Japanese *aggression*. Vestiges of the treaty system survived until abolished in 1943 by the United States and United Kingdom in the name and interest of Allied solidarity.

Suggested Reading: Rhoads Murphey, *The Outsiders* (1977).

treaty power. Article II (2) of the U.S. Constitution, which requires the president to obtain the prior "advice and consent" of the Senate, by means of a two-thirds affirmative vote in that body, before *ratification* of any treaty may be completed.

treaty state. A state which has *adhered* to a given multilateral treaty, as in "China has a direct interest in [such and such a matter] because it is a Treaty Power."

trench warfare. A form of prolonged combat characterized by opposing systems of trenches from which each side launches assaults, patrols perimeters, and tries to shelter from enemy *artillery* and gunfire. While developed by *Vauban* as an aspect of *siege warfare*, in its more modern form it resulted from application of the fruits of *industrialization* to weaponry, which gave a major advantage to defenses against frontal assault by massed formations of *infantry* or *cavalry*. Extensive trench warfare occurred in the *Crimean War* and *American Civil War*. However, the earlier and more familiar example of *Napoleon I*, and then the stunningly rapid success of Prussia in the *Austro-Prussian War* and the *Franco-Prussian War*, misled most military observers into thinking that mobility was the new standard of modern warfare. Trench warfare is most closely identified with *World War I*. From 1914 to 1918 most trenches were sodden locales of wet uniforms, lice, cold food, excrement, corpse-fattened rats, cave-ins, snipers, artillery barrages, night raids, and daily terror. Conditions were so appalling along the 475 miles of trenches in the west, and some 875 miles in the east, that diseases were named for their high incidence among the soldiery; to wit: trench fever, trench foot, trench mouth, and so forth.

German trenches tended to be deeper because intended for defense, drier because the Germans held most of the high ground in the West, much more elaborate (electric lighting, plank floors), and well-supported by carefully sighted and often concrete *machine-gun* posts. On each side of *no-man's-land*, small fortifications, machine-gun nests, spotting positions, and dense fields of barbed wire were erected. By 1916 trench systems were hugely complex, with belts of wire 50 meters wide quite common and thousands of buried telephone cables running to the rear areas. Behind the *frontline* trenches were "support" and "reserve" trenches (counterattack and jump-off trenches in the German case), and traverse supply and communication trenches leading to various headquarters. Behind the whole trench system existed a booming war economy and nearly uninterrupted civilian way of life so starkly different from life at the front that the contrast caused deep and lasting bitterness among soldiers.

After the experience of the Great War some military theorists dismissed *fortification*, believing that mobile infantry and heavy artillery could overcome any trench or fort system; others sought to perfect the trenches for defense by building them in advance, as in the *Maginot Line*. In fact, the central lesson of trench warfare in the Great War was that in the new industrial age it was necessary to destroy not just the forward elements of an enemy's war-making capacity (troops, supplies, guns), but the industrial capacity which sustained it. This brutal insight, along with unsustainably high casualty rates endured in trench warfare, led to new strategic theories which sought to evade such conflicts while still prosecuting industrial warfare, such as *Blitzkrieg* and *strategic bombing*. Nevertheless, trench warfare recurred on many fronts during *World War II* and yet again in the *Iran-Iraq War* and the *Ethiopian-Eritrean War*.

Suggested Readings: The horrors of the trenches are inimitably depicted in the classic novel by Erich Maria Remarque, *All Quiet on the Western Front* (1928), which was banned by the *Nazis* for its inherent *pacifism*. Also see the tragic, exquisite verse of Wilfred Owen in particular, along with Siegfried Sassoon and others. And see Paul Fussell, *The Great War and Modern Memory* (1975, 2000); John Keegan, ed., *The First World War* (1999).

Trent Affair. This incident during the *American Civil War* aroused widespread anti-*Union* feeling in Britain, occasioned rash and boastful threats from *Palmerston*, and led to a major crisis which almost resulted in war. Union *blockade* ships seized two *Confederate* diplomats from a British vessel (the Trent), denying them the protection of *diplomatic immunity* on the ground that they were rebels. The British chose to view this as a national affront and threatened war. The crisis was resolved when Russian *mediation* led to a Union apology, which *Seward* convinced a reluctant *Lincoln* to make, and release of the Confederate envoys into British custody.

triad. The three legs of the U.S. *strategic weapons* forces: land-based *ICBMs*, *submarine-launched ballistic missiles (SLBMs)*, and strategic *bombers*.

triangle trade. (1) The *slave trade* was triangular in nature: ships would haul slaves from West Africa to the West Indies, Brazil, or North America; slaves were exchanged for sugar, tobacco, rum, and other products, which were then sold in Boston and other ports for beans, corn, and similar food supplies used to feed slaves. The trade in slaves was originally controlled by Portuguese captains, but these were quickly joined by Dutch, French, English, and Americans. Spain mostly contracted out its slave trading. (2) To reduce the loss of specie (monetary metals), the Dutch formed a triangular trade in which slaves and textiles from India were shipped to the *Spice Islands* and sold for spices which were then shipped to Europe. (3) The English carried cotton cloth from India to China in exchange for porcelain and silks, which were then sold in Europe. Later, because silver had also been required to pay for the Chinese exports, *opium* replaced slaves and spices in this trade. *See also East India Company; Opium Wars.*

Trianon, Treaty of (June 4, 1920). The agreement formally ending *World War I* between the *Allies* and Hungary. It left Hungary truncated from its prewar position, with two-thirds of its territory and a sizeable portion of its population seized to advantage its neighbors: Czechoslovakia received most of Slovakia (Poland got the rest) and *Ruthenia,* Italy took *Fiume,* Rumania got *Transylvania,* and *Yugoslavia* (then the *United Kingdom*) took *Croatia* and *Voivodina.* Like Germany, Hungary was restricted to a small army (35,000) and made to pay proportionate *reparations. See also war guilt clause.*

tribalism. When *politics* is characterized by a shattered mosaic of loyalties to competing *tribes* or *ethnic groups.* This can lead to the worst kind of *civil war,* with overtones of *genocide. See also Bosnia; Rwanda.*

tribe. Any group of people united by common ancestry, custom, language, or religion. Politically, the difference from a *nation* or a *people* is really only one of scale. Yet the term is sometimes unconsciously used in the pejorative, as in referring in the same breath to African tribes but Asian or European peoples. It may also be used to deliberate pejorative effect, to belittle the national aspirations of a subject people (say, the *Kurds*) or an established people perceived to be acting in barbaric fashion ("the Serbian tribe," rather than nation). Under *international law,* tribe has a tightly circumscribed meaning. It is a political community which lacks full membership in the *community of nations,* in the legal sense, and hence may not exercise *sovereign* rights such as contracting binding *treaties.* More than once a colonial power or settler state such as Canada, New Zealand, or the United States made use of this distinction to deny retroactively the binding character of treaties drawn up with tribes of *indigenous peoples.* Of course, this led to bitter recrimination and much legal confusion about the international status of tribal land claims and other treaty rights which may or may not have been legally agreed to or conferred. If and when a tribe acquires a *state,* it is immediately elevated in diplomatic discourse, in international law, and usually also on the editorial pages, from the status of tribe to that of nation. *See also Manifest Destiny; Maori Wars; Zulu Wars.*

tributary. A small state which pays *tribute* (treasure, *slaves*) to a larger power as acknowledgment of its own inferior status and political subjugation, such as Vietnam to Imperial China, Cambodia to Vietnam, conquered *tribes* to the *Inca* or *Aztec*, numerous African states to other, larger African states, or Saxon Wexford to the *Vikings*. *See also equality; sovereignty.*

tribute. Treasure, as well as political homage, paid to an imperial power by a *tributary* ruler or state. Occasionally, large states may pay tribute, as when the United States paid the *Barbary pirates* not to harass its ships. Tributary relations were common in international relations, especially as conducted by empires, before the emergence of the modern *Westphalian system's* presumption of legal *equality* among *sovereign* powers. In premodern China an elaborate tribute system developed even with states which were not direct tributaries of the empire. Besides flattering and confirming the *prestige* of China's emperors as foreign emissaries did the *kowtow*, this disguised as tribute what was very often mercantile trade. Why the subterfuge? Because trade per se was despised by most of the *Confucian* scholar-elite. Nonetheless, having to trade in this dodgy fashion hampered the development of full mercantile relations. For instance, early *Qing* emperors regarded the Dutch, Portuguese, and English traders as representatives of tributary nations. In the 1680s most coastal trade restrictions were lifted and this notion was set aside. Still, later Qing emperors pretended to regard official diplomatic missions from Britain and the *East India Company* in 1793 and 1816 as supplications to become a Chinese tributary. Even so, that was a better fate than greeted another mission, when the "John Company" representative was imprisoned for three years. They kept up this harmful limitation by maintaining the *Cohong* system in Guangzhou (Canton). China also traditionally paid subsidies (bribes) to *Inner Asian* peoples such as the *Mongols* to deflect them from raiding, *pillage*, or *conquest*. Nepal paid tribute to China as late as 1908. Russia paid tribute to the Crimean khans until 1683, then turned around and over the course of the next century conquered them. *See also Ashanti; Aztec Empire; Burundi; Cambodia; Continental System; Dahomey; Ethiopia; Ifriqiya; Inca Empire; Kongo; Korea; imperialism; Lunda; Malawi; Mali; Morocco; Nerchinsk; Nubia; Nurgaci; Opium Wars;* Pax Romana; *Rwanda; Senegal; Song dynasty; Songhay; Soviet bloc; Tamerlane; Tonkin; Vietnam; Yoruba.*

Trident. American *boomers* which each carry 24 MIRVed, SLBMs (128 *warheads*). Britain also purchased several of these *nuclear weapons* platforms, but announced in 1993 it would limit its Tridents to 96 warheads each (its Polaris boats carried 48). Trident *submarines* are quite simply the most awesome, destructive weapons systems yet created.

Trieste. This historic port was a vital entry to the *Austro-Hungarian Empire*. It was made a *free city* by the Italian treaty which numbered among the several

Treaties of Paris (1947). However, Yugoslavia disputed control until 1954, causing the British and Americans to garrison the city. It was then agreed that Trieste, whose population is mostly Italian, should revert to Italy. This was confirmed in 1975.

Trilateral Commission. A group of 400 or so highly influential former policy-makers, formed in 1973 by private citizens from Japan, Europe, and North America, to foster cooperation among democratic nations at a time of apparent slippage in U.S. leadership in the wake of the *Vietnam War, Watergate,* and the *Nixon shocks.* Over the years the Commission expanded to include a Pacific Asia Group, whereas Mexicans joined the North American Group. It drafts and publishes reports on issues deemed of rising or continuing importance to international stability, peace, security, and economic cooperation. It is broadly *liberal-internationalist* in outlook and interests. The *elite* character of this association stirs deeply paranoid fears about its "real role" and suspected "secret influence" in policymaking circles, at least among the usual conspiracy theorists: inveterate *Marxists* and *postmodernists* on the far left and the "black helicopter" crowd on the far right.

Trinidad and Tobago. First charted by *Columbus* in 1498, the islands were turned into a raft of *slave labor* plantations for several centuries. Tobago became a British *protectorate* in 1763 (taken from France) and Trinidad followed in 1802: it had been taken from Spain by force in 1797 during the *Napoleon Wars* and was confirmed legally as British in the *Treaty of Amiens.* The islands were ruled as a single British *colony,* 1888–1958, when they were made part of the *West Indies Federation.* In 1962 they withdrew in favor of *independence* within the Commonwealth. In 1976 they changed to a *republican* form of government. They are rich in *oil* and other *natural resources* and are among the most prosperous of Caribbean nations. In 1990 their island peace was disturbed by a quirky revolt by 100–120 Muslim *fundamentalists,* who for six days held the prime minister and others *hostage.*

Tripartite Pact (September 27, 1940). This alliance signed by Nazi Germany, Fascist Italy, and Imperial Japan was to activate in the event any signatory was attacked by an (unnamed) third power not then at war. It was intended to deter United States entry into *World War II,* but had the reverse effect: it led most Americans henceforth to see little difference between Japan and the European *fascist* dictatorships, and it contributed to a hardening of *Franklin Roosevelt's* resolve to block Japanese *aggression* in Asia. It was later adhered to by the minor *Axis* states: Bulgaria, Hungary, and Rumania. Yugoslavia signed in March 1941, but after an anti-German coup the pact was repudiated. *Hitler* responded by invading Yugoslavia and setting up *puppet states* in Croatia and Slovakia, which also signed the Pact.

Triple Alliance. (1) An *alliance* formed originally in 1420 among the central Mexican city-states of Tecacoco and Tlacopan with Tenochtitlan, home of the imperial and rapacious Mexica, which warred against Tepaneca, and later formed the core of the *Aztec Empire*. (2) 1668: A *league* of England, the Netherlands, and Sweden, against France. (3) 1717: A league of Britain, France, and the Netherlands, against Spain. (4) 1882–1915: A secret alliance among Austria-Hungary, Germany, and Italy, pledging mutual assistance in the event of an attack by France. Unbeknown to Austria or Germany, Italy also signed a secret non-aggression pact with France in 1902. As it was Germany which attacked France in 1914, Italy was therefore within its legal rights in refusing to accept that the Triple Alliance treaty had come into effect. Then Rome performed a spectacular *reneversement des alliances* by joining the *Allies* and *declaring war* on Germany and Austria in 1915.

Triple Entente. A loose term used for the three-way British, French, and Russian cooperation between 1907 and 1914 and the military *alliance* signed on September 3, 1914, and sometimes confused with the *Entente Cordiale*. The 1914 military *pact* was disavowed by the *Bolsheviks* when they signed a *separate peace* with Germany at *Brest-Litovsk* in 1918.

Triple Intervention. Within six days of the end of the *First Sino-Japanese War* in 1895, France, Germany, and Russia "counseled" Japan to renounce the claim to the Liaodong peninsula it had just wrested from China, in exchange for an increase in its *indemnity* from China. Japan agreed to be pushed out of *Manchuria*, but regarded the *intervention* with rage and as little more than a veiled threat from imperial rivals. Within 10 years Japanese troops returned in force and stayed for 40 years. Within three years the intervening powers began the scramble for China known as *concession diplomacy*.

tripolarity. A theoretical structure for the *international system* in which three main centers of great *power*, or poles, are said to attract lesser powers into their orbit. Some theoreticians maintain that such a system would lead to extreme instability as each of the *Great Powers* would seek to be in the party of two while fearing a betrayal might leave it the party of one (a point often made, albeit in a different context, in divorce courts); these effects would be magnified for smaller powers. It is not much more than clever nonsense, of little relevance to real world affairs. *See also bipolarity; multipolarity; unipolarity.*

Tripoli (a.k.a. Tripolitania). Ancient Tripoli formed a province of the Carthaginian Empire and then of the *Roman Empire*. From the seventh century C.E. it fell under the control of several Arab and Muslim successors. It formed part of *Ifriqiya* in the thirteenth century and was the northern terminus of the shortest of the trans-Saharan *trade routes*. It was occupied by *Ferdinand* of Spain in 1511 and then given over to the *Crusading* order, the Knights of St.

John. They were expelled in 1551 by an army of the *Ottoman Empire*. By the end of the sixteenth century it was fully incorporated into that Empire, along with *Tunis* and *Algiers*. The Karamanli dynasty ruled as Ottoman pashas, 1711–1823. In the seventeenth and eighteenth centuries Tripoli was home to the *Barbary pirates*, local Muslim fiefdoms nominally under Ottoman authority but broadly *autonomous*, who preyed upon commerce in the western Mediterranean and serviced the trans-Saharan route to *Bornu*. Yusuf Karamanli (r. 1795–1830) allied with Britain against France in Egypt and thereby gained de facto independence from the Ottomans. He also extended his control south, into the Fezzan hinterland to trade for *slaves* and leather with Bornu and *Sokoto*. After his death the Fezzan broke free, and in 1835 the Ottomans reasserted their authority as a means of containing *Mehemet Ali* in Egypt. It took until 1842 to control the coast; the Fezzan remained beyond reach. Tripoli was seized from the Ottomans by Italy in the *Italo-Turkish War* (1911–1912). Interior *Bedouin* and Sanusi faithful from Tripoli and Cyrenaica put up heavy *guerrilla* resistance to conquest by Italy, into the 1930s. Tripoli became independent as *Libya* in 1951.

Tripolitan War (1801–1807). After the *American Revolution*, the U.S. *merchant marine* was no longer protected by the *Royal Navy* and quickly fell victim to predations by the *Barbary pirates*. In the mid-1790s, with a dozen ships captured and 100 (white) Americans taken as *slaves* or *hostages*, Congress agreed to pay annual ransom to the *dey* of Algiers and made similar treaties with *Tripoli* and *Tunisia (Tunis)*. All these treaties were violated by the pirates. President *Thomas Jefferson* sent a punitive expedition in 1801, but the underequipped, outgunned Americans suffered several defeats. Despite a minor victory in 1805, the United States continued to ransom its *citizens*. Jefferson withdrew the navy, which he had consistently underfunded, in 1807. After the buildup of the *War of 1812* a much stronger U.S. force returned in 1815, joined by flotillas from several European nations, and ended the *piracy*.
    Suggested Reading: Michael Kitzen, *Tripoli and the United States at War* (1993).

triumphalism. A churlish charge of "insensitivity" and "gloating" over the end of the *Cold War* made against those who thought there was every good reason to cheer the demise of the *Soviet Union* and the fact that the idea of *democracy* had prevailed over *communism*, by those who never really understood the moral and civilizational issues at stake in the first place and instead took refuge behind merely a façade of historical "*objectivity*" and assumptions of *moral equivalence*.

Troppau, Congress of (1820). The third *congress* in the so-called *Congress system*. Austria, Prussia, and Russia met, with Britain and France as observers, to deal with an outbreak of liberal *revolution* in the Italian and Iberian peninsulas. Britain agreed to Austrian *intervention* in Italy, but rejected the general premise of the three conservative powers, especially Russia, that intervention was justified to suppress any reform or revolt in Europe.

Trotskyites. Followers of the theories of *Leon Trotsky*, forming marginal groups within the wider international *Marxist* movement after 1927. Highly critical of *Stalinism*, they indulged in a *cult of personality* of their own, centered on Trotsky. Their main, historic importance was to feed *Stalin's* paranoia about a conspiracy to overthrow his regime, as they were never in power anywhere. Trotskyites became famous for arcane, doctrinal quarrels—prompting the jest that wherever one came across two Trotskyites one also found three "tendencies." Trotsky's theories continue to attract a handful of adherents on the far Left, though mainly among academics and students, notably in France.

Trotsky, Leon Davidovich, né Bronstein (1879–1940). Russian revolutionary. In 1898, at age 19, Trotsky was arrested for his *Marxist* views and subversive activities and *exiled* to the tsarist prison camp system in *Siberia*. He escaped from the camps and fled to Switzerland, where he allied with *Lenin* in 1902, but he did not yet join the *Bolsheviks*. In the *Russian Revolution of 1905* Trotsky founded and headed, at age 26, the *St. Petersburg Soviet*. Exiled once more to Siberia, once more he escaped. Trotsky now made his reputation with his pen, writing inflammatory pamphlets of the usual sort while living as a journalist and moving among the Russian émigrés communities in the West. When the *Russian Revolution* broke out in 1917, he returned to Russia and again took an activist lead in revolutionary agitation and politics. He headed the *Petrograd Soviet* and finally openly joined the Bolshevik Party. He was instrumental in the events of November (October) 1917. Appointed commissar for foreign affairs, a position he regarded as a bourgeois frivolity soon to disappear in the universal revolution to come, he provoked Germany unnecessarily by declaring a policy of "neither peace nor war." When German commanders and armies grew impatient with this nonsense and instead advanced deeper into Russia, Trotsky signed the humiliating *Treaty of Brest-Litovsk*, surrendering huge portions of Russia's population and territory and handing over its gold reserves as *reparations*. With more success, he organized and headed the *Red Army* in the *Russian Civil War*, during which he showed a capacity for ruthlessness rivaled by few, but also some real organizational and even military skills. Instinctively dictatorial, he was a firm advocate of *terror* as the basis of maintaining Soviet power, writing without blinking or apology in 1924: "The dictatorship of the *Communist Party* is maintained by recourse to every form of violence."

After Lenin's death Trotsky emerged as the main rival to *Stalin* for the political succession. They struggled fiercely over foreign policy, specifically the role of the *Comintern* in subverting *capitalist* powers and the mechanics and final purposes of cooperation with the *Guomindang* in China, rather than the then fledgling *Chinese Communist Party.* Trotsky was disdainful of the details of party organization and coalition-building among the Party leadership, whereas Stalin quietly reshaped the *apparat* and Party bureaucracy in his image and peopled it with his toadies. Stalin was also far more adept than Trotsky at maneuvering first against one leadership faction and then against another, until Trotsky (and every other potential enemy of "Koba") was utterly isolated and Stalin retained sole power. However crudely, Stalin thus was able to maneuver the more effete Trotsky out of power and out of Moscow, sending him into exile in Central Asia in 1927. Finally, he had Trotsky deported abroad in 1929. Stalin's preferred policy of *socialism in one country* thus won out over Trotsky's more romantic, *adventurist* notion of *permanent revolution.* In exile, the increasingly well-traveled Trotsky—he was welcome in few countries and was repeatedly deported—founded the *Fourth International* in 1938 to oppose *Stalinism,* which he and later followers regarded as a betrayal of the Bolshevik Revolution rather than its culmination. In 1940 Stalin sent assassins to murder Trotsky, then living a mean existence in Mexico. The deed was done by several blows to the head with an ice pick, after which Trotsky lingered awhile before dying. *See also foreign ministry; Maximilien de Robespierre.*

Suggested Readings: Francesco Benvenuti, *The Bolsheviks and the Red Army, 1918–1922* (1988); Vladimir N. Brovkin, ed., *The Bolsheviks in Russian Society: The Revolution and the Civil Wars* (1997); Alex Callinicos, *Trotskyism* (1990); Adam Ulam, *The Bolsheviks* (1998).

"The Troubles." A popular euphemism among nationalists for the confluence of events comprising the *Easter Rising* (1916), the *Irish War of Independence* (1918–1921), and the *Irish Civil War* (1922–1923). The term was revived after 1969 in reference to revived sectarian violence in *Ulster,* which continued for another thirty years.

truce. Suspension of fighting for a specified time. Unlike an *armistice,* which must be mutually agreed, a truce may be declared unilaterally. They may be general or limited to specific sectors of the front; they may be agreed for humanitarian reasons, to care for or remove the wounded or civilians before recommencing hostilities; or they may be merely political ploys. A truce may, but does not necessarily, imply that *peace* will follow. *See also war termination.*

Trucial Oman (a.k.a. Trucial States). Seven *sheikdoms* on the south, or Trucial, coast of the *Persian Gulf*: Abu Dhabi, Ajman, Dubai, Fujairah, Ras al-Kaimah, Sharjah, and Umm al-Qaiwain. They maintained a *treaty* relationship with Britain from 1853, when they were compelled to cease their *piracy* in the Gulf and to refer disputes to the British authority in India. They became a de facto British *protectorate* in 1914 after Turkey entered *World War I.* In 1971 they formed the *United Arab Emirates.* In an earlier era, they were called collectively by the British the "Pirate Coast." *See also Barbary Coast.*

Trudeau, Pierre Elliot (1919–2000). Canadian prime minister, 1968–1979, 1980–1984. Trudeau's main interest was the problem of *Québec*. In 1970 he introduced *martial law* (War Measures Act) in response to a few *terrorist* incidents in Québec. It was lifted within weeks, but had led to more than 400 arrests and was generally judged a gross overreaction to events. He tried to confirm Québec within the Canadian confederation after 1980 by *repatriation* of the Canadian constitution from Westminster. He succeeded in that, but not on obtaining Québec's agreement to the document. He spoke of finding a "Third Option" for Canada, by which he simply meant less economic and cultural reliance on the United States, and of increasing *foreign aid*. However, budgetary and domestic pressures and Trudeau's dilettantish approach to diplomacy meant that Canada never met its promised aid targets. Meanwhile, shifting national trade toward the *European Community* or the *Pacific Rim* was more easily said than done, in the face of the growing *protectionism* of the 1970s. As a result, when Trudeau left office, Canadian trade with the United States remained more or less where it had been when he became prime minister, at about 80 percent of total trade. A few years later, Canada gave up on the chimera of differentiated trade as *NAFTA* was passed and signed into law by a successor, Brian Mulroney.

One of Trudeau's first actions in foreign affairs was to cut troop commitments to *NATO* by 50 percent (1968). That was coupled with a new emphasis on promoting precise national, including economic and symbolic, interests as opposed to the postwar *liberal-internationalism* pursued by his predecessor, *Lester Pearson*. As *détente* waned, Trudeau realized that a reduced military role degraded Canadian influence in the world and reluctantly agreed to increase defense spending, paralleling a shift across all NATO countries by 1978. Unable to make real structural changes in the economy or abroad, Trudeau resorted to fashionable symbolic tweaking of the United States, a motive never far from the surface even in such apparently serious policy moves as opening diplomatic relations with *Castro's* regime in Cuba. He also enjoyed publicly insulting Great Britain, as when he spun a pirouette on camera but behind the back of *Queen Elizabeth* at an official ceremony, titillating admirers and superficial nationalists but hardly advancing Canada's real interests or serious debate about the place of the monarchy in its national constitution.

During the 1980s Trudeau's foreign policy antics became more shrill but less influential, as he fell out of step with NATO policy on missile testing and deployment. He also reacted less strongly than any other Western leader to the Soviet invasion of Afghanistan, during which he was briefly out of office, and spoke with sympathy for the dilemma faced by *Jaruzelski* in deciding to introduce martial law to Poland. As Cold War tensions sharpened during the early *Reagan* years, the always whimsical Trudeau launched a personal "peace mission" to renew *arms control* talks. Politely received abroad and domestically wildly popular in the usual corners of the Liberal Party and the academy, the effort led to no measurable or practical success. In sum,

Trudeau briefly raised Canada's international profile but also hastened a reduction in its real international influence. Still, even that reflected more the return of former Great Powers (Japan and Germany) to their former status than his or Canada's foreign policy per se.

Suggested Readings: Andrew Cohen and J. L. Granatstein, eds., *Trudeau's Shadow* (1998); Pierre Elliott Trudeau, *Memoirs* (1993).

Truk. *See Caroline Islands.*

Truman Doctrine (March 12, 1947). A promise of U.S. aid to all "free peoples who are resisting attempted subjugation by armed minorities or by outside powers." Its initial impetus was the perceived need to aid Greece against a *communist* insurgency and to psychologically prepare the American public for future engagements against the Soviet Union (including possible military *intervention* in what was otherwise peacetime) in the interests of *containment* and for a permanent military commitment to Europe and Japan. It led to a globalization and militarization of containment, which was unfortunate, but it also assured democratic and other anti-communist states that the United States would not retreat into *isolationism* but would instead accept a leadership role in the coming *Cold War* with Moscow, which was essential. *See also European Recovery Program.*

Truman, Harry S (1884–1972). U.S. vice president, 1945; *Democratic* president, 1945–1953. An autodidact, Truman was the only modern U.S. president never to attend college. He served as an *artillery* captain on the *western front* in *World War I*. Back in his home state of Missouri he failed as a small businessman (haberdashery). Adopted by the local Democratic Party boss, Truman rose through a succession of judgeships and other local offices in the 1920s until elected to the Senate in 1934. Truman first came to national prominence during *World War II* as chairman of a committee investigating fraud and abuse in wartime procurement contracts. He was selected to be *Franklin Roosevelt*'s vice presidential running-mate in the 1944 election, but once in office was kept at arms length by Roosevelt from most decision making.

Truman inherited the presidency when Roosevelt died in April 1945. He thus came to the highest office just as the key decisions on shaping the postwar peace had to be made or those already made had to be implemented. Truman immediately took a direct interest in the *San Francisco Conference*, where the *United Nations* was being officially launched—throughout his presidency he was a powerful supporter of international organization, including of the UN's innovative commitment to *human rights* promotion. That aroused bitter opposition among segregationist Democrats in the South and isolationist *Republicans* in the Midwest. Truman concurred in and actively promoted an American commitment to international economic leadership, correcting the several gross errors of foreign economic policy made before and during the *Great Depression*. He therefore endorsed Roosevelt's extant plans for development of the *Bretton Woods* institutions and oversaw implementation of the new international financial system that created and sustained. Truman took a lesser hand in framing immediate military policy toward Europe in the last days of the war, where fighting was drawing to a close. Instead, he looked to development of plans to invade Japan and thereby finish the war in the Pacific—probably in 1946, it was thought.

Within weeks of taking power Truman attended the *Potsdam Conference*, consulting on nothing less than the fate of all nations in Europe and even most nations in the world, along with the other *Big Three* decision makers, Stalin and *Churchill* (who was replaced in mid-conference by *Clement Atlee*). At Potsdam Truman told Stalin about the first successful test of the *atomic bomb* and co-issued the *Potsdam Declaration*. Also at Potsdam, and afterward, Truman was faced with enormous problems of reconstruction of a destitute, near-starving, and bombed-out continent, and problems of moral and political engagement and financial and security responsibility on a scale never before, or since, faced by an American president. The task of recovery, moreover, had to be carried out by a nation which had just come through not just the privations of the war, but of the Depression before that. It required cooperation with one ally, Great Britain, that was financially exhausted by the war. And it meant working with a deeply wounded, vengeful, and then largely uncooperative government in France. Finally, there loomed over the whole postwar settlement the enormously powerful, strangely enigmatic, brooding even, and opportunistically aggressive personality of Stalin, and the fact that the *Red Army* was already present by the millions in the heart of Europe. As a result, the political influence of the Soviet Union was expected to be correspondingly huge. In the Pacific, Truman needed to make momentous unilateral decisions, especially whether and how to use atomic bombs to end the war against Japan. He made that decision, the most difficult of his presidency, twice: concerning *Hiroshima* and again with regard to *Nagasaki*.

With the end of World War II Truman quickly canceled the wartime assistance program to allies popularly known as *Lend-Lease*—some historians say too quickly, others not. Aided by a brilliant supporting cast of talented and experienced statesmen, including *Dean Acheson, Lucius D. Clay*, and *George Marshall*, Truman oversaw the hard recovery from World War II by pushing through major postwar loans to Britain and to France, and in time also by imaginative, generous, and rapid reconstruction and rehabilitation of the *Axis* states. In Germany, that was initially done in the teeth of opposition by both France and the Soviet Union, who were keen for a harsh peace and for *reparations*, in specie or in kind. As the *Cold War* rapidly developed over Germany, Truman was firm. He oversaw commitment of American *air power* in the *Berlin airlift* to uphold the legality of the *Yalta accords* and Potsdam decisions on the administrative partition of *Berlin* and of Germany. More generally, Truman announced and implemented the critically important *Truman Doctrine*, which permanently (though in some ways unwisely) ended historic U.S. diplomatic and military isolation in peacetime and instituted the formative policy of *containment* of the Soviet Union. That set the mold for America's Cold War security policy for the next four decades. Containment at first was centered on economic recovery, to be brought about primarily through the *European Recovery Program* and the founding of NATO (1949) in Europe and a comparable aid package for Japan. Truman thus oversaw the so-called *reverse course* in U.S. postwar policy on the *zaibatsu* and other features of Japanese national life and economic development, and on *denazification* in Germany and the move to instead work closely with *Adenauer* to bring about an independent *West Germany* tied to the emerging Western alliance and trading system.

Truman won reelection in 1948, in an upset of Republican Thomas E. Dewey which surprised most political observers, and not a few friends and allies. His second term became bogged down domestically in the tragi-farce of *McCarthyism* and in foreign policy in the morass of the *Korean Conflict*. During that war Truman took the courageous decision to fire *Douglas MacArthur* for insubordination and for reckless talk about bombing China with nuclear weapons, thus preserving the crucial principal of civilian primacy. He also supported *Chiang Kai-shek* on Taiwan, but with enough deliberate restraint to prevent him trying to invade the mainland and thus provoke a wider Sino-American conflict. Truman left office deeply unpopular, but he has been subsequently judged by most historians to have been a near-great president—one of the most farsighted, courageous, and decisive American chief executives in the 20th century.

Suggested Readings: Dean Acheson, *Present at the Creation* (1969); David McCullough, *Truman* (1992); Harry S Truman, *Memoirs*, 2 vols. (1956).

trustee (a.k.a. trusteeship) powers. Seven states charged with responsibility for one or more of the United Nations *trust territories:* Australia, Belgium, Britain, France, Italy, New Zealand, and the United States.

Trusteeship Council. One of the *Principal Organs* of the *United Nations*, charged by the *United Nations General Assembly* with overseeing the *trust territories* (with the exception of the *Trust Territory of the Pacific Islands*, the sole *strategic* trust). It is technically overseen by the *Security Council*. It replaced the *mandate* authority of the defunct *League of Nations*. Membership includes all *trustee powers*, all other members of the Security Council, and other states elected by the UNGA. By 1990, most of the work of the Trusteeship Council was accomplished, including the difficult and legally tangled job of securing *independence* for *Namibia*.

trusteeship territories. The twelve *territories* so designated by Article 77 of the *United Nations Charter*. By 1950, eleven territories were in the trust of seven *trustee powers*. All but Somalia were former *mandates*: *Cameroons* (Britain), *Cameroons* (France), *Nauru* (Australia), *New Guinea* (Australia), *Ruanda-Urundi* (Belgium), *Somaliland* (Italy), *Tanganyika* (Britain), *Togoland* (Britain), *Togoland* (France), *Trust Territory of the Pacific Islands* (United States), and *Western Samoa* (New Zealand). Of these, eight achieved self-rule by 1962. By 1989 only *Palau* (from the Trust Territory of the Pacific Islands) remained in trust, and it voted for *free association* with the United States in 1993. The most difficult case was the twelfth: South Africa's refusal to submit *Namibia* (Southwest Africa) to UN authority. Even that was eventually resolved, with Namibian *independence* coming in 1990.

Trust Territory of the Pacific Islands. Some 2,100 islands spread over 3 million square miles of the Pacific. A U.S. *trust territory* from 1947, comprising the Caroline, Mariana, and Marshall Island groups recaptured from Japan. It was the only *strategic* trust. Until 1952 it was administered directly by the U.S. Navy, then handed to the Department of the Interior (save the Marianas, which remained under the navy until 1962). In 1975 a *referendum* led to formation of a Commonwealth of the Northern Marianas, in *free association* with the United States. That left only *Palau* in trust, and it too voted for free association in 1993. *See also* Guam; Micronesia (Federated States); Marianas; Marshall Islands.

truth. In international relations, as in most other realms of human activity and inquiry, truth is hard to come by. It is also not as highly valued by decision makers or as vital, as a practical matter, as one might like to think. *See also* atrocity; belligerent equality; camouflage; disinformation; double agent; doublethink; fact-finding missions; history; human rights; misperception; mole; NWICO; Pravda; propaganda; public opinion; Radio Free Europe; reparations; ruse; Tet Offensive; theory; totalitarianism; Truth (and Reconciliation) Commissions; UNESCO; war crimes; wars of religion.

Truth (and Reconciliation) Commissions. Investigative bodies set up to uncover facts about deeply contentious and divisive issues in a given society. They generally do not aim at prosecution so much as at historical clarity and national reconciliation. Amnesty may be granted to *human rights* abusers, *secret police*, and other former government (or opposition) officials in order to facilitate truthful testimony. The first was established in South Africa after the end of *apartheid*. Its acknowledged success made it a model in formation of commissions in Nigeria, Panama, East Timor, and other countries, as those societies also sought to uncover and reconcile their recent pasts. In some cases, Truth Commissions recommended that *restitution* be made.

tsar. "Caesar." Title of the emperors of Russia and some other *Slavic* rulers, as in Medieval Bulgaria.

tsarist Russia. The Russian Empire under the tsars, from the renunciation by Muscovy of its vassalage to the *Mongols* made by *Ivan III* in 1480, to the abdication of *Nicholas II* and declaration of a Russian republic in 1917. Tsarism upheld principles of *autocracy* and paternalism, even under the most able reformers. *See also Alexander I; Alexander II; Catherine II; Nicholas I; Nicholas II; Peter I; Russia; serfdom.*

Tshombe, Moïse (1920–1969). He led the revolt of *Katanga* province during the *Congo crisis*, earning opprobrium among other African leaders for his use of white *mercenaries* in support of Belgian mining interests. He had *Patrice Lumumba* murdered. Upon the reunification of Katanga with Congo, he went abroad. He returned to office briefly as prime minister of the Congo Republic, 1964–1965, but he fell out with *Mobutu* and fled again. He was condemned to death *in absentia*. He died under mysterious circumstances in an Algerian jail.

T'su Hsi (1834–1908). "The Dowager Empress." *See also Cixi.*

Tsushima Strait, Battle of (May 27–28, 1905). Known in Japan as the Battle of the Japan Sea. The Russian Baltic Fleet almost provoked a war with Britain when it mistakenly fired at fishing boats at *Dogger Bank*, as it sought urgently to make its way to the Far East after the outbreak of the *Russo-Japanese War*. Its mission was to replace the Russian Pacific Fleet which had been sunk and hemmed into the harbor by a surprise Japanese attack at *Port Arthur* in February, commanded by Admiral *Tōgō Heihachirō*. After the Dogger Bank incident, the Baltic Fleet was refused permission by the British to use the *Suez Canal*. It was thus forced to navigate around Africa, taking seven months to arrive off the coast of China. When it entered the Tsushima Strait (which runs through two small islands themselves lying adjacent to Korea and Kyushu, Japan) it was nearly entirely sunk, with heavy loss of life, during a ferocious two-day battle with the waiting Japanese war fleet, again under Tōgō Heihachirō. Russia thereafter agreed to meet to discuss terms, leading to American mediation and the *Treaty of Portsmouth*. *See also Yamamoto.*

Tuareg. A fierce, nomadic Saharan people who for centuries dominated the central portion of the great trans-Saharan *trade routes*, breeding camels and enslaving *sudanese* blacks to mine the salt deposits of the deep Sahara. They were a complex ethnic mix, with a Berber military aristocracy at the top and a black underclass descended from slaves at the bottom. What made them one people was, perhaps, the great leveling religion of *Islam* to which most converted. In the eleventh century the Tuareg helped establish caravan links from *Mali* and *Songhay* as the southern termini to *Tripoli* and *Ifriqiya* on the Mediterranean coast. In the fifteenth century they connected the *city-states* (and leather and cloth manufactures) of the *Hausa* to North Africa. Timbuktu, capital of the ancient empire of Mali, fell to the *Tuareg* in 1433. They lost it to a resurgent Songhay in 1469. Moving eastward, they established new salt mining and serviced other trade routes, establishing the state of Aïr with its capital at Agades. After Songhay fell to invading Moors, the Tuareg were largely unrestrained. They retook Timbuktu in 1787. The Tuareg violently resisted French colonization, fighting back well into the 1920s.

Tukolor Empire. The Tukolor were essentially *Fulbe* who had long settled in Muslim towns. They came to prominence under the *fundamentalist* leader al-Hajj Umar (c. 1795–1864), a Tukolor chieftain and disciple of Tijaniyya practices (the Tijaniyya were local Sufis, or *Islamic* mystics). Under this fervent preacher from Fouta-Toro, a new and more severe *Muslim* theocracy was established on the ruins of the *Mali* empire in West Africa in the 1840s and 1850s. The culminating act was a Tukolor *jihad* in 1853, the third Fulbe jihad of the nineteenth century, in which Islamic rule was imposed on the more numerous Bambara by the Tukolor. The Empire's creation was part of the more general Islamic revival which swept over much of West Africa in the early- to mid-nineteenth century. For a time, in the latter half of the nineteenth century, it resisted French colonial penetration of the riverine and also desert interior of what became *French West Africa*.

Until 1864, when al-Hajj Umar was trapped in a cave by rebels and either killed himself or was burned to death, Tukolor blocked the French from completing their conquest of the interior of Senegal. It was greatly assisted in that task by its army's access to, and solid training in the use of, modern firearms. Tukolor soldiers, many of whom were slaves trained to use rifles were organized into regular fighting corps known as "sofas." They occupied a position somewhere between the old *cavalry*-dominated military of the region and the European-style formations moving inland from the coast under the French. Militating against successful defense was the fact that the Tukolor Empire was physically vast but sparsely populated. Moreover, its religious severity led Tukolor to be intolerant of local conditions and traditions of other conquered tribes. When this combined with the usual *plunder* and *pillage* conducted by crusading and conquering armies, of whatever faith, Tukolor provoked and had to contend with much local resistance and occasional rebellion, even as the French presence and pressure grew along the border. By the 1880s the Tukolor Empire, which had been held together under the personal and charismatic authority of al-Hajj Umar, began to unravel under his son. In 1893, at the height of the *scramble for Africa*, Tukolor was overrun by French troops and colonial levies. It was subsequently incorporated into the *French Empire*. That was the culmination of many years of deliberate French planning to tie together a West African empire connecting the Senegal and Niger by force and a railway, which they began building to that explicit purpose in 1882. *See also Fulbe empire; Samori Touré; Uthman dan Fodio.*

Suggested Readings: J. F. A. Ajayi and Michael Crowder, eds., *History of West Africa*, 2 vols. (1974); John Hargreaves, *West Africa Partitioned*, 2 vols. (1974); John Hargreaves, *France and West Africa* (1969).

tuna war. *See Cod Wars.*

Tunisia (Tunis). The state of *Ifriqiya* dominated this area from the thirteenth century. European assaults were made on its coastal cities in 1270 and 1390 by French *Crusaders*. In the fourteenth century the Hafsid dynasty was sustained by Christian Spain when it came under pressure from Marind troops. In 1569 it was occupied by *corsairs* from neighboring, and from the point of view of Tunis also upstart, *Algiers*. After the Turkish naval defeat at *Lepanto* (1571), the Hafsid dynasty was briefly restored by their Spanish patrons (1571); but in 1574 they were definitively deposed and Tunis, along with *Tripoli* and Algiers, became part of the *Ottoman Empire*. Under the *beys* it was known in Europe as one of the *Barbary States*. The Hussainid dynasty, which survived into the twentieth century, took power in 1705. During most of the nineteenth century Tunis was largely autonomous within the empire, relying on alliance with Britain (1837) to fend off both the Ottomans and the French. The beys were progressive, in terms of the *Maghreb*: in 1819 *piracy* was made illegal, and *slavery* was also banned decades sooner than elsewhere in North Africa.

By 1870, however, the French presence in Algeria was also felt in Tunis. At the *Congress of Berlin* (1878) it was determined that Tunisia fell within the French *sphere of influence* in North Africa. In 1881, to forestall apparent Italian ambitions for *conquest*, France took the occasion of a minor incident on the Algerian border to invade. Upon the French capture of Tunis its *bey* signed a treaty accepting that the country was a French *protectorate*. Also during the nineteenth century, Tunisia developed an indigenous constitutional movement. In 1934, building on this tradition, Habib Bourguiba (1903–2000) formed a nationalist party dedicated to negotiating independence for Tunisia. Impending war between France and Italy, which came in 1940, forestalled serious talks. Early in the war Tunisia fell under *Vichy's* control, but in 1943 it became an *Allied* and *Free French* base for invasions of Sicily and Italy. Despite objections from the *colons* in Algeria, and after massive civil unrest and rural rebellion which began in 1954, it reemerged as an independent *monarchy* in 1956 with Bourguiba as premier.

In 1957 the bey was overthrown and Tunisia became a *republic*, with Bourguiba as president. From 1954 to 1962 Tunisia was used as a base for French operations during the *Algerian War of Independence*, which led to fighting when Tunisia tried to expel French forces in 1961. When the French military left, so too did most colons. After the Algerian war Bourguiba kept a low profile in foreign affairs, concentrating on a fairly progressive domestic agenda, by Middle Eastern or North African standards, and cultivating trade and political links with the *European Community*. His diplomatic moderation drew criticism from more radical Arab neighbors, but was appreciated by moderates. Thus, he was invited to *mediate* an end to the Jordanian-PLO war in 1970. In the early 1980s Tunisia had to fend off Libyan raids and efforts to provoke a *rebellion* of its southern population, which harbors historic grievances against the north. Political dissent rose alongside living standards, and after 1985 the demand for political freedoms could not be resisted. Bourguiba was overthrown in 1987 by General Ben Ali, and a multiparty system was set up in 1988. Like other North African states, Tunisia faced a domestic challenge to its *modernization* in the 1990s from Islamic *fundamentalists*. When an Islamic party made early electoral gains, Ben Ali moved to close down Tunisia's experiment with secular democracy, banned the fundamentalist from elections, and had himself elected by a fraudulent vote in 1994 and again in 1999.

Suggested Readings: Monir S. Girgis, *Mediterranean Africa* (1987); I. William Zartman and William Habeeb, eds., *Polity and Society in Contemporary North Africa* (1993).

Túpac Amaru II (1740–1781). "Royal Serpent." Peruvian Indian leader and rebel. He was educated by the *Jesuits*. He claimed descent from the last claimant to be the *Sapa Inca*, Túpac Amaru I (d. 1572), who had been executed by the Spanish *viceroy*. That claim to noble Inca ancestry greatly inspired many Peruvian Indians to rally round him when he called for an uprising to throw off Spanish rule in 1780; but it raised others against him among Indians who genuinely were descended from Inca nobles and among members of tribes who had resisted Inca conquest. He began the revolt by executing the Spanish *corregidor* (provincial governor) for earlier acts of cruelty to Indians (November 4, 1780). This provoked a mass uprising, which developed into the last major Indian rebellion—though some *Creoles* also participated—before independence of most of Latin America from Spain in the first quarter of the nineteenth century. Many *hacienda* were overrun and destroyed, and their owners and overseers killed. The high levels of bloodshed probably were rooted in generations of pent-up Indian anger at the *encomienda system* and other abuses of Indians, which finally took violent form—as peasant grievances similarly did in Russia, China, and other lands. Before it was crushed the rebellion spread into Indian areas of Bolivia and northern Argentina, and Túpac Amaru briefly retook the old Inca capital of Cuzco. At its vengeful climax in May 1781, Túpac Amaru's family were butchered before him by the Spanish, and then he was horribly tortured to death. The uprising exposed huge racial and class divisions in Peru, and through its great violence and racial targeting also deepened these. It thus aggravated a highland versus lowland clash of perspective and interests which survives in Peru still. Túpac

Amaru's name subsequently inspired many Indian-rights activists, as well as left-wing *guerrillas* in Uruguay in the late twentieth century (the "Tupemaros"). *See also Great Fear*; jacquerie; *Nian Rebellion*; *Pugachev rebellion*.

turbulence. *Jargon.* A term used by some theorists to describe high levels of complexity and dynamism said to be a characteristic of modern *international relations*. This, they add, qualitatively alters the efficiency and utility, and increases the permeability to outside influences, of all states. The *international system* is thus seen as in transition to global, *complex interdependence*. Note: There is much confusion in the literature about whether advocates mean this phenomenon is a *cause* of large-scale changes or an *effect* of those changes. At least one foremost proponent of the idea unapologetically uses it both ways, thereby illuminating neither side of the causal question. See *globalization*.

Turkey. Originally, the term "Turk" did not indicate ethnicity in the full sense of *nation*. Instead, it signaled a common cultural and linguistic heritage among many Central Asian tribes and peoples. This original identity was later and further cemented by conversion to a new faith, *Islam*, and then the shared imperial history of the *Ottoman Empire*, when what is now Turkey formed the core of a vast, multinational empire during many centuries of martial glory, conquest of the *Byzantine Empire* and advance even to the walls of Vienna, then still more centuries of slow decay and decline. Thus, Turks today come from a variety of ethnic backgrounds, not least of all, *Kurdish*. Modern Turkey was established after the defeat of the Ottoman Empire in *World War I*.

The *Young Turks* rejected the *Treaty of Sèvres* (1920), fighting successfully to obtain the better terms of the *Treaty of Lausanne*. The modern republic was then proclaimed by *Atatürk* in October 1923, with the deliberate intent of thereby severing Turkey from its imperial and Islamic political past as home of the *caliphate*, in order to create a modern, secular state (the caliphate was renounced in 1924). It was for this reason, and to move out of the range of British *battleships*, that Atatürk also moved the capital to Ankara in 1923 from *Constantinople* (Istanbul). Turkey was governed by Atatürk under guiding principles which came to be known as "Kemalism": republicanism, populism, statism, reformism, and secularism. His accomplishments as a national leader were many and great, most importantly the cultural transformation of Turkey into the world's most successful Muslim state. On the other had, he also ruled the new Turkish republic as an uncompromising and repressive *autocrat*. Turkey remained a *one-party state* until 1950, after which it oscillated between unstable civilian and repressive military rule for several decades. The military repeatedly intervened to put down religious parties which threatened violent resistance to Turkey's political *secularization*, notably *Hezbollah*.

In foreign affairs, Turkey remained neutral during *World War II*. Under pressure from the *Soviet Union* even in the 1930s, as in negotiations over the *Montreux Convention*, and again pressured along its northern border in the postwar period, it joined *NATO* in 1952. During most of the *Cold War*, however, its foreign policy was dominated not by anti-*communism* or direct confrontation with Moscow, but by three issues with regional and ethnic-religious, rather than ideological, origins: First, relations with Greece, which have remained bad ever since the *Greek War of Independence* in the 1820s, over the *Ionian Islands* and other territorial disputes, along with a major and ongoing conflict over control of *Cyprus*. This dispute affected Turkey's position in NATO and encouraged it to an invasion of Cyprus in 1974, where it set up the unrecognized *Turkish Republic of Northern Cyprus*. Second, relations with Armenians remained strained not just within Turkey but also with the Armenian *diaspora*, because of Turkey's continuing official refusal to acknowledge the facts of the *Armenian genocide* (1915). Turkish-Armenian relations worsened, to the degree that was even possible, in 1993 when Armenian gains in the *Armenia-Azerbaijan War* led Turkey to warn that it would not wait as it had done toward the Muslim population of Bosnia, but would *intervene* unilaterally if necessary to stop any dismemberment of Azerbaijan and to protect Muslims there. Finally, relations with Kurds in eastern Turkey worsened after 1984, when the Turkish military stepped-up operations against a Kurdish separatist movement in the southeast and worked with Iran and Syria to prevent the emergence of any Kurdish state in what had become autonomous northern Iraq after 1991.

This civil conflict in the east obscured a larger, historical truth: beneath Turkey's official nationalism there lingers an older, Ottoman pattern of folk nationalism which is deeply tolerant of ethnic and religious pluralism. In this context, many Kurds are already assimilated into the Turkish nation, and the conflict with the Kurdish separatists is thus genuinely tragic and historically probably unnecessary. Turkey did not join the *Gulf coalition*, but during the *Gulf War* it permitted coalition use of its airfields and agreed to block Iraqi oil shipments through a northern pipeline that transected its territory. It also mostly cooperated with United Nations *sanctions* against Iraq, to the end of the 1990s. The rise of *neo-Nazism* in Germany meant relations with that country were damaged by murderous attacks on Turkish nationals, or "guest workers," including firebombing deaths of women and children. Turkey hoped to join the *European Union*, but the events of 1989–1990 propelled several other countries ahead of it on the waiting list, raising suspicions among Turks that the EU had racial and/or religious prejudices against accepting them as members. In 1999 Turkey undertook a *structural adjustment* program overseen by the *International Monetary Fund*. The Kurdish PKK also called a truce in 1999.

Suggested Readings: Roderic H. Davidson, *Turkey: A Short History*, 3rd ed. (1998); Bernard Lewis, *The Emergence of Modern Turkey* (1961, 1968).

Turkish Republic of Northern Cyprus. Turkish Cypriots declared the northern 40 percent of the island independent in 1983, but this *vassal state* of Istanbul does not enjoy international *recognition. See also Cyprus.*

Turkistan. An older, geographical-cultural term referring to the vast region of *Central Asia* populated mainly by Turkic speaking peoples. It included northern Afghanistan and stretched as far as parts of southwestern China. Its main components today are Kazakhstan, Kirghizstan, Tajikistan, Turkmenistan, and Uzbekistan.

Turkmenistan. This area was overrun by successive waves of Asian nomads over the last 1,500 years, among them *Arabs,* Seljuk Turks (forerunners to the *Ottomans*), the *Mongols,* and the hordes of *Tamerlane.* For several centuries the territory of modern Turkmenistan was part of the independent Khanates of *Bukhara* and *Khiva.* It was conquered by, and incorporated into, the *Russian Empire* with the conquest and annexation of those Khanates, with the full incorporation coming in 1881. It was held in the Russian Empire during the *Russian Civil War* (1918–1921) by the *Red Army* of the *Bolsheviks.* It became a constituent "republic" of the *Soviet Union* in a reorganization made by *Stalin,* 1924–1925, whereupon it shared all the trials and torments of the perverse economic, political, and moral history of the Soviet Union during the next six decades. It declared *independence* a few months after a failed *coup* in Moscow in August 1991, but was not *recognized* until the *extinction* of the Soviet Union in December. It has rich mineral, *oil,* and gas deposits. With independence it developed its own *currency* and sought *foreign direct investment.* Politically, it changed hardly at all from the Soviet period: it remained deeply *authoritarian* with a poor *human rights* record and governed by old *apparatchiki* who learned lessons of how to maintain a *cult of personality* (centered on President Saparmurat Niyazov) and tight Party control while working for the Soviet empire: in 1999, Turkmenistan's rubber-stamp national assembly appointed Niyazov president for life.

turn-key factory. An industrial plant built and managed entirely by a foreign concern, whether an *aid* agency or a *multinational corporation* (MNC), until local management and labor are trained to take over. This is one example of *technology transfer.*

turret. A mechanized, armored encasement for heavy guns on *warships* which permitted them to be aimed at targets independently of the angle or direction of movement of the ship. Before their development in the 1860s, and deployment on the first *ironclads,* warships were forced to maneuver to bring their guns to bear, preferably in a broadside. Turrets were also developed for guns emplaced in fortified positions and latter added to tanks and other *armored* vehicles and aircraft.

Tutsi. Also Batutsi or Watusi. *See also Burundi; Rwanda.*

Tuvalu. Formerly known as the Ellice Islands, this cluster of nine Pacific atolls was a British *protectorate* from 1892 (part of the Gilbert and Ellice Islands) and a British colony after 1916. It was occupied by Japanese forces early in *World War II*, but was *liberated* by the United States, 1943–1945. A United Nations–supervised *referendum* in 1974 led to a split with the Gilberts (Kiribati), and Tuvalu was granted full independence in 1978. This tiny *microstate* (its combined land area is less than one-tenth that of an average-sized city) is isolated from all world population centers, cut off from major sea lanes, and lacks mineral resources, though it does claim a sizeable *Exclusive Economic Zone*. As a *special member* of the Commonwealth, and given its tiny population, Britain continued to represent most of Tuvalu's foreign interests after independence. As low-lying atolls (the highest peak is 15 feet over sea level), its existence could be threatened by rising seas which might result from *global warming*, should it occur. On February 17, 2000, Tuvalu was admitted as the 189th member state of the United Nations. China abstained on the vote as Tuvalu still maintained *diplomatic relations* with Taiwan.

Twelfth-imam shi'ism. *See* shi'ia *Islam.*

twelve-mile limit. Over the course of the twentieth century, agreement on the *three-mile limit* broke down, as *coastal states* extended claims to exclusive *fishing* and the *territorial sea*. Much discussion failed to resolve the problem, including lack of progress at *UNCLOS I* and *II*. During the 1960s and 1970s a number of states, including several major maritime powers, declared they would honor a twelve-mile limit. Adjusting to a *de facto* situation, *UNCLOS III* endorsed this change to the territorial sea. States may now assert their *sovereignty* to a maximum of 12 miles (some set limits less than that).

Twelve Years Truce (1609–1621). *See Eighty Years' War (1566–1648); Thirty Years' War (1618–1648).*

Twenty-one Demands. On January 28, 1915, Japan presented *Yuan Shikai* twenty-one secret demands which amounted to an *ultimatum* that China become a Japanese *protectorate*. The demands were organized into five groups, with Group Five the most far-reaching: (1) confirmation of Japan's seizure of *Shandong* from Germany; (2) extension of the *leaseholds*, soon to expire, for *Port Arthur*, Darien, and the South Manchurian Railroad from 25 to 99 years; (3) granting of Japanese industrial *monopolies* in central China; (4) nonalienation of China's coastal territory; and (5) placing Japanese overseers in key government positions, grants of interior lands to select Japanese, joint control of China's police, and Chinese arms purchases to be made solely from Japan and with Tokyo's approval. China submitted to most of the demands, granting Tokyo the rights to the previous German *sphere of influence* and extending the leaseholds. The Chinese also leaked the note, adroitly rallying international opinion to their cause. This led to British *mediation* which prevented total capitulation: Group 5 was deleted from the Japanese ultimatum. Revelation of Japan's long-term intentions toward China deepened U.S. suspicions and undermined Asian and world respect for Japan which had been earned by its earlier domestic reforms and victory over Russia. By realizing only part of its extreme ambitions, Japan lost *face*. This had consequences: it helped harden Japanese attitudes toward the United States and the role it sometimes appeared to play in Asia of protector of China. *See also Lansing-Ishii Agreement; unequal treaties.*

"two-Chinas policy." An attempt in the early 1970s by several *nations* to give *de jure* sanction to the *de facto* separation of Taiwan (*Formosa*) from China after *communist* success in the *Chinese Civil War* in 1949. The United States was especially anxious to extend *recognition* to the People's Republic of China (*mainland China*) without cutting off its close ties to the Republic of China (*Taiwan*). However, neither Beijing nor Taiping would permit joint recognition, as each claimed full *sovereignty* over the other. This ultimately forced most countries to formally downgrade their relations with Taiwan. One wag truly said of this situation that the only thing the two Chinas agreed upon was that "there was only one China." In 1981 The People's Republic proposed *union* based upon recognition of its sovereignty, but with domestic *autonomy* for Taiwan, an approach akin to the *Hong Kong* model. After 1991 intra-Chinese contacts grew, and Taiwanese introduced the slogan "one country, two political entities." No resolution of the underlying and fundamental disagreement over sovereignty was yet possible. *See also expulsion.*

two-front war. Where one has to fight two (or more) enemies on separate fronts, demanding a division of forces for both defense and offense. *Charles V* was constantly drawn back and forth among different enemies, as was *Philip II*. Two centuries later Britain found itself engaged on multiple fronts during the *American Revolution* (1775–1783). *Napoleon* found himself in a two-front war which proved fatal to his empire once he invaded Russia in 1812, while still engaged in the *Peninsular War* in Spain. A two-front war was the *strategic* nightmare of German war planners before 1914, but was a dilemma of their own making. It arose in 1890 when *Wilhelm II* and his more aggressive advisers abandoned *Bismarck's* policy of maintaining close relations with Austria and Russia in order to isolate France, and then concluded that the Franco-Russian alliance which subsequently developed meant war had become inevitable. This fear and expectation underlay and drove the design of the *Schlieffen Plan* and determined the fate of the *Reichswehr* and of Germany during *World War I*. Contemplating that fact, *Hitler* regarded fighting a two-front war as the major mistake of the Great War and was determined not to repeat it during *World War II*. Yet, that is exactly what he did: failing to finish off Britain before attacking Russia in 1941 was the decisive error, among the many he made, of that war.

The Soviets, too, feared being drawn into a two-front war, with Germany and Japan. Japan attacked softer targets to the south, however, rather than move west against *Zhukov*'s hard and tested Siberian divisions. It is noteworthy that the United States also fought a two-front (indeed, two ocean) war during World War II, although the Pacific theater played second fiddle to the European theater in terms of commitments of troops, *air power*, and *landing craft*. That contrasted with the experience of the Soviet Union, which only entered the war against Japan on August 8, 1945, three months after the *surrender* of Nazi Germany and two days after the *atomic bomb* was dropped on *Hiroshima*. It also differed from Britain, which, although at war with Japan from 1941, used mainly *Indian Army* and token naval forces in the Pacific theater until very late in the war. In the immediate post–*Cold War* period it was stated U.S. policy to maintain a military capable of fighting two *Gulf War* sized conflicts at the same time. This policy was reconsidered in 2001 by the *George W. Bush* administration and found to be beyond budgetary commitments and real-world capabilities. *See also second front; two-power naval standard; unconditional surrender.*

two-plus-four talks (1989–1990). *Negotiations* held concerning German unification, among the two Germanies (East and West) and the four *occupation* powers from *World War II* (Britain, France, the Soviet Union, and the United States). These talks were essential to rapid reunification. They concerned matters of both internal (between the Germanies) and external (between Germany and the *Allied* powers) *sovereignty*, especially the fate of some 300,000 *Red Army* troops still in *East Germany*. Full and final withdrawal of those troops took place in 1994. Mostly, they dealt with the key issue of whether the new Germany could remain in *NATO*. This eight-month flurry of extraordinary *negotiation* and innovation resulted in several *bilateral* and *multilateral treaties* on *border* issues and *arms control*. It was without peer in postwar *diplomacy* in terms of peaceful accomplishments. The agreements reached formally concluded both World War II, for Germany, and the *Cold War*, for NATO and the *Warsaw Pact*. *See also Oder-Neisse Line; Paris, Charter of (1990).*

two-power naval standard. The key to British naval policy from 1899 to 1912, a time of enormous naval construction and competition. It was Britain's stated goal, at a minimum, to maintain the *Royal Navy* at the equivalent strength of the next two largest navies combined. The standard was applied mainly to *capital warships* and then limited to *battleships, battle cruisers,* and *cruisers,* not yet the emergent technologies of *aircraft carriers* and *submarines.* In fact, the British standard was actually kept at higher than just equivalence. The revolutionary development of *dreadnoughts* and Germany's construction of a major, surface battle fleet under *Tirpitz,* meant that Britain was pressed to abandon the two-power standard in 1912, in favor of a 60 percent margin over the next largest (that is, the German) main fleet. The United States refused to accept less than equality with the Royal Navy after *World War I.* With Britain's economy damaged by the war effort and burdened with *war debts,* in 1922 the two-power standard was formally abandoned, and new ratios were accepted by London and written into the *Five Power Naval Treaty.*

Two Sicilies, Kingdom of. An intermittently independent kingdom founded by the *Normans* (*Vikings*) and existing in some form or other from 1130 to 1861, when it was incorporated into modern Italy. Toward the end, it was really the Kingdom of Naples, with Sicily kept in deep submission.

two-speed Europe. The idea that those *European Union* member states interested in rapid political, defense, and economic *integration* should push the process forward with all due speed, in the expectation that other member states will eventually have to follow or not.

two swords, doctrine of. A fifth century doctrine of the *Catholic Church* which resonated in the history of *feudal* and early modern Europe was framed by Pope Gelasius I (r. 492–496), who upheld that God had given Man two swords, one secular and the other religious, one to be held by the emperors and the other by the popes. Furthermore, of these swords the religious is the higher. In short, Gelasius was the first pontiff to affirm the supremacy of the Church over the state. This was not immediately of great consequence. It became so during the reign of Pope Gregory the Great (c. 540–604, r. 590–604), who was the first pope to claim supremacy over all Christians and all Christendom.

Typhoon. American term for a class of *Cold War* Soviet nuclear *submarine* which carried 20–24 *ICBMs* with *MIRV* capability.

tyrannicide. The killing of a tyrant. *See also assassination; wet affair.*

tyranny. (1) Unjust, arbitrary exercise of power by an absolute ruler or tyrant. (2) Laws and actions by any government which are strongly felt to be oppressive. *See also absolutism; autocracy; communism; democracy; despotism; enlightened despotism; fascism; liberalism; popular sovereignty; totalitarianism.*

U

U-2 incident (May 1, 1960). An American spy plane, the high-altitude U-2 (Utility-2), was shot down over the Soviet city of Sverdlovsk on May 1, 1960. Its pilot, Francis Gary Powers, was captured. *Khrushchev* used the incident, pretending it was a clear and deliberate U.S. *provocation*, as a pretext to break off a *summit* in Paris with *Eisenhower* scheduled for two weeks later. This embarrassed Eisenhower, who had publicly denied that such spy flights were taking place. In fact, they had been underway for years, and both Khrushchev and Eisenhower knew that: *Harry Truman* had initiated occasional espionage overflights of Soviet territory, and Eisenhower had authorized the first high-altitude overflight of Soviet airspace on July 4, 1956. Nor was Gary Powers the first (or the last) U.S. pilot downed by the Soviets: some 200 American air crew died in espionage flights over the course of the *Cold War*, before and after the 1960 incident. However, all other shoot-downs or crashes were kept secret by both sides, including from grieving families, until the Cold War ended. U-2 flights were exceptionally valuable in disproving, within the U.S. *intelligence* community, Soviet propaganda claims to have achieved a huge lead in *ICBMs* over the United States and in dispelling fears of a "bomber gap." They thus permitted Eisenhower to restrain military spending, in spite of the fact that *Kennedy* used the misleading "missile gap" issue to considerable effect in the 1960 presidential campaign against Vice President *Richard Nixon*. In retrospect, therefore, the 1960 incident mainly exposed Khrushchev's erratic policy toward the United States and his near-habitual public recklessness, along with a penchant for foreign policy *adventurism* and even *brinkmanship*. Powers was subsequently exchanged for a captured Soviet *agent* (1962). *See also NSA; Open Skies.*
Suggested Reading: Michael Beschloss, *Mayday* (1986).

Ubangi-Shari (Oubangui-Chari). The colonial name of the *Central African Republic*.

Übermensch. See *Adolf Hitler*; *National Socialism*; *Friedrich Nietzsche*.

U-boat (*Unterseeboot*). A German *submarine*, especially in *World War I* or *World War II*. See also Anglo-German Naval Agreement; Battle of the Atlantic; convoy; cruiser warfare; sea power; unrestricted submarine warfare; wolf pack; Z-Plan.

Uganda. From the sixteenth century two Bantu kingdoms, Buganda and Bunyoro, competed for control of the territory in the vicinity of Lake Victoria and for dominance of the lake itself. In the late seventeenth century Buganda—which was a more centralized and better-run kingdom—fended off the larger Bunyoro, and by the late eighteenth century it was dominant. *Swahili Arabs* first appeared in Buganda in 1844, connecting it to coastal trade. Others were on the move: driven south by the *ivory* and *slave*-raiding needs of *Mehemet Ali*, refugee Sudanese from Khartoum pressed hard on Bunyoro by 1870, when Egypt too interfered in internal Bunyoro politics. In 1874 *Gordon*'s representatives reached Buganda, and the next year *Stanley* visited. Kabaka Mutese, Buganda's leader, invited Christian *missionaries* to his court, possibly to off-set Muslim and Egyptian pressures. In 1885–1886 Christian converts were executed by the new Kabaka, Mwanga. That led to an attempted Muslim coup and a brief civil war, 1888–1890. The Christians of Buganda allied with Britain, whereas most Muslims allied with and retreated to Bunyoro. Buganda thus came under growing British *influence* after 1890, as the British East Africa Company penetrated the interior. British troops followed, as did declaration of Buganda as a *protectorate* in 1894. Bunyoro was then conquered with the help of Buganda, 1894–1899. In 1900 Buganda was rewarded with qualified recognition of its statehood, within the composite colony. Colonial government was thus a mixture of *direct* and *indirect rule*, and Uganda remained quietly within the British Empire until the "winds of change" of *decolonization* began to blow in the 1950s.

Milton Obote, founder of one of Uganda's original political parties, made a deal with the Kabaka of the Buganda which opened the door to independence. When Uganda became independent in 1962 the Kabaka became president and Obote was prime minister. In addition, Buganda was semi-*autonomous* and Bunyoro was left simmering with resentment against Buganda's territorial gains at its expense in the colonial period and ongoing constitutional privileges. In 1966 Obote carried out a *coup* which overthrew the Kabaka and the established privileges of Buganda. He ruled ineptly and corruptly, however, and was in turn overthrown in 1971 in a coup by *Idi Amin*, a career soldier from the small, northern, Kakwa *tribe*. Amin's brutal, tragic-farcical reign lasted until he provoked *intervention* by Tanzania in 1980, allowing Obote to return to office on the bayonets of the Tanzanian Army. Obote's second presidency was an economic disaster, accompanied by a national bloodbath to rival Amin's. Civil war erupted, and Obote was ultimately overthrown, fleeing abroad a second time in 1985. From 1971 to 1986 perhaps one million Ugandans perished in war, massacres, from state terror, or by *famine*.

Out of this violence and dislocation, in 1986 Yoweri Museveni led the National Resistance Army to power, seizing the capital and imposing a rough order in most provinces. With the south again ascendant politically, though still not reconciled to the north—after two decades of state and tribal terror, erosion of infrastructure, and loss of confidence and cohesion—Uganda enjoyed slow but real economic and social *reconstruction*. Its security forces mostly returned to barracks, though fighting continued along the border with Sudan until 2001. Uganda was also drawn into the fighting in Congo after 1999, as that giant neighbor collapsed into *anarchy* and became a battleground of regional warfare among a half-dozen African states. Overall, however, entering the twenty-first century Uganda was again governed by law and again began to experiment with multiparty democracy.

Suggested Reading: M. S. Kiwanuka, *A History of Buganda* (1972).

Uighur. A Turkic-speaking, largely Muslim population of Xianjiang province of western China. Throughout the 1990s they engaged in a low-level *guerrilla* war against control by Beijing, operating out of Central Asian bases in the weak, post-Soviet republics of that region. They received some support from *al Qaeda*.

ukase. A *tsarist* edict or decree. It carried the full force of law, even though it was unchecked by *popular sovereignty* or representative consultations. *See also absolutism; Peter I; Nicholas I.*

Ukraine. This vast, bountiful land hosted the first "Russian" state—Kievan Rus (c. 882–1240), which was actually founded by *Viking* settlers (the Varangians), on top of an extant *Slavic* population. Kievan Rus was a loosely organized vassalage, rather more like the latter *Holy Roman Empire* than a centralized monarchy or state, which extended far beyond Ukraine to include most of what is today Belarus and parts of western Russia. It fell victim first to chronic internal divisions and warfare among various *city-states* (Kiev, Novgorod, and others), and then to Asian nomadic invaders, culminating in 1237 when it was overrun by the *Mongols* (*Tartars*). As a result, much of Ukraine was occupied by the Golden Horde for the next 200 years. In the fourteenth century Ukraine was partly incorporated into the expanding Polish-Lithuanian *condominium*, which then dominated eastern Europe, and slowly pushed back the borders of the Golden Horde, of the Tartars of the *Crimea* and southern Ukraine, and of the *Teutonic Knights* who had invaded out of

Germany and the Baltic. Polish dominion raised a new issue in Ukrainian history, which persists still: conflict between the *Orthodox Church* (most Ukrainian peasants had converted to Orthodoxy along with their princes, when Kievan Rus was under *Byzantine* influence) and *Catholicism*, the dominate religion of Ukraine's Polish masters, but a rite shared by a sizeable portion of the peasantry in western Ukraine.

In the sixteenth century Ukrainian and Russian history began to merge as the Muscovite princes began to expand westward and southward at Polish-Lithuanian expense under *Ivan IV* (1530–1584) and several successor tsars. In addition, the *Cossacks* (many of whom were former Ukrainian serfs who had escaped to the Crimea) rebelled against Poland in the deep south (1648). In 1667 Ukraine was partitioned between Russia and Poland, but that was a temporary situation: under *Peter I*, all of Ukraine was annexed to the Russian Empire after the defeat of Sweden and Poland in the *Great Northern War* (1700–1721). The Crimea was annexed, from the *Ottoman Empire*, by *Catherine the Great*, effectively in the Treaty of Kuchuk Kainarji (1774) and formally in 1783. Ukraine was now deeply influenced by Russia, to which its major portion was connected in all aspects of its cultural and political life. Western Ukraine—Galicia—remained under Austrian dominion, however, after the *partitions of Poland*, and this exacerbated extant religious and cultural differences. Just as did most Russians, the majority of Ukrainians at this time suffered under the system of *serfdom*. Some Ukrainians willingly served the tsars; others rebelled against them. Some absorbed *Slavophile* ideas; others were ardent *Westernizers*. Many fought as conscripts in Russia's wars; others sought personal freedom in western exile.

This fundamental subservience to Russia changed briefly at the end of *World War I* with the *Treaty of Brest-Litovsk*, in which the *Bolsheviks* surrendered Ukraine to German control. During the *Russian Civil War* which followed the defeat of Germany, Ukrainian *Whites* joined with Poles to fight the Bolsheviks, while other Ukrainians joined the Bolsheviks to secure the *Russian Revolution*. Ukrainian Whites were ultimately overcome by the *Red Army*, and by a Polish invasion (1920), and Ukraine was forced back into the Russian Empire, reconstituted as one of the "republics" of the *Soviet Union*. During *Stalin's* forced *collectivization* of *agriculture* Ukraine experienced an artificial, political *famine* and slaughter of the *kulaks* which took at least 7 million lives. Then *Nazi* armies tore across it, *pillaging* and murdering from 1941 through 1944. Reflecting the wrenching and divisive experience of *Stalinism*, some Ukrainians fought the Nazis while others joined them: some helped with the extermination of the Jews; others formed divisions to fight alongside the *Wehrmacht* and *Waffen SS* in resisting the return of the Red Army to Ukraine, while yet others eagerly joined the Red Army or *partisan* groups to kill Germans. *Guerrilla* resistance to the restoration of Soviet rule lasted in remote parts of Ukraine into the early 1950s and received some support from Western *intelligence agencies*. After *World War II* new territory was added to Ukraine from Czechoslovakia, Poland, and Rumania (*Bessarabia, Bukovina*, East Galicia). The *Crimea* was added, as a "gift" from Russia in 1954.

Ukrainian independence was declared after the failed *coup* attempt in Moscow in August 1991, but not widely *recognized* until after the *extinction* of the Soviet Union on December 25, 1991. Ukraine dragged its feet on *ratification* of *START I*, retaining some 176 strategic *missiles*. Of these, 130 were SS-19s, old missiles, which leaked. Ukraine held them in order to extort economic and *disarmament* assistance monies from the West. The real problem was its 46 SS-24s, the latest and best missiles built by the Soviet Union (in a factory in Ukraine) before its demise. Each could be *MIRVed* with 10 *warheads*. Ukraine also retained a number of Blackjack nuclear *bombers*, which on paper gave it in 1992 the third largest nuclear arsenal in the world. Some argued Ukraine should keep these weapons to guarantee its *independence* through *deterrence* of a possible Russian invasion, as unlikely as that seemed. Others suggested the weapons were more likely to become targets than act as a deterrent force. The issue appeared resolved as Ukraine's economy collapsed in 1993 and high *inflation* set in. Deeply in debt to Russia, Kiev announced it would swap control of nuclear weapons for large-scale debt relief. Gains by the old, *communist* and *nationalist* right in parliamentary elections in Russia put this deal in doubt. However, in 1994 Ukraine, Russia, and the United States agreed that Ukraine had seven years to surrender its *nuclear weapons*, in exchange for a share of $12 billion committed by the United States to purchase Russian surplus *uranium* and guarantees of respect for its *territorial integrity*. Ukraine was warned that it would be excluded from *NATO*'s new *partnerships for peace* if it kept the weapons. Ukraine also argued fiercely with Russia after 1991 over the final division of the *Black Sea Fleet*. In 1993 it leased Russia the old naval base at *Sebastopol*. The status of Crimea came into question in 1994, when ethnic Russians there voted in a *secessionist* party. Eastern Ukraine, too, was a problem for Kiev, as it contained 11 million Russians and thus potentially was a secessionist area.

Post-independence Ukraine was governed at first by Leonid Kravchuk, an old *apparatchik* redressed as a Ukrainian nationalist. In 1994 he was defeated by his Prime Minister, Leonid Kuchma, a thuggish former *apparatchik* who brutally repressed the press and political opposition. Ukraine stumbled into the twenty-first century still abjuring *shock treatment* for its outmoded economy, uncompetitive internationally, and staggering under a weight of corruption and criminalization of its civil, economic, and political life.

Suggested Readings: Anatol Lieven, *Ukraine and Russia* (1999); Robert Magocsi, *A History of Ukraine* (1996); Orest Subtelney, *Ukraine: A History* (2000).

Ulbricht, Walter (1893–1973). East German statesman. He was a *communist* deputy in the *Reichstag* from 1928 until the *Communist Party* was banned by the *Nazis* in 1933, when he escaped to Paris, on to Spain, and finally to Moscow. Ulbricht returned to Germany in 1945, arriving with the other baggage while the *Red Army* was still visiting Berlin. He rose to head the German authority within the Soviet *occupation zone* and remained in charge when it became the *German Democratic Republic* in 1949. He was a stern *Stalinist* in all respects, slavishly adhering to the *party line* set out by his masters in Moscow. He thus imposed forced *industrialization* and *collectivization* of *agriculture* and ruled with *torture*, *secret police*, and endemic repression of dissent of all forms. As a result, large numbers of East Germans fled west, until erection of the *Berlin Wall* made flight nearly impossible. Ulbricht pushed hard for confrontation with the West during the *Berlin Crisis*, 1958–1961, which culminated in construction of the Wall.

ulema. See Islam.

Ulster. An independent Celtic kingdom during the Middle Ages which was somewhat larger than the modern British territory. In more recent history, it was made up of the nine northern counties of *Ireland*, but presently it comprises only six of the original nine counties. As a reward for service in Britain's wars, and as punishment for Irish *Catholic* rebellion, King James I of England (James VI of Scotland) granted Scottish and English *Protestants* the right to settle in Ulster on land *expropriated* from Irish Catholic peasants. This was the "Plantation of Ulster," remembered proudly by Protestants and bitterly by Catholics. In 1800 the province was made an integral part of Great Britain by the *Act of Union*. As the *Home Rule* movement grew in the rest of Ireland in the nineteenth century, Ulster Protestants organized strenuously to oppose it and retain their constitutional union with the *United Kingdom*. Before *World War I* they threatened armed resistance under the leadership of Edward Carson (1854–1935). His organization of a Protestant *militia* (the Ulster Volunteers) nearly brought about *civil war* in Ireland (and possibly also England) on the eve of the Great War in Europe, a near-tragedy that was averted largely by the greater tragedy of the outbreak of *World War I.*

The *Easter Rising* of 1916 in the south was put down by force of British arms and led to sharp warnings by Ulster Protestants against any similar effort to withdraw Ireland and Ulster from union with Britain. Force of arms did finally prevail in the south, however, in 1921. When the *Irish War of Independence* led to the *Anglo-Irish Treaty* (1921), which divided the island. Ulster ceded three of its most demographically Catholic counties to the *Irish Free State*, while the predominantly Protestant six counties formed a rump province of Ulster which remained in the United Kingdom. This *gerrymandered* Protestant majority ever after insisted on perpetual *union* with Britain, while for decades it also discriminated against Catholics in jobs and housing, which were in scarce supply as a result of Ulster's pronounced economic decline, especially after *World War II.*

In 1967 a new round of sectarian violence required an increased British military presence. At first, the troops protected Catholics, who patterned their *human rights* movement on the black American model of civil disobedience and provoked a similar angry response from the majority community. Then the British Army was called upon to fight the *IRA*, which seized the opportunity to escalate the crisis by attacking troops and police, as well as committing acts of indiscriminate *terrorism*. In this grand confusion of loyalties, on Bloody Sunday (January 30, 1972) 13 peaceful protesters were killed in Londonderry by panicky British troops. After that, the level of violence indulged by all sides increased, as over the next 30 years the conflict claimed some 3,200 lives. Westminster adopted *direct rule* in 1972, which made Ulster a thorny issue in British politics for the next several decades. In 1985 London agreed to give the Irish government in Dublin a direct but vaguely delineated role in peace talks concerning the north. In 1991, efforts began to return the province to home rule on the basis of a *power sharing* arrangement. Secret *peace talks* between the British government and the IRA took place in 1993. An Anglo-Irish "Framework Agreement" was signed as well, in which Britain agreed not to oppose all-Ireland union and Ireland agreed to respect a majority wish to forgo union, and to alter its constitution to meet Protestant concerns about minority rights.

The agreement aimed at new negotiating structures to help end the violence and at cooperative governance of the province. All-party talks began in 1995. The IRA announced a *cease-fire* in 1994, but ended it after 17 months with bomb attacks in London. In 1997 another cease-fire was agreed and negotiations began among the British government, *Sinn Féin* (the political wing of the IRA), and the government of Ireland. In 1998 a "Good Friday Accord" was agreed that looked to disarm all paramilitaries, withdraw British troops from Ulster, establish a separate parliament for Northern Ireland, and set up a North-South Ministerial Council concerning relations of interest to Britain, Ulster, and the Republic of Ireland. The latter subsequently formally renounced its historic claim to all the territory of the island of Ireland, to seal the agreement. During 2001 the original deal was threatened by IRA refusal to comply with its disarmament provisions.

Suggested Readings: R. F. Foster, *Modern Ireland, 1600–1972* (1989); J. Lee, *Ireland, 1912–1985* (1989); George Mitchell, *Making Peace* (1999); Connor Cruise O'Brien, *Religion and Nationalism in Ireland* (1995).

ultimate destination. Under a *blockade*, the doctrine that goods may be seized as *contraband* if their final destination is enemy territory, no matter what the ship manifest says or whether they first stop in *neutral* territory. In short, goods are required to make a continuous voyage to a neutral port, if they are to be judged neutral goods. It was originally a British doctrine, held especially against the French after 1756. The United States accepted this rule during the *American Civil War*, and its Supreme Court repeatedly upheld this doctrine in contraband cases. *See also free ships; infection.*

ultimatum. A statement by a *sovereign* state of final, often peremptory, terms of settlement of a *dispute* which, if not met, will result in a break in *diplomatic relations, sanctions,* or *armed hostilities.* Ultimata may be used to make grand, albeit highly risky, bluffs. They have also been relied upon to deliberately provoke war, as when Italy sent a set of impossible demands to Turkey in 1911 to cover its seizure of Tripoli or when Austria sent a list of impossible demands to Serbia in 1914. An ultimatum, in short, commits a state to forceful action in a way that a *diplomatic note* does not. *See also brinkmanship.*

ultramontane. Belief in the supreme moral and even political authority of the *Catholic Church* and withholding loyalty from any *state* which challenges church doctrine, authority, or interests. *See also Joseph II; Kulturkampf.*

ultra vires. In *international law,* beyond the scope or *jurisdiction* of the law.

Umayyad Caliphate (661–750). *See caliph.*

UN. *See United Nations Organization.*

unanimity rule. A fairly standard rule in *multilateral diplomacy,* whereby action may proceed only with unanimous *consent.* This protects individual state interest, but can be incapacitating to collective action because it gives each participant an effective *veto. See also qualified majority voting; weighted voting.*

unconditional surrender. An unusual demand, made only if one is, or expects to be, in an utterly overwhelming position on the battlefield. In fact, most *surrenders* take place under negotiated conditions. *Grant* demanded unconditional surrender from the *Confederates* holding Fort Donelson in 1862 and at Vicksburg in 1863. The most famous instance of unconditional surrender was the demand made of the *Axis* by *Franklin Roosevelt* at the *Casablanca Conference* in 1943, later endorsed by *Churchill* and *Stalin.* It reflected determination not to repeat the "*stab-in-the-back*" scenario about *World War I* which the *Nazis* had used to such *propaganda* advantage and to reassure Stalin that the West would not seek a *separate peace* with *Hitler* and vice versa. The policy has been criticized since then for stiffening Axis resistance and possibly prolonging the war. Alternately, it has been credited with bringing home to the defeated states the full scope of their loss and thereby setting the postwar stage for genuine reform. Applied rigorously to Germany, it was waived to permit the single condition for Japan of retention of Emperor *Hirohito,* but not until *atomic bombs* had already incinerated two cities. *See also Fourteen Points; war aims.*

underdeveloped country. An older term for *developing country*. It is no longer in wide use, at least not by the "politically correct," due to its putative insensitivity.

underdevelopment. This is a central concept in *dependency theory*. It suggests not merely that there has been a lack of economic *development* in the *Third World*, but that there is instead a history of what might be called negative development, or "underdevelopment," caused primarily by the historically exploitative forces of *imperialism* and *colonialism*. Using essentially *Marxist* categories of analysis, it was posited by some writers (not all of whom were Marxists) that for centuries *capitalism* had extracted *surplus value* from the *South* and transferred it to the *West* (*North*). From this premise several conclusions flowed: (1) continued attachment to the *world capitalist system* perpetuated unequal economic relations and *dependent development*; (2) the Third World was owed *reparations* in some form (*aid, preferential trade,* and even more radical forms of restitution); and (3) domestic and foreign policies were needed in the South which aimed to retain the domestic surplus at home so that it could be plowed back into autonomous *growth*. Classical economists in the West, and their governments, never accepted these theses. In the 1960s and 1970s the G-77 got them adopted as something of an official *ideology* for such *international organizations* as *UNCTAD* and the *UNDP*. Even as that diplomatic triumph was taking place, in light of the *oil shocks* and severe inflation of the 1970s the influence of such ideas waned sharply in the practical world of policy-making. Debate shifted in the 1980s and 1990s toward comparative streams of *reformism* and an overall embrace of market solutions to the major problems of underdevelopment. *See also debt crisis; NIEO.*

underground economy. Economic activity which goes unreported to governments, primarily as a way of avoiding taxation. *See also black market.*

understanding. (1) In *diplomacy*: A written explanation of one *state's* policy given to another, usually in the form of a memo or *diplomatic note*, for purposes of clarification. (2) In *international law*: An explanation attached to a *reservation*, which is in turn attached to the *instruments of ratification* for a *treaty*. It spells out the attaching state's interpretation of specific aspects of the treaty, but without binding the other party(ies) to that interpretation.

unequal treaties. A series of one-sided agreements with foreign powers in which Japan and China were both compelled to open to Western trade, diplomacy, and ultimately even military interests. China was forced to accept a permanent foreign presence in its coastal cities (*treaty ports*), onerous *terms of trade*, and *extraterritorial* clauses and other *capitulations* to foreign citizens and governments. The main treaties with China were *Nanjing* (1842), *Wanghia* (1844), *Tientsin* (1858), and *Shimonoseki* (1895). A spate of lesser treaties were signed in 1860, modeled on Nanjing and Wanghia, wherein China was forced to legalize the *opium* trade, open dozens of additional treaty ports, clear the Yangtze to foreign vessels and trade, permit Christian *missionaries* access to the rural interior, and accept resident ambassadors from the major European powers. The main treaty with Japan was the *Treaty of Kangawa* (1854) with the United States, soon imitated by agreements with the other *Great Powers*. Japan emerged from foreign domination fairly quickly. It sought revision of the treaties in the Iwakura mission of 1871 to 1873, which failed. The treaties expired in 1898, by which time Japan itself joined in imposition of unequal treaties on China. The *Twenty-one Demands* made by Japan on China in 1915 were not only well within the unequal treaty tradition, they were far more extreme than anything other foreign powers had ever attempted. After 1920, the *Bolsheviks* renounced Russia's special rights in China, which they could not enforce in any case, but clung to those in Manchuria, which they could sustain. Full external tariff control returned to China only in the late 1930s. Some extraterritorial provisions were not renounced by Britain or the United States until 1943, and then in behalf of their alliance with China against Japan during *World War II*.

UNESCO. *See United Nations Educational, Scientific and Cultural Organization.*

uneven development. *Growth* of sectors of a national or regional economy at varying rates, resulting in an irregular distribution of goods and benefits accruing to individuals and social classes. Uneven economic development of economic regions and countries ranks as one of the salient causes driving human affairs, alongside *war*, *technology*, and the raw power of immaterial ideas. History is replete with nations and whole civilizations whose political, social, and military fortunes rose or fell in rough, secondary correlation to the ebb and flow of the most direct consequences (starvation or plenty, poverty or prosperity) of uneven economic activity. *Dependency theory* springs directly from this observation, but then crudely and monocausally limits its explanation to the assertion that *capitalism* inevitably produces unequal and unjust distribution of benefits and burdens, both internationally and within national economies. However, such a conclusion cannot account for, among other things, the fact that uneven economic development has characterized all historical epochs, not just the modern capitalist one. *See also development; underdevelopment.*

Unfederated Malay States. Five small Malay states controlled by Britain after *World War II*, later joined to the Malaysian Federation.

unfriendly act. An action by one *state* directed against another which is hostile in intention, but not overtly illegal and not constituting a *casus belli* or an *act of war*. For instance, causing a deliberate slight to an *ambassador* or formally receiving or honoring persons, such as *terrorists* or *dissidents*, deemed objectionable by another state. *See also comity of nations.*

UNGA. *See United Nations General Assembly.*

Uniate Churches. Those which maintain a distinct Eastern liturgy and rite, but acknowledge the authority of the Catholic popes and *Ecumenical Councils* on matters of faith and doctrine and maintain a formal union with the *Catholic Church*. They are found mainly in Eastern Europe and Ukraine, but also in Armenia, Egypt, Ethiopia, Greece, Lebanon, and Syria. The Ukrainian branch, which is the largest, was founded in 1596.

UNICEF. *See United Nations International Children's Emergency Fund.*

unification of Italy. *See Camillo Benso di Cavour; Gabriele D'Annunzio;* Italia irredenta; *Italy; Giuseppe Garibaldi; Giuseppe Mazzini; mutilated victory; Papal States; Renaissance;* Risorgimento; *Roman Question; Venice; Young Italy.*

unification(s) of Germany. *See Anschluss; Bismarck; Germany; Holy Roman Empire; two-plus-four talks.*

Unification Wars (1550–1615). During the late Ashikaga period in Japan, the warlord *Nobunaga Oda* first befriended then overthrew the Ashikaga shogunate in a series of wars which ended *feudal* strife and unified about half of modern Japan under central rule. Oda formed an alliance with *Ieyasu Tokugawa* in the 1560s while still consolidating his hold over Honshu. On July 22, 1570, Oda and Ieyasu defeated all their northern enemies in the decisive Battle of Anegawa. Fighting continued, however, with Oda seeking unsuccessfully to unify all Japan under his rule. He was defeated and committed suicide in 1582. The great tyrant *Toyotomi Hideyoshi* (1536–1598) further consolidated authority and twice attempted to invade Korea. When he died, chaos returned and warfare briefly resumed. The wars of unification—which were fueled in part by the *gunpowder revolution* and paralleled centralizing and state-building developments underway in Europe at that time, in Spain, France, and Russia—continued until Ieyasu Tokugawa imposed a centralized political order on all Japan, completed with major victories at *Sekigahara* (1600) and Osaka (1615). After that, the "Great Tokugawa Peace" lasted to the 1868 *Meiji Restoration.*

unilateral act. In *international law*, a self-binding declaration by a *state* of its intention to do, or to desist from doing, something. For instance, announcing a *moratorium* on weapons testing.

Unilateral Declaration of Independence (UDI). An illegal declaration of independence made by the white-minority government of *Rhodesia* on November 11, 1965. It was rejected by Britain (the colonial power), the *Commonwealth*, and the United *Nations*, which imposed *sanctions* in 1966. In 1970 Rhodesia unilaterally declared a republic. In 1980 UDI ended with the establishment of *majority rule* in the territory, which received international *recognition* as *Zimbabwe*.

unilateral disarmament. *See disarmament.*

unilateralism. A preference for pursuing foreign policy interests independently of either the opportunities or constraints of *multilateral diplomacy*. This tendency is most pronounced among the *Great Powers*, where great *capabilities* often tempt, and sometimes actually enable, powerful states to act without restraint and in the face of broad international opposition.

unincorporated territory. A *territory* under the *sovereignty* of a larger, usually noncontiguous power, but not directly under the constitution of that power. *See also American Samoa; Guam.*

Union. The Northern states in the *American Civil War*: California, Connecticut, Delaware, Illinois, Indiana, Iowa, Kansas, Maine, Maryland, Massachusetts, Michigan, Minnesota, New Jersey, New Hampshire, New York, Ohio, Oregon, Pennsylvania, Rhode Island, Vermont, and Wisconsin. Of the *border states*, Missouri and Kentucky were held in the Union by force, as was Maryland, but their populations divided on the great question of *slavery* and many from these states thus went south to fight for the *Confederacy*. The war also created a new Union state: West Virginia carved itself out of old Virginia and hastened to join the Union, while the rest of Virginia became the keystone state of the Confederacy.

Unionists. *Protestants* dedicated to defense of the political *union* of Northern Ireland with Britain, who formed political parities and *paramilitaries* to that end. *See also Ulster.*

union of crowns. When a *dynastic marriage* (as in the pairing of *Ferdinand and Isabella*) or a succession (James I of England, who was also James VI of Scotland, in 1603) unites distinct realms at the level of the *sovereign*, but does not dissolve their separate constitutional existence or otherwise directly affect the rights and privileges of subjects. It may or may not lead to subsequent full *union*. *See also Act of Union; Union of Kalmar.*

Union of Kalmar (1397). In 1388 Queen Margaret (1353–1412), daughter of Waldemar IV of Denmark and wife of Haakon VI of Norway, was offered the crown of Sweden by that country's nobles, who were greatly displeased with their King, Albert of Mecklenburg. She agreed to the offer and invaded Sweden in order to accept it, taking Albert prisoner. In 1397 the Union of Kalmar was passed, creating a *union of the crowns* of Denmark, Norway, and Sweden, but stipulating that each should retain its own laws (domestic *autonomy*). It was dissolved by Gustav I, of Sweden, in 1523. *See also union of crowns.*

union of sovereign states. There are several types of composite, *international personality*: (1) Personal union: When states share a *head of state*, for example, previously, Denmark and Iceland; Belgium and the Congo; the *Holy Roman Empire*; Great Britain and Hanover, and less clearly, members of the *Commonwealth* sharing *Queen Elizabeth II* as head of state: Australia, Britain, Canada, etc. (2) Confederation: An interstate association in which governments volunteer to limit application of normal *sovereign* privileges in pursuit of some common aim, but keep the shared organs distant from contact with their population, and do not surrender *sovereignty*, for example, Switzerland to 1848; the *North German Confederation*; *Senegambia*; the *United Arab Emirates*. (3) Full (real) union: When states merge by *treaty*, assuming a single government and after that acting as a single entity in relations with other states and the rest of the outside world. States in a real union may remain legally sovereign and may retain a broad sphere of internal *autonomy*, but they share only one international personality in making foreign policy, for example, *Austria-Hungary* after the *Ausgleich*; *Yugoslavia*; *British Somaliland* and *Italian Somaliland*'s union as Somalia in 1960; *Tanzania*, created in 1964 by the union of *Tanganyika* and *Zanzibar*; and in 1990, merger of the Yemens into the Yemeni Republic. More often, such efforts have failed, for example, the Egyptian attempt to join with Syria in the *United Arab Republic* and Libya's several attempts in the late twentieth century seemingly to join with anyone willing. Such failures can have lasting negative repercussions, leading to deep recrimination and soured relations between once close allies. In 1996 Belarus and Russia signed a union treaty in name only because it did not seek to extinguish the international personality of the former. Some similar arrangement may yet offer a solution to the Taiwan problem. *See also federation.*

Union of Soviet Socialist Republics (USSR). The formal title of the *Soviet Union*. *See also Russia.*

unipolarity. A hypothetical *international system* in which there is only one *Great Power* or pole of *influence*. Some theorists present the *Roman Empire* as a unipolar system. That is ahistorical, even *Procrustean*, as it ignores Rome's many contacts and wars with barbarian kingdoms and with Carthage, Egypt, Nubia, and the Persian Empire (among others). Other analysts point to the "unipolar moment" of the United States in 1945, overlooking the powerful Soviet Union and other extant *empires*, or the post–*Cold War* period, neglecting Germany, Japan, China, and other Great Powers. *See also bipolarity; hegemony; preponderant power; tripolarity; multipolarity.*

Unit 731. *See biological warfare.*

unitary actor. *Jargon* for the basic and necessary assumption, made to ease discussion and permit generalization, that one may usefully speak of *states* as individual *actors* with detectible motives, interests, and fears, rather than as the extraordinarily complex, collective entities and human enterprises which they truly are.

unitary state. One in which there is a single center of supreme constitutional authority. Not a *federation. See also Thomas Hobbes; Leviathan; segmentary state; state.*

United Arab Emirates. A loose *federation* formed, 1971–1972, by the *Trucial States.* It is held together by geography and by *oil* revenues which make this per capita one of the richest countries in the world. After the *Gulf War,* it closely *aligned* with the United States and Saudi Arabia.

United Arab Republic (UAR). A *union* formed by Egypt and Syria in 1958 in the name of *pan-Arabism,* which effectively trapped *Nasser* with its rhetoric. Syria wanted a *federation* in which it still controlled domestic affairs. Egypt wanted a real union, which it fully intended to dominate, and thought it should, partly out of a sense of cultural superiority to Syrians. Because the union was both a political and economic failure, it ended in Syrian withdrawal in 1961. Egypt incongruously carried the name forward into the mid-1970s. With Yemen added, the term "United Arab States" was sometimes used.

United Empire Loyalists. During the *American Revolution* the population of Canada was swollen by an influx drawn from that third of the American public which wished to remain subjects of the British crown. Most settled in the maritime provinces or Ontario. A few settled in the eastern townships of *Québec.* In each locale, they impressed an anti-American and anti-republican mark on Canadian national life and politics.

United Irish Society. Founded in Belfast in 1791, the Society of United Irishmen was an organization of *nationalists* who followed Theobald Wolfe Tone (1763–1798), a *Protestant* barrister, in opposing British rule in Ireland. Ultimately, this led to an armed uprising, 1796–1798. The Society was inspired by the *American Revolution* and the *French Revolution.* Its members were opposed to the *ancien régime* in Ireland, socially and politically. Their demands included parliamentary reform, abolition of religious distinction (or *Catholic emancipation*), and a national government in Ireland. That drew upon ideas of the *Whigs* in England, the *Enlightenment*, and the inspiration of events in France, which also offered the possibility of material aid. By December 1796, Wolfe Tone had persuaded the *Directory* in Paris to support an Irish rebellion. The French sent a fleet of 35 ships and 12,000 men to Ireland. The fleet entered Bantry Bay on December 21st. Then a major storm blew in and scattered the fleet, which failed to land a French foot on Irish soil.

The climax came in 1798, the "Year of the French," when perhaps 100,000 Irish rose against English rule. The rebels set up a base in County Wexford in the hope and expectation that a French revolutionary army would land to aid them. They were bitterly disappointed and badly defeated, at the appropriately named Battle of Vinegar Hill. Atrocities followed on both sides. On August 22nd, a small French force landed in County Mayo, but it was too late to provide meaningful support to the remaining rebels, was quickly routed, and surrendered. Wolfe Tone was captured aboard a French ship. He committed suicide in prison: cutting his windpipe in error rather than his jugular, he took a week to die. He was buried by the British in an unmarked grave, to prevent its becoming a political rallying point for Irish nationalists. Perhaps 40,000 Irish had perished in the uprising. Others were *transported* to far-off *penal settlements*. In England, *William Pitt* responded to the uprising by pushing the *Act of Union* with Ireland through Parliament in 1800. However, he failed to resolve the *Irish Question* owing to profound royal opposition in the person of *George III* and deep division within the country over what to do about and with Catholic Ireland.

Suggested Reading: Thomas Pakenham, *The Year of Liberty* (1998).

United Kingdom of Great Britain and Northern Ireland (UK). The island of Great Britain was partially occupied by the *Romans*, 43–410 C.E. That left a lasting imprint on *England*, in particular, even as it devolved into a land of petty, warring Saxon and Celtic kingdoms over the next several centuries. From the eighth to eleventh centuries Britain and Ireland were subjected to *Viking* raids all along their coasts and to the establishment of Viking kingdoms in the north of England (the Danegeld), in the Orkneys, and in Ireland, which owed varying allegiance to the Kingdoms of Denmark and Norway. It is often said that the last foreigner to successfully cross the *English Channel* with an uninvited invading army was *William the Conqueror* (1027–1087), who made the short but difficult trip with a *Norman* army in tow, defeating the army of the Saxon kingdom of Wessex under King Harold at the Battle of Hastings (1066) and thereafter completing the Norman conquest. In fact, a study prepared in 1587 for *Philip II*, then contemplating dispatch of the *Spanish Armada*, showed that in the 500 years after the Norman invasion of 1066, England had seen nine governments fall or be seriously weakened by invasions from the sea, seven additional landings of armies in Britain, and dozens of successful coastal raids.

England slowly evolved representative institutions in isolation from the

Continent: the Magna Carta was forced on its kings by the nobility in 1215 and was then followed by unsteady extension of the right to representation in Parliament to additional social classes and the right of Parliament to raise and dispense taxation. England conquered *Wales* by 1300, but was prevented by *Wallace* and Robert Bruce (1274–1329, r. 1306–1329) from completing its attempted conquest of *Scotland*. In *Ireland*, too, most of the country continued in clannish independence from English arms and cultural isolation, though the isles were loosely connected under the Norman monarchy. For centuries the English crown was primarily interested in fighting to keep its rich, originally Norman holdings in France. However, English-Norman power was finally thrown out of France and off the continent during the *Hundred Years' War* (1338–1453), even as *new monarchies* took shape in both countries. That defeat sparked a long dynastic struggle and civil war: the War of the Roses (1455–1485). With the consolidation of Tudor rule, England enjoyed a sustained period of prosperity and rising naval and commercial power. This peace was broken by the *Protestant Reformation*, which soon propelled England into war with the Catholic powers of Europe, in alliance with the Dutch Republic during the *Eighty Years' War* (1566–1648). Imperial Spain, under Philip II, attempted to invade England in 1588, the year of the Spanish Armada. This attempt was defeated by the navy of *Elizabeth I*, last of the Tudor monarchs.

The ancient battle with Scotland ended with the *union of the crowns* under James I (1566–1625), king of England, 1603–1625, and king of Scotland as James VI, 1567–1625. The country was, uncharacteristically, radicalized and deeply divided during the English Civil War (1642–1646), which ushered in *Oliver Cromwell's* Commonwealth (1649–1660). These were also years of growing naval competition and then dominance, emerging from the *Anglo-Dutch Wars*. The Glorious Revolution (1688–1689) finally secured Britain for Protestantism by expulsion of the Catholic James II and enthronement of the Protestants *William (of Orange)* and Mary. This had a lasting significance for *Ulster*, as well, where the victory of the House of Orange is still celebrated annually by Protestants in the face of deep Catholic resentment. The Glorious Revolution also ended the Dutch wars, and enabled alliance with the Netherlands in the great contest against the newly ascendant and aggressive power of France under *Louis XIV*. Relations with *Bourbon* France and Spain were hostile for most of the seventeenth century, leading to near-continuous overseas conflict, in India and as in the *French and Indian Wars* (1689–1763). In 1707 Scotland was joined to England and the combined island power was renamed Great Britain in the *Act of Union*. Ireland had been mostly subdued by Elizabeth, and then again by Cromwell, but it presented a dual and constant strategic threat: it remained largely and even militantly Catholic, and its disaffection invited intervention by foreign armies.

Great Britain opposed the schemes for aggrandizement of Louis XIV and his successors, resulting in several wars which formed a near-seamless whole: *War of the Grand Alliance* (1688–1697), *War of the Spanish Succession* (1701–

1714), *War of the Austrian Succession* (1740–1748) and the *Seven Years' War* (1756–1763); with their North American extensions: *King William's War* (1689–1697), *Queen Anne's War* (1702–1713), *King George's War* (1744–1748), and the *French and Indian War* (1754–1760). In these wars Britain contained French power in Europe while destroying it in the Americas and India, greatly expanding the *British Empire* there in the process. The victory in the Americas, however, removed the main bond with thirteen contiguous British colonies there, and the sacrifice of colonial to imperial interests strained relations past the breaking point. The colonies rebelled, launching the *American Revolution* (1775–1783). The expense of fighting a long-distance land war in a continental-sized territory was enormous. Britain fought to preserve its only recently acquired, and hard-won, imperial preferences in America, but lost as a result of two key factors: the scale of the conflict and inability to bring superior force to bear in a decisive way given the *guerrilla* tactics of the Americans; and more importantly, French, Dutch, and Spanish naval *intervention*. This setback interrupted an otherwise spectacularly successful imperial policy, which continued apace elsewhere. In India, flag and empire followed the commercial lead and troops of the *East India Company*, acquiring support bases along the way in such places as *Aden*, *Cape Colony*, *Sudan*, and even *Egypt*. Meanwhile, in *Canada* the *Hudson's Bay Company* ruled a giant *hinterland* of rivers and fur, while the entire continent of *Australia* was claimed in the late eighteenth century and made effectively British in the nineteenth century through *penal settlements*, sheep, and sea power. Ireland was finally constitutionally joined to England in another *Act of Union* (1800).

Britain was at war with France almost without pause from the radicalization of the *French Revolution* in 1792, through the *Napoleonic Wars*, to the second and final defeat of *Napoleon I* in 1815. Shrugging off the loss of its important North American colonies, which it fought again in the *War of 1812*, it created a second and greater empire in Asia and Africa. In the first half of the nineteenth century, with the *Concert of Europe* helping to keep peace on the Continent but also nicely keeping Britain's rivals apart from one another, Great Britain emerged as the greatest power in the world and ruler of the most expansive and populous empire in history. It did so based on the superiority of the *Royal Navy*, early industrial advantage (it produced 25 percent of world industrial output), and the additional riches of its vast empire. It also succeeded as a result of the enormous tactical and strategic benefits accruing from an established and successful diplomatic tradition and a sustained and calculated policy of detachment from Continental entanglements, to whatever degree circumstances permitted. Meanwhile, the overseas Empire continued to expand: after the *Indian Mutiny*, London instituted *direct rule* in India and sought to complete construction and *modernization* of the *Rāj*, while also extending its holdings in Asia in the second half of the nineteenth century as a means of defending its core holdings in India and being drawn into repeated small wars in Africa.

As the Concert decayed in Europe in the 1850s, Britain propped up the *Ottoman Empire* against the also-expanding *Russian Empire*, helping to postpone a final answer to the *Eastern Question* by fighting the *Crimean War* and practicing *containment* of Russia in the Mediterranean and during the *Great Game* in Central Asia. Britain's industrial advantage peaked c. 1870. It was thereafter overtaken in industrial production by the United States during the 1880s, and by Germany c. 1900. It was also largely out-foxed in the later *scramble for Africa*. The so-called *Pax Britannica* waned along with relative British power at the turn of the twentieth century, mostly because other major countries caught up with or passed Britain economically and technically. Britain was deeply isolated by the *Second Boer War*, and moved to correct this under *Salisbury*, who moved from *splendid isolation* toward *rapprochements* with America, France, and Russia and framed the *Anglo-Japanese Alliance*. Relations with Imperial Germany deteriorated, however, over such episodes as the *Jameson raid*, the *Kruger telegram*, the *Boer War*, and *Agadir*, but especially over the *Anglo-German Naval Arms Race*. Then came the *mobilization crisis* of July–August 1914 and the cataclysm of *World War I*. Although still one of the world's major powers, indeed a *world power*, Britain was so wounded financially (and psychologically) by the Great War that it let Ireland break away in 1922 after the *Irish War of Independence*. And after the *Amritsar massacre* and the rise of the *Muslim League* and *Congress Party* in India, it also soon began discussions on *Home Rule* for India in the *Round Table Conferences* of the early 1930s.

Britain pursued a shoddy policy of *appeasement* of Nazi Germany until after the *Munich Conference*. Yet when it had to fight anyway, it did so doggedly. It staggered to a *Cadmean victory* in *World War II*, largely with American and Soviet help. By 1947 it started to let go of its overseas commitments, feeling the strain of *imperial overreach*. It pulled back from the eastern Mediterranean, replaced by the United States as the historic container of Russia in the early *Cold War*, when the Soviets threatened Greece and Turkey. It let India, the "jewel in the crown" of the British Empire, go free, starting a chain reaction of *decolonization* that unraveled in a single generation what had been assembled over 300 years. In the 1950s and 1960s nearly all the rest of the empire followed suit, a loss of stature not concealed by the poor cloth of the Commonwealth. The humiliation of the *Suez Crisis* aside, Britain ceased to act globally—at least, independently of the United States in its major foreign policies—during this period. In July 1967 it declared that it was withdrawing from all commitments east of Suez, abandoned *Aden*, and withdrew from the Persian Gulf. That led the United States to move into bases in the Gulf to replace British fixed positions.

Still, Great Britain remained a major nuclear power and a significant player at the United Nations and within NATO and thus continued to "punch above its weight." In 1973 the UK joined the *European Community*, but without embracing full political *union*. The *Falklands War* distracted from its main security concerns in Europe, while *Margaret Thatcher's* domestic reforms preoccupied it for most of the 1980s. In 1990–1991 it joined the *coalition* which fought the *Gulf War* and stayed to police the *no-fly zones*. It was reluctant to intervene with force in Bosnia or to develop the *WEU* as an alternative to NATO. In the mid-1990s the *Conservative Party* was turned out by the *Labour Party*, which gained the largest majority in the twentieth century. Labour was reelected with a majority in 2001. *See also Atlantic Charter; Baldwin; Balfour; Belize; Bengal; Bevin; Burma; Canning; Castlereagh; Joseph Chamberlain; Neville Chamberlain; J. Austin Chamberlain; Winston Churchill; Robert Clive; colonialism; Commonwealth; Cyprus; James Dalhousie; Benjamin Disraeli; dreadnought; Durham Report; Anthony Eden; English Channel; Falkland Islands; Fashoda; Fenians; John Fisher; George III; Ghana; Gibraltar; Gladstone; gold standard; Gurkhas; Douglas Haig; Kenya; Horatio Herbert Kitchener; Imperial Conferences; Imperial Tariff; India; India Acts; Indian Army; industrialization; Industrial Revolution; King George's War; King William's War; Liverpool; Lloyd George; Frederick Lugard; John Major; Malta; Maori Wars; Louis Mountbatten; Horatio Nelson; New France; Nepal; Newfoundland; New Zealand; Nigeria; Opium Wars; Henry John Palmerston; Pitt, the Elder; Pitt, the Younger; Princely States; racism; Rāj; Cecil Rhodes; Rhodesia; George Rodney; Royal Navy; sea power; Seven Years' War; Sikh Wars; South Africa; Sudan; Suez Canal; Sykes-Picot Agreement; Tibet; two-power standard; UDI; unequal treaties; United Kingdom; Victoria; War of 1812; War of the Austrian Succession; War of the Grand Alliance; War of the Spanish Succession; War of Jenkins' Ear; Duke of Wellington; Whig history; White Man's Burden; Harold Wilson; World War I; World War II; and specific colonies.*

Suggested Readings: *Cambridge History of the British Empire*, 2nd ed. (1963); *Oxford History of England*, 16 vols. (1936–1993); Muriel E. Chamberlain, *Pax Britannica? British Foreign Policy, 1789–1914* (1988); Muriel E. Chamberlain, *Rise and Fall of the British Empire* (1996); R. Hyam, *Britain's Imperial Century, 1815–1914* (1975); Wm. Roger Lewis, ed., *Oxford History of the British Empire*, 2 vols. (1998); Kenneth O. Morgan, ed., *Oxford History of Britain*, rev. ed. (2001); William A. Ward, ed., *Cambridge History of British Foreign Policy*, 3 vols. (1922–1923, 1971).

United Kingdom of the Serbs, Croats and Slovenes. The formal name of *Yugoslavia* from 1918 to 1929. It was run mostly by and for the Serbs.

United Nations alliance. The armed league which won *World War II* and then gave its name—coined by *Franklin Roosevelt*—to the modern security organization its members founded in 1945. *See also Allies (World War II)*.

United Nations, Charter of (1945). A multilateral treaty which serves as the constitution of the *United Nations Organization*. Its main features were hammered out in advance by the victorious *Great Powers* of World War II at the *Dumbarton Oaks* conference in 1944. It was finalized and significantly revised at the much larger *San Francisco conference*, April–June 1945. It sets out the rules and procedures governing the United Nations and its *specialized agencies*, and declares as their main aspirations: (1) maintenance of peace and international security through collective measures; (2) promotion of *self-determination* of nations and peoples; (3) encouragement of economic, social, and cultural cooperation among states; and (4) respect for fundamental *human rights* and freedoms. Difficulty in definition of both "*aggression*" and "*war*," as evidenced by the experience of the *League of Nations*, meant that both terms were avoided in the United Nations Charter. *See also Four Freedoms; lawmaking; neutral rights; Outer Space Treaty; self-defense; trust territory.*

Suggested Reading: Ruth B. Russell, *History of the United Nations* (1958).

United Nations Conference on Human Settlements (HABITAT). Held in Vancouver in 1976, it was the largest world conference ever held before the *United Nations Conference on the Environment.* Some 131 participating states focused on devising new *UNEP* machinery to deal with the problem of housing (human settlements).

United Nations Conference on the Environment and Development (UNCED). Also known as the "Earth Summit." Held in Rio de Janeiro in 1992, it was the largest conference to that point in the history of *diplomacy.* Five *conventions/declarations* were signed: (1) Agenda 21, a nonbinding action plan for environmental and development programs (only the United States refused to sign, a decision reversed by *Bill Clinton* in 1993); (2) The Rio Declaration on the Environment and Development, which called for $125 billion in new *aid* transfers to *Third World* states; (3) Declaration on Principles of Management and Sustainable Development for All Types of Forests; (4) Convention on Climate Change; and (5) Convention on Biological Diversity.

United Nations Conference on the Law of the Sea (UNCLOS) I. Held in 1958, it addressed conflict over various extensions by *coastal states* of their claims to *territorial waters, fishing* zones, and so forth. Its main innovations concerned *straight baselines* and a redefinition of *baselines* (limited to 24 nautical miles) drawn across bays entirely abutting a single country. It also led to a *convention* on rights to *oil* and natural gas under the *continental shelf,* but largely failed to resolve other looming problems of *jurisdiction.*

United Nations Conference on the Law of the Sea (UNCLOS) II. A follow-up to *UNCLOS I* held in 1960. It failed in most respects, including on whether to extend the *three-mile limit* to a *twelve-mile limit.*

United Nations Conference on the Law of the Sea (UNCLOS) III. Talks were held from 1973 to 1982. Much of the code of maritime law was overhauled to take account of new *territorial* claims and marine technologies. It set a *twelve-mile limit* and agreed to give *coastal states* 200-nautical mile *Exclusive Economic Zones* and grant them more rights to the *continental shelf*. It also dealt with new regulations concerning marine pollution, designated *international waterways*, and addressed a host of traditional concerns. Most controversial, it established an International Seabed Authority replete with Secretariat, Council, and Assembly located in Jamaica and related Tribunal located in Hamburg. It then set down that deep seabed mineral deposits are "the common heritage of Mankind," at least within the "Area" outside *territorial waters*. It gave "the Authority" *international personality* and empowered it to oversee a mining company ("the Enterprise") and *regime* which guaranteed *Third World* countries access to all available, nonmilitary mining technology. That dramatic initiative caused some states to balk. Originally not signing, for varied reasons, were: Brazil, Britain, Ecuador, Israel, Peru, Switzerland, the United States, the Vatican, Venezuela, and West Germany. As these states did not contribute to *capitalization* of the Enterprise, and as *ratifications* were slow—sixty were required for the *treaty* to enter into effect—the most radical innovations of UNCLOS III remained moot. On the other hand, most states in practice respected the majority of less controversial features of the new code, giving them status under *international customary law*. *See also baseline; common heritage principle; contiguous zone; internal waters; landlocked states.*

United Nations Conference on Trade and Development (UNCTAD). The initiative for this 1964 conference came from the *G-77.* Southern countries sought trade reform through this forum because in it they commanded a majority and hoped to have more influence than in the *General Agreement on Tariffs and Trade* (GATT) or the *International Monetary Fund* (IMF). Although they failed to significantly advance their trade agenda, they did achieve acceptance of UNCTAD as a permanent forum and a few symbolic modifications to the trade *regime*. UNCTAD quickly adopted a *dependency theory* view of the structure of the international economic system. However, the *OECD* nations declined to treat UNCTAD as a legitimate negotiating forum on trade matters. It also fell prey to internal divisions within the G-77. It has no compulsory mechanisms and may only suggest courses of action. Combined with the economic marginalism of most Southern countries, that rendered it a largely ineffective institution. *See also Integrated Program for Commodities; NIEO.*

United Nations Conferences on Population (UNCP). There were three before the close of the twentieth century: the first was held in Bucharest in 1974; the second was hosted by Mexico City in 1984; and the third, and most controversial, took place in Cairo, September 5–13, 1994. At the latter, participants included world leaders, health officials, and hundreds of interested *nongovernmental organizations*. Its main thrust was an effort to link issues of population growth with the notion of *sustainable development* and women's rights, conceived largely as rights to control reproduction through access to contraception and abortion information and services, but also refusal of unwanted sexual activity, and all within a broader context of legal extension and protection of developing international views of universal *human rights*. Most delegations focused on a perceived need to increase availability of family planning as part of broader health services. Related objectives were significantly reducing infant, child, and maternal mortality and expanding access to education for girls. The Cairo conference brought into being an alliance of the *Vatican* and several conservative *Muslim* regimes in shared opposition to abortion. The Vatican was virtually alone, however, in maintaining opposition to what it called "artificial means" of contraception.

United Nations Development Program (UNDP). To provide a new avenue for development *aid*, the *United Nations* set up a Special Fund (SUNFED) in 1959. In 1965 the *UNGA* merged SUNFED with the Expanded Program of Technical Assistance (EPTA) to form the UNDP. The UNDP now provides a single administrative center for UN *aid* and *development* projects. Its budget was small by the standards of major *donor countries*: about $1 billion in 1990, down from a high-water mark reached in 1979. If less aid in the future is delivered as *tied aid*, and if more states choose to deliver assistance through *multilateral* channels, both of which are unlikely events, then the UNDP's role will expand. Into the twenty-first century, however, despite rhetorical commitments by donor nations to multilateral delivery of aid, most state-to-state assistance remained channeled through bilateral agencies or was distributed via the *International Monetary Fund* and *International Bank for Reconstruction and Development*, where donors retained control.

United Nations Educational, Scientific, and Cultural Organization (UNESCO). A *specialized agency* set up to promote cooperation in the fields its title lists. In its early decades it was much admired as a vehicle of basic literacy education. From the 1960s it became more involved in designation and preservation of world cultural sites, including monuments, art works, and even works of music deemed of world cultural or intrinsic interest. It was immersed in controversy in the 1980s while promoting the so-called *New World Information and Communication Order* (NWICO). Criticism of the thrust of NWICO, budget overruns, and poor management were the stated reasons for *withdrawal* from UNESCO by the United States (1985) and Great Britain (1986). Other Western and some *neutral* states also criticized NWICO and UNESCO on those grounds, but remained members. UNESCO resumed more traditional support for freedom of information with the collapse of the *Soviet bloc*, which had strongly backed the censorship and propaganda provisions of the NWICO. Britain thus rejoined in 1997.

United Nations Environmental Program (UNEP). This forum became more prominent after the mid-1980s, with its support for scientific research that led to uncovering *ozone depletion* and its drafting of *conventions* on CFCs and other harmful substances. It works closely with the WMO and sponsored the *Earth Summit* in 1992 and follow-up meetings.

United Nations General Assembly (UNGA). The main deliberative body within the *United Nations system* in which all member *states* are represented on an equal basis (with the exception that during the *Cold War* the Soviet Union had three seats, one each for *Russia, Byelorussia,* and *Ukraine*). It has limited powers: it may pass nonbinding *resolutions,* issue reports, discuss and deliberate on matters of interest to the members, order missions of inquiry, and instruct (in severely limited ways) some of the *Specialized Agencies,* most of which report to it. However, the *Security Council* remains the focus of real power within the United Nations system. This caused considerable tension from the 1960s onward, as a *Third World* majority used the UNGA as a platform for demands on establishing the *NIEO* agenda and pursued other issues of specialized interest which ran contrary to the positions of one or more of the Great Powers. By the late 1980s there was a less contentious atmosphere overall. With the Cold War drawing to a close and *nonalignment* losing its original raison d'etre, the UNGA as a whole became a venue of more pragmatic rhetoric and policy. Large majorities endorsed the actions of the *Gulf coalition* in the *Gulf War* in 1990 and thereafter repeatedly endorsed Great Power and other *armed humanitarian intervention* in regional conflicts.

United Nations High Commission for Refugees (UNHCR). A position established in 1951 to replace the International Refugee Organization, a short-lived (1947–1951) *specialized agency* set up to deal with the postwar *refugee* emergency left over after the work done by the *United Nations Relief and Rehabilitation Administration* (UNRRA). Financing of the UNHCR is on a voluntary basis. Its main functions are to provide legal protection for *stateless* persons, *repatriation* or resettlement of refugees, *good offices* to other relief agencies, publicity for refugee problems, and *advisory services.* Refugees who are nationals of countries granting *asylum* do not fall under UNHCR jurisdiction. The office won the *Nobel Prize* for Peace in 1954 and again in 1981. In the 1990s the UNHCR became heavily involved in the Balkans, after which experience efforts were made by donor states to curtail its growing scope and powers in favor of a greater coordinating role for on-the-ground efforts by specialized NGOs. *See also internally displaced person.*

United Nations Human Rights Commission (UNHRC). The main body within the *United Nations* system dealing with *human rights.* Only *states* are represented, though some *nongovernmental organizations* have been granted *observer status.* It reports to ECOSOC, and thereby to the *United Nations Gen-*

eral Assembly. Its proceedings are highly political and its powers proscribed. It has a monitoring, rather than implementation, role regarding international *covenants* and *conventions.* With the *Cold War* logjam on human rights broken, a modest thematic approach emerged by which states were not singled out for political targeting, as had been the case previously, so much as general problems, such as *torture,* were addressed. Yet sharp divisions remained. The main one ran along *Southern* and collectivist notions of rights such as a right to *development* as the primary international right, as against *Northern* (Western) and individualist conceptions of civil and political liberties as a prerequisite to more just and equitable societies. Often, this debate involved sharp controversy between China and Western states. In 2001 the United States was, for the first time in the Commission's history, not reelected to membership. That resulted from clumsy diplomacy by the then inexperienced administration of *George W. Bush,* which failed to marshal support and permitted a fracturing of the *WEOG* vote. That allowed election of Sudan instead, which was governed by one of the worst human rights abusing regimes in the world. *See also anti-Semitism; World Human Rights Conference.*

United Nations Human Rights Committee (HRC). It was set up under an *Optional Protocol* to the Covenant on Civil and Political Rights, to which few states have adhered. The Protocol is notable for permitting individuals to *petition* against their own governments, directly to the Committee. Adherence to the Protocol and acceptance of the oversight role of the HRC is separate from *ratification* of the Covenant.

United Nations Industrial Development Organization (UNIDO). One of the 16 *specialized agencies* of the *United Nations,* it was approved by the *UNGA* in 1965 and actually started up operations in 1967. Its main aim is to assist in *industrialization* within the *LDCs.* It promotes research and *advisory services.* It manages a small budget and, some critics charge, is but marginally useful in a field where market forces hold most sway. It coordinates its activities with the *UNDP.* It did not formally become a specialized agency until 1985.

United Nations [International] Children's [Emergency] Fund (UNICEF). It was set up in 1946 to provide emergency relief to the child victims and *refugees* of *World War II.* "International Emergency" was dropped from the title in 1953, as UNICEF gained permanency and moved into longer term programs, beyond war-damaged Europe and Asia. UNICEF funding is on a voluntary basis by member *states* (it is not a *specialized agency*), with supplemental funds raised from millions of private individuals. Its programs focus on education, emergency *aid,* health care (including vaccinations), and nutrition. It sustains thousands of family care clinics and schools, annually servicing millions of the world's poorest and most destitute children. It won the *Nobel Prize* for Peace in 1964.

United Nations Organization (UNO). The global *peace* and *security* organization agreed upon by the *Great Powers* which headed the *United Nations alliance* that met at *Dumbarton Oaks* in 1944, and the more general founding meeting at *San Francisco*, attended by some 51 original *United Nations Charter* members (*treaty powers*); that number included Poland, whose government was still in dispute among the *Allied* governments of *World War II*. The United Nations is the linear successor of the *League of Nations*, from which it inherited some structures, programs, and affiliated bodies. Its offices are administered by the *Secretariat* under the guidance and fiscal management of a *Secretary General*. Its key security arm is the *Security Council*. It is comprised of the *permanent five (P-5)* powers which have *veto* rights over *binding resolutions*, and ten (initially, six) non-veto and non-permanent states, elected on a rotating basis from among the general membership of the *United Nations General Assembly (UNGA)* for a three-year term. The UNGA is the UN's sole forum of universal state membership. On paper, though not in fact in several cases, it oversees the various *specialized agencies*. The UN assembly halls and Secretariat were located temporarily in London, and some UNGA sessions were also held in Paris, before the main body was relocated permanently to New York City upon completion of its landmark building along the water in the 1950s.

In 1993, Macedonia, Eritrea, Monaco, and Andorra joined the UNGA, the 181st through 184th members, respectively. Several Pacific and other *microstates* were nonmembers until the late 1990s, but joined once the UNGA placed the problems of microstates on its agenda. On February 17, 2000, tiny Tuvalu was admitted as the 189th member of the United Nations. Switzerland, the *Vatican*, several *associated states*, and all non–self-governing territories remain nonmembers. However, even these entities maintained some form of observer mission in New York, either independently financed and operated, or associated with the mission of a larger and sponsoring power. In addition, many states maintained formal missions at the headquarters of this or that specialized agency which was of principal concern to them on a given issue.

The United Nations is a recognized *international personality*. Therefore, United Nations premises—wherever located—are legally immune from search, *expropriation*, or any other interference by host states or third parties. The United Nations is also immune from financial controls, though not from the practical effect of given states withholding their annual contributions or voluntary subventions, and from all taxes, duties, and other prohibitions on imported goods it deems necessary to fulfill its Charter mandate and functions. Its assets are immune from any municipal legal process, including that of host countries which house its buildings and offices. It may have unfettered access to all media and is theoretically and legally exempt from state censorship. Its *archives* are similarly immune. It may even encrypt messages and use couriers who enjoy *diplomatic immunity*. That privilege is also enjoyed by its accredited diplomats and diplomats accredited to it.

UN *Secretary-General Kofi Annan* was awarded the 2001 *Nobel Prize* for Peace, jointly with the United Nations as a whole, principally for work in advancing international concern for human rights. He was the second secretary-general to be awarded the prize (*Dag Hammarskjöld* was awarded the peace prize posthumously in 1961). During the first century of granting Nobel peace prizes, 1901–2001, the United Nations or associated agencies received the peace prize fourteen times. *See also* surrounding entries, individual secretaries-general, as well as *Bosnia*; *Cambodia*; *collective security*; *Congo crisis*; *Economic Commissions*; *El Salvador*; *embargo*; *good offices*; *Gulf War*; *Korean Conflict*; *Namibia*; *neutrality*; *peace enforcement*; *peacekeeping*; *peacemaking*; *principal organs*; *two-Chinas policy*; *Somalia*; *Suez crisis*; *veto*; *Western Sahara*.

Suggested Readings: A. Leroy Bennett, *International Organizations* (1984); Inis Claude, *Swords Into Ploughshares*, 4th ed. (1984); Adam Roberts and Benedict Kingsley, eds., *United Nations, Divided World* (1993).

United Nations presence. A term applied mainly to United Nations *peace-keeping* operations, but also to UN mediators, in-country staff or military observers, *advisory services* personnel, and other official missions.

United Nations Relief and Rehabilitation Administration (UNRRA). This agency actually preexisted the *United Nations Organization*. It was established by the *United Nations alliance* in 1943 (the UN itself was not founded until 1945). Most of its funding came from the United States. As Allied armies moved into liberated areas in 1944 and 1945, the UNRRA followed in their wake, even in some parts of Eastern Europe, where the Soviets in general denied access to all foreign observers. It brought emergency relief to the civilian populations of devastated areas and to the victims of the *concentration camps*. Innumerable lives were saved by this effort. In China, it worked until 1947 to rechannel the Yellow River, which had left its course in 1938 when *Chiang Kai-shek* ordered engineers to blast its containing dikes to flood Japanese-occupied areas during the *Second Sino-Japanese War*. Until 1949 the UNRRA continued its relief work and then began to direct some of its efforts into *reconstruction*. By then the *specialized agencies* were coming on-line to take over relief work, and reconstruction became the main task of the *Marshall Plan*. So, the UNRRA folded its tents, its job well done. Its remaining assets passed to *UNICEF*, and some of its ongoing tasks to *World Health Organization* and other *specialized agencies*.

United Nations Relief and Works Agency (UNRWA). An agency set up in 1949 in response to the *refugee* problem generated by the *First Arab-Israeli*

War. The United States was the major *donor nation.* The UNRWA was severely handicapped by the politics of the Middle East: it was unable to repatriate or resettle Palestinian refugees for several decades because neither Israel nor the Arab states accepted them as permanent residents. Instead, the UNRWA branched into provision of services such as health care and schools in the refugee camps in Lebanon and Gaza.

United Provinces. *See Low Countries; Netherlands.*

United States Agency for International Development (USAID). The main U.S. *aid* agency, in operation since 1961 and responsible for most nonmilitary aid.

United States of America (USA). (1) The Colonies: The arrival of the various peoples of Europe and Africa began after 1500, and from Asia after c. 1850. Within 100 years of the voyages of *Columbus* most of the continental United States was claimed by France or Spain, with the Dutch and English making sizeable claims too. *Slavery,* too, arrived with European settlement and lasted 350 years, as did conflict with Indians, such as *King Philip's War* (1675–1676). Slowly, thirteen of the British *colonies* in North America developed a weak sense of common destiny, at first mainly out of shared fear of France and the shared burden of empire, but also as a result of distance from the imperial government in London. They remained on the periphery of world affairs, trivial in population, and in fact and general perception but a minor extension of the *British Empire.* European wars spilled into North America as *King William's War* (1689–1697), *Queen Anne's War* (1702–1713), *King George's War* (1744–1748), and the *French and Indian War* (1754–1760). Those clashes entangled the colonies in conflicts which appeared far distant from local interests, yet when they were done they had broken French power in the hemisphere.

The pre-independence wars in America also shook the confidence of the colonists that in fighting for England their own interests were tended to as well: more than once, a *peace treaty* handed back to France *territory* hard-won in North America, in return for a concession to Britain in the Caribbean or in India. Moreover, victory proved a solvent of the bonds of empire: the end of the French and Indian Wars dissolved the natural alliance between the colonists and England born of facing a common enemy. Finally, first with war and then again with peace came higher taxes and new imperial *tariffs* needed to ensure that the colonists paid for their own defense and relieved part of the heavy financial burden of policing England's vast empire. When Britain decided also to maintain *mercantilist* tariffs against American goods, there arose an insistent demand for relief, and then for self-government, among a significant minority of the colonist population. This demand was ultimately fulfilled by the *American Revolution* (1775–1783), though not before the

American War of Independence had become yet another international entanglement for the British Empire, which finally decided to cut its losses and grant independence to the Thirteen Colonies. Not all American colonists welcomed that independence or wanted to be part of the new people called "Americans": the *United Empire Loyalists* left, or were expelled from, the new republic. Many headed to Canada, paralleling a voyage already made by defeated and forcibly expelled *Iroquois* nations from upper New York which had allied with Britain during the rebellion and after were made to pay the high price of permanent exile.

(2) The 19th century: The young republic which took shape from 1783 to 1789 was weak for many decades, as reflected in the humiliation of the *Quasi War*. The *French Revolution* and *Napoleonic Wars* bitterly divided the nation, a split personified by the dispute between *Thomas Jefferson* and *Alexander Hamilton* over whether to form a French or British alliance. *George Washington* resolved the argument by keeping his weak and fragile nation *neutral* and warning it against *entangling alliances*. That admonition was appropriate to his day, yet would hamstring policy well into the twentieth century, far past the time when *isolationism* no longer matched the country's rising power and requisite responsibilities. Moreover, as Americans were to find three more times in the next 200 years, their interest in trade and fondness for abstract principle meant they could not stay at peace when the *balance of power* and the idea of *liberty* was under challenge in Europe. With *Napoleon* commanding the continent and Britain ruling the seas, the United States had the *Louisiana Purchase* fall into its lap, but was also drawn into the chronic *Tripolitan War* with the *Barbary States* and then the much larger fiasco of the *War of 1812* with Great Britain. Postwar, the quiet future to come along the Canadian border was foretold by a demarcation settlement and *demilitarization* of the Great Lakes in the *Rush-Bagot Agreement* (1818). The rest of the eastern border was resolved after the near-run *Aroostook War*, in the *Webster-Ashburton Treaty* (1842); the northwestern *frontier*, in form of the *Oregon Question*, was addressed peacefully by 1846, leaving only a minor Pacific coast issue unresolved until 1902. Meanwhile, other than toward Canada, where British power still held sway, Americans were busy extending their isolationist and republican doctrines to the whole hemisphere with the *Monroe Doctrine*. The expansionist impulse also continued unabated in the south and west, first into the Floridas, then northwest to deliver an answer to the Oregon Question.

Most of all, Americans wanted to expand due west and southwest, which they did with annexation of *Texas* (1845). That, and related and calculated provocations by President *Polk* brought about the *Mexican-American War* (1846–1848). The huge area gained by the United States as a result of that war gave it the continental and imperial *hinterland* it long had coveted, while acquisition of *California* made it a Pacific nation. The world historical consequences of that fact were soon demonstrated by Commodore *Perry's* forcing open the door to expanded trade with Japan and a rising *missionary* and trading presence in China. The Mexican-American War did something even more fundamental: it brought to the fore of American politics the unresolved dilemma of slavery, which then tore at the vitals of a nation constitutionally (in both senses of that word) dedicated to the *liberal* proposition that all men were created equal and endowed with inalienable rights. Fundamental dedication to individualism and to liberty, in the *Enlightenment* tradition, could not forever or for long live under the same national roof with slavery. Everyone on all sides of the issue already knew that, but the outcome of the Mexican-American War forced them finally to face it. As new states applied for entry into the Union the constitutional issue arose as to whether some might adopt or retain slavery—and thus spread the "peculiar institution" deep and wide into areas other Americans saw as reserved for a *manifest destiny* to create an "Empire of Liberty" in the Western Hemisphere. The question of whether new states should enter the union as *free soil* or *slave states*, the awful question of slavery, was now to be resolved, but only by huge *Union* and *Confederate* armies grinding each other down on the sanguine battlefields of the *American Civil War*. That great contest took 620,000 American lives, more than all other American wars combined before or since, and shaped the nation into its modern form to a far greater extent than had even the American Revolution. Henceforth, the United States was in fact fully dedicated to its founding liberal principles, as promised by *Abraham Lincoln* in the *Gettysburg Address* and made indelible by the "last full measure of devotion" of the blood sacrifice of a great and truly decisive war.

The United States emerged from the Civil War a *Great Power* of the first-rank in all material measures, including population, raw industrial capacity, wealth, military capabilities, and technology. Yet, the country was not psychologically prepared to accept the new role of *world power* which victory for union and liberty had made possible, and also required. Instead, Americans sought a return only to *status quo ante bellum* simplicity and isolation. They abjured overseas expansion offered to them by *William Seward*, and they insisted on disarming and returning to their homes. American leaders also declared that nothing had changed. But it had. Other major powers recognized this, even if most Americans did not, and adjusted their policy accordingly: Russia vacated *Alaska* (1867); France abandoned its attempt to return to Mexico (1867); and Britain negotiated the *Treaty of Washington* (1870), settling all outstanding *disputes* with the United States, including the *Alabama* claims flowing from the Civil War. Although it did not seem so at the time, the stage was set for the subsequent emergence of the United States as the great, transformative nation of twentieth-century international relations—a *superpower*, even for a time a genuine *hegemon*, dedicated to a new, *liberal-internationalist* approach to world order. In the interim, Americans wanted nothing to do with the outside world. Also, they rediscovered that yet again they had spoiled the natural liberty of their wondrously endowed land—a constant motif in American national and cultural life—through a sour *Reconstruction* and in the moral failure to fully accept as citizens in spirit the newly emancipated black population which had received citizenship in law. Almost immediately, there also followed racialized *Indian Wars* in the West, accompanied by hard-hearted *ethnic cleansings* of the tribes of the Great Plains and Rocky Mountains carried out by tough veterans drawn from both sides of the Civil War.

(3) The World Wars: After several decades of quiet in foreign affairs, marred only by occasional outbursts of pugnacity toward some small Latin American neighbor, the United States broke upon the world stage during *William McKinley*'s presidency, with annexation of *Hawaii* and then the *Spanish-American War* (1898). That contest left it a somewhat reluctant colonial and imperial power. Most importantly, the acquisition of the *Philippines* projected U.S. interests deep into Asia and the Pacific—of America's five twentieth-century wars, three would begin in Asia. This new involvement was reflected immediately, though passively, in *Theodore Roosevelt*'s mediation of the *Treaty of Portsmouth*, support for construction of the *Panama Canal*, and the *Open Door notes* and general foreign policy. From 1900 to 1933 the United States *intervened* almost by reflex in Central America and the Caribbean. Yet, it found it difficult to appreciate that other Great Powers, in particular Japan, also regarded *propinquity* as justification for declaring and defending a *sphere of influence*. While conflict with Japan over its more aggressive policies toward China simmered, there arose another threat to the European balance of power and transatlantic commerce. Germany's ambitions and U.S. commercial interests led to entry into *World War I*, after which the United States was the dominant power in the world in 1919, a fact reflected in *Woodrow Wilson*'s towering influence at the *Paris Peace Conference*.

Earlier in his presidency, Wilson had declined to recognize the revolutionary government in Mexico and intervened there and in Central America repeatedly, to a greater extent than any previous president, including Theodore Roosevelt. Wilson spent three months in Paris negotiating the peace treaties and overseeing creation of the *League of Nations* and its *collective security* system. He refused to compromise with *Republican* senators during the debate over the *Treaty of Versailles* and may by that have lost a winnable fight for American entry into the League, his great hope for a lasting peace. He was a reluctant interventionist in the *Russian Civil War*, ordering American forces kept to a token level and pulling them out at the first opportunity, but also refusing to recognize *Bolshevik* victory in 1920. After Wilson's presidency, Americans again sought a return to simpler days after involvement in a major war and a burst of enthused engagement with the wider and, or so they thought, wilier world. Seeing no fundamental threat to the balance of power in Europe, the United States withdrew politically and diplomatically, while installing a nationalist tariff and pursuing an aggressive export policy. Three successive isolationist presidents then followed: *Warren Harding, Calvin Coo-*

lidge, and *Herbert Hoover*. Just as a semblance of responsible *internationalism* was returning to American diplomacy, with *Henry L. Stimson*, the *Great Depression* knocked out the smallest will to act, just as it raised up dangerous and aggressive regimes in Germany and Japan and confirmed the United States in the worst sort of *beggar-thy-neighbor* foreign economic and trade policy.

Franklin D. Roosevelt's first administration was preoccupied with the national calamity of the Depression, to which Roosevelt responded with the hundred days of New Deal legislation—public works spending and projects in agriculture and industry, social security and unemployment programs, and much else. This ameliorated some effects of the Depression, but overall his domestic efforts were undermined by a failure of his economic diplomacy, as during the *World Economic Conference* in 1933. Hard times and high unemployment continued until the United States went on a full war economy footing from 1939. In foreign affairs Roosevelt opened relations with the Soviet Union and affirmed the *Good Neighbor policy*. After 1936 he grew increasingly concerned with events in Europe and Asia, but offered only such rhetorical support as his "Quarantine" policy to proposals for collective security measures against Italy, Germany, or Japan. He funneled minor secret aid to the Republican side in the *Spanish Civil War*. Roosevelt sought to convince Britain and France to work with *Stalin* against *Hitler*, but to no avail, since he insisted at the same time that the United States would remain neutral. Roosevelt tried to stiffen American and Western resolve against the threat from Hitler, but all Congress or the public gave him to work with was words: in 1939 the U.S. Army ranked nineteenth in the world, on a par with lowly Portugal. It would take a direct attack by Japan to fully awaken America's interest in world affairs and appreciation of its new strategic vulnerability. In 1940 and 1941, however, it took creative and sustained deceit on Roosevelt's part to lead public opinion closer to a war he knew was necessary, though he sincerely wished to avoid it. By narrow margins, he secured *Lend-Lease*. Then he used his presidential prerogative to sign the *Atlantic Charter*. In secret, he also authorized the top-secret *Manhattan Project*.

Meanwhile, in the Far East Roosevelt increased pressure on Imperial Japan by applying additional *sanctions* after Tokyo joined the *Axis alliance* (1940). Ultimately, the Japanese decision for war at *Pearl Harbor* brought the United States into the conflict. Pearl Harbor meant that *World War II* would complete what World War I had started: revelation of the vast economic and latent military power of the United States to all concerned, including for the first time to most Americans themselves, and the education of its *elite* and population to the enormous responsibility for leadership which comes with *preponderant power*. Despite public pressure to concentrate on the war against Japan, Roosevelt agreed with *Churchill* and *Stalin* to concentrate on defeating Germany first. That decision was not initially popular with the American public, but was one of the most important and sound which Roosevelt ever made. On the other hand, he has been heavily criticized—mostly unfairly—for declaring the *unconditional surrender* policy at *Casablanca* which so affected the final months of the war. Roosevelt is criticized more accurately for distrusting Britain almost as much, and perhaps more on certain issues, as he did Stalin and the Soviet Union. Also, he developed an intense and personal dislike of *Charles de Gaulle*, which had a lasting negative impact on Franco-American relations. Roosevelt negotiated personally at *Tehran* and *Yalta*, for which he has received much criticism for a supposed sell-out of Eastern Europe to Stalin, when all he did was accept to live with the reality of a de facto Soviet *sphere of influence*, as any American president would have had to do. With more justice, he was criticized for overestimating the importance of *Chiang Kai-shek* to China's future and U.S. national interest, and in general for too often basing his foreign policy assessments mainly on personalities. In his last months Roosevelt pushed forcefully for creation of the *United Nations Organization*, 1944–1945.

(4) The Cold War: As World War II ended, the United States was already engaged in the task of *reconstruction*: it hosted the *Dumbarton Oaks*, *San Francisco*, and *Bretton Woods* conferences and was largely responsible for the shape taken by *General Agreement on Tariffs and Trade*, the *International Bank for Reconstruction and Development*, *International Monetary Fund*, and the United Nations. *Harry Truman* actively promoted an American commitment to international economic and political leadership. He endorsed Roosevelt's postwar economic plans and oversaw implementation of a new international financial and trading system. He also took the United States into the United Nations Organization, just weeks after Roosevelt's death. At the *Potsdam Conference*, Truman consulted on nothing less the fate of Europe and even the world. He also told Stalin about the first successful test of the *atomic bomb* and co-issued the *Potsdam Declaration*. Truman was faced with enormous problems of reconstruction of destitute, near-starving and bombed-out continents in Europe and Asia and problems of moral and political engagement and financial and security responsibility on a scale never before, or since, faced by an American president. In the Pacific, Truman needed to make momentous unilateral decisions, especially whether and how to use atomic bombs to end the war against Japan. He made that decision, the most difficult of his presidency, twice: concerning *Hiroshima*, and again with regard to *Nagasaki*.

Aided by a brilliant cast of talented and experienced statesmen, including *Dean Acheson*, *Lucius D. Clay*, and *George Marshall*, Truman oversaw recovery by pushing through postwar loans to Britain and France and, in time, also imaginative, generous, and rapid reconstruction and rehabilitation of the Axis states. In Germany, that was initially done in the teeth of opposition by both France and the Soviet Union, who were keen for a harsh peace and for reparations, in specie or in kind. As the *Cold War* rapidly developed over Germany, Truman was firm. He oversaw commitment of American air power in the *Berlin airlift* to uphold the legality of the Yalta accords and Potsdam decisions on the administrative partition of Berlin and of Germany. More generally, Truman announced and implemented the critically important *Truman Doctrine*, which permanently (though in some ways unwisely) ended U.S. historic diplomatic and military isolation in peacetime and instituted the formative policy of *containment* of the Soviet Union. That set the mold for U.S. Cold War security policy for the next four decades. Containment at first was centered on economic recovery, to be brought about primarily through the *European Recovery Program* and the founding of *NATO* (1949) in Europe and a comparable aid package for Japan. Truman thus oversaw the so-called *reverse course* in U.S. postwar policy on the *zaibatsu* and other features of Japanese national life and economic development and on *denazification* in Germany and the move to instead work closely with *Adenauer* to bring about an independent West Germany tied to the emerging Western alliance and trading system.

Truman's second term was marred domestically by the tragi-farce of *McCarthyism* and in foreign policy in the morass of the *Korean Conflict*. During that war Truman took the courageous decision to fire *Douglas MacArthur* for insubordination and for reckless talk about bombing China with nuclear weapons. At the same time, he both supported and restrained *Chiang Kai-shek* on Taiwan. This post-1945 rejection of the old isolationist tradition and acceptance that the United States was indeed a Great Power, with commensurate obligations to provide enlightened global leadership and international security was not universal, but it was powerfully embraced by the majority. Indeed, Americans sometimes took to their new role and responsibilities with more verve than *prudence*, as during expansion of the Korean Conflict into a war of national liberation of North Korea which entangled them with masses of Chinese infantry.

Globalization of containment and a heightened and forward sense of national mission converted directly to support for protracted political engagement in peripheral areas of Cold War conflict and then, most tragically, also military intervention in the *Vietnam War*. Conflict with the Soviet Union (and China) pervaded nearly all foreign policy during the *Eisenhower* administration, extending into and troubling relations with Latin America as well. During his first term Eisenhower was forced to work hard to preserve presidential discretion in foreign policy from the still isolationist "Taft wing" of his own party, governing often in cooperation with key *Democrats* in the Congress. Secretly, he encouraged trade between Japan and China subsequent to the *Chinese Revolution* (1949). He initially opposed the inclusion of West Germany in NATO, but conceded the point by 1955. He worked constantly for nuclear *arms control* but achieved limited success, mostly because of the unreadiness of the Soviet Union to deal from its position of strategic weakness. Thus, Eisenhower made imaginative proposals such as *Open Skies*, which were accepted decades later when conditions changed for the Soviet Union, only to see them come to naught. A fiscal conservative, Eisenhower kept defense spending low: in percentage terms, his defense budgets were higher than in later years; but that is deceptive as it fails to take into account an absolute increase but relative decline in defense spending as a result of huge increases in social and other government spending after 1961. He also successfully oversaw construction of the *St. Lawrence Seaway* and was a principal architect of the U.S. interstate highway system, both of which contributed greatly to the economic boom of the 1950s.

Eisenhower used *John Foster Dulles* to make tough policy declarations and public threats while he played the role of senior statesman. His administration relied on massive retaliation as its strategic doctrine and was prudent about the use of force in peripheral areas: he warned against becoming involved in another land war in Asia. Thus, although providing logistical support to the French in Indochina and then to the Republic of Vietnam (RVN, South Vietnam), when he left office there were fewer than 600 American advisers in that country and no combat troops. He was not loathe to use force, however: he supported a coup in Guatemala in 1954, sent marines into Lebanon in 1957, and twice threatened China, possibly with nuclear weapons, over *Quemoy and Matsu*. Although he oversaw a continuation of Truman's arms buildup, this did not approach levels reached under his successors. That left an opening for *John F. Kennedy* to (falsely) claim in the 1960 election campaign that Eisenhower had permitted a "missile gap" with the Soviet Union to develop. In his Farewell Address, Eisenhower warned against the rise of a *military-industrial complex*.

Upon taking office, Kennedy immediately inherited Eisenhower's plan for a proxy invasion of Cuba, by anti-*Castro* Cuban exiles supported by the *CIA*, at the *Bay of Pigs*. His greatest test came during the *Cuban Missile Crisis*. He has been alternately praised by historians for cool prudence or damned for escalating that confrontation to extremely dangerous heights. After 1962 Kennedy moved toward a limited thaw in relations with the Soviets, including setting up a *hot line* and signing the *Partial Test Ban Treaty*. Yet, he also presided over the greatest arms buildup to that point in U.S. peacetime history. His policy toward the Third World placed greater overt emphasis on promoting democracy than had his predecessors. It also emphasized economic modernization—both for its own sake and to the end of denying these areas to communist influence and penetration, in an extension of the original logic of the European Recovery Program. Kennedy also set up the *Peace Corps* and tried, with limited success, to reorder relations with Latin America in the *Alliance for Progress*. Yet, he was not loathe to use force, including attempting to have Castro killed.

Kennedy shared the consensus view on the nature of the Cold War and the nature of the threat posed by the Soviet Union and by *communism*. His view of containment, too, was a globalized one: at his Inaugural, he promised that America would "pay any price, bear any burden" in the defense of liberty against communism. Kennedy accepted, at least in part, the *domino theory* and a perceived need to oppose even local communist movements in far-flung corners of Africa and Asia. His more immediate concern was Laos, where the Soviet Union and the Democratic Republic of Vietnam (DRV, North Vietnam) had intervened in contravention of guarantees of Laotian neutrality agreed in the *Geneva Accords*. Although Kennedy inherited a limited commitment to the RVN, he greatly increased U.S. involvement in the war. In the most significant decision of his administration, he approved the coup which cost *Diem* his life and "Americanized" the Vietnam War. Thus, by the time of Kennedy's assassination (November 22, 1963) he had increased U.S. military and other personnel in the RVN over 30-fold (from 500 to 16,500), with some already engaged in combat. Kennedy was, at best, uncertain over what to do about Vietnam and appears just as intent to "stay the course" there as his successors would prove to be. His talk of withdrawal coincided with a view that the war was being won. Yet, on the very morning he was killed, he said: "Without the U.S., South Vietnam would collapse overnight."

The Cold War struggle assumed a more limited quality immediately after the *Cuban Missile Crisis*, and under *Lyndon Johnson*, who kept on most of Kennedy's key advisers and promised to fulfill his mandate, including military support for the RVN. In 1965 Johnson authorized intervention in the Dominican Republic, further eroding the Alliance for Progress. Johnson sought more than he achieved from arms control, but did set in motion the negotiating process which aided the *SALT* breakthroughs by his successors in the 1970s. He was unusually activist in domestic affairs after his landslide mandate in 1964. His legislative record was unparalleled, other than by Franklin Roosevelt, as he passed historic bills on civil rights, social welfare, and other programs which made up his Great Society, though many of these programs failed to achieve their promise. Also in 1965, Johnson began escalating American involvement in the Vietnam War, without ever telling the public the whole truth about this creeping commitment. Vietnam continuously drained his energies and the nation's resources. His conduct of the war was greatly constrained by fear that *escalation* might lead to direct intervention against the United States by China or the Soviet Union, as had happened during the Korean Conflict. As domestic opposition to the war built, Johnson asked for and received advice from the so-called *Wise Men*. They told him he was on the right course and to "stay the course" and continue the fight. In 1968, after the *Tet Offensive*, when he again asked Acheson and the other Wise Men for their views, he was told the country had turned against the war and that he should end it, but he was not told how. Confused, profoundly depressed, and beset by strong challengers for the nomination within his own party, he decided not to run for reelection and to halt the bombing in Vietnam. He left office a deeply distressed man and a widely unpopular, even despised, president. Some later sought to lay blame for the Vietnam quagmire squarely, even solely, at his door. To do so one must ignore a broad consensus within the foreign policy elite, some honorable Cassandras aside, and sustained support for the war by a majority of the American public at least until the shock of Tet.

Richard Nixon was elected president in 1968. Working intimately with *Henry Kissinger*, Nixon's aim was to wind down the war in Vietnam. He hoped thereby to reorient containment policy to its original purpose—blocking Soviet political advances into the key industrialized centers of Asia and Europe, with primary reliance on political support and economic inducements to allies rather than direct military force against the Soviet Union or its proxies. Yet, Nixon feared losing the war in Vietnam, mainly for what it would do to him politically, and he appeared also unable to learn from the prior French or American experience in Indochina. That led him to continue and then to expand Johnson's bombing campaign. Convinced that he could end the war in Vietnam without losing it, Nixon stepped up *Vietnamization* and *pacification* to enable a phased withdrawal, while conducting simultaneous peace talks with the DRV (North Vietnam) in Paris. He understood that he needed cooperation on this from China and the Soviet Union, the only states capable of bringing sufficient pressure to bear on the DRV to get Hanoi to cooperate in allowing an American pullout. Therefore, Nixon developed *détente* with the Soviets after 1970 and made his extraordinary breakthrough trip to China in 1972. To both he offered the lure of American trade and credits, but conditioned on an acceptable settlement in Vietnam. And, taking advantage of the *Sino-Soviet split*, to China he implicitly offered a counterbalance to the regional preponderance of the Soviet Union. Nixon kept up pressure on the DRV by continuing to heavily bomb the north as well as Communist bases in Cambodia and Laos and ultimately by invading Laos and Cambodia (1970) to physically cut the *Hô Chí Minh Trail*, actions for which he was severely but not always fairly criticized at the time, and since. More problematically, he authorized several new rounds of bombing of DRV cities (Linebacker I and II), including a so-called Christmas bombing in 1972 which he claimed forced the DRV back to the peace table in Paris.

On the other hand, Nixon's overall foreign policies of détente with the Soviet bloc and rapprochement with China were not merely designed to end the Vietnam War. They aimed as well at a lasting reduction in tensions with Moscow, and the communist world more generally, and at real arms control and a limit to Soviet *adventurism* in regional conflicts. He also sought to appease growing Western European (especially West German) demands for a new *Ostpolitik* toward the East bloc. He was a strong supporter of Israel, yet played tough with Tel Aviv (and Moscow) in the *Fourth Arab-Israeli War*, when the Soviets threatened to intervene directly to support their Egyptian ally. He supported *Reza Pahlavi*, viewing the Shah's Iran as an island of stability anchoring the whole Middle East. On economic policy, he shifted from *Keynesian* social spending toward fighting *inflation*, and then *stagflation*, and took the United States off the *gold standard* and raised tariffs in the *Nixon shocks* of August 15, 1971. His second term was hamstrung and then destroyed by the *Watergate* scandal. Nixon was the only president to resign (August 9, 1974), which he did in order to avoid impeachment and likely removal from office.

Although the end of U.S. involvement in Indochina forced a reconsideration of means, the main outline of American policy remained a sustained effort to block any Soviet advance, real or perceived, in Europe, Asia, Africa, or the Middle East. Therefore, the use of force by the Soviets in *Afghanistan*, which lay outside their traditional and accepted sphere of influence, provoked a strong U.S. reaction. *Jimmy Carter* began his term with a promise to move promotion of *human rights* to the center of American foreign policy. Many *conservatives*, and older *liberals*, too, met this with derision, arguing that human rights already was at the center of America's world role, as that was what containment of the Soviet Union and anti-communism was really all about. By 1978 Carter had backed away from a policy even he later conceded had not been thought through. He also retreated from his earlier proclamation that U.S. policy was too absorbed with bilateral relations with the Soviet Union and that it should look more to problems of "world order," such as *population* growth or issues of *distributive justice*. His successes were negotiating the *Panama Canal* treaties, facilitating the *Camp David Accords*, finishing the full restoration of relations with China begun by Richard Nixon, and continuing the process begun with the *Helsinki Accords*. However, Carter's handling of U.S.-Soviet relations was weak, even inept. He was unable to gain Senate consent to *SALT II*, was openly stunned by the Soviet invasion of Afghanistan, and hobbled himself with ineffective and politically damaging sanctions introduced in response. Carter was then weighed down by the *hostage crisis* in Iran, which dogged his final year and made him appear indecisive and uncertain. In addition, he faced a prolonged recession, historically high interest rates, and world inflation which followed the OPEC *oil price shock* of 1979 and was also a legacy of deficit spending on the Vietnam War. Probably his greatest accomplishment as president is one of which he was neither proud at the time, nor particularly pleased about: the decision made with the NATO allies in 1979 to carry out a deployment of intermediate-range nuclear missiles in Europe. When later implemented by the Reagan administration, this decision forced the Soviet leadership to reconsider the real-world effects of their bloated and offensive nuclear force structure and eventually also their entire political and economic relationship with the West.

Ronald Reagan took office in 1981, after a landslide over Carter. He followed *monetarism* in his economic policy, while blanket anti-communism formed the core of his approach to security policy. He was not loathe to use limited, unilateral force to advance foreign policy goals in Grenada (1983), Lebanon (1983–1984), and Libya (1986); or indirect force through aid to governments (El Salvador, Guatemala, Honduras); or *covert aid* to insurgents (the *Contras*, Afghan *mujahadeen*, and *guerrillas* in Angola and Mozambique). He relaxed

Carter-era human rights strictures on aid to Third World allies, while increasing them toward the Soviet bloc. His main concern was always the Soviet Union. During his first administration he continued the arms buildup begun in 1978 by Congress and carried over in the final Carter budget, until by 1985 both the U.S. armory and federal deficit were bulging. From 1981 to 1985 there was extreme, though mainly rhetorical, confrontation with Moscow over Afghanistan, Central America, and Poland. Also, a major leadership crisis within NATO occurred in the early 1980s over Pershing and *cruise missile* deployments. Reagan wanted to counter a prior Soviet deployment of SS-20s. At the time, Reagan was widely criticized for avoiding *summits*. He did so as a result of the rapidity with which Soviet leaders were dying and being replaced (*Brezhnev, Andropov,* and *Chernenko* all died between 1982 and 1985), but also because it was his preferred tactic to complete the arms buildup before "negotiating from strength" with Moscow.

When *Gorbachev* assumed power, he and Reagan struck a new chord in American-Soviet relations. Reagan's second term saw a winding down of the confrontation over Afghanistan and major breakthroughs in arms control and resolution of regional disputes. They achieved an *Intermediate-Range Nuclear Forces (INF) Treaty* (December 8, 1987), which eliminated all U.S. and Soviet intermediate ballistic and cruise missiles in Europe. Along with the missiles, nearly 500 U.S. and 1,600 Soviet nuclear warheads were dismantled in the first agreement to eliminate an entire class of nuclear weapons. It was badly marred, however, by the *Iran-Contra scandal* and by federal budget deficits which continued to rise, seemingly out of control. Reagan's more uncritical admirers assert that he "won the Cold War," implying that he did so single-handedly. It is true that the collapse of the outer Soviet empire began on his watch and was surely hastened by several of his policies, notably his *Strategic Defense Initiative*, but such an exclusive claim ignores decades of sustained containment by eight presidents and numerous foreign allies, all of which combined to hem in the Soviet Union until its internal economic and political contradictions led to fissures in its *legitimacy*, which then widened into canyons of social discontent. There had been great division within the United States over Reagan's policies toward and preoccupation with minor states such as Grenada, Libya, and Nicaragua, but the broad thrust of his renewed hard line toward Moscow had been received with wide elite and public support. In 1989 the Cold War began to unravel at breathtaking speed, as the Soviet bloc imploded with remarkably little violence, and *arms control* agreements rather than weapons proliferated. After 45 years of Cold War the world was again obviously and greatly complex and diverse, as it always had been beneath the surface of superpower confrontation. Yet, the world was different, too: *liberal-internationalist* principles of world order, *international law*, and *international organization* all had been installed in the workings of international relations, mainly conducing to a better world, and largely through application of American power in cooperation with its democratic allies.

(5) Post–Cold War: With the *extinction* of the Soviet Union at the end of 1991, relations with the successor state of Russia became genuinely warmer, despite worries about regional conflicts within the old Soviet sphere. In 1990–1991 *George H. Bush* assembled an unprecedented *coalition* to fight the *Gulf War*, parlaying that success into multilateral *peace talks* in the Middle East, but not electoral survival at home. Just before leaving office he also committed U.S. forces to support UN efforts in *famine* relief and social reconstruction in Somalia. Under *Clinton*, the United States faltered briefly on *NAFTA* and at first showed little interest in active involvement in Bosnia. Neither the national will nor the international climate any longer appeared conducive to clear U.S. leadership or intervention: by mid-1994 the American public and Congress had turned solidly against the Somali operation, opposed large-scale intervention in Bosnia, and wanted only limited involvement in restoring democracy in Haiti. Nor did Clinton enunciate a clear security doctrine for future engagement in regional conflicts, despite a deepening crisis with *North Korea* which briefly posed the real possibility of war. After 1995 the administration was more assertive, though in an ad hoc fashion: it intervened in Bosnia, endorsed NATO expansion, and led NATO into war and creation of a multinational *protectorate* in *Kosovo*. It also routinely but sometimes fecklessly used force against minor powers in Africa, Central Asia, and the Balkans and stumbled badly on furthering global free trade. In 2001 a new president, *George W. Bush*, retrenched from the scatter-shot foreign policy positions of the Clinton administration. The United States became far more cautious concerning long-term security relations with China, renewed an emphasis on improved hemispheric relations (especially with Mexico) and promotion of global free trade, and more actively sought a national *ballistic missile defense*, which Russia still opposed rhetorically though not in fact. Even as this important shift in priorities was underway, the *September 11, 2001, terrorist attack* occurred. This prompted Washington to reconsider its force commitments and procurement policies, its deterrent posture, and its active defenses and long-neglected homeland security. Finally, the attack provoked the United States and its core allies to adopt a proactive, anti-terrorist stance of hunting down and destroying terrorist threats with "global reach" wherever they appeared anywhere in the world, a policy shift encapsulated in the *Bush Doctrine*. Just as two generations before, Americans again proved defiant in the face of early defeat, resolute in prosecuting war to ultimate victory, and enormously magnanimous toward the long-suffering peoples of soon-to-be overturned despotic regimes. *See also Lucius Clay; Ulysses S. Grant; Robert E. Lee; William Tecumseh Sherman.*

Suggested Readings: Thomas A. Bailey, *Diplomatic History of the American People* (1980); Cohen, ed., *Cambridge History of American Foreign Relations*, 4 vols. (1993); Alexander De-Conde, *History of American Foreign Policy*, 2 vols. (1978); Norman Graebner, *Foundations of American Foreign Policy* (1985); Norman Graebner, *America As a World Power* (1984); Hunt, Michael H., *Ideology and U.S. Foreign Policy* (1987); Melvyn Leffler, *Preponderance of Power*

(1992); Arthur S. Link et al., *Concise History of the American People* (1984); Samuel Eliot Morison, *Oxford History of the American People,* (1965, 1994); *Oxford History of the United States,* 10 vols. (1928–1999, 1999–); W. Woodruff, *America's Impact on the World, 1720–1970* (1973).

Uniting for Peace Resolution. Passed during the crisis leading to United Nations intervention in the *Korean Conflict,* it authorizes the *United Nations General Assembly* to assemble on 24-hours' notice in an emergency. It has been invoked concerning: the *Suez Crisis* (1956), *Hungarian Uprising* (1956), *Lebanon* crisis (1958), *Congo crisis* (1960), Middle East (1967), *Afghanistan* (1980), *Palestine* (1980), *Namibia* (1981), *Occupied Territories* (1982), *Kuwait* (1990), and *Bosnia* (1992).

units. *Jargon.* Used in *political science* to refer "objectively" to whatever political communities are under study, which nonetheless are almost always the states. *See also Antoine-Henri Jomini; neorealism.*

Universal Declaration of Human Rights. It was adopted by the *United Nations General Assembly,* then meeting in special session in Paris, on December 10, 1948. It is a nonbinding statement of largely *liberal* principles and aspirations, but including as well *social democratic* notions of economic, social, and cultural rights. Some lawyers and activists claim it has achieved the status of *international customary law;* others dispute that claim. *See also International Bill of Human Rights.*

universalism. The view that ethical truths do not depend upon the group or individual upholding them but apply across cultures, as they derive from universal sources, alternately said to be God, human needs or nature, or reason. When applied as an adjective (to an idea, institution, *norm,* principle, or *rule*) it implies near-global acceptance, relevance, scope, or timelessness. *See also cosmopolitan values; critical theory; human rights; Immanuel Kant; natural law; relativism.*

universality (of criminal law). The doctrine that *municipal law* on criminal matters may take note of violations wherever they occur. It is heavily limited in practice. *See also jurisdiction; extraterritoriality; servitudes; territoriality of criminal law.*

Universal Postal Union (UPU). First established as a *public international union* in 1874, in 1947 it became a *specialized agency* of the *United Nations.* It operates under terms of a *convention* which is a model of successful *functionalism* at the international plane. It standardizes postal service and overall makes handling the world's huge volume of public and private mail a remarkable story of international cooperation and success—appearances to the contrary in one's local post office notwithstanding. Its headquarters is in Bern, Switzerland. *See also diplomatic immunity; Spanish Road.*

unrestricted submarine warfare. When *World War I* began, the United States remained *neutral*. As it wished to continue trade with all *belligerents*, it asserted a traditional doctrine of *neutral rights* and narrow respect for the *Declaration of Paris*. However, neutral trading rights clashed with the British and German *blockades*. Furthermore, the Paris code in practice favored Britain's superiority in surface *warships*. It took no account of *submarines* because it had been drafted before their significant development or effective use in naval warfare and because ever since the *Navigation Acts* Britain had been the principal draftsman of the *law of the sea*. Unanticipated by any strategist, it was the German *U-boats*, not *dreadnoughts*, that became the main threat to the *Royal Navy*. In short order, Germany grew desperately dependent on its U-boats to strangle Britain, as both before and after *Jutland* the bulk of its surface navy was bottled up in its Baltic home ports. That neutral merchants were sometimes sunk in the course of U-boat combat was, from the German point of view, simply part of the fortunes of war. Most Americans, not fully appreciating the degree to which the combat in Europe had become a no-holds-barred affair, were outraged. That reaction was aggravated by the failure of U-boats to observe the established rules on *cruiser warfare*, which required warnings to merchant ships and provision of aid to their passengers and crew. Germany ceased these practices after surfaced U-boats were fired upon by armed merchants or rammed. Also, there was hardly room on a World War I submarine for its own crew, let alone *POWs* or *civilians*. This practice led to charges of *piracy* and also inflamed American *public opinion* against Germany, a development greatly encouraged by British propaganda agents secretly and highly effectively at work in the United States.

The British blockade of the *Central Powers* gripped Germany hard by early 1915: by the end of the war nearly 750,000 German civilians would die of starvation as a result of the Allied blockade. The German *High Command*, stymied on land by the failure of its great offensive strategy, the *Schlieffen Plan*, and fighting a tough Russian enemy in the east, ordered all-out submarine warfare. This sharply altered relations with the United States, which had been on a fairly good footing. *Woodrow Wilson* and *William Jennings Bryan* now took a hard line on neutral rights. Then, on May 7, 1915, the passenger liner Lusitania was sunk, off Ireland, leading to a diplomatic crisis which threatened war. Tensions lasted until early 1916 (see *Lusitania Notes*). Other liners were sunk even after Germany made a formal apology for the Lusitania sinking in early 1916. Wilson protested in the strongest terms. Not yet willing to add America to a formidable list of enemies, Germany backed down and restricted its U-boat campaign, even though *Falkenhayn* and *Tirpitz* wished to resume it.

On January 9, 1917, at an Imperial Conference concerning the future conduct of the war, *Hindenburg* and *Ludendorff* rolled what *Bismarck* once called "the iron dice of war." They ordered resumption of all-out submarine warfare, knowing this would tumble the United States into the fight in Europe. This was the great gamble taken by the German High Command: if they defeated Russia in the east and starved Britain into submission in the west, they thought they could force France to terms before an aroused United States brought its millions and its industrial might to bear and decided the conflict in favor of the *Allied and Associated Powers*. On February 1, 1917, the U-boat war duly resumed. Meanwhile, the British gave Wilson a secret intercept, the famous *Zimmermann Telegram*, and on March 15th the United States began to arm its merchant fleet. On April 2nd, enraged and convinced that he could delay no more, Wilson asked Congress for a *declaration of war* on Imperial Germany. The U-boat onslaught was terrible. Sinkings rose dramatically until Allied adoption of the *convoy* system in April. After the war, a number of U-boat captains were brought up on *war crimes* charges, but it was a desultory process and they were all allowed to "escape" by their German jailors.

No amendments were made to the rules of cruiser warfare between the wars, partly because the British thought they had ensured an end to the Kriegsmarine in the *Treaty of Versailles* (1919). Also, the German fleet had been scuttled at Scapa Flow. Britain had then vitiated its own interest by accepting the *Anglo-German Naval Agreement* in 1935. *Hitler* helped save the British from themselves by concentrating on building superbattleships and otherwise restoring the German surface fleet, when he should have been building submarines. Admiral *Karl Dönitz* had other ideas. He headed a secret group within the German high command which spent the 1920s in U-boat research and planning. When the Anglo-German Naval Agreement lifted the U-boat ban contained in the Versailles Treaty, Dönitz oversaw construction of the new fleet. At the start of *World War II*, Nazi Germany adopted a policy of unrestricted submarine warfare from the first moment. The result was the hugely important *Battle of the Atlantic*. This time, *isolationist* opinion in the United States militated against protest, as many Americans became convinced that the best way to stay out of Europe's latest war was not to support claims of neutral rights against any belligerent. People and goods therefore sailed at their own risk. After the war, Dönitz was tried at *Nuremberg* as a major war criminal on the charge that he had ordered submarine captains to ignore the rules of cruiser warfare and not to stop to rescue crew from ships they sank. He was only censured for that order, however; his 10-year sentence was for planning a war of *aggression*—the lightest sentence received by any defendant. Even hypocrisy has its limits: immediately upon entry into the Pacific War, in late 1941, the United States had quietly adopted a policy of "sink on sight" of all Japanese shipping in the Pacific theater and had then carried this out to devastating effect from 1942 to 1945. The British, also, had employed sink-on-sight tactics with their submarines in the Mediterranean and elsewhere. *See also Third Ypres.*

Untermenschen. "Lesser (literally, "under") men." In *Nazi* race theory, the non-*Aryan* peoples and races, such as Jews or *Slavs*, considered racially and culturally inferior to the so-called *Herrenvolk. See also Friedrich Nietzsche.*

untouchability. In *Hinduism*—and specifically in the classical *caste system* of the Vedic tradition of four "varna" classes of brahman, kshatriya, vaishya, and shudra, each ranked morally and socially by the degree of "pollution" which attached to its members at birth—the class of untouchables developed later, as a lower-ranking fifth caste or "out caste" ("panchamas"). These were originally shudra ("dasas") who were also Hindus, but fell outside the four varna categories because they served in occupations considered spiritually polluting, including slaughterhouses, tanneries, night soil clearance, and so forth, or they were forest dwellers who lived wholly outside the village structure and caste system. In harsher times and areas, "outcastes" were required to carry small bells to warn devout Hindus of their "polluting presence." One could easily slip into this status from the shudra caste through economic misfortune which forced one into a "polluting" occupation. Elevation from the outcaste state was much harder, possible only through devotion to duty ("dharma") or, in later centuries, through entry into a respectable military caste such as the *Rajputs.* Any rebellion against servility would build up evil "karma" and condemn the rebel to more earthly suffering in future lives.

Deeply abused and openly discriminated against for millennia as a result of these doctrines and social mores, some 50 million or more untouchables were finally brought into India's national politics (and renamed "harijans," or "children of God") by *Mohandas Gandhi.* Many in the top leadership of the *Congress Party* opposed this emphasis on reform of untouchability and uplift of the harijans, considering it an unwarranted distraction from the primary goal of national independence from British rule—and for some, also as an interference with a traditional social hierarchy of which they privately approved. Gandhi was surely both inspired and right, however, to insist upon Indians reforming themselves as a prerequisite to, and an integral part of, making a new nation. In terms of Hindu theology, Gandhi looked past the multiple origins of the caste system, including its distantly past but real racial component, to argue idealistically that there was no proper basis in Hinduism for a fifth caste, and that harijans should instead be considered as shudra. Believing all work was honorable and that caste was essentially a designation of occupation, he argued for a change in moral regard for the social value of even the most menial and "spiritually polluting" physical tasks. To make this point, he and his followers, of whatever educational attainment or caste background, spun humble cloth, fed goats, emptied bed pans and cleaned toilets, and freely mixed with, ate with, and touched "untouchables."

Of course, attitudes rooted in many centuries of Indian history did not change overnight, but slowly they did begin to change following Gandhi's inspiration and model. Harijans were separately represented at the *Round*

Table Conferences as among the "depressed classes," where they won a guarantee of proportional representation in any provincial parliaments and were made—over Gandhi's strenuous objections—a separate electorate. Untouchability was made illegal in postindependence, secular India (1955), though it remained a widespread social practice. In the 1990s harijans gained a large share of state jobs through a federal affirmative action program, along with "set-asides," or reserved public contracts, causing much resentment among other castes and social classes. In 1999 large-scale violence against harijans by other castes occurred in parts of India. At the turn of the twenty-first century, their numbers had grown to some 150 million. From the 1970s the secular and more expansive term "dalit" ("oppressed") was widely used in place of Gandhi's "harijans." This classification comprised close to one-third of India's population.

Suggested Readings: A. L. Basham, *The Wonder That Was India* (1963); John Keay, *India: A History* (2000); Percival Spear, ed., *Oxford History of India*, 4th ed. (1981); Burton Stein, *A History of India* (1998); Stanley Wolpert, *A New History of India*, 6th ed. (2000).

Upper Canada. A British *colony*, 1791–1840, comprising southern Ontario and named for its inland location on the *St. Lawrence River*. It received the bulk of the migrating *United Empire Loyalists* after the *American Revolution*. It was briefly invaded by American forces during the *War of 1812*. It was the locale of a failed rebellion against the British in 1837 which had eclectic support from Irish-Americans (*Fenians*) and some northerners. *See also Lower Canada; William Lyon Mackenzie*.

Upper Peru. "Alto Perú." The eighteenth-century name for what is today Bolivia. It was also known as "Charcas."

Upper Volta. Former name of *Burkina Faso*.

uranium. *See Auzou strip; Axis; nuclear weapons; plutonium; radiological weapons*.

Uruguay. Settled by Europeans later than most South American areas, the Spanish did not begin deliberate settlement or displace the Indian population until 1625. Portuguese southward encroachment from Brazil was violently resisted and ended by the Spanish in 1724. Like other Latin states, Uruguay rebelled against Spain during the *Napoleonic Wars*. There was periodic fighting from 1810 until effective *independence* in 1825, with full *sovereignty* coming in 1828 after a period of contested government between Brazil and Argentina. In the case of Uruguay, the independence struggle thus also involved breaking free of Argentine control and avoiding Brazilian conquest. When this was achieved, Uruguay became a *buffer zone* between Brazil and Argentina, though its ties were clearly closer to the latter. Uruguay was split by civil war between

Blancos and Colorados, 1830–1851, which ended only with Argentine intervention. In 1864 Brazil invaded Uruguay to force it to pay *compensation* for *damages* incurred during the civil war. This sparked the *War of the Triple Alliance* (1864–1870). The liberal Colorado Party ruled Uruguay without interruption for 86 years (1872–1958), until defeated by its ancient rival the Blancos. After 1963 a left-wing *guerrilla* group, the Tupemaros (named for *Túpac Amaru II*), conducted a random, anarchic campaign of *terrorism* which was not entirely put down until the late 1970s, and then at considerable cost to civil liberties as the military took effective control, 1973–1985, and conducted a campaign of counterterror and extrajudicial killings. The economy declined through much of the 1960s and 1970s, and Uruguay's external debt rose with the *oil shocks* and a falloff in *foreign direct investment* as a result of the ongoing *guerrilla* campaign. Civilian rule was restored in 1985. Uruguay made better economic, political, and *human rights* progress as its larger, surrounding neighbors also returned to civilian rule. In 1991 Uruguay joined *Mercosur*, a regional *free trade* association led by Argentina and Brazil.

Suggested Readings: Burns E. Bradford, *Latin America*, 6th ed. (1994); Thomas Skidmore, *Modern Latin America* (1997).

Uruguay Round (1986–1993). The eighth round of GATT negotiations. It was to have ended in 1990, but lasted to the end of 1993. It brought the hitherto excluded sectors of *agriculture, services* (worth $4 trillion in 1993), and intellectual property under the GATT. It also reformed GATT's institutions and further reduced general *tariffs*. Additional features included: an agreement on farm trade which replaced *quotas* with tariffs ("tariffication"); major cuts in tariffs on tropical produce; a 10-year phaseout of tariffs on *textiles* and *clothing* (an end to the multifiber arrangement which previously managed trade in these areas); weak, but additional, rules on *anti-dumping laws* and *subsidies*; and an effort to limit use of *voluntary export restraints* (VERs) and other *nontariff barriers* (NTBs), such as import *investment* and local procurement rules. Lastly, there was discussion of transforming GATT into (and renaming it) a Multilateral Trade Organization. Entrenched disagreements and a papered-over, last-minute compromise between the United States and the *European Union* reduced the planned freeing of financial *services*; kept very high tariffs on agricultural imports; and excluded films and television ("audio-visuals") from the agreement on the basis of a French assertion of the need to protect national "culture" (language, film, and printing).

Urundi. Former name of *Burundi.*

USSR. *See Soviet Union.*

Ussuri River clashes (1966 and 1969). *See Sino-Soviet split.*

Uštaše. A Croat *fascist* and *nationalist* movement which collaborated with the Nazi occupation of Yugoslavia in a *puppet state* in Croatia, 1941–1945. The Uštaše pursued a number of quixotic projects, including splitting the Serbo-Croatian language. Mainly the Uštaše pursued *genocide* and *ethnic cleansing* against Jews, Gypsies, Muslims, and Serbs. They massacred as many as they could of both the *Chetniks* and *Tito's* Communist *partisan* units, who answered tit-for-tat. They may have murdered as many as 500,000 in all, in their *concentration camp* at Jasenovac. They fought a war-within-a-war against other Yugoslavs during *World War II*. After *liberation*, 1944–1945, Tito had some 200,000 Uštaše hunted down and killed in reprisal.

U Thant (1909–1974). Burmese and world statesman. *Secretary General* of the *United Nations*, 1961–1971. He succeeded *Dag Hammarskjöld* when the latter was killed during the *Congo crisis*, which U Thant finally helped *mediate* to an end in 1964. He also oversaw the sending of UN *peacekeeping* forces to *Cyprus* that year. However, the limits of his office were made clear during the *Cuban Missile Crisis*, the *Third Arab-Israeli War*, the *Nigerian Civil War*, the *Vietnam War*, and other major conflicts where he exercised little influence.

Uthman dan Fodio (1754–1817). "Shehu." "Commander of the Faithful." Spiritual leader of the great nineteenth-century *jihad* by the *Fulbe* of West Africa, and first sultan of *Sokoto*. Born in Gobir, one of the lesser *city-states* that housed a new monarchy which had only recently expanded its control over the local *Hausa* peasantry, Uthman studied in the *Tuareg* desert capital of Agades before becoming tutor to the Gobir King, Bawa, who disappointed him with his lack of personal piety. In 1804 Uthman and his followers retreated to a small village—perhaps consciously, but certainly symbolically, mimicking the Prophet's "Hegira," or flight from the pagans of *Mecca* in 622 C.E. Fulbe and some Tuareg warriors, *mujahadeen* filled with piety and intent on *plunder*, gathered around the great mallam (teacher) and urged him to make a *jihad* against Gobir, a *holy war* of return as Muhammad had done in Mecca. The target would be the moral laxity of the rich, Hausa cities—which were Muslim, but could be characterized at a minimum as lapsed, from the point of view of such desert devouts. There was social revolution afoot, too. Uthman was supported by lower class Hausa intent on breaking centuries-old labor bondage in the agricultural slave system which supported the Hausa city-states, and others who resented the newly imposed rule of Gobir. The warriors gathered, and Uthman sent them out to conquer in the name of Allah and with his blessing: Zaria fell in 1804; Kano and Katsina, the major Hausa trading cities, in 1807; and Gobir submitted in 1808. After his armies overran the major Hausa cities, Uthman retired to scholarship, settled in Sokoto, and left further conquest to his sons. War between and among the Hausa, Fulbe, and Tuareg continued for decades. Some Hausa peasants, enjoying their new freedom, did not submit to the new theocracy until the

1830s, and the Tuareg remained fiercely independent to the north and occupied with a jihad of their own. Uthman's influence was felt widely throughout more than a dozen successor emirates—including into northern *Oyo*—
and well into the twentieth century.

Suggested Reading: Murray Last, *The Sokoto Caliphate* (1967).

uti possidetis. An ancient principle of *international law* which calls for respect
for inherited *frontiers*. It originated in efforts by the *Roman Empire* to settle
outstanding *border* disputes and legally dispose of conquered territory. During
the era of European overseas expansion it was adapted to endorse *de facto*
possession of territory as a legitimate basis for *sovereign* claims, in order to
avoid or resolve disputes among competitive colonial powers. It was adapted
again in Latin America after independence (c. 1825) to forbid European re-
colonization of even uninhabited parts of that continent based upon claims
of "effective occupation" of so-called *territorium nullius*. Secondarily, uti possidetis was invoked to resolve boundary conflicts among the *successor states*
to the Spanish Empire in the Americas. This originally subsidiary purpose
spread, to became the primary function of the doctrine in the twentieth century during the *decolonization* of Africa and Asia, and still later concerning
the successor states of the former *Soviet Union*. In sum, the principle seeks to
secure international legal acceptance of extant administrative boundaries as
international borders at the moment a territory becomes independent. Once
a new state comes into existence uti possidetis is displaced by the principle
of *territorial integrity*.

utopian. Any scheme, proposal, or idea based upon imagined conditions of
economic, legal, political, or social perfection. Usage is almost always pejorative, implying an intellectual primitivism untempered by hard realities. The
word entered the language with publication of "Utopia" (1516) by Thomas
More (1478–1535), a book which described an imaginary island whose inhabitants lived harmonious lives under perfect laws. More coined the word,
which is a Greek pun meaning "no place." Similarly, Samuel Butler entitled
his 1872 "utopian" work "Erewhon" ("nowhere," spelled backwards). These
works of fiction had many imitators in many languages. Tragically, they also
had would-be imitators in the real world. And real-world experience of attempted utopias—of *Robespierre's* "Republic of Virtue," or Stalin's *collectivized*
Soviet Union, or *Mao's* China—led to another new word, the antonym of
utopia, which is "dystopia." These are evil or negative utopias, inevitably
corrupted utopias such as depicted famously and brilliantly in the novel
"1984" and the equally luminous satire "Animal Farm," both by George Orwell (1903–1950). As Orwell shows so well, all would-be utopias are inherently coercive and become more so as the gap between ideal construction
and real-world effort widens. Bad builders, utopians ineluctably turn to blam-

ing their materials: the "crooked timbers of humanity." *See also conservatism; fundamentalism; Khmers Rouges; liberalism; Marxism; Russia; Taliban.*

utopian socialism. This derisory term was applied by *Karl Marx* to all non-*Marxist* visions of new social relations claiming to be *socialist*, especially those which called for a voluntary shift from unregulated early *capitalism* to more cooperative methods of production, and various schemes of collective endeavor and ownership. He used this derision to elevate his own theories, which he claimed derived from scientific insight into the "laws of history" which predicted an ineluctable movement toward violent *class struggle*. Among the notables so dismissed were French thinkers Claude Henri Saint Simon (1760–1825) and François Marie Fourier (1772–1837) and the Welsh reformer Robert Owen (1771–1858). However, by the end of the twentieth century it was *democratic socialists* who fairly claimed a record of real-world political achievement and humane accomplishment, contrary to the appalling dystopias constructed by hard-line Marxists in Cambodia, China, and throughout the *Soviet bloc*.

Utrecht, Treaty of (1713). A singular name often used for a collection of treaties negotiated between 1713 and 1714, including Utrecht (1713) and Rastadt (1714), which put an end to the ambitions of *Louis XIV*. Together, they gave *Gibraltar* to England and gravely weakened *New France* by also giving England *Newfoundland*, Nova Scotia (*Acadia*), and title to the vast *Hudson's Bay* region. The Dutch gained a measure of security and independence from France. Permanent separation of the Spanish and French monarchies was confirmed (the *casus belli* of the *War of the Spanish Succession*); the Protestant succession in England was formalized; and Spain lost the *Spanish Netherlands* and additional territories in Italy (Naples, Sardinia) to the *Austrian Empire*. In the east, *Frederick II* was confirmed in the right to style himself king and his Prussian lands a kingdom and gained some new lands into the bargain. Louis' ambitions for *hegemony* were utterly frustrated, and English power was henceforth ascendant: over the rest of the century, much of what was left of the French empire overseas would pass to England. Moreover, France was exhausted and would not try for domination in Europe again until its power was inflated by the *French Revolution* and its better sense again dazzled by *Napoleon I*.

Uzbekistan. This region of Central Asia was overrun by the *Mongols* under the "Great Khan," Ghengis Khan himself, in the thirteenth century. It subsequently became the center of an independent Mongol empire (under the Timurids, descendants of *Tamerlane*) which held sway over the Turkmen, Tadjik, and other Central Asian peoples. In the sixteenth through eighteenth centuries it broke into separate *feudal* Khanates. Thus weakened, it was conquered by, and incorporated into, the *Russian Empire* in a series of *expansionist* wars in the nineteenth century. Held in the Russian Empire by the *Red Army* under the *Bolsheviks*, it was briefly administratively joined with Tajikistan within the *Soviet Union*, before becoming a separate "autonomous republic" in 1925. It declared *independence* after a failed *coup* attempt in Moscow in August 1991, but was not widely *recognized* as *sovereign* until December 25, 1991, when the Soviet Union became *extinct*. The most populous of the Central Asian republics, Uzbekistan regards itself as the historic and cultural leader of the whole region—an image of its role not necessarily shared by other Central Asians. Upon independence the old Uzbek *apparatchiki* retained power. In 1993 they joined Russia in sending troops into Tajikistan. Uzbekistan's post-Soviet regime also shared with Russia an antipathy to Muslim *fundamentalism*: Islamic parties were banned and political opposition generally repressed. In 1994 it signed an agreement with Kazakhstan allowing freer movement of *labor, goods, and services*. In the late 1990s it faced an Islamist *guerrilla* opposition in the countryside, based among the Uzbek population of Tajikistan. This was partly brought on by internal repression and in part externally sponsored by the fundamentalist *Taliban* in Afghanistan. *See also Aral Sea;* cordon sanitaire.

Suggested Readings: *Journal of Central Asia*; S. A. M. Adshead, *Central Asia in World History* (1994); Martha B. Olcott, *Central Asia's New States* (1996).

V

V-1 and V-2 rockets (*Vergeltungswaffe*). "Reprisal (or vengeance) weapon."
The V-1 was a subsonic "flying bomb" (a crude precursor to the *cruise missile*);
the V-2 was the first true *ballistic missile*. Both were developed by *Nazi* scientists at *Peenemünde* during *World War II*. They were used as terror weapons
against British cities before the invasion of Normandy and then to hammer
the port of Antwerp after its liberation by the invading *Allies* in 1944. Some
35,000 V-1s were produced by slave laborers worked to death in underground
factories located in converted mines. As a result of their limited range, shortened further by the Allied advance inland during 1944, only about 9,000
were fired on Great Britain. Nearly half of these slow "buzz bombs" were shot
down by fighters or antiaircraft guns before reaching their targets. About
1,300 V-2s hit London during 1944–1945, fired mainly from the Netherlands.
Winston Churchill considered using *poison gas* to retaliate, but was dissuaded
from taking this course. The Germans were near completion of the world's
first *ICBM*, the revolutionary A10 which had a range of 2,800 miles and
might have been able to hit even the United States, when their factories and
research facilities were overrun. The final barbarian act of Nazi overseers was
to burn alive more than 1,000 slave laborers. The German rocket program
was an expensive military failure, but it greatly contributed to the later missile
programs of the victorious Allies: after the war, captured V-2s were shipped
to the United States, United Kingdom, and Soviet Union, to form the basis
of early *Cold War* research on missiles and rockets. *See also Werner von Braun;
space age.*

validity. The degree to which a *treaty* is binding on states giving their *signature* and *ratification*. Theoretically, treaties are fully binding. Yet, circumstances may arise which erode this quality and deplete treaty obligations. Thus, the validity of treaties may be brought into question if the person(s) who negotiated them are later shown to have lacked proper authority, or to have exceeded their authority, to act on behalf of the *states* concerned. Treaties also may be invalidated: if forced upon one party (agreed "under duress"); if bribery is discovered to have influenced the agent(s) of one state; if one of the parties lacks standing under *international law* to make a binding agreement (e.g., a *tribe*); if treaty rights of a third state, stemming from a prior agreement, are abridged without that state's *consent*; if there is a fundamental conflict with established, basic principles of *international law*; if the agreement aims at an illegal or immoral object; or due to *error. See also* clasula rebus sic stantibus; pacta sunt servanda.

Valley Forge (1777–1778). *See American Revolution; Marquis de Lafayette; George Washington.*

Valois dynasty. The *Capetian dynasty* ruled much of France directly from its founding by Hugh Capet in 987 until 1328, when the House of Valois, a branch of the Capetians based in the province of Valois, took the throne. A Valois monarch then governed France from 1328 (Philip VI) to 1589, or from the *Hundred Years' War* (1337–1453) from which the modern nation-state of France finally emerged, to the end of the French *Wars of Religion*. Having done with the English by 1453, for the next 150 years the Valois led France in a prolonged struggle against *Habsburg* domination of Europe. In 1589 the last of Catherine de Médici's three royal sons, and the last Valois king of France, King Henri III (1551–1589), was murdered. The path to the French throne was thus finally clear for the head of a rival branch of the Capetian family tree, the House of *Bourbon,* to supplant the House of Valois: the great *Henri IV* became the first Bourbon king of France.

Vance-Owen peace plan. *See Third Balkan War.*

Vandenberg, Arthur (1884–1951). U.S. *Republican* senator and statesman. Originally a leader among Senate *isolationists*, during *World War II* he was persuaded by events (and by *Franklin Roosevelt*) of the need for an American commitment to postwar *reconstruction* and *security* through the *United Nations*. He served on the U.S. delegation at *San Francisco*, authored the *Vandenberg Resolution*, and steered financial and other support in the Senate to back the *Truman Doctrine* and the *European Recovery Program*. His death left Congressional Republicans bereft of conservative-internationalist leadership, even as the party captured the *White House* for the first time in 20 years.

Vandenberg Resolution (June 11, 1948). It paved the way for U.S. participation in *NATO*, relying in part on Article 51 of the *Charter of the United Nations*, enshrining a right of collective *self-defense*. With *Arthur Vandenberg's* support it passed with just four votes against. That took most *Cold War* issues out of the 1948 presidential campaign and laid the basis for two decades of *bipartisan* foreign policy. *See also containment.*

Van Diemen's Land. The original British name for Tasmania, changed in 1855. It was later joined to Australia. *See also penal settlement.*

vanguard. (1) In military usage: Troops at the head of a moving army. (2) In *Marxism-Leninism*: A ruthless, self-designated revolutionary *elite* which guides the *proletariat* and wields power once the *revolution* succeeds. *See also Four Cardinal Principles; Vladimir Lenin.*

Vanuatu. "Our Land." Formerly the New Hebrides. In 1887 France and Britain agreed to a Naval Commission to administer the islands. In 1906 they set up a joint *condominium* to forestall *annexation* by Germany. This island group thus divided into *Anglophone* and *Francophone* communities, as full colonial administration and education systems took hold. The 1970s saw belated national sentiment overcome linguistic barriers. It was the only *South Pacific* territory to witness violence during the *decolonization* process, and then only on Espiritu Santo and Tannu, where Papua New Guinea sent troops to repress an attempt at *secession* in 1980. *Independence* came under the name Vanuatu, which for a time was one of the most *radical* of the region's *microstates*. Stiffly anti-nuclear, until 1988 it was the only regional member of the *Nonaligned Movement*. It also opened relations with Libya, Cuba, Nicaragua, North Korea, the PLO, and Vietnam, then all Soviet allies or friendly to the *Soviet Union*, and twice expelled a French ambassador, in 1981 and 1987. Vanuatu claims two dependent islands of, and supports independence for, the French possession of *New Caledonia*. Despite this diplomatic tweaking, France remains an *aid* donor.

variable. In traditional statistical analysis this terminology is used without pretension. In methodologically pretentious social science, however, it is *jargon* intended to give a "scientific" veneer to works which often have minimal or no value. Thus, in *quantitative* approaches to the study of international relations, a "variable" is anything apt or able to vary, which is subject to measurement, and which might bear a causal relation to another variable one is attempting to explain. The "dependent variable" is any phenomenon for which an interpretive hypothesis is proposed; or, in plain English, it is the "effect"—some social, economic, or political event—which one tries to explain by examining its underlying *causation*. The "independent variable" is the main agent thought to explain change (variation) in the dependent variable; in other words, it is the primary cause proposed to explain the effect one seeks to understand. A supporting role is played by "intervening variables" which modify the relation of the independent variable to the dependent variable; that is, secondary or tertiary causes are suggested to explain changes in the effect (the thing being studied) which cannot be traced directly to the primary cause. "Correlation analysis" is the quantified search for associations between a dependent variable and an independent variable over time, which proponents believe suggests a causal relationship. When more than one independent variable is used the technique is called, prosaically enough, "multiple correlation analysis." (This begs the question, of course, of whether a mere correlation is also a cause.) An "autonomous variable" is one not entirely dependent on "objective factors" being studied, but also on immeasurable vagaries of *volition*, and psychological, religious, ideological, or other thoroughly human motivation. Similarly, an "indeterminate solution" is a term resorted to by researchers when the outcomes in their models cannot be predicted owing to random changes in the variables (in other words, it means they are left just guessing, but can't admit it). A "control experiment" is when one variable is supposedly "held constant" (considered unvarying, which ought to mean it is not a variable) in order to observe and measure the effects it has on all other variables. When social scientists discuss—usually in somber tones and with deadly earnestness—how to "operationalize a variable" they mean no more, though very often they achieve a great deal less, than that they think they have found some way to "measure" and "test" the relations of cause and effect they suspect are in play and about which they have proposed a set of best educated guesses ("modeled the problem"). Since most of these points are seldom made clear—because to do so would expose too many research agendas as little more than "formal modeling" of what is already known, or obvious, or trivial—legions of graduate students continue to suffer unduly from intellectual and methodological confusion caused by this *obscurantist* terminology. *See also falsification; null hypothesis; rational choice theory; scientism.*

variable sum game. *See game theory.*

Vasco da Gama (1469–1524). *See Age of Exploration; Sri Lanka.*

vassal state. A synonym for *puppet state.*

Vatican. "State of the City of the Vatican." This legally unique statelet occupies 108.7 acres within central Rome. Its population consists of the residents and employees of Vatican City, which is the rump of the former *Papal States* still controlled by the *Catholic Church.* Its military is strictly ceremonial—Swiss Guards, a pale reminder of days before and during the *Renaissance* when warrior popes led *mercenary* armies and were a power on the Italian peninsula, and beyond. Its major international associations are the OSCE and the *Universal Postal Union*. It also maintains an *observer mission* at the United Nations. The Vatican has a small fire department, police force, and jail, but the latter was so little in demand at the end of the twentieth century it had been filled with overflow books. The last reported murder in the Vatican was in 1848. The attempted *assassination* of Pope *John Paul II* in 1981 took place in St. Peter's Square, which is the only part of the Vatican its police regularly patrol. In this case, the investigation was beyond the means of the Vatican, so at its request the crime was investigated by Italian police and courts. To investigate possible crimes within the Vatican which have external connections, such as the Vatican Bank (Banco Ambrosiano) scandal in 1982 in which illegal financial transactions and networks snaked in and out of the Vatican, Italian police must first obtain official permission from Vatican officials.

In 1871 the Papal States were annexed by Italy, causing a 58-year breach in relations between the papacy and Italian state. An annual allowance set aside by Italy for the popes remained in *escrow* all through this quarrel, unclaimed as a matter of disputed principle. On February 11, 1929, *concordats* (the *Lateran Treaties*) were signed recognizing The State of the City of the Vatican as a *city-state* distinct from Rome and Italy, and *establishing* Catholicism as the state religion of Italy; this clause was annulled in 1976. The *sovereign* of the Vatican is the pope, who is pledged to perpetual *neutrality* in temporal affairs; that is, neutrality concerning the merits of international disputes among nations over issues such as territory and legal or military conflict, with the exception of performing *arbitration* when asked to do so. That is a request made less commonly than previously, though it can be important still, as during the *Beagle Channel dispute*. As spiritual leader of a billion Catholics, any pope has moral and political influence beyond the sharp limits of the Vatican. However, this influence has often been limited by doctrinal disputes or even *schism* within the Church and by external criticism over selective moral stances. Any claim to papal authority on moral issues of international significance was severely tested during the *Holocaust*, when *Pius XII* failed to speak forthrightly against *Nazism* and *anti-Semitism*. On the other hand, the Vatican conducted an anti-*communist* crusade after the founding of the *Soviet Union* and all during the *Cold War*.

General, post-*Westphalia* self-denial of involvement in *temporal* issues does not prevent Vatican comment when secular laws touch upon "matters of faith, morals, or doctrine." Nor has it prevented the establishment of *diplomatic relations* with more than 100 states. Initially, the United States abjured relations—barred by an 1867 Act of Congress, arising mainly from anti-Catholic bigotry. During *World War II* a special U.S. envoy resided in Rome and reported directly to *Franklin Roosevelt*, who needed papal help to prepare American Catholics to accept *Lend-Lease* to the Soviet Union. The United States did not establish diplomatic relations with the Vatican until 1984.

Other "Protestant" powers which had severed relations with the papacy over one quarrel or another pertaining to the *Protestant Reformation*—among them Denmark, Great Britain, Norway, and Sweden—established full diplomatic relations with the Vatican in 1982. Papal relations with China were sorely tested in the sixteenth century over the *rites controversy*, and in the nineteenth century over the activities of *missionaries*. China's relations with the Vatican State were severed in 1951, after the *Chinese Revolution* of 1949. In 2000 the Vatican's move to canonize "martyred" missionaries provoked a bitter Chinese response. Strained relations with Israel improved in the 1980s, with a papal apology by John Paul II for the historic anti-Semitism of the Church and many Catholics, and over deferral of resolution of the status of *Jerusalem*. In 1993 Israel and the Vatican agreed to move toward mutual recognition, but relations deteriorated again in 2000 over the Vatican's push to beatify (a stage on the road to canonization and sainthood) Pius XII. Relations with Russia—previously strained by the official atheism of the Soviet state—improved when religious freedom was restored after 1991, but were strained again in 2001 when Pope John Paul II visited Ukraine and was greeted with hostility by many *Orthodox*, and was refused an invitation to Russia by the Patriarch in Moscow. In 1993 the Vatican publicly criticized Sudan for severe persecution, enslavement, and indeed *genocide* of Christians by a *fundamentalist* Islamic regime. The Vatican was also closely interested in the independence movement and fate of *East Timor*, where most of Indonesia's Catholic minority lived. *See also extraterritoriality; Holy See; Roman Question; Sovereign Military Order of Malta; United Nations Conferences on Population; Vatican Councils.*

Suggested Readings: Eric Hanson, *The Catholic Church in World Politics* (1987); Thomas Reese, *Inside the Vatican* (1996).

Vatican Councils. There were two great *Ecumenical Councils* in the modern era, each with a significant impact on the lives of hundreds of millions of people in dozens of countries.

(1) First Vatican Council (1869–1870): Its most controversial doctrine was proclamation of the "infallibility" of the popes "on matters of faith and doctrine" (the notion that God would not let the "true faith" fall into theological error). That was a refined and restated version of an old idea, one long in tension with a competing and even older (fourth through eighth centuries) assertion of conciliar infallibility. It thus hardened an already deep doctrinal division, rooted in the original *schism* over papal authority, from the *Orthodox Church*. It also led to new and sustained conflict with secular authorities in several nations, especially Prussia. It was followed by the incorporation of Rome into Italy, which began a 58-year dispute between the popes and the Italian state, settled only with negotiation of the *Lateran Treaties* (1929). The first Vatican Council may be understood as a constitutional response by the Church hierarchy (the pope and Curia) to the insistent challenge of secular modernity

and the growing attraction of democratic and national ideas for Catholic laity. It was hoped by the Curia that the faithful would rally around a centralized papacy which governed in doctrinal and administrative matters. For this, the role of *concordats* was highly significant.

(2) Second Vatican Council (1962–1965): Modernist calls for local and national diversity within the Church had been temporarily repressed by the infallibility edict of the First Vatican Council and, later, by the unifying challenge of international *communism* (the problem of *fascism* was another matter). Socially and politically activist, lay Catholicism resurfaced after World War II and turned to questions about Church doctrine as well, in spite of strenuous efforts by the Curia at containment of doctrinal challenge and dissent. The Second Vatican Council broke sharply with the old policy and sought instead a fundamental reform and modernization of the *Catholic Church* to meet growing demands by lower-ranking clergy and many lay Catholics for enhanced involvement in governance, and for "greater relevance" of doctrine to the great changes and apparent new requirements of modern life. The Second Council adapted by making changes to liturgy, moving from Latin to vernacular languages in services, and stressing *ecumenism* in relations with other Christian faiths. It did not retreat from the claims for papal authority asserted in 1870, which left the door open to more *conservative* Popes to reassert central authority in later years. Moreover, the reform pope who called the Council, *John XXIII*, died early. He was succeeded by two centralizing, *authoritarian* popes: Paul VI and *John Paul II*. Whether the reforms of Vatican II succeed in the longer term is still a matter of evolving history. In short, the centuries-long struggle of the papacy against urges to local autonomy and the formation of national churches continues, just beneath the surface unity of the modern Catholic world. *See also Kulturkampf; Lord Acton; Pius IX.*

Suggested Reading: Adrian Hastings, ed., *Modern Catholicism* (1991).

Vattel, Emerich de (1714–1767). Swiss philosopher and jurist. He had some experience as a *diplomat*, serving (1746–1758) as minister in Bern in behalf of the Saxon court. His permanent influence arose from a single work of philosophy and law, "Droit des gens" (1758). This was a treatise fundamentally on *natural law* which popularized and publicized the partially *Grotian* ideas about international law of Samuel Freiherr von Puffendorff (1632–1694), who had stressed the naturalist side of Grotius' work, and the sharp rationalism of *Frederick the Great's* favorite international lawyer, Johann Christian von Wolff (1679–1754). Vattel directly applied the natural law tradition to consideration of the relation of *sovereigns* to the *nations* they governed, but diminished its importance relative to what he called "voluntary law," or the law of pure consent by states. His often contradictory theories both elaborated and gave real impetus to the idea of *popular sovereignty* and, ultimately, also philosophical justification for acts of *revolution*. It became the standard work referred to among rulers in the actual conduct of interstate legal affairs. As a theorist, his reputation has gone into sharp and perhaps terminal decline. As a historical figure who had a profound impact on the actual affairs and habits of states, he remains important.

Vauban, Sébastien le Prestre de (1633–1707). French military engineer; the progenitor of modern theories of *fortification*. Vauban was captured by the French while in the Spanish service (1653) and, convinced by *Mazarin* to sign with France, by 1658 he had been made the deputy chief military engineer in the French service. He spent nearly a decade fortifying Dunkirk. In his career, he built some 154 major fortifications to defend France. He was good at knocking things down, too. In the War of Devolution (1667–1668) Vauban helped reduce fortifications at Lille and was made France's top military engineer in reward. During the *Dutch War* (1672–1678) he took part in no fewer than 17 sieges of Dutch defensive positions and one defense of a French fortification. In his lifetime, he directed 50 important sieges over 52 years—which exemplifies the nature of late seventeenth century warfare in Europe.

At Maastricht (1673), Vauban introduced the method of approaching and reducing a fortified position via parallel trenches. In 1687 he invented the socket *bayonet*, revolutionizing the relationship of *infantry* to *cavalry*. The next year he invented ricochet fire, wherein a reduced charge allowed a cannonball to ricochet in multiple directions, creating a lethal hazard to man and beast on any battlefield or inside a fortress. In 1703 his career peaked with promotion to the rank of marshal. Vauban actively promoted military schools, including scientific training for officers in the *artillery* and engineering corps. His foray into the political economy of *Louis XIV's* war finances was less well received: his analysis was banned from publication (1707). Shortly thereafter, he died. Had this work been better read by the king, Louis might have learned that Vauban anticipated much of the financial crisis which policies of heavy taxation to finance prolonged wars was severely aggravating, a crisis which would cost France its overseas empire to the better economically managed *British Empire* over the course of the eighteenth century, and which in the century's last decade would bring down the French monarchy.

Vauban is most famous for his development of siege warfare, the dominant form of land warfare at the end of the seventeenth century in Europe, and especially in the Dutch War. Much of Vauban's thinking about war reflected that of the Age of *Enlightenment*, in the sense of an attempt to apply reason and science to military problems, but also an aesthetic of rationality of form. Hence, in defense Vauban evinced a prejudice in favor of geometric regularity, as dictated by science applied to war, in his selection of the regular polygon as the keystone structure for all fortification, because its sides permitted covering and crossfire one to the other. Vauban also moved beyond reliance on a single *enceinte*, to an early form of the strategy of *defense-in-depth*. On the attack, he used temporary fortifications (usually, earthworks) to protect the attacking troops, while engineers prepared to blow the defenses or artillery maneuvered into range under cover. He thus approached a siege by having sappers dig a main trench toward the fortress, but also parallel trenches at advanced points to serve as assembly areas from which new approaching trenches zigzagged toward the main fortress. Many of these essential fortification techniques and methods of attack were replicated over the next 200 years of warfare, including by all sides in the *trench warfare* of the *Crimean War* and *World War I*. More generally, he began the deliberate, calculated application of science and technology to warfare that has marked it ever since. *See also Hugo Grotius; Niccolò di Bernardo Machiavelli.*

Suggested Readings: Peter Paret, *The Makers of Modern Strategy* (1986); F. J. Hebbert and G. A. Rothrock, *Soldier of France* (1990).

VE (Victory in Europe) Day. May 8, 1945, the day *Nazi Germany* surrendered to the *United Nations alliance.*

velvet revolution. The disintegration of *communist* rule in Czechoslovakia, 1989–1991. The term derives from the fact that after initial repression of a mass demonstration on November 17, 1989, there was little violence. The *Communist Party* simply stood aside, and democracy was established under *Václav Havel.*

Suggested Reading: Bernard Wheaton and Zdenek Kavan, *The Velvet Revolution* (1992).

Vendée rebellion (1793–1800). The *Catholic* peasants of this region of western France, led by their clergy, rebelled against the *secularism* of the *French Revolution.* The *Jacobins* put down the initial rebellion with their usual brutality and raw use of force, in the form of twelve columns of "blues" sent into the region in February 1794, and with little to no effort to win the hearts and minds of the peasants. About 25 percent of the population of the Vendée were butchered, or some 160,000 persons. For generations, this fact was ignored or downplayed by historians and other propagandists favorable to an idealized view of the French Revolution. More recent historical work suggests that revolutionary reprisals taken in the Vendée were so horrific they approached *genocide,* with tens of thousands summarily shot and others massdrowned. Discontent and opposition remained deeply rooted until 1800 and took the form of a protracted *guerrilla war,* when *Napoleon* sent an army to hammer peasant resistance flat while buying off the church hierarchy with symbolic concessions nationally.

Venezuela. First charted by *Columbus* in 1498 and mapped by Amerigo Vespucci (1451–1512) in 1499, it became part of the *Habsburg* holdings in South America when in 1528 *Charles V* commissioned the Wesler Bank (of Augsburg, in the *Holy Roman Empire*) to settle it. In 1548 Charles revoked the license, which had not borne out the promised profits. Thereafter, incremental settlement took place from surrounding Spanish colonies. With the *Peninsular War* underway in Europe, nationalist *Creoles* struck for effective independence from the French-dominated court in Madrid, forming a *junta* in Caracas and proclaiming for the deposed Ferdinand VII on April 19, 1810. This nominal loyalty to the Spanish king then captive in France was really a de facto assertion of independence from Madrid. *Francisco de Miranda* (1750–1816) took command of its army, only to surrender to the Spanish in 1812. In 1821, with victory in the Battle of Carabobo, *Simón Bolívar* enabled Venezuela to secure independence from Spain as part of the larger state of *Gran Colombia*. In 1830 Venezuela became a separate *republic*. It was then governed by a man of humble origins from its cattle country, José Antonio Páez (1790–1873), who had emerged as an anti-Spanish *guerrilla* fighter during the war for independence. He had joined forces with Bolívar in 1818, and his "Ilaneros" troops had played a key role in liberating the country, but he took Venezuela out of the Bolívarian experiment of Gran Colombia in 1829. He was president from 1831 to 1835, from 1839 to 1843, and after a long exile in the United States, again from 1861 to 1863. From 1895 to 1896 Venezuela was involved in a serious dispute with Britain over its border with *British Guiana*, in which Venezuela was robustly supported by the United States, much to the surprise of Britain. From 1902 to 1908 Venezuela was under *blockade* by several European powers for declining to pay *compensation* sought for their nationals for various injuries. That dispute too was *mediated* by the United States. In the 1920s it began to exploit its *oil* reserves, becoming a major exporter in the 1940s–1960s. In 1959 it returned to civilian rule after several decades of government by *junta*. In 1960 it instigated the founding of OPEC. In the 1970s and 1980s it squandered much of its oil revenue on wasteful megaprojects and unregulated development. Riots ensued in 1989 after a strict austerity program was put in place. Two coup attempts failed in 1992. In 1994 Venezuela signed a *free trade* agreement with Mexico and Colombia. It also suspended certain constitutional rights and imposed price and *foreign exchange* controls. In 2001, under the populist Hugo Chavez, Venezuela crept closer to open civil conflict. National strikes and creeping authoritarianism marked its politics, as Chavez adopted radical and sometimes confiscatory economic policies and the global price of oil declined. Venezuela maintains a standing claim to part of Guyana.

Suggested Reading: John Lombardy, *Venezuela* (1982).

Venice. Cut off from the mainland of Europe in the sixth century by the Lombard invasion of north Italy, Venice turned to maritime trade, mainly with the *Byzantine Empire* but reaching as far afield as Persia, India, and even China. For nearly 800 years Venice was the commercial center of the Western Mediterranean, serving also as a conduit of ancient Greek and contemporary Muslim learning to Europe. It eventually became a military, and even a small imperial, power in its own right. For 300 years the Venetians defied the

Ottomans in de facto alliance with *Constantinople*. In the fourteenth century Venice ran the great "Flanders Fleets" to Bruges and sent its merchants overland into France, the Baltic *Hansa*, and as far east as Poland. Venice reached an apex of commercial and secular influence as one of the main peninsular powers of the Italian *Renaissance*. For some 400 years it controlled a miniature empire of its own outside Italy, in *Dalmatia* and several smaller holdings. Its successful republican constitution, and the shrewd and worldly merchant class which ran the Venetian Republic, bequeathed much to the history of politics, navigation, and banking. Venice ceased to be effectively *sovereign* soon after the French invasion of Italy at the close of the fifteenth century. Its formal independence was ended with conquest by *Napoleon I* in 1797. It was ceded to Austria after 1815. In 1848 it briefly declared itself a republic again, but that movement for independence was crushed by Austrian arms. In 1866 it was ceded to the newly unified Italy by *Bismarck*, as a reward for Italy's aid in the *Seven Weeks' War. See also Camillo Cavour; Giuseppe Garibaldi.*

Suggested Reading: Gary Wills, *Venice: Lion City* (2001); Larry Wolff, *Venice and the Slavs* (2001).

Venizelos, Eleutherios (1864–1936). Greek prime minister, 1910–1915, 1917–1920, 1924, 1928–1932, 1933. He declared the *union* of Crete with Greece in 1905 and led Greece in the *Balkan Wars*, gaining control of *Macedonia*. He tried to bring Greece into *World War I*, siding with the *Allies*, but was dismissed from office. He returned from *exile* in 1917, deposed the king, and *declared war* on Germany and Bulgaria. He represented Greece at the *Paris Peace Conference*, but his efforts to seize part of *Anatolia* from Turkey led to more war and final defeat. Out of office in 1935, he staged an abortive uprising which led to a brief *civil war*, after which he fled to *exile* in France.

venture capital. Also called "risk capital." High-risk *investments* in new ventures made in search of high *profits*. Venture capital played an important part in international relations at least since the South Sea Bubble (1720). Among other projects, it backed the various *East India Companies*, the construction of the *Suez Canal*, opened *Siberia* and the American West, built *railways*, and was in play behind many a colonial adventure, such as that of *Rhodes* in southern Africa. It can be a critical component of national *power* because it supports economic *competitiveness*. The global demand for venture capital grew at a tremendous pace at the end of the 1980s, as new market opportunities opened in the former *Soviet bloc* countries, Chinese opportunities continued, and certain *Third World* economies entered periods of rapid *growth. See also patient capital.*

Verdun, Battle of (February 21–December 16, 1916). After winning at *Gorlice-Tarnow* in the east, Germany transferred forces to a quiet sector of the *western front* to attack the French lines at the ancient fortress complex (it had been a Roman fort) of Verdun. From the French point of view this was the worst battle of *World War I*, and perhaps in French military history—bloody victory though it eventually was. It was fought bitterly and often hand-to-hand for more than 300 days. Nearly three quarters of a million men were casualties in this war of deliberate *attrition* between distant generals, *Falkenhayn* (who promised to "bleed white" the French Army) for the Germans and *Pétain* for the French, neither of whom showed much concern for casualties. As Falkenhayn foresaw, the French fed men into the charnel house of Verdun, along what became known as the "Voie sacrée"—the sole road into the salient capable of carrying heavy truck traffic. The initial German effort to destroy the French within a narrow front without themselves suffering massive losses failed, so they attacked instead along a broad front (April 9th), using massed artillery, massed infantry, and chlorine *gas*. They made initial progress but then, as so often in the trenches of the Great War, the attack bogged down. By July the Germans ceased their offensive. In October and December, French counterattacks recaptured much of the lost ground. The battle destroyed French morale, contributed to the *French Army mutinies* of 1917, and rendered the French incapable of independent offensive action. Yet it may have cost Germany the war: it consumed precious *reserves* and compelled the *High Command* to make the decision, in January 1917, to resume *unrestricted submarine warfare* which brought the full power of the United States down upon them in 1918. Falkenhayn was dismissed when his strategy failed to finish the French. Pétain became one of the greatest French heroes of the war, but never again had the stomach for a fight. His *defeatism* pervaded the French military during the 1920s and 1930s; he *surrendered* to Germany at the first available opportunity in 1940. In 1984 Chancellor *Kohl* of Germany and President *Mitterand* of France met at Verdun in a ceremony of reconciliation between their nations.

Suggested Reading: Alistair Horne, *The Price of Glory: Verdun 1916* (rev. ed., 1993).

Vereeniging, Treaty of (May 31, 1902). *See Second Boer War.*

verification (regime). Any set of agreed rules, procedures, and mechanisms, cooperative or independently operated (e.g., *fixed satellite* surveillance) used to verify that each party is actually complying with the *terms* of a *treaty*. It is used especially about *arms control* agreements. *See also continuity of safeguards; CSBMs; IAEA; inspection; intelligence; National Technical Means of Verification; Open Skies.*

Verona, Congress of (1822). Austria, France, Prussia, and Russia met, with Britain as observer, in the last full meeting of the *Congress system*. *Castlereagh* was to have attended, but committed suicide before his scheduled departure. The main issue was a French proposal to invade *Iberia* to repress *liberal* rebellion. *Metternich* of Austria agreed, in part hoping to prevent a Russian army from marching across Europe, as *Alexander I* was threatening. The British were opposed, not so much from principle as because Portugal was an ally. They also wanted to see Spanish ports remain open to free commerce and so contested a royal *restoration* in Iberia or Latin America. The possibility of Russian *intervention* in the Americas led *Canning* to approach *John Quincy Adams*, and by that route to the proclamation of the *Monroe Doctrine*.

Versailles. The great palace built by *Louis XIV*, outside Paris. On January 18, 1871, the German Second Reich was proclaimed at Versailles in the closing days of the *Franco-Prussian War* (1870–1871). "Versailles" is often used as shorthand for the *Paris Peace Conference*, held there and in Paris from January 1919 to January 1920. It may be used, interchangeably, to refer to the peace conference as a whole or just to the *Treaty of Versailles*, one of several war-ending instruments negotiated at Paris.

Versailles, Treaty of (June 28, 1919). Negotiated at the *Paris Peace Conference*, this *peace treaty* (the first instrument where English received equal status with French) formally ended *World War I* between the *Allies* and Germany. The United States *signed* but failed to *ratify* it: a first vote went against the Treaty of Versailles in the U.S. Senate in November 1919, and it went down to a second and final defeat in March 1920. The United States therefore concluded a separate peace treaty with Germany in August 1921, legally ending the *state of war*. Versailles was concluded not least because, after the *Armistice* of November 11, 1918, the *Allied and Associated Powers* kept up their *blockade* throughout the negotiations, bringing slow starvation to parts of Germany.

Its terms: (1) Territorial adjustments included: *Alsace-Lorraine*, to France; all German colonies were relinquished and converted to *mandates*; *Danzig* was made a *free city* under *League of Nations* administration and connected to Poland via the *Polish corridor*; much of historically German *East Prussia* and *Silesia*, to Poland; *Eupen and Malmedy*, to Belgium; *Memel*, to Lithuania; and northern *Schleswig*, to Denmark after a *plebiscite*; (2) *Anschluss* with Austria was forbidden; (3) the *Rhineland* was *demilitarized*; (4) the *Saar* was to be administered by the League of Nations as a *condominium*, while France was permitted to extract its coal resources as *reparations*-in-kind for French mines which the *Reichswehr* had flooded while retreating in 1918; (5) large-scale *reparations* were exacted, with the amount set by commission; (6) an upper limit of 100,000 was set for the armed forces of Germany, and no *General Staff* was permitted; (7) a ban was introduced on any German air force, *conscription, gas weapons, armor, capital warships* more than 10,000 tons, and *U-boats*, with the German fleet at *Scapa Flow* to be surrendered to Britain; and (8) a right-of-way *servitude* was placed on the Kiel Canal. Among more controversial provisions, the treaty contained a so-called *war guilt clause* and called for *war crimes trials* of *Wilhelm II* and the *High Command*. These never took place, although some lesser officers were tried.

Versailles also contained the *Covenant of the League of Nations*, an inclusion with manifold and deleterious effects on later events. Lastly, Germany was barred from the League until it passed a period of probation. These *terms* weighed heavily on the *Weimar Republic* without entirely satisfying British or especially French *public opinion* or *security* concerns. Long before the *Nazis* took power, the German military devised ways to evade the disarmament provisions, for instance, by secret training in Russia after *Rapallo*. And without British or American support, France alone was unable to enforce the harsher clauses. *Hitler* disemboweled the treaty after 1933.

The Treaty of Versailles was much criticized, at the time and after, for putative harshness. Maybe so, but it hardly compares with the brutal treatment meted out to Germany in 1945. Besides, there is nothing inherently unwise or morally reprehensible about a harsh peace. If a gentle settlement works (keeps the peace), well and good. If a harsh one is necessary to the same purpose, so be it. The point should always be, does the settlement work? If it does, then a harsh peace will be a practical and moral good; if it does not, then a gentle peace may lead to the far greater evil of another round of fighting necessary to resolve disputes left in abeyance, or papered over, or not fathomed in the first place. In this light, the real problem with the Treaty of Versailles was that it was too harsh to be a truly generous peace, but far too generous to have had the positive (that is, deterrent) effect on Germans that a harsher peace might have had after 1919. *See also Anglo-German Naval Agreement; Georges Clemenceau; defeat; diplomacy; entangling alliance; Ferdinand Foch; German East Africa; Lloyd George; "stab-in-the-back"; Gustav Stresemann; Woodrow Wilson.*

Suggested Readings: Michael Dockrill and J. Good, *Peace Without Promise* (1981); Erik Goldstein, *Winning the Peace* (1991); William R. Keylor, *The Legacy of the Great War* (1998); Arno Mayer, *Politics and Diplomacy of Peacemaking* (1933, 1967); Alan Sharp, *The Versailles Settlement* (1991); Arthur Walworth, *Wilson and His Peacemakers* (1986).

vertical escalation. *See escalation.*

vertical proliferation. Quantitative increases in available weapons systems. *See also horizontal proliferation.*

vertical takeoff and landing (VTOL). A (self-descriptive) genus of aircraft designed for forward, battlefield conditions, where full-length airfields are in short supply. They also permit design of short-deck *aircraft carriers.*

veto. A by-product of situations in which the *unanimity rule* is in effect, whereby any one state refusing *consent* blocks or invalidates an agreement. This rule may be qualified according to the organization concerned. Under terms of the *United Nations Charter* it is a right limited to the five *permanent members of the Security Council*, the only states empowered to stop substantive—but not procedural—decisions simply by casting a negative vote. On procedural issues, nine votes are required to pass. However, the veto applies when voting on the advance matter of whether an issue is to be treated as substantial or procedural. This is sometimes called the "double veto." Mere abstention on a recorded vote by a permanent member never constitutes a veto, though it may make impossible the accumulation of sufficient votes for a positive outcome. Nor can a negative vote in the Security Council block a resolution passed in the *United Nations General Assembly*, where the P-5 vote in legal *equality* with the discontented, the middling, and the powerless among nations. *See also* liberum veto; *qualified majority voting; weighted voting.*

viceroy. A ruler of a country, as in British colonial India, who serves in lieu of a distant or absent *sovereign*. In *Spanish America*, two viceroys served the Spanish Monarchy into the eighteenth century, located in Mexico City, *New Spain*, and Lima, *Peru*. In 1739 *New Granada* was elevated to a Viceroyalty, and in 1776 so was the *Río de la Plata*.

Vichy. Unoccupied France, plus its overseas possessions, July 1940–November 1942. It was named for its capital, the provincial town of Vichy where the national government moved in 1940 (the Germans were visiting Paris at the time). Contrary to comforting myths of a special, limited French form of *collaboration*, the Vichy regime in fact willingly collaborated to a high degree with Nazi occupiers. Some Vichy commanders fired on the *Allies* during invasions of French colonial territories, while domestically many Vichy police aided the *Gestapo*, and Vichy officials helped deport French citizens—workers, political prisoners, and *Resistance* fighters—to *forced labor* camps, and French Jews to the *death camps*. It was anti-*republican* and at least partly *fascist* itself. *Pétain's* declared reason for heading it, that it would preserve at least part of France from direct *occupation*, was invalidated in November 1942 when the Germans occupied the whole country. The Pétain myth of a "National Revolution" was exposed when he and other top Vichyites continued to collaborate until forced to flee to Germany by advancing Allied forces in July 1944. The full extent of Vichy's collaboration has never really been admitted within France, which instead tends to look on *World War II* through the rosier lens of the revered Resistance. *See also Jean Louis Darlan; Charles de Gaulle; Free French; Greater East Asia Co-Prosperity Sphere; French Indochina; Pierre Laval; François Mitterand.*

Suggested Readings: Sarah Fishman et al., eds., *France at War* (2000); Robert Paxton, *Vichy France* (1972).

Vicksburg, Surrender of (July 4, 1863). *See American Civil War; Ulysses S. Grant; Abraham Lincoln; William T. Sherman.*

Victor Emmanuel III (1869–1947). King of Italy. On the throne for 46 years, 1900–1946, he watched as Italy abandoned the *Central Powers* to enter *World War I* on the *Allied* side, hoping for territorial gain, only to be humiliated in the field and denied *Italia irredenta* at the *Paris Peace Conference*. He collaborated with *Mussolini* and the Italian *fascists* and accepted to become Emperor of Ethiopia in 1935. He tried to distance himself from them when they brought Italy to *defeat* and foreign *occupation* during *World War II*. He then agreed to dismiss Mussolini as part of the coup which brought *Bodoglio* to power. Widely viewed as having served too many masters too easily, he was deposed in 1946.

Victoria (1819–1901). Queen of the *United Kingdom*, 1837–1901; empress of India, 1876–1901. Upon Victoria's accession to the throne, Britain's link with *Hanover* was severed, as that state's Salic law did not permit a woman to reign. Her efforts to interfere with foreign affairs were easily deflected, and her reign saw the complete and final subordination of the British *monarchy* to parliamentary authority. In 1840 she married Prince Albert of Saxe-Coburg-Gotha. They were devoted to each other. Albert took a real interest in foreign policy and was, by the standards of the day and of his class and position, a *liberal* with a refined social conscience. Albert died in 1861, moving Victoria into a prolonged widowhood of forty years. Before his passing they had nine children together, which in itself suggests rather urgently that her reputation for sexual prudery is overdone. She was a devoted wife, if a distant mother, and then a grieving widow. In short, she was in sexual matters, as in so much else, no more or less than a representative of her class and day. Victoria was not always popular with the public in her early years, but she was viewed with great fondness late in her reign.

Victoria's children, grandchildren, and diverse in-laws occupied many of the thrones of Europe before *World War I*. They included George V of England, *Wilhelm II* of Germany, the queen of Spain, the kings of Greece and Norway, and the tsar of Russia, as well as other *dynastic marriages* establishing ties to the monarchies of Denmark and Rumania. That and her constitutional position meant that Victoria associated with several of the greatest British prime ministers, including *Palmerston* and *Gladstone*. The latter she did not like. She vehemently disapproved of his liberal policies on imperial questions, *Home Rule* for Ireland, and disestablishment of the Irish Church. *Disraeli* was Victoria's favorite. He flattered her often and successfully as a "fellow author," paid her many small attentions, and elevated her to be Empress of India. For students of *international relations*, Victoria remains notable mainly as a symbol of British power at its greatest and most detached imperial height. For students of human relations, there is much to contemplate about the interaction of an ordinary, essentially decent personality bred for duty and then thrust into an extraordinary station in life at a tender age and at a remarkable

juncture in the history of the *British Empire*. Victoria died on January 22, 1901. *See also Boer War; Cetewayo; Charles Gordon; Gurkhas; Cecil Rhodes.*
Suggested Reading: Stanley Weintraub, *Victoria* (1992).

victor's justice. When *victors* in war convict and punish leaders or soldiers of the *defeated* side, which may or may not mean that real justice is done. The term is usually meant as a pejorative. *See also war crimes trials.*

victory, in war. When an enemy concedes one's superiority in combat by asking for *terms*, with the consequence that one's interests in the *dispute(s)* occasioning the war are advanced at the expense of the loser. That qualified definition should not surprise. No victory is absolute, though some defeats are, because all wars are inherently political as well as military. Hence, they reflect competing interests and continuing opposition to the absolute triumph of any one group, nation, or idea, regardless of momentary ascendancy in matters of combat. As a general rule, even apparently spectacular military victories tend over time to be seen as partial, or even as defeats, unless they also lead to a lasting peace settlement. *See also defeat; pyrrhic victory; war.*
Suggested Reading: Brian Bond, *The Pursuit of Victory* (1998).

Vienna, Congress of (September 1814–June 1815). The meeting of the four main victors over *Napoleon* and France: Austria, Britain, Prussia, and Russia. Its main purpose was to discuss a host of questions pertaining to territorial settlement, *restoration* of the monarchs of Europe deposed by the *French Revolution* and by Napoleon, and other questions left in the wake of French *defeat*. It was interrupted by Napoleon's return for the *Hundred Days*. When it resumed, France received less generous terms than before, including some minor loss of territory. Yet, although France was not fully accepted back into the fold, under *Talleyrand*'s masterful diplomacy it was still treated with the respect accruing to a *Great Power*. Vienna was the first, and most important, of the meetings of the *Congress System*. It laid out a comprehensive settlement after a quarter century of war, based on the twinned principles of *containment* of France and of *revolution* and the idea of *compensation*. In so doing Vienna set the basic mold of Great Power relations which would last until its system of Great Power alliances and cooperation broke down in the *Crimean War*, leading to German and Italian unification and a whole new *balance of power* in the second half of the nineteenth century.

(1) Territorial provisions: It set up a *cordon sanitaire* of *buffer states* to contain France through creation of a united kingdom of Belgium, Luxembourg, and the Netherlands, confirmation of the independence of several Italian states, restoration of the *Papal States*, and establishment of the *German Confederation*. It confirmed Britain's capture of the Cape of Good Hope (*Cape Colony*), Ceylon, *Heligoland*, *Malta*, Mauritius, St. Lucia, and Tobago; united Norway to Sweden (to punish the Danes); reinstated and made *neutral* the

Swiss Confederation; confirmed control of *Venice* and parts of the *Balkans* by Austria; and accepted yet another partition of *Poland* by Russia (which got the larger share) and Prussia; and granted *Danzig* and other Baltic areas to Prussia. Prussia was denied Saxony (another buffer state) and instead accepted compensation in the *Rhineland*.

(2) Other clauses: It denounced the *slave trade*; recommended constitutional protections for Jews in Germany; *internationalized* the Rhine and the Meuse; barred France from involvement in the politics of the Italian peninsula (a traditional French *sphere of influence*); and revamped diplomatic procedures and *protocol*, regularizing the titles, rights, and duties of *ambassadors, ministers, envoys,* and *chargés*. Unlike the *Paris Peace Conference* a century later, Vienna did not enunciate general principles and then apply them with varying degrees of integrity. Instead, it made deals and arrangements which flowed from *power* and political realities, from which later observers extrapolated principles said to govern the *Concert of Europe. Liberals* came to view the Congress of Vienna with general disdain, for its territorial adjustments which took little or no regard of *self-determination*. For instance, *Woodrow Wilson* said at Paris that he wished to avoid the "odor of Vienna." And it is quite true that *nationalism* was not just ignored at Vienna: it was despised, and feared, by Russia and Austria in particular. *Conservative* observers, in contrast, have admired and acclaimed the settlement for its *realism* about Great Power relations and for helping keep the *peace* for several decades.

Suggested Readings: Henry Kissinger, *A World Restored* (1957); Harold Nicholson, *The Congress of Vienna* (1946); Paul W. Schroeder, *The Transformation of European Politics, 1763–1848* (1994).

Vienna Convention on Consular Relations (1961). Negotiated alongside the more important *Vienna Conventions* listed below, it regularized and codified the rights, duties, and status of *consuls* and *consulates*.

Vienna Convention on Diplomatic Privileges, Intercourse and Immunities (1961). Drafted in 1961, it came into effect in 1964. It codified much extant *international customary law* on the status and functions of *diplomats* and *embassies*, carrying forward the clarifying and regularizing work begun at the *Congress of Vienna* (1815). It affirmed the rights of all *sovereign* states to *representation*, to *recall an ambassador*, or to break *diplomatic relations*. It also affirmed the ranking of diplomats, as follows: (1) *ambassadors* and *high commissioners*; (2) *envoys, envoy extraordinary, minister plenipotentiary*; (3) *ministers resident*; and (4) *chargés*. Below these ranks are quasi-diplomatic positions: (5) *attaché*, and (6) *consul*. Finally, it confirmed the principle of *diplomatic immunity* by which diplomats (and their families) are immune from criminal prosecution and civil liability for crimes they may be charged with or commit, unless their government chooses to waive *extraterritorial* immunity to permit their prosecution.

Vienna Convention on the Law of Treaties (1969). It was drafted at an international conference on the law of *treaties* held from March 26th to May 24th, 1968. France voted against it, while the entire *Soviet bloc* abstained. It codified well-established *international customary law* governing treaties, including reaffirmation of the basic principle of *pacta sunt servanda*. It entered into force for *ratifying* states on January 27, 1980. *See also validity; violation.*

Viêt Cong (*Viêt Nam Công San*). A South Vietnamese and American pejorative for "Vietnamese Communists" (VC). Their self-designation was "National Liberation Front" (NLF). This *guerrilla* army was drawn from committed *communist* volunteers as well as *conscripts* dragooned from the villages of the Republic of Vietnam (RVN, South Vietnam). From 1959 they fought against the armed forces of the RVN, the United States, and other armies of the anti-communist alliance which intervened in the *Vietnam War*. The VC were a determined foe with significant *logistical* and political backing from the Democratic Republic of Vietnam (DRV, North Vietnam), which was in turn heavily supported by China and the Soviet Union. The VC were largely eliminated as a fighting force during the *Tet Offensive*, after which People's Army of Viêt Nam (PAVN), or North Vietnamese, regulars took their place. After Tet the NLF was reconstituted as a Provisional Revolutionary Government (PRG) and by 1975 had 60,000 guerrillas in the RVN, but the main communist fighting force after 1968 remained the PAVN.

Viêt Minh (*Viêt Nam Dôc Lâp Dông Minh Hôi*). "Vietnamese Independence League." The Communist-nationalist organization, led at first by *Hô Chí Minh*, which spearheaded resistance to the Japanese occupation of Vietnam, 1941–1945, with some help from the OSS. From its base in the Democratic Republic of Vietnam (DRV, North Vietnam) it fought the bitter *French-Indochina War* (1946–1954). It fought against anti-communist Vietnamese in the prolonged civil war which underlay the *Vietnam War*, 1954–1975; and it fought and defeated the United States, 1964–1972. It governed Vietnam as a *one-party state* after unification in 1975.

Vietnam (*Nam Viêt*). Nam Quôc or "the Southern Nation." In 207 B.C.E. a Chinese *warlord* conquered the Vietnamese (Kinh) state of Au Lac in northern Indochina, to form Nam Viêt, a province governed from Guangzhou (Canton). In 111 B.C.E. Nam Viêt was overrun by a Chinese imperial army and became a *vassal state* of the *Han Empire*. Chinese occupation lasted on and off for 1,000 years. A major revolt broke out in 39 C.E. but ended in defeat at Láng Bac in 42, followed by a southern Han, punitive expedition in 44. In the far south, a Hindu kingdom at Fu-nan traded with both India and China. Indian influence declined after 192. A new coastal kingdom, *Champa* (Lin-i), was established which lasted in some form into the nineteenth century. In the north, a Kinh revolt against China lasted from 542 to

570. The second *Tang* emperor reasserted Chinese control over north Vietnam. Other revolts occurred in 687, 722, 766–791, and 819. The Vietnamese finally achieved significant autonomy after defeat of a large Chinese force at the Battle of the Bach-Dăng River (938). For five centuries more, they had to fight off Chinese efforts to reconquer them, not always succeeding. They fought off a Chinese invasion in 980 and two massive invasions by the *Mongols* in 1285 and 1287–1288, defeating the Mongols in a second Battle of the Bach-Dăng River (1288). Meanwhile, they progressively expanded south and west, into Champa and the Khmer Empire. China's *Ming* emperors sought to reconquer northern Vietnam (*Tonkin*), intervening in 1407. This invasion was repelled by 1428, and the Ming *recognized* Tonkin as an independent *tributary* state in 1431.

After 1471 the Vietnamese steadily increased their control of Champa; they would not eliminate it entirely until 1822. A long internal war divided Vietnam for nearly two centuries after c. 1527. In the north the Trinh ruled, later helped by the Dutch; in the south the Nguyên held sway, later in alliance with Portugal, and made war on the Khmers for control of the rich Mekong River delta. (Portuguese ships had first arrived in 1535, and Dutch traders in 1636. French traders and *missionaries* set up shop in 1680.) By 1658 the Nguyên had captured most of the delta; Saigon (Sài Gòn) fell in 1672. In 1623 the Vietnamese intervened in Cambodia, by invitation, against the Siamese. In 1660 Cambodia became a tributary of Vietnam. Siamese counterintervention in 1717 forced a switch of Khmer allegiance to Siam. From 1739 to 1749 the Khmer failed to dislodge the southern Vietnamese from the Mekong delta. In 1755–1760 Vietnam expanded deeper into Cambodia. From 1769 to 1773 it fought Siam, once again over the issue of hegemony in Cambodia. From 1773 to 1785, the Nguyên were slowly overwhelmed by an armed revolt, led by three brothers and known as the Tây Són Rebellion. The Trinh took advantage briefly in the north, while Siam invaded the Mekong. The Tây Són stunned the Siamese in 1785, forever ending Siam's penetration into Vietnam. They then moved north in 1786 to defeat the Trinh. When China invaded in 1788, to take advantage of the chaos, one of the Tây Són brothers, Nguyên Huê (or Quang Trung, d. 1792) defeated them in a series of historic battles remembered as the Ngoc Hôi-Dông-Da (1789). China recognized him as king of *Annam*, but civil war soon resumed. In 1802 Nguyên Ánh defeated the Tây Són with the help of foreign *mercenaries*, founded the Nguyên dynasty which ruled Vietnam until 1945, and gave the country its modern name of Nam Viêt, or Vietnam.

Vietnam and Siam fought again over Cambodia, 1831–1845. Conflict with France predominated after 1847 as the French began to penetrate to the interior. Between 1858 and 1884, France progressively extended its dominion over what it knew as Annam, *Cochin China*, and Tonkin. Saigon fell in 1858, and by 1867 all of Cochin China was taken; Hanoi (Hà Nôi) capitulated in 1873; the rest of Tonkin succumbed in the *Tonkin Wars*. The *Treaty of Tien-*

tsin (1885) formally ended China's historic claim to Vietnam and established it as a French *protectorate*. France then combined its Vietnamese conquests with Laos and Cambodia in the composite colony called *French Indochina* (1887). A revolt broke out in 1930–1931, but was repressed. In September 1940 Japan forced French *Vichy* authorities to cede military bases in Indochina, which Tokyo used in 1941 to complete its own conquest of the peninsula. The *Việt Minh* fought the Japanese, 1941–1945. On March 11, 1945, Japan allowed Emperor *Bao Dai* to declare Vietnam's independence, mostly to frustrate the returning French. Chinese troops intervened in the north in 1945–1946. The Việt Minh were crushed by Japanese and later French troops in the south, but held the north and with Chinese and Soviet aid defeated France in the *French-Indochina War* (1946–1954). The *Geneva Accords* then temporarily divided Vietnam at the 17th parallel, into the Democratic Republic of Vietnam, or North Vietnam, and the Republic of Vietnam, or South Vietnam. These states eyed each other with barely suspended hostility until 1959, when the climactic phase of the long nationalist-communist struggle—known as the *Vietnam War*—broke out.

(1) Democratic Republic of Vietnam (DRV): *Hô Chí Minh* was the guiding light of the DRV, proclaimed on August 16, 1945, the day after Japan surrendered. This state was maintained against the French and its *legitimacy* was confirmed in 1954 in the Geneva Accords. Hô and the Việt Minh introduced a modified *Stalinist* system in the DRV in the 1950s, including forced *collectivization* of the villages and massacres of "landlords" (reclassified, better-off peasants). When economic collapse threatened and rural rebellion broke out in 1956 the Việt Minh called in the army and backtracked on reform, with Hô admitting "some errors have been made." The DRV aligned with China and the Soviet Union and kept ties with both despite the *Sino-Soviet split* over other issues. It drew upon the larger communist powers for assistance in industrialization, but mainly it called upon their military prowess and weaponry to build itself into a formidable martial state. During the Vietnam War it took a terrific pounding from the U.S. Air Force without flinching from its core determination for reunification of all Vietnam under communist rule. It achieved that objective in 1975.

(2) Republic of Vietnam (RVN): Former Annam Emperor Bao Dai was *head of state*, 1949–1955, when he was deposed and South Vietnam was declared a republic by *Ngo Dinh Diem*. After 1957 it faced a loss of control over the countryside as the *Việt Cong* murdered thousands of local officials. It also suffered from illegitimacy in the eyes of many Buddhists. The *Kennedy* administration responded by raising the number of U.S. advisers from approximately 600 to more than 16,500 just before Kennedy was assassinated in November 1963. Diem's response was too timid for some of his own military, and apparently also for Washington. At first supported by the United States, Diem was overthrown in a *coup* approved by Kennedy (though Kennedy did not approve of Diem's murder) on November 1, 1963. A succession of failed

governments gave way to Nguyên *Cao Kỳ* and *Thieu*, who shared power in the south from 1965 onward. Under *Lyndon Johnson* the number of U.S. advisers soared and after the *Tonkin Gulf Resolution* the United States became directly involved in large-scale combat. The American phase of the war raged until 1973 and the *Paris Peace Accords*. The RVN thereafter fought on alone, succumbing to a full-scale DRV invasion in 1975, whereupon the RVN became *extinct*. A political *purge* followed, including some killings, with about one million former RVN officials and soldiers sent to "*reeducation*" camps.

(3) After Unification: Finally united after 30 years of war, Vietnam was renamed the "Socialist Republic of Vietnam" and bent to the task of *reconstruction*. It was hamstrung by a U.S. *embargo* which lasted until 1994, but far more so by ideological insistence on *collectivization* of industry and agriculture. It was aided somewhat by the Soviet Union and joined COMECON in 1978. However, that organization had little to offer beyond *barter* markets and limited choice and supply. Rigid ideology, gross economic mismanagement, the embargo, and new wars with Cambodia and China ushered in two more decades of grinding poverty, while elsewhere in southeast Asia former colonies emerged as prosperous *Asian Tigers*. In 1978, after running border skirmishes with its former ally, the *Khmers Rouges*, Vietnam invaded Cambodia and became bogged down in the *Cambodia-Vietnam War* (1977–1991). That long occupation set Vietnam at odds with *ASEAN* and with China: Hanoi fought the *Sino-Vietnam War* with China in 1979, and battled Thai troops on the Cambodia border in 1985. Meanwhile, from 1975 large numbers of *boat people* were forced out.

Facing famine and economic collapse by 1986, Vietnam reluctantly followed China's lead by experimenting with "Đôi mói" ("economic renovation") market reforms. With its economy in shambles and its Soviet ally collapsing, Hanoi pulled its forces from Cambodia. In 1990 *inflation* surpassed 1,100 percent per annum. In 1992 Vietnam signed the Treaty of Amity and Cooperation with *ASEAN*, a first step toward membership. Hanoi maintained an ancient claim to the *Paracels* and *Spratlys*, where its forces clashed with Chinese naval and marine units in 1992. In 1993, it signed an agreement with China renouncing the use of force over such border disputes. Relations with the United States remained constrained by a lack of full *diplomatic relations*, and American insistence on a satisfactory accounting (whatever that means, and if it is still physically possible) by Vietnam of all American *POWs* and *MIAs* from the war. In mid-1993 the United States lifted a ban on joint business ventures and ended a veto on *World Bank* loans. In 1994 *Clinton* ended the embargo over objections from MIA families, but with support from the U.S. business community. Diplomatic relations were restored in 1995, an American ambassador arrived in 1997, and Clinton visited in 2000. *See also Montagnards.*

Suggested Readings: Oscar Chapuis, *A History of Vietnam* (1995); Oscar Chapuis, *The Last*

Emperors of Vietnam: From Tu Duc to Bao Dai (2000); Spencer Tucker, *Vietnam* (1999); Nguyûn Khăc Viên, *Vietnam* (1993).

Vietnamization. A policy announced by *Richard Nixon* as a key to phased American withdrawal from the *Vietnam War*, but actually initiated by the *Johnson* administration after the *Tet Offensive*, and essentially also pre-1964 practice. It called for arming and training of more South Vietnamese (Army of the Republic of Vietnam, ARVN) soldiers in sufficient numbers and to levels of skill which would permit replacement of American GIs in the field, and for *pacification* of the RVN countryside. That was supposed to allow the United States to remain committed to RVN security only with naval and *air power.* Nixon later grumbled that Congress gutted his efforts by cutting large-scale military aid to the RVN after 1972 and prohibiting the use of American air power against DRV *incursions.* He asserted, in short, that the war was still winnable (the RVN could survive) even after U.S. withdrawal. It seems highly unlikely that a downsized bombing campaign could have saved the RVN where the most intensive bombing in all history, and an eight-year commitment of up to 550,000 U.S. troops, had not. Nor is it likely that the determined, fanatical leadership of the DRV could have been stopped short of complete *victory* by anything other than ultimate force (*atomic weapons*), which was never used by the United States. Note: The French had a similar policy, which they called "jaunissement" ("yellowing") of their forces in Indochina. It, too, failed. *See also Nixon Doctrine.*

Vietnam syndrome. A popular culture/journalistic term for America's deep reluctance to wage another ground war like the *Vietnam War*. It spoke especially to a perceived fear at both the public and policy-making levels to endure casualties or to commit forces in areas of peripheral strategic interest. It is generally conceded to have lasted from 1975 until the triumph of the *Gulf War*, though vestiges of the attitude were still detectable in U.S. foreign policy debates and strategic planning into the twenty-first century.

Vietnam War (1959–1975). Fighting in Vietnam spanned the period 1940–1975. Led by *Hô Chí Minh*, the *Viêt Minh* and other nationalists fought against invading Japanese during *World War II*. In 1946 the *French-Indochina War* broke out when France tried to return to Indochina as colonial overlord. After 1950 China and the Soviet Union lent military aid to the Viêt Minh. That—and the outbreak of the *Korean Conflict*—drew the United States into the region: Washington aided France as part of an extended *containment* of international communism. The French phase of the war ended with a decisive Viêt Minh victory at *Dien Bien Phu*, which led to the *Geneva Accords*. Fighting soon broke out between the *Viêt Cong* (VC), or NLF (National Liberation Front), under the direction of the leadership of the Democratic Republic of Vietnam (DRV), or North Vietnam, and the armed forces of the Republic of

Vietnam (RVN), or South Vietnam. Low-level *guerrilla* warfare and assassination campaigns began in 1957 and continued until heavy fighting broke out in 1959. The war escalated steadily from 1960 to 1963. It entered a new phase with large-scale intervention by American ground and air forces after 1964, and yet another with southward infiltration of large PAVN (People's Army of Viêt Nam), or NVA (North Vietnamese Army), units after 1968. The fighting spread to neighboring countries in Indochina and dominated United States foreign policy for the next decade. It did not subside until complete communist victory in 1975.

(1) Before *Tet*: In 1957 *cadres* of Viêt Minh began coordinated armed attacks on the institutions and officials of the RVN. Some Viêt Minh had remained in the south to implement the Geneva Accords. Along with new NLF recruits, they stayed restlessly quiet on orders from Hô until sufficient strength was built up to threaten the *Diem* regime. Attacks began in 1957. By 1961 the NLF had assassinated about 10,000 RVN officials (teachers, doctors, social workers) and village heads. In response, some 500 U.S. military and civilian advisors were dispatched by *Eisenhower*. Economic aid and a U.S. military presence was significantly escalated under *Kennedy*: U.S. advisors multiplied 32-fold to 16,500 and took on additional tasks, even participating in combat. Kennedy approved the coup against Diem which politically, morally, and militarily was the critical moment in Americanizing the war in Indochina. Large-scale U.S. combat units were committed by *Lyndon Johnson* after the *Tonkin Gulf Resolution*, so that by 1964 the war was fully Americanized in its direction, strategy, and weapons. This remained true despite combat contingents also arriving from Australia, New Zealand, Korea, and the Philippines and noncombat commitments to the RVN by some 44 nations. Also in 1964, the DRV decided to escalate, sending the first PAVN units south and directly attacking U.S. personnel. The United States began to bomb Laos, which ultimately was more heavily bombed even than the DRV. In June, General *William Westmoreland* took charge of U.S. forces. By 1965 some 200,000 U.S. troops were "in-country." The number reached 540,000 by 1968, when Westmoreland asked for 200,000 more and was refused by an administration grown confused, internally divided, and deeply unpopular.

The U.S. military firmly believed in *air power*, launching major bomber offensives with code names such as "Rolling Thunder" (1965–1968) and "Linebacker" (I and II, 1972–1973). Air Force General Curtis LeMay framed the problem bluntly in 1965: "They've got to draw in their horns and stop their aggression or we're going to bomb them into the Stone Age." What was not anticipated was that the DRV would both match the American ground escalation and escalate even further in response to the bombing, as well as import from the Soviet Union the most sophisticated air defense system in the world. By war's end, the United States had lost 3,000 aircraft over Vietnam. On the ground, the NLF/PAVN strategy was elegantly if brutally simple: make Vietnam ungovernable by anyone but the Viêt Minh. To accomplish this end they employed highly effective, albeit savage, tactics of terror and assassination at the village level. They infiltrated supplies and reinforcements down the ever-expanding *Hô Chí Minh Trail*, recruited in the south and drew strength from the manpower reserves of the DRV, and depended on large-scale logistical and technological support from China and the Soviet Union.

U.S. forces and the Army of the RVN (ARVN) tried to defeat the NLF and PAVN conventionally through *search-and-destroy* missions, politically through village *pacification*, and unconventionally with borrowed tactics of assassination and guerrilla warfare overseen by the CIA. Meanwhile, the United States penalized and tried to coerce the DRV via massive bombing strikes along the Hô Chí Minh Trail, including secret bombing of the Trail's Cambodian and Laotian ancillaries, and against DRV *infrastructure*. That meant killing large numbers of DRV civilians as *"collateral damage,"* and provoking popular resistance to the war back home. Some battles were traditional, such as in the Ia Drang Valley (October 23–November 20, 1965), the first major encounter between U.S. and PAVN forces. Most combat (96 percent for the United States) took place at company strength or less. PAVN commander *Giáp* wished to fight a protracted war, but also hoped to draw U.S. forces away from the coastal cities into the interior, where he might repeat the success of Dien Bien Phu. To this end there was bloody fighting in Quang Tri Province in 1966, and again at Khe Sanh, Lôk Ninh, and Dak Tô in 1967. By the end of 1967 the U.S. military claimed, truly believed, and probably actually was winning the war against the NLF. The crucial political and psychological context of the war changed dramatically with the 1968 Tet Offensive, which proved *tactically* disastrous for the NLF but propagandistically, and ultimately *strategically*, decisive for the PAVN and DRV.

(2) After Tet: Giáp laid costly siege to a Marine firebase at Khe Sanh in early 1968, but was repulsed. U.S. forces and ARVN then moved into areas denuded of NLF/PAVN troops by Tet, including the A Shau Valley. Westmoreland's request for more troops to drive home the defeat of the NLF and win the war was denied because of the new political context in the United States. By the end of 1968 the decision was made in Washington to phase out American involvement in the war and to return to a policy not of "graduated response" (escalation), but pre-1965 denial of victory to the DRV. The American *home front* had folded, *McNamara* had resigned, PAVN was still a powerful and determined enemy, and *victory* looked both more distant and indefinable than before. Publication of the "Pentagon Papers," a secret summary of U.S. decision-making, raised suspicions about the truthfulness of government statements and further undermined public confidence. After mid-1968, the argument was over how fast—not whether—the United States should withdraw.

The Paris Peace Talks began on May 13, 1968; they would continue until 1973, the five years in which the United States both took and inflicted the most casualties in the war. In 1969 *Richard Nixon* stepped-up *Vietnamization*, reversing the pattern of Johnson's escalation, and subsequently traveled to Moscow and Beijing to obtain agreement to a prolonged truce, or what *Henry Kissinger* called in private "a decent interval" between U.S. withdrawal and *defeat* of the RVN. In the interim, Nixon was not loathe to strike out at the DRV with large-scale force. He thus authorized a secret U.S. and ARVN *incursion* into eastern Cambodia, in an extended "search-and-destroy" mission in 1970. And several times he, like Johnson, renewed and halted bombing of DRV installations and mining of DRV harbors. Those actions, continuing DRV infiltration of the RVN, and ongoing fighting in the fields and jungles took place while *peace talks* were underway in Paris, 1969–1972.

During 1971–1972 ARVN held the initiative in battle, as PAVN rebuilt its strength after Tet and Cambodia and trained on new Chinese and Soviet heavy weapons. By the end of 1971, U.S. forces were drawn down to 175,000, with just 75,000 of those being combat troops. Meanwhile, ARVN had become overextended when it intervened in Laos in 1971, there to lose fierce battles with heavy PAVN units. On March 30, 1972, Giáp launched a massive conventional invasion of the RVN. Just back from Beijing, Nixon ordered resumption of bombing of the DRV, including the first use of *smart weapons*, and mining of northern harbors to prevent seaborne resupply. Then he left for a *summit* in Moscow. The PAVN offensive was halted, at great cost to the DRV, and peace talks resumed in July. In October, Kissinger announced that "peace is at hand," but Thieu scuttled the deal and on December 13th talks broke down. On the 18th Nixon ordered a massive, B-52 "Christmas bombing" (Linebacker II) of the DRV. On the 28th talks resumed, culminating in the *Paris Peace Accords* on January 23, 1973.

Withdrawal of all American ground forces was completed in March 1973. Fighting between ARVN and PAVN continued, however: in 1973 ARVN lost more than 25,000 KIA (killed in action) and in 1974 it lost 31,000 KIA. In April 1975, greatly assisted by several disastrous decisions by Thieu, the Viêt Minh and PAVN completed via a conventional invasion of the RVN what had begun as a guerrilla campaign 30 years earlier: unification of all Vietnam under their iron rule. The United States evacuated Cambodia on April 12th. Its last personnel left by helicopter from the roof of the embassy in Saigon on April 29th. The next day, PAVN forces entered Saigon. The war was finally over. Roll call of the dead: 6,000 from the minor allies of the RVN; 58,000 Americans (47,000 KIA); 200,000 ARVN; some 1.1 million NLF and PAVN regulars, the official DRV figure; and two million civilians, also a DRV number. Many, many more on all sides were terribly wounded, in body, mind, or soul. *See also Clark Clifford; containment; domino theory; national liberation, wars of; mutiny; My Lai massacre; Nixon Doctrine; Wise Men.*

Suggested Readings: E. Irving, *The First Indochina War, 1945–1954*; George C. Herring, *America's Longest War* (1979); Anthony Joes, *The War for South Vietnam, 1954–1974* (rev. ed., 2001); David Kaiser, *American Tragedy* (2000); Stanley Karnow, *Vietnam* (1984); Robert McNamara, *In Retrospect* (1995); Andrew Rotter, *Path to Vietnam* (1987); Robert D. Schultzinger,

A *Time for War: The United States and Vietnam, 1941–1975* (1997); Marilyn Young, *The Vietnam Wars* (1991).

Vikings. "Northmen" or "Norsemen." Viking kingdoms arose out of the deeply divisive and bloody internal politics of Scandinavia in the first millennia C.E., only slowly coalescing into the recognizable modern divisions of the kingdoms of Denmark, Norway, and Sweden. The Vikings were fierce, pagan nomads from Scandinavia who used long boats (*galleys* modified with sails, with some capable of oceanic as well as coastal navigation) to raid the Atlantic and Mediterranean coasts of *Christian* Europe and the British Isles from the ninth to the eleventh centuries. They also sailed into the mid-Atlantic and settled Iceland and, less happily, Greenland. Briefly, they explored and attempted to settle parts of the east coast of North America. Less well known, they also traveled overland, so far south in fact that they helped found the first Russian state, *Kievan Rus*, in the ninth century. Thereafter, they conducted a rich Russian trade which stretched some 2,000 miles south and hundreds of miles eastward. They were driven outward from Scandinavia by the internal pressures of a warlike culture and factional politics, but especially by a rising population which could not be supported by Scandinavia's poor soils and long winters. They were also drawn southward by the sheer, simple lure of opportunities to *plunder* the far richer, more settled communities of Medieval Europe. Vikings captured the Orkney Islands, which from 875 to 1231 formed a Viking earldom under the crown of Norway. And they repeatedly raided into Scotland, even while warring among each other in Scandinavia. Other Viking adventurers settled, to set up fortified towns in Ireland (Dublin, Wexford, and other coastal cities began as Viking strongholds), in northern England and in Normandy.

Danish Vikings hammered for decades at the several Saxon kingdoms of England until they overran several. A truce was agreed with Alfred of Wessex (849–899), the last Saxon state in England, which left the Danes in control of north England and in receipt of a heavy annual *tribute* known as the "Danegeld." Vikings raided and ravaged, and then settled, in northern France, establishing there a powerful Castilian kingdom. These people later became known as the *Normans*, the greatest warrior nation of the Medieval Age. It was these Normans who launched the last successful invasion of England, under William the Conqueror, in 1066. Viking raiders also scoured the Baltic and penetrated deep into Germany. And they plundered and marauded all along the Atlantic coast of Iberia, and the Mediterranean coasts of Spain and Italy. A late Viking (Norman) kingdom was established in Sicily in the early twelfth century. As they settled, they adopted the ways of the peoples they conquered, including most importantly the *Christian* faith. Once the Scandinavian homeland itself converted to Christianity it became more fully integrated with Western Europe. With the rise of new sources of trading wealth among the Baltic cities of the *Hansa,* Viking raiding ebbed, and finally stopped.

Suggested Readings: J. B. Brondsted, *The Vikings* (1965); W. W. Fitzhugh and E. I. Ward, eds., *Vikings* (2000); P. Foote and D. M. Wilson, *The Viking Achievement* (1970); Gwyn Jones, *A History of the Vikings* (1968, 2001); Else Roesdahl, *The Vikings* (2nd ed., trans. 1998); P. H. Sawyer, *The Age of the Vikings* (1972).

Villa, Francisco (1877–1923). "Pancho." *Mestizo* bandit leader and Mexican revolutionary. He was a former muleteer, miner, and cattle rustler. He fought against *Díaz* in 1910 and 1911 and led peasant forces in northern Mexico during the *Mexican Revolution.* In 1914, he captured much northern territory for the constitutionalists. He opposed *Venustiano Carranza* after it became clear the latter's dedication to *agrarian reform* was shallow. In November 1914 Carranza left Mexico City for Veracruz, and Villa occupied the capital, where he was soon joined by *Zapata.* The U.S. supplied Carranza with weapons which gave him a distinct advantage. Villa retired to the north, but was pursued, and at the Battle of Celaya Villa's forces were defeated by Carranza's. Back in the north country, Villa's army fell apart and, although he kept up an intermittent *guerrilla* campaign for several years, he never again threatened to take power. However, he deliberately provoked U.S. *intervention* in Mexico by attacking a Texas town in 1916, in the apparent belief he could then play the role of defender of all Mexico against the "Yankee." *Woodrow Wilson* took the bait, so that much of the U.S. Army had to be recalled from chasing Villa when war was declared on Germany in April 1917. *See also George Patton; John J. Pershing.*

Suggested Reading: Frank McLynn, *Villa and Zapata: A Biography of the Mexican Revolution* (2000).

Vilna (Vilnius). The ancient *capital* of Lithuania. It was seized by Poland in 1920, but returned in 1939 as part of the settlement in the *Nazi-Soviet Pact.*

Vimy Ridge, Battles of. (1) First Vimy Ridge, 1915: The French Army launched a bloody, unsuccessful assault on this shoulder of the Somme front, suffering thousands of casualties. (2) Second Vimy Ridge, 1917: As part of the larger *Battle of Arras*, this was a spectacularly successful assault on April 16, 1917, by the Canadian Corps. Attacking entrenched, hill-top positions, the Canadians took the ridge where French troops had failed in 1915, and with remarkably few casualties. They suffered many more as the offensive sputtered out and the Germans recovered and counterattacked. This battle helped arouse both pride and an interest in an independent foreign policy for Canada after the war, the intent being to avoid repeating such carnage on behalf of Britain, for reasons so little understood. *See also Gallipoli.*

violation. When one party to a *treaty* acts against one or more of the *terms* of the agreement. This gives ground for *termination* by the other party(ies). *See also grave breaches.*

la violencia. *See Colombia.*

Virgin Islands of the United States. These three Caribbean islands were discovered by *Columbus* in 1493. They were claimed by the Spanish, who went on to utterly destroy the native population by 1596, supplanting it with European settlers. In 1917 the islands were purchased by the United States for naval use and then made an *unincorporated territory*. In 1927 residents were granted U.S. *citizenship*. In 1973 they received limited, non-voting representation in the U.S. House of Representatives.

visa. A permit or pass stamped or written on the *passport* of one country by a *consul* or *customs* official of another, allowing the bearer to enter or exit the second country. Visas may allow passage but still place considerable restrictions on the bearer, such as excluding areas which may be visited, compelling currency *exchange* at set government rates, prohibiting censored literature, or, in many Muslim countries, barring importation of alcohol or pornography. Visas may be temporary (*tourist*, transit, or work visa) or permanent (*immigration* visa).

visé. To issue, or to check, a *visa*.

Visegrad countries. The Czech Republic, Hungary, Slovakia, and Poland.

visible trade. Trade in tangible *goods*; not *services*.

visit and search. (1) The right of a *belligerent* to stop on the *high seas* and search for *contraband* any or all *neutral* shipping. (2) The right of any *state* to stop and inspect a foreign merchant ship if it suspects that ship of *piracy*, engaging in the *slave trade*, or concealing its *nationality* under a flag of false registration.

vis major. *See* force majeure.

vital interests. Any *national interest* which is, or is deemed to be, indispensable to the prosperity, future *development*, and, most of all, the *security* of a given *state*. A vital interest might be virtually anything perceived in such terms, including but not limited to access to markets or a *strategic* commodity such as *oil*, preventing encirclement by enemy powers, or preempting another state's acquisition of a *weapon of mass destruction*. When a state declares that it regards such-and-such as among its vital interests, it is indicating that it is prepared to use *force* to defend those defined interests. *See also self-help.*

VJ (Victory in Japan) Day. August 15, 1945 (GMT), when Japan indicated it would *surrender* to the *United Nations alliance.* The instruments of surrender were signed two weeks later, aboard the U.S.S. Missouri in Tokyo Bay.

Voice of America. A division of the United States Information Agency which makes worldwide shortwave broadcasts in multiple languages. During the *Cold War* its broadcasts were a supplement to the more clearly political work of *Radio Free Europe.*

Voivodina. Once part of the *Austro-Hungarian Empire*, it was ceded to *Yugoslavia* in the *Treaty of Trianon.* As an "autonomous region" it was attached to *Serbia* while both were part of Yugoslavia, except briefly during *World War II* when Hungary *occupied* and *annexed* it. It was retained by Serbia after the breakup of the Yugoslav federation. It has a large Hungarian minority.

volition. Choices made or decisions taken by freely willing individuals. Whether decisions are heavily conditioned by circumstance or not, *decision makers* always operate within a realm where some free choice is possible, and hence where moral and political accountability remain active. *See also determinism; rational choice theory.*

Volksdeutsche. Germanness, ethnically defined. For *Hitler*, "Volk" and "völkische" conveyed all the meanings of the English words "folk" and "race," while adding the German sense of "Kultur" (a superior civilization, and in *Nazi* terms also "blood," which was imbued with a historic, Hegelian "soul"). The Volk was supposedly rooted in the "Volksgemeinschaft," or "organic community." These terms were used by the Nazis to define *nationality* in terms of ethnicity rather than *citizenship*, and thus included Germans living beyond the borders of the *Reich* while excluding others living in-country (such as *Roma* or Jews). Alleged repression of the rights of the outer Volksdeutsche then became a favored ploy in agitating German-speaking populations against governments in Austria, Poland, and Czechoslovakia. The Volksdeutsche were heavily recruited into the SS. In postwar Germany, ethnically defined rights of citizenship continued, which meant that a Turk who had lived always in Germany had more difficulty securing citizenship than an ethnic German from Polish *Silesia* or Russia, who had never before set foot on German soil. An effort to reform this nationality law was made by Chancellor Gerhard Schroeder in 1998. *See also Fifth Column*; jus sanguinis; jus soli; *Minorities Treaties; naturalization.*

Voltaire, né François Marie Arouet (1694–1778). French "philosophe." Educated by the *Jesuits*, whom he frequently skewered, he was a leading figure in the *Enlightenment*. He corresponded with and advised *Catherine the Great*, *Frederick the Great*, and other monarchs, and greatly helped advance the career of *Jean-Jacques Rousseau*. He was alternately praised and exiled by these leaders, beaten and persecuted, spied upon and a paid spy (for the French, against Frederick), widely read and cited, or his many works censored, banned, and burned. Beginning in 1717, he spent nearly a year in the Bastille for having penned verses offensive to the regent to the young king of France. For 42 years he corresponded with Frederick, and after spying on him for a time later became a fawning courtier in Berlin. He never liked Prussia, describing it as "Athens in the morning, Sparta in the afternoon." Such wonderful insults to Prussian dignity and pretension was why Frederick finally lost patience and had him taken to the border, stripped, beaten badly, and kicked out of the kingdom. Voltaire's writings had such an impact that his history of *Louis XIV*, "Siècle de Louis Quatorze," gave the name of that brilliant, brooding king to the Age itself. His novel "Candide" likewise did much to expose the myth of benevolent *colonialism* through its savage honesty about conditions on the plantations of the Americas. Voltaire had Candide, seeing a mutilated, dying slave, unforgettably recognize that "this is the price of sugar in Europe." Of the *Holy Roman Empire* he famously, and accurately, said: "It is neither holy, nor Roman, nor an empire." During the *rites controversy* he wrote influential books on China, noting how its *Confucian* civilization seemed to have got on quite nicely over the ages in the absence of Christian "revelation," relying instead on the light of reason and philosophy. Voltaire's satire was biting, his pen acid, his irreverence subversive of authority in the best possible sense, his wit infectious and politically penetrating, and his influence lasting. His motto: "au fait!" ("to the facts!").

voluntary export restraints (VERs). Also called voluntary restraint agreements (VRAs). These are actually involuntary export restrictions which everyone agrees to pretend are voluntary in order to limit the political fallout from a serious trade *dispute*. The first major industry affected by VERs, which are a form of *nontariff barrier*, was steel. Japanese automobiles were targeted for VERs by the United States and *European Community* starting in the 1980s. Japan agreed to curtail its exports and to negotiate VER limits under threat of unilateral, mandatory *quotas*. This led to application of VERs to other industries where *trade wars* threatened to break out or where the importing nation threatened to close its market to specified goods. A near-synonym is "orderly market arrangements." *See also protectionism.*

voting, in international bodies. *See qualified majority voting; unanimity rule; veto; weighted voting.*

"voting with their feet." (1) A coinage of *Lenin's*, in response to queries about the democratic legitimacy of the *Bolshevik* regime. He maintained, radical tongue planted firmly in cheek, that Russia's soldiers and peasants had voted for *revolution* "with their feet" when they threw down their rifles and walked home from the *eastern front*. By the same token, erecting the *Berlin Wall* and drawing down the *Iron Curtain* demonstrated how little Soviet leaders trusted their chances of reelection. (2) Any similar mass movement, especially a *migration*, which effects basic political change without formal consultation.

Vukovar. An ethnic Serb *enclave* forming part of eastern Slavonia, in modern Croatia. It is known regionally for its agricultural bounty and minor *oil* reserves. It was the scene of heavy fighting during Croatia's war of *secession* from Yugoslavia, 1991–1995. The Yugoslav (Serbian) Army shelled Vukovar for three months in 1991, destroying much of the ancient city and killing 10,000 Croats. Nearly 100,000 Croats were later expelled by the occupying Serbs. Serbian military fortunes slowly waned as a result of battlefield losses and international *sanctions*. The United Nations mediated a gradual handover to Croatia, completed in December 1997.

vulnerability. Under *interdependence*, when changes in economic conditions within one state have sharply adverse consequences for another. This is true of most small powers on most issues in their relations with larger powers. It also applies to *Great Powers* on issues such as access to foreign reserves of *strategic resources* or sudden fluctuations in *exchange rates* as a result of a change in *interest rates* set by a major trading partner.

Vyshinsky, Andrei Yamuareivich (1883–1954). Soviet foreign minister, 1949–1953. He was a front man for *Stalin*, both as commissar for foreign affairs in the 1940s and earlier, when he carved out a noxious reputation for baiting and vilifying defendants during the *Yezhovshchina* and *show trials*. Nightmare states such as Stalin's could not stand if they did not rest on pylons sunk into the small talents and perverse loyalties of such gray functionaries as Andrei Vyshinsky. *See also Mikhail Kalinin.*

W

Wadai. A small Central African sultanate located between *Bornu* and *Dafar*. Nominally Muslim, into the nineteenth century it lived off *ivory* trade in the deep interior and *slave*-raiding of less advanced animist and *stateless* populations to the south.

Waffen SS. *See Schutzstaffel.*

Wahhabi. A puritanical Islamic sect founded in eighteenth century Arabia by Abd al-Wahhab (1703–1792). The Wahhabi follow the Hanbali legal tradition, the strictest and most militant within *Islam*. As a political movement Wahhabism emerged from deep desert isolation in the 1760s, to launch a *jihad* against other Muslims they considered to be followers of less pure forms of Islamic observance. During the first decade of the nineteenth century they conquered most of Arabia. They invaded the south of modern Iraq in 1802 and then overran the *Hejaz*, capturing *Mecca* (1803) and Medina (1805). *Mehemet Ali* was sent by the Ottomans to deal with the Wahhabi uprising. They were thrown out of Mecca and back to the deep desert by 1818, but remained a threat to the new desert power into the 1840s. In the twentieth century the Wahhabi supported *Abd al-Aziz ibn Saud* in his bid to regain control of the Hejaz and thereafter sustained the Saudi *dynasty* in its control of the Islamic holy lands against challenges from Iraq, from radical *shi'ites* in Iran, and from other *tribes* of the interior of Arabia. In the latter twentieth century Wahhabism spread as an influential, *fundamentalist* reform movement even in non-Arab lands. It took deepest and most disastrous root in Sudan and Afghanistan. In the former, it sustained a brutal jihad against Christian and animist tribes in the south, including a revived *slave trade*; in the latter, radical Wahhabis took power in the 1990s under the *Taliban* in cooperation with *al Qaeda*, ultimately bringing down on that country the wrath of the United States after the *September 11th, 2001 terrorist attack on the United States*. *See also Oman.*

Waitangi, Treaty of (1840). Agreed with approximately 500 *Maori* chiefs, this treaty gave Britain *sovereignty* over most of New Zealand in exchange for protection of Maori land claims from white settlers. When the British failed to uphold this guarantee, the first *Maori War* began. *See also tribe; validity.*

Wake Island. Located on the Hawaii-to-Hong Kong *trade route*, this Pacific island was claimed by the United States in 1898. It was captured by Japan early in *World War II*, but was later retaken. It had no *indigenous population*. After 1972 it was administered by the U.S. Air Force. *Guam* claims Wake, as does the *Marshall Islands*.

wakō. Mostly ethnic Japanese *pirates* who, in the fourteenth through sixteenth centuries, plundered the coasts of China, Japan, and Korea. Sometimes wakō fleets landed several thousand armed brigands. On the other hand, as in Europe at that time, *piracy* and *trade* were closely linked, with pirates often enjoying governmental protection and encouragement. *See also Taiwan.*

Waldheim, Kurt (b. 1918). *Secretary general* of the *United Nations*, 1971–1982; Austrian foreign minister, 1968–1970; president, 1986–1992. He was ineffective at the United Nations because of his election as a compromise candidate, a chronic impasse in the *Security Council*, and his passive personality. Files released in the mid-1980s showed he had covered up his war record (he had been an *intelligence* officer in the *Wehrmacht* during *World War II*). In 1988 an international panel of historians concluded that Waldheim had known of *war crimes* committed in *Yugoslavia* during the war and, although not participating himself in the killings, did nothing to stop them. A highly unusual diplomatic *boycott* of Austria ensued, with many states, led by Israel, refusing to maintain full *diplomatic relations* as long as Waldheim remained president. He stayed popular at home, however, where local opinion grew more defiant even as *world public opinion* became more critical. In 1994 Israel's recently improved relations with the *Vatican* deteriorated again over the latter's award of a public honor to Waldheim for his supposed "safeguarding [of] *human rights*" as secretary general.

Wales. This southwestern part of the island of *Great Britain* was peopled by Celts for centuries before the Roman conquest of Britain. It regained its independence after the Roman withdrawal. It was conquered and annexed to England in 1286 by Edward I ("Longshanks") after a six-year campaign. It was governed as an integral part of England's interior empire for the next 700 years without experiencing rebellions and oppressions similar to those in Scotland or Ireland. In 1999 it was given limited *autonomy*, under a regional assembly, within the *United Kingdom*.

Walesa, Lech (b. 1943). Polish statesman. Former worker and trade union leader in the *Gdansk* shipyards, he founded and led *Solidarity* from the 1970s, through its banned period under *martial law*, and then to electoral victory in 1989 and 1990, with himself elected as president of Poland. He was awarded the *Nobel Prize* for peace in 1983. Admiration for him in the West, and his close relationship with Pope *John Paul II*, raised Poland's importance and influence in international relations. In 1992 he apologized to all Jews, and to Israel, for remarks he made as president which were tainted with *anti-Semitism*. In 1993 he resigned from Solidarity, citing its refusal to accept his reform proposals. His influence declined as Poland left the struggle against *communism* and the broad Solidarity movement behind, sought greater integration with the West, and resumed the normal politics of factional and policy division.

Walker, William (1824–1860). *Filibuster* extraordinaire. Short, small, but intensely fierce in his personal habits and politics, in 1853 Walker sailed from San Francisco with just 45 men, many of them rootless and restless "Forty-niners," determined to seize and colonize Baja, California. He easily captured La Paz and proclaimed himself president of a "Baja Republic." Joined by additional recruits eager for more easy spoils, he next proclaimed the annexation of neighboring Sonora province from Mexico, which he promptly invaded. His small force met mainly with disease, desertions, and defeat. Walker and a handful of survivors fled back across the Rio Grande. Now famous and widely popular in *California, Texas,* and the *slave* South, Walker was nonetheless arrested and tried for violation of U.S. *neutrality* laws. Unfortunately, he was acquitted by a jury of eight *nullifiers* who ignored all evidence in their eagerness (they deliberated for less than 10 minutes) to acquit a man who was fast becoming a hero of American expansionism, especially within the *slave states.*

Walker's next expedition was even more ambitious, backed as it was financially by the *railway* tycoon Cornelius Vanderbilt, who wanted the filibusterers to seize Nicaragua so that he could build a pan-isthmian canal there. In May 1855, Walker sailed with the first allotment of 57 American adventurers to join the rebel side in an ongoing civil war in Nicaragua. Walker's men and the rebels together defeated the Legitimist forces and took power. Walker named himself commander-in-chief of the Nicaraguan Army and in the months which followed recruited or was joined by another 2,000 Americans. In addition to the usual frontier *mercenaries* and freebooters, among these recruits were many fire-eating Southerners eager to seize Central America for

"The Cause" of expanded *slavery*. In contrast, most of the northern papers and population regarded Walker as anything but a hero and closer to the pirate and petty dictator which he was in fact. In 1856 the pro-slavery government of President Franklin Pierce *recognized* Walker's regime. That same year the *Democratic Party*—then dominated by Southern slave interests—adopted a national plank endorsing an American imperium over the whole Gulf of Mexico, which leading opinion in the old South had come to regard as an area "natural" for expansion of the "peculiar institution" which Northern *Whigs*, and now also *Republicans*, had succeeded in blocking from westward advance.

The other governments of Central America rightly feared this American intrusion and organized to topple Walker. They were backed by none other than Vanderbilt, whom Walker had alienated over a business matter. When the rebel president of Nicaragua defected to the Central American alliance, Walker installed himself as president. This compelled even the Pierce administration to withdraw *diplomatic recognition*. Throwing in his lot entirely with the "slave power" of the South, on September 22, 1856, Walker revoked the 1824 constitution by which slavery had been abolished in Nicaragua. The South predictably rallied to his support, but the Central American armies defeated him in battle anyway. Walker and his men surrendered to the U.S. Navy and thus were carried to New Orleans on a U.S. warship. They left more than 1,000 dead Americans, and many more dead Nicaraguans, behind them. In November 1857, an unrepentant Walker sailed back to Nicaragua to reclaim his "presidency." This time, the U.S. Navy intercepted him and returned him to New Orleans to again stand trial for violation of U.S. neutrality laws. A Southern, nullification jury acquitted him for a second time.

Febrile demonstrations of Southern support persuaded Walker to try to invade Nicaragua yet again. He departed from Mobile in 1858, but the ship hit a reef some 60 miles offshore. Walker was returned to the United States by a British warship, which had picked up survivors. This humiliation dampened Southern enthusiasm for new expeditions. Yet, Walker tried a fourth time. Just under a hundred Southern boys agreed to join what proved to be his last invasion. They planned to join together in Honduras and then invade Nicaragua, but they were quickly captured. Walker surrendered to a British naval captain, expecting to be returned to the United States. Instead, he was handed over to the Honduran government. On September 12, 1860, he met his deserved end before a Honduran firing squad. *See also Hernando Cortés*; *Nicaragua*.

Wallace (a.k.a. Walays, Wallensis), William (c. 1274–1305). Patriot, *guerrilla* leader, and Guardian of Scotland. His origins and education are shrouded in speculation and myth. His first confirmed appearance was in 1297, the year after the English sack of Berwick, when he emerged as a brilliant guerrilla leader, at first mainly of his own clansmen, later of most common Scots. At

Lanark, his small band burned an English fort and slew the sheriff and garrison after the murder of Wallace's wife. His father had also been killed by the English. He led a Scottish army to victory over the king's men at Stirling Bridge (September 11, 1297), where a heavy, Victorian stone monument stands today. At Stirling, he put an end to the rule of heavy *cavalry* which had dominated late *feudal* warfare for several centuries. The English retreated from Scotland, but Wallace followed, leading punitive raids through the north country. When he returned to Edinburgh he was elected by the Scottish nobles "Guardian of Scotland." In 1298 Edward I ("Longshanks") invaded Scotland with a huge army—by the standard of that day—of nearly 90,000 men. Wallace and the Scots met Edward's English troops at Falkirk (July 22, 1298), but the Scottish nobles and cavalry abandoned the field and the remaining peasant *infantry* were mown down by superior Welsh archers using a deadly new weapon, the longbow; English swordsmen and Irish infantry finished the job. Wallace went to France, and possibly also to Norway and to Rome, to seek assistance. He was absent during the Comyn Wars (1297–1304). He reappeared in Scotland in 1304 and resumed his guerrilla campaign, until betrayed and arrested in 1305. He was convicted of *treason* in London, though he was the one Scottish rebel never to have sworn allegiance to England's king, and was savagely tortured, hanged, drawn, quartered, and beheaded. In accordance with the usual English practice, the quarters of his body were dispatched as a warning to the four corners of the kingdom: Newcastle, Stirling, Berwick, and Perth. "He has no tomb. He needed none."

Wallenstein, Albrecht Wenzel von (1583–1634). Bohemian *mercenary* and *Habsburg* general. From first to last, in his lucrative marriages and prolonged wars, Wallenstein was motivated by exceptional ambition for power, titles, and estates. He achieved all three, beyond that of any other man of the Age, but also lost it all in bloody betrayal. He married great wealth in 1614 and married again for new estates when his first wife died. When the *Thirty Years' War* broke out, he spurned the entreaties of *Protestant* rebels in Bohemia, instead raising troops from his vast estates for the Habsburgs of the *Holy Roman Empire*. In 1625 he was given command of all Imperial armies by *Ferdinand II* of Austria. In coordination, but also in constant rivalry, with the other great Habsburg general of that war, *Johan Tilly*, he fought many battles in behalf of imperial authority and *Catholic* rights (though he was himself an agnostic mystic), but always with an eye to his own aggrandizement, power, and wealth. He drove Hungary from the war in 1627, joined Tilly to defeat Christian IV of Denmark in 1628, and occupied much of Germany. His unquenchable ambition, constant intrigue, and growing independence posed a real threat to the monarchy. He was accordingly dismissed by Ferdinand in 1630. He retired to his estates, but was recalled in 1631 as Catholic armies fled from the Swedish army of *Gustavus Adolphus*. Wallenstein stopped the Swedes from occupying Vienna. He thus rose even further in power and potential, until he was badly beaten at Lützen in 1632 by Adolphus, who died of wounds received in the battle. Ferdinand decided to finish Wallenstein for good in 1634 when he learned that—ever the *mercenary*—he was intriguing with other Catholic and even Protestant powers to hire out his services and his army and force Ferdinand to make an unwelcome peace. Wallenstein learned of the plot against his life—he was charged with *treason*—and fled toward Swedish lines. He was tracked down and murdered by Scottish and Irish captains working for the Habsburgs.

Suggested Reading: Golo Mann, *Wallenstein* (1976).

Wallis and Fortuna Islands. Once a *colony* of *Tonga*, these sparsely populated archipelagoes became French *protectorates* in 1887. In 1957 they voted to become French *overseas territories.*

Wall Street crash. *See Black Tuesday.*

Walpole, Robert (1676–1745). He was chancellor of the Exchequer on several occasions, including after 1721 when the *South Seas Bubble* burst. As the first prime minister of Great Britain, 1724–1742, he pursued a conservative, restrained, and pacific foreign policy which was deeply unpopular, but also inexpensive. He kept Britain out of the *War of the Polish Succession*, but after initial resistance he was compelled to make war on Spain during the *War of Jenkins' Ear.*

Walvis Bay. A British *colony* deep inside Southwest Africa (Namibia), annexed to *Cape Colony* in 1878. In 1910 it was incorporated as an *exclave* of the Union of South Africa. In 1993 it was ceded to Namibia.

Wanghia, Treaty of (1844). Negotiated between China and the United States in the immediate aftermath of the *First Opium War*, it mimicked the terms of the *Treaty of Nanjing* (1842), but added new clauses expanding foreign rights and immunities under the doctrine of *extraterritoriality*. These clauses were subsequently added by other foreign powers to treaties negotiated with China, progressively stripping it of *sovereign* control of its trade and ports, and restricting the reach of its *municipal law* on its own territory. All that contributed to a growing anti-foreigner component in Chinese nationalism, along with growing anger with the *Qing dynasty* for its acceptance of legal *capitulations* and symbolic humiliations.

Wang Jingwei (Ching-wei, 1883–1944). Chinese traitor. A founding member of the *Revolutionary Alliance* and one of *Sun Yixian's* key lieutenants, he was prominent during the *Chinese Revolution* (1911). In the 1920s he was on the left of the *Guomindang*, but then joined *Chiang Kai-shek*. He headed the regional government in Wuhan from 1927 and then served as head of the administrative council and as party president, 1932–1935. He was nearly assassinated in 1935; he fled to *Hong Kong* in 1938. After the Japanese invasion he *collaborated*, becoming a vassal prime minister of a *puppet state* in occupied central China, with his "capital" in the same city where the Japanese butchered probably 300,000 civilians during the *rape of Nanjing*. He died in Japan in 1944. *See also Benedict Arnold; Konoe Fumimaro; Pierre Laval; Vidkun Quisling.*

Wanli emperor (r. 1572–1620). Reign name of Zhu Yijun (1563–1620), *Ming* emperor. After 1500 China suffered from recurring ossification of the central government and scholar-elite into both endemic corruption and a rigid *Confucianism* which ultimately was unable to adapt the rural economy to the expanding population. This crisis was aggravated by, and personified in, the progressive isolation and unreality of Wanli's reign, once he withdrew from public service in the 1580s into the *Forbidden City*, leaving administration to corrupt advisers and imperial eunuchs, who numbered near 10,000. Once responsible and keen, as he aged he increasingly shirked most of his duties, retreating into a semi-private and monkish life of study and reflection in the Forbidden City. In response, some Confucian scholars led the "Donglin reform movement" to curb eunuch power, but this was violently crushed by the eunuchs, 1624–1627.

Wannsee conference (January 20, 1942). The *Nazi* conference hosted by *Eichmann* and *Heydrich* at which the "*final solution to the Jewish problem*" was planned by leaders of the *SD* and *SS*. There never was before in history such a chilling meeting: functionaries of one of the world's great nations sat at a conference table and coldly, clinically, and methodically planned the mass murder of millions of fellow human beings. They talked as though the issues at stake were nothing more than logistics—of transport, rail schedules, personnel and morale issues, pay rates, construction contracts, and engineering specifications for the *death camps* and other instruments of industrial butchery of an unarmed people, along with their own advancement should they complete the task at the speed requested and to the full satisfaction and pleasure of their masters in Berlin. When these murderous gangsters were done, three years later, more than six million Jews, and several million more non-Jews, had been sacrificed at the altars of their hatred, twisted ambition, and evil loyalty to *Hitler* and the Nazi regime. *See also anti-Semitism; Auschwitz; concentration camps; Dachau; ethnic cleansing; genocide; Gestapo; Herman Göring; Heinrich Himmler; Holocaust; National Socialism.*

war. War's distinguishing characteristic is organized mass violence. In its conduct it is, as *Clausewitz* explained so well, an admixture of three essential ingredients: violence, chance, and rational purpose. In more precise terms, it is armed conflict within, between, or among states (or other political communities, such as *ethnic groups* or *tribes*) in which basic economic, political, or other public outcomes are decided primarily by superior force, not in accordance with principles of law or justice, by the light of reason, or moderate negotiation. By convention, outbreaks of mass political violence are termed wars (as opposed to riots or "communal violence") when 1,000 or more are killed and opposing camps are organized into regular formations whose purpose is to oppose violence by, or inflict murder upon, the other side. War is also a legal state of open and declared hostility between or among states, wherein they may use any force deemed fit or effective, subject only to the *laws of war* and perhaps to notions of *just war*. In this sense, war is the ultimate *self-help* device. The narrowest meaning of the term is the art and science of military operations, including *logistics*, *strategy*, and *tactics*. Discourse on war classifies the phenomenon according to an ascending scale of participation, thus: *rebellion, insurrection, insurgency, guerrilla war, civil war, regional war*; and then three synonyms, global war, *systemic war*, and *world war*. Or war may be typed by the main weapons used to conduct it, as in *conventional war* or *nuclear war*. Or it may be ranked by scope, objectives, and targeting, as in *limited war* and *total war*.

At its most basic level, war is simply the use of massive force to compel an enemy to do one's will. At the other extreme, armed conflict may aim at some higher good such as achievement of an improved *peace*—one that is more stable and just. War has driven the largest social, economic, political, diplomatic, demographic, and other changes in history. It built and broke empires, ancient and modern. It made and unmade tyrants, and whole nations and peoples. And it made the modern *state*, which used it to suppress internal rebellion and private force, usually under a strong centralized monarch, but then was faced with other powerful states like itself and thus was forced to further centralize bureaucracy and administration, raise new taxes and revenues, and sustain large *standing armies* and navies. War has also changed during the modern period. Starting in c. 1500, for reasons largely technological and administrative, European states experienced a radical expansion in the scale and destructiveness of war. Referred to by some historians as a *revolution in military affairs* (RMA), this shift ended Europe's ancient vulnerability to invasion and conquest—by *Normans, Magyars, Mongols, Arabs*, and others whose very social structures were organized for war and *plunder*. It then helped launch Europe on its own path of world conquest, *colonialism*, and *imperialism*. Thus began a new phase in warfare in which it was closely intertwined with *exploration* and *trade*, constituting a new phase of world history also, which lasted to the mid-twentieth century. Only then did non-Europeans—Japanese, Americans, Soviets—equal and then surpass European states in military power and proficiency.

Globally, during this 500-year period the most important effect of war was to force nation-building and technological innovation—first and most dramatically among Europe's *Great Powers*, but ultimately in all successful societies—by threatening all communities with fear, insecurity, and destruction. Subsequent RMAs, in the nineteenth and twentieth centuries, and the process of *diffusion*, spread advances in military technology across the globe. War also sparked major social reform, as when improving national health and education levels became policy in nineteenth-century Britain upon the discovery that too many conscripts were illiterate or sickly. In these ways and many others, war has concentrated the mind and focused the political will of individuals and whole communities as has no other human endeavor, and thus it has had deeper and more lasting effects than any other phenomenon in history.

War is highly organized, purposeful, political violence. It thus has important legal ramifications as well. At a more sophisticated level than that of mere or unadulterated *power politics*, it has two recognizable legal objectives, especially when undertaken by one or more of the Great Powers: (i) it is a device for enforcing political claims based on asserted legal rights; and (ii) it is a means of overturning an existing legal order, either to unilaterally alter it to one's own advantage, as in Iraq's 1990 attempt to deny Kuwait's *sovereignty* by *occupation* and *annexation*, or China's 1962 affirmation by force of its preferred border with India; or to compel other states to adjust to fundamentally changed conditions in the *international system* of which the law has not yet taken account, such as *Bismarck's* reordering of the *balance of power* in Europe, first in fact and then in law, through demonstration of its *preponderance* in successful wars. Among lesser legal ramifications of war, it severs *diplomatic relations*, if accompanied by a *declaration of war*. War has a mixed effect on *treaties*, dissolving some, but simply placing most in abeyance (*suspension*), while calling others related to the laws of war into operation and effect. War also severs legal relations among citizens of *belligerent* states. Thus, war must be understood not simply as the moral crudity of superior physical power carrying the day on a given dispute, but as a complex of legal, economic, psychological, and political motives, tactics, and effects.

As for causation, the crudest cause of war is also its most frequent: organized theft. War may result when one side, or both sides, in a conflict over scarce resources or territory decides to seek some comparative economic gain—land, population, raw materials, markets—by resort to force. Other factors in the decision to make war may include the belief (mistaken or not) that it will serve the dynastic, social, religious, ideological, or other partisan purposes of rulers or elites. Or it may be undertaken to gratify the collective egoism ("honor") of national, ethnic, or tribal groups. Or it may arise from civil strife and economic desperation, compounded by social and economic inequalities in a given society. Thus understood, it emerges that war is seldom primarily the result of accident, miscalculation, the "structure of the system," evil genius, or the inevitable consequence of "human nature" or "anarchic" political conditions. All of the above may and do conduce to war, but at the end of the day the decision to resort to armed conflict is always a conscious act initiated by deliberate choice: war is the political instrument selected, somewhere, by someone, in preference to peace. Often (mis)quoted on this aspect of war, as essentially a continuation of political struggle by violent means, is Clausewitz.

Theories about the root causes of war abound, many characterized by crude and oversimplified generalization, some by genuine insight, and others by a pose of objectivity or by intellectual but *scientistic* sophistication. Some ideas about the origins of war are clearly and demonstrably false, but that does not deny them adherents. The most commonly argued, and sometimes mutually exclusive, theses on the general cause of war are the following:

(i) War is inevitable. It arises from an ineluctable human nature, which we see produce similar patterns of conflict across all history and diverse cultures. Classically, this assumed common nature is regarded as innately self-seeking and aggressive. A more recent anthropological and behavioral variant sees it as inherently territorial. Philosophically as well as temperamentally, this view tends to deep pessimism about all proposed solutions for "perpetual peace," to suggest short-term solutions only, such as the balance of power (as a policy) or building up one's defensive strength, and at the extreme exhibits a profound fatalism about the eschatological destiny of the species.

(ii) War results from conspiracy. Various *devil theories of war* focus on the role of evil leaders, and/or secret and manipulative special interests, who are said to seek war as an instrument of personal, clique, or class gain. War can, in this view, be easily ended—everywhere and forever—simply by barring from power the special interests which favor and profit from it. However, the means of removal may themselves involve great violence, amounting even to war, which is always justified as the necessary price of perpetual peace. Two common subsets of this thesis are: (a) if only we could root out and destroy the identified conspirators (say, a racial, religious, or ethnic minority, or some social or economic elite) whose interests war serves, there would be no more war; and (b) we should make all politics, domestic and international, so utterly uniform and transparent that the "natural pacifism" of plain folks, or proletarians, or the faithful, will ensure lasting peace.

(iii) War is a systemic phenomenon. It results mainly, and for more rigid *international relations theorists*, even exclusively, from interstate or other political animosities which are determined by how world order is arranged (how power is distributed) and states are arrayed, at any given historical moment. There are numerous variants of this thesis, of more-or-less sophistication, all of which locate the fundamental causation of war in international "structure," including: (a) war as a product of shifting and competing political and military forces (*power transition theory*), or of *imperialism* (as conceived in *Marxism-Leninism*), or some disequilibrium in the balance of power; (b) economic scarcity, as was the view both in *mercantilism* and of it, by liberal critics such as *Adam Smith* or, more crudely, *Jeremy Bentham*; or (c) unbridled monopoly capitalist competition (*world capitalism*), a more recent variant on item (a) above. In all such variations the *structure* of the *international system* is said to be determinative, the underlying and unseen force which increases or decreases *tension*, helps to identify and determine enemies, and exacerbates *conflicts* by turning otherwise resolvable disputes into a *zero sum game* in which each side fears the *defection* of the other and so is driven to strike first.

(iv) Wars occur by accident. In this view, unforeseen events or the confrontational structure of this or that *crisis* may conduce to *misperception* of an opponent's intentions by *decision makers* acting under stress, lead to faulty decision-making, and then to "unintended" armed conflict. Immersed in accident, confusion, misinformation, and overexcited advisers presenting worst case scenarios, events will tend to spin out of control so that no one leader makes a fully informed or deliberate decision to go to war, and adversaries instead stumble over the precipice together. This is a widely popular explanation of war, including of the origins of specific wars such as *World War I*. True or not of some wars, and in most cases it is not an accurate depiction, this proposition does not speak to the causes of war as a general phenomenon because it says nothing at all about the many conflicts in which naked *aggression* and other deliberate decisions are the clear cause of fighting.

(v) War results from parochial thinking. Versions of this thesis include the idea that a lack of global imagination (or for Marxists, "false consciousness") leads to failure to recognize the putative, general, or *cosmopolitan* interest of all humanity (or the *proletariat*) and hence to conflict which "right thinking" ("class consciousness") would avoid. Such reflection about war and peace may take an apocalyptic form, in which it is assumed that rather than material or territorial interests at stake the real conflict with an enemy regime or society is a conflict of incompatible, even Manichean, belief systems (*fascism, communism*, muscular *Christianity*, *Islam*, and so on), or ethnic or cultural identities (*Volk, nation, tribe*). Conversely, exclusionary ideologies are said to animate, some other community to seek domination over, or even extermination of one's own, owing to the nature of its ideological worldview. If this conviction about the origin of war is adopted, the proposed solution is nearly always to reconstruct regional or world order in accordance with some presumed genuinely universal principle of political, social, or economic justice. The problem is agreeing on which universal principle to employ, and what to do with recalcitrants from the other side who refuse to reform or conform.

Over the centuries theocrats of different cast proposed idealized systems of universal justice they claimed to know directly from the mind of God (Jehovah, Allah, the Buddha, Shiva, etc.). For early liberals it was such theocrats who were the main problem, along with the hoary aristocracies and monarchies whose legitimacy they upheld. Late eighteenth-century liberals instead proposed a universal, rational humanism based upon the moral, psychological, and scientific insights of the *Enlightenment* and upheld by representative government and material prosperity born of *free trade*. No one said this better than *Kant*. By the middle of the nineteenth century, Marxists were pointing to the hypocrisy of early liberal capitalism as the core problem because it permitted severe class and other economic disparities at home and appeared to encourage colonial exploitation of non-European peoples. In this latter conclusion, at least, they were mostly wrong. Mercantilism had been far more conducive to the construction of overseas empire. Because they were simultaneous processes, Marxists mistook the expansion of European dominion over most of the world for capitalism, when the former arose from the deeper *great divergence* brought about after c. 1500 by still precapitalist technological and organizational changes in Europe.

Then Marxists offered to substitute for markets and free trade a far more radical, apocalyptic even, but still secular, solution to the problem of war: the universal brotherhood of proletarians. This was achievable, said Marx, only through violent class and international conflict which would end in perpetual peace under world *communism*. This cosmopolitan pretension was paid lip service by real-world communism in the twentieth century. Mostly, it was deployed as an adjunct to more narrow imperial interests of Russia, both out of ideological sincerity and once the *Bolsheviks* felt threatened by neighboring non-communist (and later, also communist) political and religious communities which they had done much to provoke to animosity. Ultimately, the idea of the Soviet Union as the flag bearer of a universal socialist brotherhood which promised eventual world peace was rejected by the *community of nations*, including all other socialist states.

At the end of the *Cold War*, Marxist claims were shelved almost everywhere and liberal governing principles were reaffirmed by the majority of states, including most Great Powers. They had in any case already been formally lodged in international treaties, enshrined in *international law*, and embedded in the constitutions of major international organizations and other multilateral instruments, including the *United Nations Charter*, the *Helsinki Accords*, and the *Charter of Paris*. In every quarter of the globe, almost especially where they were not respected in fact, these principles were declared to be self-evident and universal in morality and application, and to support perpetual peace. Whether or not this rhetorical triumph of Kantian idealism constituted the *end of history* was moot, but it certainly did not end all wars. Post–Cold War, small wars proliferated as states formerly propped up by superpower competitors were allowed to collapse, and regions of marginal strategic interest and value dropped back to reality from prior heights to which they had been inflated during the long global contest. As for perpetual peace, as *Clemenceau* said of the great expectations raised throughout Europe nearly a century ago by the *Fourteen Points*, "we shall see."

In any essay, however compact, on the nature of war, the last word belongs by right to warriors who have seen and suffered its consequences directly. The final say here, therefore, goes to generals on different sides of different wars, not simply because they are more famous than ordinary soldiers but because they spoke simply and directly to profound truths about one or another aspect of war. *Wellington*, at *Waterloo*: "Nothing except a battle lost can be half so melancholy as a battle won." *Robert E. Lee*, upon seeing a Union charge repulsed at Fredericksburg: "It is well that war is so terrible, else we should grow too fond of it." And especially *William T. Sherman*, recalling the great carnage of the *American Civil War*: "War is at best barbarism. . . . Its glory is all moonshine. It is only those who have neither fired a shot nor heard the shrieks and groans of the wounded who cry aloud for blood, more vengeance, more destruction. War is hell." *See also accidental war; active defense; act of war; airborne; airburst; aircraft carrier; airdrop; air power; angary; anti–ballistic missile, missile (ABM); anti-personnel weapon; antisatellite weapons (ASAT); anti-submarine warfare (ASW); area defense; armed hostilities; armed neutrality; armistice; armor; arms race; arsenal; artillery; atomic bomb; atomic demolition mine (ADM); attrition; ballistic missile; ballistic missile defense (BMD); barrage balloon; battle cruiser; battle fatigue; battleship; beachhead; belligerency; belligerent rights; besiege; billets; binary weapons; biological warfare; blast effects; Blitzkrieg; blockade; blue water navy; bomb; bombardment; bomber; booty; bridgehead; bus; C³; C³I; camouflage; campaign; cannon; cannon fodder; capital warships; capture; carpet bombing; case shot; casus belli; cavalry; cease-fire; chemical and biological warfare; chemical agents; civil defense; civilian; cobelligerency; coercion; collaboration; collateral damage; combat area; commando; conquest; conscription; convoy; counterattack; counterinsurgency; crimes against humanity; crimes against peace; cruise missile; cruiser; D-Day; death squad; defeat; defeat-in-detail; defeatism; defense; defense area; defense-in-depth; defilade; demilitarized zone (DMZ); demonstration; depth charge; destroyer; deterrence; dimension of war; disengagement; diversionary war; dog fight; Dreadnought; dynastic war; élan vital; emplacement; enceinte; enemy prisoner of war (EPW); enfilade; entrench; envelopment; escalation control; escalation dominance; ethnic cleansing; feint; field artillery; fighter; fighter-bomber; firebreak; first line; first strike; first use; flagship; flak; flank; foot soldiers; force; fortification; forward defense; fraternize; friction; friendly fire; frigate; frontline; gas weapons; General Staff; Geneva Conventions; Geneva Protocol; genocide; grapeshot; guerre couverte; guerre mortelle; guerrilla warfare; guided missile; gunnery; Hague Conferences; Hague Conventions; heavy (bomber, cruiser, missile etc.); high command; home front; hostilities; hot war; hunter-killer; hydrogen bomb; impressment; incendiary weapons; incursion; indiscriminate bombing; infantry; inter bellum et pacem; Intercontinental Ballistic Missile (ICBM); interdiction; internment; intervention; intrawar deterrence; intrusion; invasion; ironclads; jihad; kamikaze; landing craft; land mine; land power; launcher; launch on warning; letters of marque; levée en masse; liberation; limited nuclear war; limited war; line officer; living off the land; low-intensity conflict; Luftwaffe; manned penetrator; man-of-war; measures short of war; mercenary; military government; military law; military necessity; military objective; military ranks; military science; military units; militia; MIRV; mobilization; mortar; munitions; mustard gas; Napoleonic warfare; navy; necessities of war; necessity; nerve weapons; neutrality; neutralization;*

neutral rights and duties; neutron bomb; no-fly zone; no-man's-land; noncombatants; nuclear agents; nuclear winter; occupation; officer; officer corps; ordnance; outflank; pacification; pacifism; Panzer; paramilitary; Paris, Declaration of; partisan; passive defense; peace; penetration aids; pike; pillage; piracy; PLA; plutonium; pocket battleship; poison; police action; pontoon bridge; postwar; preemptive strike; preventive war; prisoner of war; privateer; prize; prohibited weapons; proportionality; proxy wars; prudence; psychological warfare; quarantine; radiation effects; radiological weapons; rake; rampart; qui desiderat; *rationing; rear echelon; rear guard; recognition; reconnoiter; Red Army; Red Cross; redoubt; refugees; regular army; reprisal; requisition; resistance; retaliation; rifled bore; Royal Navy; rules of engagement; ruse; sabotage; salvo; scorched earth; sea mine; sea power; search-and-destroy; second strike; self-defense; sentry; shell shock; ship-of-the-line; shock troops; siege; sloop-of-war; smooth bore; staff officer; standards of civilized behavior; state of war;* status mixtus; *strategic bombing; Strategic Defense Initiative (SDI); strategic nuclear response; strategic nuclear weapons; submarine; summary execution; superior orders; supply lines; surface-to-air; surface-to-surface; surface-to-underwater; surgical strike; surrender; tactical nuclear weapons; targeting doctrine; task force; technology; terminal defense; terms, ask for; territorial defense; theater nuclear weapons; thousand bomber raids; topography; torture; TOW; tracer; traumatic stress disorder; trench warfare; truce; two-front war; two-power naval standard; U-boat; unconditional surrender; unrestricted submarine warfare; V-1 and V-2 rockets; vanguard; vertical escalation; victory; visit and search; war aims; war avoidance strategy; war chest; war contagion; war crimes; war debts; warfare; war fighting strategy; war games; warhead; warlord; warmongering; warplane; war planning; warship; wars of independence; war termination; war treason; war weariness; war zone; weapons of mass destruction; Wehrmacht; withholding strategy; wolf pack; yield; zeppelin; zero hour.*

Suggested Readings: Geoffrey Best, *Humanity in Warfare*, 2nd ed. (1983); Jeremy Black, ed., *War and the World* (1998); Peter Calvocoressi et al., *Total War* (1989); Karl von Clausewitz, *On War* (1818); J. A. de Moor and H. L. Wesseling, eds., *Imperialism and War: Essays on Colonial War in Asia and Africa* (1989); Ferdinand Foch, *Principles of War* (1919); Lawrence Freedman, ed., *War* (1994); Paul Fussell, *Wartime* (1989); Paul Fussell, *The Great War and Modern Memory* (1975, 2000); Ulysses S. Grant, *Personal Memoirs* (1885); Michael Howard, *War in European History* (1976); Michael Howard, *The Causes of Wars* (1983); Michael Howard, ed., *The Theory and Practice of War* (1965); John Keegan, *A History of Warfare* (1993); John Keegan, *The Face of Battle* (1974); John Keegan, ed., *The Book of War* (1999); W. Murray et al., eds., *The Making of Strategy* (1994); Peter Paret, ed., *Makers of Modern Strategy* (1986); Martin van Creveld, *Supplying War* (1977); Martin van Creveld, *Command in War* (1985); Hew Strachan, *European Armies and the Conduct of War* (1983); Charles Townshend, ed., *The Oxford History of Modern War* (2000); Kenneth Waltz, *Man, the State, and War* (1959); Quincy Wright, *A Study of War* (1964).

war aims. The declared and secret economic, political, and *strategic* goals and ambitions a *state* engages in war to fulfill or advance.

war-avoidance strategy. A *strategic* posture where one does not attempt to fight or win (survive) a *nuclear war*, but instead seeks to avoid such a conflict altogether through a *deterrent* posture of threatening *massive retaliation*. In *just war* terms, the morality of this position inheres in its avoiding all war by making the prospect of any war too terrible to rationally consider. *See also mutual assured deterrence; war-fighting strategy.*

War Between the States. Colloquial for the *American Civil War*, at least below the *Mason-Dixon line*. For those southerners who remain utterly unreconstructed the preferred term is the "War of Northern Aggression."

war chest. "Kriegskasse." Before the development of modern economies and systems of taxation and expenditure, national leaders literally kept chests of *gold* and other precious metals to finance their wars. This practice contributed to *bullionism* and related *mercantilist* policies, but it abated in Western Europe after c. 1500. Still, as late as the 1750s *Frederick the Great* kept a literal war chest. *Napoleon*, too, kept a separate source of funds from which he could raise reserves and reward loyal service.

war communism. The *Bolshevik* policy of *nationalization* of finance and industry, and artificially low prices for agricultural produce, which lasted from 1918 until adoption of the *New Economic Policy* in 1921 following a *mutiny* of sailors at *Kronstadt*. It relied centrally on *terror* and became a euphemism for *forced labor* and brutal and often bloody *requisition* of grain and other foodstuffs from peasants during the *Russian Civil War*. *See also Vladimir Lenin; Leon Trotsky.*

war contagion. A common metaphor likening *war* to a disease and implicitly warning against allowing it to spread by contact or neglect. By extension, it implies that one ought to pursue an interventionist *diplomacy*, in which measures are taken to lance the conflict (or cut out the canker, depending on one's chosen image). *Franklin Roosevelt* was fond of this metaphor, which he made famous in his *Quarantine* speech of 1937. *See also* cordon sanitaire.

war correspondent. A journalist reporting on a war, from near the field of battle. The first worked for "The Times" of London, to which he sent dispatches reporting on the *Crimean War*.

war council. *See council of war.*

war crimes. The third in a category of criminal acts concerning war, along with *crimes against humanity* and *crimes against peace*, for which individuals (military or civilian) may be held accountable. War crimes may be a violation of either *international criminal law*, as laid out in the *Hague* and *Geneva Con-*

ventions, or of the municipal law of the place the act was committed. Traditionally, there were two defenses against a charge of war crimes: *act of state* and *superior orders*. However, this has changed since 1945. New principles were developed at the *war crimes trials* at *Nuremberg* and *Tokyo*, and in treaties such as the *Genocide Convention*, in which for certain acts defined as war crimes the defenses given above did not sway tribunals and no longer appear to convince most legal thinkers. In addition to normally criminal acts (murder or *torture*) which take place in wartime, certain acts are classed as war crimes: (1) killing or wounding enemy *combatants* who ask to *surrender*; (2) firing on a flag of *truce*; (3) abusing a *flag* of truce or request for mercy to gain a military advantage and continue hostilities; (4) using *ruses de guerre*, such as hiding military targets under the emblem of the *Red Cross* or *Red Crescent* or otherwise abusing the privileges attached to those emblems, such as firing from the sanctuary of a hospital; (5) hiding among a *civilian* population by discarding one's uniform and wearing civilian clothes, if done in order to better commit hostile acts (not if done to effect escape); (6) killing, wounding, or maliciously neglecting *prisoners of war* (POWs) or using them for medical or other experimentation; (7) killing or wounding civilians, unless as a form of *collateral damage*; (8) using *prohibited weapons* of war, such as *biological*, *chemical*, *gas*, or *nerve agents*; (9) targeting militarily insignificant areas; (10) *pillaging*; (11) using POWs as slave or *forced labor* on military installations; (12) accepting *surrender* terms, then disregarding them; (13) using torture to elicit information about the enemy from its civilian population; (14) abusing the dead in any way; (15) sacking hospitals or similarly protected buildings; (16) performing deliberate *terror* attacks on a civilian population; (17) forcing a POW to serve in one's own armed forces, or auxiliary units, against his or her former comrades; and (18) concealing oneself in the uniform of the enemy, for purposes of deceit and advantage in combat.

With appropriate adjustments, the same rules apply to naval and air warfare: no false flag or markings, no firing from or on hospital ships or planes, no indiscriminate *bombardment* or bombing, no killing after surrender by lowering the flag, and so on. Additional prohibited acts were added by an International Tribunal set up in 1993 to try war criminals from the *Third Balkan War*. It added new prohibitions on *ethnic cleansing* and *rape*. *See also Armenian, Cambodian, and Rwandan genocides*; aut punire aut dedire; *biological warfare; Martin Bormann; denazification; depredation; Karl Dönitz; extradition; Hans Frank; Gestapo; Herman Göring; Hirohito; Holocaust; in absentia; International Criminal Court; Alfred Jodl; just war; Kellogg-Briand Pact; Konoe Fumimaro; Krupp family; Slobodan Milošević; My Lai massacre; rape of Nanjing; nullum crimen; Potsdam; Pu Yi; Red Terror; Joachim Ribbentrop; Albert Speer; Tōjō Hideki; Trail of Tears; Versailles; victor's justice; Kurt Waldheim; war crimes trials; war treason; Yalta; Yamashita Tomoyuki.*

Suggested Readings: Geoffrey Best, *War and Law Since 1945* (1994); Yoram Dinstein and

Mala Tabory, eds., *War Crimes in International Law* (1996); Theodor Meron, *War Crimes Law Comes of Age* (1998); A. Neier, *War Crimes* (1998).

war crimes trials. Before the twentieth century the acts and decisions of statesmen were regarded as beyond the reach of *international law*, under the principle of *state immunity*. Thus, even so despised a figure as *Napoleon* was exiled to St. Helena without trial, while *Murat* was executed by France for *treason* rather than war crimes, all despite their central parts in a quarter century of destructive, and at times also merciless, warfare. The first international proceedings to lay charges of *war crimes* were set up after *World War I* by the *Treaty of Versailles* in the vain hope of trying *Wilhelm II* and other top German leaders for "a supreme offense against international morality and the sanctity of treaties." U.S. opposition to this procedure—then failure to *ratify* the treaty—combined with German obstruction to turn the proceedings into a farce. In the end, from a list of 890 suspects drawn up by the Allies, a mere handful of junior officers, mainly from *U-boats*, were convicted in trials held in Leipzig. Even these few were conveniently allowed to escape by their German jailors. Britain also briefly detained some Turks accused of complicity in the *Armenian genocide*, but later swapped them for some of its own *prisoners of war*.

Two international, and multiple national, war crimes tribunals were set up after *World War II*, with mixed success. The international courts sought convictions of top leaders of the *Axis* states deemed to have committed *crimes against humanity* and *crimes against peace*, in addition to war crimes. Top German and Austrian officials faced the *Nuremberg war crimes* tribunal. Key Japanese civilian and military leaders faced a tribunal in *Tokyo*. A separate tribunal for Japanese officers met in the Philippines. These proceedings were spectacular—dozens of the principal Nazi and Japanese leaders were tried—but short-term and limited. It was actually national military tribunals and civilian courts which brought most war criminals to justice: by 1960 the Western *Allies* tried some 5,000 accused German and Austrian war criminals, executing nearly 500 of those convicted; the Soviets tried more than 10,000 Germans after WWII, executing a high proportion. West Germany tried even more of its own citizens, while Israel hunted down those major German criminals, most notably *Eichmann*, who had escaped justice at Nuremberg. In Asia, 5,570 Japanese were tried by various Allied courts.

Most occupied countries tried their own citizens for *collaboration* in German, Italian, or Japanese war crimes, but not usually their own military for war crimes committed against the enemy. There is minimal legal controversy over trials and convictions on strict charges of war crimes. However, the introduction at Nuremberg and Tokyo of charges of "crimes against peace" and "crimes against humanity" provoked two main criticisms of the proceedings, then and since: (1) no specific laws about crimes against humanity or peace existed before the war, and therefore no crime, in a legal sense, could have taken place, however reprehensible the moral transgressions of the defendants; and (2) the tribunals represented *victor's justice*, as only persons from or allied with the *defeated* nations were tried (e.g., no Soviet was tried for the *Katyn massacre*, nor Allied crew or commander for, as some later suggested they might have been, *carpet bombing* of Axis cities. Yet, the evidence against most defendants was so overwhelming that the mere presence of national judges could not have made a real difference, and, anyway, few among the convicted were condemned solely on the basis of a charge of crimes against humanity—most were also convicted for war crimes. Proponents of international war crimes tribunals assert that the cause of *peace* may be fortified by the deterrent threat of punishment of leaders; trials properly locate the blame for criminal acts of individuals rather than entire ethnic groups or peoples; they may help *purge* evil leaders from defeated populations, allowing for faster recovery and reconciliation; and at the least, they vitiate spurious moral claims or defenses by the prior regime by exposing the truth of its inner evil. All that may be true, but it is too soon to say so with lasting confidence.

Other examples: (i) In 1971 Bangladesh began proceedings against some 200 West Pakistanis, but dropped the charges upon return of its detained POWs. (ii) The United States court-martialed a handful of its own men for the *My Lai massacre*; this was a war crimes trial in spirit, if not strictly so in law. (iii) In 1988 a *naturalized* American *deported* to Israel for trial for crimes dating to WWII was convicted and sentenced to death. The judgment was overturned in 1993 when new evidence showed that a mistake in identity had occurred. (iv) In 1993 the *United Nations General Assembly* authorized the *secretary general* to develop rules and procedures to open war crimes trials concerning the *Third Balkan War*. A recommendation from a five-nation commission named top Serbs (and others) as suspected war criminals, including *Slobodan Milošević*, for atrocities in Bosnia and Croatia. This was the first international advance warning that leaders would be held accountable for their decisions—during WWII the Allies warned *Axis* leaders of postwar retribution, but as the warning came from a hostile alliance it did not carry the sanction or authority of the full *community of nations*. The commission also recommended guidelines: no trials *in absentia*; for the first time, *rape* was to be punishable as a war crime; and *ethnic cleansing* was deemed a war crime. In 1995 war crimes trials under the new Tribunal began at The Hague, both of low-level killers and some senior commanders and politicians, but culminating in the 2001 arrest and *extradition* of Milošević for trial at The Hague. (v) In 1993 Canada tried several of its UN peacekeepers on charges of *torture* and murder of civilians in Somalia. Like the My Lai trials, these were not war crimes trials per se. They were marked by an attempt to revive the defense of *superior orders*. (vi) In 1994 Ethiopia set up a national tribunal to punish those behind the *Red Terror*. (vii) In Rwanda, several thousand Hutu were tried for the 1994 *genocide* against the Tutsi; many were convicted and executed. (viii) In 1999 Cambodia agreed to try top *Khmers Rouges* commanders, but vacillated and obfuscated in practice. (ix) In 1998 three members of the Guatemalan "civilian patrols," *death squads* sponsored by the army during that country's protracted civil war, were sentenced to death for war crimes. In 1998 a multilateral treaty was signed to set up the *International Criminal Court*, with standing jurisdiction over individuals charged with war crimes, crimes against humanity, or genocide.

Suggested Readings: Gary Bass, *Stay the Hand of Vengeance* (2000); European Commission, *Law in Humanitarian Crises*, 2 vols. (1995), especially the article "Laws of War," by Adam Roberts; Norman Tutorow, *War Crimes, War Criminals, and War Crimes Trials* (1986).

war debts. Debts accumulated by heavy borrowing to pay for a *war*. War debts add greatly to the general burden of *reconstruction*. After *World War I* the United States was owed huge amounts by Britain and France and lesser sums by Russia. Britain and France tried to use German *reparations* to repay the United States until the *Hoover moratorium* of 1931, after which both countries defaulted. The *Bolsheviks* repudiated Russia's war debts, which mostly hurt its largest creditor, France. *See also Calvin Coolidge.*

war economy. Placing the full resources of a nation at the disposal of military production in the interests of waging *total war*.

warfare. Actual hostilities, not merely a legal state of affairs. For example, North and South Korea remained legally at war for many decades after the *Korean Conflict*, but, other than harassing actions, could not accurately be said to have been at war or engaged in warfare. Similarly, after 1973 Israel was for many years legally at war with a number of Arab states, but without engaging in actual hostilities with some. *See also peace treaty.*

war-fighting strategy. A *strategic* posture by which one's ability to fight and win (survive) a *nuclear war* denies the opportunity of *victory* to the adversary, thereby reinforcing *deterrence*. Some analysts said this was the main posture of the Soviet military, c. 1947–1989. In *just war* terms, the morality of this position inheres in its maintenance of targeting distinctions for as long as possible. *See also war-avoidance strategy.*

war games. Military exercises simulating combat conditions, used to train *officers* and troops and test operational plans and strategies. *See also maneuvers.*

war guilt clause. A popular but misleading characterization of Article 231 of the *Treaty of Versailles*, which did not actually use the phrase "war guilt." It read: "The Allied and Associated Governments affirm and Germany accepts the responsibility of Germany and her Allies for causing all the loss and damage to which the Allied and Associated Governments and their nationals have been subjected as a consequence of the war imposed upon them by the *aggression* of Germany and her Allies." This identification of Germany's responsibility for *World War I* was not intended primarily as a moral assertion, but to provide a legal basis for collecting *reparations*. It has been argued that the psychological harm done to the *Weimar Republic* by the clause outweighed any good or justice obtained by including it in the treaty, although an argument for inclusion on such grounds might be made. In fact, it was the Weimar government which obstructed payment of reparations and likely deliberately chose to *hyperinflate* the German economy in order to make devalued payments. Moreover, while Article 231 appeared to create an open-ended German liability, Article 232 limited this liability to civilian damage. Finally, virtually the same clause was included in treaties with Austria and Hungary. *See also stab in the back.*

warhead. The business end of a *missile*, rocket, or torpedo. It can be *conventional* or *nuclear*, or contain *chemical, biological,* or *nerve agents*, and it can be a single device or part of a *MIRVed* system.

warlord. (1) A local or national leader whose power derives from, and whose survival may depend upon, a continuing ability and willingness to wage war. Important warlords of this type included: *Cortés, Hideyoshi, Hitler, Jiang Jieshi, Moctezuma II, Napoleon, Nurgaci, Yuan Shikai, Samori Touré,* and *Shaka.* (2) A military commander who has seized political power over part or all of a country, as in China, 1916–1949; Russia, 1918–1921; Somalia, after 1988; Afghanistan after 1988; or Angola after 1975. China had several periods of "warlordism" in its long history, in which powerful generals rebelled and sometimes themselves sought to establish a new dynasty, as in the time of *Kangxi.* The most recent began in 1916, as Republican China was still divided among seven foreign powers occupying coastal *treaty ports* and *concession areas,* as well as hundreds of Chinese warlords in control of large parts of the interior. Not all were bad rulers or bad men. Some were loyal to the idea of a unified and strong China, but governed their provinces in an era in which central authority and legitimacy had collapsed, and for long periods no one emerged deserving of their loyalty. Others were mere *filibusterers* or even drug lords. Heavy fighting in the north ended with *Chiang Kai-shek's* victory over that region's warlords in 1928. Other warlords were simply bought off or paid nominal allegiance to the central government, and some subsequently rebelled again. There were still intermittent warlord rebellions until 1937 and during *World War II.* In fact, warlord China was not completely defeated until unification under the *Communists* in 1949 and attendant crushing of all remaining private and regional forces in Shanxi. In 1996 Charles Taylor, a vicious warlord in West Africa—another region with a long history of warlordism—took control of Liberia and subsequently spread death, destruction, and instability to Sierra Leone and Guinea as well. *See also* generalissimo; *Ming dynasty; shogun.*

Suggested Readings: Ch'i Hsi-sheng, *Warlord Politics in China, 1916–1928* (1976); Donald Sutton, *Provincial Militarism and the Chinese Republic* (1980).

war matériel. Arms, ammunition, vehicles, ships, aircraft, communications equipment, and any other raw or manufactured material supplies necessary to conduct military operations.

warmongering. Advocating or attempting to precipitate an *aggressive* or otherwise needless war.

warm-water port. One which does not become unusable by freezing in the winter. Not having access to enough warm-water ports was a major geopolitical problem for Russia, especially as its Crimean outlets could be—and were—sometimes made useless by Britain's corking the Black Sea bottle at the *Bosporus* and *Dardanelles*. *See also Port Arthur; Straits Question.*

War of 1812 (1812–1814). This entirely avoidable conflict between the United States and Great Britain sprang from the strain the British and French *blockades* of *neutral* trade with Europe placed on the U.S. economy. Additional grievances included the *impressment* of U.S. citizens into the *Royal Navy* and rumors that the British in Canada were stirring trouble among the frontier Indian tribes. Having allowed the navy built by *John Adams* to rot in port, *Madison* could not strike at the most valuable British possessions, those in the Caribbean; so he hit the British the only way and place he could, overland in Canada. This divided American opinion. Nonetheless, American *militia* invaded from New York, in ragtag fashion, in 1812. During a second invasion, in 1813, American troops set fire to the capital and parliament at York (Toronto). In retaliation, in 1814 British troops set fire to Washington, including the *White House*, when they counterinvaded. Canadian militia and some Indian allies also skirmished with American militia farther west. A hastily constructed inland navy cleared the British from the Great Lakes, and American *privateers* raided English commerce in the Caribbean and elsewhere. The British held onto Québec City and Montréal, while blockading the east coast, greatly pressuring American maritime trade.

The war ended indecisively, with a settlement *mediated* by Russia. That saved the United States from having to face the seasoned veterans of the *Napoleonic Wars*, perhaps under *Wellington* himself, just freed by victory over *Napoleon*. Terms were agreed at *Ghent*, Belgium, in December 1814, after which a bloody and entirely useless battle was fought at *New Orleans* (January 8, 1815). The peace treaty avoided all points at issue in the war, as befitted a stalemate. That left serious questions between Britain and the United States unresolved for decades more. Americans and Canadians alike still tend to exaggerate and even misinterpret this conflict: the former as a spirited and decisive victory over Britain, and even as a "second War of Independence,"

though it was neither, the latter as evidence of supposedly simmering Yankee plans for *annexation*, when the furthest American thinking went along those lines was some Southerners who wanted to use Canada as a bargaining chip to be traded for some more valuable British colony in the Caribbean, such as Jamaica. The British view the war more for what it actually was: an unfortunate and avoidable side action to their much larger and more important conflict with France. *See also Andrew Jackson; Winfield Scott; Zachary Taylor.*
Suggested Reading: J. C. A. Stagg, *Mr. Madison's War* (1983).

War of American Independence. *See American Revolution.*

War of Attrition (March 1969–June 1970). Egypt and Israel engaged in this conflict along the *Bar-Lev Line* in the manner its name suggests. It was announced with promises of *victory* by *Nasser*, who hoped to use Egypt's larger army to wear down Israeli morale by inflicting a stream of casualties the smaller country would find unacceptable. Instead, Egyptian casualties reached unsustainable levels fast, and the campaign thereafter faded into sporadic violence and futility.

War of Devolution (1667–1668). *See Louis XIV.*

War of Jenkins' Ear (1739–1740). This minor naval conflict between England and Spain derived its freakish name from the story of Captain Robert Jenkins, who testified to the Commons that in 1738 Spaniards captured his ship, tied him to his own mast, and cruelly hacked off his ear—which he carried around in a finely decorated snuff box to amaze the curious. Clamor for war was growing in Europe already, since the *War of the Polish Succession*. The motive force behind rising war fever was fiercely competitive overseas trade and colonial conflicts—*mercantilist* ideas were still much in vogue, war and trade seemed natural extensions one of the other, and Spain's exposed position in its weak American colonies might be exploited in war. *Robert Walpole* believed that any war in favor of the interests of London traders in *slaves*, sugar, tobacco, and other *smuggled* goods would be a boon to the merchants but a tragedy for Britain and Europe. He was ahead of his time, but also out of touch with the public mood for war. By 1739 *William Pitt,* most members of parliament, and the people wanted war. And so, against Walpole's wishes, Britain *declared war* on Spain. This avoidable war with a silly name was important for two reasons: (1) it was the first major conflict among European powers which began as a dispute about overseas possessions; and (2) it said much about the wider European mood, which was rapidly shifting away from a desire for peace in the wake of the spilled blood and exhaustion of 1713, back toward the old game of the *balance of power*, of fighting to retain or expand overseas *colonies*, and aggrandizements within Europe itself. All that was needed to light a larger fire was a spark struck from the flint of international tensions and an aggressor willing to apply that spark to the tinder of war. The man and the moment met in October 1740, when *Frederick the Great* of Prussia struck in a bid for Austrian *Silesia*, setting off the *War of the Austrian Succession* (1740–1748), which would subsequently lead to the even more destructive *Seven Years' War* (1756–1763).

Suggested Reading: Michael Morpurgo, *The War of Jenkins' Ear* (1995).

War of the Austrian Succession (1740–1748). Multiple conflicts merged as Austria, England, Hanover, Hesse, Saxony, and the Netherlands fought France, Prussia, Bavaria, and Spain for control of Austrian (*Habsburg)* provinces and parts of the *Holy Roman Empire*, while Sweden fought Russia in the north and France and Britain fought on several continents beyond Europe. The conflict was touched off by the death of Austrian and Holy Roman Emperor Charles VI in 1740, which raised rival claims to the Imperial succession from royal houses in Bavaria, Saxony, and even Spain. Charles had sought since 1717 to gain Europe's acceptance of the *Pragmatic Sanction* securing the succession to his daughter, *Maria Theresa*. The perception of real weakness at the center of the Habsburg empire tempted *Frederick the Great* to seize *Silesia*, and this naked *aggression* by Prussia set off the conflagration. France supported Prussia while Britain (and Hanover), Saxony, and other parts of the Holy Roman Empire backed Austria. Prussia secured Silesia from Austria in 1742 (First Silesian War), but then had to defend against a renewed Austrian onslaught in 1742–1745 (Second Silesian War). This brief peace was agreed between Prussia and Austria (after France and Russia shocked Vienna by signing a treaty) in 1742, but their war resumed in 1744 because neither Frederick nor Maria Theresa would or could compromise on Silesia.

That year, Prussia invaded Bohemia, but lost a bloody contest of *attrition* to Austrian *partisans*. France and Britain also clashed in 1744, spreading the fighting to North America, the West Indies, the Middle East, and India. In early 1745 France scored a major victory over the Dutch and English at Fontenoy, and the *Catholic* "Bonnie Prince Charlie" landed in Scotland, causing a panicky English Parliament to recall its Army from *Flanders*. Meanwhile, Austria and Saxony invaded Silesia, but lost badly to Frederick at Hohenfriedberg (June 4, 1745) and Soor (September 30, 1745). Every side began to feel the financial strain. On Christmas Day, 1745, the Peace of Dresden ended the Austro-Prussian-Saxon War, leaving Silesia in Frederick's hands. The Austro-French and Anglo-French wars continued. The wider war ended formally with the *Peace of Aix-la Chapelle* (1748), but that is somewhat misleading, as other than Prussia, which kept Silesia, no major power was satisfied with the final settlement. This conflict was among the first modern wars in that it ended as one fought among emergent *nations*, though it masqueraded still as a *dynastic* and imperial conflict. Fighting continued in India even after settlement of the succession question, which in the end went to

Maria Theresa after all. Prussia consolidated its gains, and Austria and Spain licked their wounds. England and France resumed their global fight in the *Seven Years' War*, linking struggles over North America and India with the age-old contest in Europe. The general round of fighting which began in 1740 was thus not truly resolved until the *Peace of Paris* in 1763. *See also diplomatic revolution; East India Company; King George's War; War of Jenkins' Ear.*

Suggested Readings: Matthew S. Anderson, *The War of the Austrian Succession, 1740–1748* (1995); Reed S. Browning, *The War of the Austrian Succession* (1995).

War of the Bavarian Succession (1778). There was little actual fighting in this war between Austria and Prussia. It began in August and was over by November, after Russian *mediation*. Its real importance was to signal Prussia's clear acceptance as a member of the *Great Power* club, something *Frederick the Great* had not achieved in any of his earlier, larger wars. It ended with the Treaty of Teschen (May 1779).

War of the First Coalition, Second Coalition, etc. *See French Revolution; Napoleon I; Napoleonic Wars.*

War of the Grand Alliance (1688–1697). *See War of the League of Augsburg.*

War of the League of Augsburg (1688–1697). Sometimes called the War of the Grand Alliance, as well as the Nine Years' War, *King William's War* is the usual American designation for its North American theater of operations. *Bavaria, Brandenburg-Prussia, England,* the *Holy Roman Empire,* the *Netherlands,* the *Palatinate, Savoy, Spain,* and *Sweden* all allied to oppose *France* under *Louis XIV.* There was desultory fighting until 1692, when Louis raised an invasion army aimed at England. Before it could sail, his fleet was savaged by an Anglo-Dutch fleet at Barfleur-La Hogue. After that, the war at sea was one of raids and *attrition* along the major *trade routes,* much of it by *privateers* under *letters of marque,* including the brutal Cpt. William Kidd (c. 1645–1701). This long sea war brought economic despair to most participants and *famine* to France. The war on land, however, was large and bloody. Armies reached the then unprecedented size of a quarter million each. It ended when Savoy defected from the Alliance, meaning that this war, too, ended in *stalemate.* This fact was reflected in the *Treaty of Ryswick,* which satisfied most Dutch concerns but also restored all conquests to their prior owners and thereby helped set the stage for more Anglo-French conflict in the years ahead. Louis was thus again at war with Europe within four years, in the *War of the Spanish Succession. See also Dutch War; John Churchill Marlborough; William of Orange.*

Suggested Readings: G. N. Clark, *The Dutch Alliance and the War Against French Trade, 1688–1697* (1923, 1971); Stewart Philip Oakley, *William III and the Northern Crowns During the Nine Years War, 1688–1697* (1987).

War of the Pacific (1879–1884). The main issue was control of the Atacama Desert region, which was valued by all as a source of fertilizer because it was rich in centuries of accumulated bird guano and nitrates, then becoming widely used in the international explosives industry. In 1878 Bolivia raised taxes on Chilean nitrate exporters mining in its territory, in violation of a prior agreement on exploitation of the resource. Chile seized Bolivia's coastal province, leading to a secret alliance between Bolivia and Peru and then a full-scale war. Most of the fighting was over by 1881, but the war was not formally ended until the United States *mediated* two *peace treaties*, in 1883 and 1884. Chile was the main victor, keeping in the peace treaties all the Bolivian territory it had seized in battle. That made it a third again as large as it had been before the war. Subsequently, export of the purloined nitrates became a mainstay of the Chilean economy, raising newly enriched families into its governing oligarchy.

Suggested Reading: Bruce Farcau, *The Ten Cent War* (2000).

War of the Polish Succession (1733). This was a short war born of the fact that Poland's monarchy was elective and the legitimate succession fell into dispute upon the death of the old king, and of the more important fact that Poland remained hostage to a fractious internal politics of squabbling aristocratic families. The argument over the succession opposed a French candidate to an Austrian favorite. The war ended when a joint Austrian-Russian intervention took Warsaw and the French candidate fled to *Danzig*. In the west, France attacked Lorraine and marched into north Italy and across the Rhine into the *Holy Roman Empire*. The war ended with a compromise in which the Austro-Russian candidate, the Saxon Elector, became King August III of Poland while the French candidate became King Stanislaus of a French *protectorate* in Lorraine. In return, France guaranteed the *Pragmatic Sanction*. A major reason the war remained limited was that Prime Minister *Robert Walpole* kept Great Britain out, proudly telling Queen Caroline that of the 50,000 men killed in Europe that summer, not one was an English soldier. The war had little wider consequence, but demonstrated that the generational exhaustion which had followed *Louis XIV* was about over, as a new generation not yet sated with blood and glory strained at the reins of power and champed for battle. The chance for war came again at the end of the decade, with the *War of Jenkins' Ear* and the *War of the Austrian Succession.*

Suggested Reading: John L. Sutton, *The King's Honor & the King's Cardinal* (1980).

War of the Spanish Succession (1701–1713). Some call this conflict the first of the modern "world wars." Austria, England, the Netherlands, Portugal, and Prussia allied against France and Spain. This was the last and greatest of the wars sparked by the hegemonic ambitions of *Louis XIV*. When it broke out, *Peter I* of Russia—recently defeated by *Charles XII* of Sweden at *Narva* (November 30, 1700) and in desperate need of time and relief—wrote to an adviser: "Long may it last! God willing." The most important of its many battles was fought in 1704 at *Blenheim*, which saved Austria from defeat, drove Bavaria out of the war, and shook the French Army to its roots. Other coalition victories came at sea at Malaga (1704) and on land at Ramillies (1706), which cleared the French from the southern Netherlands, and at Oudenarde (1708), which prevented the French from reoccupying Belgium. At Malplaquet (1709) the Allies won a costly victory, which exacted so high a price it partially reversed French fortunes and prolonged the war. This last of Louis' wars broke the French treasury and his power, leaving France intact but exhausted and utterly frustrated in its ambition for dominance. Britain emerged as the major winner, once more expanding its overseas holdings as the continental powers fought to a standstill. It gained mainly in Canada at the expense of *New France*, but also in the Mediterranean and the West Indies. The Dutch and the *Habsburgs* also gained territory (the *Spanish Netherlands*, Naples, Sardinia) and a measure of security. This was all codified in the *Treaty of Utrecht* (1713) and the Treaty of Rastadt (1714). Its major, lasting effect was to establish a *Bourbon* connection between Spain and France and thus leave them allied for most of the eighteenth century. *See also Gibraltar; John Churchill Marlborough; William of Orange.*

Suggested Readings: David Francis, *The First Peninsular War, 1702–1713* (1975); John B. Hattendorf, *England in the War of the Spanish Succession* (1987); Henry Kamen, *The War of Succession in Spain, 1700–15* (1969).

War of the Three Feudatories (1673–1681). *See Kangxi emperor.*

War of the Thousand Days (1899–1902). A war of *secession*, in part prompted and aided by the United States but mainly reflecting the genuine national sentiment of many in Panama, in which Panama broke free of Colombia. It was followed by a swift agreement with the United States to build the *Panama Canal. See also Theodore Roosevelt.*

War of the Triple Alliance (1864–1870). "The Paraguayan War." In this, the deadliest of all Latin American interstate wars, Paraguay fought Argentina, Brazil, and Uruguay. Brazil had sent a punitive raid into Uruguay to compel *compensation* for *damages* it claimed it had suffered during Uruguay's prolonged civil war, and in support of the Colorados in Uruguay. The dictator of Paraguay, Francisco Solano López, who had supported the losing Blancos in the Uruguayan civil war, sent an army across Argentine territory to attack the Brazilians in Uruguay. That act propelled Argentina into alliance with Brazil and the now Brazilian-controlled and supported Colorado regime in Uruguay. Nearly 100,000 alliance troops died over five years of fighting, but in the end Paraguay lost far more. In addition to losing huge portions of its original territory (about 40 percent), by some early estimates it lost 65–70 percent of its population to a combination of battle deaths, epidemic disease, and annexation by other states of lands occupied by erstwhile Paraguayans. More recent research suggests the figure was closer to 20 percent—still a catastrophic loss for any nation to absorb and which understandably left Paraguay in a state of turmoil for decades. Brazil gained a large section of northern Paraguay, while Argentina took two large pieces in the south. In Brazil, the fine performance by slave soldiers reopened the old and divisive issue of *slavery,* and in 1871 the law was reformed so that children born to slaves would be free. In 1888, all slaves were freed.

Suggested Readings: Pelham Horton Box, *The Origins of the Paraguayan War* (1929, 1967); Charles J. Kolinski, *Independence or Death!: The Story of the Paraguayan War* (1965).

warplane. Any aircraft armed for combat or designed for other military functions, such as *espionage* or transport.

war plans. Preparation by a *general staff* of details of *mobilization, logistics, tactics,* and *strategy,* in the event *war* should occur or as part of the advance work in launching a war of *aggression.* All military powers make and update various war plans which seek to anticipate future contingencies, with some more equal than others. War planning at sea has an ancient pedigree, originally relating to utilization of trade winds and oceanic currents. The era of modern war planning on land dates to the revolutionary development of *railways* and, to a lesser degree, also the *telegraph.* These permitted (and demanded) advance mobilization and troop deployment timetables, made direct command and control of combat units more ready to the high command, and amplified the role and effectiveness of professional war and staff colleges and the general staff. For examples, *see Adolf Hitler; mobilization crisis; Schlieffen Plan; Yamamoto Isoroku; Z-Plan*

Suggested Readings: Paul Kennedy, *War Plans of the Great Powers, 1880–1914* (1979); B. J. C. McKercher and Roch Legault, *Military Planning and the Origins of the Second World War in Europe* (2001).

War Powers Resolution (1973). Of the U.S. Congress. It sought to limit the independent ability of the president to commit armed forces to combat. It required notification of military commitments to Congress within 60 days (extended to 90 on request), after which the president must ask Congress for a *declaration of war* or withdraw the forces. It arose in response to executive abuse of the *Gulf of Tonkin Resolution* and the sense that an "imperial presidency" had overcommitted the United States militarily, and to misguided and fruitless conflicts. It has been mostly ignored by presidents from both parties. That defiance has not gone unchallenged politically, yet the law did not find support in the courts, which instead found its reporting and withdrawal provisions an unconstitutional burden on presidential authority. This was not really surprising, as the Supreme Court has consistently found in favor of the executive in foreign affairs.

Warring States (403–221 B.C.E.). The second half of the *Eastern Zhou* dynastic period witnessed emergence of about 170 *city-states* in north central China, ultimately reduced by war, conquest, and merger to fewer than ten, and then to one: *Qin*, which began the classical period of Imperial China, in the traditional periodization. In the final century of fighting the sequence of consolidation was (all dates are B.C.E.): Zhongshan, conquered by Zhao in 296; Song destroyed in 286; Lu defeated by Chu in 256; Zhou overrun in 256; Han suppressed by 230; Zhao conquered in 228; Wei submitted in 225; Chu destroyed in 223; Yan absorbed in 222; and Qi annexed to Qin in 221. The period also witnessed the introduction of new weapons, including the crossbow and iron (rather than bronze-age) swords and armor.

Warsaw Ghetto. Under the *Nazi* occupation, nearly 400,000 Jews were forced into a tiny ghetto in Warsaw (a few square miles in size), just as Jews were ghettoized in other East European cities. They were kept there until *Hitler* settled on the *"final solution,"* and the trains began running to *Auschwitz*. Some 100,000 died of starvation and disease in the Ghetto. In 1942 most of the rest were shipped to one or another of the *death camps*. In April and May 1943, the remaining 70,000 Jews resisted a final sweep of the Ghetto by German and Latvian units of the *Waffen SS* and some Polish police. Minimally armed Jewish fighters, men and women, rose against their mass murderers. At first they inflicted heavy casualties on SS units, which entered the Ghetto carelessly and with their usual arrogant swagger, singing blood-thirsty songs about murdering Jews. For 42 days fierce, and often suicidal, fighting continued. In the end almost all Jews were killed; by one estimate, fewer than 100 survived or escaped. The uprising enraged Hitler. It later became a symbol of resistance for all Jewish people the world over, captured in the fighting slogan: "Never again!"

Suggested Reading: Reuben Ainsztein, *The Warsaw Ghetto Revolt* (1979).

Warsaw Pact. *See Warsaw Treaty Organization.*

Warsaw Rising (1944). When the *Red Army* advanced on Warsaw in the early summer of 1944 it asked the Polish *resistance* to rise and harass the German rear to hasten the Soviet advance. The Poles seized most of Warsaw. Then the Red Army, commanded by *Rokossovsky*, stopped in its tank treads. The Germans moved in reinforcements to systematically destroy Warsaw and slaughter about 10,000 resistance fighters. For 63 days, despite pleas from *Roosevelt* and *Churchill* and the Polish fighters, the Soviets sat and watched from across the Vistula as the Germans eliminated the only force which might resist the imposition of Moscow's authority over Poland. Some 200,000 Polish civilians died, many butchered by special SS units of criminals and non-German turncoats organized by *Himmler*. It was a cynical betrayal of the first order, and smolders still in Polish national memory. *See also Katyn massacre.*

Warsaw Treaty Organization (WTO). The military alliance formed by the *Soviet bloc* in 1955 in response to rearmament of *West Germany* and its inclusion in *NATO*. It gave legal sanction to an already existing state of affairs: the presence of Soviet troops in several East European countries. Where NATO was essentially a *deterrent* guarantee of U.S. military aid to Western Europe, the WTO was merely a guarantee of *Eastern Europe's* enforced allegiance to the Soviet Union. Thus, when Hungary announced the next year that it would withdraw, the Soviets invaded and crushed the *Hungarian Uprising*. Similarly, the WTO invaded Czechoslovakia in 1968, crushing the *Prague Spring*. Only Albania, because it was buffered by the interposed territory of *Yugoslavia*, left the Pact without suffering an *invasion* in consequence— and it did so only because it found the Soviets insufficiently *Stalinist* after 1958! The WTO ceased to be an effective alliance by fall 1989. In 1990 it signed the *Charter of Paris* with NATO. It was dissolved on March 31, 1991. Its membership: Albania (ceased participation in 1962, withdrew formally in 1968), Bulgaria, Czechoslovakia, East Germany, Hungary, Poland, Rumania, and the Soviet Union.

Suggested Readings: Neil Fodor, The Warsaw Treaty Organization (1990); Charles Gati, *The Bloc that Failed* (1990).

warship. Any government-commissioned ship armed for combat which displays national colors and markings, is captained by a *commissioned officer*, and is operated by a navy crew. Such a ship enjoys total immunity from *visit and search* or any other oversight by any government whatsoever, except its own, while on the *high seas*. Other ships may arm for defense, such as merchant craft refitted with deck guns or *depth charges*, but any vessel using offensive force which does not meet the criteria above may be classed as engaged in *piracy*. *See also aircraft carrier; battle cruiser; battleship; brigantine; capital warship; caravel; cruiser; destroyer; frigate; galleon; galley; man-of-war; minesweeper; pocket battleship; privateer; ship-of-the-line; sloop-of-war; submarine; torpedo boat.*

War(s) of Independence. *See* particular wars, listed by country.

wars of intervention. *See intervention.*

wars of observation. *Clausewitz* used this term (some prefer "armed observation") for conflicts in which the struggle was not perceived or pursued as a matter of life-or-death, but more as a form of strategic fencing. *See also Cold War; proxy wars.*

wars of religion. (1) On the thirty-year French civil war usually known as the "Wars of Religion," *see France; Edict of Nantes; Henri IV; Huguenots; Armand Richelieu.* (2) On religion and major wars or international conflicts, *see Arab-Israeli Wars; Aztec Empire; Byzantine Empire;* conquistadores; *Counter*

Reformation; Crimean War; Oliver Cromwell; Crusades; Eighty Years' War; Gustavus Adolphus; Habsburgs; holy war; India; Indian Mutiny; Indo-Pakistani Wars; Ireland; Jacobites; jihad; *Livonian Order; manifest destiny; mission, sense of; Ottoman Empire; Peace of Westphalia; Protestant Reformation;* Reconquista; requerimiento; *Russo-Turkish Wars; Sikhism; Sovereign Order of Malta; Soviet Military Order; Taiping Rebellion (1850–1864); Teutonic Knights; Thirty Years' War; Johan Tilly; Ulster; Albrecht Wallenstein; White Lotus Rebellion (1796–1804).*

Wars of the French Revolution. *See Wars of the First and Second Coalition,* under *Napoleonic Wars.*

Wars of the Roses (1455–1485). *See England.*

war termination. The process of making the transition from combat to *negotiation,* and ultimately to *peace.* As a general rule, fighting in most wars— perhaps all wars—continues well past when it should rationally end. This is because passions are deeply engaged by bloodletting, communications usually break-down in the *fog of war,* and the political significance of a final advance or sudden halt is almost never clear at that moment and may not be seen clearly for months or years. That said, once the decision to end a war has been made, the first task is to physically disengage *combatants,* usually through a *cease-fire* agreement which (i) stops fighting at a designated time; (ii) builds in a waiting period to satisfy all sides that the enemy is not seeking to use the pause for resupply or some other tactical advantage, with an eye to resuming the fighting; and (iii) moves *frontline* troops back a specified distance, so they avoid direct contact which risks accidentally restarting the fighting. After that the assessment of who, if anyone, has "won the war," and the degree of respective *victory* and *defeat,* will drive negotiations over *terms* governing an *armistice.* This will include such questions as whether and how the parties will *demobilize,* whether any *territory* will be *occupied,* and whether existing governments will remain in place or give way to acceptable (to the victors) substitutes. Much later, there may be a formal *peace treaty* to legally end the *state of war;* spell out permanent territorial adjustments, if any; whether there are to be *war crimes trials;* the amount and schedule of *reparations,* if any; and resolve other *casus belli* which led to war in the first instance. However, quite a few wars end without the states involved proceeding to reestablish peace, in the legal sense of that word, or taking many years to reach agreement. Such wars still end, in fact, by simple cessation of the fighting without any formal agreement or with a local cease-fire which does not lead to detailed agreements. Even major conflicts may end without advancing from a cease-fire to a peace treaty, such as *World War II* and the *Korean Conflict,* the main instrument which legally ends a state of war between or among surviving *international personalities.* It is also possible for a war to end legally by *conquest* followed by *subjugation*, in which no need for a peace treaty arises as one party has become *extinct*. It usually takes a great deal of time for other states to accept the extinction of a fellow member of the *community of nations*. *See also surrender*.

war treason. "Kriegsverath." Acts seen as criminal by most states in times of war and usually carrying a death sentence. These include giving information to the enemy, enticing soldiers to desertion, harboring enemy personnel, and all *sabotage*. Where this is applied solely to one's own citizens or subjects it might be deemed reasonable. However, during *World War I* and again in *World War II*, Germany retrieved this ancient concept from the files to use as justification for punitive tactics of intimidation against populations whose territory it was *occupying*. This sometimes included taking *hostages*, and related acts of *reprisal* amounting to *atrocity*, to discourage *resistance*. This rendered the concept highly controversial and caused many theorists to reject it outright. *See also treason; war crimes.*

war weariness. (1) Fatigue with the privation and death attendant on war, which undercuts *national morale* during a prolonged armed conflict. (2) The idea that after a long and bloody war a nation will avoid bellicose policies and be more amenable to negotiated settlements, at least until the next generation of leaders and young men (and now, perhaps, young women too) begin to romanticize about national glory and yearn to test their mettle in combat. For instance, immediately after the *Napoleonic Wars* Europeans exhibited a generalized longing for *peace* and *international order* which may even have helped sustain the *Concert of Europe*. After several generations of peace, and forgetfulness, troops who volunteered in 1914 marched off to the sounds of marching bands and cheering crowds, scenes not repeated in 1939, but seen again on a smaller scale in Britain during the *Falklands War*. Similarly, after the *American Civil War* most Americans opposed new annexations (the purchase of *Alaska* was widely dismissed as "*Seward's* Folly") and resisted calls to fight Spain in aid of a *rebellion* in Cuba. Yet, thirty years later a new generation demanded war with Spain over a similar Cuban rebellion.

war-widening strategy. A synonym for horizontal escalation. See *escalation*.

war zone. (1) A synonym for *combat area* or any place where *armed hostilities* are underway. (2) A zone on the *high seas* where normal rights of *neutral* shipping are suspended by declaration of a *belligerent*. *See also Lusitania Notes; theater of war.*

Washington, George (1732–1799). American general; first United States *president*, 1789–1797. Educated as a surveyor and master of a large Virginia plantation, Washington joined the Virginia *militia*, in 1752. As a young officer, from 1753 to 1754 he assessed French forts and defensive lies along the Ohio River, skirmishing with French units who beat him in the race to take and hold Fort Duquesne (Pittsburgh), upon the outbreak of the *French and Indian War*. At a hastily prepared *fortification* he christened "Ft. Necessity," Washington was defeated and surrendered to the French (July 3–4, 1754). He was *paroled* back to Virginia soon after. Serving under English General Edward Braddock, Washington marched back to Fort Duquesne in the summer of 1755. The British were overwhelmed by a well-planned French and Indian ambush: Braddock was killed and English regulars and colonial troops alike took heavy losses. For the next two years Washington, now in command of all Virginia militia, built a fortified line along the frontier. In 1758 he was part of a third, and finally successful, effort to capture Fort Duquesne.

Washington spent the next half decade in prosperous civilian life. He represented Virginia at the First Continental Congress (1774) and again at the Second Continental Congress (1775). In May 1775 Washington took command of the Continental Army, then a ragtag force of ill-disciplined militia, and immediately blockaded the British in Boston. He led the Continental Army throughout the *American Revolution*, often losing battles but overall doing just well enough in the field to encourage the European *intervention* which proved decisive to the outcome. He lost part of the army and New York City to the British in the summer of 1776, in the Battle of Long Island (August 27–29, 1776), and a fighting retreat through upper New York. Washington recovered with a daring assault across the Delaware River (on Christmas Day, 1776), catching by surprise and soundly defeating a regiment of Hessian *mercenaries* at Trenton, New Jersey. Two weeks later he won again, against British troops, at Princeton (January 3, 1777). Washington was defeated by General Richard Howe at Brandywine Creek, Pennsylvania (September 11, 1777), but again showed tactical imagination in organizing a surprise though desultory counterattack at Germantown (October 4, 1777). With his command of the army coming under question in Congress, he quartered his badly beaten and demoralized army at Valley Forge during the winter of 1777 to 1778, where nearly 2,000 men died of sickness, cold and hunger, and many deserted as Congress dithered about funding and strategy.

Washington used the time to retrain and emerged from winter quarters to fight General Henry Clinton to a tactical draw at Monmouth, New Jersey (June 28, 1778). In 1779 he sent an expedition to burn out the *Iroquois* nations of upper New York, which were allied with Britain; his orders were carried out with ruthless dispatch, leaving many Indians dead or starving and homeless. An Iroquois exodus to Canada resulted, where the Indians sought and received British protection. In 1780 France at last committed to the war on the American side. French regulars arrived to reinforce the Continental Army, while the French Navy undercut Britain's great advantage in holding, blockading, or bombarding American coastal cities. Washington now planned and carried through a major campaign which eventually led to a decisive victory over General Charles Cornwallis at *Yorktown* (October 19, 1781). Subsequently, Washington renewed a siege of New York. The war was won with French (and Dutch and Spanish) naval intervention, especially in Europe where Britain had more *vital interests*. The *Peace of Paris* was negotiated in 1783. It is widely agreed that Washington, by sheer moral force and strength of character, saved the American Revolution from the usual decay and betrayal into factionalism and dictatorship which successful revolutions usually undergo. He utterly astonished Europe, and many of his compatriots, by laying down the sword rather than using it to take personal power, as would *Napoleon* in France a few years later, *Bolívar* in South America after that, and so many others.

Instead, Washington accepted election as president by the Constitutional Convention in 1787 and then was twice elected by the nation, in 1789 and 1792. He declined a third term, establishing a two-term custom which survived until 1940. In that and other ways, he left a permanent and defining imprint on the office. As president, Washington strove to govern above faction and did so without recourse to party. He leaned toward *Alexander Hamilton* and *Federalist* plans for construction of a stronger central government, but he opposed their *Anglophilia*. Similarly, he appointed *Thomas Jefferson* to his cabinet even while blocking his efforts to align the United States more closely with France. Washington ultimately adopted a policy of *neutrality* toward the great contest unfolding between France and Britain as a consequence of the *French Revolution*, but a policy tempered by prudent preparation for war and by reliance on *deterrence* through construction of a serious navy. In his vaunted Farewell Address (1796), he warned: "'Tis our true policy to steer clear of permanent alliances, with any portion of the foreign world." That was subsequently mistaken by *isolationists*, who were fond of quoting the passage, as a prohibition against all alliances. It was not: it was instead a practical expedient by a small power faced with maintaining neutral rights and trading interests during a quarter century of mortal clash among foreign titans. While successful in Washington's time, this advice proved inappropriate as a guideline for American diplomacy after the United States emerged as an unquestioned *Great Power* after the *American Civil War*. *See also entangling alliance; revolution on horseback.*

Suggested Readings: Ethan Fishman et al., eds., *George Washington* (2001); Robert F. Jones, *George Washington* (1986); Esmond Wright, *Washington and the American Revolution* (1957).

Washington Naval Conference (November 1921–February 1922). Conference on the Limitation of Armament. This gathering of the principal naval powers dealt with naval *disarmament* and Asian *security* issues. It was attended by all the major naval and/or Asian powers, among which the most important were Britain, France, Italy, Japan, and the United States. It arrived at nine *treaties* and 12 *resolutions* on Asian affairs. The three key agreements were the *Five Power Naval Treaty*, the *Four Power Treaty*, and the *Nine Power Treaty*.

These understandings replaced the security system which had been based on the *Anglo-Japanese Alliance* since 1902 and maintained stability in Asia for 10 years. The Japanese were far more conciliatory than in previous years: nearly 50 percent of their national budget was being consumed by military expenditures, and for the moment the hard-liners were pushed aside. In the end, however, besides codifying a number of miscalculations about the future strengths of various *capital warships*, these agreements were reliant on *good faith* to maintain the *balance of power* and international *peace*. But good faith—like *oil*, rice, rubber, and patience—was increasingly in short supply in Tokyo after 1927. *See also aircraft carrier; London Naval Treaty/Disarmament Conference; Shandong; two-power standard.*

Suggested Readings: Erik Goldstein and John Maurer, eds. *The Washington Conference, 1921–22* (1994), Akira Iriye, *After Imperialism* (1965).

Washington, Rules of (1871). Laid out in the *Treaty of Washington*, they spelled out rights of *neutrals* in sea warfare, laying to rest a long and bitter dispute between Britain and the United States. They reflected a fresh U.S. appreciation of Britain's historic defense of *belligerent rights*, born of the *Union's* experience with *blockade*, and the new U.S. status as a major *sea power*.

Washington, Treaty of (1871). This agreement represented a major advance for *arbitration* as a mechanism of resolving non-vital *disputes*. There were four sets of long-standing disagreements to be resolved: (1) The main issues involved Britain's claims about its *neutral rights* to have traded with the *Confederacy* against U.S. assertions of *belligerent rights* in enforcing its *blockade*. Britain conceded most of the points at issue in advance in order to set a precedent with Washington on interpretation of belligerent versus neutral rights. That was clever: London knew that, as the world's greatest *sea power*, and given America's penchant for *isolationism*, the future was likely to reverse roles and place Britain in the position of making belligerent claims against U.S. assertions of neutral rights. And that is just what happened from 1914 to 1917 and again from 1939 to 1941. (2) A *fisheries* agreement was signed concerning the United States–Canada maritime border, where Canadians had shut out American fishermen in *retaliation* for high U.S. *tariffs* on other goods. The border was set by an arbitration commission. (3) The issue of ownership of the San Juan Islands, in the Strait of Juan de Fuca off Vancouver Island, was sent to arbitration. (4) The *Alabama claims* were resolved by an ad hoc international tribunal in exchange for Britain assuming the obligation to make financial redress of Canada's grievance over *Fenian* raids launched from U.S. soil, 1866–1868. This treaty cleared away the accumulated dross of decades of animosity and distrust between the United States and Britain, thereby opening the path to the great *rapprochement* which was vital to the history of the twentieth century and to the success of liberty. It also fortified

Canada–United States relations as entirely peaceful and increasingly harmonious.

Washington, Treaty of (April 4, 1949). *See NATO.*

wastage. The loss of troops in any military formation unrelated to battle casualties, as by desertion, disease, or accidental death.

water. (1) Fresh water: Water, as a *vital interest* and source of conflict, is often overlooked. Yet water (or more precisely, water shortage) has the potential to send states to war. The availability of potable water is the determining factor in distinguishing in *international law* between an *island* and an *islet*, which may have major consequences as to where the boundary of the *territorial sea* is drawn and the extent of the *Exclusive Economic Zone* which may be claimed. Lack of fresh water for agriculture and/or competition over hydroelectric power generation underlie several political fault lines in the modern *Middle East*, including settlements in *Palestine* and relations between Jordan and Israel. For example, in 1960 the *Arab League* denounced as "an act of *aggression*" Israel's plans to divert some of the Jordan River to irrigate the Negev Desert. From time to time, water rights have been a major issue in relations between Egypt, Sudan, and Ethiopia, concerning damming and diverting the Blue Nile, and between India and Bangladesh over sharing the Ganges. Large numbers of people now live and grow crops where fresh water does not flow in abundance (*North Africa*, the Middle East, *Sahel*, *California*) and desalination *technology* is at best a limited solution. Conversely, most of the world's fresh water—which is only 3 percent of all water on the planet—is located where there are no, or almost no, people. About 70 percent of all fresh water is frozen into the *Antarctic* ice sheet and cap, a resource currently forbidden to *exploitation* by the rigors of nature and the *terms* of the *Antarctic Treaty system*. Other sources flow unused, or are trapped as ice sheets, over the various *Arctic nations*. Some 10 percent of world supplies of fresh water flow largely unexploited over northern Canada. Yet, most suggestions that such waters might be rechanneled and sold for use elsewhere raise loud protests from environmental or nationalist groups. (2) The Oceans: Access to the great oceanic *trade routes* and to *warm water ports* has driven much of international history, especially during and after the *Age of Exploration*. Oceanic issues are covered by the *law of the sea*. *See also Aral Sea; Euphrates River; Bosporus; Dardanelles; English Channel; geopolitics; Alfred Thayer Mahan; Halford Mackinder; Panama Canal; sea power; slave trade; Straits Question; Suez Canal; Third Arab-Israeli War; West Bank*

Watergate scandal. An essentially domestic crisis, arising from *Nixon's* personality and political abuses, but one also rooted in the *Vietnam War*, secret diplomacy, and secret bombing of People's Army of Vietnam (PAVN, North

Vietnam) bases in Cambodia. When these actions were revealed by the "New York Times" in 1969, Nixon authorized wiretaps and abused his presidential authority in ways which ultimately led to compiling of an "enemies list" and illegal manipulation of the Federal Bureau of Investigation and the Internal Revenue Service. The crisis so eroded Nixon's ability to govern after 1972 that it had serious foreign policy implications as well. During the summer lead-in to the 1972 presidential election, a group of five *White House* "plumbers" (so-called because they were tasked to fix information "leaks") were caught inside the *Democratic Party* National Headquarters in the Watergate Hotel complex in Washington. A spate of denials of White House involvement was followed by revelations that "hush money" was paid to keep the plumbers quietly in prison. A sorry tale then unraveled of "dirty tricks," illegal wiretaps of opponents of the administration, and, most damaging of all, a cover-up of these activities which was directed out of the Oval Office itself. Nixon's top aides and attorney general were indicted, and later convicted, on various charges related to obstructing justice. The crisis peaked during the *Fourth Arab-Israeli War*, when Nixon fired Special Prosecutor Archibald Cox, Attorney General Elliot Richardson resigned, and Congress initiated impeachment hearings. For 18 months, as the nation was transfixed on itself, Nixon was hamstrung and profoundly preoccupied. That left control of U.S. foreign policy in the hands of *Henry Kissinger*.

The conspiracy to cover up the "dirty tricks" campaign unraveled when some White House staff—notably Counsel to the President John Dean—testified before Congress as to their role in the cover-up and revealed that Nixon had a secret taping system in the Oval Office (which had been installed and used by several earlier presidents). Its output, it seemed clear, could settle most evidentiary questions. A titanic legal struggle ensued, with Nixon asserting "executive privilege" over the tapes. The Supreme Court finally ordered him to surrender recordings of his Oval Office conversations concerning Watergate. Despite an infamous "18-minute gap" in one crucial tape, these recordings revealed that, although Nixon had not known of the burglary, he was directly involved in obstructing investigations by the Justice Department and Senate committees. Moreover, they displayed the baser parts of his character—suspicion bordering on paranoia, a Manichean approach to political disagreement, low cunning about how to "pay back" those he typed as "political enemies," and almost casual abuse of power as he deployed assets of the Federal Government to harass or monitor those identified as his foes. Impeachment proceedings continued apace, and now looked unstoppable. The *Republican* leadership in Congress went to see Nixon and admonished him to resign for the good of the Party and the country. On August 9, 1974, Richard M. Nixon resigned, the only president ever to do so. The next five years witnessed a newly "imperial congress" attempt to displace the "imperial presidency" from its lead role in foreign policy, and attach hitherto unheard of constraints on presidential prerogatives in foreign affairs.

Waterloo, Battle of (June 18, 1815). The bitter, final battle of the long *Napoleonic Wars*. It was fought within earshot of Brussels and constituted the climax of the *Hundred Days*. A scattered, Anglo-Flanders army led by *Wellington* had fought the French at Quatre Bras (June 16th). United at Waterloo, it met the main French force under *Napoleon* and fought brilliantly. Nevertheless, it was nearing defeat by early evening. The day was saved for the Allies when the Prussian Army under *Gebhart von Blücher* arrived from the flank. It had outrun and evaded a pursuing French corps, which had been ordered by Napoleon to prevent the Prussians from linking with Wellington's army. The advent of the Prussians on the field of battle panicked even the most seasoned French veterans. When even the Imperial Guard broke and ran, which it had never done before, the battle was won for the Allies and Napoleon's career as *warlord* and emperor was finally at an end. He abdicated, for the second and last time, four days later. In a famous commentary, upon viewing the carnage of the field of battle Wellington said: "Nothing except a battle lost can be half so melancholy as a battle won."

Suggested Readings: Lord Chalfont, ed., *Waterloo: Battle of Three Armies* (1980); Peter Hofschröer, *1815: The Waterloo Campaign* (1998); Henry Lachouque, *Waterloo* (trans. 1975).

weapons-grade material. Elements which can sustain an uncontrolled *fission* or *fusion* reaction and are thus suitable for making *atomic bombs*. *See also plutonium.*

weapons of mass destruction. Ever since the *World War I* experience with *poison gas*, there have been sustained legal efforts to limit the production and use of weapons which can kill indiscriminately and on a vast scale. The motive forces behind that effort included a complex mix of pragmatic and moral concerns. In addition to concern with *nuclear weapons*, attention has also focused on *chemical, biological,* and *nerve weapons*, all capable of destroying whole populations. Actually, only nuclear weapons are capable of mass destruction, to the point of wiping out civilization itself; the other types might be better termed "weapons of mass death." *See also ballistic missile defense; just war tradition; prohibited weapons.*

Weber, Max (1864–1920). German political economist. Weber was enormously influential in framing the basic approaches of academic disciplines that later developed into sociology, political science and political economy, and economic history. Weber sharply opposed *Marxist* approaches to understanding society and economics, though he shared *Marx's* distorting German predilection for thinking in "ideal types," or grand historical models, into which he then tried to squeeze all known societies, as did Marx with his idea of *modes of production*. Unlike Marx, however, Weber had a reasoned and refreshing distrust of *economic determinism* or other single-factor explanations of large social and historical phenomena, placing particular emphasis on the role of religion and ideology and of charismatic leaders as *agents* of change. He also wrote cogently on the role of *bureaucracy* in modern societies and the need to restrain its growth and influence. Weber is best remembered for his thesis on the presumed relationship between *Protestantism*, in its *Calvinist* form, and modern *capitalism*. In "The Protestant Ethic and the Spirit of Capitalism" he argued that the piety, and more so the core asceticism, of early Calvinists made them more "thrifty" than *Catholics* or *Lutherans*, which led to a greater savings rate (accumulation of capital), and that worldly material success was then read backward into their notion of the "elect" (those predestined by God for eternal salvation) to produce a virtuous circle of thrift, investment, prosperity, and more saving.

In fact, the thesis does not stand up. Many early capitalists were not Calvinists, and the reverse was also true. It is more likely that the special connection between Calvinism and capitalism, insofar as there even was one, had more to do with the urban concentration of most Calvinists in France and the Low Countries, in particular. Thus, they were disproportionately involved in the economic changes toward capitalism and an expansion of commerce which matured first in the larger cities. Also, Calvinists were concentrated in the rising Atlantic states of northwest Europe rather than in the declining states of the Mediterranean and Iberia, which again associated them with areas where capitalism first took root. Yet, even those provisos do not account for the fact, any more than Weber did, that recognizable capitalism was first evident in the *city-states* of the Italian (Catholic) *Renaissance*. Even though Weber's thesis failed to account for the full complexity of the extraordinary phenomenon known as capitalism (no one thesis or single causal factor does), it was bold and ambitious, rich in its apparent explanatory power, and for many years also widely influential.

Suggested Reading: David Beetham, *Max Weber and the Theory of Modern Politics* (1985).

Webster-Ashburton Treaty (1842). Most immediately prompted by the *Aroostook War*, and negotiated by U.S. Secretary of State Daniel Webster and Baron Ashburton (Alexander Baring) of Great Britain, this treaty settled a long-standing border dispute between the United States and Great Britain over where to draw the boundary between Maine and Canada, and in parts of the Great Lakes area. It also spoke to joint suppression of the *slave trade*, which was contributing to the "Underground Railroad," by which American blacks sought and received personal freedom in Canada, and other, minor issues. *See also Oregon Question; Rush-Bagot Agreement (1818).*

Wehrmacht. "Armed power." The regular German military, 1933–1945. In 1937 it fell under the OKW (Oberkommando der Wehrmacht), which *Hitler* personally headed. His conviction after 1941 that he knew better than his generals how to wage *total war* helped the *Allies* win *World War II*. The

Wehrmacht's great rival was the *Schutzstaffel* (SS), especially its *Panzer* (and pampered) formations in the "Waffen SS." Senior Wehrmacht officers later maintained that the SS, and not they or their men, implemented the *"final solution"* and other wartime atrocities. This claim has been thoroughly discredited by historians. In fact, many German officers—most—were deeply implicated at the very least by their passivity in the face of rank atrocity and bestiality, and not a few had been enthusiastic murderers. Overall, as in other areas of German society and other national institutions, the Wehrmacht underwent deep Nazification during World War II. As the war progressed and losses mounted, it also underwent massive destruction, becoming less well-equipped, and even less modern. Ultimately, it was totally defeated. *See also Ardennes Offensive; Barbarossa; Bundeswehr; Battle of France; Kursk; Heinz Guderian; Leningrad; Erich von Manstein;* Reichswehr; *Erwin Rommel; Stalingrad.*

Suggested Readings: Wilhelm Deist, *The Wehrmacht and German Rearmament* (1981); Andris J. Kursietis, *The Wehrmacht at War, 1939–1945* (1999); Alfred M. de Zayas, *The Wehrmacht War Crimes Bureau, 1939–1945* (1989).

weighted voting. Where the principle of *equality* is waived so that states making the greatest financial contribution to the *International Monetary Fund*, or some other *international organization*, have the most influence in deciding how funds are used or other decisions are made. Depending on the forum, voting may also be weighted by *population, size,* or some other criterion. *See also qualified majority voting.*

Weimar Republic. Popularly named for the city where its constituent assembly met, its official name was the German Federal Republic. It lasted from 1918 to 1933. *See also Germany: Weimar Republic.*

Weizmann, Chaim (1874–1952). First president of Israel, 1948–1952. His real importance came as a *Zionist* leader before the founding of Israel, particularly his success in obtaining British recognition of the *Jewish Agency* and issuance of the *Balfour Declaration.* He opposed the use of *terror* and other indiscriminate and anti-British tactics of groups such as *Irgun* and the *Stern Gang.* He negotiated directly with *Harry S Truman* for U.S. recognition of Israel.

Wellesley, Richard (1761–1848). *See East India Company.*

Wellington, Duke of, né Arthur Wellesley (1769–1852). "The Iron Duke." British field marshal and statesman. He was named Viscount Wellington in 1809 and Duke in 1814. Like many young aristocrats, Wellesley purchased a commission in the army. As a major landowner, he served in the Irish Parliament. From 1793 to 1795 he fought in the Netherlands, but the campaign went badly and Wellesley resigned his commission. In 1796 he rejoined the army and led a regiment to India, where he fought to victory in Mysore (1799) and in Poona (1803). The important war was back in Europe, however, so Wellesley returned to England in 1805 and fought in the ill-fated Hanover campaign. In 1806 he was elected to the English Parliament and served as secretary for Ireland in 1807. He fought next in an expedition to Denmark in 1807. He saddled his military reputation in Portugal during the early *Peninsular War* (he would cinch it in Flanders in 1815), where he defeated a succession of *Napoleon's* best marshals before invading Spain in 1811. It was in Iberia that he first showed a great talent for engineering, logistics, and the use of field intelligence. During 1812, while Napoleon was in Russia, Wellington finished clearing Portugal and Spain of the French (his descendants still control a good deal of sherry production in Spain) and threatened to invade France. He was promoted to field marshal in 1813, as his army crossed the French border. He was *ambassador* to the restored *Bourbon* monarchy in 1814 and replaced *Castlereagh* at the *Congress of Vienna* in early 1815. It was there that Wellington heard of the start of Napoleon's *Hundred Days* and rushed to Flanders to take command of allied forces. With *Gebhard von Blücher* of Prussia, he planned a second invasion of France. As always, Napoleon struck first, forcing a battle in Flanders in the hope of yet again dividing the gathering and quarrelsome Allies. Wellington and his men fought brilliantly and courageously on the bloody field of *Waterloo* on June 18, 1815, but he and they were almost certainly saved by the early evening arrival of the Prussian Army, which routed the French from the field.

Wellington's at times crippling class prejudice was well-captured in his cavalier remark that "the battle of Waterloo was won on the playing fields of Eton." In fact, it was won more in the working-class clubs of the several peoples of the British Isles. Wellington next commanded the Allied *occupation* of France, 1815–1818, moderating others' suggestions for a more punitive policy. He attended several meetings of the powers within the *Congress system*, but *statecraft* was never his forte. He took overall command of the army in 1827. As prime minister, from 1828 to 1830, he completed *Catholic Emancipation*. His natural *conservatism* caused him to oppose further reform of Parliament, and on this issue he lost office. He was prime minister again for just two months in 1834, but was more comfortable as foreign secretary, 1834–1835, and commander-in-chief, 1842–1852. Some blame him for failing to adopt military reforms after 1815, for instead clinging to an eighteenth-century army and tactics, and hence for early debacles suffered by British arms during the *Crimean War*, and for the army's retrograde professionalism deep into the nineteenth century. Yet, the deeper defect was national complacency born of the great victories over France of 1792–1815, more than any one man's prejudice or administrative failings. In any case, the weakness went mostly unnoticed in Britain's smallish colonial wars. Even once it had been exposed on the larger battlefields of the Crimea, national smugness reigned;

thus, until 1871 British Army commissions still could be purchased by the wealthy or well-born, rather than earned solely by professional training or demonstrated merit.

Suggested Readings: Lord Chalfont, ed., *Waterloo: Battle of Three Armies* (1980); Peter Hofschröer, *1815: The Waterloo Campaign* (1998); Jac Weller, *Wellington in the Peninsula* (1962); Jac Weller, *On Wellington* (1998).

Weltpolitik. "World policy." (1) A term first applied to Kaiser *Wilhelm II's* foreign policy of making Germany a first-rank *world power*. It abandoned *Bismarck's* caution and satisfied continentalism in favor of overseas *adventurism*, shrill insistence upon *prestige* and "national honor," construction of a navy to rival Britain's, and belated joining in the *scramble for Africa* and for *spheres of influence* in China. It contributed to the belief of many in the German elite before 1914 that the nation's destiny required an ultimate military confrontation with Russia, and perhaps also with France and Great Britain, as these nations stood in the way of Germany's achieving its rightful status as a world power. It was fed by theories of *social Darwinism*, in which the only other alternative to dominance was seen as decline, or "Weltmacht oder Niedergang!" ("World Power or Downfall!"), as some Germans put it. Its main effects to provoke formation of the *Triple Entente*, raise international tensions, and earn Germany a reputation for bluster and bullying. (2) An overarching concern in foreign policy with geopolitical *strategy* and *prestige*, as opposed to regional stakes and interests. *See also Bernhard von Bülow.*

West. (1) Historically: European civilization, and its many colonial extensions, extending into the Middle East under the *Byzantine Empire* and as far east as the vast Christian lands of Russia before *Mongol* conquest cut off that nation from further intercourse with the Latin world. (2) In common usage: The industrial democracies of the Atlantic region, but also including Japan and Turkey after *World War II*, and New Zealand and Australia. *See also OECD; westernize.*

West Africa. *See Africa.*

West Asia. Asia west of the Hindu Kush in the Himalayas: from Afghanistan through *Central Asia* and including all the states of the *Middle East* lying east of the *Suez Canal*.

West Bank. The part of *Palestine* west of the Jordan River. It was occupied by *Transjordan* in 1948 and *annexed* in 1950, over international objections. Captured by Israel in 1967, it was the larger part of the *occupied territories*. Jordan renounced its claim in 1974, in favor of the *Palestine Liberation Organization*. Two of Israel's three main aquifers lie under the West Bank. Even so, in the 1990s a general accord was achieved between Israel and the PLO on forming an *autonomous* Palestinian area from the West Bank and *Gaza*. *See also Jerusalem*.

West Berlin. The combined American, British, and French *occupation zones* in Berlin, 1945–1994, located some 110 miles inside the surrounding Soviet occupation zone which became *East Germany*, until that state became *extinct* in 1990 and East and West Berlin were politically and administratively reconnected. *See also Berlin; Berlin airlift; Berlin, division of; Berlin Wall*.

Western Europe. A cultural/geographical term used for nearly 1,000 years to refer basically to the successor territories of Carlos Magnos (Charles the Great, or *Charlemagne*, 742–814 C.E.), king of the Franks and "Emperor in the West." These lands extended to the Elbe in the east, the *frontier* with historic *Slav* lands; the south shores of the Baltic in the North, excluding Denmark and other *Viking* lands; and the Mediterranean in the South, excluding most of Iberia, which was then occupied by Moors from the competing civilization of *Islam*. During the Middle Ages, as the *schism* from the *Orthodox Church* deepened and widened, these areas of common culture and overarching political and religious institutions—the *Catholic Church* and *Holy Roman Empire*—were known as the *res publica Christiana*. Iberia was added with the slow *Reconquista* of its Muslim states, concluding with the surrender of *Granada* in 1492. *Scandinavia* was slowly drawn in as well, as Vikings settled in France and Britain and *Christianity* spread northward. This process of incorporation spread to western Russia as well and may be said to have been "completed" after the *Renaissance* and during the *Thirty Years' War*. For the next four centuries, Western Europe was that region of the world which experienced the most sustained and dynamic *growth* and *development*. The core of the modern world economy was formed in this region, and from it waves of successful *imperialist* expansion connected the globe politically and militarily and then drew it into repeated *systemic wars*. The central ideas of modern *international law*, *diplomacy*, the *balance of power*, and the states system took shape and root first in Western Europe and then spread globally—carried along by European *imperialism* and *colonialism*—to the wider world. *See also Europe*.

Western European and Other Group (WEOG). A *caucus group* of Western states in the United Nations and other forums of *multilateral diplomacy*. "Other" referred to the United States and Canada. The United States did not always caucus with WEOG, depending on the forum or issue. *See also United Nations Human Rights Commission*.

Western European Union (WEU). It was formed as a follow-up to the *Brussels Treaty* in a compromise with France to permit West Germany and Italy to rearm under close supervision after 1955. It lay dormant for three decades until in the mid-1980s European federalists sought to revive it as the core of an independent *European Community* military. Portugal and Spain joined in 1988. By 1994 it contained all *European Union* countries except Greece, Denmark, and Ireland; it subsequently added most *NATO* and former *Warsaw Pact* states as associate members. Britain wanted it to become the European pillar of NATO, France wished it disconnected from the United States and to serve as the defense arm of the EU, and Germany vacillated between those alternatives. In 1992 the WEU agreed to help enforce *sanctions* against Serbia, coordinating operations with NATO. Under the Petersburg Declaration (1992) the WEU took on the less militarily onerous tasks of *peacekeeping* and *crisis management*, leaving the real job of collective defense to NATO. The European Security and Defense Identity (ESDI), an extension of the *Maastricht Treaty's* call for a Common Foreign and Security Policy (CFSP), was located in the WEU. This involved the use of Combined Joint Task Forces with NATO, in which assets in communications, intelligence, and logistics were to be shared. In 1995 its *EUROCORPS* became operational. After 1999 it moved further in the direction desired by France, toward becoming the security arm of the European Union.

western front. (1) In *World War I:* The frontline—of near-constant length and position—between the armed forces of the Western *Allied and Associated Powers* and those of Germany. From September 1914 until the summer of 1818 it ran 475 miles from the Atlantic coast of Belgium to the Franco-Swiss border. (2) In *World War II:* The frontline—of greatly varying length and position—between the armed forces of the Western *Allies* and those of *Nazi Germany*. It ran from the Belgian border south along the *Maginot Line* to the Swiss frontier, 1939–1940, during the *Phony War*. It went madly active when the Low Countries and France were invaded by Germany in May 1940, the *Battle of France* was fought, and the British Army was forced to evacuate from the Continent at *Dunkirk*. It was re-established on June 6, 1944 (D-Day), and during the *Normandy campaign* expanded out of the Normandy beachhead (and from a second landing made later in the south of France) in a widening arc which ultimately took Allied armies through southern Germany into western Czechoslovakia, as well as to Paris and the frontier, and north into the *Low Countries* and across the Rhine. In neither war was the western front considered to include the extensive fighting between the Western powers and Germany which occurred in Italy, North Africa (WWII only), and the Balkans. *See also Ardennes Offensive; Champagne; French Army mutinies; Frontiers; Loos; Marne; Neuve-Chapelle; no-man's-land; race to the sea; second front; Somme; trench warfare; Verdun; Ypres.*

Suggested Readings: Richard Holmes, *The Western Front* (2000); John Terraine, *The Western Front, 1914–1918* (1965).

westernize. (1) To establish political control by the *West* over non-Western areas of the world. (2) To imbue with the values, practices, and habits of mind of Western civilization. It refers in particular to the West's modern emphases on *individualism* and *secularism*, its preference for *market economics*, and its liberal-democratic values and institutions. Although westernization in the first sense clearly waned during the twentieth century, with retreat from empire, in the second sense it may be advancing still. *See also cosmopolitan values; end of history; human rights; liberalism; liberal-internationalism; modernization.*

Westernizer. A designation of a Russian intellectual and cultural tradition holding that values drawn from the *West*, including modes of economic, political, and social organization, are necessary and proper for Russian *modernization*. Among leaders identified with this tradition are *Peter I* (the Great), *Alexander II*, *Gorbachev* and *Yeltsin*. *See also Slavophile.*

Western Sahara. Formerly *Spanish Sahara*. Spain withdrew in 1976 and this territory was immediately *partitioned* between Mauritania and Morocco, an action not recognized by the *OAU* or *United Nations*. By 1979 *POLISARIO* forced Mauritania to abandon its claim, but Morocco then seized that portion of Western Sahara as well. The fighting continued for 12 years. King *Hassan II* of Morocco persisted in opposing POLISARIO in defiance of most African and international opinion, even constructing hundreds of miles of wall in the desert to block access by the nomad population of Sahrawis who supported POLISARIO and to present barriers to the *guerrillas*. In 1984 the OAU admitted POLISARIO as if it was the government of an established *state* in Western Sahara (the "Sahrawi Arab Democratic Republic"). That led to Morocco's *withdrawal* from the organization. In 1988 a United Nations special *envoy* was sent to mediate a *cease-fire* between the guerrillas and Morocco. An agreement was signed which called for a *referendum* on the future of the territory. The OAU agreed to appointment of the *secretary general* as "the sole authority over all issues related to the referendum," and the UN set up an *observer mission*. By 1991 hundreds of United Nations observers were in place. Disputes over the census continued, with Morocco preventing nomads from voting by claiming they were not "permanent residents," while simultaneously diluting the Sahrawi vote by adding names from Moroccan tribal groups known to oppose Sahrawi independence. In 1998 *James Baker* was appointed to get the referendum process restarted and solve the issue of the census.

Suggested Reading: R. Adloff, *The Western Saharans* (1989).

Western Samoa. *See Samoa.*

West Germany. *See Germany.*

West Indies. The three island groups forming a large archipelago lying between the American continents, comprising the *Greater Antilles*, the *Lesser Antilles*, and the *Bahamas*.

West Indies Associated States. The smaller *colonies* in the eastern part of the *West Indies* which became *associated states* with Britain in 1968: Antigua, Dominica, Grenada, St. Kitts–Nevis-Anguilla, and St. Lucia.

West Indies Federation (1958–1962). An *extinct* effort at forming a *federation* of the British *colonies* in the *West Indies*, out of concern that individually *independence* was not viable. It comprised Barbados, Jamaica, Trinidad, Tobago, the Windward and Leeward Islands, and the *West Indies Associated States*. It collapsed when Jamaica withdrew, out of reluctance to subsidize the poorer island members. It was quickly followed out by Trinidad and Tobago. *See also Organization of Eastern Caribbean States (OECS).*

West Irian. *See Irian Jaya.*

Westminster, Statute of (1931). An act of the British Parliament granting powers over foreign affairs well beyond the domestic *autonomy* already enjoyed by the main *Dominions*: Australia, Canada, Eire (Irish Free State), New Zealand, Newfoundland, and South Africa. Despite this, the Dominions still coordinated policy with Britain, to the point of again joining its war effort in 1939 (except for Eire, which remained *neutral*) after pro forma gestures of independent decision-making. Real independence in foreign policy came after *World War II*, that crucible to burn away old sentimentalities about the imperial tie, excepting South Africa, whose *Boers* had never felt much regard for things British and who broke away even more sharply with the introduction of *apartheid* in 1949. *See also Durham Report.*

Westmoreland, William (b. 1914). U.S. commander during the *Vietnam War*, 1964–1968. He had a distinguished combat career during *World War II*, fighting in North Africa, Sicily, Normandy, and Germany. He also fought in the *Korean Conflict*. In 1958 he took command of the 101st Airborne Division, one of the most famous and decorated units in the U.S. Army. He was also superintendent of West Point. On June 20, 1964, he took overall command of U.S. forces in Vietnam. For the next four years he worked with *Lyndon Johnson* to build up American forces and conduct a "big war" of *attrition* against the *Viêt Cong* (VC), or National Liberation Front (NLF), and People's Army of Vietnam (PAVN, North Vietnam) regiments infiltrated south by the Democratic Republic of Vietnam (DRV, North Vietnam). In settling on a strategy of attrition, he seriously underestimated both the *logistics* capability of the DRV and the willingness of his enemy to continue the fight despite taking huge—and to Americans, also unacceptable—losses. In 1967 he asked for a call-up of U.S. reserves and an additional 200,000 troops in-country (for a total of 670,000) to take the war into Laos and Cambodia. This was refused. Still, at the end of 1967, he said: "I hope they [the NLF and PAVN] try something, because we are looking for a fight." What he got was the *Tet Offensive*. Yet, if Westmoreland overall chose the wrong strategy, and even that is moot, it was the civilians (*Kennedy, Johnson, McNamara, Rusk,* et al.) who chose the fight in the first place, overcommitting the United States to what many came to see as the wrong war, against the wrong enemy, in the wrong country, whatever the arguable justice of the cause. Westmoreland was relieved of field command in Vietnam after Tet. He served as army chief-of-staff, 1968–1972. In 1986 he won a bitter libel suit against CBS News, which had accused him of deliberate falsification of casualty reports during his time in Vietnam. *See also Nguyễn Võ Giáp; search and destroy.*

Suggested Reading: Samuel Zaffiri, *Westmoreland* (1994).

West Pakistan. From 1947 to 1971 it dominated *East Pakistan*, which is now Bangladesh. After the *secession* of East Pakistan most references to West Pakistan simply dropped the geographical indicator.

Westphalian system. The modern, state-centered international political system, first codified in the form of key secular principles laid out by the powers in the *Peace of Westphalia* (1648), which upheld the absolute local authority of discrete *states* in international relations as against any and all universal claims or pretensions, whether based on imperial or religious authority. Despite their historically Western European origins, Westphalian principles were subsequently confirmed by all or most states in their common practice, agreed statutes, *international organizations*, and formal *treaties*. Its central ideas and pillars remain: *diplomacy, equality, nonintervention, sovereignty,* and the rule of *international law.*

Westphalia, Peace of (1648). A set of discrete Treaties of Westphalia (*Münster* in January 1648 and *Osnabrück* in October 1648) which settled the *Thirty Years' War,* the *Eighty Years' War,* and a number of lesser conflicts. Taken together as the Peace of Westphalia, these treaties codified key rules of a still slowly emerging *nation-state* system. Thereby, they legally sanctioned with the aura of *legitimacy* the shift long underway in real-world power from the universalist claims of popes and emperors to the now fully ascendant nation-states. The process would take another 100 years and was at first confined solely to *Catholic* and *Protestant* powers. It excluded not just the great *Islamic* empire of the *Ottomans,* who were already a de facto major player in the European states system, but virtually all *Orthodox* kingdoms as well. This changed 50 years later with the ascent of Russia under *Peter I,* who demanded entry into the Westphalia system after the *Great Northern War* (1700–1721).

Still, 1648 serves as a useful marker of a truly fundamental change in world history and politics.

As for Germany itself, the Thirty Years' War had left no single German state in a position to dominate the others, a situation France's *Mazarin* appreciated and worked to sustain, and *Louis XIV* after him. The terms of Osnabrück, which was the German or *Holy Roman Empire* treaty, elevated Sweden and France to formal guarantors of Germany's security and made all of Germany's many discrete political entities fully *sovereign*. That cleared the way for a century of French intrusion into German affairs, while also ensuring that no German concentration of power existed for another 200 years. Sweden would also interfere, until it fell from the ranks of the *Great Powers* early in the eighteenth century, a victim of the excessive ambition of its young king, *Charles XII*, but more of the rise of Russia under Peter.

The principle of *sovereignty* permeated the various settlements, raising with it as absolute standards of interstate conduct subordinate principles such as *nonintervention* in all *internal affairs*, and especially on religious matters. The wars occasioned by the great ideological *schism* of previous centuries within *res publica Christiana* were ended with affirmative and universal ratification at Westphalia of the great settlement principle of the *Peace of Augsburg*, decided in 1555 and briefly bringing peace to Germany, but ignored thereafter: "cuius regio, eius religio" ("who rules, decides the religion"). Indeed, *secularism* was to be the new order in international, though not yet all internal, politics. The states, which still meant mostly princes and kings, or *sovereigns*, rather than government based on *popular sovereignty*, and not religious authorities, were henceforth supreme in temporal matters. The quasi-*feudal* relations and pretensions to universal empire of the Holy Roman Empire were also mostly dismissed, though the Empire continued a truncated role as a pan-German institution. The popes, too, were henceforth ignored by the political world, including by Catholic powers at least as jealous of their sovereign prerogatives as were Protestant counterparts. So angry did this make Pope Innocent X, he condemned all articles of the treaties which pertained to religious matters as perpetually "null and void, invalid, iniquitous, unjust, condemned, rejected, frivolous, without force or effect, and no one is to observe them, even when they be ratified by oath."

Rail as the enraged pontiff might, the *Reformation* and the *Counter Reformation* had alike failed to achieve doctrinal exclusivity, and the passions they once aroused were now faded for all but a few. In their place, an age of absolute sovereignty began. With it came a new pattern of international politics, one of Great Powers lording it over small, and elevation of new principles of statecraft and action, of *raison d'etat*, the *balance of power*, and *power politics*. Not until the *French Revolution* tempted the continent's greatest power, France, to revive the old ambition to universal political dominion would European civilization again so badly and bloodily divide against itself over ideology. *See also community of nations; Edict of Nantes; Armand Jean Richelieu.*

Suggested Reading: Derek Croxton and Anuschka Tischer, *The Peace of Westphalia* (2001).

wet affair. Intelligence slang for *assassination*, in reference to the spilling of blood.

whaling. Whaling is an ancient, local occupation, notably in northern countries along the great migratory routes. It became a major international industry in the eighteenth century (brilliantly and evocatively recalled in Herman Melville's classic novel of the American whaling industry, "Moby Dick"), as whale oil products rose in great demand for use in light industrial lubrication and tanneries. Before the discovery of, and switch to, ground *oil* by industrial countries, faux oil from animal and whale fats were widely used for lighting. In addition, some nations developed a taste for whale meat and blubber. International reforms and state action in the nineteenth century aimed mainly at protecting whalers, not whales. Concern grew, however, as stocks of valued species were depleted. Still, what saved entire whale species from being hunted to extinction was not early conservation, but the discovery of petroleum as a substitute for whale products. Conservation did play a hand, however, especially after *World War II* and concerning specific species of whale. An International Whaling Commission (IWC) was set up in 1946, charged with deciding the length of hunting seasons for individual whale species and setting out national quotas. In the 1960s scientists warned that certain whale species were on the verge of extinction. Many countries announced unilateral hunt *moratoria*, but historic whaling nations such as Iceland, Japan, Norway, and the Soviet Union refused to submit to a general ban, despite building international and scientific pressure for a 10-year moratorium.

In 1979 the IWC banned whaling in the Indian Ocean. In 1980 the major whaling nations accepted highly restrictive quotas, but not yet a global moratorium. Canada resigned from the IWC in 1982, asserting it was no longer a whaling nation. Bans were then introduced on a species-by-species basis. Beginning in 1986 a worldwide ban was imposed by the IWC, though with a loophole permitting Iceland, Japan, Norway, and South Korea to hunt a limited number of whales, ostensibly for scientific purposes. Even this limited hunt was vehemently protested by *Greenpeace*, among other *nongovernmental organizations*. And some small whaling states (such as Mauritius) pulled out of the IWC, as a result of the decision. In 1993 Norway, a major whaler, announced it was resuming commercial whaling in violation of the IWC ban. In 1994 the IWC declared a kill-free zone around *Antarctica*, though of questionable enforceability. In 1996 Canada's Inuit embarrassingly killed a whale with automatic weapons fire in the Arctic, then watched the carcass sink out of sight. They had lost old skills and mostly forgotten old Inuit methods of hunting. Two years later the Inuit completed their first successful whale hunt in over 50 years, harpooning a bowhead whale in the Arctic. The Inuit hunt was approved by the Canadian government essentially as a cultural activity and was tightly regulated and limited. In 1997, in open revolt against international regulation of the whaling industry, Iceland withdrew from the IWC. In 1999 the Makah Indians of Washington State resumed their traditional hunt of gray whales in the historical manner, from canoes. In 2001 Norway openly defied the IWC by resuming export of whale products.

Suggested Reading: Bjørn Basberg et al., eds., *Whaling and History* (1993).

Whig. (1) In Great Britain: A major political "party" from 1679 to 1832, though that was an era when party affiliation was far looser than in later periods and policy differences correspondingly greater within parties. Still, the English Whigs generally favored reform and a strong parliament as a check on the prerogatives of the monarch, in the spirit of the Glorious Revolution of 1688. Dominant in the early eighteenth century, the Whigs were repeatedly blocked from power in the later eighteenth and early nineteenth centuries by *George III* and by the success of *William Pitt*. Many joined the successor Liberal Party, wherein erstwhile Whigs favored *free trade* and supported manufacturing interests. (2) In the United States: (i) A supporter of the 1776 *American Revolution* against rule by Britain; (ii) A major political party, 1834–1855. Western and northern-based, it was founded in opposition to *Andrew Jackson*. It opposed the *Mexican-American War* and any expansion of *slavery* into new states carved from Mexican lands. It also pushed for a high national *tariff* to protect industry. Its demise was followed by the ascendance of the *Republican Party* under *Abraham Lincoln*, a one-time Whig. (3) In Liberia: The True Whig Party, formed in 1878, was comprised mostly of descendants of freed slaves who governed as a de facto aristocracy over native Liberians. The party was overthrown in a coup in 1980. *See also protective tariffs; Alexander Hamilton; Winfield Scott; Zachary Taylor; United Irish Society.*

Whig history. A tendency among British *liberal* historians in the nineteenth century to overread the success of the *British Empire* of their day deep into the study of the past, identified and denounced by Herbert Butterfield in his great work "The Whig Interpretation of History" (1931). In particular, the Whig historians tended to identify the source of British imperial success with the internal development of principles and institutions of constitutional liberty.

White Dominions. An informal, but formerly oft-used term, for those British *Dominions* with large white populations: Australia, Canada, the Irish Free State (from 1921), Newfoundland, New Zealand, and South Africa. They were given foreign policy *autonomy* within the evolving British Commonwealth by the *Statute of Westminster* (1931). *See also Durham Report.*

White Fleet. *See Great White Fleet (1907–1909).*

Whitehall. A common, shorthand reference for the British government and its policies, derived from the location of the major government offices on Whitehall Street in London. *See also Foggy Bottom; Forbidden City; Kremlin; Quai d'Orsay; Sublime Porte; White House.*

White Highlands. The highland areas of Central Africa, where European settlement was encouraged and extensive in the colonial period. Alienation of African populations from these fertile lands led to prolonged, and often violent, land wars.

White House. (1) The working residence of the president of the United States, containing the Oval Office. It was burnt by the British during the *War of 1812.* The term is used as a shorthand reference for the *executive* power and policies of the United States. (2) The former Soviet-Russian Parliament. It was used as a headquarters by *Boris Yeltsin* during the August 1991 *coup* attempt by the *communist* old guard and elements of the *Red Army.* In 1993 he abolished the old, Soviet-era parliament and sent troops against the White House when hardcore members and their supporters holed up within and called for a nationwide political and military revolt. *See also Duma; Foggy Bottom; Forbidden City; Kremlin; Quai d'Orsay; Sublime Porte; Whitehall.*

White Lotus Rebellion (1796–1804). A smaller rebellion by White Lotus Buddhists had taken place in 1774, when poorly armed peasants had been easily overwhelmed by *banner troops* and local militia with *artillery* and fire-arms. This time, a millenarian peasant uprising against the *Qing* came just at the end of the long reign of the *Qianlong emperor* and was massive. It sprang from: (1) tax and food supply pressures built up in previous decades by an unchecked population increase in China (without a corresponding rise in food production or urban employment) which marginalized peasants on already overworked land; (2) the ever-growing distance of the *Manchu* emperors from the mass of people; and (3) the ideology of the rebels, which looked to an earthly apocalypse and which was particularly attractive to women, who were received into the cult with more tolerance than they found in the surrounding society. The *Buddhist* White Lotus Society dated from *Mongol* times. White Lotus was one of many secret sects in China, which was forced into secrecy in good part by the absence of a tradition of "loyal opposition" within *Confucianism.* Its adherents in the eighteenth century vaguely hoped for a mystical restoration of the *Ming dynasty.* At first the rising was virtually uncontained, spreading from province to province and tying down whole Imperial armies. However, using *concentration camps,* Qing generals systematically isolated and exterminated the rebels over time. Occasional defeats at the hands of White

Lotus *militia* revealed that Manchu banner troops could be beaten, and this further weakened the dynasty. *See also agricultural revolution; Taiping Rebellion (1850–1864).*

Suggested Reading: Philip Kuhn, *Rebellion and Its Enemies in Late Imperial China, 1796–1864* (1970).

"white man's burden." A phrase from the heyday of European *imperialism* which was widely used in English-speaking nations, c. 1900–1945, to refer to the ostensible historical and moral obligation of the "white nations" to guide and govern the nonwhite, colonized peoples of Africa and Asia. It was borrowed from a bit of doggerel of the same title written in 1899 by the bard of English imperialism, Rudyard Kipling (1865–1936). Kipling hoped to exhort the United States to join the major imperial nations by *annexation* of the territories it had just captured from Spain. He wrote to Americans: "Take up the White Man's burden, send forth the best ye breed; Go, bind your sons to exile, to serve your captive's need." One ruthlessly honest British newspaper printed this alternative rhyme to the couplet: "Pile on the brown man's burden, to satisfy your greed." *See also manifest destiny;* mission civilisatrice.

White Mountain, Battle of (November 8, 1620). This was the opening battle of the *Thirty Years' War* (1618–1648). The majority population of Bohemia, and then an army of Bohemian *Protestant* rebels, stood against the election of *Ferdinand II* as *Holy Roman Emperor*—Bohemia exercised the seventh and deciding vote. Instead, the Bohemian Diet chose a Protestant prince, Frederick of the Palatinate (1596–1632), as king. Ferdinand was a zealous *Catholic* dedicated to the repression of Protestantism throughout his Austrian domains and the Holy Roman Empire, by application of the *Inquisition* and by brute force of arms. Fear that his election would lead to similar methods in Bohemia provoked Frederick's election and the revolt to sustain that choice. However, the Protestant Army was destroyed at the Battle of White Mountain by the Imperial Army and its allies in the Catholic League, under the command of the great imperial general, *Tilly.* Subsequently, Ferdinand did indeed repress Protestantism in Bohemia: rebel leaders were executed or exiled, and their lands and titles stripped from them. Frederick, too, was driven from Bohemia, and into history, where he is remembered as the "Winter King" for his brief sojourn in Bohemia. This harsh Catholic and Imperial intolerance in the Czech lands, backed by *Habsburg* power from Austria and Spain, helped spread confessional warfare throughout Germany and beyond. Bohemia was cemented to the Holy Roman Empire, and Czechs restored to Catholicism, to which most remain attached to the present day, by the battle and its *Counter Reformation* aftermath.

White Russia. *See Byelorussia; Belarus.*

White Russians. (1) Sometimes used for natives of Belarus. (2) Anti-*Bolshevik* Russians during the *Russian Civil War*. *See also Whites*.

Whites. (1) The Royalist supporters of the *exiled* kings of France, who opposed the *French Revolution*; taken from the white flag of the House of *Bourbon*. (2) Tsarist *officers*, aristocrats, *Cossacks*, nationalists, and others who opposed in arms the Bolshevik dictatorship (often preferring one of their own) during the *Russian Civil War*.

"white slavery." A term often mistaken to mean traffic in women or girls for use in forcible prostitution. In fact, the victims of this repugnant trade may be of either sex and of any color or "race." The term originated in the nineteenth century in distinction from the main abolitionist effort which aimed at ending the *slave trade* in blacks (of both sexes) exported from Africa. An international abolitionist *congress* met on this issue in Geneva in 1877, with additional congresses in 1899 and 1904. A *convention* was drafted in 1910 making traffic in human beings for purposes of the sex trade an international crime, punishable under domestic jurisdiction wherever committed. *See also "comfort women"; crimes against humanity; rape*.

White Terror (1794–1797). A counterterror, under the *Directory*, which aimed to extirpate *Robespierre* and all other *Jacobins* who conducted *The Terror* during the climactic *radical* phase of the *French Revolution*. Although it began with guillotining in Paris, it was most extensive in the provinces. In several cities, it was marked by roving gangs of extravagantly dressed, prosperous youths ("jeunesse dorée") who roamed the streets searching out and killing those accused of radicalism, or just for sport. The term later took on a generic meaning of *counterrevolutionary* violence, whether reactive or preemptive in nature. *See also Shanghai massacres*.

Wilberforce, William (1759–1833). English evangelical and humanitarian. Friends with *William Pitt*, though not a man of any political party, he entered Parliament at age 21 (1780). He served there, for various boroughs, until 1825. In 1788 he began an evangelically inspired parliamentary and public campaign, which lasted nearly two decades, to end the *slave trade* within the *British Empire*. He secured Pitt's support before the latter's death and succeeded in having the law altered in 1807. He then turned to abolition of the foreign slave trade. The British delegation tried to achieve this at the *Congress of Vienna*, but was deflected by the other powers, who feared licensing *visit and search* by the *Royal Navy*. Wilberforce spent the remainder of his life in the effort to extend the ban on slaving to the non-British trade, contributing to Britain's obtaining agreements instituting bilateral bans. He also launched the reform movement to end *slavery* itself, everywhere. His was an extraordinary contribution to the real betterment of the condition of the least fortunate. The great slogan of the anti-slavery movement was "I am a man and a brother."

Wilhelm II (1859–1941). *Kaiser* of Germany and king of Prussia, 1888–1918. Often caricatured as either a bloodthirsty *autocrat* or a bumbling fool, he was famously erratic and unpredictable—probably as a result of brain damage during his birth, when he was deprived of oxygen for several minutes. As a child, he was a precocious narcissist who grew up oblivious to his many limitations. As an adult, he was an intelligent and well-educated fool with no discernible diplomatic skills. He often behaved as a crass, pompous martinet, was easily flattered, and was vain beyond justification about his strategic and military judgment. Early on he was an avid Anglophile: he was a grandson of Queen *Victoria*, a colonel of the 1st Dragoons, and an admiral in the *Royal Navy*, but he became evermore relentlessly Anglophobic after 1895. In 1890 he forced the cautious *Bismarck's* resignation, preparatory to endorsing a reckless foreign policy of *Weltpolitik* which contributed much to the outbreak of *World War I*. On the other hand, he fell increasingly under the military's influence and authority and directed affairs of state but little during the war. On November 10, 1918, he went into exile in the Netherlands; he abdicated formally on November 28th. The *Allied and Associated Powers* wanted to bring him to trial (for "a supreme offense against international morality and the sanctity of treaties") but the *neutral* Dutch refused *extradition*. In 1940 *Hitler* invited him to transfer his retirement home to Germany, but he refused. *See also adventurism; Kruger Telegram; First Moroccan Crisis.*

William I (1027–1087). "William the Conqueror." Duke of Normandy, 1035–1087; first *Norman* king of England, 1066–1087. Having put down a rebellion by Norman nobility in western Normandy, 1047–1051, with the aid of the *Capetian* king of France, Henri I, Duke William visited England and was promised the succession to Edward the Confessor (c. 1003–1066). While he awaited Edward's death, he fended off two invasions of Normandy from France. When Edward died (January 1066), Harold of Wessex (1022–1066) claimed the English crown, possibly in violation of an earlier oath of fealty to William, who now sought and received the pope's approval of his *legitimate* succession. Anglo-Saxon England was now doubly invaded, by William in the south in alliance with an army from Norway. The Norwegian King, Harold Hardrada, was killed and his army destroyed by Harold's Wessex army at Stamford Bridge (September 25, 1066). Four days later, William landed, at Pevensey, and Harold swung south to meet the new threat. The Saxon and Norman armies met at a field near Hastings on October 14, 1066. At the end of a sanguinary day, a Norman feigned retreat drew out the Wessex forces and they were then pounced upon and beaten; Harold was killed by an arrow through the eye. The last Saxon kingdom of England had finally fallen to men from the "North." William was crowned on Christmas Day, 1066. It took another two years to subdue the West of England and Wales. In 1069 the north revolted, leading William to conduct a punitive campaign to burn out rebellion in a wide swath of his new kingdom. With order restored, the heavy peace of the Norman monarchy and *feudal* system was imposed. In 1072 William made a vassal of the king of Scotland, portending many battles to come between rival kingdoms sharing a single isle. In 1079 his son, Rupert, rebelled against his authority in Normandy, and in 1083 William was again at war with France—another long pattern in the foreign policy and politics of the Norman monarchy. He died of a fall from his horse while burning out the French city of Mantes. His descendants, the Norman kings of England, held vast swaths of territory in France until pushed from these at the end of the *Hundred Years' War* (1337–1453).

Suggested Reading: Frank Barlow, *William I and the Norman Conquest* (1965).

William III, Prince of Orange (1650–1702). Stadholder of the Netherlands, 1672–1702; king of England, 1689–1702. He led the United Provinces in a drawn-out conflict with *Louis XIV* of France, forcing Louis to make peace (albeit, briefly) in 1678. He was the principal opponent of Louis XIV as long as he lived, first in the *War of the League of Augsburg* and then in the *War of the Austrian Succession*. In 1688 he landed a *Protestant* army at Torbay, in England, cementing the Anglo-Dutch alliance in the Glorious Revolution which overthrew the *Catholic* king, James II (1633–1701). Within a year, William and his wife Mary were proclaimed king and queen of England. James fled to France, there to form a Catholic army among exiles and supporters. Catholic armies held out against William in parts of Scotland and Ireland, but were decisively defeated in Ireland by William at the *Battle of the Boyne* (1690) and everywhere else in the realm by 1691. William's victory over Catholic power in the British Isles proved permanent. *See also John Churchill Marlborough.*

Suggested Readings: S. Baxter, *William III* (1976); G. M. Trevelyan, *The English Revolution* (1967).

Wilsonian. Of, or like, the *liberal-internationalist* policies pursued by *Woodrow Wilson*, especially insofar as these include an aspiration to universal principle as a determinant of the *national interest*; a rejection of traditional security notions such as the *balance of power*, *spheres of influence*, and colonial *empires*; reliance on an expectation of collective versus unilateral action by the *Great Powers*; support for *international law* as a mechanism for resolving serious disputes among nations; and a general tendency to see economic and other material inducements or *sanctions* as more important in driving the affairs of nations than military prowess, *prestige*, or the will to power of tyrants and bloody-minded nationalism. The term is alternately used as a pejorative, or in praise, in accordance with the speaker or writer.

Wilson, James Harold (1916–1995). British statesman. *Labour* prime minister, 1964–1970, 1974–1976. In foreign affairs he was preoccupied with repairing the damage done by *de Gaulle's* veto of his application for British entry into the *European Community* and by several messy endings to British imperial rule in Africa. Of these the most bloody was the *Nigerian Civil War*, in which Wilson never wavered from support for the Federal cause despite widespread popular belief (later proved false) that *genocide* was occurring in *Biafra*. The most troublesome was *Rhodesia*, where he faced calls for British military *intervention* from African leaders and domestic opinion split along ugly, racially informed lines. Wilson supported restrictions on *immigration* from *Commonwealth* countries and announced that the United Kingdom would withdraw all military forces "east of Suez." In short, he presided over the painful but inescapable retreat of Britain from the status of great imperial power to that of modest, European *regional power*. Domestically, he met a crisis over the shrinking value of sterling with *devaluation*, but also higher taxes and interest rates. In 1974 he was drawn into the crisis over Cyprus, resulting from Turkish invasion of the island.

Wilson, Thomas Woodrow (1856–1924). *Democratic* president of the United States, 1913–1921. Wilson was elected in 1912 when *Theodore Roosevelt* ran on an independent "Bull Moose" ticket, thereby splitting the *Republican* vote with *William Howard Taft*. A progressive reformer, Wilson remarked in private that it would be a great irony should his administration become concerned primarily with foreign affairs. It did. In 1913 he refused to recognize the revolutionary government in Mexico, the first time *recognition* was withheld based upon the internal nature of a *regime*. He also intervened in Mexico and Central America repeatedly, to a greater extent than any previous president, including Theodore Roosevelt. Wilson tried to keep to a policy of strict *neutrality* after *World War I* started in Europe in 1914, but his own sympathies and that of the public leaned increasingly toward the *Allies*. His offers of impartial *mediation* were repeatedly rebuffed by both sides. Wilson almost made the decision for war in 1915, during the first *U-boat* crisis with Germany. He returned to impartiality, though he was not as strict about it as before, when Germany pulled back from *unrestricted submarine warfare*. When that policy was resumed in February 1917, and after interception of the *Zimmermann Telegram*, he took a largely unprepared America into war in April, pronouncing it necessary to "make the world safe for democracy." Wilson welcomed the *March Revolution* in Russia. He was disappointed but not overly concerned by the *November Revolution* because he believed *Bolshevism* to be an absurd doctrine which would soon fail as a result. He was only half right. Wilson's later authorization of a minor U.S. military intervention in the *Russian Civil War* mostly arose out of concern over what Japan was up to in *Siberia*.

In January 1918, Wilson announced the *Fourteen Points*, which became the basis for the *Paris Peace Conference*, which he dominated as a major figure in his own right and the president of what was then already and clearly the most powerful country in the world. He was the first president to leave the country for an extended period, traveling to Paris for three months to negotiate the *peace treaties* and oversee creation of the *League of Nations* and its *collective security* system. He tried to bring the various Russian factions into the *peace* process, but the effort went nowhere. He refused to compromise with Republican senators during the debate over the *Treaty of Versailles* and may by that have lost a winnable fight for American entry into the League, his great hope for a lasting peace. [Note: Wilson's peace proposals are discussed at greater length under the entry, *Paris Peace Conference*.] He was a most reluctant interventionist in the Russian Civil War, ordering American forces kept to a token level and pulling them out at the first opportunity, but also refusing to recognize Bolshevik victory in 1920. He was awarded the 1919 *Nobel Prize* for Peace in 1920. He suffered two strokes during his second term; the second left him nearly incapacitated, and much policy was made secretly by his personal secretary, Joseph P. Tumulty, and his wife, Edith. Many of his initiatives went down in ruins in the *interwar* period (but then, whose did not?). Yet, as the twentieth century closed, he was clearly a more lastingly important and historically influential figure than his contemporary, and rival visionary, *Lenin*.

Suggested Readings: Lloyd Ambrosius, *Wilsonian Statecraft* (1991); Kendrick Clements, *Woodrow Wilson* (1987); Robert H. Ferrell, *Woodrow Wilson and World War I, 1917–21* (1985); Thomas Knock, *To End All Wars* (1992); Arthur S. Link, *Woodrow Wilson* (1979).

Windsor, House of. The British Royal House; previously Saxe-Coburg-Gotha. The name was changed to Windsor, after the castle where the family summers, during *World War I* (1917), to better conceal the German lineage of the Royal Family.

Winter Battle (1915). *See Second Masurian Lakes.*

Winter War (1939). *See Finnish-Soviet War.*

Wisconsin school. An economic interpretation of American history and foreign policy first promulgated at the University of Wisconsin by Fred H. Harrington and then his student, William Appelman Williams. It borrowed heavily from *Marxist* notions, but was mostly rooted in the American radical tradition. Its basic assumption was that *capitalist* countries are inherently *expansionist* and *aggressive*. American foreign policy thus could be usefully understood as the more or less rapacious pursuit of the *Open Door*, and the United States was to be seen as an "imperial democracy" from its founding, or even before in some accounts. This school argued that American *imperialism* was different from the British, French, German, or Russian kind: it sought markets, not *colonies*. It was thus only superficially anti-imperial, in that its drive for new markets required the prior breakdown of the *mercantilist* systems of old *empires*, and other closed economies such as China and Japan, and substitution for formal empire of informal mechanisms of American *hegemony* such as the "Open Door" and *dollar diplomacy*. Thus, individual *decision makers* became relatively unimportant: *Polk, Wilson, Roosevelt, Johnson*, yes even *Lincoln* took the country to war to gain or preserve access to foreign markets or, in Lincoln's case, to crush the last domestic resistance to capitalism, and they made peace always in ways which expanded "American empire." The United States was fundamentally responsible for the *Cold War*, too, adherents argued, because out of greed and the expansionist character of capitalism the United States tried to force open the door to *Eastern Europe*, which lay within Russia's legitimate *sphere of influence*. The response of *Stalin* in consolidating that sphere—with the *Red Army* and proxy *Communist Parties*—was thus understandable, hardly more than a defensive reaction. This view of the origins of the Cold War did not survive the light of exposure of Soviet archival information which confirmed that Stalin indeed had singularly ideological and aggressive intentions. On the other hand, the Wisconsin School's larger thesis about the sources of American conduct remains highly influential among academic historians, though just as highly moot.

Suggested Readings: Robert Maddox, *The New Left and The Origins of the Cold War* (1973); Robert W. Tucker, *The Radical Left and American Foreign Policy* (1972); William Appleman Williams, *The Tragedy of American Diplomacy*, 2nd ed. (1972).

"Wise Men." An informal designation for six American *statesmen*, all friends and/or old classmates, who laid the intellectual foundations for, and then constructed, U.S. *Cold War* policy and early policy in the *Vietnam War: Dean Acheson*, Charles Bohlen, *Clark Clifford, George Kennan, W. Averell Harriman*, Robert Lovett, and *John McCloy*. *See also Lyndon Johnson.*

Suggested Reading: Walter Isaacson and Evan Thomas. *The Wise Men: Six Friends and the World They Made* (1986).

withdrawal. Owing to the rights and nature of *sovereignty*, a state may withdraw from an *international organization* any time, bound only by legal requirements (should they exist in a given *treaty*) to give formal *notification* and wait the required period. Withdrawal may carry little or very heavy political penalties. Germany (1933), Japan (1933), and Italy (1937) all withdrew—as did some minor powers, such as Brazil—from the *League of Nations* without consequence to themselves, though with great consequence for the League. Only one state withdrew from the *United Nations*, Indonesia in 1965, and it rejoined in 1966. Less important organizations and/or alliances experienced more withdrawals. *See also expulsion; suspension.*

withholding strategy. A theory of *nuclear war* fighting, proposing that by not striking at all the enemy's targets in the first wave of *missiles* launched one might preserve enough of value to the adversary nation to provide it with an incentive to join in mutual de-escalation of the conflict.

Witte, Serge (1849–1915). Russian statesman. He constructed the trans-Siberian railroad and the Chinese Eastern Railroad in *Manchuria* and guided a surge in industrial development. He was displaced by *imperialists* in such a hurry to acquire Manchuria they provoked the *Russo-Japanese War*. In 1905 he was brought back to negotiate the *Treaty of Portsmouth* with Japan. He served briefly as prime minister but again fell victim to court intrigues. After this final dismissal he remained out of office, and in rather a bad temper, for 10 years. He opposed Russia's entry into *World War I*.

wolf pack. In *World War I* and again in *World War II*, this term referred to *U-boats* acting in unison, coordinating their patrols and attacks in response to the Allied *convoy* system. It was a tactic developed by *Dönitz* and nearly turned the *Battle of the Atlantic* in Germany's favor. It was designed to counteract convoys by setting up a picket line of U-boats to improve the chances of contact with the enemy and then concentrate the submarine fleet to co-ordinate hit-and-run attacks so that the Allied escorts were confused and exhausted. It worked, but only for a time.

women, in international relations. *See Amazons; Benazir Bhutto; Battle of Berlin; Gro Harlem Bruntland; caste system; Catherine II; Catholic Church; civilians; Cixi; "comfort women"; Dahomey; death camps; Elizabeth I; female circumcision; foot-binding; human rights; Hakka; Hanover; Hinduism; honey trap; Indira Gandhi; Mohandas Gandhi; Indian Mutiny; Iran; Iranian Revolution; Islam; John Paul II; jus civile; Ruhollah Khomeini; Horatio Kitchener; Kuwait; manifest destiny; Maria Theresa; Nanjing massacre; Jawaharlal Nehru; Netherlands; noncombatant; population; power; rape; restitution; salt march; sati; Saudi Arabia; shi'ia Islam; slavery; Albert Speer; Switzerland; Taiping Rebellion (1850–1864); Mao Zedong; Margaret Thatcher; United Nations Conference on Population; Victoria; White Lotus Rebellion (1796–1804); World Health Organization; war crimes; war weariness; white slavery; World War I; Yahya Khan.*

working class. *See proletariat.*

world affairs. A plain-spoken synonym for *international relations*, much preferred by those historians who do not wish to be mistaken as endorsing the more specious and *scientistic*, *jargon*-laden, *obscurantist* sort of work done by many political scientists.

World Bank. *See International Bank for Reconstruction and Development.*

world capitalist system. In *dependency theory*, this is the underlying economic structure which supposedly determines all important relations of the *core* with the *periphery*. The theory posits the dominance of a global *capitalist* class with powerfully shared interests and is entirely dismissive of the role played by individual *states* (except as putative instruments of controlling economic interests) or by the *states system*. It focuses instead on what it sees, and hopes for, as efforts of the mass of the population of the periphery to break free of the *exploitation* of its resources and labor by the dominant *elite* controlling the core, aided in repression by bought servants in the *comprador classes* running the periphery. *See also war.*

world community. (1) All *states* and, in some ill-defined and immeasurable sense, their publics too. (2) On occasion, a euphemism to avoid saying "the West," when what is meant in a discussion of the "norms of the world community" is the prevailing values of Western states and their political and legal traditions. *See also community of nations.*

World Council of Churches. A *transnational* organization founded in the Netherlands in 1948 to pursue *ecumenism* among the *Christian* churches, and in particular to bridge the historic divide among the *Catholic Church*, various *Protestant* churches, and the *Orthodox* churches of Eastern Europe, the Balkans, and then *Soviet Union.* From the 1960s it increasingly moved beyond doctrinal matters, possibly because ecumenism was making little headway, and partly in response to wider social unrest, toward public policy concern with *disarmament, human rights,* and *North-South issues.*

World Court. The informal, journalistic, and popular name for the *International Court of Justice* and, before that, the *Permanent Court of International Justice.*

World Disarmament Conference (1932–1934). *See Disarmament Conference, Geneva (1932–1934).*

World Economic Conference (1933). One of the twentieth century's more spectacular diplomatic failures, this conference of dozens of participating states convened in London to seek a solution to the *Great Depression.* The major powers—the United States, France, and the United Kingdom—could not agree on *exchange rate* stabilization, and after several fruitless weeks the conference disbanded when *Franklin Roosevelt* ordered the U.S. delegation home. This had lasting effects: the U.S. and United Kingdom treasuries became mutually hostile and, instead of international cooperation, other states—including Nazi Germany, Italy, and Japan—pursued *autarky* and ultimately *aggression*.

world federalism. The idea, fluctuating in popularity among theorists (and the public) from decade to decade, of a global *federation* in which the existing *states* merge at the political level first, with *integration* to follow on *functional* lines. *See also world governance; world government.*

World Food Program (WFP). This United Nations food *aid* program was first set up, 1961–63, jointly by the *Food and Agriculture Organization* and the *United Nations General Assembly.* Subsequently, it coordinated *multilateral* relief during *famines*, channeling short-term relief to needy populations in response to "food emergencies." It also became involved in agricultural and other rural *development* projects in numerous *Third World* countries. It is based in Rome and operates under a series of Food Aid Conventions adopted by member states of the United Nations.

world governance. The art and necessity of somehow governing world affairs in the absence of any *world government.* This demands and receives a high degree of cooperation among states through the decentralized mechanisms they have developed for this grand task: the *balance of power, diplomacy, international law, international organization, moral norms, sovereignty*, and *spheres of influence.* Increasingly, world governance has begun to include *nonstate actors* in advisory roles, as well. *See also anarchical society; anarchy; classical school (of international relations); international society.*

world government. The idea of a lawmaking and enforcing supreme global authority to replace the present system of *states.* Although usually spoken of hopefully as a democratic and federal model, it is conceivable that a world government might take the form of a global *tyranny.* In either case, it should be clearly understood that the *United Nations system* is not even the beginning of a world government, just as the *World Court* is not a supreme court for the world. For good, for ill, or more likely for both, *sovereignty* remained the fundamental principle of international political life at the start of the twenty-first century. That said, the United Nations does represent an aspect of *world governance.*

World Health Organization (WHO). This *specialized agency* of the *United Nations* has more members (*states* and *territories*) than the United Nations itself. It was founded in 1948, absorbing its *League of Nations* predecessor as well as several non-League, health-oriented *international governmental organizations.* It is headquartered in Geneva. It provides medical *advisory services* as well as occasional direct assistance, sponsors research into numerous health issues, and conducts educational programs which have helped eradicate several epidemic diseases and brought others under some measure of control. By 1977 it had helped eradicate smallpox and therefore targeted six other major child killing diseases: diphtheria, measles, polio, tetanus, tuberculosis, and whooping cough. By the mid-1990s nearly 80 percent of the world's children were vaccinated against these diseases under WHO's Expanded Program of Immunization. WHO played a smaller role in the *Children's Vaccine Initiative*. Its record is not unblemished, however, or without controversy. Under pressure from *Islamic* and some *African* nations, until the 1980s it failed to even discuss *female circumcision* as a medical issue. During two terms under Director General Hiroshi Nakajima (1988–1998), WHO was severely criticized for mismanagement, corruption, and favoritism in its administration and in decisions about medical priorities and research. With broad European and American support (the United States provided 25 percent of WHO's budget), *Gro Harlem Bruntland* was elected in 1998 with a mandate to reform WHO's finances and shift its research toward such areas as resurgent tuberculosis, *AIDS*, resistance of bacterial infections to antibiotics, maternal and child health, and eradication of polio.

World Human Rights Conference, Beijing (June 1993). This was the first global conference on *human rights* since a meeting held in Tehran in 1968. It confirmed a continuing, fundamental split between those nations (mostly, though not exclusively, in the *West*) which saw human rights as centering on the individual, and those in the developing world which argued—sincerely, or as a cover for privileged classes and repressive *regimes*—that individual rights must be subordinated to collective rights, such as a "right to *development*." A major shift from the *Cold War* period came when Russia supported a High Commissioner for Human Rights, leaving China alone among the *P-5* opposing that initiative. As host, China also blocked an appearance before state delegates by the *Dalai Lama*; he was relegated to speaking to a lesser meeting of *NGOs*.

World Intellectual Property Organization (WIPO). A forum devoted to standardization of the highly diverse laws governing copyright on intellectual property, importantly related to trade in hi-tech *services*. It failed to perform this function, forcing the issue into *GATT* as part of the *Uruguay Round*.

World Island. In the theory of *Halford Mackinder*, the adjoining continents of *Africa*, *Asia*, and *Europe*.

World Meteorological Organization (WMO). A *specialized agency* of the United Nations set up in Geneva in 1947 to coordinate information about climate, weather patterns, and related phenomena. It built upon the work of the International Meteorological Organization which was established in 1873 to provide accurate weather information critical to maritime commerce. The

WMO worked quietly and effectively for years, coming to general public attention only in the late 1980s by coordinating and publicizing research revealing that *ozone depletion* had caused holes to appear in the ozone layer over both poles. It is also concerned with setting up a global climate data bank concerning *global warming*.

world politics. A near-synonym for *international politics* and *international relations*, but implying for some less emphasis on the central role played by *states*.

world power. A state capable of moving events on a global scale and seeing itself as having worldwide *national interests*. Not even all the *Great Powers* qualify as world powers, which emerged in the seventeenth through eighteenth centuries with the expansion of European *imperialism* into Latin America, Asia, and Africa, and in the nineteenth century with the *Industrial Revolution* and comparable revolutions in communications and transportation technology. World powers to date have been, in rough order: Spain, France, Great Britain, Germany, the Soviet Union, and the United States. After 1991 only the United States qualified. China, Japan, and India may yet emerge as world powers, though into the early twenty-first century all of those states still gave an extraordinary stress to regional affairs in their diplomacy. *See also hegemon; hyperpower; superpower; Weltpolitik.*

world public opinion. An amorphous concept, varying with (and usually saying most about) the user. (1) It may be employed as a rhetorical device to claim universal support for one's own position, based on some immeasurable and unsubstantiated sense of how "plain folks" the world over must regard an issue. It is usually wielded in conjunction with that other resort of the incompetent debater or the scalawag, the appeal to "common sense" (after all, relying on our common senses should lead us to the uncommon belief that the sun revolves around the earth). Any claim to know what opinions the world holds is, of course, an imaginative leap of the first order of arrogance. It also makes the rather large assumption that most people in the world actually have opinions on international affairs, when national polling data from various countries suggests only a minority in each has anything more than a superficial knowledge of, or low interest in, world politics. (2) The term is sometimes used, with only slightly more accuracy, to mean the collective opinion of the world's governments, usually as voiced in *resolutions* in the *United Nations General Assembly* and *Security Council* or this or that regional organization—in which case, it would be more factual to say just that. *See also Woodrow Wilson.*

world religions. *See Buddhism; Christianity; clash of civilizations; Confucianism; Hinduism; Islam; religion, in international affairs.*

world slump. Common contemporary slang for the *Great Depression* (1929–1939).

world socialist system. A *Soviet* term for those states (16 in all) proclaiming *Marxist-Leninist* principles and under the firm control of *Communist parties*, including at various times China, Cuba, and all members of the *Warsaw Pact*. It did not include some *Third World* allies of the Soviet Union, such as Afghanistan or Ethiopia, which were clearly in the socialist camp but which, in Soviet "development theory," had not yet advanced to the level of mature *communist* states.

world society. *See international society.*

world system theory. A late-twentieth-century variant of *Marxist* theory which views the world as a single, *capitalist* system, with an international division of labor wherein *core* states monopolize capital-intensive industries and exploit resources and *labor* of the *periphery*. In this view, substantial *convergence* of different national societies is enforced by markets, but is never completed because of the huge inequalities necessary to operation of the system. Its essential historical argument is that the transition to capitalism succeeded in the West because those economies were advantaged by *colonialism* and *imperialism*, which permitted them to accumulate capital for their own development by extracting it in an exploitative manner, and for nearly 300 years, from states and societies of the periphery which otherwise might have made similar advances themselves. This school sometimes seems fixated on the role of imports as a means of productive knowledge. *See dependency theory; Smithian growth.*

World Trade Center, terrorist destruction of. *See September 11, 2001, terrorist attack on the United States.*

World Trade Organization. *See GATT.*

world war. A great war involving all or most of the *Great Powers*, which overturns the old *balance of power* and sets up a new one. Even Great Powers may be destroyed in such wars. *See also Cold War; Thirty Years' War; War of the Spanish Succession; Seven Years' War; Wars of the French Revolution; Napoleonic Wars; systemic war; World War I; World War II.*

World War I (1914–1918). The Great War and "the war to end all wars." Through the streets, farms, and cafés of Europe in the summer of 1914 there whispered the old lies about glory in combat. Few young men knew or cared about the carnage which had been seen in the trenches of the *Crimean War* or the killing fields of the *American Civil War*. Most dreamed of the offensive, of storybook charges and rapid promotion, of honor and glory; few understood what it meant to truly "meet one's *Waterloo*." Even the *general staffs* of the major protagonists thought little of defense. Their secret *war plans*, too, were visions of great sweeping assaults, *envelopments*, national revenge, and rapid victories. *Mobilization* was accompanied by bands and parades, by wives and parents cheering the departing troops, in country after country. "Ausflug nach Paris!" "Au Berlin!" "Victory by Christmas!" Such were the illusions, the eagerness, and excitement with which Europe plunged the world into the greatest war humanity had yet suffered through. In the first two weeks of 1914 millions of men entrained for the front. In nearly every sector what met them was not glory, but mass death amid barbed wire, bayonets, grenades, *artillery barrages*, *machine gun* nests, *poison gas*, shell holes, muddy trenches, and corpse-fattened rats.

Except for a brief phase of movement in the summer and fall of 1914, and again in 1918, for more than three years—despite one major *campaign* after another—the *western front* moved no more than 10 miles; it was joined after 1915 by an Italian-Austrian front, which similarly bogged down in alpine valleys and passes. The *trench warfare* went on and on, summer into winter into spring, for four awful years. On the *eastern front* things were more fluid because wider spaces made a war of movement more possible, but in the end it amounted to the same thing: World War I killed at least 15 million, mostly soldiers, and wounded and maimed in body or mind many millions more. Two million of the dead were German; another 1.5 million were from the Austro-Hungarian Empire. Some 1.7 million French died, and a million more from the *British Empire*. About 500,000 Italians fell, along with hundreds of thousands from Australia, Belgium, Canada, the Ottoman Empire, the United States and a dozen more nations. Russian losses were about 1.8 million dead, with another five million captured. In all those countries in 1918, millions of widows grieved alongside millions more mothers, and fathers, brothers, and sisters, and a whole generation bent to tend to millions of wounded survivors—five million in France alone. Uncountable millions of civilians died—as always in war, the very young and very old or infirm went first—from malnutrition and disease. After it was over another 20 million or so civilians died from pestilence, in part carried worldwide by returning soldiery and made more deadly by years of *home front* deprivation and economic contraction.

The Great War would ultimately draw in 32 nations—28 *Allied and Associated Powers* and the four *Central Powers*. It ended four historic dynasties: *Habsburg, Hohenzollern, Ottoman,* and *Romanov* and encouraged challenges to monarchy in a dozen more countries. It broke apart three *multinational* empires (the *Austro-Hungarian, Ottoman,* and *Russian*), spilling their diverse and quarrelsome peoples into new and untidy arrangements in the Balkans, Central and Eastern Europe, and the Middle East, and stripped all overseas colonies from a fourth (Germany). It introduced to twentieth-century Europe mass death on a scale that continent had not seen since the *Mongols* or *Tamerlane* or the near-genocidal conquests of the Slavic lands by the *Teutonic Knights*. In later decades, the world would consummate this practice in pitiless industrialization and obscenely rational calculation of the *death camps*, in Germany and Poland, but also in the Soviet *GULAG* and the killing fields of Cambodia. And the First World War would leave behind a global legacy of unrequited bitterness such that it would take a Second World War to quell.

Indeed, it may be seriously argued that most of the major evils that followed over the course of the twentieth century are directly traceable to the catastrophe of World War I: the ascent to power of the *Bolsheviks* and of that monstrously disruptive and *totalitarian* state, the Soviet Union; then the ascent to power of *warlords* such as *Mussolini* and later, also *Tōjō*, but especially *Adolf Hitler*—who was twice wounded in WWI and emerged from its trenches and field hospitals determined to mobilize Germany for "the big revenge"; the spread of *fascist* and *totalitarian* thought, thugs, and politics, to levels of real influence in dozens of other countries; a precipitous decline of prior norms of *civilized states* and world order, hidden by the states with a more public screen of international legality and higher organization; devastation of whole nations and regional economies which set back development by decades; the collapse into anarchy of entire societies, with attendant brutalizing effects on their civil society and individual citizenry which lingered for several generations; lasting damage to the idea of civilization itself and to belief in and pursuit of moral as well as material progress; and lastly, and most immediately, nearly 200 million violent deaths and mammoth disruption of the normal lives of hundreds of millions more innocent people on every inhabited continent.

Through all the blood, mud, fire, murder, lethal ideology, and bombast, from 1914 to 1918 the inscription on the belt buckles of German soldiers read "Gott mit uns" ("God is with us"). That expressed an arrogance common to all *propaganda* of the Great War, though it may be doubted whether more than a handful of conscripts, though rather more civilians, were fooled. After all, Russians, too, fought for "God and the Tsar," the British said they battled for "God, King and Country" and the "rights of small nations," and Americans felt called upon by Providence itself to "make the world safe for democracy." Such claims remembered a past era, of *Crusades* for ostensibly noble and sacred causes, whipped up yet again to service the thoroughly secular purposes of the self-sacralized states of the European system. All who believed they marched, and killed or maimed, in the footsteps of the deity might have learned from *Frederick the Great*, a man who knew war: "God," he once observed, "is always with the strongest battalions." And so, it was to be the big battalions, grinding against each other over four years of cold, bloody murder, which were to decide the greatest of wars to that time.

The proximate cause of World War I was a prolonged crisis in the Balkans driven by territorial disputes, as evident in the *First* and *Second Balkan Wars*. The immediate cause was Austrian resistance to Serbian *provocation*, the Serb assassination of *Francis Ferdinand*, heir to the Austrian throne, which drew in the other *Great Powers* during the *mobilization crisis* of June–August 1914. The more fundamental causes are moot. Many historians from the Allied and Associated Powers later wrote, of course, victors' history, assigning most responsibility for starting the war to Germany. An early generation of American historians tended to blame all Europe (and the *"merchants of death"*) for tricking the United States into an unnecessary war. Predictably, *Marxists* wrote that capitalism itself was to blame, as the war sprang from a scramble for overseas markets and deadly competition among decaying, monopoly economies desperate to export their surpluses. In contrast, and perhaps in frustration, some historians argued that the war was accidental, that no one had really planned or wanted it, that instead the Great Powers had stumbled into it through misperception and ineptitude. Meanwhile, German nationalist (as well as Nazi) historians argued that Germany had been "encircled" by enemies and denied its "proper place in the sun." Then another German historian, Fritz Fischer, shook the profession with a landmark study which argued Imperial Germany had plotted war to serve its long-term imperial interest (the "Fischer Thesis"). This argument rested on impressive documentary evidence that German leaders decided—at a Prussian crown council on December 8, 1912—that the weakening of their *Triple Alliance* partners and strengthening of France and Russia meant that Germany's window of opportunity to establish hegemony over Europe would shortly close, and so fighting a decisive war sooner rather than later was in the *national interest*.

Fischer did not render the last word on the causes of the war or end the argument among historians, but at the least he put the lie to *Bethmann-Hollweg*, who said of the reasons why on the night of Britain's *declaration of war*, "if we only knew." Among all men, on that awful night, he and the German and Austrian high commands knew better than most the essential truth that the crisis of July 1914 had provided the context, but also a pretext, for a long-planned war of conquest and aggrandizement. For the central fact conducive to war that summer was the abiding dissatisfaction of the two major German peoples of Europe with their relative standing among the Great Powers, even if the proximate cause of fighting was a more widely shared responsibility for excessive secrecy, blunder, and delusion, underwritten by a continent-wide fear. In addition, German belligerency was matched by Britain's resistance to any fundamental change in its dominant global position. And it was the engagement of the British Empire, with its worldwide interests and possessions (and scattered *Dominions* automatically committed to war by any declaration made by London) which ensured that what started as just another Balkan squabble widened into a European war, to finally become a world war.

Although not all views are reconcilable, there has emerged general agreement that the main antecedents of the war were shifts in relative power and serious unresolved disputes among the Great Powers, as well as lesser powers, with roots deep in the nineteenth century, including: (1) The slow fading of

Ottoman power, which left a power vacuum in the Balkans and opened contentious territorial issues (see the *Eastern Question*); (2) a corresponding decline of Austrian power, which Vienna was desperate to arrest, compounded by the archaic and unsustainable character of Vienna's multinational empire in an emergent era of insistent *nationalism*; (3) a comparable internal weakness and fear—and thus aggressiveness and sensitivity to slights against "national honor"—within the Russian Empire, recently exacerbated by the *Russian Revolution* (1905) and the humiliating loss of the *Russo-Japanese War*; (4) the still sharply bitter legacy in France of Germany's territorial acquisitions after the *Franco-Prussian War* and the depth of French *revanchism*; (5) the dangerous *Weltpolitik* and ideas of *social Darwinism* pursued by Germany after 1890, and the unsettling belief of its civilian and military leaders that a window of opportunity existed to use its power for *aggrandizement* which would close by c. 1920, or "Weltmacht oder Niedergang!" ('World Power or Downfall!') as too many Germans put it; (6) Britain's reluctance to adjust to a relative decline in its status vis-à-vis Germany, especially the challenge made to the *Royal Navy*, and its traditional dominance of the world's oceans, by Germany and other rising naval powers; (7) the existence of broad *alliances* or near-alliances which helped spread the war beyond the Balkans; (8) abrasive colonial rivalries; and (9) a series of key *crises* and war scares which raised international tensions, c. 1900–1914, worsened animosities, and inflamed conflicts.

Even deeper causes were volcanic social and economic tensions in Europe and the widespread reality of political *reaction*, beneath which moved a magma of frustrated national ambitions, ethnic and minority resentments, and religious and social hatreds, all surging toward eruption beneath a cone of frustrated promises of political *liberalism* and industrialized prosperity. World War I was, therefore, not merely a war over the *balance of power*, or between social classes, or over control of economic resources and interests, or among ambitious colonial empires and muddled *imperialisms*, or the result of bumbling by inept rulers or the evil ambitions of others. It *was* all that. Yet, it was, too, a long-awaited (and in some locales, also longed-for) clash of *nations* and *peoples* which had for decades harbored deep enmities and conflicting views of society and of progress—"civilization" for France and Britain, "Kultur" for Germany, "Slavic values" for Russia, and so on—and had then built the military means to enforce these. Once the drift to war began, statesmen and generals thus found it could not be easily channeled or arrested: too many Europeans wanted war, for one reason or another—though probably none wanted the holocaust they actually got. Its course is described below.

(i) The West: In accordance with the *Schlieffen Plan*, a powerful German thrust was made through Luxembourg and Belgium, while the French dashed pell-mell into Alsace-Lorraine; that led to the *Battle of the Frontiers*. The Germans tried to swing past Paris but were stopped by logistical problems and an Allied counterattack in force at the *First Battle of the Marne*. After that, both sides tried *flanking* maneuvers which took them to the Atlantic in the so-called *race to the sea*. The Germans dug in first, along the Meuse and Aisne and then from Belgium to the Alps. By November, France had lost more than 500,000 men, including 306,000 dead; Germany had lost 240,000 men; Belgium mourned 30,000 dead, as did Britain. The result was an unbroken line of trenches stretched 475 miles from the North Sea to the Swiss border. Germany would hold this line for the next four years against repeated Allied efforts to break through, starting with *First Ypres*. Facing a *two-front war*, in 1915 *Falkenhayn* drained units from the west to face Russia in the east. Meanwhile, *Foch* and *Joffre* divided the western front into "passive" (Flanders, Meuse, Argonne) and "active" (Arras, Somme, Champagne) sectors, thinning defenses in passive sectors for reinforced attacks in active ones. The First Battle of Artois (December 14–24, 1914) was inconsequential, as was the Winter Battle at *First Champagne* (December 20, 1914–March 17, 1915). The Allies would repeatedly launch new offensives against the shoulders (*Vimy Ridge* and *Champagne*) of the German salient, starting in the spring of 1915 (*Neuve-Chapelle, Second Ypres*), and again in the fall (*Loos, Second Champagne*); they failed again in 1917 (*Arras-Vimy Ridge, Chemin des Dames, Third Ypres, Cambrai*), attacking with success only in 1918. The Allies also tried to flank the entire front by drawing Italy into the war, aiding Serbia, and attacking the Ottomans. These efforts only added to their burden.

In 1916 the Germans attacked at *Verdun*, intending to exhaust the French by attrition, but were stopped by a dogged French defense under *Pétain*. To relieve this terrible pressure new armies of conscripts and Commonwealth troops, assembled in Britain by *Kitchener* and now commanded by *Douglas Haig*, struck at the *Somme*. This was the only assault on the deadly center of the German trench line and led to the bloodiest defeat in British military history. Indeed, the slaughter everywhere that summer was unprecedented. Germany resumed *unrestricted submarine warfare* on February 1, 1917, to try to break Britain's industrial and financial resources, which sustained the Allied cause; Germany simultaneously withdrew 20 miles along the Somme front to the *Hindenburg Line*. The U-boat war, German subversion campaigns in America, and the *Zimmermann Telegram* offer of a German alliance in a Mexican war with the United States finally brought that sleeping giant into the conflict in April 1917. The U.S. Navy engaged the U-boats at sea immediately, but on land the United States needed almost a year to retrieve its army from Mexico, where it was chasing *Pancho Villa*, and then train and arm its millions of raw volunteers and conscripts.

In the interim, the Allies nearly collapsed: two *Russian Revolutions* in 1917 cracked, and then broke open, the eastern front. *French Army mutinies* ended French offensive action for a full year, even though the lines held. After that, only the British attacked in 1917, again without success. Berlin's all-or-nothing gamble came to a head in a final German offensive launched on March 21, 1918. Preceded by a gas and artillery barrage, Germany sent 76 crack divisions (many transferred to the west after the collapse of Russia) against 28 British divisions along the 50-mile Somme front. By the end of the first week the British had suffered their worst defeat of the war, and Germany threatened to divide the Allied armies. By April, German momentum stalled. The *Reichswehr* had lost 420,000 men, and some units refused any more attacks. The Allied and Associated Powers also took heavy casualties but, whereas they called up fresh American *reserves*, the Germans had none. Then *Ludendorff* launched the *Second Battle of the Marne* on July 15th, a bloody failure which broke the German Army. On August 7th the Allied and Associated Powers struck at Amiens: supported by tanks, Canadian and Australian divisions broke through, in places reaching the Hindenburg Line. That September the American Expeditionary Force (AEF) launched its first offensive, supported after the 26th by British and French attacks. On the 28th, Ludendorff told *Hindenburg* that all hope was lost and warned that Germany must seek terms.

(ii) The East: A massive Russian advance (98 oversized infantry divisions and 37 cavalry divisions) into *East Prussia* in 1914 drew troops away from the western front; this helped save Paris, and perhaps France. By autumn, having divided its forces and exposed them to *defeat-in-detail*, Russia was driven back by Ludendorff, with major battles fought at *Tannenberg* and the *Masurian Lakes*. The Austrians and Russians shared a 300-mile front in Galicia stretching from Austrian Poland to neutral Rumania. The fighting began with an *encounter battle* at Lemberg, in which the Austrians at first prevailed. They were soon driven back after a loss of 400,000 men (300,000 prisoners) and a zone of Austrian territory 150 miles deep. This Austrian collapse along the Carpathian front meant that Hungary and German Silesia lay open to the Russians. Ludendorff chose to strike first, advancing toward Warsaw. At the Battle of Augustow (September 29–October 5, 1914) Russian reinforcements from Siberia attacked, but were stalled. Ludendorff pulled back from Warsaw, while his Austrian ally was badly beaten at Ivangorod (October 22–26, 1914), losing 40,000 men. A second, indecisive battle was fought at Lodz in late November, after which Germany transferred four corps to the east. The Austrians blocked a Russian advance on Budapest at Limanowa-Lapanow, the last solo Austrian victory of the war. Vienna had lost 1.3 million men (one-third of its mobilized troops); Russia had lost 1.5 million, but had two million still under arms and nearly 10 million in reserve. An ill-advised winter offensive in the Carpathians cost Austria another 800,000 by the end of March 1915; and a long-besieged fortress garrison of 150,000 at Przmysl surrendered to the Russians on March 22nd. Austria was finished as an offensive force: it remained in the war only with massive logistical and strategic support from Germany.

Russia's losses had reached two million with the war barely six months old, but it still had vast reserves. The question of the eastern front thus remained open, along an 875-mile line of trenches dividing the several armies of the east. Germany and Austria broke through at *Gorlice-Tarnow* later in 1915, keeping Austria in the war while savaging the Tsarist Army, many of whose troops literally went into battle carrying no weapon. Rapid *industrialization* in Russia made up for matériel shortfalls in shells and rifles, and the opening of the Italian front with Austria permitted the Stavka (Russian *high command*) to launch a successful attack in 1916—the *Brusilov Offensive.* Russia's victory, the British presence at Salonika, and false promises of territorial gains made to Bucharest brought Rumania into the war on the Allied side on August 27, 1916. The Rumanians attacked into Hungary, but were quickly counterinvaded by Bulgarian, Austrian, German, and Turkish forces. Bucharest fell on December 5, 1916. The rump of Rumania's Army retreated to Moldavia, leaving 300,000 casualties behind and delivering Rumania's oil and food stocks to the Central Powers. Greece joined the Allied and Associated Powers in June 1917, but it too proved more of a drain than a benefit to the alliance. In March 1917, the tsarist regime collapsed, but Russia promised to stay in the war. That summer it launched the *Kerensky Offensive.* Its failure broke the morale of the Russian Army, finished it as a fighting force, and hastened the collapse of Kerensky's government and the subsequent *Bolshevik Revolution.* As soon as they seized power, the Bolsheviks declared an immediate *armistice,* which was agreed to by Ludendorff and Hindenburg. In March 1918, with the German Army again advancing, Lenin and Trotsky bent to reality and formally took Russia out of the war in a *separate peace* signed with the Central Powers at *Brest-Litovsk.* Isolated and beaten, Rumania also sued for a *Carthaginian peace.*

(iii) The South: In August 1914, Austria was set on crushing Serbia, which it underestimated. It immediately launched a *demonstration* to draw out Serbia's 400,000-man army and then attacked eastward out of Bosnia. By August 24th, however, the Serbs had successfully repelled the Austrians and themselves advanced into eastern Bosnia. They stayed just over one month, until driven back in turn. On December 2nd the Austrians took Belgrade. The next day a Serb counteroffensive began which drove the Austrians out of the country within two weeks. The Ottoman Empire joined the Central Powers on October 31st, attacking Russia in the Crimea and the Caucasus, where fighting contributed to the *Armenian genocide* in 1915. Meanwhile, British/ Indian units threatened the Euphrates. Italy entered the war against Austria (but not Germany) on May 23, 1915, under terms of the secret *Treaty of London* (1915), in a naked grab for territory both in Europe and Africa. Hopes that Italian intervention would crack open the southern front quickly faded, as undertrained and under-armed Italians met stiff Austrian resistance on an impenetrable alpine front: over the next three years, 12 distinct Battles of *Isonzo* were fought to little or no strategic gain. The Ottomans also held off British, French, and ANZAC forces at *Gallipoli,* inflicting terrible damage on the Australians, in particular, as well as to the career of First Lord *Winston*

Churchill. That encouraged Bulgaria to join the Central Powers in October 1915.

Things had been quiet on the Balkan front until then, but now Serbia was overrun by armies from Germany, Austria, and Bulgaria, sending the rump of the Serb Army over the mountains to Albania and then by ship to Corfu. An Anglo-French expedition to aid Serbia was imposed on neutral Greece, too late to help Serbia; but the Allies stayed in Salonika anyway. The whole southern strategy thus drained Allied resources—the opposite of its intended effect. Austria launched a futile but bloody attack toward the River Po in May 1916, while Italy repeatedly attacked at Isonzo. Vienna mourned the death of *Franz Josef* in November 1916. More importantly, the war sorely and increasingly tested the *"Kaisertreu"* sentiment of non-Austrians. In March 1917, Vienna secretly asked Paris to open negotiations. Rather than bringing peace, this initiative was received as a sign of Austria's impending collapse, and so encouraged Allied hopes of victory and hardened Allied negotiating positions. *Woodrow Wilson,* too, offered to *mediate* a general settlement, but he was rebuffed by all sides. Then disaster befell the Italian Army at *Caporetto* (October 24–November 12, 1917). Instead of accepting Austria's defeat and dictating its withdrawal from the war, Britain and France found themselves shipping troops that were desperately needed on the western front to bolster the collapsing southern front instead, and thereafter effectively took over the defense of Italy. Austria hung on for another year, but it was incapable of pressing home an offensive victory, and Germany had no reserves to spare, as it was husbanding all men and weapons for a final offensive in the west. After an Allied offensive that broke through at Vittorio Venito (October 24–November 3, 1918), with all reserves exhausted and the Kaisertreu loyalties of non-German peoples of the empire wholly wilted and fallen, Vienna at last asked for terms.

(iv) The Middle East: The Ottoman Empire's entry into the war, in October 1914, opened a whole new front in the Middle East. Britain immediately separated Kuwait from Ottoman control, proclaimed a *protectorate* over Egypt, and closed the *Suez Canal* to the Central Powers. The Ottomans attacked Suez, but were repulsed. They were then pushed back from southern Palestine and Syria by *Ibn Ali Hussein, T. E. Lawrence,* and the *Arab Revolt,* launched in support of British forces in 1916. However, the main fighting was in Mesopotamia against the *Indian Army* and in Palestine against Anglo-Egyptian forces. Mesopotamia fell in 1917; *Jerusalem* was captured on December 9, 1917. The British broke through Ottoman lines in northern Palestine on September 19–20, 1918, and Constantinople sued for peace.

(v) Asia: German Samoa was taken by New Zealand on August 29, 1914. Papua New Guinea fell to the Australians on September 17th. Japan declared war on Germany on August 23rd, in nominal accordance with the renewed *Anglo-Japanese Treaty* (1911), but in reality to take advantage of Europe's difficulty to seize territory in Asia. Japanese forces occupied the Carolines,

Marianas, and Marshall Islands by October 1914. There was more serious fighting over the German concession in China, *Kiaochow*, where Japanese and British forces combined to lay siege until the base fell on November 7, 1914.

(vi) Africa: Limited fighting occurred in West Africa, where Togo was overrun by August 27th by French and British forces. *Kamerun* (Cameroon) was separately invaded by Britain and France, but its interior German garrison held out until February 1916. *German Southwest Africa* (Namibia) was overrun by British and *Boer* forces by July 1915. Heavier fighting occurred in *Tanganyika* (Tanzania) in 1914, including elements of the Indian Army. The Germans conducted an effective irregular campaign through 1915. Heavy South African, Belgian, and Portuguese reinforcements (Portugal joined the Allies in March 1916) arrived under the command of *Jan Smuts*, but bush fighting continued in *German East Africa* into 1918. The last Germans were defeated in Africa only a few days before the *Armistice* in Europe.

(vii) At Sea: Individual German *cruisers* raided Allied commerce in the Pacific and Caribbean, until sunk. A fleet of five German cruisers defeated a small British fleet off the Chilean coast, at Coronel (November 1, 1914). British revenge came in December in the Battle of the Falkland Islands, where four German warships were sunk. That ended surface combat in both the Pacific and Atlantic. Other surface action took place, however, in the Adriatic (Austria versus Italy), the Baltic (Germany versus Russia), and the Black Sea (Russia versus Turkey). The great British and German battle fleets faced each other in the North Sea. They skirmished with cruisers and *destroyers* at Heligoland Bight (August 28, 1914) and with *battle cruisers* at the Dogger Bank (January 23, 1915). There was only one major surface battle involving *battleships* (*Dreadnoughts*), at *Jutland* in 1916. There was a final surface encounter at Heligoland (November 17, 1917). The main naval action involved *submarines*, in the form of *unrestricted submarine warfare* waged by Germany. The *U-boats* compelled reintroduction of the Atlantic *convoy* system last used by Britain during the *Napoleonic Wars*, saw the development of *escort carriers*, and finally brought the United States into the Great War. Also at sea, Britain blockaded all German trade beyond Europe, and with Italy and France also blockaded Austria and Turkey in the Mediterranean. Nearly 750,000 German civilians would die of starvation as a result of the British blockade.

(viii) End Game: On September 29, 1918, Bulgaria asked for terms. On October 4, 1918, the Austrian and German Empires opened negotiations with the Allied and Associated Powers, even as fighting continued. It was already too late for the Austro-Hungarian Empire, however: all its non-German provinces broke away during the next three weeks. On October 30th the Ottomans signed a cease-fire agreement. On November 4th Austria itself *surrendered*. In Germany, a naval mutiny and civic rebellion hastened the end. On November 10th Kaiser *Wilhelm II* left for exile in Holland. The next day, an Armistice was signed between Germany and the Allied and Associated Powers. The German Army marched home, largely unbowed, to disband.

The Allied and Associated Powers then marched into the *Rhineland*. Finally, all was "quiet on the western front." *Peace treaties* with the Central Powers or their *successor states* were signed at the *Paris Peace Conference* (1919–1920). Fighting continued elsewhere, however. For several years more, wars of independence or civil wars springing from the Great War raged in the Caucasus, Turkey, Ukraine, Poland, Finland, the Baltic States, and throughout the former Russian Empire, from Murmansk to Sebastopol and from Moscow to Vladivostok. Just 20 years later the Great War essentially resumed, on an even vaster scale of destruction of lives and property, as World War II. *See also Agadir; armed neutrality; Bosnian crisis; William Jennings Bryan; Georges Clemenceau; Constantinople Agreement; Fourteen Points; Lloyd George; Edward Grey; Entente Cordiale; Jean Jaurès; Alexander Kerensky; London, Treaty of (1839); Lusitania Notes; Moroccan crises; Military Conversations; Helmut von Moltke; mustard gas; mutilated victory; no-man's-land; Nicholas I; Vittorio Orlando; Gregori Yefimovich Rasputin; stab-in-the-back; Sykes-Picot Agreement; Alfred von Tirpitz; Triple Entente; Treaties of Neuilly, St. Germain, Trianon, and Versailles; war guilt clause;* and other participant states and leaders.

Suggested Readings: Hugh Cecil and Peter Liddle, eds., *Facing Armageddon* (1996); Paul Fussell, *The Great War* (1975); John Keegan, *The First World War* (1999); Basil Liddell Hart, *History of the First World War* (1970); Hew Strachan, ed., *World War I* (1999); Hew Strachan, *The First World War* (2001).

World War II (1939–1945). World War II was in many vital respects a continuation of the unfinished business of *World War I*. Yet, this even greater conflict (five times as many died as in the First World War, and because it was fought more in cites, its physical and cultural destruction was also more vast) had distinctive roots as well. The social origins of the war lay in the *Great Depression*. That was the sine qua non of the rise to power of German *fascism*, a contributing factor to the growth of *militarism* in Japan and national bombast in Italy, and the great handicap on a dynamic response by the democratic states. The Depression did not of itself cause World War II. The central, political origin of the war in Europe was German unwillingness, intensified after 1933, to continue to live within the strictures laid down in the *Treaty of Versailles*. At first Germany was opposed, albeit meekly, by all the *Great Powers* of Europe, including Italy and the Soviet Union. However, by 1936 a combination of political division (most notably, mutual distrust between the West and *Stalin*, but also the rise of Italy's own ambitions to empire) and adroit Nazi diplomacy prevented those states from forming a solid front against German *revisionism*. With the failure of the *Stresa front* and the shift of Italy into the German camp, the western democracies turned to a policy of *appeasement*. That encouraged the Soviet Union to return to its earlier, brooding *isolationism*. Meanwhile, from the United States arrived empty moral exhortation, but no demonstration of willingness to commit to *collective security* or just mutual defense against an emerging alliance of fascist powers. A series of deep crises followed: the *Abyssinian War*, the *Rhineland crisis*, the *Spanish Civil War*, and lastly, *Hitler's* direct threat to the *territorial integrity* of Czechoslovakia which culminated in the ultimate spectacle of Western appeasement at the *Munich Conference*.

After Munich, Western opinion and policy finally began to harden, and a full-scale *arms race* against Germany (and Japan) got underway. Stalin's thinking was changing too, toward the prospect of a separate and secret deal with Hitler, which came in the *Nazi-Soviet Pact* in August 1939. At the same time, a distinct conflict in Asia had been brewing. After their defeat of China in 1895, Japan's leaders increasingly acted in Asia on the assumption that a growing population on a resource-poor cluster of islands required the seizure of large, wealthy, and productive portions of the adjacent (Chinese and Manchurian) mainland. Japan was tempted to this conclusion because of China's extreme weakness and internal divisions during the first half of the century, and because the Western imperial powers were vitally preoccupied with events in Europe after 1914 and withdrew military resources from Asia. In 1915 Japan revealed its long-term ambitions when it presented the infamous *Twenty-one Demands* to China. American and British diplomatic intervention forestalled a victory by Tokyo or complete Chinese subservience. Japan felt rebuffed again by *Woodrow Wilson* at the *Paris Peace Conference*, though in fact it achieved most of its goals there. After intervening in *Siberia* to take advantage of Russian weakness, 1918–1922, Tokyo concentrated on *Manchuria* from 1931 (*Mukden incident*) and launched a direct assault on China in 1937 (*Marco Polo Bridge incident*). That led to ever-increasing tension with the United States. *Franklin Roosevelt's* insistence, 1937–1941, on a tightening economic *embargo* on trade in strategic materials with Japan, which aimed at curtailing Tokyo's aggression, brought Japan into clear and ultimately violent conflict with the United States. Japan's attack at *Pearl Harbor* on December 7, 1941, and Hitler's odd declaration of war against the United States four days later, united two hitherto distinct and widely separate wars into the second "great war" of the twentieth century. Before it was done, World War II would engage dozens of countries, which in 1945 together fielded fully 45 million men and women under arms.

(1) Europe, 1939–1941: On September 1, 1939, Hitler asserted that Polish troops had attacked a German border post and launched a long-planned invasion of Poland. Britain and France issued *ultimata* demanding Germany pull out; when they expired at midnight on September 3rd, three of the Great Powers were again at war (Japan, Italy, the Soviet Union, and the United States all remained *neutral*). The Polish Army was torn apart within days and all resistance crushed within a month—the Western Allies had hoped Poland would hold out six months or more—first by the German *Blitzkrieg* and then by Soviet units, who attacked into eastern Poland on September 17th in accordance with a secret protocol to the Nazi-Soviet Pact. What followed on the *western front* has been caustically called the *Sitzkrieg*, or *Phony War*, al-

though at sea the vitally important *Battle of the Atlantic* was being fought in deadly earnest. To the west, the nations which had been constant attackers in World War I—Britain and France—waited in dread defense, all *élan* exhausted, while the army which had defended from late 1914 through early 1918 was now determined to avoid a repeat of the *trench warfare* of the Great War and instead sought a crushing *battle of encounter*. In the interim, in November 1939, Russia attacked Finland, beginning the discrete but related *Finnish-Soviet War*. Germany watched with interest as the *Red Army* initially floundered in the Karelian snows, but it still had to deal with the western Allies. In April 1940, the *Wehrmacht* attacked, overran, and *occupied* Denmark and Norway. On May 10th it attacked Belgium, the Netherlands, and into France, its lead units of ten *armored* and motorized *infantry* divisions rolling through the Low Countries in days, to be followed by the greater weight of the German army which smashed through Belgian, British, and French defensive lines and compelled *surrender* within just seven weeks. During the *Battle of France* the French Army mostly hunkered down inside the *Maginot Line*, which the Germans had circumvented by unexpectedly attacking through the Ardennes Forest. The British Army was thrown back, to depart the continent—sans most of its equipment—at *Dunkirk* (May 25–31, 1940).

Meanwhile, in the east the Soviets forced Rumania to cede *Bessarabia* and annexed the *Baltic States*. And to the south, *Mussolini* had declared war on Britain and France (June 10th), trying to pick up what he thought would be easy spoils on the Italo-French border. In fact, Italy was bloodied badly by French frontier troops before France surrendered to Germany. Still, it looked, and it was widely assumed, that the war was over, handily won by the Nazis who now occupied Paris and dictated terms to *Vichy* (June 19th). Britain refused to bend or barter, however, and this made all the difference. German plans to invade Great Britain had to be abandoned with defeat of the *Luftwaffe* in the *Battle of Britain*. That turned Hitler's attention back east, where his main interest always lay. Mussolini invaded Greece, but found the going much rougher than expected, as he also did in North and East Africa, while the Italian Navy was savaged by Britain's Mediterranean flotillas—and by biplane torpedo-bombers at Taranto (November 1940). The British enjoyed their few early successes in Africa, routing the Italians. In early 1941 Hitler came to his friend's aid, throwing the British out of Crete in the first *paratroop* invasion in history, sending the Afrika Korps to Tripoli, and himself reinvading Greece and Yugoslavia, with Bulgaria as an ally. Operation *Barbarossa*, the German attack on Russia which was to give the conflict an additional character of a *genocidal* race war against Slavs and Jews, was launched on June 22, 1941. By the first week of December, the Germans (along with their Finnish, Hungarian, Italian, and Rumanian allies) had captured three million Soviet soldiers, shattered and destroyed entire armies, overrun Minsk, Kiev—where they were initially welcomed as liberators—and dozens of lesser cities, besieged Leningrad, and shelled Moscow. It seemed that the flags of fascism were destined to fly over the *Kremlin* itself. Hitler's empire stretched from the Atlantic to the heart of European Russia, and from the Baltic to North Africa. That same week, however, Japan attacked Pearl Harbor and four days later Germany and the United States were also at war. The Japanese thereby brought about what Roosevelt, *Churchill,* and even Adolf Hitler had not achieved in two prior years of fighting: the joining of otherwise separate Atlantic and Pacific conflicts through provocation of the American *intervention* which would prove decisive for both.

(2) Africa and the Middle East: Hitler's rapid defeat of France left most of the French Empire in the hands of Vichy. The British attacked and severely crippled the main French fleet at Mers-el-Kebir (July 3, 1940), killing more than 1,300 sailors. That embittered enough French servicemen that the Armée d'Afrique on occasion offered resistance to subsequent Allied invasions, particularly during the campaign in Syria in 1941 and the Operation Torch Anglo-American landings in North Africa in 1942. The war in Africa started, however, with Italian entry into World War II. In July–August 1940, Mussolini used his base in Ethiopia as a springboard to attack the British in the *Anglo-Egyptian Sudan* and *British Somaliland.* In September, *de Gaulle* led a *Free French* force in a failed effort to capture Dakar, Senegal, from Vichy. Cameroon, Chad, and the French Congo rallied to the Free French cause and provided forces to successfully invade Gabon. Bit by bit, the French Empire in West Africa either joined or was forced into de Gaulle's camp. British colonial reinforcements from such imperial outposts as Egypt, Nigeria, and South Africa, joined by a Belgian force from the Congo, attacked and overran the Italian Empire in Ethiopia, and an amphibious assault from *Aden* recaptured British Somaliland. Free French forces attacked into southern Libya in 1941, but the bulk of French forces in Africa—those in Morocco, Algeria, and Tunisia—remained loyal to Vichy, at least until the Allied invasion of North Africa in November 1942. After initial resistance, most French troops in Africa and the Middle East laid down their arms, and some even changed sides. Next, the British intervened in Iraq to counter a German-inspired coup, and shortly thereafter British Army and Free French forces moved against a Vichy garrison in the Levant. So bitter was the division among the French during the war that units of the *Foreign Legion* sometimes fought on different sides, as in Lebanon.

Meanwhile, the main fighting in Africa was in Tunis, Libya, and Egypt, from September 1940, when the Italians invaded Egypt from Libya. They were stopped by the British at Sidi Barani and thrown back (December 1940). The harder Germans of the Afrika Korps under *Erwin Rommel* arrived in Libya to bolster the Italian effort, and the war turned for awhile in favor of the Axis powers. Fighting washed back and forth along an archipelagic, coastal, and desert battlefield 1,200 miles long but effectively just 45 miles wide. Rommel ignored his Italian superior officers and often failed to coordinate with Italian units while on the move. Striking with stunning speed, he forced the British back to Egypt, cutting off and besieging in his rear a predominantly Australian garrison (the "Desert Rats") at Tobruk (March 1941). A British counteroffensive drove the Afrika Korps back to El Agheila (January 1942). But then a German counterattack took Benghazi and forced the British into a strictly defensive posture. Rommel sent his armor against the hastily constructed British line at Bir Hachim (May–June 1942), forcing another British retreat to a new defensive line drawn in front of Alexandria—with minefields, foxholes, bayonets, and sheer guts—from the coastal village of El Alamein to the interior Qattara Depression, which was impenetrable by armor. Meanwhile, Tobruk finally fell to the Germans (June 21, 1942). The climax of the North African campaign came at the decisive *Battle of El Alamein* (October–November, 1942), won by the British Eighth Army under a new commander, *Bernard Montgomery*. As the Afrika Korps retreated pell-mell back to Tunisia, an Anglo-American force landed in Algeria in the first week of November 1942. After more heavy fighting, North Africa was finally cleared of Axis forces, with large numbers of German and especially Italian prisoners taken. Africa now became a secure base for Allied invasions of Sicily and Italy, for clearance of Axis forces from elsewhere in the Middle East, and for bombing and other harassment of Axis positions in the Mediterranean and the Balkans.

(3) Europe, 1942–1945: At first 1942 looked like it would bring more German victories. Rommel was still bedeviling the British, soon to be joined by the Americans, in North Africa. Meanwhile, new thrusts were made into the *Crimea* and deeper into Russia. Leningrad refused to fall, Hitler's legions were pushed slowly back from Moscow, and in October the British inflicted the major defeat of El Alamein. Then, in January 1943, the German Sixth Army was annihilated at *Stalingrad*. The tide turned. Anglo-American forces pushed the Germans out of North Africa by May 1943 and then invaded Sicily and Italy, toppling Mussolini and taking Italy out of the war by September. The Soviets, too, moved over to the offensive in 1943, winning an enormous victory at *Kursk*—one of the largest, most destructive, and decisive battles of the entire war. Less effectively, *partisans* resisted the Nazis, in Norway, France, Yugoslavia, Greece, and deep within the *Pripet Marshes* region of western Russia. The Western Allies opened a *second front* in Western Europe when they landed in France on D-Day (June 6, 1944), commencing the *Normandy campaign*, in which they were aided by the French *Resistance* and by *Free French* regular formations. After weeks of consolidation of the beachhead, the Americans, under *Patton*, broke out and raced through southern France and toward the *Ziegfried Line* while British and *Commonwealth* troops, under Montgomery, moved up the coast into Belgium and Holland toward the Rhine. Nazi Germany had been pounded by Anglo-American *thousand bomber raids*, and other bombing, since 1942. Now it was engaged in an all-out *two-front war* on the ground. By midwinter its once triumphant, swaggering, murderous armies were fighting desperately on their own soil in both east and west.

A sense of looming defeat among the most fanatic Nazis hastened the mass killing program of the *concentration camps*, as the Nazi *Holocaust* reached for the darkest depths yet known to human history. The advance of the Red Army, which was determined on exacting the last full measure of revenge from Germans—any Germans, the innocent along with the guilty—for the ineffable atrocities which had been carried out in the east, encouraged a pitiless combat on all sides all along the *eastern front*. Warsaw was razed to the ground. Millions were raped; hundreds of thousands of civilians were summarily murdered, by all armies engaged. Twelve million German refugees fled their homes, to no safe place in particular (there was none), joining many millions more Czech, Polish, Baltic, Russian, Jewish, and other refugees on the move all over eastern Europe. A last-ditch effort to divide the Allies by an attack in the west was made by Hitler in the *Ardennes Offensive*. That spent Germany's final *reserves* and finally broke the morale of its defenders. The Wehrmacht and even the *Waffen SS* began to surrender en masse in the west and south, where the Americans moved through Bavaria into Czechoslovakia; yet they fought a still-disciplined, house-by-house and town-by-town retreat in the east, against the advancing Soviets. The Allies, so soon to fall out, would not do so (openly) however, while Hitler and his senior henchmen yet lived and plotted in Berlin. Instead, they demanded *unconditional surrender* and pressed on with invasion of the *Third Reich* from all fronts. The Red Army thrust toward the heart of the beast, expending 100,000 lives in the *Battle of Berlin* to take that benighted city. On April 30, 1945, with fighting going on barely 100 meters from his subterranean bunker, Hitler and several others of the Nazi leadership killed themselves; others were captured, or not, in later days and weeks. On May 2nd Berlin fell, and on May 8th Germany *surrendered* unconditionally. Over the next three days the last fragments of German holdouts surrendered in Norway, Courland, Dunkirk, and finally, Heligoland. The "Thousand Year Reich" had lasted but 12 years, but to bring it and its allies down required the combined forces of more than 40 nations, and took at least 55 million lives in the most violent and brutal ways yet seen in warfare.

(4) The Pacific War, 1939–1945: The main prewar tension was between the United States and Japan over ongoing Japanese aggression against China, dating to the *Second Sino-Japanese War* which began in 1937 with the horror of the *Rape of Nanjing*. It also arose from American suspicions of larger Japanese ambitions such as the "*Greater East Asia Co-Prosperity Sphere*." Still, from 1919 to 1939 most American leaders appeased Japan and acquiesced in its imperialism in Asia because no U.S. *vital interests* were seen as at stake in Asia. However, when Japan became an ally of Nazi Germany in the *Anti-Comintern Pact*, that changed. The outbreak of war in Europe in 1939 presented Tokyo's *warlords* with a strategic dilemma: the army was being drawn deeper into the China *quagmire*, but ultimately wanted to strike the Soviets in *Siberia*. The navy was drawn south, toward the ripe pickings of now lightly

defended European colonial empires in Southeast Asia, especially after the Nazi conquest of France and Holland and the drawing back of British forces from *Burma, Hong Kong,* and *Singapore.* In other words, the Japanese had to choose whether they wanted to fight a land war against the Soviet Union ("hokushin," or "northern advance"), then desperately fending off a ferocious Nazi onslaught, but with 40 superb winter divisions in reserve in Siberia under Marshal *Zhukov,* who had bloodied the Japanese in an undeclared border war in August 1939. Or they might fight an oceanic war against the United States ("nanshin," or "southern advance"), the only power with sufficient naval resources, but perhaps not the will, to stand against a naval thrust toward Southeast Asia and even India. With the fall of France, Tokyo forced the Vichy regime in *French Indochina* to accept onerous terms and put great pressure on Britain, too, overstretching its naval resources and weakening its ability to resist Germany. Such easy conquest helped the navy view prevail within the war party in Japan, and the pressure on the UK changed minds in Washington.

During 1940 and 1941 Washington offered a diplomatic and strategic accommodation, but on terms which included Japan's withdrawal from China, something deemed unacceptable by Japanese imperialists. The United States therefore imposed an ever-tighter *embargo* on Japan's purchase of *war matériel,* including oil. When Japan occupied the remainder of French Indochina in July 1941, Roosevelt froze Japanese assets. Tokyo saw this and the oil embargo as unfairly constricting its national ambitions and economic needs, and as threatening its war effort in China and plans for further expansion in Asia. On September 6th, an Imperial Conference concluded that war with the United States was inevitable, though victory was uncertain; military preparations began for an attack in October. *Tōjō Hideki* replaced *Konoe* as prime minister on October 18th, as Japan made a final peace overture. The terms offered were little changed and still amounted to acceptance of Japanese hegemony in Asia. This was rejected by Washington, partly out of fear that such a deal might free Tokyo to attack the Soviet Union in Siberia, which threatened far greater United States interests in Europe—a psychological and strategic linkage of the two theaters of war which sprang from Japan's accession to the Axis alliance. On December 7, 1941, the Imperial Japanese Navy struck directly at the United States at Pearl Harbor.

Within days, for reasons which remain murky, Germany and Italy declared war on the United States. Japan at first enjoyed victory after victory in its sea-borne Blitzkrieg: on Guam and Wake; in the consolidation of its hold on Indochina; against the British in *Hong Kong, Burma,* and *Singapore;* and against American and Filipino troops in the *Philippines.* In many places, these conquests were accompanied by Japanese atrocities against civilian and soldier alike, such as the *Bataan death march,* extensive and genocidal use of *biological warfare* against Asian civilian populations, and the most heinous medical experimentation on, and vivisection of, *prisoners of war* and civilians. The

Japanese were stopped by ANZAC and American forces in New Guinea and then suffered a series of naval setbacks starting with *Coral Sea*, where American naval air power prevented Admiral *Yamamoto* from successfully luring the U.S. Navy into a battle in which Japan's *battleships* could destroy it. Japanese home front complacency was shattered by the *Doolittle Raid*, which helped prompt Yamamoto into making a major mistake: an amphibious assault on Midway Island escorted by his main *carrier* fleet. The strategic loss of four Japanese carriers at the *Battle of Midway* (June 4–5, 1942), within just six months of the triumphs at Pearl Harbor and Singapore, threw the Japanese onto the strategic defensive. The Americans then adopted *Chester Nimitz's* "island-hopping" strategy, by which they bypassed and isolated Japanese island garrisons while progressing toward the recapture of more important territories from which their *strategic bombers* could pound the Japanese *home islands*.

The United States also outbuilt Japan, achieving a staggering advantage in war matériel, to go along with their greater numbers of conscripts and volunteers. For instance, in 1943 Japan built just 122 warships to America's 2,654, of all types; in 1944 Japan built four new aircraft carriers to 90 commissioned by the United States. The United States also conducted *unrestricted submarine warfare* to devastating effect against Japan's *merchant marine*, strangling its overseas island garrisons of supplies and the home islands of food and fuel. Overall, the United States defeated Japan while expending just 15 percent of its total war effort in the Pacific theater of operations. Meanwhile, in awful jungle fighting, British and *Indian Army* troops threw the Japanese back from Bengal and India's northeastern frontier and began to drive them from Burma as well, though some Indians, in the *Indian National Army*, fought alongside Japan against the British. The fall of Saipan, in July 1944, was another turning point, allowing round-trip bombing of Japan from the *Marianas* and toppling Tōjō's government. The Philippines was retaken by American forces under *Douglas MacArthur* after the spectacular battle of *Leyte Gulf* and vicious and prolonged fighting, 1944–1945, including house-to-house fighting which destroyed most of Manila. Fighting continued in the Philippine hills until Japan's final surrender. The other theater of land warfare in Asia was China, where Allied *air power* supported Chinese *Guomindang* and *Communist* armies, as after the *Xi'an incident* those old and bitter enemies paused the *Chinese Civil War* to fight the foreign invader. The sinking of Japan's merchant marine by U.S. submarines cut off its outward island garrisons and slowly but decisively strangled the island empire, intercepting virtually all resupply by early 1945.

The *carpet bombing* of Japan's cities from March 1945, threat of imminent invasion, and "demodernization" (through combat) of its armed forces, pushed Japan to desperate measures, including air and naval *kamikaze* attacks at Okinawa. The Japanese military began to prepare for a final, cataclysmic bloodbath to greet any invasion of the *home islands*, to salvage their "national honor" (which was not possible, after the type of war Japan had fought) and more so to influence surrender negotiations. Meanwhile, American planners set November 1st as the date for invasion of Kyushu. Some in Tokyo were already considering capitulation when the United States dropped *atomic bombs* on *Hiroshima* and *Nagasaki*, on August 6 and 9, 1945, respectively, and President *Harry Truman* promised to bring down upon Japan a further "rain of death never equaled in history" if the *militarists* in Tokyo did not surrender. In fact, the *Manhattan Project* had not produced any additional bombs, though the leadership in Tokyo did not know that. The Soviet Union entered the Pacific War on November 8th, between the atomic attacks. It assaulted the Japanese on a massive scale, smashing their armies in Manchuria and northern China. The atomic bombs persuaded Japan's military leaders that, since the Allies possessed such awesome weapons, they would not need to invade the Japanese home islands after all. Therefore, the final and bloody defense of Japan—which the militarists had hoped might be used to extract concessions from the Allied powers—was no longer a viable option, and the Japanese military decided upon surrender instead. On August 10th the first formal peace feelers were sent out, and on August 15th Japan agreed to *terms*. Even then, after the instant incinerations of two Japanese cities, and the conventional fire-bombing and destruction of most others, and facing a whole new front and a determined and vastly more powerful enemy, there was still last-ditch resistance by thousands of fanatic Japanese officers who opposed surrender. Some junior officers attempted a coup, to forestall Emperor *Hirohito*'s surrender announcement, but it was foiled. Japan at last surrendered on August 15, 1945 (August 20th in Korea), with the United States in the end conceding the continued reign (*kokutai*) of Hirohito. On September 2, 1945, representatives of Imperial Japan signed the instrument of surrender to the Allied powers aboard the battleship U.S.S. Missouri in Tokyo Bay, in the presence of Allied representatives from many nations and liberated prisoners of war, including commanding officers who had experienced the Bataan death march.

(5) Legacy: The toll of the dead in World War II was, at the least: 25 million Soviets (some estimates suggest 45 million); 8 million Germans; 6 million Jews (including 3 million Polish Jews); 5 million Chinese; 3 million Japanese; 3 million non-Jewish Poles; and several millions more from two score of other combatant or occupied nations. The war was so vast, so truly global in its conduct and effects, that it is next to impossible to summarize its full legacy. In parts of the world where basic public order broke down—indeed, where civilization itself was reversed—fighting simply continued: civil wars broke out or resumed in China, French Indochina, Greece, Indonesia, Palestine, and Yugoslavia. Fighting also continued in Ukraine and elsewhere within the Soviet Union, as the Red Army was forced to fight to reestablish Stalin's writ where bitter, anti-Soviet populations feared it should run again. Hundreds of the world's greatest cities lay in utter ruin, their populations

scattered and forlorn, and many of its greatest architectural and artistic treasures had been forever lost to bombs or fire. The global economy was shattered and would have to be rebuilt and reoriented to civilian production if millions more were not to starve or perish from cold, disease, or despair. Property damage was far greater than in World War I because, whereas the first great war had been fought mainly in the countryside, the second was largely urban. Transportation systems—railways, ports, roads, canals and dykes, and thousands of bridges in dozens of countries—lay in ruin, bombed from existence or destroyed by retreating armies practicing *scorched earth*. Defeated Germany and its main allies, Italy and Japan, were disarmed and occupied, their surviving leaders tried and some executed. Some 30 million persons were forcibly displaced by massive *ethnic cleansing* in eastern and central Europe; millions more were forced from their historic homelands in Asia, Africa, and the Middle East.

The political systems and postwar character of entire societies and economies were decided not by choice, or reason, or national will, but by whichever army—Soviet or Western Allied—occupied their territory. According to prior agreement at *Tehran, Yalta,* and *Potsdam,* or just the fortunes of war, Korea was divided, Austria was divided, Germany was divided, and Europe was divided; all precursor to the coming division of the world into hostile armed camps during the long, chill peace of the *Cold War.* The main victors of World War II quickly disagreed over division of the territorial and geopolitical spoils, *reconstruction, reparations,* and *ideology.* Vital and unbridgeable divisions had appeared within the *United Nations alliance* even before the war was won. This meant that no general peace conference was ever held—there was no equivalent of the *Congress of Vienna* or of the *Paris Peace Conference.* Instead, peace treaties with the vanquished were settled, or left in abeyance, state-by-state between individual vanquished and victors. The United States found itself the clear, *preponderant power* in world affairs, and in effective mastery of the Western hemisphere, Western Europe, Japan, and much of the Pacific, and quickly set about reconstruction in a mostly benign manner. The Soviet Union, the other great victor of the war, malignantly bestrode Eurasia for the next four decades, brooding over a vast empire which began to decay and resist from the moment it was acquired.

Yet, beneath the surface postwar dominance of the superpowers, other forces were at work. For also shattered by the fighting was the post–World War I international consensus which had deferred to the Great Powers in matters of peace and security. Replacing it was a radical assertion not just of the right of all peoples and nations to *self-determination* and self-government, but a right of all states to equal representation in the determinative councils of world affairs. In the Far East the disruption of the *ancien régime* was so extensive that returning European occupiers, such as the British under *Mountbatten* in Burma, felt compelled to use just surrendered Japanese troops to quell nationalist unrest and restore public order and imperial rule. In India,

West Africa, the Middle East, and other territories which had remained loyal to the metropolitan countries, demands for independence no longer could be ignored. The will to empire was gone, broken on the wheels of the First and Second World Wars. Even *Mao* in China and *Hô Chí Minh* in Vietnam later conceded that Japan's initial defeat of the Western colonial powers, rather than the irresistible march of proletarian history, had advanced the cause of revolution in their nations.

After World War II, great and small imperial powers alike at first tried to return to their possessions. Within 20 years, however, Great Britain, Belgium, and Holland learned to tack with, instead of against, the winds of change and withdrew from enforced empire back to their national homelands, retaining only those overseas territories which desired continuing *association*. It took several bitter, anti-colonial wars to drive the same lesson home in Paris and then in Lisbon, but it was finally learned and adjusted to all the same. On the other hand, it would still require a long Cold War to teach that same lesson to the great empire centered on Moscow, with bloody stops along the way in the *Korean Conflict, Vietnam War, Afghan-Soviet War*, and many others. This was perhaps the greatest, and also wholly unintended, consequence of World War II: together with World War I it halted, and then reversed, a European imperial expansion and global mastery underway for more than 400 years, which at its apex had encompassed most of the globe. Such huge disruption and dislocation of individual, national, and international life caused by these closely related wars make them the Himalaya range of modern history. They overshadowed and influenced all subsequent events, and do so still. *See also Atlantic Charter; Pietro Badoglio; Cairo conference; Wilhelm Franz Canaris; Casablanca conference; Neville Chamberlain; Chetniks; Galeazzo Ciano; English Channel; "final solution"; Four Freedoms; Josef Goebbels; Herman Göring; Japanese Peace Treaty; Katyn massacre; Lansing-Ishii Agreement; Morgenthau plan; National Front governments; Nazism; Neutrality Acts; Nuremberg trials; Pact of Steel; Treaties of Paris (1947); Joachim "von" Ribbentrop; Konstantin Rokossovsky; Saar; Second Sino-Japanese War; Wladislaw Sikorski; Tito; Tripartite Pact; V-1 and V-2 rockets; war crimes trials; Warsaw Rising; Yamashita Tomoyuki;* and selected military and political leaders and participating countries.

Suggested Readings: P. M. H. Bell, *The Origins of the Second World War in Europe* (1986); Gunter Bischof and Robert Dupont, eds., *The Pacific War Revisited* (1997); Winston Churchill, *The Second World War*, 6 Vols. (1953); Paul Fussell, *Wartime* (1989); Martin Gilbert, *Second World War* (1989); Akira Iriye, *Power and Culture* (1981); John Keegan, *The Second World War* (1989); Basil Liddell Hart, *History of the Second World War* (1999); Alan Milward, *War, Economy, and Society, 1939–45* (1987); W. Murry and Alan Millett, *A War to Be Won* (2000); R. A. C. Parker, *Struggle for Survival* (1989); A. Seaton, *The Russo-German War, 1941–45* (1971); Ronald Spector, *Eagle Against the Sun* (1988). A quirky but influential interpretation is A. J. P. Taylor, *Origins of the Second World War* (1963). It should be read in combination with Wm. Roger Louis, ed. *The Origins of the Second World War* (1972).

WTO. *See* (1) *Warsaw Treaty Organization*; (2) *World Trade Organization*.

Wu (625–705). *See Tang dynasty.*

Wu Sangui (1612–1678). This Chinese general and *warlord* played an extraordinary role in ending one great dynasty in China and launching another, which he then rebelled against in the War of the Three Feudatories (1673–1681). During that drawn-out conflict he proclaimed himself emperor and sought to establish a new Zhou dynasty. This effort failed, but only after much blood had been shed and at great cost to China's prosperity and stability. *See also Kangxi emperor; Ming dynasty; Qing dynasty.*

X

X article. In July 1947, *Foreign Affairs* magazine published an article entitled "The Sources of Soviet Conduct," identifying the author only as "X." In fact, it was by *George Kennan*, writing under a pseudonym owing to his position as a government official. Kennan pointed to the Soviets as the central threat to global *security* and proposed a strategy of flexible *containment* to forestall a new shift in the *balance of power*—so recently restored by *World War II*, at great cost in lives and treasure—out of America's favor. He argued that the United States should aim at keeping the two remaining centers of great industrial capacity, Western Europe and Japan, free of Soviet control. As these regions were struggling to recover from the war, it was imperative for the United States to oppose the threat of takeover by local *communists* supported by the Soviet Union with diplomatic, political, and, most important, economic aid. Containment thus was not conceived as an offensive strategy, nor was it a military one, at first or essentially. Kennan did not believe the Soviet Union had the clear intention of invading Western Europe with the *Red Army*. Rather, he wanted the United States to ensure that Moscow was never presented with the temptation to do so, through a perceived or real failure of resolve in Washington or neglect of the need to rapidly restore social, economic, and political order—under Western and democratic tutelage—in Germany and Japan.

Counterforce might have to be used on occasion, but *deterrence* was always to be the preferred course and policy. Most important was to deny political opportunity to the Soviets through direct support for, and guarantees of, the continuation of liberal-democracy in those countries which already enjoyed it and long-term cultivation of democratic virtues and habits of mind in the defeated *Axis* states. This could be accomplished through application of the anaesthetic of prosperity to Western Europe and Japan in the form of a U.S.-led and underwritten *aid*, *trade*, and credit *regime*. That was, of course, something entirely in American economic interests as well: a fulfillment of its long-standing interest in the *Open Door*. Kennan was supremely confident. He regarded the West as by far the stronger party, which in fact it was, and recognized that the Soviet Union was so full of systemic and structural contradictions it must surely collapse if further expansion was denied its ideologically driven, and thoroughly paranoid and economically inept, leadership. "No mystical, messianic movement can face frustration indefinitely," he wrote, "without eventually adjusting itself in one way or another to the logic of that state of affairs." The Soviet state and system might not fall soon, but given time and containment, it would surely fail and then fall. The same year he penned the "X Article," Kennan was sent off to Japan to tell *MacArthur* it was time to *reverse course*. *See also Cold War*; *domino theory*; *double containment*; *Iron Curtain*; *Long Telegram*; *Paul Nitze*; *NSC-68*; *peaceful coexistence*.

xenophobia. An unreasonable fear of foreigners and/or of foreign cultures and values. *See also chauvinism*; *cosmopolitan values*; *ethnocentrism*; *isolationism*; *jingoism*; *liberalism*; *nationalism*; *pluralism*; *racism*; *Slavophile*.

Xhosa. The second-largest *ethnic group* in South Africa, after the *Zulu*, against whom they fought desperate wars in the time of *Shaka Zulu* and the *Mfecane*. The Xhosa also fought the British and the *Boers*, both of whom were *migrating* northward from the Cape after 1800. These "Kaffir Wars" were waged intermittently before 1880, ending in Xhosa defeat and subordination, 1877–1878. Under *apartheid*, many Xhosa were herded into *Bantustans*, where they subsequently became ardent supporters of the *African National Congress*.

Xi'an incident (December 1936). In the midst of the *Chinese Civil War*, Nationalist and Manchurian troops grew angry that *Chiang Kai-shek*, head of the *Guomindang* and generalissimo of the Nationalist Army, continued to pursue military efforts against the Chinese *Communist Party* and *Red Army* instead of concentrating on expelling the Japanese invaders from *Manchuria*. A Manchurian unit broke into Chiang's headquarters on December 13, 1936, killing his guards. They held him captive for nearly two weeks, while he met with *Zhou Enlai*, who arrived at Xi'an by plane on December 16th, and the commander of the local Nationalist forces. On December 25th Chiang agreed to join forces with the Communists against the Japanese and issued a proclamation establishing (on paper) a united front of all Chinese factions. This tenuous and coerced contract was hardly adhered to during the next few years of the *Second Sino-Japanese War* and then collapsed completely c. 1941 as Nationalist and Communist forces resumed heavy fighting after the "New Fourth Army Incident" in January 1941, where Chiang ordered an ambush of Communist forces. Nonetheless, the kidnapping oddly confirmed Chiang as a popular defender of China against the Japanese and relieved immediate Nationalist pressure on Communist bases in the north.

Xianjiang. "New Territories." A vast, semi-*autonomous* region in northwest China, home to several non-*Han* peoples, including the Uighurs. Among other exploitative uses, it has been the locale of China's *nuclear weapons* testing program.

XYZ Affair. U.S. President *John Adams* wanted to defuse a growing crisis with France which faced his new administration in 1797, rooted in *blockade* running and *smuggling*, and send a delegation to Paris. The delegates were asked for a bribe by the wily *Talleyrand* before he would even receive them, but they did not have the money and the mission failed. Adams was shocked at the slight and considered *war*, but announced only limited hostilities. He told Congress of the bribe demand, substituting the initials "X," "Y," and "Z" for names of the French *agents*. National indignation resulted which fueled conflict with France for years and built public support for the first significant appropriations to build the U.S. Navy. *See also Quasi War.*

Y

Yahya Khan, Agha Muhammad (1917–1980). President of Pakistan, 1969–1971. His troops repressed an *uprising* of the Awami League (a Bengali political party) in *East Pakistan* with such *genocidal* intent and cruelty that a full-scale civil war broke out. The refugees pouring into India numbered more than 10 million, destabilizing the whole region and threatening to provoke a wider war. He refused to quell the violence or to placate India, partly from a mistaken belief in the superiority of Pakistan's armed forces. When *Indira Gandhi* delivered an ultimatum, he fumed that such an insult should come from a woman and sent 85 aircraft to attack India. That stimulated a punishing Indian reprisal against *West Pakistan*, defeat in the ensuing *Third Indo-Pakistani War*, and national dismemberment as Bangladesh became independent. India also emerged from the war as the *preponderant power* in southeast Asia.

Yalta Conference (February 4–11, 1945). A wartime *summit* held in the *Crimea*, attended by *Winston Churchill, Franklin Roosevelt, Josef Stalin*, and their top advisers. It was critical to the shape of the postwar world and to the origins of the *Cold War*. They discussed some military matters concerning the final phases of *World War II*, but focused on four main postwar topics: (1) What to do with Germany: It was decided to demand *unconditional surrender*, hold *war crimes trials*, and impose military *occupation*. It was not agreed to divide Germany, however, other than into administrative zones: the longer term division of Germany resulted from the Cold War, not directly from World War II. (2) What to do about Asia: As the *atom bomb* was yet untested and the *invasion* of Japan promised to be very costly in American and British lives, Roosevelt and Churchill urged Stalin to bring Russia's vast reserves of troops into the Asian war. They offered the *Kurile Islands, Sakhalin Island, Outer Mongolia*, and restoration of Russia's pre-1904 rights in *Manchuria* as an incentive and agreed as well to a large territorial concession in Poland, all out of a desire to bring Russia's might to bear on the Japanese military. Stalin agreed to attack Japan three months after Germany *surrendered*, a promise he kept. In return, he recognized the *Nationalists* in China. It was also decided to jointly occupy Korea. (3) What to do about *Eastern Europe*: This proved the most difficult and controversial of issues. It was agreed to join the Polish *government-in-exile* in London with the Soviet-backed Lublin Poles, pending free elections in Poland and other *liberated* countries as promised in the *Declaration on Liberated Europe*. Elsewhere, it was agreed that Stalin should have *"friendly states"* on his borders, but what that meant on the ground was left ill-defined. (4) What about the United Nations? The scope of the *veto* and other unsettled issues were discussed, pending final resolution at the *San Francisco Conference*. Within three weeks of the Yalta conference serious disagreements broke out and mutual charges of violations were exchanged. The main points of controversy concerned unilateral Soviet actions in Rumania and Poland, Moscow's refusal to permit Western observers into those areas, and Soviet neglect of liberated Allied *prisoners of war*. By *Potsdam*, the wartime *alliance* was crumbling fast. Over the next two years it completely fell apart. *See also Casablanca; containment; Long Telegram; Tehran; X article.*

Suggested Readings: Edward M. Bennett, *Franklin D. Roosevelt and the Search for Victory: American-Soviet Relations, 1939–1945* (1990); Russell Buhite, *Decisions at Yalta* (1986); Herbert Feis, *Churchill, Roosevelt, Stalin* (1957).

Yamagata Aritomo (1838–1922). Japanese statesman. Minister of war, 1873; prime minister, 1889–1893, 1898–1900; *éminence grise*, 1900–1921. After *Itō Hirobumi*, he was the most important of the *Meiji* leaders. He held a command in the Restoration War, 1868–1869. A convert to *modernization*, he built up the Japanese Army but kept it out of politics. He then oversaw its operations in the *Sino-Japanese War* (1894–1895), headed the *Guandong Army*, served in occupied Korea, and fought again during the *Russo-Japanese War*. As home minister after 1883, he set up the national police and local governments, both in an authoritarian fashion. He remained an influential member of the *genrō* to the end of his life.

Yamamoto Isoroku, né Takano (1884–1943). Japanese admiral. He saw action as a young *officer* at the *Battle of Tsushima Straits* (1904) during the *Russo-Japanese War*. He studied at Harvard University, 1919–1921 and was greatly impressed with the dynamism and latent power of American society. In 1923 he returned to the United States on a tour of inspection, and from 1925 to 1928 he was naval *attaché* at the Japanese embassy in Washington. He then briefly commanded the aircraft carrier Akagi. In 1929 he was promoted to rear admiral. He headed the Japanese delegation to the *London Naval Disarmament Conference*, 1934–35, where he opposed the official Japanese position insisting on naval parity with the United States and Great Britain, but dutifully pressed it nonetheless. This was a pattern in his official life: private dissent but public obedience. He had lived, studied, and worked in the United States and opposed proposals for war with America. He also opposed Japan joining the *Axis* alliance. When the order for war came, he argued forcefully that it was essential to attack the U.S. Pacific Fleet in Hawaii, lest it interfere with expansion into southeast Asia, and set about putting his considerable *tactical* and *strategic* talents to work on behalf of Japanese *imperialism*. He personally commanded the fleet which attacked *Pearl Harbor* and directed follow-up Japanese naval operations in the Pacific theater. Yet he suffered from forebodings of *defeat*. Immediately after Pearl Harbor, when he learned that Japan's *declaration of war* had come only after the attack began, he said of America: "I fear all we have done is awaken a sleeping giant, and fill him with a terrible resolve." He carried out successful invasions of sundry territories in southeast Asia and the Pacific. As he had foreseen, this "happy time" was brief. Japanese forces were pushed back at the *Coral Sea*, and Yamamoto's battle plan for *Midway* went badly awry. His old carrier, the Akagi, was sunk along with three others, largely because American and British *intelligence* had broken some Japanese codes, but partly owing to the varying luck and/or courage of pilots and commanders on both sides. When U.S. intelligence intercepted a message saying precisely where and when Yamamoto would be on April 17, 1943, his plane and escorts were duly intercepted by an entire U.S. *fighter* squadron and shot down. In later years many Americans came to regard Yamamoto as having been an "honorable enemy."

Suggested Reading: Hiroyuki Agawa, *The Reluctant Admiral* (1979).

Yamani, Ahmad Zaki (b. 1930). Saudi *oil* minister, 1962–1986. Harvard educated, he was the leading individual behind the creation and management of *OPEC*, including its use of oil *embargoes* in 1973 and 1979. He was ousted in 1986 after a six-year drop in world oil prices, which continued into the late-1990s, before world prices rose again after 2000.

Yamashita Tomoyuki (1885–1946). "Tiger of Malaya." Japanese general. He served as a military attaché in the 1920s in Switzerland, Germany, Austria, and Hungary. An ultranationalist, he was active in the anti-democratic politics of the Imperial Way faction throughout the 1930s. He was in command of a unit in Korea in 1937 before moving to northern China. In 1940 he headed a mission to *Nazi Germany* sent to study *Blitzkrieg* tactics which had proved so successful in the war in Europe. In 1941 he briefly commanded the *Guandong Army*. He next led the invasion of Malaya and Singapore, where he accepted the humiliating British and Commonwealth surrender on February 15, 1942. He then took command of the Japanese *campaign* in the

Philippines, capturing Bataan and Corregidor and shooing *MacArthur* from the islands. The *Bataan death march* took place under his command. He was again in command when MacArthur and Allied forces returned and was captured. His troops committed numerous *war crimes* and *atrocities* against the Philippine population, especially during 1944 and 1945, when it became clear that Japan was losing the war. He was therefore tried as a war criminal and convicted and hanged in Manila. His death sentence and execution remains controversial, as no direct evidence existed that he ordered the atrocities and some believe that he simply lost control of his disintegrating army. The court held that, as the overall commander, he should have known what his troops were doing and he should have stopped them from doing it. *See also command responsibility.*

Yankee. (1) Originally, residents of New England, especially those of Puritan descent. (2) Residents of the northern states of the United States, especially those which formed the *Union* during the *American Civil War*. (3) Internationally, a colloquialism—and sometime pejorative—for any American.

Yaoundé Convention (1969). Some 18 African states signed this *preferential trade* and *aid* agreement with the *European Community*. It was superseded by the *Lomé Conventions.*

Yap Island. In the Caroline chain, and originally a German possession, it caused friction between the United States and Japan in the 1920s when it was run by Tokyo as a *mandated territory*. At the *Washington Conference* it was agreed to give the United States cable and other rights equal to Japan's, in return for *recognition* of Japanese mandates north of the equator. Discrete recognition was necessary, as the United States was not a *League of Nations* member and hence had not formally approved the mandate system.

Yazidis. *See Kurds.*

"Yellow peril." The pre–*World War II* fear, springing from *racism* but also from more legitimate *security* concerns, that Japan might try to overrun territories such as Australia or the west coast of North America which were settled by whites (who had themselves earlier overrun the native populations). It gained currency after Japan's surprising success in the *Russo-Japanese War.*

yellow press. Media which indulge in and/or encourage shrill *nationalism* or *jingoism*, especially in times of *crisis* and *war*. The term was originally applied to U.S. newspaper baron William Randolph Hearst (1863–1951), whose several newspaper chains whipped up war fever before the *Spanish-American War.*

Yeltsin, Boris Nikolayevich (b. 1931). Russian statesman. *Gorbachev* promoted him to head the Moscow party in 1985, viewing him as an ally. After 1987 he grew openly critical of Gorbachev, pushing him toward more radical and faster reform. Yeltsin won an overwhelming popular victory in May 1990, as president of the Russian Federation (or Russia, as opposed to the *Soviet Union*, of which Gorbachev remained president). When Yeltsin joined other republic leaders in calls for decentralization under a new Union Treaty, Gorbachev floundered and briefly turned to the old *communist* right. During the August 1991 *coup* attempt by reactionary elements of the Party and the *Red Army*, Yeltsin acted bravely and decisively—at one point, taking command while standing atop a tank whose crew had switched sides—to emerge as the undisputed spokesman for Russia and dispatcher of the old Soviet Union. He later deliberately and publicly humiliated Gorbachev, while pushing for creation of the *CIS* and thereby the end of any supranational role for the Soviet Union; *extinction* of the old Union duly took place on Christmas Day, 1991. Yeltsin subsequently cooperated extensively with the West on *arms control*, the *Gulf War*, and even toward *Bosnia*, where Russian "conservatives" preferred to support the Serbs. In return he received extensive *aid*. He improved relations with China, but quarreled with Ukraine over many issues and could not resolve the old impasse with Japan over the *Kurils*. He showed up uninvited at the *G-7* summit in Tokyo in July 1993. He was politely received, and, although not allowed to attend the meetings, he walked away with another $3 billion in aid. His biggest battles were back home. From 1991 he was locked in a mortal struggle with the entrenched interests of the old Soviet system, in particular over the division of powers between the presidency and parliament in any new constitution, and the pace and depth of economic reform. In October 1993, he moved to settle the question by forcibly crushing an armed *rebellion* by supporters of the old parliament, which refused his order to disband. After shelling the *White House*, he replaced the *Duma* old assembly with a new State Duma. He next pushed through a new constitution granting the presidency unprecedented powers, even as he saw his Duma supporters lose ground to both *fascists* and old-guard communists. His declining power—along with his vanity, personal crudeness, ill-health, worsening alcoholism, and tolerance of massive corruption upon which his political base finally rested—dominated Russian politics in the second half of the 1990s, while the nation as a whole drifted in a chaotic and semi-lawless condition. By the end of Yeltsin's presidency he was widely seen—at home and abroad—as unstable and wholly ineffective. Russian relations with the West had also deteriorated badly over *NATO* expansion and intervention in *Kosovo* and Russian brutality in the war in *Chechnya*. Yeltsin left much of Russia essentially unreformed, with its financial markets and economy near outright bankruptcy and in the hands of a new *kleptocracy*. His was mostly a chronicle of wasted years. *See also Katyn massacre; MIAs; Vladimir Putin.*

Yemen. An ancient, strategically located territory with a history traceable to the days of trade with Pharaonic Egypt and the *Roman Empire*, when it was the source of frankincense and myrrh and its sailors alone knew the secret of the monsoon trade winds. It declined as Rome and other trade competitors developed direct links with India and as demand for its products fell. Its tribes fed hordes of warriors into the *Islamic* armies which poured over and then out of Arabia in the seventh and later centuries, before Yemen itself sank back into relative, desert obscurity. For 400 years it was a province of the *Ottoman Empire* (1517–1918). From 1833, the British secured the port of *Aden* as a refueling stop for their ships en route to India. The rest of Yemen became an independent *monarchy* in 1918 with the collapse of the Ottoman Empire. It spent several decades more in tribal quarrels (it had more than 1,400 tribal groups). After the assassination of its first king in 1948, a son took Yemen into the camp of *radical* Arab states, associating closely with *Nasser* and then approaching the *Soviet bloc* directly and supporting anti-British rebels in Aden. Saudi Arabia *intervened* on the royalist side against *Nasser*'s Yemeni protégées in a succession struggle in 1962, when a *republic* was declared. That widened and prolonged a civil-tribal war which lasted until 1970, in which as many as 70,000 Egyptian troops were involved. The United States *recognized* the new Yemeni regime, but the United Kingdom at first refused. After a radical *rebellion* in Aden in 1967, the British withdrew and the People's Republic of Yemen (also known as South Yemen) was set up, absorbed Aden, and drew assistance from the Soviet Union and China. In 1979 it fought a brief war with its neighbor, and ethnic kin, provoked in part by several hundred thousand *refugees* who fled southern socialism for the wilder and freer north. It then signed a *friendship treaty* with Moscow, leading to stationing of Soviet troops in South Yemen and stalling an Arab League effort to bring about unification of the Yemens. In 1986 an uprising in South Yemen broke the Soviet tie, and in 1990 the erstwhile enemies formed a *union*. During the *Gulf War* Yemen lent diplomatic support to Iraq. That strained already uneasy relations with Saudi Arabia, which expelled one million Yemeni workers. In 1993 Yemen was accused by Egypt and the United States of fomenting *terrorism* by *fundamentalist* Muslims. The union was unstable: the urban and more cosmopolitan south had 3 million people and some *oil* reserves, and so was at odds with the 10 million Yemenis of the mostly rural, fundamentalist north. This cleavage led to another bloody civil war in 1994, as the south tried to secede. It was stopped from doing so by a fierce northern assault on Aden. Yemen entered the twenty-first century as one of the poorest societies in the world, largely dependent on remittances from expatriate citizens working abroad.

Yenan (Ya'anan). The large provisional area on China's western frontier which was controlled by, and served as the main base for, the Chinese *Communist Party* after the *Long March*. *See also Chinese Civil War.*

Yezhovshchina. "The Time of Yezhov." There were several terrible *purges* in Russia during the 1930s, all accompanied by huge *propaganda* campaigns, elaborate legal paraphernalia, and spectacular *show trials*, as well as many more secret trials. The bloodiest lasted from 1934 to 1938 and was named for Nikolai I. Yezhov (1894–1939), head of the *NKVD*, 1936–1938. Under *Stalin's* close direction, Yezhov slaughtered the top ranks of the *Communist Party* and beheaded the *Red Army* by savaging the *officer corps*. The principal victims were those senior officers associated with *Leon Trotsky's* command of the army, dating back to the *Russian Civil War*. Many of the new officers Stalin appointed were dolts or ideologues, or both. For instance, the head of *ordnance*, G. I. Kulik, opposed the use of automatic weapons by Soviet troops, issuing them only rifles instead, and banned outright the production of anti-tank and anti-aircraft guns. His ambition was to convert the Red Army into an all-infantry force supported by horse-drawn carts. Another post-Yezhovshchina appointee forbade the development of a Soviet tank corps, whereas still others simply had no idea how to command a modern division, corps, or army. The reduction in Soviet military effectiveness was dramatic. This was first exposed by initial and bloody failure of the Soviet assault on the *Mannerheim Line* during the *Finnish-Soviet War*. It nearly proved fatal to the regime in 1941: when *Hitler* launched his massive invasion of the Soviet Union (code-named *Barbarossa*) on June 22, 1941, the Red Army which faced the multiple *Panzer* divisions of three Nazi *armored* spearheads, and the massed and mechanized infantry of the lead units of the *Wehrmacht* and *Waffen SS*, was largely a weak-firepower infantry force near-totally dependent on horses for its transport and resupply. The result was mass encirclement, mass surrender, and mass panic in Soviet ranks during the first weeks and months of the *Great Patriotic War*. The purges also eliminated nearly all the *Old Bolsheviks*, wiped out whole classes of "state enemies" real or imagined, and utterly terrorized the populace. After serving as Stalin's willing and eager executioners, Yezhov and other top NKVD officers were themselves purged. Estimates vary, but Stalin's purges as a whole probably took 10 million lives (*Khrushchev's* number). A later KGB report said 20 million were arrested, of whom seven million had been shot. Overall, Stalin killed perhaps 20–25 million (consensus Western estimates) in purges, deliberate *famines*, and the forced labor camps of the *GULAG archipelago*; but he may have slaughtered as many as 40 million—that shocking figure is Soviet, compiled by the *KGB* and first released in 1989. *See also Lavrenti Beria; Sergey Kirov; Vyacheslav Molotov; Andrei Vyshinsky.*

Suggested Reading: Robert Conquest, *The Great Terror* (1990).

yield. A measure of the energy released by, and therefore the destructive power of, a *nuclear weapon* or any other explosive. *See also kiloton; megaton.*

Yom Kippur War. *See Fourth Arab-Israeli War.*

Yorktown, Battle of (October 19, 1781). After failing to pacify the Carolinas, a British Army under Cornwallis (1738–1805) moved into Virginia, specifically to the York peninsula. Cornwallis *fortified* Yorktown and settled in to await the arrival of reinforcements under Sir Henry Clinton, expected to arrive from New York. Meanwhile, a French battle fleet under De Grasse evaded *Rodney* in the Caribbean and sailed uncontested to Virginia, where it *blockaded* Chesapeake Bay and defeated a British squadron attempting to relieve Cornwallis. *Lafayette* was left in New York to hold off Clinton's men, while the main Continental Army under *George Washington*, reinforced by French allied troops, hurried to Yorktown to trap and besiege Cornwallis there. On Oct. 17, 1781, Cornwallis *asked for terms* and accepted to *surrender* two days later.

Yoruba. A West African people who, along with the *Ibo* and *Hausa*, are one of three dominant *tribes* in modern Nigeria. Yoruba also live in neighboring Benin and Togo. By 1400 the Yoruba were already organized in a complex system of *city-states* (Ekiti, Ijebu, Ife, Owu, Oyo), among which Ife was the oldest and culturally and religiously most significant. In 1535 the northern city-state of Oyo was overrun by Nupe, and its ruling family forced into nearly a century of exile in Borgu. In the mid-seventeenth century, however, possibly with aid from Borgu (to whose rulers the Oyo kings were related by *dynastic marriage*), Oyo developed a *cavalry* force which freed the city. Oyo then went on to conquer other Yoruba, as well as conquer south toward the *Slave Coast*, paralleling the forest where its cavalry lost the advantage. In the eighteenth century Oyo exacted *tribute* from *Dahomey*, which it first invaded and devastated, 1726–1730. In the early nineteenth century the rapid decline of Oyo occurred mainly as a result of a succession dispute that divided its governing classes and fed its people into the slave ships then still departing Lagos and other Slave Coast ports. Southern Yoruba states like Egba, Ijebu, and Ondo grew in strength from their coastal trade, while Ilorin declared its independence from Oyo in the 1790s and then maintained this assertion by calling upon *Hausa* and *Fulbe* mercenaries to hold off the Oyo counterattack. Ilorin's independence cut off Oyo from the northern trade as well. As its economy collapsed, additional Yoruba cities in the north came under Fulbe influence as a result of the great *jihad* of *Uthman dan Fodio*. In 1817 the outer cities broke their ties to Oyo, which was itself subsequently overrun by the now thoroughly Islamicized Yoruba city-state of Ilorin. Inter-city warfare among the Yoruba continued to feed the late Atlantic *slave trade*, as prisoners from the Yoruba wars were sold into *slavery* by their enemies. As that trade was progressively shut down, Yoruba slaves were transported to the desert markets up north. Many northern Yoruba converted to Islam as a result of the continuing power and jihads of the Fulbe through the remainder of the nineteenth century. Out of the breakup of the old Oyo empire two new cities were founded which grew to dominate Yorubaland culturally and economically during the twentieth century: Abeokuta and Ibadan. During the *Nigerian Civil War* the Yoruba (Western) region supported the Federal side. In 1993 there was great unrest among Yoruba over northern and military cancellation of the clear victory of one of their own as president, and wild rumors of possible secession. These came to naught.

Suggested Readings: J. F. A. Ajayi and Michael Smith, *Yoruba Warfare in the 19th Century* (1964); Robin Law, *The Oyo Empire, 1600–1836* (1977).

Yoshida Shigeru (1878–1967). Japanese prime minister, 1946–1947, 1949–1954. He served as a minor diplomat at the *Paris Peace Conference* and later as ambassador to Great Britain. Along with *Konoe*, from 1944 he tried to negotiate an end to *World War II*. After the war, he was a principal architect of pro-Western foreign and domestic policies, working closely with *MacArthur*. That led to astonishing electoral success for the *Liberal Party* in Japan and, more importantly, to a remarkable national recovery under conditions of exceptional economic and political difficulty. Like *Eisenhower*, his historical reputation improved after he left office, as appreciation of his real role and accomplishments set in. He accepted the *Japanese Peace Treaty* in 1951. The "Yoshida Doctrine" largely shaped Japan's postwar foreign policy. This saw Japan as highly constrained by the *Cold War* and ties to America and argued for carving out a niche in which Japan relied on economic power and diplomacy, rather than its military, to develop beneficial and stable relations with most major powers.

Suggested Reading: Richard Finn, *Winners in Peace* (1992).

Young Italy (Young Ireland, etc.). "Giovine Italia." Romantic, nineteenth-century nationalist and *liberal* movements in several European countries, all modeled on the original movement founded by *Mazzini*, which sought to establish independent, liberal *republics. See also Revolutions of 1848; Young Turks.*

Young Plan (1929). Named for Owen Young (1874–1962), an American who headed an international committee on German *reparations*, charged with revising the *Dawes Plan*. It proposed a further reduction of the amount owed by Germany and spacing out payments until 1988. The *Great Depression* rendered it moot, as the payment schedule was overtaken by a severe capital shortage and then *Nazi* refusal in 1933 to make any more reparations payments whatever. The Nazis used popular opposition to the Young Plan to great effect in two election campaigns before 1933.

Young Turks. "Committee on Union and Progress." (1) The movement of Turkish army officers founded c. 1889, which sought rapid *modernization* of the *Ottoman Empire*. In 1908 they took power, deposing the *sultan* from real authority while leaving him as a figurehead. Led by *Enver Pasha*, they intended to strengthen and revive the empire but instead took charge just in time to preside over its greatest humiliations: the loss of Bulgaria and Bosnia-Herzegovina in the *Balkan Wars* and then the catastrophe of *World War I*, as the Young Turks led the Empire into alliance with the *Central Powers*. That climactic war brought on the *Arab Revolt* and witnessed the *Armenian genocide*, though the Turks fought well at *Gallipoli* under *Atatürk*, and elsewhere, and led to final imperial defeat and dismemberment. Many participated in and indirectly led the *secularization* of Turkish politics and society after World War I. Some Armenian scholars blame the Young Turks above all others for the Armenian genocide, 1915–1922. (2) Anyone, especially if quite young, who is aggressive in advocating rapid social or political change.

Suggested Reading: Sükrü Hanioglu, *Preparation for a Revolution* (2000).

Ypres Salient, Battles of. From 1914 to 1918 this small, walled Belgian town witnessed three bloody battles over a loop in the lines which formed an Allied salient, overseen by German trenches on the heights of Passchendale and Gheluvelt.

(1) First Ypres (October 8–November 22, 1914): The Belgians fell back from Antwerp, flooded the area, and dug in alongside the *British Expeditionary Force* (BEF) just as the Germans attacked. The battle which ensued was near-continuous over six weeks and fought for ground which would be bloodied futilely twice more before the war's end. The main contest pitted 14 German volunteer divisions against seven British, including three dismounted cavalry divisions. When it was over, 50,000 Germans, mostly college student volunteers, were dead (this is remembered in Germany as the "Kindermond bei Ypern"). First Ypres is also bitterly remembered by British, who lost 24,000 killed, and Canadians and Indians, who also took heavy losses. First Ypres finished the prewar British regular army: Britain had to refill the empty ranks of the BEF with volunteers, and later with conscripts.

(2) Second Ypres (April 22–May 1, 1915): The German attack was designed to disguise a larger transfer of troops to the east. It commenced with the first ever use of lethal *gas* (chlorine, loosed from cylinders), which broke the line held by French Zouave and Algerian units; Canadian troops held, however, both on the evening of the 22nd and two days later when they were again gassed by the Germans. A third gas attack was launched against British troops on May 1st, but they also held their line.

(3) Third Ypres (July 31–November 10, 1917): Also known as "Passchendaele." With Russia leaving the war and the *French Army mutinies* paralyzing the French sectors, Britain alone struck at Germany. *Lloyd George* wanted to wait for American reinforcements, but *Douglas Haig* was unconvinced, even by his colossal defeat at the *Somme*, that frontal assault by massed infantry against an *entrenched* enemy was fatal mainly to the attackers. He therefore sent tens of thousands more to fruitless death in this rain-soaked, mud and blood offensive which focused on the village of Passchendale and saw attack

after attack come to naught. By September the brunt of "British" casualties were being taken by ANZAC and Canadian divisions. In addition to sheer bloodiness, the battle was notable for the first use of *mustard gas* on the *western front*, by the Germans. The Allies lost 70,000 dead and 170,000 wounded; the Germans lost about the same. *See also Bernard Montgomery.*

Suggested Readings: First Ypres: Anthony Farrar-Hockley, *Death of an Army* (1968, 1998); Second Ypres: Daniel Dancocks, *Welcome to Flanders Fields* (1988); Third Ypres: Robin Prior and Trevor Wilson, *Passchendaele* (1996); Nigel Steel and Peter Hart, *Passchendaele: The Sacrificial Ground* (2000); Leon Wolff, *In Flanders Fields* (1958, 1980).

Yuan dynasty (1279–1368). In 1211 Chinggis (Ghengis) Khan (1162–1227) launched the *Mongol* conquest of China, as well as its frontier neighbor the Jin Empire. Most of northern China was overrun between 1217 and 1223, with the Jin Empire succumbing in 1234. The Mongols conquered the *Southern Song* in 1279 and thereafter ruled all China until 1368. The first Yuan emperor was Kubilai Khan (1214–1294), grandson of Chinggis. The Mongols were seen by the Chinese—and with good reason—as barbarians, and were never accepted as possessors of the *mandate of heaven.* They racially classified the population, they favored Lama *Buddhism* and Shamanism in China over Chinese belief in *Confucianism* and *Daoism*, and they allowed the country to stagnate, not themselves having the wit to appreciate the sophistication and accomplishment of Chinese civilization. Efforts to rehabilitate their reputation are mostly unpersuasive: they took much and gave back nothing. Under the Mongols China's population declined precipitously, for reasons which are not entirely clear but must have related in part to inept administration, agriculture disturbed by constant warfare leading to famine, and forced migrations southward. The Mongols badly neglected China's infrastructure, failing to manage the Yellow River properly so that it catastrophically flooded in 1344, and allowing the Grand Canal to silt up. They ruled China for less than 100 years, through a corps of collaborators and by brute force, just as they ruled the rest of their vast empire. The Chinese imperial system was inherently despotic, but it was made more cruel by the Mongols, as the reign of their successor, *Hongwu* quickly demonstrated. The Yuan dynasts also used that huge land as the launch pad for a series of unsuccessful amphibious invasions of Japan—these were restless, nomadic fighters, not sedentary governors—as well as attempted invasions of northern Vietnam, Burma, Siam, and even Java. Their rule did have the effect of partly sinifying Mongolia, which they continued to govern. The Yuan dynasty collapsed under the weight of simultaneous Chinese peasant uprisings against them (Red Turban Rebellion) and a civil war among their own impoverished and unhappy horde. They were driven from China by the resurgent *Ming* in 1368. *See also culturalism.*

Suggested Readings: J. Langlois, ed., *China Under Mongol Rule* (1981); David Morgan, *The Mongols* (1986).

Yuan Shikai (1859–1916). "Father of the *warlords*." A minor *Qing* official in Korea, he rose to prominence and power as the trainer of China's New Army, which replaced the *banner troops* from 1901 under Dowager Empress *Cixi*, whom he assisted in suppressing the *Hundred Days* reform movement. Always the opportunist, he also suppressed the *Boxers* once it was clear they were going to lose to the foreign armies which had intervened in China. He used the position to seed the army with personal loyalists, and by 1910 he commanded the most professional force in China. Jealous of his growing influence in the army, the Qing court compelled him to retire in 1910. Qing officials turned to him for aid in their moment of darkest crisis, however, as an army *mutiny* broke out in Wuhan in 1911. Instead, he counseled and then arranged the abdication of *Pu Yi*. He replaced *Sun Yixian* as provisional president of the Chinese republic on February 13, 1912. Into 1913 he struggled with the new National Assembly, then engineered the assassination of the parliamentary leader of the Nationalist Party and seized full dictatorial powers for himself in March. He then abolished the National Assembly. In 1914 he further consolidated his power by abolishing all provincial assemblies. He failed to reign in provincial warlords, however, who began to challenge his—and then all—central authority over China. He ingratiated himself with Western powers and gained international *recognition* of his regime by pandering to their interests in *missionaries* and Chinese *Christian* converts, and specifically by formally acknowledging in late 1913 to the British the *autonomy* from China of Tibet, and to Russia the autonomy of Outer Mongolia. His reputation in China was damaged by the Japanese 1914 seizure of the German concession in *Shandong*; it was nearly shattered by the blow delivered by Tokyo when it presented him with the *Twenty-one Demands* the next year. Despite these humiliations, and in part owing to them, in 1915 he tried, but failed, to make himself emperor. Military governors declared their independence from his regime, as earlier they had done regarding the Qing. He tried to revoke his coronation, but to no avail. In the midst of the crisis he generated, he died of natural causes.

Suggested Reading: Ernest Young, *The Presidency of Yuan Shih-k'ai* (1977).

Yugoslavia. "South Slav State." It was created after *World War I* when the *Slav* areas of the *Austro-Hungarian Empire* (Bosnia, Croatia, and Slovenia) were free to attach themselves to Serbia and Montenegro, which formed the core of Yugoslavia. The country was put together in the *Pact of Corfu*, creating the United Kingdom of the Serbs, Croats and Slovenes, which was dominated by the Serbs. The name was officially changed to Yugoslavia in 1929. During the 1930s Yugoslavia drifted toward association with German policy, although it remained *neutral* in 1939. Because Yugoslavia stood between Germany and Greece, which *Mussolini* had invaded unsuccessfully, and following a Serbian coup which had pro-British implications, Germany and Italy invaded Yugoslavia on April 6, 1941. Within days, the country broke apart. Croats and Slovenes both declared independence of the Serb-dominated Yugoslav government and made a separate peace with *Hitler*. The army, one million strong, simply collapsed. Some units deserted to the new Croat and Slovene states, and almost no effective resistance was mounted against the *Nazi* invasion (fewer than 200 Germans soldiers were killed). During the remainder of *World War II*, however, resistance grew. Serb nationalist partisans (*Chetniks*) took to the mountains and fought the Germans, but they later also fought Serb communist partisans, led by *Tito*, who emerged in 1942 to also fight the Germans. During the war 1.5 million Yugoslavs were killed, the vast majority by fellow Yugoslavs. The British coordinated *Allied* policy in Yugoslavia. At first, London supported the Chetniks but later switched to Tito's communists. Meanwhile, *fascists* set up a Nazi *puppet state* in Croatia, setting off a vicious multisided civil war which was fought within the parameters of the larger conflict with Germany and Italy. Yugoslavia was divided among the *Axis* powers: Germans, Italians, Bulgarians, Hungarians, Croats, and Slovenes all took a slice.

With British aid and Allied *recognition*, at war's end Yugoslavia was restored and Tito—who was well placed with the Allies, especially the British, to set himself up as postwar leader—brutally and bloodily repressed all Chetnik and Croatian resistance and united the South Slavs in a federal, communist dictatorship. It was made up of six republics: *Bosnia, Croatia, Macedonia, Montenegro, Serbia,* and *Slovenia*. Yugoslavia's postwar communist regime had taken power under its own steam, without prior Soviet *occupation*. Hence, throughout the *Cold War* it maintained an agenda more independent of Moscow than any other European communist state, except for neighboring Albania. Its refusal to toe Stalin's *party line* after 1948 undermined support it gave Greek communists, then fighting in the Greek Civil War, and at times threatened to lead to a Soviet invasion. Tito's break with Stalin was much praised in the *West*, but little exploited with direct aid or imaginative diplomacy. In 1953, with *Stalin's* death, Yugoslav-Soviet relations *thawed*. Yugoslavia disputed control of *Trieste* with Italy until 1954 and then relinquished its claim. After 1955 Tito took a leading role in the *nonaligned movement*. Violence erupted among the various *ethnic groups* in 1968 and again in 1981 in *Kosovo*. Within a few years of Tito's death, during 1990–1991, Yugoslavia unraveled: Slovenia, Croatia, Bosnia, and Macedonia all dumped their communist governments and then severed ties to Serbia and Montenegro. There, communists recloaked as nationalists under *Slobodan Milošević* clung to power through a decade of war, international *sanctions*, and collapsing economic conditions, until overthrow of Serbia's communist regime in 2000. In *international law*, Serbia together with Montenegro retained legal title to the name "Yugoslavia," even after the departure of the other constituent republics meant that in everyday discourse the union was taken to be effectively defunct by c. 1995. The name was formally abandoned in 2002. *See also ethnic cleansing; Third Balkan War; successor states.*

Suggested Readings: Jasper Ridley, *Tito* (1994); Richard West, *Tito and the Rise and Fall of Yugoslavia* (1995).

Z

zaibatsu. Great industrial and banking *cartels*, semi-*feudal* in organization, which first appeared in Japan during the *Meiji* period and grew to dominate its economic life through the middle of the twentieth century, among them Mitsubishi, Mitsui (the oldest), Nissan, Sumitomo, and Yasuda. During the *Second Sino-Japanese War* (1937–1945), the zaibatsu were an integral part of Japan's imperial exploitation of Manchuria, Korea, and China, including the use of *forced labor*. After *World War II* American *occupation* authorities in *SCAP* sought to break up the zaibatsu, which they saw as an obstacle to rapid economic growth and political democracy. By 1947 this effort was set aside as U.S. policy shifted (*reverse course*) from fundamental reform of Japanese national life and political culture toward rapid *reconstruction* of the economy, so that a rebuilt Japan might serve as a bulwark against Soviet and *communist* penetration of Asia. In the end, of 1,200 zaibatsu slated for breakup only 28 were fully dismantled. Even so, the day of the zaibatsu passed. In their place rose new concentrations of corporate power (Honda, Sony, Toyota, and others) known as "keiretsu." *See also* chaebol; *Manchukuo; MITI.*

Zaire. From "Nzadi," the local name of the Congo River. Belgium constructed a huge colony in the former Kingdom of *Kongo*, known as "the Belgian Congo" until its independence as *Congo*. This name was changed to "Zaire" by *Mobutu* in 1971. It was changed back to Congo in 1997.

zakat. The main *Islamic* tax, required of all the faithful, payment of which constitutes one of the cardinal pillars of the faith. *See also* jizya.

Zambia. It was acquired for Britain by the machinations of *Cecil Rhodes*. As the *colony* of Northern Rhodesia, it was under the control of the British South Africa Company, 1889–1924. In 1924 it was made a crown *protectorate*. It was later merged into the *Federation of Rhodesia and Nyasaland*. The drive for Zambian independence was led by Kenneth Kuanda (b. 1924), who wished to break with white *settlers* who controlled Southern Rhodesia (later known as Rhodesia, then Zimbabwe). The *sovereign* republic of Zambia thus emerged in 1964. For its first several decades of independence Zambia was handicapped by being one of the *frontline states*, first concerning *UDI* in Rhodesia, then *apartheid* in South Africa. For decades, Kuanda ran Zambia as a *one-party state*, albeit a relatively moderate and gentle one. With the economy failing, in 1991 he was voted out, in favor of Frederick Chiluba. Nothing so became Kuanda's political life as the leaving of it: he departed office with considerable grace, indeed he provided something of a model for peaceful transition. He became a respected statesman and Zambia looked to its first multiparty political system. However, Chiluba quickly fell into the old, bad habits of tribal and urban favoritism and ingrained party corruption. The country also wrestled with *International Monetary Fund* insistence on basic economic reforms (*structural adjustment*), beginning in the 1990s. In 1998 Zambia strove to remain outside a building regional war in Congo, but it was drawn in after the MPLA government in Angola—an old regional adversary—sponsored a series of bomb attacks in Lusaka.

Suggested Reading: Andrew Roberts, *A History of Zambia* (1976).

Zanzibar. This east African island was home to the *Swahili Arabs*, who for 1,000 years controlled the East African *slave trade* with the Gulf States and India. It was managed by the local *sultans* who had close ties to *Oman*. Even *Ming* Chinese junks reached Zanzibar in the fifteenth century. In the sixteenth century Portuguese traders from Fort Jesus ran the Zanzibar trade. A rebellion occurred in 1632, but by 1635 Portuguese were back in control. An Omani fleet captured Zanzibar in 1652. Omani sultans then laid siege to Mombasa (Fort Jesus) in 1695, finally taking it in 1698. Portugal recaptured it briefly, 1728–1730, before it reverted to Arab control. Seyyid Said (r. 1806–1856), of Oman, introduced clove cultivation to Zanzibar and greatly diversified the economy. He also stepped up slave-raiding in the interior, while signing the Moresby Treaty (1822) with Great Britain prohibiting slaving east of a line drawn from the southernmost perimeter of his African holdings. He accepted this because he had to—the *Royal Navy* stood ready to act against the Indian Ocean trade—and thereby to save his ability to keep slaving west of the line. He reasserted Omani authority over Zanzibar's coastal possessions on the mainland, retaking Mombasa from local Arab potentates in 1837. In 1840 he transferred his capital there from Muscat. In 1845 Britain imposed further restrictions on Zanzibar slaving, and yet more in 1873.

From the 1860s to the 1890s, under *Tippu Tip*, Zanzibar's authority and influence nonetheless briefly penetrated deep into the interior in search of *ivory* and slaves. In 1873 the British persuaded the sultan to abolish *slavery* in his domains, which in turn encouraged Britain to support Zanzibar's territorial claims on the mainland. The British and Germans competed for trade concessions (cloves and clove oil replaced slaves) until 1890, when a British *protectorate* was established over Zanzibar in exchange for *concession on Heligoland* in the *Anglo-German Agreement*. Throughout the colonial period Britain technically "leased" the Kenya coast from the sultans; this ended with Kenya's independence. In 1963 Zanzibar, along with Pemba, joined the *Commonwealth* as a newly independent state. Within months the sultanate was overthrown by a *Marxist* coup. That led to a brief civil war, in which *Nyerere* intervened. Zanzibar then joined *Tanganyika* in the *union* of *Tanzania*. That gave it distinct advantages: it gained privileged access to the resources of the mainland without having to surrender its local *autonomy*: Tanganyikans by law could not hold office or own land on Zanzibar, but the reverse was not true. In 1993 it was learned that Zanzibar had secretly joined the *Islamic Conference*, violating the union constitution. *Julius Nyerere* mediated and persuaded Zanzibar to withdraw. The issue raised doubts about the permanence of the union.

Zapata, Emiliano (c. 1877–1919). Mexican revolutionary, agrarian reformer, and *guerrilla* leader, 1911–1916. A southern peasant by background, he fought independently from the other revolutionary leaders in the *Mexican Revolution*, though he cooperated importantly with *Pancho Villa*. He opposed *Venustiano Carranza* after it became clear the latter's dedication to *agrarian reform* was shallow. In November 1914 Carranza left Mexico City for Veracruz, and Villa occupied the capital, where he was soon joined by Zapata. The U.S. supplied Carranza with weapons which gave him a distinct advantage. Villa retired to the north. Meanwhile, Zapata withdrew his forces from Mexico City to his home province of Morelos. He retired from active fighting after 1916 to concentrate on his land reforms in the south. His rallying cry was: "Men of the south! It is better to die on your feet than to live on your knees!" Carranza's troops entered Morelos in 1916, and low-level fighting continued there for another three years. Zapata was ambushed and killed by troops loyal to *Carranza*, whom Zapata opposed. In 1994 peasant rebels in south Mexico (Chiapas province) styled themselves "Zapatistas" in memory of the agrarian revolution of bygone days. *See also Spanish Civil War.*

Suggested Readings: Samuel Brunk, *Emiliano Zapata: Revolution and Betrayal in Mexico* (1995); Frank McLynn, *Villa and Zapata: A Biography of the Mexican Revolution* (2000).

zealot. A Jewish resistance fighter opposed to rule of *Palestine* by the *Roman Empire*. *See also fanatic.*

Zeitgeist. The spirit of a given time or place, as in "the Zeitgeist of *interwar* France was one of *defeatism* and willful denial."

zemstvo. A system of local government set up in Russia by *Alexander II* after the abolition of noble councils in 1864. It promised, but never delivered, representative government. It was swept aside by the *Russian Revolutions of 1917*.

zeppelin. A class of large, hydrogen-filled dirigibles, named for its German inventor (Ferdinand von Zeppelin, 1838–1917). They were used in *World War I* for bombing missions against the English coast until 1916, in violation of the ban promulgated at the first *Hague Conference*. They were militarily ineffective, killing mainly *civilians*, and anti-zeppelin defenses soon made them too costly in crew lives to continue. However, the experience of city bombing further lowered *jus in bello* expectations and hardened attitudes toward the eventual *peace*. Their use as civilian passenger liners ended with the Hindenburg tragedy in Lakehurst, New Jersey, on May 6, 1937, which killed 36.

zeriba system. *See Mehemet Ali.*

zero hour. The time set to begin an attack.

zero population growth (ZPG). When the birth rate reaches replacement levels which match the death rate. In the 1990s *Malthusian* calamities in Africa ranging from floods and drought to the *AIDS* epidemic and multiple wars pushed the continent close to ZPG.

zero-sum game. *See game theory.*

Zhirinovsky, Vladimir Wolfovich (b. 1944). Russian politician and *fascist* buffoon. In elections in 1993, his Liberal Democratic Party (the name an utter malapropism) gained the most seats in post-Soviet Russia's first freely elected parliament (the State *Duma*), marshaling about 25 percent of the national vote and more in the army. That sent shock waves through Russia's reformers and Western capitals, as Zhirinovsky's views were both fascist and *imperialistic*. The latter did not matter in the short run, as Russia's ability to project *power* beyond the *near abroad* was more limited than before and historically discredited. His views boded ill, however, for hopes of democracy in Russia—which some began to compare to *Weimar Germany*. Also, his reckless speeches raised tensions in the *CIS* and made it less likely that Ukraine would give up its *nuclear weapons* and agree to *START*. One sample of his bombast was a threatening assertion that, if Japan demanded the *Kurils*, "I would bomb the Japanese. . . . If they so much as chirped I would nuke them." Within weeks he was expelled from Bulgaria for interfering in its politics and barred from Germany for associating with *neo-Nazis* and other reprobates. On the Duma's first day, he got in a fist fight in the cafeteria. By the end of the 1990s his political star had fallen. His name was still invoked, but mainly as a symbol of Russia's persistent backwardness and occasional fatal attraction to thuggish leaders.

Zhivkov, Todor (1911–1998). Leader of the Bulgarian *communist Party*, 1954–1989, and the most powerful man in Bulgaria for most of four decades, first as party leader, 1954–1962, next as premier, 1962–1971, and lastly as president, 1971–1989. He was the longest-surviving East European communist leader. He led the communist coup against the Bulgarian monarchy in 1944 and thereafter rose through the *apparat*, and in the favor of Moscow, to whose *party-line* he always tightly adhered. He cooperated closely with Soviet foreign policy. His doctrinaire socialism kept his country among the most *hard line*, and therefore also backward, of all *Soviet bloc* states. Zhivkov tried to develop a *cult of personality*, but he just didn't have the personality to pull it off. He was forced out on November 10, 1989, during the *revolutions of 1989*. Convicted of corruption in 1992, he was pardoned—officially for reasons of ill-health—in 1996.

Zhou Enlai (1899–1976). Prime minister of China 1949–1976; foreign minister, 1949–1958. He was from a *Confucian*-educated family, but also studied briefly in Japan, France, and Germany, where he took a German mistress (with whom he later corresponded for more than 40 years) and fathered a child. In 1924 he returned to China and joined the Whampoa Military Academy, then commanded by *Chiang Kai-shek*. He was a *Communist Party* (CCP) organizer in Shanghai, leading up to the *Shanghai massacres* in April 1927. In 1935, during the *Long March*, he entered a role he played the rest of his life: the main adviser to *Mao Zedong*, who had been his military subordinate. Henceforth, he was also the principal *Communist* envoy in negotiations with the Nationalists and with any foreign powers. He met with the detained Chiang Kai-shek during the *Xi'an incident* (December 1936), finally persuading him to join forces against Japanese *aggression*. He then served as CCP liaison to the *Guomindang* during the *Second Sino-Japanese War* and *World War II*, and to the United States delegation in China, 1945–1947. With the *Chinese Revolution* (1949), his face and voice became nearly synonymous with China's foreign policy for nearly three decades. He played a key role on the Chinese side during the *Korean Conflict*, in negotiating the *Geneva Accords*, where he dealt directly with *John Foster Dulles*, at *Bandung*, and during the long *Vietnam War*. He moved China away from alliance with the Soviet Union as the *Sino-Soviet split* widened.

Once seen in the West as a gentler Chinese leader and a moderating influence, it later became clear from documentary evidence that he had in fact acted as Mao's attack dog in party power struggles and played a full role in instigating and carrying out several bloody purges. He also welcomed many aspects of the *Great Proletarian Cultural Revolution*, though he did act to restrain radicals such as the *Gang of Four* and eventually headed the more pragmatic wing of the Party. Given that background, even Zhou could be seen as a moderate, *realist*, and pragmatist in foreign policy. That view was confirmed for the West when he, *Richard Nixon*, and *Henry Kissinger* engineered a *détente* between the United States and China in 1972. In 1973 he anointed *Deng Xiaoping* to be his successor as premier. Zhou died just nine months before Mao. At his *funeral*, the *Gang of Four* tried to block public celebrations of his life achievements and briefly *purged* Deng Xiaoping. The Chinese public felt differently, gathering in his memory during the *Tiananmen Square incident* of April 4, 1976. In the end Zhou's policies won out, under Deng. Zhou's 48 years on the *Politburo* were unmatched by any Communist leader, anywhere. His adopted son, *Li Peng*, rose to become premier of China, 1988–1998. *See also biological warfare.*

Suggested Readings: Thomas Kampen, *Mao Zedong, Zhou Enlai and the Evolution of the Chinese Communist Leadership* (2000); Kuo-kang Shao, *Zhou Enlai and the Foundations of Chinese Foreign Policy* (1996); Dick Wilson, *Zhou Enlai* (1984).

Zhu De (1886–1976). He spent time in the Imperial Army, and then as a *mercenary* in the service of northern *warlords*. During the chaos of the *Chinese Revolution* of 1911 he led an invasion of Sichuan province. As a warlord himself after the death of *Yuan Shikai*, Zhu was rich, powerful, and an *opium* addict. He eventually overcame the addiction and traveled to Europe to study modern military methods. In Germany he met *Zhou Enlai* and became a *communist*. He next helped found and commanded the *People's Liberation Army*. He joined *Mao's* faction in 1928 and commanded in the *Jiangxi Soviet*. There he developed successful *guerrilla* tactics to defend against the *bandit suppression campaigns* launched against the Communists by the Nationalist Army under *Chiang Kai-shek*. At first quite successful, Zhu was ordered to fight a set piece battle against the Nationalists in 1934. His troops suffered a major defeat and were thus forced to begin the epic *Long March* to safe havens in northern China. Zhu took charge of the Eight Route Army during the march, leading it on a meandering, 5,000-mile retreat which stands as one of the most remarkable feats of recorded military history. He remained in command of Communist forces during the *Second Sino-Japanese War*. His "hundred regiments" campaign against the Japanese was no more successful than his earlier effort at *conventional warfare* against the Nationalists, and he turned back to tested guerrilla tactics. His army eventually numbered close to one million troops. He fought the *Guomindang* again when the *Chinese Civil War* resumed from 1945 to 1949. Under Mao, Zhu was minister of defense, 1949–1955. He oversaw the dispatch of hundreds of thousands of Chinese "volunteers" to the *Korean Conflict*. He became a marshal of the People's Republic in 1955. Despite his stellar record, he was publicly criticized and shamed during the *Great*

Proletarian Cultural Revolution. He subsequently underwent *"rehabilitation." See also Lin Biao; Nguyên Võ Giáp; Giorgii Zhukov.*

Zhukov, Giorgii Konstantinovich (1896–1974). Soviet marshal. Zhukov served as a conscript in the Imperial Russian Army during *World War I.* He fought well and was twice decorated for bravery. During the *Russian Civil War* he joined the *Bolsheviks,* fighting with the *Red Army.* He studied secretly in Germany during the 1920s. He defeated the Japanese in an undeclared border war along the Khalka river in July–August 1939. Thereafter, Tokyo's imperial ambitions turned from *Siberia* toward Southeast Asia. He became one of the preeminent commanders of *World War II,* directing the defense of Smolensk and Leningrad during the onslaught of *Operation Barbarossa* in 1941. He also designed the massive, desperate Russian counterattack at Moscow, starting on December 8th, 1941. And he planned and commanded in the several great Russian *counterattacks* of 1942–1945, including *Stalingrad* and *Kursk.* In those huge battles, where *armor* and *artillery* played a major role, he made brilliant use of the instruction in tank warfare he had gained from German officers during the secret German-Soviet military cooperation of the 1920s. Not all his plans worked, however: he suffered a terrible defeat in 1942 in Operation Mars, losing more than 300,000 men; he also took heavy casualties during the *Battle of Berlin.* He accepted the German surrender in behalf of the Soviet Union on May 8, 1945. After the war he oversaw the Soviet *occupation zone* in Germany, getting along well with his American counterpart, *Lucius Clay.* Zhukov was rewarded for his enormously important national service with a demotion, which was far less than had happened to *Stalin's* other prominent generals and potential rivals during the terrible years of the *Yezhovshchina.* Zhukov rose to become minister of defense under *Khrushchev,* 1955–1957. He probably saved Khrushchev's premiership in June 1957, when he used military aircraft to fly in supporters and forestall an anti-Khrushchev vote in the Central Committee of the *Communist Party.* Zhukov was abruptly sacked by Khrushchev within a few months anyway; just like Stalin, most successive Soviet leaders feared prominent, potential rivals in the military. Zhukov lived his last 17 years in dull retirement. *See also Lin Biao; Nguyên Võ Giáp; Zhu De.*

Suggested Readings: Otto P. Chaney, *Zhukov,* 2nd ed. (1996); David M. Glantz, *Zhukov's Greatest Defeat* (1999); Georgii K. Zhukov, *Memoirs of Marshal Zhukov* (1969).

Zia ul-Haq, Muhammad (1924–1988). President of Pakistan, 1978–1988. He led the *coup* which toppled *Zulfikar Ali Bhutto,* whom he had hanged despite widespread international protests. He established a ruthless dictatorship, which routinely used *torture* and killings of political opponents. He further *Islamicized* Pakistan, introducing elements of the *sharia.* He did not go as far as revolutionary regimes in Iran or Sudan. Despite a turn to the Islamic right, after the Soviet Union's invasion of Afghanistan he quickly moved to improve relations with the United States, agreeing to act as a transit for arms to the Afghan *mujahadeen*. In exchange, Pakistan became a major recipient of U.S. *aid*, running into the billions of dollars, some of which Zia used to finance secret research into the production of *nuclear weapons*. For that, Washington cut off aid in 1990. Zia was assassinated on August 17, 1988: his plane was blown out of the sky, by a bomb or a *surface-to-air missile*. The U.S. ambassador and many top Pakistani military and civilian leaders were also killed. It is still not known, publicly, who the assassins were.

Ziegfried Line. A line of fortified positions protecting Germany itself, along the *western front* in *World War II*. It was feared by the *Allies* that punching through it would be terribly costly, but when they got there they found its defenses had been neglected, or stripped down to feed the German war effort on other fronts. It did not significantly slow the advance of *Patton's* American Third Army into southern Germany, and on to western Czechoslovakia.

Zimbabwe, Republic of. Formerly called Southern Rhodesia, then Rhodesia, and finally renamed for *Great Zimbabwe. Cecil Rhodes* first penetrated the area in 1891. It was made into a *charter colony* in 1897 after subjugation of the African population. It was run by and for the British South Africa Company until taken over by Britain in 1923. Thereafter it was linked to two other British colonies, Northern Rhodesia (Zambia) and Nyasaland (Malawi). Godfrey Huggins (1883–1971) was prime minister of Southern Rhodesia, 1933–1953, and of the Central African Federation, 1953–1956. He was a strong supporter of the tie to Britain, but also of cooperation with neighboring black-ruled states, this in spite of his personal racial prejudice. His successors did not display the same flexibility or imagination, or his ability to overcome their baser racial views. Instead, they reserved most land for whites-only ownership, progressively impoverishing and disenfranchising a growing population. In 1961, with winds of change blowing over Africa, Rhodesia's whites (about 220,000 versus an African population of four million) entrenched their privileges in a revised constitution. Their intransigence led to the breakup of the *Federation of Rhodesia and Nyasaland.*

On November 11, 1965, prime minister Ian Smith made a *Unilateral Declaration of Independence* (UDI), to preempt a proposed settlement by Britain which would have enfranchised the black majority. Britain obtained United Nations agreement to *sanctions*, at first on *oil*, but by 1968 on all trade. London resisted calls for military intervention. Several black *guerrilla* groups waged a campaign against the illegal Smith regime, which was supported by South Africa and Portugal, until the latter's collapse into domestic revolution in 1974, powers which also refused to support the sanctions. By 1978 the independence of Portuguese Africa, the corrosive effect of even partial sanctions, and escalation of the conflict by the guerrillas forced a *power-sharing* agreement on the whites. Independence, under the name "Zimbabwe," followed in April 1980, accompanied by considerable United Nations political assistance. The most unreconstructable whites departed the country, emigrating mainly to Australia, Britain, Canada, or South Africa, in each of which their unrepentant attitudes worsened race relations. Black *majority rule* was qualified by a quota of reserved seats for whites. Race-based representation was ended in 1987. Joshua Nkomo led his Ndebele people in the struggle against UDI in Rhodesia, but he lost the 1980 election to a self-proclaimed *Marxist* and fellow guerrilla leader, *Robert Mugabe*, under whom Zimbabwe was converted into a *one-party state*.

For a time, constitutional agreements were kept, but during the 1990s they were discarded in favor of Mugabe's personal and party dictatorship. Nonetheless, Zimbabwe gained prestige within Africa as a leader among *frontline* states in the struggle against *apartheid*, and in the *Commonwealth* regarding British reluctance to introduce full sanctions against South Africa. In 1990 the *state of emergency* he had earlier declared was ended, but thereafter his authoritarian rule actually worsened. In 1998 Zimbabwe's economy collapsed under the weight of the regime's gross mismanagement, extensive corruption, and Mugabe's expensive intervention in a regional war centered in Congo. The cost in lives and treasure of this *adventurism* caused violent demonstrations in Harare. By 2000 the country was in a deep crisis, worsened by forced and illegal seizures of (third- and fourth-generation) white-owned farms by "war veterans," rural and tribal thugs backed by Mugabe whose main target was really black political opposition in the cities.

Zimmermann Telegram (1917). A poorly coded message sent on January 19, 1917, by the German Foreign Minister, Arthur Zimmermann (1864–1940), to his ambassador (Bernstorff) in Mexico City. It was intercepted by British naval *intelligence* and given to the *State Department* (which had intercepted it independently) on February 24th. In the event of an American-German war, Berlin offered Mexico a formal alliance and recovery of territories lost in the *Mexican-American War*, to wit: Arizona, California, and New Mexico, as well as Texas. The message also hinted at a Japanese alliance, suggesting to the Mexicans that the United States might find itself in a three-front war (Europe, Mexico, and the Philippines). Its transparent intention was to tie down American forces, and public opinion, in a local war in order to forestall a decisive U.S. intervention in *World War I* in Europe. Germany had some reason to hope for this outcome, as the enormous turmoil attendant on the *Mexican Revolution* (1911) had already twice drawn in United States forces: in 1914 *Woodrow Wilson* had occupied Veracruz, and in 1916 he ordered the U.S. Army to chase *Pancho Villa* back into Mexico, where it remained into 1917. Moreover, Wilson was already deeply concerned about Japan's aggressive intentions toward China, as revealed in Tokyo's infamous *Twenty-one*

Demands (1915). Having sincerely tried to play honest broker to the Great Powers of Europe, including Germany, he was appalled by Zimmermann's misguided and hostile missive. He responded by ordering arming of the U.S. *merchant marine*, a forward measure he had resisted even after Berlin's earlier announcement (January 31, 1917) of resumption of unrestricted submarine warfare. Publication of the "Zimmermann Telegram" on March 1st further aroused anti-German feeling, already stirred up over unrestricted submarine warfare, until the national mood built to a war pitch. Wilson asked Congress for a *declaration of war* on Germany on April 2nd and received it four days later.

Suggested Reading: Barbara Tuchman, *The Zimmermann Telegram* (1959).

Zinoviev, Gregori (1883–1936). *Old Bolshevik.* A prominent activist and aide to *Lenin*, he was appointed to head the COMINTERN in 1918. He reputedly wrote the "Zinoviev Letter" (which most likely was fraudulent) to British Communists and Labour leaders, urging them to foment *revolution*. That had a positive impact on the *Tory* vote in the 1924 election which brought down Labour. After Lenin's death Zinoviev briefly formed a triumvirate with Stalin and Lev Borisovich Kamenev (né Rosenfeld, 1883–1936). He broke with Stalin in 1926, allying with *Trotsky*. He recanted in 1928, but was purged anyway in 1935 on a (darkly ironic) charge of making foreign plots and of complicity in the murder of *Kirov*. He was shot in 1936.

Zionism. A cultural-political movement for the establishment of a national homeland for Jews, which spoke to the deep yearnings of millions. Migration from Europe began spontaneously in response to the *pogroms* against Jews conducted in Russia from 1881 onward, with increasing ferocity. Those outrages would eventually drive nearly two million Jews out of Russia, over a 30-year period, with most settling in the United States. Movement to settle in *Palestine* was at a trickle until Theodore Herzl (1860–1904) published "The Jewish State" in 1896, partly in response to the revelation by the *Dreyfus Affair* of just how deep was *anti-Semitism* in France as well, at the close of the nineteenth century. Zionism was not a uniform movement: it had secular and religious variants, as well as *conservative* and *socialist* ones. Ultimately, enough Jewish emigrants *voted with their feet* for the historic homeland, Palestine, that their numbers were noticed and the idea of a Jewish homeland there started to look achievable. The movement was greatly spurred by the *Balfour Declaration* (1917), and its main goal was of course achieved with creation of the State of Israel in 1948. Zionism—which continued to inspire a minority of world Jewry to emigrate to Israel under the *law of return*—was condemned as a "form of racism" in a contentious and propagandistic *United Nations General Assembly* resolution passed in 1975, which outraged many in the West. The resolution was repealed in 1991. There are also some Christian Zionists, who tend to be *fundamentalists* and biblical literalists who support Jewish migration

to Israel in expectation that re-establishment of the Jewish state is in fulfill-ment of Biblical prophesy, and presages both the imminent occurrence of Armageddon and their own elevation come the Judgment Day. *See also David Ben-Gurion; Jewish Agency; Irgun; Stern Gang; Chaim Weizmann.*
   Suggested Reading: Benny Morris, *Righteous Victims* (1999).

Zog I (a.k.a. Zogu I), né Ahmed Bey Zogu (1895–1961). He served in the Austrian Army in *World War I*; Albanian minister of war, 1921; premier, 1922–1924; president, 1925–1928; and king, 1928–1939. He pursued a policy of close collaboration with *Mussolini*, which did not save him or Albania from Italian *invasion* in 1939. He lobbied the *Allies* for *recognition* and restoration of the monarchy, but events on the ground in Albania (a successful com-munist *guerrilla* campaign against the *Axis* occupiers) prevented his return after *World War II.*

Zollverein. "Toll Union." (1) A *customs union* set up by Prussia with its neighbors in a formal treaty in 1833 and deeply influenced by the economic theories of Friedrich List (1789–1846). It had begun to germinate in 1818, when Prussia enacted a common *tariff* and nearby German states adjusted their tariffs to the Prussian rates. The 1833 treaty abolished all internal tolls within the common market it created and erected a common external tariff, aimed in good measure at excluding Austria from Germany's economic de-velopment. The Zollverein also facilitated *railway* and road construction across borders. This helped launch a period of German economic advance under Prussian leadership characterized by deliberate emulation of the legal, intellectual, and industrial order taking shape in Britain, Belgium, and France, including building of the core *infrastructure* which made modern Germany a leading industrial nation. Under *Bismarck* it came to include all the North German states, and after the *Seven Weeks' War*, the south German states as well. (2) A proposed customs union in 1931 between Austria and Germany, which was forbidden by the treaties of *Versailles* and *St. Germain*. The case was taken to the *Permanent Court of International Justice* at the Hague, which decided against union.

"zone of peace." Any region or grouping of states where the expectation of war is negligible, as a result of the *"democratic peace."*

Zone of Peace, Freedom and Neutrality (ZOPFAN). In 1971 ASEAN pro-claimed the subregion made up of its members to be such a (vaguely defined) zone, in an effort to insulate it from both the *Cold War* and the *Vietnam War*. In 1992 ASEAN proposed another ZOPFAN for the *Spratlys*. The one for ASEAN proper did not require *demilitarization*, whereas that for the Spratlys would have barred China from claiming *uti possidetis*. Both zones thus are little more than a hybrid of *propaganda* and wishful thinking. *See also buffer zone; DMZ; neutral zone.*

Z-Plan. In 1935 the *Anglo-German Naval Agreement* freed Germany from most prior constraints on the size of its surface fleet. In 1938 *Hitler* threw away all remaining reservations and laid out his Z-Plan—which violated the 1935 agreement—for construction of a surface fleet capable of challenging the *Royal Navy* for supremacy in the North Sea and Atlantic. Happily, this was a major strategic mistake on Hitler's part, as it wasted years of production time which Germany might have used building *submarines* (*U-boats*). It was only when *Dönitz* took command of the Kriegsmarine that construction of major surface ships was stopped and all production and combat crews shifted into creation of a 300-strong fleet of *U-boats*. *See also Anglo-German naval arms race; Battle of the Atlantic; convoy; dreadnought.*

Zulu. A composite *Nguni* people of southern Africa originating as a small group in Natal within the domain of Dingiswayo (r. 1800?–1818), king of the Mthethwa. In 1816 the Zulu were united under *Shaka*, a lieutenant and regimental commander under Dingiswayo and a member of the Zulu royal family. Shaka had grown up as an impoverished and shunned youth, and the Zulu as one of many small groups conquered by Dingiswayo. Through blood and war, Shaka forged the Zulu into a dominant Nguni nation and a military despotism. Like the Swazi, the Zulus had responded to regional overpopulation in the late eighteenth century by organizing into regiments ("impi"), whose members were not permitted to marry until they retired from the service at about age 40. Shaka inherited this system and reformed it to establish a severe military dictatorship and state. Shaka took the impi organization, infused it with his own ruthless military genius, and inflicted the *Mfecane* on the other Nguni peoples of the region. The Zulu later fought the *Boers* of the *Great Trek*, and under *Cetewayo*, fought the British in the *Zulu Wars*. In the decade after their defeat by the British the Zulu fell out in a protracted civil war. Some Zulu impi even joined with British troops to defeat other Zulu. Born in war and dynastic conflict, the Zulu never settled their internal differences and therefore faced the Boer and the British throughout the nineteenth century always as a divided and internally unstable nation. The Zulu nation thus succumbed toward the close of the nineteenth century as much to their own internal divisions as to the superior military technology and greater firepower of European arms. Absorbed into the *Union of South Africa*, under *apartheid*, and after, these divisions continued. Some Zulu, mainly those still concentrated in Natal province of South Africa and in KwaZulu, one of the former tribal *Bantustans*, supported *Inkatha*. Many others preferred and joined the non-tribal *African National Congress*.
Suggested Reading: John Laband, *The Rise and Fall of the Zulu Nation* (1998).

Zululand. Part of northeast Natal, now in South Africa.

Zulu Wars. The *Zulu* nation was born out of intertribal conflict in southern Africa, then hardened by *Shaka* in the great and bloody upheaval known as the *Mfecane*. There followed intermittent conflict with Boer settlers during and after the *Great Trek*. Boer ascendancy was driven home at Blood River (1838), where 3,000 Zulu warriors fell to Boer rifles. A regional *Pax Britannica* was maintained until the 1870s, when three more Zulu wars broke out. Under King *Cetewayo*, Zulu warriors raided Boer settlements in the *Transvaal*. The Boers appealed to the British in *Cape Colony* and *Natal* for protection. On his own initiative, the British *high commissioner* sent an armed expedition against the Zulu. It was surprised and its full complement (1,600 men) wiped out at the Battle of *Isandlwana* (1879). Meanwhile, a small contingent of Welsh held off a Zulu force of some 5,000 at nearby Rorke's Drift. Isandlwana provoked British public opinion, forcing the hand of a reluctant government in London. Some 17,000 British regulars were sent as reinforcements to southern Africa. With their superior firepower—rifles, artillery, and *machine guns* versus the Zulu "assagai" (short, stabbing spear) and rawhide shields—these troops exacted the Queen's revenge for Isandlwana, and then some. There were minor conflicts in 1888 and again in 1906, but in fact by 1880 the Zulu were already beaten.

    Suggested Readings: David Clammer, *The Zulu War* (1973, 1989); John Laband, *Kingdom in Crisis: The Zulu Response to the British Invasion of 1879* (1992); J. D. Omer-Cooper, *The Zulu Aftermath* (1966).

Select Bibliography

SERIAL PUBLICATIONS

Africa Today (1991–).
American Journal of International Law.
British Yearbook of International Law.
CIA World Factbook (1981–).
Current History.
Diplomacy and Statecraft.
Diplomatic History.
The Economist.
Ethics and International Affairs.
Foreign Affairs.
Foreign Policy.
International History Review.
International Journal of African History.
International Security.
Jane's Armor and Artillery (1980–).
Jane's Fighting Ships (1897–).
Jane's Intelligence Review (1991–).
Journal of African History.
Journal of Asian Affairs.
Journal of Asian Civilizations.
Journal of Asian History.
Journal of Central Asia.
Journal of European Studies.
Journal of Pacific History.
Journal of Southeast Asian Studies.
Le Monde diplomatique (1954–).

New York Times.
New York Times Electronic Archive.
Russian Review.
Slavic Review.
Wall Street Journal
World History Bulletin.

GENERAL HISTORIES

Cambridge Economic History of India, T. Raychaudhuri and Irfan Habib, eds., 2 vols. (1982).

Cambridge History of Africa, J. D. Fage and Roland Oliver, gen. eds., 8 vols. (1975–1986).

Cambridge History of American Foreign Relations, Warren I. Cohen, ed., 4 vols. (1993).

Cambridge History of the British Empire, 2nd edition (1963).

Cambridge History of British Foreign Policy, William A. Ward, ed., 3 vols. (1922–1923; 1971).

Cambridge History of Early Inner Asia, Denis Sinor, ed. (1990).

Cambridge History of India (1922).

Cambridge History of Iran, 7 vols. (1968–1991).

Cambridge History of Islam, 2 vols., P. M. Holt, Ann K. S. Lambton, and Bernard Lewis, eds. (1970).

Cambridge History of Japan, 6 vols., John W. Hall et al., gen. eds. (1989–1999).

Cambridge History of Latin America, vols. 1–5; vol. 6, pt. 1; vols. 7–8, vol. 11, Leslie Bethell, ed. (1984–1995).

Cambridge History of Modern France, 8 vols. (1983–1993).

Cambridge History of the Pacific Islanders, Donald Denoon, ed. (1997).

Cambridge History of Southeast Asia, 2 vols., Nicholas Tarling, ed. (1999).

Chambers's Biographical Dictionary, J. O. Thorne, ed., new edition (1961; rev. 1963).

Jane's Air War (1997).

Jane's Historic Military Aircraft (1998).

Jane's Strategic Weapons Systems (1999).

Jane's War at Sea, 1897–1997 (1997).

New Cambridge History of India, Gordon Johnson, gen. ed. (1987–).

Oxford History of the American People, Samuel Eliot Morison (1965; 1994).

Oxford History of Australia, 2nd edition, Geoffrey Bolton, gen. ed. (1996–).

Oxford History of Britain, rev. ed. Kenneth O. Morgan, ed. (2001).

Oxford History of the British Empire, 2 vols., Wm. Roger Lewis, ed. (1998).

Oxford History of Christianity, John McManners, ed. (1993).

Oxford History of the Classical World, John Boardman et al., eds. (1988–).

Oxford History of the Crusades, Jonathan Riley-Smith, ed. (1999).

Oxford History of England, 16 vols. (1936–1993).

Oxford History of the French Revolution, William Doyle, ed. (1989).

Oxford History of India, 4th ed., Percival Spear, ed. (1981).

Oxford History of Islam, John Esposito, ed. (1999).

Oxford History of Italy, George Holmes, ed. (1997).

Oxford History of Medieval Europe, George Holmes, ed. (1992).

Oxford History of the Roman World, John Boardman et al., eds. (1991).
Oxford History of South Africa, 2 vols., Monica Wilson and Leonard Thompson, eds. (1969–1971).
Oxford History of the Twentieth Century, Michael Howard and Wm. Roger Louis, eds. (1998).
Oxford History of the United States, 10 vols. (1928–1999; 1999–).

OFFICIAL PUBLICATIONS

European Commission, *Law in Humanitarian Crises*, 2 vols. (1995).
Soviet Union, *Soviet Documents on Foreign Policy, 1917–1941*, 3 vols. Jane Degras, ed. (1951).
United Nations. *Official Records.*
———. *Treaty Series.*
———. *Yearbook of the United Nations.*
———. Department of Public Information. *The Blue Helmets: A Review of United Nations Peacekeeping* (1990; 1996).
United Nations Educational, Scientific, and Cultural Organization (UNESCO). *General History of Africa*, 2 vols. (1981).
United States, Department of State. *American Foreign Policy: Basic Documents.*
———. *American Foreign Policy: Current Documents.*
———. *The Brest-Litovsk Peace Conference.* GPO (1918).
———. *Bulletin.*
———. *Country Reports on Human Rights Practices.*
———. *Current Policy.*
———. *Digest of International Law.*
———. *Nazi-Soviet Relations: Documents From The Archives of the German Foreign Office.* GPO (1948).
———. *Notes Exchanged on the Russian-Polish Situation.*
———. *Papers Relating to the Foreign Relations of the United States* (1867–).
———. *Postwar Foreign Policy Preparation, 1939–1945.* GPO (1948).
United States, President. *A Compilation of the Messages and Papers of the Presidents.*
———. *Public Papers of the Presidents of the United States.*
———. *Report on the United Nations* (1946+).
United States, Secretary of State. *Treaties and Other International Acts Series.*
———. *United States Foreign Policy: Documents.*
World Bank. *Annual Reports.*

SECONDARY WORKS

Abernethy, David. *Dynamics of Global Dominance* (2000).
Abir, Mordecai. *Ethiopia in the Era of the Princes, 1769–1855* (1968).
Abu-Lughod, Ibrahim, ed. *The Transformation of Palestine* (1971; 1987).
Acheson, Dean. *Present at the Creation* (1969).
Adams, W. Y. *Nubia: Corridor to Africa* (1977).
Adeleye, R. A. *Power and Diplomacy in Northern Nigeria, 1800–1906* (1972).
Adloff, R. *The Western Saharans* (1989).

Adshead, S. A. M. *Central Asia in World History* (1994).

Agawa, Hiroyuki. *The Reluctant Admiral: Yamamoto and the Imperial Navy* (1979).

Ahmed, A. S. *Jinnah, Pakistan, and Islamic Identity* (1997).

Ajayi, J. F. A., and Michael Crowder, eds. *Historical Atlas of Africa* (1985).

———, eds. *History of West Africa*, 2 vols. (1974).

———, and Michael Smith. *Yoruba Warfare in the 19th Century* (1964).

Alam, Muzaffar, and Sanjay Subrahmanyan. *The Mughal State, 1526–1750* (1998).

Alba, Victor. *Peru* (1977).

Aldcroft, Derek, and Anthony Sutcliffe, eds. *Europe in the International Economy, 1500–2000* (1999).

Alden, John. *A History of the American Revolution* (1969).

Aldrich, Robert. *Greater France* (1997).

Alexander, John. *Catherine the Great* (1988).

Alexander, Martin. *French History Since Napoleon* (1999).

Allen, Paul C. *Phillip III and the Pax Hispanica, 1598–1621: The Failure of Grand Strategy* (2000).

Allen, Peter. *The Yom Kippur War* (1982).

Allmand, Christopher. *The Hundred Years' War* (1988).

Almedingen, E. *The Emperor Alexander II* (1962).

Alpers, A. *Ivory and Slaves in East Central Africa* (1975).

Alter, Peter. *The German Question and Europe* (2000).

Ambrose, Stephen. *Nixon* (1987).

———. *Eisenhower*, 2 vols. (1984).

Ambrosius, Lloyd. *Wilsonian Statecraft* (1991).

Amitai-Preiss, Reuven, and David Morgan, eds. *The Mongol Empire and Its Legacy* (1999).

Andaya, Barbara, and Leonard Andaya, *A History of Malaysia*, 2nd ed. (2001).

Anderson, Fred. *The Crucible of War: The Seven Years' War and the Fate of Empire in British North America, 1754–1766* (2000).

Anderson, Matthew S. *The War of the Austrian Succession, 1740–1748* (1995).

———. *The Eastern Question, 1774–1923* (1966; 1987).

Andersson, Ingvar. *A History of Sweden* (1975).

Andrew, Christopher. *Intelligence and International Relations* (1987).

———, and Oleg Gordievsky. *KGB* (1990).

———, and Vasili Mitrokhin. *The Sword and the Shield: The Mitrokhin Archive and the Secret History of the KGB* (1999).

Andrien, Kenneth, and L. L. Johnson. *Political Economy of Latin America in the Age of Revolution, 1750–1850* (1994).

Angold, Michael. *The Byzantine Empire, 1025–1204* (1997).

Anstey, Roger. *The Atlantic Slave Trade and British Abolition, 1710–1810* (1975).

———. *King Leoplod's Legacy: The Congo Under Belgian Rule, 1908–1960* (1966).

Anzulovic, Branimir. *Heavenly Serbia: From Myth to Genocide* (1999).

Armstrong, David. *Revolution and World Order* (1993)

———, and Erik Goldstein, eds. *The End of the Cold War* (1991).

Armstrong, J. A. *Soviet Partisans in World War II* (1964).

Aron, Raymond. *Clausewitz: Philosopher of War* (1985).

———. *An Explanation of De Gaulle* (1965).

————. *The Century of Total War* (1954).

Asch, Ronald. *The Thirty Years' War* (1997).

Ascher, A. *The Revolution of 1905* (1988)

Ashe, Geoffrey. *Gandhi: A Biography* (2000).

Ashton, T. S. *The Industrial Revolution* (1968).

Ashworth, William. *A Short History of the World Economy* (1987).

Asprey, Robert. *Frederick the Great* (1999).

————. *War in the Shadows: Guerrillas in History* (1994).

Ausland, John C. *Kennedy, Khrushchev, and the Berlin-Cuba Crisis, 1961–1964* (1996).

Austin, M. M. *The Hellenistic World from Alexander to the Roman Conquest* (1981).

Aveling, John. *The Jesuits* (1982).

Axelson, Eric. *Portugal and the Scramble for Africa, 1875–1891* (1967).

Ayalon, David. *The Mamluks and Naval Power: A Phase of the Struggle Between Islam and Christian Europe* (1965).

Baer, G. *Test Case* (1976).

Bagnasco, Erminio. *Submarines of World War Two* (2000).

Bailey, Thomas A. *Diplomatic History of the American People* (1980).

Baird, Henry Martyn. *The Huguenots and Henry of Navarre* (1886; reprint, 1970).

Baker, Ray Stannard. *Woodrow Wilson and the World Settlement*, 2 vols. (1922–1923).

Baker, R. W. *Egypt's Uncertain Revolutions Under Nasser and Sadat* (1979).

Ball, S. J. *The Cold War* (1998).

Bark, Dennis, and David Gress. *A History of West Germany*, 2nd ed., 2 vols. (1993).

Barlow, Frank. *William I and the Norman Conquest* (1965).

Barman, Roderick. *Brazil: The Forging of a Nation, 1798–1852* (1988).

Barston, R. P. *Modern Diplomacy* (1988).

Bartov, Omar. *Mirrors of Destruction* (2000).

Basham, A. L. *The Origins and Development of Classical Hinduism* (1989).

————. *The Wonder That Was India* (1963).

Bass, Gary. *Stay the Hand of Vengeance* (2000).

Bassiouni, M. Cherif, ed. *International Criminal Law*, 2nd ed., 3 vols. (1999).

Bauer, Yehuda. *Rethinking the Holocaust* (2001).

Baugert, W. V. *A History of the Society of Jesus* (1972).

Baumgart, Winfried. *The Crimean War, 1853–1856* (2000).

————. *Imperialism: The Idea and Reality of British and French Colonial Expansion* (1982).

————. *The Peace of Paris, 1856* (1981).

Baxter, S. *William III* (1976).

Bayly, C. A. *Empire and Information: Intelligence Gathering and Social Communication in India, 1780–1870* (1996).

Bazant, Jan. *A Concise History of Mexico, From Hidalgo to Cárdenas, 1805–1940* (1977).

Beach, D. N. *The Shona and Zimbabwe, 900–1850* (1989).

Beasley, W. G. *The Japanese Experience: A Short History of Japan* (2000).

Beaumont, R. *War, Chaos and History* (1994).

Beck, Roger B. *History of South Africa* (2000).

————. *Christian Missionaries and European Expansion, 1450 to the Present* (1999).

Beckwith, Christopher. *The Tibetan Empire in Central Asia: A History of the Struggle* for *Great Power Among Tibetans, Turks, Arabs, and Chinese During the Early Middle Ages* (1987).

Bederman, David J. *International Law in Antiquity* (2001).

Beeching, Jack. *An Open Path: Christian Missionaries, 1515–1914* (1980).

Beetham, David. *Bureaucracy*, 2nd ed. (1996).

——. *Max Weber and the Theory of Modern Politics* (1985).

Beevor, Anthony. *Stalingrad* (1998).

Belich, James. *Making Peoples: A History of the New Zealanders, from Polynesian Settlement to the End of the Nineteenth Century* (2001)

——. *The New Zealand Wars and the Victorian Interpretation of Racial Conflict* (1986).

Bell, Coral. *The Reagan Paradox* (1990).

Bell, J. Bower. *The Secret Army: The IRA*, 3rd ed. (1997).

Bell, P. M. H. *The Origins of the Second World War in Europe* (1986).

Beloff, Max. *Thomas Jefferson and American Democracy* (1948).

Bemis, Samuel Flagg. *John Quincy Adams and the Foundations of American Foreign Policy* (1949; 1973).

——. *The Diplomacy of the American Revolution* (1957; 1983).

Benedictus, David. *Lloyd George* (1981).

Bennet, Edward M. *Franklin D. Roosevelt and the Search for Security: American-Soviet Relations, 1933–1939* (1985).

——. *Franklin D. Roosevelt and the Search for Victory: American-Soviet Relations, 1939–1945* (1990).

Bennett, A. Leroy. *International Organizations* (1984).

Bentley, Michael. *Companion to Historiography* (1997).

Benvenuti, Francesco. *The Bolsheviks and the Red Army, 1918–1922* (1988).

Berlin, Isaiah. *Crooked Timbre of Humanity* (1992).

——. *Against the Current: Essays in the History of Ideas* (1980).

——. *Age of Enlightenment* (1956).

Berman, Marshall. *Adventures in Marxism* (1999).

——. *All That Is Solid Melts Into Air: The Experience of Modernity* (1988).

Best, Geoffrey. *War and Law Since 1945* (1994).

——. *Humanity in Warfare: The Modern History of the International Law of Armed Conflicts*, 2nd ed. (1983).

Bethell, Leslie, ed. *Latin America: Politics and Society Since 1930* (1998).

Billings-Yun, M. *Decision Against War* (1988).

Bingham, Woodbridge. *The Founding of the T'ang Dynasty: The Fall of Sui and Rise of T'ang* (1970).

Birmingham, David. *Trade and Conflict in Angola* (1966).

——, and Phyllis M. Martin. *History of Central Africa* (1983).

Bischof, Gunter, and Robert Dupont, eds. *The Pacific War Revisited* (1997).

Bishop, Denis, and Keith Davis. *Railways and War Before 1918* (1972).

——, and Keith Davis. *Railways and War After 1918* (1972).

Biskupski, M. B. *The History of Poland* (2000).

Bix, Herbert. *Hirohito and the Making of Modern Japan* (2000).

Black, Cyril, ed. *The Modernization of Inner Asia* (1991).

Black, Jeremy. *A History of the British Isles* (2000).

——. *War and the World* (1998).

————. *Culloden and the '45* (1990).

Blake, Robert. *Disraeli* (1966; 1987).

————. *Disraeli and Gladstone* (1969).

Blanning, T. C. W. *The French Revolutionary Wars, 1787–1802* (1996).

Blight, James et al. *Cuba on the Brink* (1993).

Bluche, François. *Louis XIV* (1990).

Blum, J. *Lord and Peasant in Russia* (1961).

Bond, Brian. *The Pursuit of Victory* (1998).

————, and Nigel Cave, eds. *Haig: A Reappraisal* (1999).

Booth, Peter. *Yankees in the Land of the Gods* (1990).

Boulden, Jane. *Peace Enforcement: The United Nations Experience in Congo, Somalia, and Bosnia* (2001).

Bovill, E. W. *Caravans of the Old Sahara* (1933).

————. *Golden Trade of the Moors*, new ed. (1968).

Box, Pelham Horton. *The Origins of the Paraguayan War* (1929; 1967).

Boxer, C. R., ed. *Portuguese Commerce and Conquest in Southern Asia, 1500–1750* (1985).

————. *The Portuguese Seaborne Empire* (1969).

Boyle, John. *China and Japan at War, 1937–1945* (1972).

Bradford, Burns E. *A History of Brazil* (1970).

————. *Latin America: A Concise Interpretive History*, 6th ed. (1994).

Bradford, E. *The Shield and the Sword* (1973).

Brading, D. A. *The First America: The Spanish Monarchy, Creole Patriots, and the Liberal State, 1492–1867* (1991).

Bradley, John. *Allied Intervention in Russia* (1968).

Bradley, Peter. *The Lure of Peru: Maritime Intrusion into the South Sea, 1598–1701* (1989).

Brands, H. W. *The Wages of Globalism* (1997).

————. *TR: The Last Romantic* (1998).

Brenner, Michael, ed. *NATO and Collective Security* (1998).

Brett-James, A. *1812: Napoleon's Defeat in Russia* (1966).

Breuer, William. *Race to the Moon* (1993).

Brodie, Bernard. *Naval Strategy* (1942).

Brodie, Heinrich. *Tippu Tip* (2000).

Broers, Michael. *Europe Under Napoleon* (1996).

Brondsted, J. B. *The Vikings* (1965).

Brookhiser, Richard. *Alexander Hamilton, American* (1999).

Brovkin, Vladimir N., ed. *The Bolsheviks in Russian Society: The Revolution and the Civil Wars* (1997).

Brown, Archie. *The Gorbachev Factor* (1996).

Brown, Dee. *Bury My Heart at Wounded Knee: An Indian History of the American West* (1971; 2001).

Brown, Judith M. *Gandhi: Prisoner of Hope* (1989).

Brown, Michael E. et al., eds. *Rational Choice and Security Studies* (2000).

————, ed. *The International Dimensions of Internal Conflict* (1996).

Browning, Robert. *The Byzantine Empire* (1992).

————. *Justinian and Theodora* (1971).

Browning, Reed S. *The War of the Austrian Succession* (1995).

Brunk, Samuel. *Emiliano Zapata: Revolution and Betrayal in Mexico* (1995).

Bryce, James. *The Holy Roman Empire* (1892; reprint 1978).

Brzezinski, Zbigniew. *The Grand Chessboard* (1997).

———. *The Grand Failure* (1989).

———. *Power and Principle* (1983).

Buchanan, Brenda J. *Gunpowder: The History of an International Technology* (1996).

Buhite, Russell. *Decisions at Yalta* (1986).

Buisseret, David. *Henry IV* (1984).

Bukey, Evan. *Hitler's Austria, 1938–1945* (2000).

Bull, Hedley. *The Anarchical Society* (1975).

———. *International Theory* (1996).

———, ed. *Intervention in World Politics* (1984).

———. *The Control of the Arms Race* (1961).

Bullock, Alan. *Parallel Lives: Hitler and Stalin* (1991).

Bullough, D. *The Age of Charlemagne* (1966).

Bundy, William. *A Tangled Web* (1998).

Burke, Edmund. *Reflections on the Revolution in France* (1792).

Burkhardt, Jacob. *Civilization of the Renaissance in Italy* (1995).

Burleigh, Michael. *The Third Reich* (2000).

Burman, Edward. *Templars* (1986; 1990).

Bury, J. P. *France, 1814–1940*, 5th ed. (1985).

Bush, George H., and Brent Scowcroft. *A World Transformed* (1998).

Cahill, T. *How the Irish Saved Civilization* (1995).

Callahan, David. *Dangerous Capabilities* (1990).

Callinicos, Alex. *Trotskyism* (1990).

Calvocoressi, Peter et al. *Total War* (1989).

Cameron, Rondo, ed. *Banking and Economic Development* (1972).

Cannon, Lou. *Role of a Lifetime* (1991).

Caputi, Robert. *Neville Chamberlain and Appeasement* (2000).

Carley, Michael. *Revolution and Intervention: The French Government and the Russian Civil War, 1917–1919* (1983).

Carman, Philip. *The Lost Paradise: The Jesuit Republic in South America* (1976).

Carment, David, and Frank Harvey. *Using Force to Prevent Ethnic Violence* (2001).

Carr, E. H. *What Is History?* (1961).

Carr, Raymond. *Spain, 1808–1975*, 2nd ed. (1982).

Carsten, F. *The Origins of Prussia* (1954).

Carter, C. H., ed. *From the Renaissance to the Counter-Reformation* (1965).

Carter, James. *Keeping Faith* (1982).

Cassese, Antonio. *International Law* (2001).

Catton, Bruce. *The Centennial History of the Civil War*, 3 vols. (1961–1965).

———. *U. S. Grant and the American Military Tradition* (1954).

Caven, Brian. *The Punic Wars* (1980).

Cecil, Hugh, and Peter Liddle, eds. *Facing Armageddon: The First World War Experienced* (1996).

Chadwick, Owen, series ed. *Pelican History of the Church*, six vols. (1970–).

———. *The Popes and European Revolution* (1981).

———. *The Reformation* (1972).

Chamberlain, Muriel E. *Pax Britannica? British Foreign Policy, 1789–1914* (1988).

Chambers, J. D., and G. E. Mingay. *The Agricultural Revolution* (1966).

Chan, Anita. *Children of Mao* (1985).

Chandler, David. *Voices From S-21* (2000).

———. *A History of Cambodia* (1983, 2000).

Chaney, Otto Preston. *Zhukov*, 2nd ed. (1996).

Chang, Gordon. *Friends and Enemies* (1990).

Chapuis, Oscar. *The Last Emperors of Vietnam: From Tu Duc to Bao Dai* (2000).

———. *A History of Vietnam* (1995).

Charlton, Michael. *The Little Platoon: Diplomacy and the Falklands Dispute* (1989).

Chase, James. *Acheson* (1998).

Chen, Jian. *China's Road to the Korean War* (1994).

Chibnall, Marjorie. *The Normans* (2001).

Chidester, David. *Christianity* (2000).

Choueiri, Youssef M. *Arab Nationalism, A History: Nation and State in the Arab World* (2000).

Churchill, Winston S. *The Second World War*, 6 vols. (1953).

Cimant, James. *The Kurds* (1996).

Cimbala, Stephen J. *Clausewitz and Chaos: Friction in War and Military Policy* (2000).

Cipolla, Carlo. *Economic History of World Population*, 7th ed. (1978).

———. *Guns and Sails* (1965).

Clammer, David. *The Zulu War* (1973; 1989).

Clarence-Smith, Gervase. *The Third Portuguese Empire, 1825–1975* (1985).

Clark, G. N. *The Dutch Alliance and the War Against French Trade, 1688–1697* (1923; 1971).

Claude, Inis. *Swords Into Ploughshares*, 4th ed. (1984).

———. *The Balance of Power* (1965).

Clausewitz, Karl von. *On War* (1818).

Claven, Patricia. *The Failure of Economic Diplomacy, 1931–36* (1997).

Clayton, Gerald. *Britain and the Eastern Question* (1971).

Clemenceau, Georges. *Grandeur and Misery of Victory* (1930).

Clements, Kendrick. *Woodrow Wilson* (1987).

Clendinnen, Inga. *Aztecs* (1991).

Clodfelter, Marc. *The Limits of Air Power: The American Bombing of North Vietnam* (1989).

Clogg, R. *A Short History of Modern Greece* (1988).

Coats, A. W. *The Classical Economists and Economic Policy* (1971).

Cobban, Alfred. *A History of Modern France*, 3 vols., 3d ed. (1966–1967).

Cohen, Andrew, and J. L. Granatstein, eds. *Trudeau's Shadow: The Life and Legacy of Pierre Elliott Trudeau* (1998).

Cole, Donald B. *The Presidency of Andrew Jackson* (1993).

Collier, Simon, and William F. Sater. *A History of Chile, 1808–1994* (1996).

Collingwood, R. G. *The Idea of History* (1946).

Collins, Richard H. *Theodore Roosevelt's Caribbean* (1990).

Collins, Roger. *Charlemagne* (1998).

Conquest, Robert. *Stalin: Breaker of Nations* (1991).

————. *The Great Terror* (1990).

————. *Harvest of Sorrow* (1986).

————. *The Soviet Police System* (1969).

Conrad, David. *The Songhay Empire* (1998).

Conrad, Geoffrey, and Arthur Demarest. *Religion and Empire: The Dynamics of Aztec and Inca Expansionism* (1984).

Coogan, Tim Pat, and George Morrison. *The Irish Civil War* (1998).

————. *The IRA*, 4th ed. (1995).

Cook, Sherburne, and Woodrow Borah. *Essays in Population History*, 3 vols. (1971–1979).

Cooper, Duff. *Talleyrand* (1932; 2001).

Cooper, John Milton. *The Warrior and the Priest: Woodrow Wilson and Theodore Roosevelt* (1983).

Cooper, William. *Jefferson Davis, American* (2000).

Cordesman, Anthony H. *The Gulf and the West: Strategic Relations and Military Realities* (1988).

Cornell, John. *Hitler's Pope* (1999).

Courtois, Stéphane et al. *The Black Book of Communism* (1997; 1999).

Cox, John K. *The History of Serbia* (2002).

Cracraft, James, ed. *Peter the Great Transforms Russia* (1991).

Craig, Gordon. *Germany, 1866–1945* (1978).

Crampton, R. J. *A Short History of Modern Bulgaria* (1989).

Creighton, D. G. *The Story of Canada* (1959; 1971).

Crossley, Pamela K. *A Translucent Mirror: History and Identity in Qing Imperial Ideology* (1999).

Crowder, Michael. *The Story of Nigeria*, 4th ed. (1978).

Croxton, Derek, and Anuschka Tischer. *The Peace of Westphalia: A Historical Dictionary* (2001).

Cumings, Bruce. *Korea's Place in the Sun* (1997).

————. *Origins of the Korean War* (1981; 1990).

Curtis, Michael, ed. *Anti-Semitism in the Contemporary World* (1985).

Curtiss, J. S. *Russia's Crimean War* (1979).

Cust, R., and Ann Hughes, eds. *The English Civil War* (1997).

Daaku, K. Y. *Trade and Politics on the Gold Coast, 1600–1720* (1970).

Daborn, John. *Russia: Revolution and Counter-Revolution, 1917–1924* (1991).

Dakin, D. *The Unification of Greece, 1770–1923* (1972).

Dallek, Robert. *Flawed Giant* (1998).

————. *Franklin D. Roosevelt and American Foreign Policy* (1979).

Daly, M., ed. *Cambridge History of Egypt*, 2 vols. (1998).

Dame, Frederick William. *History of Switzerland* (2001).

Danchev, Alex, and Dan Keohane, eds. *International Perspectives on the Gulf Conflict, 1990–91* (1994).

Dancocks, Daniel. *Welcome to Flanders Fields* (1988).

Davenport, T. R. H., and Christopher Saunders. *South Africa: A Modern History* (2000).

Davidson, Miles H. *Columbus Then and Now* (1997).

Davidson, Roderic H. *Turkey: A Short History*, 3rd ed. (1998).

————. *Reform in the Ottoman Empire, 1856–1876* (1973).

Davies, Norman. *The Isles: A History* (2000).

Davis, Colin, and Peter Lineham, eds. *The Future of the Past: Themes in New Zealand History* (1991).

Davis, D. *The Problem of Slavery in Western Culture* (1966).

de Bary, William T., ed. *The Buddhist Tradition in India, China, and Japan* (1972).

————. *The Trouble With Confucianism* (1991).

DeConde, Alexander. *History of American Foreign Policy*, 2 vols. (1978).

de Gaulle, Charles. *War Memoirs*, 3 vols. (1955–1960; rep. 1984).

————. *Memoirs of Hope* (trans. 1972).

de Hartog, Leo. *Ghengis Khan* (1989).

de Madariaga, I. *Catherine the Great* (1990).

————. *Russia in the Age of Catherine the Great* (1981).

de Moor, J. A., and H. L. Wesseling, eds. *Imperialism and War: Essays on Colonial War in Asia and Africa* (1989).

Deng, Gang. *Chinese Maritime Activities and Socioeconomic Development* (1997).

Dennett, Tyler. *Americans in Eastern Asia* (1922).

Derfler, Leslie. *The Dreyfus Affair* (2002).

Desai, Sar. *Legacy of Nehru* (1992).

de Silva, Chandra. *Sri Lanka: A History*, 2nd rev. ed. (1997).

de St. Jorre, John. *The Nigerian Civil War* (1972).

De Vries, Jan, and Ad Van Der Woude. *The First Modern Economy* (1997).

Dinstein, Yoram, and Mala Tabory, eds. *War Crimes in International Law* (1996).

Divine, Robert. *The Johnson Years* (1990).

————. *Eisenhower and the Cold War* (1981).

————. *The Reluctant Belligerent* (1965; 1979).

————. *Roosevelt and World War II* (1969).

————. *Second Chance* (1967).

Dobson, Alan. *U.S. Wartime Aid to Britain, 1940–1946* (1986).

Dockrill, Michael, and J. Good. *Peace Without Promise* (1981).

Donald, David. *Lincoln* (1995).

Dorn, F. *The Sino-Japanese War* (1974).

Dorrill, Stephen. *MI6* (2000).

Douglas, David C. *The Norman Achievement, 1050–1100* (1969).

Dower, John. *Embracing Defeat: Japan in the Wake of World War II* (1992).

Downing, Brian. *The Military Revolution and Political Change* (1992).

Doyle, Michael. *Empires* (1986).

Doyle, William. *Origins of the French Revolution*, 3rd ed. (1999).

Drescher, Seymour. *From Slavery to Freedom* (1999).

Drew, Daniel. *The Lost Chronicle* (2000).

Duffy, M. *The Military Revolution and the State, 1500–1800* (1980).

Duiker, William. *Ho Chi Minh* (2000).

Dunn, Walter S. *Kursk: Hitler's Gamble, 1943* (1997).

Duus, Peter et al., eds. *The Japanese Wartime Empire, 1931–1945* (1996).

Dutton, David. *Anthony Eden* (1997).

Eastman, Lloyd. *The Nationalist Era in China* (1991).

————. *Seeds of Destruction* (1984).

————. *The Abortive Revolution* (1974).

Eber, Irene. *Confucianism* (1986).

Eccles, W. J. *The French in North America, 1500–1783* (1998).

Eckes, Alfred. *A Search for Solvency* (1975).

Eichengreen, Barry, ed. *The Gold Standard in Theory and History* (1985).

Eisenhower, Dwight D. *Waging Peace: 1956–1961* (1965).

————. *Mandate for Change: 1953–1956* (1963).

Eisenhower, John S. *Agent of Destiny: The Life and Times of General Winfield Scott* (1997).

————. *So Far From God: The U.S. War with Mexico* (1989).

————. *The Bitter Woods* (1969).

Elliot, J. H., ed. *Hispanic World, Civilization, and Empire: Europe and the Americas* (1991).

————. *Richelieu and Olivares* (1984).

————. *Imperial Spain, 1469–1716* (1964, 1970).

————. *Europe Divided, 1559–1598* (1969).

Ellis, J. *American Sphinx* (1997).

Ellwood, Sheelagh. *Franco* (2000).

Elton, G. *Reformation Europe* (1963).

Emmerson, J. *Rhineland Crisis* (1977).

Endacott, G. B. *A History of Hong Kong* (1973).

Epps, Valerie. *International Law*, 2nd ed. (2001).

Esdaile, Charles. *The Wars of Napoleon* (1995).

Evans, Eric J. *Thatcher and Thatcherism* (1997).

Evans, Richard. *Deng Xiaoping and the Making of Modern China* (1997).

Evans, Richard J. *In Defense of History* (1999).

Evans, Robert. *The Revolutions in Europe, 1848–49* (2000).

Fage, J. D. *A History of Africa* (1995).

————. *Ghana: A Historical Interpretation* (1959; 1983).

Fahmy, Khaled. *All the Pasha's Men* (1997).

Fairbank, John. *China* (1992).

Farrar-Hockley, Anthony. *Death of an Army* (1968; 1998).

Farcau, Bruce. *The Ten Cent War: Chile, Peru, and Bolivia in the War of the Pacific, 1879–1884* (2000).

Fay, Peter. *The Opium War, 1840–42* (1975).

Feis, Herbert. *Europe: The World's Banker, 1870–1914* (1965).

————. *Between War and Peace: The Potsdam Conference* (1960).

————. *Churchill, Roosevelt, Stalin* (1957).

Fergusson, Niall. *The House of Rothschild*, 2 vols. (1998–1999).

Fernández-Armesto, Felipe. *Columbus* (1991).

Fero, N. *Nicholas II* (1991).

Ferrell, Robert H. *The American Secretaries of State and Their Diplomacy: Marshall* (1966).

————. *American Diplomacy in the Great Depression* (1957).

————. *Woodrow Wilson and World War I, 1917–21* (1985).

Fieldhouse, D. K. *Economics and Empire, 1830–1914* (1973).

Fifer, J. Valerie. *Bolivia: Land, Location, and Politics Since 1825* (1972).

Filtzer, Donald. *The Khrushchev Era* (1993).

Finer, S. E. *The History of Government From the Earliest Times*, 3 vols. (1997).

Finn, Richard. *Winners in Peace* (1992).

Fisher, John. *Economic Aspects of Spanish Imperialism in America* (1997).

Fishman, Sarah et al., eds. *France at War* (2000).

Fitzhugh W. W., and E. I. Ward, eds. *Vikings* (2000).

Fitzpatrick, Sheila. *The Russian Revolution*, 2nd ed. (1994)

Fleming, Thomas. *Duel: Alexander Hamilton, Aaron Burr and the Future of America* (1999).

Flint, John. *Cecil Rhodes* (1976).

Foch, Ferdinand. *Principles of War* (1919).

———. *Memoirs* (1931).

Fodor, Neil. *The Warsaw Treaty Organization* (1990).

Fogel, Joshua, ed. *The Nanjing Massacre* (2000).

Foot, Rosemary. *The Wrong War* (1985).

Foote P., and D. M. Wilson. *The Viking Achievement* (1970).

Foote, Shelby. *The Civil War*, 3 vols. (1958–1974).

Foreman-Peck, J. *History of the World Economy* (1983).

Foster, R. F. *Modern Ireland, 1600–1972* (1989).

Fowler, Jeaneane. *Hinduism: Beliefs and Practices* (1997).

Fowler, K. A. *The Age of Plantagenet and Valois* (1967).

Fox, Robert. *Alexander the Great* (1986).

Francis, David. *The First Peninsular War, 1702–1713* (1975).

Frank, Richard. *Downfall: The End of the Imperial Japanese Empire* (1999).

Fraser, David. *Frederick the Great* (2000).

Freedman, Lawrence. *Kennedy's Wars* (2000).

———, ed. *War* (1994).

Friedrich, Otto. *Blood and Iron* (2000).

Fromkin, David. *A Peace to End All Peace* (1989).

Fuglestad, F. *A History of Niger, 1850–1960* (1983).

Fulbrook, Mary. *German History Since 1800* (1997).

———. *Anatomy of a Dictatorship: Inside the GDR, 1949–1989* (1995).

———. *Divided Nation* (1992).

Fuller, J. F. C. *The Conduct of War, 1789–1961* (1962).

———. *Armaments and History* (1946).

Furet, François. *The Passing of an Illusion: The Idea of Communism in the 20th Century* (1999).

Fussell, Paul. *Wartime* (1989).

———. *The Great War and Modern Memory* (1975; 2000).

Fyfe, Christopher. *A History of Sierra Leone* (1962).

Gaddis, John et al., eds. *Cold War Statesmen Confront the Bomb* (1999).

———. *We Now Know* (1997).

———. *The United States and the End of the Cold War* (1992).

———. *The Long Peace* (1987).

———. *Strategies of Containment* (1982).

Garthoff, Raymond. *Detente and Confrontation* (1985).

Garton Ash, Timothy. *The Polish Revolution* (1983; 1991).

Gash, G. *Renaissance Armies* (1975).

Gates, David. *The Napoleonic Wars, 1803–1815* (1997).

———. *Spanish Ulcer* (1986).

Gati, Charles. *The Bloc That Failed* (1990).

———. *Hungary and the Soviet Bloc* (1986).

Garlake, Peter. *Great Zimbabwe* (1973).

Garraty, John, and Peter Gay. *Columbia History of the World* (1981).

Gay, Peter. *The Enlightenment* (1968).

———, and R. K. Webb. *Modern Europe* (1973).

Geiss, Immanuel. *Panafricanism* (1974).

Gelber, Yoav. *Palestine: 1948* (2001).

Gernet, Jacques. *China and the Christian Impact* (1985).

Getzler, I. *Kronstadt, 1917–1921* (1983).

Giáp, Võ Nguyên. *Dien Bien Phu* (1994).

Gibbon, Edward. *The Decline and Fall of the Roman Empire*, abridged to 2 vols. by D. M. Low (1960; 1985).

Gilbert, Martin. *The Second World War* (1989).

———. *Winston Churchill* (1991).

Gill, G. *Stalinism* (1990).

Girgis, Monir S. *Mediterranean Africa* (1987).

Glaeser, Bernhard, ed. *The Green Revolution Revisited: Critique and Alternatives* (1987).

Glahn, Gerhard von. *Law Among Nations*, 6th ed. (1992).

Glamann, Kristof. *Dutch-Asiatic Trade* (1958).

Glantz, David M. *Zhukov's Greatest Defeat: The Red Army's Epic Disaster in Operation Mars, 1942* (1999).

———, and Harold Orenstein, eds. *The Battle for Kursk, 1943: The Soviet General Staff Study* (1999).

———. *Stumbling Colossus: The Red Army on the Eve of World War* (1998).

Gleason, Abbott. *Totalitarianism* (1995).

Glete, Ian. *Navies and Nations: Warships, Navies, and State-Building in Europe and America, 1500–1860* (1993)

Glover, Jonathan. *Humanity: A Moral History of the Twentieth Century* (2000).

Glover, M. *The Peninsular War* (1974).

Goldblat, Jozef. *Arms Control: A Guide to Negotiations and Agreements* (1994).

Goldstein, Erik. *Wars and Peace Treaties* (1991).

———. *Winning the Peace: British Diplomatic Strategy, Peace Planning, and the Paris Peace Conference, 1916–1920* (1991).

———, and Igor Lukes, eds. *The Munich Crisis, 1938* (1999).

———, and John Maurer, eds. *The Washington Conference, 1921–22: Naval Rivalry, East Asian Stability and the Road to Pearl Harbor* (1994).

Goldsworthy, Adrian. *The Punic Wars* (2001).

Good, David. *Economic Rise of the Habsburg Empire, 1750–1914* (1984).

Goodman, D. *Spanish Naval Power, 1589–1665: Reconstruction and Defeat* (1996).

Goodwin, Jason. *Lords of the Horizons: A History of the Ottoman Empire* (1999).

Gopal, S. *Jawaharlal Nehru*, 3 vols. (1975–1984).

Gordon, Andrew, ed. *Postwar Japan As History* (1993).

Gormley, James. *From Potsdam to the Cold War* (1990).

Gorodetsky, Gabriel. *Grand Delusion: Stalin and the German Invasion of Russia* (1999).

Götz, Aly. *"Final Solution": Nazi Population Policy and the Murder of the European Jews* (1999).

Goubert, Pierre. *The Ancien Régime* (1969).

———. *Louis XIV and 20 Million Frenchmen* (1966).

Gould, Louis L. *The Presidency of Theodore Roosevelt* (1991).

———. *The Spanish-American War and President McKinley* (1982).

———. *The Presidency of William McKinley* (1980).

Graebner, Norman. *Foundations of American Foreign Policy* (1985).

———. *America As a World Power* (1984).

———. *Age of Global Power* (1979).

———. *Empire on the Pacific* (1955).

Graham, Hugh F. *Ivan the Terrible* (1981).

Grann, L. H., and Peter Duignan, eds. *Colonialism in Africa*, 5 vols. (1969–1975).

Grant, Michael. *From Rome to Byzantium* (1998).

———. *Constantine the Great: The Man and His Times* (1994).

———. *Founders of the Western World: A History of Greece and Rome* (1991).

———. *Fall of the Roman Empire: A Reappraisal* (1990).

———. *History of Rome* (1978).

———. *Ancient Mediterranean* (1969).

———. *Julius Caesar* (1969).

———. *The Climax of Rome: The Final Achievements of the Ancient World A.D. 161– 337* (1968).

Grant, Ulysses S. *Personal Memoirs* (1885).

Gray, Christine. *International Law and the Use of Force* (2000).

Gray, Colin. *Leverage of Sea Power* (1992).

Gray, J. M. *A History of The Gambia* (1966).

Gregor, A. James. *The Faces of Janus: Marxism and Fascism in the Twentieth Century* (2000).

Green, Peter. *Alexander of Macedon, 356–323 B.C.: A Historical Biography* (1991).

Grew, Raymond. *Food in Global History* (1999).

Grewal, J. S. *The Sikhs of the Punjab*, rev. ed. (1998).

Grey, Edward. *Twenty-Five Years, 1892–1916* (1926).

Grey, Ian. *Ivan III and the Unification of Russia* (1964).

Griffith, Paddy. *The Art of War of Revolutionary France, 1789–1802* (1998).

Grimsted, P. K. *The Foreign Ministers of Alexander I* (1969).

Gromyko, Andrei. *Memoirs* (1989).

Guilmartin, John F. *Gunpowder and Galleys* (1974).

Gulick, Edward. *Europe's Classical Balance of Power* (1955).

Gungwu, Wang. *China and the Overseas Chinese* (1991).

Gustafson, Lowell, ed. *Thucydides' Theory of International Relations* (2000).

Guy, R. *The Emperor's Four Treasuries* (1987).

Haig, Alexander. *Caveat* (1984).

Haldon, John. *Byzantium* (2000).

Hale, John R. *War and Society in Renaissance Europe, 1450–1620* (1986).

———. *The Age of Exploration* (1974).

————— et al. *Europe in the Late Middle Ages* (1965).

—————. *Machiavelli and Renaissance Italy* (1960).

Hall, J. et al., eds. *Japan Before Tokugawa* (1981).

Hall, John. *Liberalism* (1988)

Halliday, Fred. *Revolution and World Politics* (1999).

Hamill, Hugh. *The Hidalgo Revolt* (1966).

Hamilton, A. *The Appeal of Fascism* (1971).

Hamilton, E. P. *The French and Indian Wars* (1962).

Hammond, Richard. *Portugal and Africa, 1815–1910* (1966).

Hamnett, Brian. *Juárez* (1994).

Hampson, Norman. *The Enlightenment* (1982).

Hancock, W. K. *Smuts*, 2 vols. (1962; 1968).

Handy, J. *A Gift of the Devil: A History of Guatemala* (1984).

Hanioglu, Sükrü. *Preparation for a Revolution: The Young Turks, 1902–08* (2000).

Hanson, Eric. *The Catholic Church in World Politics* (1987).

Hardie, F. *The Abyssinian Crisis* (1974).

Hargreaves, John. *West Africa Partitioned*, 2 vols. (1974).

—————. *France and West Africa* (1969).

—————. *West Africa: The Former French States* (1967).

Harriman, W. Averell. *Special Envoy to Churchill and Stalin* (1975).

—————. *America and Russia in a Changing World* (1971).

Harris, Sheldon H. *Factories of Death* (1994).

Harrison, G. A., ed. *Famine* (1988).

Hart, Peter. *The IRA and Its Enemies: Violence and Community in Cork, 1916–1923* (1998).

Hasegawa, T. *The February Revolution: Petrograd, 1917–1918* (1981).

Haslip, Joan. *The Crown of Mexico* (1971).

Hassan, Y. F. *The Arabs and the Sudan* (1967).

Hastings, Adrian, ed. *Modern Catholicism* (1991).

Hattendorf, John B. *England in the War of the Spanish Succession* (1987).

Hatton, R. *Louis XIV and Europe* (1976).

Haydon, Colin, and William Doyle, eds. *Robespierre* (1999).

Hayes, P. *Fascism* (1973).

Haynes, John. *Venona: Decoding Soviet Espionage in America* (1999).

Headrich, D. *Tools of Empire* (1981).

Hebbert, F. J., and G. A. Rothrock. *Soldier of France: Sèbastien LePrestre de Vauban, 1633–1707* (1990).

Heckscher, Eli. *Mercantilism*, (1965).

Heder, Stephen. *Propaganda, Politics, and Violence in Cambodia* (1996).

Heer, Friedrich. *The Holy Roman Empire* (1968).

Heilbroner, Robert L. *The Worldly Philosophers*, 7th rev. ed. (1999).

—————, and Lester Thurow. *Economics Explained*, rev. ed. (1998).

Heinl, Robert, and Nancy Heinl. *Written in Blood: The Story of the Haitian People, 1492–1995*, 2nd ed. (1996).

Hemming, John. *Red Gold: The Conquest of the Brazilian Indians* (1978).

Henao, Jesús María, and Gerardo Arrubla. *History of Colombia*, 2 vols. (1938; trans. 1972).

Henkin, Louis. *The Age of Rights* (1990).

Herdt, Robert, and Grant Scobie. *Science and Food* (1988).

Herring, George C. *LBJ and Vietnam* (1995).

———. *America's Longest War: The United States and Vietnam, 1950–1975* (1979).

———. *Aid to Russia* (1973).

Hervey, J. B. *Submarines* (1994).

Herzstein, R. E., ed. *The Holy Roman Empire in the Middle Ages* (1966).

Hess, Gary. *Vietnam and the United States* (1990).

Higginbotham, D. *The War of American Independence* (1977).

Higgins, Trumbull. *The Perfect Failure: Kennedy, Eisenhower, and the CIA at the Bay of Pigs* (1987).

Hilberg, Raul. *Destruction of the European Jews*, 3 vols. (1985).

Hill, Christopher. *Lenin and the Russian Revolution* (1971).

Hill, D. J. *A History of Diplomacy* (1921).

Hill, Roland. *Lord Acton* (2000).

Hillen, John. *The Blue Helmets: The Strategy of UN Military Operations* (2000).

Hillenbrand, Carole. *Crusades: Islamic Perspectives* (2000).

Hilton, Ann. *The Kingdom of the Kongo, 1641–1718* (1983).

Hinsley, F. H. *Sovereignty*, 2nd ed. (1986).

———, ed. *British Intelligence in the Second World War* (1979).

———. *Power and the Pursuit of Peace* (1962).

Hiro, Dilip. *The Longest War: The Iran-Iraq Military Conflict* (1991).

Hitchcock, William. *France Restored* (1998).

Hochschild, Adam. *King Leopold's Ghost* (1998).

Hodgson, Marshall. *Rethinking World History* (1993).

———. *The Gunpowder Empires and Modern Times* (1974).

———. *The Classical Age of Islam* (1974).

———. *Expansion of Islam* (1974).

Hoff, Joan. *Nixon Reconsidered* (1994).

Hoffman, Bruce. *Inside Terrorism* (1998).

Hoffman, Stanley. *Duties Beyond Borders* (1982).

Hogan, Michael J. *The Marshall Plan* (1987).

———. *History of Modern Germany* (1959).

———, ed. *Republic to Reich* (1973).

Holborn, Hajo. *Germany and Europe* (1970).

Holmes, Richard. *The Western Front* (2000).

Holt, P. M. *Age of the Crusades* (1986).

———. *Egypt and the Fertile Crescent, 1516–1922* (1966).

———. *The Mahdist State in the Sudan, 1881–98* (1958).

Hook, Sidney. *Marxism and Beyond* (1983).

Horden, Peregrine, and Nicholas Purcell. *The Corrupting Sea: A Study of Mediterranean History* (2000).

Horne, Alistair. *The Price of Glory: Verdun 1916*, rev. ed. (1993).

Hourani, Albert. *History of the Arab Peoples* (1997).

———. *Arabic Thought in the Liberal Age, 1798–1939* (1983).

Howard, Michael. *The Invention of Peace* (2001).

———. *The Franco-Prussian War* (1961; 1981).

————. *The Causes of War and Other Essays* (1983).

————. *Clausewitz* (1983).

————. *War and the Liberal Conscience* (1978).

————. *War in European History* (1976).

————. *Theory and Practice of War* (1975).

————, ed., *Restraints on War* (1979).

———— et al., eds. *The Laws of War* (1994).

Howe, Anthony. *Free Trade and Liberal England* (1997).

Hsi-sheng, Ch'i. *Warlord Politics in China, 1916–1928* (1976).

Hsu, Immanuel. *Rise of Modern China*, 4th ed. (1990).

Htin Aung, U. *A History of Burma* (1967).

Hucker, Charles. *China's Imperial Past* (1975).

Hughes, J. M. *To the Maginot Line* (1971).

Hughes, Lindsey. *Russia in the Age of Peter the Great* (1998).

Hulme, Peter. *Colonial Encounters: Europe and the Caribbean, 1492–1797* (1986).

Hunt, Edwin, and James Murray. *A History of Business in Medieval Europe, 1200–1550* (1999).

Hunt, Michael H. *Ideology and U.S. Foreign Policy* (1987).

Huntington, Samuel P. *The Clash of Civilizations and the Remaking of World Order* (1996).

————, and Clement Moore. *Authoritarian Politics in Modern Society* (1970).

Hussey, J. M. *The Orthodox Church in the Byzantine Empire* (1986).

Hutton, Ronald. *The British Republic, 1649–1660* (2000).

Hyam, R. *Britain's Imperial Century, 1815–1914* (1975).

Ienaga, Sabur. *The Pacific War* (1978).

Iliffe, John. *A Modern History of Tanganyika* (1979).

Immerman, Robert. *John Foster Dulles* (1999).

————, and Robert Bowie. *Waging Peace* (1998).

Inalcik, H. *The Ottoman Empire* (1978).

Iriye, Akira. *Cultural Internationalism and World Order* (1997).

————. *China and Japan in the Global Setting* (1992).

————. *Across the Pacific* (1967; 1992).

————. *Origins of the Second World War in Asia and the Pacific* (1987).

————. *Power and Culture: The Japanese-American War* (1982).

————, ed. *Origins of the Cold War in Asia* (1977).

————. *After Imperialism* (1965).

Irokawa, Daikichi. *The Age of Hirohito* (1995).

Irving, Ronald E. *The First Indochina War, 1945–1954* (1975).

Isaacson, Walter, and Evan Thomas. *The Wise Men: Six Friends and the World They Made* (1986).

Israel, Jonathon. *Conflicts of Empires: Spain, the Low Countries, and the Struggle for World Supremacy, 1585–1713* (1997).

————. *The Dutch Republic: Its Rise, Greatness and Fall, 1477–1806* (1995).

————. *The Dutch Republic and the Hispanic World, 1606–1661* (1982).

Jackson, Robert. *The Global Covenant* (2000).

————. *Quasi States* (1990).

————, and Carl G. Rosberg. *Personal Rule in Black Africa* (1982).

————, ed. *Politics and Government in African States, 1960–1985* (1986).

Jacques, Kathryn. *Bangladesh, India, and Pakistan* (2000).

Jagchid, Sechin, and V. J. Symons. *Peace, War, and Trade Along the Great Wall* (1989).

James, Lawrence. *Raj: The Making and Unmaking of British India* (1998).

————. *Rise and Fall of the British Empire* (1996).

————. *Imperial Rearguard: Wars of Empire, 1919–1985* (1988).

————. *Savage Wars: British Campaigns in Africa, 1870–1920* (1985).

James, Robert. *Anthony Eden* (1987).

————. *Gallipoli* (1965).

Jansen, Marius. The *Making of Modern Japan* (2000).

————. *The Emergence of Meiji Japan* (1995).

————. *Japan and China* (1975).

Jelavich, Barbara. *Russia's Balkan Entanglements, 1806–1914* (1991).

————. *The Great Powers, the Ottoman Empire, and the Straits Question, 1870–1887* (1973).

Jeremy, David. *International Technology Transfer, 1700–1914* (1991).

Joes, Anthony. *The War for South Vietnam, 1954–1974*, revised ed. (2001).

Johnson, C. *MITI and the Japanese Miracle* (1982).

Johnson, James Turner. *Just War Tradition and the Restraint of War* (1981).

Johnson, John J. *Simón Bolívar and Spanish American Independence, 1783–1830* (1968).

Johnson, Lyndon B. *The Vantage Point* (1971).

Jones, E. L. *Growth Recurring: Economic Change in World History* (1988).

Joseph, William et al. *New Perspectives on the Cultural Revolution* (1991).

Johnson, Eric. *Nazi Terror* (2000).

Johnson, James T., and John Kelsey. *Cross, Crescent and Sword* (1990).

————. *Ideology, Reason, and the Limitation of War: Religious and Secular Concepts, 1200–1740* (1975).

Jomini, Antoine-Henri. *Treatise on Grand Military Operations*, 5 vols. (1804–1810).

————. *Military Critique of the Wars of the Revolution* (1819–1824).

————. *Summary of the Art of War* (1830; 1862).

Jones, E. L. *The Agricultural Revolution* (1974).

Jones, Gwyn. *Denmark: A Modern History* (1986).

————. *A History of the Vikings* (1968; 2001).

Joseph, William et al. *New Perspectives on the Cultural Revolution* (1991).

Kagan, Donald. *The Western Heritage* (2001).

————. *The Fall of the Athenian Empire* (1987).

————. *The End of the Roman Empire* (1992).

————. *Problems in Ancient History* (1975).

Kahn, Harold. *Monarchy in the Emperor's Eyes* (1971).

Kaiser, David. *American Tragedy* (2000).

Kajima, Morinosuke. *The Diplomacy of Japan, 1894–1922*, vol. I (1976).

Kamen, Henry. *The Spanish Inquisition* (1998).

————. *Philip of Spain* (1997).

————. *Imperial Spain* (1983).

————. *The War of Succession in Spain, 1700–15* (1969).

Kampen, Thomas. *Mao Zedong, Zhou Enlai and the Evolution of the Chinese Communist Leadership* (2000).

Kane, Brian. *Just War and the Common Good* (1997).

Kann, R. *History of the Habsburg Empire, 1526–1918* (1974).

Kant, Immanuel. *Perpetual Peace* (1795).

Kaplan, Karel. *The Short March* (1987).

Kaplan, Lawrence. *Thomas Jefferson* (1999).

Karnes, T. L. *The Failure of Union: Central America, 1824–1960* (1961).

Karnow, Stanley. *Vietnam* (1984).

Karsh, Efraim. *Empires of the Sand* (1999).

———, and Inari Rautsi. *Saddam Hussein: A Political Biography* (1991).

Katz, Mark, ed. *Revolution* (2000).

Keatinge, Richard, ed. *Peruvian Prehistory* (1988).

Keay, John. *India: A History* (2000).

Keddie, N. R. *Religion and Politics in Iran* (1983).

Kedward H. R. et al., eds. *France in World Politics* (1989).

Keegan, John, ed. *The Book of War* (1999).

———. *The First World War* (1999).

———. *A History of Warfare* (1993).

———. *The Second World War* (1989).

———. *The Face of Battle* (1974).

Kennan, George F. *Nuclear Delusion* (1982).

———. *Memoirs*, 2 vols. (1967; 1972).

———. *Russia and the West under Lenin and Stalin* (1961).

———. *American Diplomacy, 1900–1950* (1951).

Kennedy, Hugh. *Muslim Spain and Portugal* (1996).

———. *The Prophet and the Age of the Caliphates* (1986).

Kennedy, Paul. *Rise and Fall of British Naval Mastery* (1986; 1998).

———. *Grand Strategies in War and Peace* (1991).

———. *Rise and Fall of the Great Powers* (1988).

———. *Rise of Anglo-German Antagonism, 1860–1914* (1987).

———. *Strategy and Diplomacy, 1870–1945* (1983).

———. *War Plans of the Great Powers, 1880–1914* (1979).

Kennedy, R. G. *Burr, Hamilton, and Jefferson* (1999).

Kent, Bruce. *The Spoils of War: Politics, Economics, and Diplomacy of Reparations, 1918–1932* (1989).

Keohane, Robert. *Neorealism and Its Critics* (1986).

Kershaw, Ian. *Hitler*, 2 vols. (1999; 2000).

———. *The Nazi Dictatorship* (1985).

Kessler, Lawrence. *K'ang hsi and the Consolidation of Ch'ing Rule, 1661–1684* (1978).

Keylor, William R. *Twentieth Century World*, 4th ed. (2000).

———, ed. *The Legacy of the Great War: Peacemaking, 1919* (1998).

Khadduri, Majid, and Edmund Ghareeb. *War in the Gulf, 1990–91: The Iraq–Kuwait Conflict and Its Implications* (1997).

Khrushchev, Nikita S. *Khrushchev Remembers*, 3 vols. (1971; 1974; 1990).

Kicza, John, ed. *The Indian in Latin American History* (1993).

Kiernan, Ben. *The Pol Pot Regime* (1996).

Kimball, Warren. *The Juggler* (1991).

Kindleberger, Charles. *Keynesianism vs. Monetarism* (1985).

———. *The World in Depression, 1929–1939* (1973).

Kirby, D. G. *Finland in the 20th Century* (1979).

Kissinger, Henry. *Years of Renewal* (1999).

———. *Diplomacy* (1994).

———. *American Foreign Policy* (1982).

———. *Years of Upheaval* (1982).

———. *White House Years* (1979).

———. *A World Restored* (1957).

Kitzen, Michael. *Tripoli and the United States at War* (1993).

Kiwanuka, M. S. *A History of Buganda* (1972).

Kleeblatt, Norman L. *The Dreyfus Affair: Art, Truth, and Justice* (1987).

Klein, Herbert. *The Atlantic Slave Trade* (1999).

Klier, J., and S. Lamboza, eds. *Pogroms* (1991).

Knight, Alan. *The Mexican Revolution*, 2 vols. (1990).

Knock, Thomas. *To End All Wars* (1992).

Knott, Stephen. *Secret and Sanctioned* (1996).

Knox, MacGregor. *Common Destiny: Dictatorship, Foreign Policy and War in Fascist Italy and Nazi Germany* (2000).

———. *Mussolini Unleashed, 1939–41* (1982).

———, and Williamson Murray, eds. *The Dynamics of Military Revolution, 1300–2050* (2001).

——— et al., eds. *Making of Strategy: Rulers, States, and Wars* (1994).

——— et al., eds. *German Nationalism and European Response, 1890–1945* (1985).

Koebner, Richard, and Helmut Schmidt, *Imperialism* (1964).

Kolinski, Charles J. *Independence or Death!: The Story of the Paraguayan War* (1965).

Kortepeter, C. M. *Ottoman Imperialism During the Reformation* (1992).

Kossmann, E. H. *The Low Countries, 1780–1940* (1978).

Kramer, Lloyd. *Lafayette in Two Worlds* (1996).

Krauze, Enrique. *Mexico* (1998).

Kreyenbroek, Philip, and Stefan Sperl, eds. *The Kurds* (1992).

Kuhn, Philip. *Rebellion and Its Enemies in Late Imperial China, 1796–1864* (1970).

Kunz, Diane. *Economic Diplomacy of the Suez Crisis* (1991).

Kwanten, Luc. *Imperial Nomads: A History of Central Asia, 500–1500* (1979).

Kyle, Keith. *Suez* (1991).

Laband, John. *The Rise and Fall of the Zulu Nation* (1998).

———. *Kingdom in Crisis: The Zulu Response to the British Invasion of 1879* (1992).

Lacouture, J. *De Gaulle*, 2 vols. (1990–1992).

Lafeber, Walter. *The Clash: US-Japan Relations Throughout History* (1997).

Landes, David. *The Wealth and Poverty of Nations* (1998).

Langlois, J., ed. *China Under Mongol Rule* (1981).

Laquer, Walter. *The Uses and Limits of Intelligence* (1993)

———. *Guerrilla* (1977).

———. *Terrorism* (1977).

Large, David. *Berlin* (2000).

Last, Murray. *The Sokoto Caliphate* (1967).

Latner, R. *The Presidency of Andrew Jackson* (1979).

Lauren, Paul G. *The Evolution of International Human Rights* (1998).

———. *Power and Prejudice: The Politics and Diplomacy of Racial Discrimination* (1988; 1996).

Lauterpacht, Hersh. *International Law and Human Rights* (1968).

Law, Robin. *The Oyo Empire, 1600–1836* (1977).

Lawrence, T. E. *Revolt in the Desert* (1927).

———. *Seven Pillars of Wisdom* (1926).

Lawson, Philip. *The East India Company* (1993).

Leckie, Robert. *A Few Acres of Snow: The Saga of the French and Indian Wars* (1999).

Ledonne, John. *The Russian Empire and the World, 1700–1917* (1997).

Lee, J. *Ireland, 1912–1985* (1989).

Lefebvre, Georges. *Napoleon*, 2 vols. (1969).

Leffler, Melvyn. *Preponderance of Power* (1992).

Leggett, G. *The Cheka* (1981).

Lensen, G. *Russia's Eastward Expansion* (1964).

Lentin, Anthony. *Lloyd George, Woodrow Wilson, and the Guilt of Germany* (1984).

Lesch, Ann. *The Sudan* (1998).

Leslie, R. F. *The History of Poland Since 1863* (1980).

Levine, Stephen. *Anvil of Victory* (1987).

Levtzion, N. *Ancient Ghana and Mali* (1973).

Levy, Richard. *Anti-Semitism in the Modern World* (1991).

Lewin, R. *American Magic* (1982).

Lewis, Bernard. *The Emergence of Modern Turkey* (1961; 1968).

Lewis, Daniel K. *The History of Argentina* (2001).

Lewis, I. M. *Modern History of Somaliland*, 2nd ed. (1979).

Lewy, Guenter. *The Nazi Persecution of the Gypsies* (2000).

Libæk, Ivar, and Øivind Stenersen. *A History of Norway from the Ice Age to the Age of Petroleum*, 3rd rev. ed. (1999).

Libenow, J. Gus. *Liberia: The Evolution of Privilege* (1969).

Liddell Hart, Basil. *History of the Second World War* (1999).

———. *History of the First World War* (1970).

Lieven, Anatol. *Ukraine and Russia* (1999).

Lieven, Dominic. *Empire: The Russian Empire and Its Rivals* (2001).

Lincoln, W. Bruce. *Sunlight at Midnight: St. Petersburg and the Rise of Modern Russia* (2001).

———. *Red Victory: A History of the Russian Civil War* (1989; 1999).

———. *Conquest of a Continent: Siberia and the Russians* (1994).

———. *Nicholas I* (1978; 1989).

Linderman, G. F. *The Mirror of War* (1974).

Lindsay, Jack. *The Normans and Their World* (1974).

Link, Arthur S. et al. *Concise History of the American People* (1984).

———. *Woodrow Wilson and a Revolutionary World* (1982).

———. *Woodrow Wilson* (1979).

———, ed. *The Papers of Woodrow Wilson*, 69 vols. (1966–1994).

Linn, Brian M. *The Philippine War, 1899–1902* (2000).

Litwak, Edward. *Détente and the Nixon Doctrine* (1984).

Liu, Xinru. *Ancient India and Ancient China: Trade and Religious Exchanges* (1994).

Lloyd George, David. *The Truth About the Peace Treaties*, 2 vols. (1938).

———. *War Memoirs* (1933–1936).

Logan, Rayford W. *Haiti and the Dominican Republic* (1968).

Lombardy, John. *Venezuela* (1982).

Lossky, A. *Louis XIV and the French Monarchy* (1994).

Louis, Wm. Roger, and Robert Owen, eds. *Suez: 1956* (1989).

———, and Robert W. Stookey, eds. *The End of the Palestine Mandate* (1986).

———. *Ruanda-Urundi, 1881–1919* (1979).

———, ed. *The Origins of the Second World War: A. J. P. Taylor and His Critics* (1972).

Lovejoy, Paul. *Transformations in Slavery: A History of Slavery in Africa* (1983).

Low, D. *Congress and the Raj* (1977).

Lukes, Igor, and Uri Ra'anan, eds., *Inside the Apparat* (1990).

———. *Gorbachev's USSR* (1990).

Lunenfeld, Martin. *1492: Discovery, Invasion, Encounter* (1991).

Luttwak, Edward. *Strategy* (1990).

———. *Coup d'Etat* (1979).

———. *The Grand Strategy of the Roman Empire* (1976).

Lydon, James G. *Pirates, Privateers, and Profits* (1970).

Lynch, John. *The Spanish American Revolutions, 1808–1826* (1986).

Lyons, Martyn. *Napoleon Bonaparte and the Legacy of the French Revolution* (1994).

MacFarquhar, Roderick. *The Great Leap Forward, 1958–1960* (1983).

Macfie, A. L., ed. *Orientalism: A Reader* (2000).

Macintosh, John M. *Juggernaut: A History of the Soviet Armed Forces* (1967).

Mackay, James. *Michael Collins: A Life* (1996).

MacKenzie, David. *Serbs and Russians* (1996).

Mackie, J. D. *A History of Scotland* (1964; 1974).

MacMillan, W. M. *Bantu, Boer and Briton* (1964).

MacMullen, Ramsay. *Roman Government's Response to Crisis, 235–337 AD* (1974).

Madden, T. *A Concise History of the Crusades* (1999).

Maddox, Robert. *The New Left and The Origins of the Cold War* (1973).

Magocsi, Robert. *A History of Ukraine* (1996).

Mahan, Alfred Thayer. *The Influence of Sea Power Upon History, 1660–1783*, 3 vols. (1890–1892).

Makiya, Kanan. *Republic of Fear: The Politics of Modern Iraq* (1998).

Malcolm, Noel. *Bosnia: A Short History* (1994).

Malia, Martin. *The Soviet Tragedy* (1994).

Mallet, M. *Mercenaries and Their Masters* (1976).

Mandelbaum, Michael. *The Nuclear Revolution* (1981).

Mango, Andre. *Atatürk* (2000).

Mann, Golo. *Wallenstein* (1976).

———. *History of Germany Since 1789* (trans. 1968).

Mannix, Daniel. *Black Cargoes* (1978).

Manz, Beatrice. *The Rise and Rule of Tamerlane* (1989).

Marais, J. S. *The Fall of Kruger's Republic* (1961).

Marius, Richard. *Martin Luther* (1999).

Marks, Frederick W. *Power and Peace: The Diplomacy of John Foster Dulles* (1995).

Marks, Sally. *Illusion of Peace* (1976).

Marr, Phoebe. *The Modern History of Iraq* (1985).

Marrus, Michael. *The Holocaust in History* (1987).

Marshall, P. J. *Bengal—The British Bridgehead: Eastern India, 1740–1828* (1987).

Martin, C. J., and Geoffrey Parker. *The Spanish Armada* (1988).

Martin, Simon, and Nikolai Grube. *Chronicle of the Maya Kings and Queens* (2000).

Marwick, Arthur. *War and Social Change* (1974).

Marx, Karl. *Capital* (1869; trans. 1919).

———, with Friedrich Engels. *The Communist Manifesto* (1848; trans. 1968).

Massie, R. *Dreadnought* (1991).

Massie, Robert. *Peter the Great* (1980).

Mastny, Vojtech. *The Cold War and Soviet Insecurity* (1996).

———, ed. *Helsinki, Human Rights, and European Security* (1986).

Masur, Gerhard. *Simón Bolívar* (1966).

Matmatey, V. S. *Rise of the Habsburg Empire, 1526–1815* (1978).

Matsusaka, Yoshihisa. *The Making of Japanese Manchuria, 1904–32* (2000).

Matthias, P. *The First Industrial Nation* (1969).

Mattingly, Garrett. *Renaissance Diplomacy* (1955).

Mawdsley, Evan. *The Russian Civil War* (2000).

May, Ernest. *Strange Victory* (2000).

———. *American Cold War Strategy* (1993).

———. *Knowing One's Enemies* (1984).

———, and P. Zelikow, eds. *The Kennedy Tapes* (1997).

Mayer, Arno. *Politics and Diplomacy of Peacemaking* (1967).

Mayer, Hans. *The Crusades* (trans. and rev. ed. 1988).

Mayers, David A. *The Ambassadors.* (1998).

———. *George Kennan and the Dilemmas of US Foreign Policy* (1988).

———, ed. *Reevaluating Eisenhower* (1987).

Mazower, Mark. *Dark Continent: Europe's 20th Century* (1999).

McCullough, David. *John Adams* (2001).

———. *Truman* (1992).

McDougal, Walter A. *The Heavens and the Earth: A Political History of the Space Age* (1997).

———. *France's Rhineland Diplomacy* (1978).

McFarlane, Anthony. *Colombia Before Independence* (1993).

McKercher, B. J. C., and Roch Legault. *Military Planning and the Origins of the Second World War in Europe* (2001).

McLellan, David. *Karl Marx* (1974).

McLeod, W. H. *Sikhism* (1997).

McLynn, Frank. *Villa and Zapata: A Biography of the Mexican Revolution* (2000).

McNamara, Robert. *In Retrospect* (1995).

McPherson, James. *Battle Cry of Freedom* (1988).

Meany, Neville. *Search for Security in the Pacific* (1976).

Medvedev, Roy A. *Let History Judge: The Origins and Consequences of Stalinism* (1989).

Meisner, Maurice. *Mao's China and After* (1986).

———. *Marxism, Maoism, and Utopianism* (1982).

Melissen, Jan. *Innovation in Diplomatic Practice* (1999).

Merk, Frederick. *The Monroe Doctrine and American Expansionism* (1966).

————. *Manifest Destiny and Mission in American History* (1963).

Meron, Theodor. *War Crimes Law Comes of Age* (1998).

Millward, Alan. *War, Economy, and Society, 1939–45* (1987).

————. *Reconstruction of Western Europe, 1945–1951* (1984).

Miscamble, Wilson. *George F. Kennan* (1992).

Misiunas, R. et al. *The Baltic States* (1983).

Moin, Baqer. *Khomeini* (2000).

Molotov, Vyacheslav. *Molotov Remembers* (1993).

Monod, Paul. *The Power of Kings* (1999).

Morgan, David. *The Mongols* (1986).

Morgenthau, Hans J. *Politics Among Nations*, 5th ed. (1948; 1978).

————. *Scientific Man vs. Power Politics* (1946).

Mori, Jennifer. *William Pitt and the French Revolution, 1785–1795* (1997).

Morley, James William. *The China Quagmire: Japan's Expansion on the Asian Continent, 1933–1941* (1983).

————. *Fateful Choice: Japan's Advance Into Southeast Asia, 1939–41* (1980).

————. *Final Confrontation: Japan's Negotiations With the United States, 1941* (1994).

————. *Japan's Thrust Into Siberia, 1918* (1957; 1972).

————, ed. *Japan Erupts: The London Naval Conference and the Manchurian Incident, 1928–1932* (1984).

Moro, Rubén E. *History of the South Atlantic Conflict: The War for the Malvinas* (1989).

Morpurgo, Michael. *The War of Jenkins' Ear* (1995).

Morril, J. S. *Oliver Cromwell and the English Revolution* (1990).

Morris, Benny. *Righteous Victims: A History of the Zionist-Arab Conflict, 1881–1999* (1999).

Morris, Richard B. *The Peacemakers* (1965).

————. *Forging of the Union* (1987).

————. *The Indian Wars* (1985).

Morris, Stephen J. *Why Vietnam Invaded Cambodia: Political Culture and the Causes of War* (1999).

Morrow, J. *The Great War in the Air* (1993).

Morse, W. *Alexander II and the Modernization of Russia* (1962).

Mortimer, Edward, and Robert Fine, eds. *People, Nation, and State: The Meaning of Ethnicity and Nationalism* (2000).

Moykr, Joel. *Twenty-Five Centuries of Technological Change* (1990).

Muldoon, James. *Empire and Order: The Concept of Empire, 800–1800* (1999).

Mullineux, A. W. *Business Cycles and Financial Crises* (1990).

Mungeam, G. H. *British Rule in Kenya* (1968).

Murphey, Rhoads. *The Outsiders* (1977).

Murray-Brown, Jeremy. *Kenyatta* (1972).

Murray, J. L. *History of Switzerland* (1985).

Murray, W. et al., eds. *The Making of Strategy* (1994).

————, and Alan Millett, *A War to Be Won* (2000).

Musicant, Ivan. *Empire by Default: The Spanish-American War and the Dawn of the American Century* (1998).

Nahm, A. C. *Korea: Tradition and Transformation* (1988).

Naimark, Norman. *Fires of Hatred: Ethnic Cleansing in 20th Century Europe* (2001).

Nakane, Chie, and Shinzabur Oishi, eds. *Tokugawa Japan: The Social and Economic Antecedents of Modern Japan* (1990).

Nardin, Terry, and David Mapel, eds. *Traditions of International Ethics* (1992).

Nasr, J. Abun. *A History of the Maghreb* (1971).

Nasson, Bill. *The South African War* (1999).

Näth, Marie-Luise, ed. *The Republic of China on Taiwan in International Politics* (1998).

Naylor, R. T. *Canada in the European Age, 1453–1919* (1988).

Neave, Airey. *Nuremberg* (1978).

Newitt, Malyn. *Portugal in Africa: The Last Hundred Years'* (1981).

Newbury, C. W. *The Western Slave Coast and Its Rulers* (1961).

Newsom, David. *The Diplomacy of Human Rights* (1986).

Nicholson, Harold. *Evolution of Diplomatic Method* (1954).

———. *The Congress of Vienna* (1946).

———. *Peacemaking, 1919* (1933).

Neier, A. *War Crimes* (1998).

Neillands, Robin. *The Hundred Years' War* (1990; 2001).

Ninkovich, Frank. *The Wilsonian Century* (1999).

———. *Modernity and Power* (1994).

Nish, I. *Japan's Foreign Policy, 1869–1942* (1978).

———. *The Anglo-Japanese Alliance* (1966).

Nitze, Paul. *From Hiroshima to Glasnost* (1989).

Nolan, Cathal J. *Principled Diplomacy* (1993).

———. *Longman Guide to World Affairs* (1995).

———, ed. *Ethics and Statecraft* (1995).

———, ed. *Notable U.S. Ambassadors Since 1775* (1997).

———, and Carl Hodge, eds. *Shepherd of Democracy? America and Germany in the 20th Century* (1992).

Northrup, David. *The Atlantic Slave Trade* (1994).

Nussbaum, A. *A Concise History of the Law of Nations* (1953).

Nyrop, Richard F. *Saudi Arabia* (1984).

———. *Jordan*, 3rd ed. (1980).

———. *Turkey* (1980).

———. *Syria* (1980).

Oakley, Stewart Philip. *William III and the Northern Crowns During the Nine Years War, 1689–1697* (1987).

Oberdorfer, Don. *Tet!* (2001).

———. *From the Cold War to a New Era: The United States and the Soviet Union, 1983–1991* (1998).

———. *The Two Koreas: A Contemporary History* (1997).

O'Brien, Connor C. *Religion and Nationalism in Ireland* (1995).

O'Brien, D. P. *The Classical Economists* (1975).

O'Carroll, J., and J. Murphy, eds. *De Valera and His Times* (1986).

O'Connel, Daniel. *The Influence of Law on Sea Power* (1975).

Okey, Robin. *The Habsburg Monarchy* (2000).

Olcott, Martha B. *Central Asia's New States* (1996).

———. *The Kazakhs* (1987; 1995).

———, and Anders Aslund, *Russia After Communism* (1999).

Oliver, Roland. *The African Experience* (1991).

———, and J. D. Fage. *A Short History of Africa* (1962; 1995).

Olmstead, A. T. *History of the Persian Empire*, 2nd ed. (1969).

Olson, Mancur. *Power and Prosperity: Outgrowing Communist and Capitalist Dictatorships* (2000).

O'Malley, John W., ed. *The Jesuits: Cultures, Sciences, and the Arts, 1540–1773* (1999).

Omer-Cooper, J. D. *The Zulu Aftermath* (1966).

Omissi, David. *The Sepoy and the Raj: The Indian Army, 1860–1940* (1994).

O'Phelen Godoy, Scarlett. *Rebellions and Revolts in 18th Century Peru and Upper Peru* (1985).

Orlow, Dietrich. *Common Destiny: A Comparative History of the Dutch, French and German Social Democratic Parties, 1945–1969* (2000).

———. *A History of Modern Germany*, 4th ed. (1999).

———. *The History of the Nazi Party*, 2 vols. (1969–1973).

O'Rourke, Kevin, and Jeffrey Williamson. *Globalization and History: The Evolution of a 19th Century Atlantic Economy* (2000).

Osborne, Harold. *Bolivia: A Land Divided* (1964; 1985).

O'Sullivan, Noel. *Conservatism* (1976).

Overy, Richard J. *The Battle* (2000).

———. *The Air War, 1939–1945* (1980).

Packer, Ian. *Lloyd George* (1998).

Padfield, P. *Guns at Sea* (1973).

———. *The Battleship Era* (1972).

Pagden, A. R. *Lords of All the World: Ideologies of Empire in Spain, Britain and France, c. 1500–c. 1800* (1995).

Pakenham, Thomas. *The Year of Liberty: The Great Irish Rebellion of 1798* (1998).

———. *The Boer War* (1979).

Palmer, David Scott. *Peru: The Authoritarian Tradition* (1980).

Palmer, Robert. *Rome and Carthage at Peace* (1997).

Paludan, Ann. *Chronicle of the Chinese Emperors* (1998).

Pan, Lyn. *Sons of the Yellow Emperor* (1990).

Pangle, Thomas, and P. Ahrensdorf. *Justice Among Nations* (1999).

Papacosma, S. Victor et al., eds. *NATO After Fifty Years* (2001).

Paraskevas, J., and F. Reinstein. *The Eastern Orthodox Church* (1969).

Parekh, Bhikhu. *Gandhi* (1997).

Paret, Peter. *The Makers of Modern Strategy* (1986).

Parker, Geoffrey. *The Grand Strategy of Philip II* (1998).

———. *The Military Revolution: Military Innovation and the Rise of the West, 1500–1800* (1988; 1996).

———, ed. *The Thirty Years' War* (1987).

———. *The Dutch Revolt*, rev. ed. (1985).

———. *The Army of Flanders and the Spanish Road, 1567–1659* (1972).

Parker, R. A. C. *Struggle for Survival* (1989).

Parker, Richard B., ed. *The Six-Day War: A Retrospective* (1996).

Parry, J. H. *Trade and Dominion* (1971).

Parsons, Lynn. *John Quincy Adams* (1998).

Patterson, Thomas C. *The Inca Empire* (1991).

Patterson, Thomas G. *Contesting Castro* (1994).

———, ed. *Kennedy's Quest for Victory* (1989).

———. *Meeting the Communist Threat* (1988).

Paust, Jordan J. et al. *International Criminal Law*, 2nd ed. (2000).

Paxton, Robert. *Vichy France* (1972).

Payne, Stanley. *Fascism in Spain, 1923–1977* (2000).

Pennell, C. R. *Bandits at Sea: A Pirates Reader* (2001).

Pepper, Suzanne. *Civil War in China* (1978).

Pérez, Louis. *The War of 1898* (1998).

Perroy, Édouard. *The Hundred Years' War* (1951).

Perry, Elizabeth. *Rebels and Revolutionaries in North China, 1845–1945* (1980).

Peters, Marie. *The Elder Pitt* (1998).

Peterson, M. *Recognition of Governments* (1997).

Pflanze, Otto. *Bismarck and the Development of Germany* (1963).

Phillip, Thomas, and Ulrich Haarmaan, eds. *The Mamluks in Egyptian Politics and Society* (1998).

Phillips, Hugh. *Between Revolution and the West* (1992).

Phillips, William, and Carla Rahn. *The Worlds of Christopher Columbus* (1992).

Phillipson, David. *Ancient Ethiopia* (1998).

Pike, Frederick. *The Modern History of Peru* (1967).

Pipes, Richard. *A Concise History of the Russian Revolution* (1996).

———, ed. *The Unknown Lenin: From the Secret Archive* (1996)

———. *Russia Under the Bolshevik Regime* (1994).

———. *The Russian Revolution* (1991).

Pirenne, Henri. *Muhammad and Charlemagne* (1939).

———. *Medieval Cities* (1925).

Pletcher, David. *The Diplomacy of Annexation* (1973).

Pogue, Forrest. *George C. Marshall* (1987).

Pollard, Michael. *The Red Cross and the Red Crescent* (1994).

Pomeranz, Kenneth. *The Great Divergence: Europe, China, and the Making of the Modern World Economy* (2000).

Popper, Karl. *The Poverty of Historicism* (1957).

Porch, Douglas. *The French Foreign Legion* (1992).

———. *The Conquest of the Sahara* (1984).

———. *The Conquest of Morocco* (1982).

Porter, Roy. *The Greatest Benefit to Mankind: A Medical History of Humanity from Antiquity to the Present* (1997).

Potter, E. *Sea Power* (1981).

Prange, Gordon. *At Dawn We Slept* (1981).

Presseisen, E. *Amiens and Munich: Comparisons in Appeasement* (1978).

Preston, Paul. *Franco* (1994).

Prior, Robin, and Trevor Wilson. *Passchendaele* (1996).

Prosterman, Roy, and J. Reidlinger, *Land Reform and Democratic Development* (1987).

Polvinen, Tuomo. *Between East and West* (1986).

Quigley, John. *Palestine and Israel* (1990).

Quinn, Frederick. *The French Overseas Empire* (2000).

Quirk, Robert. *Fidel Castro* (1993).

————. *The Mexican Revolution, 1914–1915* (1963).

Raack, R. C. *Stalin's Drive to the West, 1938–1945* (1995).

Rady, Martyn. *The Emperor Charles V* (1988; 1995).

Radzinsky, Edvard. *The Rasputin File* (2000).

Raeff, M. *Michael Speransky* (1961).

Rajaee, Farhang, ed. *Iranian Perspectives on the Iran-Iraq War* (1997).

Ramsey, Paul. *Just War* (1983).

Ranelagh, John. *The Agency* (1986).

Rashid, Salim, ed. *The Clash of Civilizations? Asian Responses* (1997).

Ratchnevsky, Paul. *Ghengis Khan: His Life and Legacy* (1992).

Rawski, Evelyn. *The Last Emperors* (1999).

Read, Piers. *The Templars* (2000).

Reese, Thomas. *Inside the Vatican: The Politics and Organization of the Catholic Church* (1996).

Reich, Robert. *The Work of Nations* (1991).

Reische, Diana. *Arafat and the Palestine Liberation Organization* (1991).

Regan, Richard. *Just War: Principles and Cases* (1998).

Remini, R. V. *Andrew Jackson* (1999).

————. *Andrew Jackson and the Course of American Empire, 1767–1821* (1977).

Reynolds, Clark. *Navies in History* (1998).

————. *Command of the Sea* (1974).

Rhodes, Richard. *Dark Sun: The Making of the Hydrogen Bomb* (1995).

————. *Making of the Atomic Bomb* (1986).

Riasanovsky, Nicholas. *A History of Russia* (1984).

————. *Nicholas I and Official Nationality in Russia, 1825–1855* (1959).

Rice, Geoffrey W., ed. *Oxford History of New Zealand*, 2nd ed. (1992).

Rickett, Richard. *A Brief Survey of Austrian History*, 5th ed. (1975).

Ridley, Jasper. *Tito* (1994).

Riley, James C. *The Seven Years War and the Old Regime in France* (1986).

Riley-Smith, Jonathon. *A History of the Crusades* (2000).

————. *Hospitallers: History of the Order of St. John* (1999).

————. *The Crusades* (1990).

Ritter, E. A. *Shaka Zulu: The Rise of the Zulu Empire* (1957).

Ritter, G. *The Schlieffen Plan* (1958).

Roberts, Adam, and Benedict Kingsley, eds. *United Nations, Divided World* (1993).

Roberts, Andrew. *A History of Zambia* (1976).

Roberts, J. A. G. *A Concise History of China* (1999).

Roberts, J. M. *The French Revolution* (1997).

Roberts, M. *The Swedish Imperial Experience, 1560–1718* (1979).

————. *Gustavus Adolphus and the Rise of Sweden* (1973).

Robinson, David. *The Holy War of Umar Tal* (1985).

Robinson, I. H. *Henry IV of Germany, 1056–1106* (1999).

Robinson, R. H. *The Buddhist Religion*, 3rd ed. (1982).

Robinson, Ronald et al., *Africa and the Victorians* (1982).

Robinson T., and D. Shambaugh. *Chinese Foreign Policy* (1994).

Roche, Daniel. *France in the Enlightenment* (1998).

Rock, Stephen. *Appeasement in International Politics* (2000).

Rodríguez, Jaime. *The Independence of Spanish America* (1998).

Roesdahl, Else. *The Vikings*, 2nd ed. (trans. 1998).

Roger, N. A. M. *The Safeguard of the Sea: A Naval History of Britain* (1997).

Rogers, George. *The Transportation Revolution, 1815–1860* (1951).

Rong Syamananda, *A History of Thailand* (1981).

Rosberg, Carl G., and John Nottingham. *The Myth of the Mau Mau* (1967).

———, and William Friedland, eds. *African Socialism* (1964).

Rose, J. E. *Bismarck* (1987).

Rosenberg, H. *Bureaucracy, Aristocracy, and Autocracy* (1958).

Rosenthal, Joel. *Righteous Realists* (1991).

Rossabi, Morris. *Khubilai Khan* (1988).

———. *China Among Equals* (1983).

———. *China and Inner Asia From 1368* (1975).

Rostow, W. W. *The World Economy* (1978).

Rothenberg, Gunther E. *The Napoleonic Wars* (1999).

Rotter, Andrew. *Path to Vietnam* (1987).

Rowse, A. L. *The Elizabethan Renaissance* (2000).

———. *The Use of History* (1963, 1985).

———. *The Expansion of Elizabethan England* (1955).

———. *England of Elizabeth* (1950, 1978).

Rubin, Barry. *The Transformation of Palestinian Politics* (1999).

Rudy, T. M., ed. *Charting an Independent Course* (1998).

Rundell, John. *Origins of Modernity: Social Theory from Kant to Hegel to Marx* (1987).

Rusk, Dean. *As I Saw It* (1990).

Russell, Peter. *Prince Henry "the Navigator"* (2000).

Russell, Ruth B. *History of the United Nations* (1958).

Russell-Wood, A. J. R., ed. *From Colony to Nation: Essays on the Independence of Brazil* (1975).

Ryder, Allan. *Benin and the Europeans, 1485–1897* (1969).

Sachar, Howard M. *Israel and Europe* (1999).

———. *History of Israel* (1996).

———. *The Course of Modern Jewish History*, rev. ed. (1990).

Said, Edward. *Culture and Imperialism* (1993).

———. *Orientalism* (1978).

Sampson, Anthony. *Mandela* (1999).

Samuelson, Paul, and W. Nordhaus. *Economics*, 16th ed. (1997).

Sawyer, P. H. *The Age of the Vikings* (1972).

Schaller, Michael. *Douglas MacArthur* (1989).

———. *American Occupation of Japan* (1985).

Schama, Simon. *History of Britain* (2000).

———. *Citizens* (1989, 1990).

Scherrerl, Christian. *Genocide and Crisis in Central Africa* (2001).

Schiffren, Harold. *Sun Yat-sen and the Origins of the Chinese Revolution* (1970).

Schom, Alan. *Napoleon Bonaparte* (1997).

Schreuder, D. M. *The Scramble for Southern Africa* (1980).

Schroeder, John H. *Mr. Polk's War* (1973).

Schroeder, Paul W. *The Transformation of European Politics, 1763–1848* (1994).

Schroeer, Dietrich, and Mirco Elena, eds. *Technology Transfer* (2000).

Schuker, Stephen. *American "Reparations" to Germany, 1919–1933* (1988).

Schultz, George P. *Turmoil and Triumph: My Years As Secretary of State* (1993).

Schultzinger, Robert D. *A Time for War: The United States and Vietnam, 1941–1975* (1997).

Schwabe, Klaus. *Woodrow Wilson, Revolutionary Germany, and Peacemaking, 1919–20* (1985).

Schwarcz, Vera. *The Chinese Enlightenment* (1986).

Schwartz, Thomas. *America's Germany* (1991).

Schwarz, Solomon M. *The Russian Revolution of 1905* (1967).

Sciolino, E. *Persian Mirrors: The Elusive Face of Iran* (2000).

Scobie, James. *Argentina: A City and a Nation* (1964).

Seaton, A. *The Crimean War* (1977).

———. *The Russo-German War, 1941–45* (1971).

Sebag, Simon. *Prince of Princes: The Life of Potemkin* (2000).

Segal, G. *Defending China* (1985).

Sellassie, Sergew H. *Ancient and Medieval Ethiopia* (1972).

Sen, Amartya, *Development As Freedom* (2001).

———. *Beyond the Crisis* (1999).

———. *Africa and India* (1988).

———: *On Ethics and Economics* (1987).

——— et al. *Political Economy of Hunger* (1995).

Service, Robert. *Lenin* (2000).

———. *Russia: A History* (1998).

Seton-Watson, Hugh. *The Russian Empire, 1801–1917* (1990).

Shafer, Michael. *Deadly Paradigms* (1988).

Shakya, Tsering. *Dragon in the Land of Snows* (1999).

Shannon, Albert C. *The Medieval Inquisition* (1991).

Shannon, Richard. *Gladstone*, 2 vols. (1984; 1999).

———. *The Age of Disraeli, 1868–1881: The Rise of Tory Democracy* (1992).

———. *The Crisis of Imperialism, 1865–1915* (1976).

Shao, Kuo-kang. *Zhou Enlai and the Foundations of Chinese Foreign Policy* (1996).

Sharp, Alan. *The Versailles Settlement* (1991).

Shaw, Malcolm N. *International Law*, 4th ed. (1997).

Shaw, Stanford, and E. K. Shaw. *History of the Ottoman Empire and Modern Turkey*, 2 vols. (1977).

Shay, Robert. *British Rearmament in the Thirties: Politics and Profits* (1977).

Shearer, David. *Private Armies and Military Intervention* (1998).

Sheehan, James J. *German History, 1770–1866* (1989).

Sherwin, Martin. *A World Destroyed* (1987).

Shevardnadze, Eduard. *The Future Belongs to Freedom* (1991).

Shinkichi Eto and Harold Schiffrin, eds. *The 1911 Revolution* (1984).

Showalter, Dennis. *The Wars of Frederick the Great* (1996).

———. *Tannenberg: Clash of Empires* (1991).

———. *Railroads and Rifles: Soldiers, Technology, and the Unification of Germany* (1975).

Shu Zhang. *Mao's Military Romanticism* (1995).

Sih, Paul, ed. *Nationalist China During the Sino-Japanese War, 1937–45* (1977).

Simpson, B. D. *Ulysses S. Grant* (2000).

Simpson, Leslie. *The Encomienda in New Spain* (1966).

Singh, Simon. *The Code Book: The Evolution of Secrecy from Mary, Queen of Scots, to Quantum Cryptography* (1999).

Singleton, F. *Short History of Finland* (1989).

Sinor, Denis. *Studies in Medieval Inner Asia* (1997).

Skidelsky, Robert. *John Maynard Keynes*, 3 vols. (1983–2000).

Skidmore, Thomas. *Modern Latin America* (1997).

Skilling, H. Gordon. *Czechoslovakia's Interrupted Revolution* (1976).

Slugglett, Peter, and Marion Farouk-Slugglett. *Iraq Since 1958: From Revolution to Dictatorship* (1990).

Smith, D. Mack. *Mussolini* (1982).

Smith, Gaddis. *Last Years of the Monroe Doctrine* (1994).

———. *Morality, Reason, and Power* (1986).

———. *American Diplomacy During the Second World War* (1985).

———. *Dean Acheson* (1972).

Smith, Gene. *Until the Last Trumpet Sounds: The Life of General of the Armies John J. Pershing* (1998).

Smith, Jean. *Lucius D. Clay* (1990).

———. *Grant* (2001).

Smith, John Holland. *Constantine the Great* (1971).

Smith, Tony. *America's Mission* (1994).

———. *The Pattern of Imperialism* (1981).

Sokolski, Henry. *Best of Intentions: America's Campaign Against Strategic Weapons Proliferation* (2001).

Solzhenitsyn, Alexandr. *The Gulag Archipelago, 1918–1956*, 3 vols. (1973–1976).

Sontag, Sherry, and Christopher Drew. *Blind Man's Bluff: The Untold Story of American Submarine Espionage* (1998).

Sørensen, George, ed. *Democracy and Democratization* (1998).

Souchek, Svat. *A History of Inner Asia* (2000).

Spector, Ronald. *Eagle Against the Sun* (1988).

Speer, Albert. *Inside the Third Reich* (1970).

Speer, Thomas. *The Swahili* (1985).

Spence, Jonathan. *Treason by the Book* (2001).

———. *Mao Zedong* (1999).

———. *God's Chinese Son: The Taiping Heavenly Kingdom of Hong Xiuquan* (1996).

———. *The Search for Modern China* (1990).

———, and John Wills, *From Ming to Ch'ing* (1979).

———. *Emperor of China* (1974).

Spring, D., ed. *The Impact of Gorbachev* (1991).

Spruyt, J., and J. B. Robertson. *History of Indonesia*, rev. ed. (1973).

Stagg, J. C. A. *Mr. Madison's War* (1983).

Stavrianos, Leften. *The Balkans Since 1453* (1958).

Stavrou, T. G., ed. *Russia Under the Last Tsar* (1969).

Steel, Nigel, and Peter Hart, *Passchendaele: The Sacrificial Ground* (2000).

Steele, Ian. *Warpath: Invasions of North America* (1994).

Stein, Burton. *A History of India* (1998).

Steinberg, S. H. *The "Thirty Years' War" and the Conflict for European Hegemony, 1600–1660* (1966).

Stephens, A. *The War in the Air, 1914–1994* (1994).

Stern, Fritz. *Gold and Iron* (1977).

Stern, Jessica. *The Ultimate Terrorists* (1999).

Stone, L. *Causes of the English Revolution* (1972).

Stone, N. *The Eastern Front, 1914–1917* (1975).

Story, R. *History of Modern Japan* (1982).

Strachan, Hew. *The First World War* (2001).

———, ed. *World War I* (1999).

———. *European Armies and the Conduct of War* (1983).

Strachey, Lytton. *Eminent Victorians* (1918).

Stremlau, John. *The International Politics of the Nigerian Civil War* (1977).

Stueck, William. *The Korean War* (1995).

Subtelney, Orest. *Ukraine: A History* (2000).

Sudoplatov, Pavel et al., *Special Tasks* (1994).

Sugar, P. F. *A History of Hungary* (1991).

Sumner, B. *Peter the Great and the Emergence of Russia* (1940).

Sumption, J. *The Hundred Years' War* (1991).

Suny, R. *The Making of the Georgian Nation* (1988).

Sutherland, N. M. *The Massacre of St. Bartholomew and the European Conflict, 1559–1572* (1973).

Sutton, Donald. *Provincial Militarism and the Chinese Republic* (1980).

Sutton, John L. *The King's Honor & the King's Cardinal: The War of the Polish Succession* (1980).

Suvanto, Pekka. *Conservatism From the French Revolution to the 1990s* (1997).

Swartz, Thomas. *America's Germany* (1991).

Tan, Samuel. *A History of the Philippines* (1987).

Taylor, A. J. P. *Bismarck* (1955; 1987).

———. *The Struggle for Mastery in Europe, 1848–1918* (1954, 1971).

———. *Origins of the Second World War* (1963).

———. *The Habsburg Monarchy* (1948).

Taylor, Arthur. *Laissez-faire and State Intervention in 19th Century Britain* (1972).

Taylor, John. *East Timor* (2000).

Taylor, Peter. *Behind the Mask: The IRA and Sinn Féin* (1998).

Taylor, Telford. *Anatomy of the Nuremberg Trials* (1992).

———. *Munich: The Price of Peace* (1979).

Terraine, John. *The Western Front, 1914–1918* (1965).

Thomas, Hugh. *Conquest* (1993).

———. *Armed Truce* (1986).

———. *The Spanish Civil War* (1961).

Thompson, J. M. *Robespierre and the French Revolution* (1973).

Thompson, William. *Khrushchev* (1995).

Thornton, J. K. *The Kingdom of the Kongo* (1983).

Tibawi, Abdul L. *British Interests in Palestine, 1800–1901* (1961).

Tibi, Bassam. *Arab Nationalism: A Critical Enquiry*, 2nd ed. (trans. 1990).

Tilchin, William N. *Theodore Roosevelt and the British Empire* (1997).

Toby, R. *State and Diplomacy in Early Modern Japan* (1984).

Tocqueville, Alexis de. *The Ancien Régime and the French Revolution* (1856).

———. *Democracy in America*, 2 vols. (1835–1840).

Tolentino, Paz Estrella. *Multinational Corporations: Emergence and Evolution* (2000).

Torpey, John. *The Invention of Passports* (2000).

Totman, Conrad. *Early Modern Japan* (1993).

Towle, Philip. *Arms Control and East-West Relations* (1983).

Townshend, Charles, ed. *The Oxford History of Modern War* (2000).

Trachtenberg, Marc. *Reparation in World Politics: France and European Economic Diplomacy, 1916–23* (1980).

Trani, Eugene. *The Treaty of Portsmouth* (1969).

Trebilcock, C. *Industrialization of the Continental Powers, 1780–1914* (1981).

Trevelyan, G. M. *The English Revolution* (1967).

Troyat, Henri. *Ivan the Terrible* (1984).

Trudeau, Pierre Elliott. *Memoirs* (1993).

Truman, Harry S. *Memoirs*, 2 vols. (1956).

Tucker, Robert C. *Stalin in Power* (1990).

———, ed. *Stalinism* (1977).

———. *Stalin As Revolutionary* (1974).

Tucker, Robert W. *The Just War* (1960; 1978).

———. *The Radical Left and American Foreign Policy* (1972).

———. *Principles of International Law* (1966).

———, and David Hendrickson. *Empire of Liberty: The Statecraft of Thomas Jefferson* (1990).

———, and David Hendrickson. *Fall of the British Empire: Origins of the War of American Independence* (1982).

Tucker, Spencer. *Vietnam* (1999).

Tuchman, Barbara. *Stilwell and the American Experience in China, 1911–1945* (1970; 2001).

———. *The Proud Tower: A Portrait of the World Before the War, 1890–1914* (1966; 1996).

———. *Distant Mirror: The Calamitous 14th Century* (1978).

———. *August 1914* (1962).

———. *The Zimmermann Telegram* (1959).

Tutorow, Norman. *War Crimes, War Criminals, and War Crimes Trials* (1986).

Tuveson, Ernest. *Redeemer Nation* (1968).

Tyler, Royall. *The Emperor Charles the Fifth* (1956).

Ulam, Adam. *Understanding the Cold War* (2000).

———. *Bolsheviks* (1998).

———. *The Communists, 1948–1991* (1992).

———. *Stalin: The Man and His Era* (1989).

———. *Dangerous Relations: The Soviet Union in World Politics, 1970–1982* (1983).

———. *Russia's Failed Revolutions* (1981).

———. *History of Soviet Russia* (1976).

———. *Expansion and Coexistence: Soviet Foreign Policy, 1917–1973* (1974).

Urquart, Brian. *Hammarskjöld* (1972; 1984).

Vance, Cyrus. *Hard Choices* (1983).

van Creveld, M. *Technology and War From 2000* B.C. *to the Present Day* (1989).

———. *Command in War* (1985).

———. *Supplying War* (1977).

van der Vat, Dan. *The Good Nazi: The Life and Lies of Albert Speer* (1997).

Van Dyke, Carl. *The Soviet Invasion of Finland* (1997).

Vansina, Jan. *Kingdoms of the Savannah* (1966).

Vatikiotis, P. J. *A Modern History of Egypt*, 2nd ed. (1980).

Viên, Nguyûn Khăc. *Vietnam* (1993).

Viljoen, S. *Economic Systems in World History* (1974).

Vincent, R. J. *Human Rights and International Relations* (1986).

———. *Nonintervention and International Order* (1974).

Vital, David. *A People Apart: the Jews in Europe, 1789–1939* (1999).

Vogelsang, Willem. *The Afghans* (2001).

Vologonov, Dmitri. *Lenin* (1994).

Waites, R. *Vanguard of Nazism* (1952).

Waldron, Arthur. *The Great Wall of China* (1990).

Walker, David. *Anxious Nation* (1999).

Walker, E. A. *The Great Trek* (1934; 1960).

Walker, G. *Armenia* (1980).

Walker, Thomas W. *Nicaragua: The Land of Sandino*, 3rd ed. (1991).

Wallerstein, Immanuel. *The Modern World System* (1980).

Walsh, Warren B. *Readings in Russian History*, 2 vols. (1963).

Walt, Stephen. *Origins of Alliances* (1987).

Walters, F. P. *History of the League of Nations*, 2 vols. (1952).

Walters, Ronald W. *Pan-Africanism in the African Diaspora* (1993).

Waltz, Kenneth. *Man, the State, and War* (1959).

Walworth, Arthur. *Wilson and His Peacemakers* (1986).

Walzer, Michael. *Just and Unjust Wars* (1977; 1992).

Wang, Zhongshu, *Han Civilization* (1982).

Ward, Chris. *Stalin's Russia*, 2nd ed. (1999).

Watson, David. *Clemenceau* (1974).

Watts, Arthur. *International Law and the Antarctic Treaty System* (1992).

Watts, David. *The West Indies: Patterns of Development, Culture and Environmental Change Since 1492* (1987).

Watts, Sheldon. *Epidemics and History* (1998).

Wawro, Geoffrey. *Warfare and Society in Europe, 1792–1914* (2000).

———. *The Austro-Prussian War* (1996).

Webster, C. *Foreign Policy of Castlereagh* (1931).

Weinberg, Albert. *Manifest Destiny* (1935).

Weinstein, Alan, and Alexander Vassiliev. *The Haunted Wood: Soviet Espionage in America—the Stalin Era* (1999).

———. *Perjury: The Hiss-Chambers Case* (1978).

Weintraub, Stanley. *MacArthur's War* (2000).

———. *Disraeli* (1993).

Weissman, Benjamin M. *Herbert Hoover and Famine Relief to Soviet Russia, 1921–1923* (1974).

Welfield, John. *An Empire in Eclipse* (1988).

Weller, Jac. *On Wellington* (1998).

———. *Wellington in the Peninsula* (1962).

Wernham, R. *The Making of Elizabethan Foreign Policy, 1588–1603* (1980).

———. *The Return of the Armadas: The Last Years of the Elizabethan War Against Spain, 1595–1603* (1994).

West, Nigel. *Venona: The Greatest Secret of the Cold War* (1999).

West, Richard. *Tito and the Rise and Fall of Yugoslavia* (1995).

Westwood, J. N. *Endurance and Endeavor: Russian History, 1812–1992* (1973; 1993).

———. *Russia Against Japan* (1986).

Wheatcroft, Andrew. *The Habsburgs* (1996).

———. *The Ottomans* (1993).

Wheaton, Bernard, and Zdenek Kavan. *The Velvet Revolution: Czechoslovakia, 1988–1991* (1992).

Wheeler, James. *Cromwell in Ireland* (1999).

White, J. *The Diplomacy of the Russo-Japanese War* (1964).

White, Jonathan R. *Terrorism: An Introduction*, 3rd ed. (2001).

White, Lynn. *Policies of Chaos* (1989).

Wight, Martin. *Power Politics* (1946; 1979).

Wilks, Igor. *Ashante in the 19th Century* (1975).

Williams, E. *The Ancien Régime in Europe, 1648–1789* (1979).

Williams, Neville. *The Sea Dogs: Privateers, Plunder and Piracy in the Elizabethan Age* (1975).

Williamson, Samuel R. *Austria-Hungary and the Origins of the First World War* (1991).

Wills, John. *Pepper, Guns and Parlays: The Dutch East India Company and China, 1662–1681* (1974).

Wilson, Charles. *The Dutch Republic* (1969).

Wilson, Dick. *Zhou Enlai* (1984).

Winter, D. *Haig's Command* (1991).

Withey, L. *Voyages of Discovery: Captain Cook and the Exploration of the Pacific* (1989).

Wohlstetter, Roberta. *Pearl Harbor* (1962).

Wolf, J. *Emergence of the Great Powers, 1685–1715* (1951).

Wolff, Larry. *Venice and the Slavs: The Discovery of Dalmatia in the Age of Enlightenment* (2001).

Wolff, Leon. *In Flanders Fields* (1958; 1980).

Wolpert, Stanley. *A New History of India*, 6th ed. (2000).

———. *Nehru* (1997).

Wong, J. Y. *Deadly Dreams: Opium, Imperialism, and the Arrow War (1856–1860) in China* (1998).

Wong, R. Bin. *China Transformed* (1997).

Wood, A., and R. French. *Development of Siberia* (1989).

Wood, Michael. *Conquistadors* (2001).

Woodham-Smith, Cecil. *The Great Hunger* (1962).

Woodruff, W. *America's Impact on the World, 1720–1970* (1973).

Wortman, Miles. *Government and Society in Central America, 1680–1840* (1982).

Wright, Arthur. *The Sui Dynasty* (1978).

Wright, Esmond. *Washington and the American Revolution* (1957).

Wright, Quincy. *A Study of War* (1964).

Wright, Robin. *The Last Great Revolution* (2000).

———. *In the Name of God* (1989).

———. *Sacred Rage* (1985).

Wucker, Michele. *Why the Cocks Fight: Dominicans, Haitians, and the Struggle for Hispaniola* (1999).

Wyden, Peter. *Bay of Pigs* (1979).

Yamamoto, Masahiro. *Nanking* (2000).

Yang, B. *From Revolution to Politics* (1990).

Young, Ernest. *The Presidency of Yuan Shih-k'ai* (1977).

Young, Louise. *Japan's Total Empire* (1998).

Young, Marilyn. *The Vietnam Wars* (1991).

Yuan, Gao. *Born Red: A Chronicle of the Cultural Revolution* (1987).

Yuwen, Jen. *The Taiping Revolutionary Movement* (1973).

Zartman, I. W. et al., eds. *Peacemaking in International Conflict* (1997).

———, and William Habeeb, eds. *Polity and Society in Contemporary North Africa* (1993).

Zhukov, Georgi K. *Memoirs of Marshal Zhukov* (1969).

———. *Marshal Zhukov's Greatest Battles* (1969).

Ziegler, Philip. *The Black Death* (1969).

Zubok, Vladimir, and Constantine Pleshakov. *Inside the Kremlin's Cold War* (1996).

Index

(bold page numbers indicate a main entry)

deterrence and, 426; diplomacy and, 434; dowager empress and, 449; drug trade and, 452; East India Companies and, 462; Eisenhower and, 482, 1747–48; *fait accompli* and, 532; famine and, 535; fascism and, 537; feudalism and, 542; five-year plans and, 552; Flying Tigers and, 555; food and, 557; footbinding and, 558; Ford and, 560; foreign ministry and, 562; Four Modernizations and, 565; Four Power Treaty and, 565; French-Indochinese War and, 585; friendly fire and, 591; friendship treaty and, 592; fundamentalism and, 598, 599; General Agreement on Tariffs and Trade and, 611; Gordon and, 638; Grand Canal and, 641; Great Leap Forward and, 647–48; Great Proletarian Cultural Revolution and, 651–52; Great Wall and, 654; Greater East Asia Co-Prosperity Sphere and, 646; Guandong Army and, 666; Guangzhou (Canton) trade system and, 666–67; *guanxi* and, 667; *Guomindang* and, 677–78; Gurkhas and, 678; Hakka and, 688; Han dynasty and, 691–92; Hasegawa Yoshimichi and, 696; Heath and, 698; Hegel and, 699; hegemonic stability theory and, 700; Hirohito and, 711; history of, 278–79; Hô Chí Minh and, 722; Honecker and, 730; Hong Kong and, 731; Hongwu and, 731; Hoover and 732; Hoover-Stimson Doctrine and, 732–33; Hoxha and, 736; Hu Yaobang and, 750; Hull and, 739; Hundred Days and, 743; Hundred Flowers campaign and, 744; hydrogen bomb and, 750–51; hyperinflation and, 751; Imperial China and, 756; imperial, 279–80; Inchon battle and, 762; India and, 770; Indo-Chinese War and, 779; Indonesia and, 780; Indo-Pakistani War and, 782; industrialization and, 784; Inner Asia and, 788;

Intelligence Bureau and, 752; Intercontinental Ballistic Missiles and, 796; internal colonialism and, 797; Internationals and, 808–9; intervention and, 812; Iran-Iraq War and, 821; iron rice bowl and, 829; isolationism and, 835; Jackson-Vanik Amendment and, 847; Japan and, 850–51, 852, 853, 855, 856, 858; Japanese Peace Treaty and, 859; Jesuits and, 863; Jiang Zemin and, 865; Jiangxi Soviet and, 865–66; Johnson and, 871; *kamikaze* and, 886; Kashmir and, 890; Khrushchev and, 901; Kiaochow incident and, 901; Kissinger and, 906; Kokand and, 909; Konoe Fumimaro and, 910–11; Korea and, 911–13; Korean Conflict and, 914, 915–16; *kowtow* and, 918–19; land power and, 931; Lansing-Ishii Agreement, 932; legitimate government and, 945; Lend-Lease and, 946; Leninism and, 949; Li Hongzhang and, 961–62; Li Peng and, 968–69; liberalism and, 956; Lie and, 961; Lytton Commission and, 986; Macao and, 987–88; Macartney mission and, 989; Madagascar and, 996; Manchukuo and, 1008; Manchuria and, 1008–9; Manchus and, 1008; mandate of heaven and, 1009–10; Mao Zedong and, 1014–16; Marco Polo bridge incident and, 1019; Marshall and, 1023; Marx and, 1024; Marxism and, 1027; May 4th movement and, 1033; McCarthyism and, 1036; McMahon Line and, 1038; mercenaries and, 1045; migration and, 1057; Ming dynasty and, 1062–64; mission, sense of, and, 1068, 1069; missionaries and, 1067; Mongolia and, 1078; Mongols and, 1079; most-favored-nation and, 1089; multipolarity and, 1095; mutiny and, 1101; Nagasaki and, 1103; Nanjing treaty and, 1106–7; Nanjing, Rape of, and, 1106; nationalism and, 1124;

About the Author

CATHAL J. NOLAN is Executive Director of the International History Institute at Boston University. An award-winning teacher, he has guest taught at several universities in Canada, the United States, and in Buenos Aires. He held a Barton Fellowship in Peace and Security from the Department of Foreign Affairs, Canada, in 1993. His books include *Shepherd of Democracy? America and Germany in the 20th Century* (Praeger, 1992), *Principled Diplomacy: Security and Rights in U.S. Foreign Policy* (Praeger, 1993), *Ethics and Statecraft* (Praeger, 1995), *The Longman Guide to World Affairs* (1995), and *Notable U.S. Embassadors Since 1775* (Greenwood, 1997), which was selected by *Choice* as an "Outstanding Academic Book of 1998."